WITHDRAWN

GWION

GWION

© 2000 Könemann Verlagsgesellschaft mbH
Bonner Str. 126, D-50968 Köln

Narratives editing & observations: Jeff Doring

Project management: Sally Bald
Coordination: Sabine Gerber, Robert von Radetzky
Song translation into English: Tony Redmond
German translation: Gabi Kempf-Allié, Manfred Allié
French translation: Apolline Kohen, Eric Wittersheim
Contributing editors: Dr Graeme K. Ward and Dr Michael Scuffil (English),
  Dr Corinna Erckenbrecht (German), Pierre Brochet (French)
Layout and design: Jeff Doring
Layout and typography: Pierre Brochet
Typesetting: argus Korrekturservice, Cologne
Production: Mark Voges
Reproductions: Typografik, Cologne
Printing and binding: MOHN Media · Mohndruck GmbH, Gütersloh
Printed in Germany

ISBN 3-8290-4060-1
10 9 8 7 6 5 4 3 2 1

WITHDRAWN

GWION

GWION

Ngarjno   Ungudman   Banggal   Nyawarra

WITHDRAWN

KÖNEMANN

DULWAN   MAMAA

SECRET AND SACRED PATHWAYS   GEHEIME UND HEILIGE PFADE   CHEMINS SECRETS ET SACRÉS

Preface

This book is dedicated to **Ngarjno... Ungudman... Nyawarra...** and especially the man who started it all, **Banggal.**

I began working with these four **munnumburra** in 1992 at their request, when they decided that they wanted to reveal **junjun** (evidence of the antiquity of **Ngarinyin** culture). At **Alyaguma** they asked me to film them talking on their **dulwan nimindi** (pathway of knowledge). The first icon that we recorded was the **guloi** tree painting, an ancient visual metaphor for the transmission of knowledge from generation to generation, which they also call **dulwan** (pathway). With the shared aim to record such meanings active in the land, we initiated the Pathway Project.

This book has three interrelated elements.

At its core are the narratives of four senior **Ngarinyin** law men – **munnumburra.** These narratives are connected to the images and are accompanied by observations.

The narratives are edited to reflect their dialogue as **worri-unbin** (flowing words). Under their direction, we follow them along the pathways where these narratives were recorded, so these words were spoken when and where the photographs of their evidence were taken.

The meanings of key **Ngarinyin** words in the narratives are discussed in the observations located within five titled sections. These observations on the paintings and themes developed in the narratives are titled in red, from the keywords listed in the page of contents.

The book concludes with a glossary, introduced by a note on the transcription of the narratives, and on the reading of translations of songs.

The narratives are preceded by an introduction to the four **Ngarinyin munnumburra** and the socio-historical context of their revelations.

Just before delivering the final text to the publishers, **Nyawarra** and I visited remote country belonging to the senior **munnumburra Ngarjno.** As a cyclonic storm approached, **Nyawarra** found a rock shelter and spontaneously painted a **Gwion** figure wearing a long **mudurra** (wig) and with various other shaped extensions to the basic human form. Each of these are rich with different **mamaa** (sacred connections and secret meanings). It will take us years to record enough graphic evidence and translate all the meanings related to the significant elements in this one painting. It also reminds us how much there is to learn and how, as a result of our experience, knowledge circulates in our time and proceeds across generations through art.

The **guloi** tree painting at **Alyaguma** illustrates this idea, and demonstrates the continuity of the **Ngarinyin** narrative.

Jeff Doring
Origma Creek, Sydney, February 2000

Vorwort

Dieses Buch widme ich **Ngarjno ... Ungudman ... Nyawarra ...** und vor allem **Banggal,** dem Mann, mit dem alles anfing.

Meine Arbeit mit diesen vier **munnumburra** begann im Jahr 1992; damals hatten sie beschlossen, das Geheimnis der **junjun** (sichtbare Zeugnisse für das Alter der Kultur der **Ngarinyin**) zu lüften. In **Alyaguma** baten sie mich, sie dabei zu filmen, wie sie auf ihrem **dulwan nimindi** (Pfad des Wissens) über ihre Traditionen sprachen. Das Erste, was wir aufnahmen, war das Bild des **guloi**-Baumes, eine uralte Bild-metapher für die Überlieferung des Wissens von Generation zu Generation, die sie auch als **dulwan** (Pfad) bezeichnen. Unser gemeinsames Ziel war es, mehr von dem festzuhalten, was das Land an Bedeutung birgt, und deshalb riefen wir das Pathway-Projekt ins Leben.

Das Buch besteht aus drei eng miteinander verknüpften Elementen.

Im Mittelpunkt stehen die Erzählungen der **munnumburra,** der vier Gesetzeshüter der **Ngarinyin.** Diese Erzählungen werden illustriert mit Fotografien und begleitet von kommentierenden Texten.

Das Layout der Dialogpassagen versucht, ein Gefühl für den **worri-unbin** (Redefluss) zu vermitteln. Unter ihrer Führung wandeln wir auf ihren Pfaden, dort, wo diese Erzählungen und Fotos zur selben Zeit entstanden, als sichtbare Zeugnisse der Vergangenheit.

Die Bedeutung der Schlüsselbegriffe aus der **Ngarinyin**-Sprache, die in den Erzählungen vorkommen, wird in kurzen kommentierenden Texten am Ende eines jeden der fünf Abschnitte erläutert. Die Erläuterungen bieten Informationen zu den Bildern und Themen, die in den Dialogpassagen zur Sprache kommen. Sie haben einen roten Kolumnentitel und beziehen sich auf die Schlüsselwörter im Inhaltsverzeichnis.

Die im Buch fett gesetzten Begriffe werden im Glossar erläutert. Vor dem Glossar finden sich Bemerkungen zur Transkription der Dialogpassagen und Hinweise zur Übersetzung der Lieder.

Am Anfang des Ganzen steht eine Einführung zu den vier **munnumburra** und eine kurze Einordnung in den sozial-geschichtlichen Zusammenhang.

Unmittelbar vor der Abgabe der letzten Manuskript-fassung besuchte ich zusammen mit **Nyawarra** ein entlegenes Gebiet, das unter der Obhut von **Ngarjno,** dem ältesten der **munnumburra,** steht. Als ein Wirbelsturm aufzog, suchte **Nyawarra** Schutz unter einem Felsvorsprung und malte spontan eine **Gwion**-Figur mit einer langen Perücke und einer Reihe von seltsam geformten Fortsätzen. Diese Fortsätze sind so reich an geheimen und heiligen **(mamaa)** Assoziationen, dass es Jahre dauern würde, die Bedeutung dieses einen Bildes zu erfassen und mit Worten wiederzugeben. Es erinnert uns auch daran, wie viel es zu lernen gibt und wie wir durch unsere Beobachtungen dazu beitragen, dass das Wissen in unserer Zeit und von Generation zu Generation dank der Malereien weitergegeben wird.

Das Bild des **guloi**-Baums in **Alyaguma** ist ein schönes Beispiel für diese Idee, und es versinnbildlicht das Fortbestehen der Geschichte der **Ngarinyin.**

Jeff Doring
Origma Creek, Sydney, Februar 2000

Préface

Ce livre est dédié à **Ngarjno ... Ungudman ... Nyawarra ...** et surtout à l'homme par qui tout a commencé : **Banggal.**

J'ai commencé à travailler avec ces quatre **munnumburra** à leur demande, en 1992, quand ils décidèrent de révéler les **junjun** (les preuves de l'ancienneté de la culture **Ngarinyin**). À **Alyaguma**, ils me demandèrent de les filmer marchant sur leur **dulwan nimindi** (leur chemin de la connaissance). La première image filmée fut la peinture de l'arbre **guloi**, une métaphore visuelle ancienne de la transmission de la connaissance de génération en génération ; ils l'appellent aussi **dulwan** (chemin). Nous initiâmes le Pathway Project (« le projet du chemin ») avec la volonté partagée d'enregistrer ces connaissances encore effectives dans le pays.

Ce livre est constitué de trois éléments étroitement liés.

En son cœur se trouvent les récits des quatre anciens gardiens de la loi **Ngarinyin** ou **munnumburra.** Ces discours sont associés aux images et sont accompagnés d'observations.

Les récits sont présentés de manière à restituer la forme sous laquelle ils ont été transmis : celle d'un dialogue, d'un flot de mots **(worri-unbin).** Sous leur direction, nous suivons les chemins au long desquels ces récits ont été transmis ; leurs mots ont été enregistrés au moment et à l'endroit mêmes où étaient prises les photographies des preuves.

La signification des mots-clés **Ngarinyin** contenus dans les récits est discutée dans les observations figurant au sein de chacune des cinq sections. Ces observations sur les peintures et les thèmes évoqués dans les récits sont signalées en rouge, comme les mots-clés cités dans la table des matières.

Tous les mots en gras sont expliqués dans le glossaire. Le glossaire est précédé d'une note sur la transcription des récits et sur la manière de lire les traductions des chants.

Les récits sont précédés par une introduction aux quatre **munnumburra Ngarinyin,** et au contexte sociohistorique qui entoure leurs révélations.

Juste avant de donner le texte final à l'éditeur, **Nyawarra** et moi, nous avons visité une région isolée appartenant à **Ngarjno,** un des anciens **munnumburra.** Alors qu'une tempête cyclonique s'annonçait, **Nyawarra** trouva un abri sous roche et peignit spontanément une image **Gwion** portant une longue coiffe avec plusieurs formes prolongeant la forme humaine. Ces formes sont riches en significations secrètes et sacrées **(mamaa).** Il nous faudrait des années si l'on voulait recueillir suffisamment de preuves visuelles et traduire toutes les significations en rapport avec les éléments contenus dans cette peinture. Cela nous rappelle combien nous avons ici à apprendre et comment la connaissance se transmet de génération en génération grâce à l'art.

L'image de l'arbre **guloi** à **Alyaguma** illustre cette idée, et souligne la continuité de l'histoire **Ngarinyin.**

Jeff Doring
Origma Creek, Sydney, février 2000

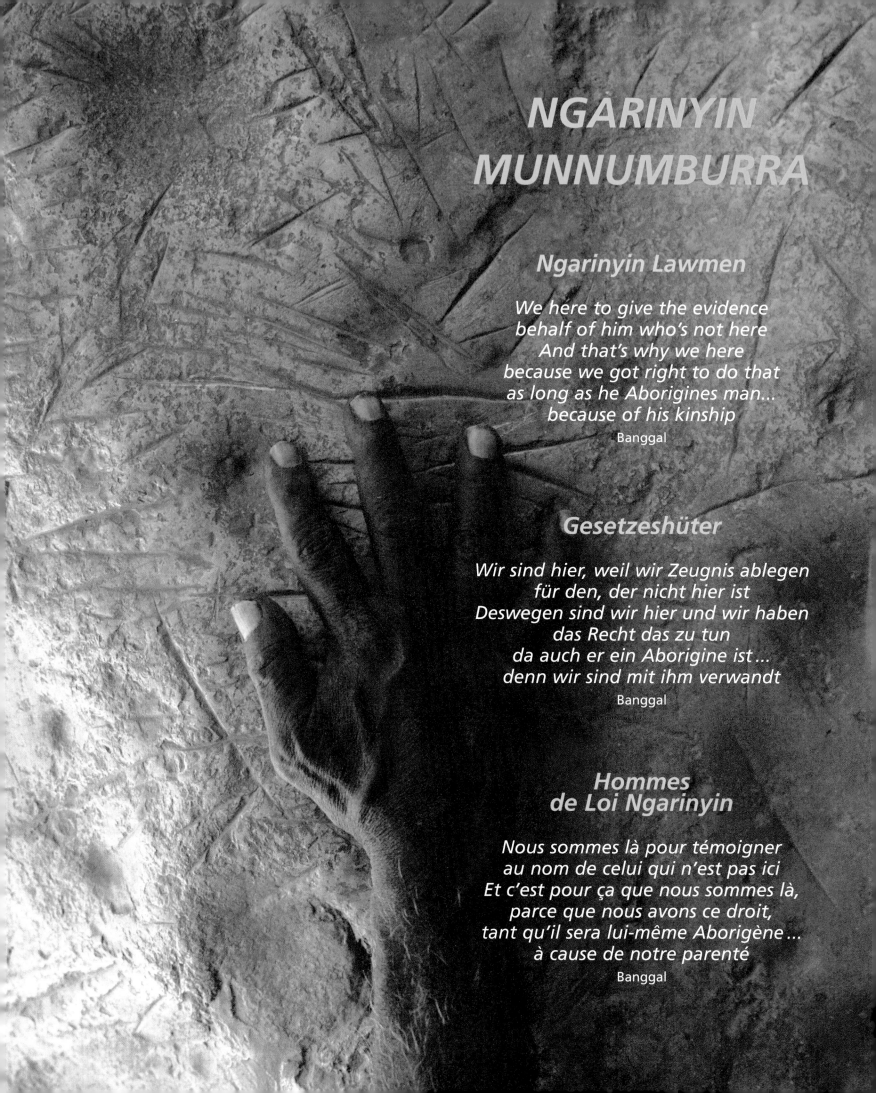

NGARINYIN MUNNUMBURRA

Ngarinyin Lawmen

We here to give the evidence
behalf of him who's not here
And that's why we here
because we got right to do that
as long as he Aborigines man...
because of his kinship

Banggal

Gesetzeshüter

Wir sind hier, weil wir Zeugnis ablegen
für den, der nicht hier ist
Deswegen sind wir hier und wir haben
das Recht das zu tun
da auch er ein Aborigine ist ...
denn wir sind mit ihm verwandt

Banggal

Hommes de Loi Ngarinyin

Nous sommes là pour témoigner
au nom de celui qui n'est pas ici
Et c'est pour ça que nous sommes là,
parce que nous avons ce droit,
tant qu'il sera lui-même Aborigène ...
à cause de notre parenté

Banggal

The **Ngarinyin** people are custodians of the oldest known figurative art in north-western Australia that records a distinct society. The fine, blood-coloured paintings of graceful people that are preserved in sandstone rock-shelters throughout their homeland create a rare cultural resonance and residue of extraordinary antiquity. Every painting is a story, every painting is an ancestor, every painting marks a place of cultural significance. When **Ngarinyin** gives the name of the artists, they say **Gwion Gwion**.

The vibrant bush and sandstone terrain where the paintings are preserved is a fertile world. Expanses of eucalypt woodland and savannah grassland clothe vast undulating plateaux that spread from horizon to horizon. Where the sun goes down, everything is embraced by a rugged coastline of mangrove-lined inlets and archipelagos with many isolated bays where saltwater marks the eastern margin of the Indian Ocean. Where the sun rises from the sandy deserts of central Australia, this tropical area of more than 420,000 square kilometres becomes an elevated patchwork of vegetation, typical of dry sclerophyll forest, but with traces of the desert visible wherever spiky spinifex grows among sandstone crumbling in the heat.

During most of the year when the weather is dry and very hot, the higher, open plateaux forested by various acacias and eucalyptus are rich with life. Their grassy slopes are criss-crossed by meandering strings of freshwater lagoons and deep waterholes, which are full rivers in the tropical wet season. These inland networks of permanent, fresh drinking water, so rare in the driest continent on earth, provide more than basic resources for survival. Each pool defines the landscape for humans during the two main seasons: the long "dry", good for hunting kangaroo on the higher plateaux, and the short "wet", when shelter is found in the rock-shelters among the many deep ravines and gorges.

After many months of scorching heat, the hard sandstone outcrops and eroded boulders are cooked under the sun until thunder-clouds move across the sky and cyclonic storms travel across the parched country. Flooding rains then flush the many rivers, lined with pandanus and paperbark, that snake across the high plateaux. The floodwaters are channeled into gorges that carve their way through the ramparts of stone that form the rugged edges of the plateau along the saltwater coast. This country, now known as the "remote Kimberley" of north-western Australia, is the homeland of the **Ngarinyin** people and their neighbours, the **Wororra, Wila Wila** and **Wunambul** peoples; all are closely related in language and history. The **Ngarinyin** and their coastal relatives are blessed with abundant fresh water and identify themselves as "wanjina water people". When meeting each other, the **Ngarinyin** recognise each other's "shining forehead".

Die **Ngarinyin** sind die Hüter der ältesten bekannten Bilddarstellungen einer eindeutig bestimmbaren Kultur im Nordwesten Australiens. Die schönen blutroten Malereien von anmutigen Menschen, die sich in Höhlen und unter Felsvorsprüngen in den Sandsteinformationen ihrer Heimat erhalten haben, künden von einer außerordentlich fernen Zeit. Jedes Bild ist eine Geschichte, jedes Bild ist ein Ahnenwesen, jedes Bild markiert einen bedeutsamen Ort. Wenn die **Ngarinyin** von ihnen sprechen, nennen sie die Künstler **Gwion Gwion**.

Das abwechslungsreiche, von Sandsteinfelsen durchbrochene Buschland, in dem sich die Malereien verbergen, ist eine fruchtbare Welt. Sanft hügelige Hochflächen erstrecken sich von Horizont zu Horizont, bedeckt von weiten Eukalyptuswäldern und grasbewachsenen Savannen. Wo die Sonne untergeht, umspülen die salzigen Fluten des Indischen Ozeans eine zerklüftete Küste aus mangrovengesäumten Flussmündungen und kleinen Inseln mit zahllosen einsamen Buchten. Wo die Sonne über den Sandwüsten Zentralaustraliens aufgeht, geht die Vegetation dieser mehr als 420 000 Quadratkilometer großen tropischen Region in einen lockeren Flickenteppich aus Hartlaubgewächsen und typischen Wüstenpflanzen wie dem stachligen Spinifexgras über, das auf dem von der Gluthitze brüchig gewordenen Sandstein wächst.

Die meiste Zeit des Jahres herrscht trockenes, sehr heißes Wetter, und die höher gelegenen offenen Plateaus mit ihren Akazien- und Eukalyptuswäldern wimmeln vor Leben. Ein weit verzweigtes Netz aus Süßwasserlagunen und tiefen Wasserlöchern, aus dem sich in der tropischen Regenzeit reißende Flüsse entwickeln können, überzieht die grasbewachsenen Hänge. Diese ständig in den Landesinneren vorhandenen Süßwasservorräte – eine Seltenheit auf dem trockensten Kontinent der Erde – garantieren nicht nur das Überleben. Jeder Tümpel ist für die Menschen zugleich auch ein wichtiger Orientierungspunkt in den beiden Hauptjahreszeiten: in der langen „Trockenzeit", in der sich auf den höheren Plateaus gut Jagd auf Kängurus machen lässt, wie in der kurzen „Regenzeit", in der man unter den Felsvorsprüngen der vielen tiefen Schluchten Zuflucht findet.

Monate sengender Hitze bringen die harten Sandsteinformationen und verwitterten Felsbrocken zum Glühen, bis schließlich Gewitterwolken am Himmel aufziehen und tropische Wirbelstürme über das ausgedörrte Land fegen. Heftige Regenfälle lassen die zahlreichen Flüsse der Hochplateaus anschwellen und über die mit Pandanus- und Paperbark-Bäumen (so genannt wegen ihrer weißen papierartigen Rinde) bestandenen Ufer treten. Die Fluten ergießen sich in enge Schluchten und fressen sich tief in das Gestein der zerklüfteten Felsen ein, von denen die Hochfläche wie von einem steinernen Wall gesäumt ist. Dieses Land, die so genannte „entlegene Kimberley-Region" Nordwestaustraliens, ist die Heimat der **Ngarinyin** und ihrer Nachbarn, der **Wororra, Wila Wila** und **Wunambul**. Sie alle sind sprachlich und geschichtlich eng miteinander verwandt. Die **Ngarinyin** und die Bewohner der benachbarten Küstenstriche kennen keinen Mangel an Süßwasser und beschreiben sich selbst als die „Leute des Wasser-**wanjina**". Wenn sie sich treffen, begrüßen die **Ngarinyin** die „glänzende Stirn" des anderen.

Les **Ngarinyin** sont les gardiens du plus ancien art figuratif connu du nord-est australien perpétuant la mémoire d'une société. Les magnifiques peintures ocres de ce peuple raffiné, qui sont conservées dans des abris sous roche gréseux sur toutes leurs terres, sont d'une résonance culturelle unique, vestiges d'une très haute antiquité. Chaque peinture est une histoire, chaque peinture est un ancêtre, chaque peinture est la marque d'un lieu culturel important. Quand les **Ngarinyin** citent le nom des artistes, ils disent **Gwion Gwion**.

Les peintures sont situées dans des lieux retirés du monde fertile et plein de vie du bush, au milieu des terrains de grès. Les étendues boisées d'eucalyptus et la savane recouvrent les vastes plateaux ondulés qui s'étendent d'un bout à l'autre de l'horizon. Le couchant est enlacé par une côte accidentée de criques bordées de mangroves et d'archipels aux nombreuses baies isolées où l'eau de mer marque la rive est de l'océan Indien. Au levant, du côté des déserts de sable de l'Australie centrale, cette région tropicale de plus de 420 000 km² devient un patchwork de végétation, composé d'une typique forêt sèche sclérophylle mais avec des poches désertiques visibles partout où le spinifex à pointe pousse au milieu du terrain de grès qui se délite avec la chaleur.

La majeure partie de l'année, le temps est sec et très chaud, en altitude, et les plateaux boisés de diverses espèces d'acacias et d'eucalyptus sont la source d'une vie abondante. Les pentes herbeuses sont entrecoupées d'une enfilade de cours d'eau sinueux allant de lagons d'eau douce en trous d'eau profonds qui deviennent de véritables rivières pendant la saison tropicale humide. Ces réseaux intérieurs permanents d'eau potable, si rares dans le continent le plus aride de la terre, offrent bien plus que les seules ressources minimales nécessaires à la survie de l'homme. Chaque bassin d'eau délimite le paysage humain durant les deux principales saisons : la saison sèche, la plus longue, bonne pour chasser le kangourou sur les hauts plateaux et la courte saison humide, durant laquelle on trouve refuge dans les abris sous roche au milieu des nombreux ravins profonds et des gorges.

Après de nombreux mois d'une chaleur torride où les affleurements de grès durs et les blocs de pierre érodés sont brûlés par le soleil, c'est le temps des nuages orageux et des cyclones qui traversent le pays desséché. Les pluies diluviennes font dévaler les rivières bordées de pandanus et de paperbark (arbres typiques d'Australie dont l'écorce, comme celle des bouleaux, pèle en feuilles de façon constante) qui traversent les hauts plateaux. Les torrents d'eau passent en force dans des gorges profondes qui s'enfoncent entre les remparts de pierre formant les bords accidentés du plateau le long de la côte maritime. Ce pays, aujourd'hui appelé la région « reculée » du Kimberley du nord-ouest de l'Australie, est la terre du peuple **Ngarinyin** et de leurs voisins, les **Wororra**, les **Wila Wila** et les **Wunambul** ; tous sont étroitement apparentés linguistiquement et historiquement. Les **Ngarinyin** et leurs voisins côtiers bénéficient d'eau douce en abondance et s'identifient au « peuple d'eau » **wanjina**. Lorsqu'ils se rencontrent, pour se saluer, les **Ngarinyin** utilisent souvent une expression qu'on peut traduire par « je vois ton front brillant ».

"amalad minia"... that one man

and you say "guru.amalad minia"
to the whole world...
welcoming everybody
Nyawarra

„amalad minia"... das ist ein Mann

und man sagt „guru.amalad minia"
zur ganzen Welt...
damit begrüßt man alle zusammen
Nyawarra

On dit « amalad minia »... à cet homme-là,

et « ... guru.amalad minia »
au monde entier...
pour souhaiter la bienvenue à tous
Nyawarra

So when you welcome anybody
friendly with everybody you know
you may be watching one lady coming up
you probably saying that
"yamalad minia"
and they saying **"yamalad minia"** to you

So we say **"guru.amalad minia"**
"I'm saying hello to everybody"
welcome to everybody
the ladies, the kids, the mans
that the word say **"guru.amalad minia"**
Nyawarra

Wenn man also jemanden begrüßt
freundlich, jemanden den man gut kennt
wenn zum Beispiel eine Frau auf einen zukommt
dann sagt man wahrscheinlich
"yamalad minia"
und sie antwortet **"yamalad minia"**

Und wir sagen **"guru.amalad minia"**
Ich begrüße alle
damit begrüßen wir alle,
die Frauen, die Kinder, die Männer
das bedeutet **"guru.amalad minia"**
Nyawarra

Quand vous saluez quelqu'un
que vous êtes amical avec quelqu'un
que vous connaissez
vous verrez peut-être une femme venir vers vous
vous lui direz sans doute « **yamalad minia** »
et elle vous dira « **yamalad minia** »

Et nous disons « **guru.amalad minia** »
« bonjour à tout le monde », bonjour à tous
les femmes, les enfants, les hommes
voilà, c'est ce ça que veut dire
« **guru.amalad minia** »
Nyawarra

This book was initiated at the suggestion of four **Ngarinyin** elders and men of law **(munnumburra)**; **Ngarjno, Banggal, Ungudman** and **Nyawarra.**

The narrative and photographic material was recorded and produced under their direction to present their own **junjun,** evidence of their history and culture. To appreciate the context and their motive, we cannot ignore the tragic results of colonisation experienced by the people who inform us in this book.The Kimberley region of the continent was the most remote from the first British colony on the eastern coast more than 3000 kilometres away. Fortunately for the **Ngarinyin,** their distance from advancing prospectors and pastoralists meant that they were one of the last groups of indigenous Australians to be invaded by force. By the time of the First World War, as the old world order was falling apart in Europe, the **Ngarinyin** way of life had come under attack. It was a tragic confrontation of spear against rifle. The invasion of a century ago produced a social upheaval disrupting the dynamic stability of what is now recognised as the most durable of cultures. They were violently subjugated by foreigners with no knowledge of their land or its all-embracing laws, the **Wunan.**

The expanding land-grab of the cattle industry was encouraged by governments that dispatched mounted police to help the few pastoralists remove numerous indigenous people from the vast areas of the Kimberley. Newspapers portrayed the mounted police as heroes, whereas the **Ngarinyin,** fighting back on foot, were described as traitors by the new "nation-builders"; thus were sown seeds of urban prejudice and ignorance that still plague the young nation. **Ngarinyin** resistance was widespread but, ultimately, futile against bullets. The "wild red men" of the Kimberley were made famous by reports of their athletic elusiveness, but these "treacherous renegades" were gaoled for defending their country, and many died from the trauma of being imprisoned. Virtually all the **Ngarinyin** and their neighbours were rounded up at gunpoint and marched in chains to the coast.

The remoteness of the Kimberley ensured many racially motivated murders went unreported until the infamous Forrest River massacre of 1926 prompted enough public outcry to restrain the more blatant frontier violence. Survivors of the initial invasion were then expected to work as virtual slaves for the new "kings in grass castles", or they would be "civilised" in the Christian missions being established on the coast. No rural industry in the region would have developed without the sweat of cheap labour: stockmen and ringers like Paddy Neowarra **(Nyawarra)** and Paddy Wamma **(Ungudman),** and wharf-labourers like Laurie Gawanali **(Ngarjno).** A refugee child born under a coastal mission tree was the late David Mowaljarlai **(Banggal),** whose father was **Ngarinyin** from inland and mother **Wororra** from the coast. Although both these language groups intermarried, he was a member of the first generation growing up away from his father's traditional **dambun** family estate. Like many deported **Ngarinyin,** he ignored the pastoralists' fences, travelling widely across the Kimberley to maintain his cultural commitments to both his parents' country.

Die Anregung zu diesem Buch kam von vier **Ngarinyin**-Ältesten und Hütern des Gesetzes **(munnumburra):** **Ngarjno, Banggal, Ungudman** und **Nyawarra.**

Die Texte und Fotografien entstanden unter ihrer Anleitung und dokumentieren ihre **junjun,** die sichtbaren Zeugnisse ihrer Geschichte und Kultur. Wenn man das Umfeld und ihre Motive verstehen will, darf man die tragischen Folgen der Kolonisation nicht außer Acht lassen, denn sie haben die Menschen, die sich in diesem Buch vorstellen, geprägt. Die Kimberley-Region lag weitab von der ersten britischen Kolonie an der Ostküste, mehr als 3000 Kilometer. Ein Glück für die **Ngarinyin,** denn dank ihrer großen Entfernung von den immer weiter vordringenden Landvermessern und Viehzüchtern waren sie eine der letzten Gruppen australischer Ureinwohner, die mit Gewalt unterworfen wurden. Zu Beginn des 20. Jahr-hunderts und in der Zeit des Ersten Weltkriegs, als in Europa die alte Weltordnung zugrunde ging, geriet auch die traditionelle Lebensweise der **Ngarinyin** unter Beschuss. Es war ein tragischer Kampf, mit Speeren gegen Gewehre. Die nun ein Jahrhundert zurückliegende Invasion führte zu gesellschaftlichen Umwälzungen und zur Zerstörung der dynamischen Stabilität einer Kultur, von der man heute weiß, dass sie eine der beständigsten überhaupt war. Die **Ngarinyin** wurden unterjocht von Fremden, die weder das Land noch sein allumfassendes Gesetz kannten, das **Wunan.**

Australische Regierungen unterstützten den unersättlichen Landhunger der Viehindustrie durch den Einsatz von berittenen Polizisten, die den zahlenmäßig unterlegenen Schafzüchtern bei der Vertreibung der einheimischen Bevölkerung aus den Weiten der Kimberley-Region helfen sollten. Zeitungen feierten die berittenen Polizisten als Helden, die **Ngarinyin** hingegen, die sich zu Fuß gegen die Angriffe zur Wehr setzten, wurden von den neuen „Baumeistern der Nation" als Verräter diffamiert. Damals säten die Siedler die Saat der Vorurteile und der Unwissenheit, unter der die junge Nation bis heute leidet. Die **Ngarinyin** leisteten erbitterten Widerstand, konnten aber auf Dauer gegen die Gewehre nichts ausrichten. Die „wilden roten Männer" der Kimberley-Region waren berühmt dafür, dass sie schwer zu fassen waren, aber man steckte sie als „treulose Verräter" ins Gefängnis, weil sie ihr Land verteidigten. Viele von ihnen überlebten die traumatische Erfahrung der Haft nicht. Fast die gesamten **Ngarinyin** und ihre Nachbarn wurden mit Waffengewalt zusammengetrieben und in Ketten an die Küste verschleppt.

Da die Kimberley-Region so abgelegen war, blieben viele rassistisch motivierte Morde ungesühnt, und erst 1926 sorgte das berüchtigte Massaker am Forrest River für so viel Empörung in der Öffentlichkeit, dass die schlimmsten Gewaltexzesse der Kolonisten fortan unterbunden wurden. Die Überlebenden der ersten Invasion mussten Sklavenarbeit für die neuen „Könige in ihren Schlössern aus Gras" leisten, oder sie wurden in den neu errichteten christlichen Missionsstationen an der Küste „zivilisiert". Ohne den Schweiß dieser billigen Arbeitskräfte, von Viehtreibern und Schafscherern wie Paddy Neowarra **(Nyawarra),** Paddy Wamma **(Ungudman)** und von Werftarbeitern wie Laurie Gawanali **(Ngarjno)** hätte sich die Wirtschaft dieser ländlichen Region nicht entwickeln können. Der mittlerweile verstorbene David Mowaljarlai **(Banggal)** war ein Flüchtlingskind, das unter einem Baum in einer Missionsstation an der Küste das Licht der Welt erblickte. Sein Vater war ein **Ngarinyin** aus dem Landesinneren, seine Mutter eine **Wororra** von der Küste. Heiraten zwischen diesen beiden Sprachgruppen waren nicht selten, doch er gehörte zur ersten Generation, die fernab vom traditionellen Stammesland **(dambun)** seines Vaters aufwuchs. Wie viele andere verschleppte **Ngarinyin** missachtete auch er die Zäune der Viehzüchter und wanderte kreuz und quer durch die Kimberley-Region, um seinen rituellen Verpflichtungen gegenüber dem Land beider Elternteile nachzukommen.

Ce livre a pris naissance à la suggestion de quatre Anciens **Ngarinyin** et gardiens de la Loi **(munnumburra)**: **Ngarjno, Banggal, Ungudman** et **Nyawarra.**

Les dialogues et les photographies recueillis sont publiés sous leur direction afin de présenter leur propre **junjun,** c'est-à-dire le témoignage de leur histoire et leur culture. Pour apprécier à sa juste valeur le contexte et leur motivation nous devons prendre en compte les effets tragiques de la colonisation sur ceux qui nous ont informé pour ce livre. Située à plus de 3000 km, la région du Kimberley était la plus éloignée de la première colonie britannique de la côte est. Par chance pour les **Ngarinyin,** leur éloignement des prospecteurs et éleveurs qui avançaient dans le territoire leur a permis d'être un des derniers groupes indigènes d'Australie envahi par la force. C'est seulement au début du siècle, au moment de la Première Guerre mondiale, lorsque le vieil ordre du monde se désagrégeait en Europe, que le mode de vie **Ngarinyin** fut mis en péril. Ce fut une tragique confrontation entre la lance et le fusil. L'invasion, vieille d'un siècle, a produit un bouleversement social qui a perturbé l'équilibre de ce qui est aujourd'hui reconnu comme la plus ancienne et la plus stable des cultures. Les **Ngarinyin** furent violemment assujettis par des étrangers qui n'avaient aucune idée de ce qu'étaient leur rapport à la terre et leurs lois: les **Wunan.**

La mainmise croissante de l'industrie du bétail sur les terres a été encouragée par les différents gouvernements, qui envoyaient la police montée pour aider quelques éleveurs à chasser de nombreux groupes indigènes des vastes étendues des Kimberley. Les journaux présentaient en héros les policiers montés alors que les **Ngarinyin** se défendant à pied étaient perçus comme des traîtres par les « fondateurs » de la nouvelle nation: ainsi furent semées les graines du racisme urbain et de l'ignorance qui minent encore ce jeune pays. La résistance **Ngarinyin** a été générale mais finalement vaine contre les balles. Les « sauvages hommes rouges » du Kimberley acquièrent la réputation d'être maîtres dans l'art de l'insaisissabilité mais ces « éléments incontrôlables » étaient emprisonnés pour avoir défendu leur terre, et beaucoup moururent du traumatisme de l'enfermement. Pratiquement tous les **Ngarinyin** et leurs voisins furent raflés sous la menace des armes et durent marcher enchaînés vers la côte.

L'isolement des Kimberley a permis à de nombreux crimes racistes de ne pas être signalés jusqu'à ce que l'abominable massacre de Forrest River, en 1926, provoque assez d'indignation publique pour atténuer la violence la plus criante. Les survivants de cette invasion initiale furent tenus de travailler virtuellement comme des esclaves pour les nouveaux « rois dans leurs châteaux d'herbe » ou bien furent « civilisés » dans des missions chrétiennes établies sur la côte. Aucune industrie rurale n'aurait pu se développer sans le labeur pénible de cette main d'œuvre bon marché que furent les bouviers et tondeurs de moutons comme Paddy Neowarra **(Nyawarra)** et les travailleurs aux entrepôts maritimes comme Laurie Gawanali **(Ngarjno).** David Mowaljarlai **(Banggal),** aujourd'hui décédé, était un enfant réfugié né sous un arbre d'une mission côtière; son père était un **Ngarinyin** de l'intérieur et sa mère une **Wororra** de la côte. Bien que ces deux groupes linguistiques se mariaient entre eux, **Banggal** a appartenu à la première génération qui a grandi loin des **dambun** (terres familiales) du côté paternel. Comme beaucoup de **Ngarinyin** déportés, il n'a pas tenu compte des clôtures des éleveurs de bétail et a beaucoup voyagé dans les Kimberley pour entretenir ses obligations culturelles sur les terres de ses deux parents.

*All Aborigines was shot and mustered up
... the knowledge was taken away*
Banggal

*Alle Aborigines haben sie erschossen
und zusammengetrieben
... ihnen das Wissen geraubt*
Banggal

*Tous les Aborigènes ont été tués et parqués
... tout notre savoir a été emporté*
Banggal

Ngarinyin found that foreign cattle, instead of humans, now drank at sacred waterholes, seriously degrading the very substance humans rely on for survival in this hot land. In a short time, these heavy-footed beasts had destroyed the pockets of rainforest secluded in ravines, and consumed all the stands of native bamboo valuable for manufacturing straight spear-shafts. **Ngarinyin** men and women also have many social responsibilities to maintain around places of permanent water. These include repainting **wanjina** icons to refresh the colour of their image and to renew their intimate spiritual connections with the origin of their ancestors.

Following the visits of the English explorer, James Cook, the British had presumptuously occupied the new continent and systematically denied the rights of its various peoples. During the early chaotic years of foreign settlement, guerrilla warfare had failed to stem the tide of squatters, convicts, sheep and cattle. To bring some order to the pastoral expansion, the new colonies issued generous pastoral leases over much of the continent, thus creating huge private estates that took control of the land. Legislation continued to deny that Aborigines had any civil awareness or system of law. This meant they could neither legally own land themselves nor get a loan from a bank to do so. When **Guringi** stockmen took strike action for equal pay, most were refused re-employment. As other pastoralists refused to pay them equal wages, many Aboriginal families were forced from the country where they had worked with little reward apart from the opportunity to visit significant cultural places. Injustices suffered by Aboriginal Australians have been progressively addressed by de jure measures, but they still experience de facto discrimination in many ways.

Australian Aboriginal painting on canvas is now established as a profitable element of the world art market. Aboriginal cultures are romanticised as examples of ancient "wisdom" but the colonial mind had no place for people labelled as "missing links" in human evolution. Popular accounts once arrogantly dismissed such cultures as without intelligence and their art as "primitive"; they were "living specimens" of the Palaeolithic past. Demand for physical remains for study in the museums of the world resulted in a gruesome trade in flesh and bones. While their knowledge supported some early anthropological careers, **Ngarinyin** informants of outsiders working in the Kimberley gained few benefits to assist their survival. Until researchers became more respectful, and began to work with local experts as equals, the patronising cultural bias was hardly challenged. After a century of disruption – from warfare and introduced diseases to alcohol, amid great social turmoil and in the face of the accelerating intervention of mining and tourism – acculturation still poses significant challenges to traditional values. But nothing has been able to crush the morale of the **munnumburra** or erase their faith in the ethics of their **Wunan** law and cultural beliefs.

Die **Ngarinyin** mussten mit ansehen, wie anstelle von Menschen nun fremdes Vieh aus den heiligen Wasserlöchern trank und damit ausgerechnet das Element verdorben wurde, ohne das die Menschen in diesem heißen Land nicht überleben können. Binnen kurzem hatten diese Tiere mit ihren Hufen die kleinen, verborgenen Regenwaldinseln in den Felsschluchten zertrampelt und den einheimischen Bambus abgefressen, der für die Herstellung von geraden Speerschäften von so großer Bedeutung war. Zudem haben die Männer und Frauen der **Ngarinyin** eine Reihe von Pflichten an diesen permanenten Wasserstellen zu erfüllen. Dazu gehört das Erneuern der **wanjina**-Bilder, damit die Farben immer frisch sind und die enge spirituelle Verbindung zum Ursprung ihrer Ahnen gewahrt bleibt.

Nach den Erkundungsreisen des englischen Entdeckers James Cook hatten die Briten den neuen Kontinent skrupellos in Besitz genommen und die Einheimischen systematisch ihrer Rechte beraubt. In diesen frühen, wirren Jahren der Kolonisation war es den Aborigines nicht gelungen, der Flut der Siedler, Sträflinge, Schafe und Rinder durch ihre Guerillataktik Einhalt zu gebieten. Um eine gewisse Ordnung in die Landnahme der Viehzüchter zu bringen, gewährte die neue Kolonie günstige Pachtverträge für große Teile des Kontinents, damit das Land in die Hände von Großgrundbesitzern kam. Die Gesetzgebungsorgane leugneten hartnäckig, dass die Aborigines etwas wie staatsbürgerliches Bewusstsein oder ein Rechtssystem hätten. Die Folge war, dass sie weder selbst Land besitzen noch einen Kredit bei einer Bank aufnehmen konnten, um Land zu erwerben. Als die Viehtreiber von **Guringi** in Streik traten und gleiche Bezahlung verlangten, verloren die meisten von ihnen ihre Arbeit. Da andere Viehzüchter sich ebenfalls weigerten, ihnen gleichen Lohn zu zahlen, mussten viele Aborigine-Familien das Land verlassen, wo sie für ihre Arbeit nicht viel mehr bekommen hatten als die Möglichkeit, ihre heiligen Orte zu besuchen. Im Laufe der Jahre sind viele Missstände de jure abgestellt worden, aber de facto sind die Aborigines nach wie vor Opfer einer Vielzahl von Diskriminierungen.

Aborigine-Malereien auf Leinwand lassen sich mittlerweile auf dem internationalen Kunstmarkt mit gutem Profit verkaufen. Die Kultur der Aborigines wird romantisch verklärt und gilt als Beispiel für uralte „Weisheit", aber im Denken der Kolonisten war kein Platz für Menschen, die man als „Vorstufen" der menschlichen Evolution ansah. Populäre Berichte bescheinigten solchen Kulturen damals einen Mangel an Intelligenz und bezeichneten ihre Kunst als „primitiv"; sie galten als lebende Relikte einer steinzeitlichen Kultur. Die rege Nachfrage nach menschlichen Überresten als Studienmaterial für Museen in aller Welt führte zu einem grausigen Handel mit Körpern und Knochen. Obwohl so mancher frühe Anthropologe seine Karriere ihrem Wissen verdankte, hatten die **Ngarinyin**, die fremden Forschern in der Kimberley-Region Informationen lieferten, nur wenig Nutzen davon für ihr eigenes Überleben. Heute zeigen Wissenschaftler mehr Respekt und behandeln die einheimischen Fachleute als gleichberechtigte Partner, doch über lange Zeit wurde die weiße Voreingenommenheit und die damit einhergehende soziale Ungleichheit nur selten in Frage gestellt. Nach einem Jahrhundert der Zerrüttung – durch Kriege und eingeschleppte Krankheiten ebenso wie durch Alkohol, begleitet von tief greifenden sozialen Umwälzungen und angesichts der immer rascheren Zerstörung durch Bergbau und Tourismus – ist die Eingliederung der Aborigines in die westlich geprägte australische Gesellschaft noch immer eine große Herausforderung an die überlieferten Werte. Aber die Moral der **munnumburra** ist ebenso ungebrochen wie ihr Glaube an die Grundsätze des **Wunan** und ihre überlieferte Kultur.

Les **Ngarinyin** découvrirent que le bétail importé s'était mis à boire aux points d'eau sacrés à la place des hommes, dégradant ainsi sérieusement l'élément essentiel sur lequel les hommes peuvent compter pour leur survie sur cette terre brûlante. En peu de temps, ces bêtes aux lourds sabots détruisirent les poches de forêt tropicale abritées dans les ravins et consommèrent tous les bosquets d'un bambou indigène précieux pour la fabrication des manches de lance. Les hommes et les femmes **Ngarinyin** ont beaucoup d'obligations sociales à remplir près des points d'eau permanents. Cela inclut entre autres le fait de repeindre les peintures **wanjina,** pour en rafraîchir les couleurs mais aussi pour renouveler leurs attaches spirituelles profondes avec l'origine de leurs ancêtres.

Après les visites de l'explorateur anglais James Cook, les Britanniques ont occupé le nouveau continent en niant systématiquement les droits des différentes populations qui l'occupaient. Pendant les premières années chaotiques de la colonisation, la guérilla n'a pas réussi à endiguer le flot de squatters, de bagnards, de moutons, de bétail … Pour mettre un peu d'ordre dans l'expansion pastorale, les nouvelles colonies ont émis de vastes baux fonciers sur presque tout le continent, créant ainsi d'énormes propriétés privées qui prirent le contrôle de la terre. La législation continua à nier le fait que les Aborigènes aient une quelconque conscience civique ou un système juridique. Cela voulait dire qu'ils ne pouvaient légalement ni posséder de terres ni obtenir un prêt bancaire pour en acquérir. Quand les bouviers de **Guringi** firent grève pour obtenir une paie égale aux Blancs, la plupart se virent refuser le réemploi. Comme les autres éleveurs de bétail ne voulaient pas leur payer des salaires égaux, beaucoup de familles aborigènes furent refoulées hors des régions où ils avaient travaillé pour bien peu de récompense hors celle d'avoir la possibilité de se rendre sur leurs sites culturels importants. Les injustices subies par les Aborigènes australiens n'ont été que progressivement corrigées par des mesures légales mais ils subissent encore une discrimination dans de nombreux domaines.

L'art aborigène sur toile est aujourd'hui rémunérateur sur le marché de l'art international et on a une vision romantique des cultures aborigènes, maintenant présentées comme exemplaires d'une ancienne « sagesse », alors qu'il n'y avait aucune place dans l'esprit colonial pour ces peuples considérés comme le « chaînon manquant » de l'évolution humaine. Les récits populaires des Européens niaient sans vergogne leur intelligence, décrivant leur art comme « primitif » et parlant d'eux comme de spécimens d'un âge paléolithique disparu. Pour les étudier, des musées du monde entier demandèrent des échantillons humains, ce qui eut pour résultat un macabre trafic de chair et d'os. Alors que leurs connaissances aidaient la carrière de certains des premiers anthropologues, les informateurs **Ngarinyin** travaillant dans le Kimberley recevaient en retour peu d'avantages contribuant à leur survie. Jusqu'à ce que les chercheurs deviennent plus respectueux et travaillent avec ces experts locaux sur une base égalitaire et les traitent comme leurs contemporains, peu de choses mirent en doute la valeur du paternalisme culturel et social. Après un siècle de troubles dus à la guerre, aux maladies importées par les colons et à l'alcool, au cœur d'un terrible marasme social et confrontés à l'expansion de l'industrie minière et du tourisme, l'acculturation est encore un défi majeur aux valeurs traditionnelles. Mais rien n'a pu détruire la confiance en eux des **munnumburra** ou atténuer leur foi dans l'éthique de leur loi **Wunan** et de leurs croyances culturelles.

Charcoal there today from that time
I don't know what date that was
when Aborigine was mustered away
from their country
They still here... we still see them today

this **wanjina**
He's happy when he see people
long side him all the time
and he's sad when nobody round here
and that's very very shame
Banggal

Holzkohle ist heute da, von damals her
ich weiß nicht, wann das war
als sie die Aborigines verschleppt haben
aus ihrem Land
Sie sind noch da ... wir sehen sie heute noch

dieser **wanjina**
Der ist glücklich, wenn er Leute sieht
er will sie immer um sich haben
er ist traurig wenn niemand da ist
und das ist wirklich eine Schande eine Schande
Banggal

Ce charbon est là depuis ce moment
je ne sais pas quelle date c'était
quand les Aborigènes ont été parqués
loin de leur pays
Mais il est toujours ici ...
on le voit encore aujourd'hui

ce **wanjina**
il est heureux quand il voit des gens
près de lui tout le temps
mais il est triste quand il y a personne par ici
et ça vraiment... vraiment c'est une honte
Banggal

During the violence of invasion many senior women were spared because it was wrongly presumed they were sub-servient and without authority. Old men were targeted for murder because of their obvious status and influence in **Ngarinyin** society. It is a great irony that many men had their wrists and ankles slashed so that they would have to crawl on all fours and slowly bleed to death. Blood on the earth is sacred evidence in Aboriginal law.

Guli (blood) is the living proof of ancestors. Blood and name connect past and present across generations; they are the universal bonds between parent and child, and between the sexes. Family heritage and personal identity are defined through knowledge of both maternal and paternal land, so that, to claim his heritage, a young man must know exactly where his father was initiated with blood. When confirming his shift from adolescence to manhood with circumcision, a new man's blood is given to the soil with solemn reverence as a sacred act of belonging to that land. Signal stones mark the very place where each is bled for the first time as a man. Youthful blood given to the land indelibly marks each individual's belonging to their own family, place and name. Adult men must continue to put their blood into the earth and onto each other as part of a graduated series of secret rituals of the **Wunan.** As a custodian of the law, **Banggal** declared:

> *Spills his blood on the earth... on earth*
> *to look after the whole country*
> *That is the **munnumburra** – lawman*
> *because he the elder he's a **munnumburra***
> *he already spilled his blood on the earth*
>
> ***mamaa**... name mean holy place*
> *like it's a blood place that's why it's **mamaa***
> *blood is there covered up*
> *and that blood is there forever*
> Banggal

The near genocide of the **Ngarinyin** occurred during living memory and some elders narrate a modern history from personal experience. Survivors recall that the new settlers manacled men with donkey chain, then crushed their skulls with blows from branding irons to save precious bullets. In recollecting his experiences of those cruel times, **Ngarjno** remembers being chained and beaten beside a friend who later died of his stomach wounds. He denied feeling pain as his back was chain-whipped except whenever the length of chain came flicking over his shoulder to catch the tip of his cheekbone, because "that did hurt". But **Ngarjno** has refused to succumb to hatred and revenge, insisting that such tragic accounts "belong to the **gadiya** (white men)" and should not displace traditional stories or dissip-ate their value for everyone.

Bei aller Brutalität der Invasion wurden viele alte Frauen verschont, weil die europäischen Siedler fälschlich davon ausgingen, dass sie von untergeordneter Bedeutung waren und keinerlei Autorität besaßen. Im Gegensatz dazu waren alte Männer wegen ihres offensichtlichen Rangs und Ein-flusses in der Gesellschaft der **Ngarinyin** bevorzugte Mord-opfer. Es ist eine große Ironie, dass die Mörder vielen Männern die Pulsadern aufschnitten und die Sehnen an den Fußgelenken durchtrennten, so dass sie auf allen vieren kriechen mussten und langsam verbluteten. Blut, das auf die Erde fließt, ist nach dem Gesetz der Aborigines heilig.

Guli (Blut) ist der lebende Beweis für die Existenz der Ahnen. Blut und Name verbinden Vergangenheit und Gegenwart über die Generationen hinweg; sie sind die universellen Bindeglieder zwischen Eltern und Kindern und zwischen den Geschlechtern. Das Erbe der Familie und die Identität des Individuums erwachsen aus dem Wissen um das Land von Mutter und Vater, und wenn er sein Erbe antritt, muss ein junger Mann daher genau wissen, wo das Blut seines Vaters bei der Initiation geflossen ist. Wenn durch die Be-schneidung besiegelt wird, dass ein Junge zum Mann ge-worden ist, schenkt dieser neugeborene Mann sein Blut in einem feierlichen Akt der Erde – ein Sinnbild dafür, dass er fortan zu diesem Land gehört. Gedenksteine markieren den genauen Ort, an dem ein Mann sein erstes Blutopfer als Erwachsener dargebracht hat. Durch das Blut, das der junge Mann dem Land gibt, setzt er ein unauslöschliches Zeichen der Zugehörigkeit zu seiner Familie, seinem Land und seinem Namen. Erwachsene Männer müssen der Erde und einander auch weiterhin Blutopfer bringen; das ist Teil einer Stufenfolge von geheimen, durch das **Wunan** vorgeschriebenen Ritualen. Dazu erklärte der Gesetzeshüter **Banggal:**

> *Er lässt sein Blut auf die Erde fließen... auf die Erde*
> *so sorgt er für das ganze Land*
> *Das ist der **munnumburra** – der Hüter des Gesetzes*
> *weil er ein Ältester ist, ist er ein **munnumburra***
> *er hat sein Blut schon auf die Erde fließen lassen*
>
> ***mamaa**... heiliger Ort heißt das*
> *weil es ein Ort des Blutes ist, deswegen ist es **mamaa***
> *Blut ist da in der Erde*
> *und das Blut bleibt für immer da*
> Banggal

Die Geschichte der nahezu vollständigen Ausrottung der **Ngarinyin** ist noch in lebendiger Erinnerung, und manche Ältesten kennen die Ereignisse aus eigener Erfahrung. Über-lebende wissen noch, wie die neuen Siedler die Männer mit Eselsketten fesselten und ihnen mit Brandeisen den Schädel einschlugen, weil sie keine wertvollen Kugeln ver-geuden wollten. Wenn er an seine Erlebnisse in diesen grausamen Zeiten zurückdenkt, dann erzählt **Ngarjno,** wie er an der Seite eines Freundes, der später seinen inneren Verletzungen erlag, angekettet und geschlagen wurde. Er sagt, er habe keinen Schmerz gespürt, als man seinen Rücken mit einer Kette auspeitschte; nur wenn das Ketten-ende ihm über die Schulter schlug und seine Wangen-knochen traf, habe es „wirklich wehgetan". Aber **Ngarjno** lässt es nicht zu, dass Hass und Rachegefühle ihn über-wältigen; für ihn steht fest, dass solche Erinnerungen „den **gadiya** (den Weißen) gehören" und die traditionellen Geschichten nicht verdrängen, die für alle gelten.

Lors des violences de l'invasion, beaucoup des aînées parmi les femmes **Ngarinyin** furent épargnées car on pensait à tort qu'elles étaient des subordonnées et n'avaient aucune autorité. En revanche, les anciens étaient les principales cibles des meurtriers à cause de leur statut évident et de leur influence dans la société **Ngarinyin.** Quelle ironie du sort de savoir que tant d'hommes eurent leurs poignets et chevilles tailladés, obligés de ramper à quatre pattes jusqu'à ce qu'ils soient saignés à mort, quand on sait que le sang répandu sur le sol est une preuve sacrée dans la loi aborigène.

Guli (le sang) est une preuve vivante des ancêtres. Le sang et le nom sont le fil conducteur entre les générations et constituent les liens absolus entre parent et enfant et entre les deux sexes. L'héritage familial et l'identité personnelle sont définis par la connaissance de la terre maternelle et paternelle de telle sorte que, pour pouvoir affirmer son héritage spirituel, un jeune homme doit savoir exactement où le sang versé à l'initiation de son père a été caché. Quand on confirme le passage de l'adolescence à l'âge adulte par la circoncision, du sang du « nouvel » homme est donné à la terre solennellement en tant qu'acte sacré marquant l'appartenance à celle-ci. Des pierres indiquent l'endroit précis où chacun a versé son sang pour la première fois en tant qu'homme. Le sang des jeunes donné à la terre marque de façon indélébile l'appartenance de chaque individu à sa famille, à son territoire et à son nom. Les hommes adultes doivent continuer à déposer leur sang sur la terre et sur eux mutuellement, cela fait partie des rituels secrets et gradués des lois **Wunan. Banggal,** lui-même gardien de la Loi, déclare :

> *Il a fait couler son sang sur le sol... sur la terre*
> *ça veut dire qu'il est responsable de tout le pays*
> *C'est le **munnumburra**... le gardien de la Loi*
> *parce que lui cet Ancien, un **munnumburra***
> *il a déjà fait couler son sang sur la terre*
>
> ***mamaa**... ce nom-là c'est « endroit sacré »*
> *c'est un endroit où on a fait couler du sang*
> *c'est pourquoi c'est **mamaa***
> *y a du sang ici qui est recouvert*
> *et ce sang est là pour toujours*
> Banggal

Du génocide presque total des **Ngarinyin** il reste encore des témoins vivants et certains anciens relatent une histoire moderne à travers leur expérience personnelle. Des survivants se souviennent que les nouveaux colons menottaient les hommes avec des chaînes pour les ânes et qu'ils leur écrasaient le crâne à coups de barre de fer pour économiser des balles. Se remémorant les expé-riences qu'il a vécues en ces temps cruels, **Ngarjno** se sou-vient d'avoir été enchaîné et battu à côté d'un ami qui mourut plus tard de ses blessures à l'estomac. Il a fait comme s'il ne sentait pas la douleur lorsqu'il a été frappé à coups de chaîne, sauf lorsque le bout passant au-dessus de ses épaules lui cognait la mâchoire parce que « ça fai-sait mal ». Malgré tout, **Ngarjno** a refusé de céder à la haine et à l'esprit de vengeance et insiste sur le fait que de telles histoires tragiques « appartiennent aux **gadiya** (hommes blancs) » et ne doivent pas occulter les récits traditionnels et atténuer leur valeur pour tout le monde.

That colour will change
when you just looking at it in the cave
when you are sitting quiet
you see his face will change
When you looking very hard
you see it get brighter... he really happy
Nyawarra

Die Farbe verändert sich
je nachdem, ob man es nur kurz in der Höhle
ansieht
oder ob man in Ruhe davor sitzt
sieht man, wie sich sein Gesicht verändert
Und wenn man ganz genau hinsieht
kann man sehen, wie es strahlt...
so glücklich ist er dann
Nyawarra

Sa couleur va changer
quand tu le regardes dans cette grotte
en étant assis tranquillement
tu vas voir son visage va changer
Quand tu regardes fixement
tu vas voir il va s'éclaircir...
c'est qu'il est content
Nyawarra

Government policy of forced adoptions of Aboriginal children continued until recently with disastrous emotional and social results. This patronising form of genocide was belatedly exposed in *The Stolen Generation*, a landmark report of 1997. Despite mourning the death of many relatives in distant towns, the **Ngarinyin** have been determined to repatriate all dispossessed land and build new communities in their tribal homelands. **Munnumburra** have pursued Native Title claims for many years as senior members of the **Kamali Land Council** ("Native Title" describes the interests and rights in common law "of indigenous inhabitants in land, whether communal, group or individual, possessed under the traditional laws acknowledged by and the traditional customs observed by the indigenous inhabitants"). Colonial ignorance persists with the presumption that all indigenous Australians were once nomads wandering around constantly searching for food, without laws of land tenure or any concept of sovereignty. To make Native Title claims, the **Ngarinyin** had to prove that they are truly "natives" and that their land is under law.

Munnumburra may not change any detail of law; they must faithfully reproduce the ancient regional boundaries created by their ancestors to demarcate **dambun** (family regional land). They are compelled by tradition to follow the original family titles over land mutually as agreed by the **Kamali Gwion** when they ceased to be nomadic thousands of years ago. After a century of struggle to repatriate their homelands, they remain frustrated by external influences, a succession of remote courts, governments, and tribunals, but most perplexing are constantly changing laws. The response of **Nyawarra,** the current Chairman of the **Kamali Land Council,** is firm:

It very important to protect this land
so we want that land back to us
so we can protect it and talk about it
and show the other people say like Europeans
can understand our ways... what we think
and how this thing was written in Australia
this is our evidence so we giving this to them
this junjun evidence
so everybody can understand
about this land business

Well people don't believe it
say like Europeans don't believe
most of the time they say "no evidence"
well that's our evidence
that's how it is... this is our law
so we try and protect it in our land
that's our real title

And all the tribal people thats their title too
whether it's Wunambul... Wororra... Ngarinyin
this is our title... the way it was written
Everything was written in this painting thing here
that's how it was written...
and it stays that way we can't change it

Well we have to protect it somehow
we don't know what sort of law we got
We got European law coming in
we got Aborigine law standing there
We don't know which law we gonna stay on
But I wish... I think...
it should be the Aboriginal law in this ground

and stay with that law
It started from the beginning... until the end
Nyawarra

Die Praxis der Zwangsadoption von Aborigine-Kindern blieb bis in die jüngste Vergangenheit in Kraft und hatte katastrophale emotionale und soziale Folgen. Diese arrogante Variante des Völkermords wurde mit großer Verspätung erst 1997 in dem Aufsehen erregenden Bericht *The Stolen Generation* („Die gestohlene Generation") angeprangert. Trotz des Todes vieler Verwandter in den fernen Städten, sind die **Ngarinyin** nach wie vor entschlossen, das geraubte Land zurückzugewinnen und in ihrem ursprünglichen Stammesgebiet neue Gemeinschaften aufzubauen. Die **munnumburra** sind seit Jahren Mitglieder des **Kamali Land Council** und setzen sich dort für die Native Title ein. Der Begriff Native Title bezeichnet die Ansprüche, die die Aborigines nach den Grundsätzen des Gewohnheitsrechts auf das Land haben, und zwar „als Gemeinschaft, Gruppe oder Individuum, auf der Grundlage traditioneller Gesetze und Gebräuche, die von der indigenen Bevölkerung anerkannt und eingehalten werden". Die falsche Sichtweise der Kolonisten hat sich bis heute in der Vorstellung gehalten, die Ureinwohner Australiens seien ursprünglich Nomaden gewesen, die auf der Suche nach Nahrung ständig umherzogen und weder Gesetze hatten, die den Landbesitz regelten, noch überhaupt eine politische Ordnung kannten. Um ihre Ansprüche auf das Land geltend machen zu können, mussten die **Ngarinyin** nachweisen, dass sie tatsächlich „Ureinwohner" sind und dass in ihrem Land Gesetze existierten.

Die **munnumburra** dürfen das Gesetz in keinem Punkt verändern, sie müssen genau die alten Grenzen beachten, mit denen ihre Ahnen das als **dambun** bezeichnete Land der einzelnen Familien einst abgegrenzt haben. Sie sind verpflichtet, die traditionellen Landansprüche der Familien zu wahren, wie die **Gwion** der **Kamali** sie festlegten, als sie ihr Nomadendasein aufgaben. Nach einem Jahrhundert vergeblichen Kampfes um die Rückgabe ihres Landes sind die Aborigines noch immer Opfer widriger Umstände, weit entfernter Gerichtshöfe und Tribunale, wechselnder Regierungen und werden immer wieder neu in die Irre geführt durch ständige Gesetzesänderungen. **Nyawarra,** derzeit Vorsitzender des **Kamali Land Council,** erklärt mit Nachdruck:

Das ist sehr wichtig, dass wir dieses Land schützen
deshalb wollen wir das Land zurück
damit wir es schützen und davon sprechen können
es anderen zeigen können den Europäern zum Beispiel
damit sie uns verstehen – verstehen wie wir denken
und wie wir in Australien so etwas festgehalten haben
das sind unsere Belege deshalb zeigen wir sie ihnen
unsere junjun damit alle verstehen
wie das mit dem Land geregelt ist

Aber die Leute glauben uns nicht
die Europäer zum Beispiel, die glauben uns nicht
sie sagen immer nur „keine Beweise"
aber das sind doch unsere Beweise
so ist das bei uns … das ist unser Gesetz
das wollen wir in unserem Land schützen
das ist unser Anspruch

Das gilt für alle Stämme sie haben alle Anspruch
ob es Wunambul, Wororra oder Ngarinyin sind
das sind unsere Belege … so wird das bei uns festgehalten
Alles ist hier in diesem Bild aufgezeichnet
so schreiben wir das auf … und das bleibt für immer so
wir können es niemals ändern

Und das müssen wir irgendwie schützen
wir wissen nicht welche Gesetze gelten
Die Europäer wollen uns ihr Gesetz aufzwingen
doch das Gesetz der Aborigines bleibt
Wir wissen nicht an welches Gesetz wir uns halten sollen
Aber ich wünsche mir … ich finde …
es sollte das der Aborigines sein, das Gesetz dieser Erde

diesem Gesetz sollten wir treu sein
es war vom ersten Tag da und wird da sein bis zum letzten
Nyawarra

La politique gouvernementale des adoptions forcées d'enfants aborigènes a continué jusqu'à très récemment, avec des résultats désastreux sur le plan psychologique et social. Cette forme paternaliste de génocide n'a été que tardivement dénoncée dans *The Stolen Generation* (« La génération volée »), un rapport qui constitua un événement marquant en 1997. Bien que rendant un culte aux morts dans des villes éloignées, les **Ngarinyin** sont déterminés à regagner toutes dans les terres d'où ils furent expropriés et à y construire de nouvelles communautés. Depuis des années, les **munnumburra** ont lancé des revendications foncières basées sur leurs « Native Title » en tant que membres doyens du **Kamali Land Council** (le terme Native Title désigne dans le droit civil australien « les intérêts et les droits des indigènes habitants une terre, quelle soit habitée en communauté, en groupe ou individuellement, possédée au titre des lois traditionnelles qui font autorité et des coutumes traditionnelles qu'observent les habitants indigènes »). La négation coloniale persiste et présuppose toujours que tous les Indigènes étaient des nomades errant constamment à la recherche de nourriture, sans loi d'occupation des terres et sans aucun concept de souveraineté. Pour formuler leurs revendications, les **Ngarinyin** durent prouver qu'ils étaient de « vrais indigènes » et que leurs terres étaient soumises à une loi.

Les **munnumburra** ne peuvent changer aucun détail de la Loi, ils doivent fidèlement suivre les frontières des **dambun** (la terre familiale) créées par leurs ancêtres. Ils sont obligés de suivre les délimitations territoriales telles quelles ont été définies par les **Gwion Kamali** il y a des milliers d'années quand ils ont cessé d'être nomades. Après un siècle de lutte pour être rapatriés, ils restent contrés par des influences extérieures, une avalanche de cours de justice, de gouvernements et tribunaux éloignés, mais le plus déroutant reste les changements constants des lois. **Nyawarra,** président actuel du **Kamali Land Council** est ferme :

Il est vraiment important de protéger ce pays
donc on veut que ce pays nous revienne
comme ça on pourra le protéger et en parler
et montrer aux autres aux Européens par exemple
comment comprendre nos coutumes, ce qu'on pense
et comment tout cela s'est écrite en Australie
c'est notre preuve donc on la leur donne
à eux la preuve, c'est junjun
comme ça tout le monde peut comprendre
l'histoire de ce pays

Mais les gens ils nous croient pas
les Européens par exemple ils nous croient pas
la plupart du temps ils disent « pas de preuves »
eh bien c'est ça nos preuves
c'est comme ça … c'est notre Loi
donc on essaie de la protéger dans notre pays
c'est notre vrai titre de propriété

Et pour tous les gens des tribus comme nous
c'est pareil c'est leur titre aussi
que ce soit les Wunambul les Wororra les Ngarinyin
c'est notre titre de propriété …
la manière dont ça s'est fait
Tout était écrit dans ces choses peintes
c'est comme ça que s'était écrit
et ça reste comme ça, on ne peut pas le changer

Il faut bien qu'on se protège
on ne sait pas ce qu'on a comme loi
On a la loi européenne qui est arrivée
on a la loi aborigène qui est là
On ne sait pas quelle loi on doit suivre
Mais j'espère … je pense que ça doit être
la loi aborigène sur cette terre

et on doit garder cette loi elle était là tout au début …
elle sera là jusqu'à la fin
Nyawarra

Galeru.ngarri joi iri…
Galeru.ngarri my tribe name
Ngin daligunda Nyawarra…
I this one Nyawarra

When they say "Native Title"
whose native titles they talking about?
We are the natives…
this law been given to us
Wunan… It stays that way
we can't change to another way of thinking

Galeru.ngarri joi iri…
Galeru.ngarri, so heißt mein Stamm
Ngin daligunda Nyawarra…
Das bin ich, Nyawarra

Wenn sie von „Native Title" reden
wessen Rechte meinen sie dann?
Die Einheimischen sind wir…
das ist unser Gesetz
Wunan… Es bleibt wie es ist
wir können nicht plötzlich anders denken

Galeru.ngarri joi iri…
Galeru.ngarri – le nom de ma tribu
Ngin daligunda Nyawarra…
je suis celui-là, Nyawarra

Quand ils disent « Native Title »
ils parlent de quels titres indigènes?
C'est nous les indigènes…
cette Loi nous a été donnée
le Wunan… il reste comme ça, on peut pas
le changer pour une autre manière de penser

Nyawarra

The **Wunan** is a set of prescriptive and proscriptive rules of civilised behaviour controlling land and marriage. **Wunan** is the most prized possession of a **Ngarinyin** adult in a hostile world. For people so long denied their inheritance, there is a strong value in the civil process of belonging to **Wunan**. **Wunan** functions as received law rather than as an imposed statute. Described by **munnumburra** as a **lulwa** (gift), the receiving of law as knowledge has a subtle but profound honour attached that sustains dignity and morale. Because **Wunan** laws create social bonds between people and land by the invocation of ancestral connections, cultural networks have endured despite invasion, dispossession and assimilation. **Ngarinyin** people are resilient and will accommodate change, but **Wunan** law never changes.

Native Title rights were barely understood by the general public until the 1992 High Court of Australia decision in the seminal "**Mabo** case". While the **Kamali Land Council** applied to the new Native Title Tribunal, the 1996 High Court decision of the Wik people's claim recognised that Native Title and pastoral leases could co-exist, but that, where dispute arose between the two, the rights of the pastoralist would take precedence. Once again, about a hundred years after the arrival of the **gadiya** in the Kimberley, cattle would come before culture.

Despite difficulties in adapting to the current cash economy, **Ngarinyin munnumburra** have determinedly vitalised a wide range of cultural events to strengthen the role of **Wunan** law in their community. The wider **Ngarinyin** community continues rituals of the **walu.ngarri** (ring-dance) and **wir.nganyen** (circumcision initiations) as recorded at **Marranba.bidi** in 1995.

Munnumburra know that music for the **walu.ngarri** was first composed by **Wiji.ngarri,** whose repertoire of law songs could have the longest provenance of any still sung in the world. Following the archaic tradition of the **walu.ngarri,** first performed at **Wudmangu,** the **Ngarinyin** men began by placing in the middle of a dance-ring a new stone seat for the senior songman. From this central position, **Ngarjno** would lead the performance of the ring-dancers. They danced around him over several days to his tightly controlled performance of the series of **Wunan** songs composed by **Wiji.ngarri.** After it was all over, the new stone seat was left to stand, marking the middle of the sacred ground, and to be remembered with the name **Duduk.ngunga.**

Individual cultural authorship is very encouraged by the **munnumburra**. **Ngarinyin** composers like Scotty Martin, express personal visions in **junba** (staged musical performances). **Junba** are proliferating across the Kimberley, becoming popular with the young, who now climax performances with their own popular music. Perhaps the full identity of an "Indigenous Australian" remains with one whose imagination is born within the bush, who is intimate with the origins of his culture and is always intimate with the life of the land.

Das **Wunan** ist ein Verhaltens- und Verbotsregelwerk zu den Bereichen Land und Heirat. Es ist der wertvollste Besitz des erwachsenen **Ngarinyin** in einer feindlichen Umwelt. Für Menschen, denen man ihr Erbe so lange Zeit vorenthalten hat, ist das Gefühl der gemeinschaftlichen Zugehörigkeit zum **Wunan** von großer Bedeutung. Das **Wunan** enthält allgemein anerkannte Rechtsgrundsätze, keine von einer äußeren Autorität auferlegten Vorschriften. Die **munnumburra** beschreiben es als ein Geschenk (**lulwa**); wer das Wissen über die Gesetze empfängt, dem wird damit eine große Ehre zuteil, die seine Würde und Moral stärkt. Da sich die Gesetze des **Wunan** auf die Ahnen berufen, schaffen sie soziale Bindungen zwischen den Menschen und dem Land, und auf diese Weise konnte die traditionelle Kultur trotz Invasion, Vertreibung und Assimilation fortbestehen. Die **Ngarinyin** sind flexibel und werden sich auch weiterhin veränderten Lebensbedingungen anpassen; die Gesetze des **Wunan** hingegen sind unveränderlich.

Vor der bahnbrechenden **Mabo**-Entscheidung des Obersten Gerichtshofs im Jahr 1992 hatte die australische Öffentlichkeit keine rechte Vorstellung davon, was es mit den Landrechten der Ureinwohner auf sich hatte. Der **Kamali Land Council** machte seine Ansprüche bei dem neu eingerichteten Native Title Tribunal geltend, doch inzwischen war das so genannte Wik-Urteil von 1996 gefallen, in dem der Oberste Gerichtshof gegen die Ansprüche dieses Stammes festlegte, dass sich Landrechte der Aborigines einerseits und Pachtverträge über Weideland andererseits nicht grundsätzlich ausschlössen, sondern durchaus nebeneinander bestehen könnten, dass aber die Rechte der Pächter von Weideland im Streitfall Vorrang haben sollten. Auch 100 Jahre nach dem Auftauchen der **gadiya** in der Kimberley-Region waren Viehherden mehr wert als die Kultur der Aborigines.

Doch nicht einmal von der Macht der herrschenden Wirtschaftsordnung lassen sich die **munnumburra** der **Ngarinyin** beirren: Sie haben ein breites Spektrum von Traditionen wieder aufleben lassen, um die Rolle der **Wunan**-Gesetze in ihrer Gemeinschaft zu stärken. Unbeirrt führen die **Ngarinyin** die Initiationsrituale des Kreistanzes (**walu.ngarri**) und der Beschneidung (**wir.nganyen**) fort, wie die Aufnahmen belegen, die 1995 in **Marranba.bidi** entstanden.

Die **munnumburra** wissen, dass die ursprüngliche Musik für den **walu.ngarri** von **Wiji.ngarri** stammt, und es dürfte auf der ganzen Welt kaum ein heute noch gesungenes Repertoire von Rechtsgesängen geben, dessen Wurzeln weiter in die Vergangenheit zurückreicht. Nach den uralten Regeln des **walu.ngarri,** wie er erstmals in **Wudmangu** getanzt wurde, errichteten die Männer der **Ngarinyin** zunächst in der Mitte des Tanzplatzes einen neuen Steinsitz für den Vorsänger. Von dieser zentralen Position aus dirigierte **Ngarjno** die Tänzer. Sie umtanzten ihn mehrere Tage lang, während er nach genau festgelegten Regeln die von **Wiji.ngarri** komponierten **Wunan**-Lieder vortrug. Als die Zeremonie zu Ende war, blieb der neue Steinsitz zur Erinnerung in der Mitte des heiligen Ortes stehen und erhielt den Namen **Duduk.ngunga.**

Die **munnumburra** sind auch aufgeschlossen gegenüber schöpferischen Weiterentwicklungen der alten Traditionen. So bringen heutige Komponisten der **Ngarinyin** wie Scotty Martin ihre persönlichen Vorstellungen in musikalischen Aufführungen (**junba**) zum Ausdruck. Solche **junba** gibt es in großer Zahl in der Kimberley-Region, und sie erfreuen sich wachsender Beliebtheit bei Jugendlichen, die als Höhepunkt der Aufführungen mittlerweile ihre eigene populäre Musik spielen. Wohl kein Aborigine wird seine Identität als „australischer Ureinwohner" ganz verlieren, so lange seine Vorstellungswelt im Busch verwurzelt ist und er in Verbindung bleibt mit den Ursprüngen seiner Kultur und dem Leben des Landes.

Les **Wunan** sont une série de règles des rapports humains consacrés par la coutume et concernant la terre et le mariage. Les **Wunan** sont le bien le plus précieux pour un **Ngarinyin** adulte dans un monde hostile. Pour ces gens dont on a nié pendant si longtemps l'héritage, il est important, pour le développement personnel, d'appartenir aux **Wunan**. Les **Wunan** fonctionnent comme des lois reçues plutôt qu'imposées. Décrites par les **munnumburra** comme un cadeau (**lulwa**) le fait de recevoir les lois comme un savoir est empreint d'un subtil mais profond honneur qui maintient la dignité et la confiance en soi. Les réseaux culturels sont restés malgré l'invasion, les dépossessions et l'assimilation, car les **Wunan** créent des liens sociaux entre les individus et la terre par l'invocation des liens ancestraux. Les **Ngarinyin** sont résilients et s'accommodent des changements, mais les lois **Wunan** ne changeront jamais.

Les droits inhérents aux Native Title furent peu compris du public jusqu'à l'arrêt de la Haute Cour de justice australienne en 1992 dans un cas sans précédent, le « Mabo case ». Le **Kamali Land Council** s'adressa au nouveau tribunal appliquant le Native Title en 1995, l'année même où la Haute Cour, dans un arrêt concernant la revendication du peuple Wik, admettait que Native Title et droits de propriété pastorale pouvaient coexister mais que, dans le cas d'une contestation, ce serait les droits pastoraux qui auraient le dernier mot. Encore une fois, près de cent ans après l'arrivée des **gadiya** dans le Kimberley, le bétail prime sur la culture.

Malgré les contradictions culturelles de l'ordre économique actuel, les **munnumburra Ngarinyin** ont animé avec détermination de nombreux événements culturels pour renforcer le rôle de la loi **Wunan** dans leur communauté. L'ensemble de la communauté **Ngarinyin** continue à pratiquer les rituels de la danse de l'anneau (**walu.ngarri**) et des cérémonies de circoncisions (**wir.nganyen**) comme cela s'est fait à **Marranba.bidi** en 1995.

Les **munnumburra** savent que la musique du **walu.ngarri** a été composée par **Wiji.ngarri,** dont le répertoire de chants célébrant les lois pourrait être le plus ancien de tous ceux encore chantés dans le monde. En suivant la tradition archaïque de **walu.ngarri,** exécutée pour la première fois à **Wudmangu,** les hommes **Ngarinyin** commençèrent par placer au milieu du cercle de danse un nouveau siège de pierre pour le doyen des chanteurs. De cette place centrale, **Ngarjno** dirigea l'exécution de la danse de l'anneau. Ils dansèrent autour de lui pendant plusieurs jours au son des chants **Wunan** composés par **Wiji.ngarri** et exécutés avec la plus grande minutie. Après la cérémonie, le nouveau siège de pierre fut laissé en place, marquant ainsi le milieu du sol sacré ; on en garde le souvenir par l'appellation **Duduk.ngunga.**

Être auteur est culturellement très encouragé par les **munnumburra**. Les compositeurs **Ngarinyin,** comme par exemple Scotty Martin, expriment leurs visions dans des **junba** (performances musicales et théâtrales). Ces **junba** se développent dans toute la région du Kimberley et sont populaires auprès des jeunes qui aujourd'hui s'épanouissent dans les représentations en y mettant leur propre musique populaire. Peut-être peut-on dire que la « véritable » identité d'un Aborigène australien perdure chez celui dont l'imagination est née dans le bush, reste imprégnée par lui, et qui reste ainsi intimement lié aux origines de sa culture et à la vie de sa terre.

My name Paddy Wamma...
Paddy white man name
black fella name... **Ungudman**

Ich heiße Paddy Wamma ...
Paddy, das ist ein weißer Name
der schwarze Name ist ... **Ungudman**

Mon nom c'est Paddy Wamma ...
Paddy c'est un nom de Blanc
mon nom de Noir... c'est **Ungudman**

Ungudman

Until recently, most publications stated that the indigenous people of the Kimberley had no cultural connections with the artists or the scenes portrayed in **Gwion** art that abounds throughout the region. These ancient human images, delicately painted on rock, had been named "Bradshaw figures" after the explorer who first described them to the outside world. While colonial attitudes denied any depth to indigenous Australian culture, ignorant observers could not attribute such finely painted images to Aboriginal hands. It is ironic that Bradshaw himself noted obvious physical similarities between the **Gwion** figures wearing wigs and the people who he observed near the Prince Regent River in 1892:

"Two or three of them had imposing head gears, made I imagine from the pliable bark of the papyrus tree. We noticed one man in particular who had two huge appendages extending upwards and obliquely outwards from the top of his head, about 3 ft. long; but whether they were made from the wings of a large bird, or pieces of bark we could not ascertain, as he kept in the background far up the range."

The men wearing long wigs observed by Bradshaw probably were members of the **Gubu.ngarri** clan living at the time around **Wudjawudja.ngarri dambun** area. The wigs are one distinguishing motif of **Gwion** art, but all **Gwion** paintings are described as **junjun** (indelible evidence of ancestors). These images are therefore **mamaa** (sacred).

Because their knowledge of the motifs and motives of **Gwion** art was key evidence for their Native Title claim, exposing the extensive meaning behind the imagery was problematic. When we began working together, the **munnumburra** explained the cultural reasons for the previous embargo on exposing their traditional connection with **Gwion** art. Paintings were created by ancestors who originated law, and reflect their images.The four principal **munnumburra** declared in unison that the true meaning of the paintings:

is a secret to protect...
arri guli Wunan
man... blood... law
Ngarjno Ungudman Banggal Nyawarra

They directed the recording of their own evidence to show their relationship with the **Gwion** artists and to demonstrate to all the origin of their law:

because we only got little time –
older people – and when older people go
we got it already in a book or in a film
it'll be translated and documented
Banggal

As an individual progressively acquiring knowledge of **Wunan** law throughout life, you must journey to observe vital signs in nature and identify evidence on **dulwan** (pathways) created by ancestors. To visit sacred sites you must follow the footsteps of the **Gwion** originators of law. Arriving at any sanctuary with paintings, you must proceed only after completing the required protocol. After introducing yourself to the host **wanjina**, you must announce your intentions, and remain quiet and calm. You must never swear or damage anything alive and growing on the path or tamper with anything old and **mamaa.**

Noch bis vor wenigen Jahren gingen die meisten Publikationen davon aus, dass es keine Verbindung zwischen den Aborigines des Kimberley-Gebiets und den Künstlern oder Motiven der überall in der Region anzutreffenden **Gwion**-Malereien gebe. Nach dem Forscher, der sie zuerst beschrieben hatte, nannte man diese uralten, fein gemalten Felsbilder „Bradshaw-Figuren". Da die Kultur der Aborigines im Denken europäischer Kolonisten keinerlei tiefere Dimension hatte, kamen unwissende Betrachter auch nicht auf die Idee, dass diese kunstvollen Malereien von den Aborigines stammen könnten. Dabei berichtet Bradshaw selbst von den offensichtlichen Ähnlichkeiten zwischen den Perücken tragenden **Gwion**-Figuren der Felsbilder und den Menschen, denen er 1892 in der Nähe des Prince Regent River begegnet war:

„Zwei oder drei von ihnen trugen einen imposanten Kopfschmuck, der vermutlich aus der weichen Rinde des Papyrusbaums gefertigt war. Ein Mann fiel uns besonders auf, denn seinen Kopf zierten zwei schräg nach außen ragende Aufsätze, etwa drei Fuß hoch (ca. 90 cm). Ob sie aus den Flügeln eines großen Vogels gemacht waren oder aus Rinde, konnten wir nicht feststellen, denn er kam nicht näher heran."

Die Männer mit den hohen Perücken, von denen Bradshaw berichtete, dürften Mitglieder des **Gubu.ngarri**-Clans gewesen sein, der damals im **Wudjawudja.ngarri dambun** ansässig war. Die Perücken sind ein charakteristisches Motiv der **Gwion**-Kunst, wobei alle Bilder der **Gwion** als **junjun** (unauslöschliche Zeugnisse des Wirkens der Ahnenwesen) gelten. Die Bilder sind daher **mamaa** (heilig).

Da ihr Wissen um die Gegenstände und Hintergründe der **Gwion**-Malereien entscheidend für ihre Ansprüche auf das Land waren, mussten sie die tiefere Bedeutung der Bilder enthüllen, was problematisch war. Zu Beginn unserer Zusammenarbeit erläuterten die **munnumburra,** warum sie die Verbindungen ihrer Kultur zu den Felsbildern der **Gwion** zuvor geheim gehalten hatten. Die Bilder sind Werke und Abbild derselben Ahnenwesen, auf die auch die Gesetze zurückgehen. Wie aus einem Munde erklärten die vier Stammesältesten, die wahre Bedeutung der Bilder sei:

ein Geheimnis, das geschützt werden muss
arri guli Wunan
Mensch … Blut … Gesetz
Ngarjno Ungudman Banggal Nyawarra

Sie selbst wollten, dass ihre Aussagen festgehalten wurden, weil sie ihre Beziehung zu den **Gwion**-Künstlern dokumentieren und zeigen wollten, woher ihre Gesetze kommen:

denn wir haben nur wenig Zeit –
wir Alten – und wenn die Alten gehen
dann haben wir es in einem Buch oder in einem Film
es wird übersetzt und festgehalten
Banggal

Im Laufe seines Lebens erfährt ein Aborigine immer mehr über die Gesetze des **Wunan,** doch dazu muss er sich auf die Reise begeben, muss lernen, die Zeichen der Natur zu lesen und die Spuren der Ahnenwesen auf den von ihnen geschaffenen Pfaden **(dulwan)** zu entdecken. Wer die heiligen Orte aufsuchen will, muss auf den Fußspuren der **Gwion** wandeln, die die Gesetze geschaffen haben. Wer einen Ort mit Felsbildern betritt, muss sich an eine bestimmte Etikette halten: Nachdem der Besucher sich dem gastgebenden **wanjina** vorgestellt hat, trägt er leise und ruhig sein Anliegen vor. Er darf niemals fluchen, keinem Lebewesen und keiner Pflanze auf dem Pfad Schaden zufügen und sich nie an etwas vergreifen, was alt und **mamaa** ist.

Jusqu'à récemment, la plupart des publications affirmaient que les populations du Kimberley n'avaient pas de liens culturels avec les artistes ou les scènes peintes de l'art **Gwion** qui abondent dans toute la région. Ces anciennes figures humaines peintes sur la roche ont été nommées « figures Bradshaw » du nom de l'explorateur qui les a décrites en premier. Alors même que l'état d'esprit colonial refusait de voir une quelconque profondeur dans la culture indigène australienne, les observateurs dans leur incompétence ne pouvaient attribuer l'exécution d'images peintes aussi raffinées à des mains aborigènes. Il est assez ironique que Bradshaw lui-même ait remarqué des similarités physiques évidentes entre les figures **Gwion** portant des coiffes et les gens qu'il observa près de la rivière Prince Regent en 1892 :

« Deux ou trois d'entre eux avaient d'imposants accoutrements sur la tête, faits j'imagine d'écorce souple de paperbark. Nous avons remarqué en particulier un homme qui avait deux énormes appendices dépassant vers le haut et vers l'extérieur de sa tête et mesurant à peu près trois pieds de long (90 centimètres) ; étaient-ils faits avec des ailes d'un gros oiseau ou des bouts d'écorce, on ne pouvait en être certain, car il resta en arrière, au-delà d'une bonne vision. »

Les hommes portant ces longues coiffes qu'observa Bradshaw étaient probablement des membres du clan **Gubu.ngarri** qui vivaient à cette époque près de **Wudjawudja.ngarri dambun.** Les coiffes sont un des motifs distinctifs de l'art **Gwion,** mais toutes les peintures **Gwion** sont décrites comme **junjun** (preuve ineffaçable des ancêtres). Ces images sont donc **mamaa** (sacrées).

Si la connaissance des motifs et des thèmes de l'art **Gwion** était une preuve capitale pour leurs revendications foncières, dévoiler la signification de l'imagerie posait problème. Quand nous commençâmes à travailler ensemble, les **munnumburra** expliquèrent les raisons culturelles de leur refus antérieur d'exposer leurs liens traditionnels avec l'art **Gwion.** Les peintures furent crées par les ancêtres qui sont les auteurs de la Loi et elles reflètent leurs images. Les quatre représentants principaux des **munnumburra** déclarèrent à l'unisson que le vrai sens de ces peintures était :

un secret à protéger
arri guli Wunan
l'homme … le sang … la Loi
Ngarjno Ungudman Banggal Nyawarra

Ils dirigèrent l'enregistrement de leur discours pour montrer leur lien avec les artistes **Gwion** et pour démontrer à tous l'origine de la Loi :

Il nous reste plus beaucoup de temps
à nous les vieux
et quand les plus vieux s'en iront
ça sera déjà dans un livre ou un film
ça sera traduit et documenté
Banggal

Comme l'individu acquiert progressivement la connaissance de la loi **Wunan** tout au long de sa vie, il lui faut voyager pour observer les signes vitaux dans la nature et retrouver les preuves des sentiers **dulwan** créés par les ancêtres. Pour pouvoir visiter les sites sacrés, il faut suivre les pas des auteurs **Gwion** de la Loi. En arrivant à n'importe quel sanctuaire de peintures, on ne peut pénétrer qu'après avoir accompli le cérémonial exigé. Après s'être présenté à l'hôte **wanjina,** on doit annoncer ses intentions, puis demeurer silencieux et calme. On ne doit jamais blasphémer ou abîmer quoi que ce soit de vivant ou qui pousse sur le chemin, ni toucher à quelque chose d'ancien et **mamaa.**

We call it now Pathway Project
because where all the tracks
of **wanjina** and kangaroo and emu
everything that walked put their track
and that is the project now
we following the history

All that education belong here to this area
People can respect all different area
when he got his own story
I can't go stealing another man's story
no way!
This story only belong here... one place

Wir nennen es das Pathway-Project
weil all die **wanjina** und Kängurus und Emus
ihre Spuren hinterlassen haben auf diesen Pfaden
und das ist unser Projekt
wir folgen den Spuren der Geschichte

Alles was wir wissen gehört zu diesem Land
Jeder respektiert das Land des anderen
wenn er eine eigene Geschichte kennt
Ich kann nicht die Geschichte eines anderen stehlen
das geht nicht!
Diese Geschichte gehört nur hierher …
jede hat ihren Platz

On l'appelle maintenant le Pathway Project
à cause de toutes ces traces
de **wanjina,** de kangourou et d'émeu
de tout ce qui marche et qui a laissé des traces
c'est ça le projet aujourd'hui
on suit les traces de l'histoire

Tout cet enseignement appartient à cet endroit
On peut respecter les autres peuples
quand on connait sa propre histoire
Je peux pas aller voler l'histoire d'un autre
c'est pas possible !
Cette histoire c'est celle d'ici… seulement d'ici

Banggal

The Pathway Project was initiated at the suggestion of the four **munnumburra** when they took me to view one ancient painting at **Alyaguma**. This is the remarkable **guloi** tree icon of knowledge they described as a **dulwan** or "pathway". Their expressed aim was to record enough essential evidence from their pathway in the bush, to connect their knowledge of **Gwion** art to **Wunan** law and to the land. With a dual motive to preserve the knowledge of elders and to hand on substantial narrative and photographic evidence to the next generation, there is also the immediate need for the **munnumburra** to educate the outside world about their culture from within their country. Using new media to convey their message also brings them onto the digital pathways of new technology. These many aspects of message and meaning are all combined as a new educational path for **Ngarinyin** knowledge today. By their choice of the word pathway they invite outsiders to enter and explore the multi-dimensional realms of **Ngarinyin** cosmology, but the term also has implications for a personal moral direction; **Nyawarra** cogently insists that culture demands:

"One road a clean place... one road
We go to the one road"
that's what the song means
Nyawarra

Knowledge must travel. When **munnumburra** of the **Ngarinyin** Aboriginal Corporation decided to reveal their ancestral association with **Gwion** art, and initiated the Pathway Project recordings in 1992, they acted to reveal something of the secret pathways **(dulwan mamaa)** to the origins of their history. This resulted in the photographic exhibition at the Musée Nationale d'Histoire Naturelle and a UNESCO forum on their cultural evidence, both held in Paris in 1997.

As laws begin from birth, secrets act as seeds of knowledge at each stage of learning. **Wunan** laws, infused with secrets, stimulate moral development and focus religious experience. **Ngarinyin** education involves walking through the bush, directly learning from experience and respecting evidence rich with secrets located on their **dulwan nimindi** (pathway of knowledge). But we should never intrude where we are not invited. So we follow by invitation, walking behind them, guided and informed by these four **munnumburra**, as **Nyawarra** confirmed:

He very dangerous in the law
secret things... he on that path... on that path
Nyawarra

Das Pathway-Projekt wurde von vier **munnumburra** angeregt, die mir ein altes Gemälde in **Alyaguma** zeigten. Dieses bemerkenswerte Bild zeigt den **guloi**-Baum, ein Symbol des schrittweise erworbenen Wissens, das sie als **dulwan** (Pfad) oder „pathway" beschrieben. Ihr Ziel war es, auf ihrem „Pfad" durch den Busch Belege zu sammeln, um eine Verbindung zwischen der **Gwion**-Kunst, den **Wunan**-Gesetzen und dem Land herzustellen. Es ging den **munnumburra** nicht nur darum, das Wissen der Ältesten zu bewahren und in Erzählungen und Fotografien an die nächste Generation weiterzugeben, sondern auch darum, der Welt draußen einen Begriff von ihrer Kultur, die sich aus ihrem Land erklärt, zu geben. Sie nutzen neue Medien für ihre Botschaft und finden damit Zugang zu den digitalen Pfaden der Zukunft. Botschaft und Bedeutung in vielerlei Gestalten verbinden sich in einem neuen Pfad. Mit dem Wort „pathway" laden sie ein, das vieldimensionale Reich der **Ngarinyin**-Kosmologie kennen zu lernen und zu erforschen; doch das Wort „pathway" legt auch ein persönliches, moralisches Element nahe – Kultur fordert, wie **Nyawarra** sagt:

„Eine Straße ... das ist eine klare Sache ... nur die eine
Wir gehen zur Straße"
das bedeutet das Lied
Nyawarra

Wissen muss weitergegeben werden. Als die **munnumburra** der **Ngarinyin** Aboriginal Corporation sich entschlossen, ihre Verbindung zur **Gwion**-Kunst zu enthüllen, und 1992 den Anstoß zum Pathway-Projekt gaben, erklärten sie sich bereit, etwas preiszugeben von den bis dahin geheim gehaltenen Pfaden **(dulwan mamaa)** zu den Wurzeln ihrer Geschichte. Das führte zu der Fotoausstellung im Musée Nationale d'Histoire Naturelle und zu einer Präsentation der Zeugnisse ihrer Kultur bei der UNESCO, beides 1997 in Paris.

Da man von Geburt an den Gesetzen unterliegt, tragen die überlieferten Geheimnisse auf jeder Stufe des Lernens den Keim des Wissens in sich. Die **Wunan**-Gesetze, die voller Geheimnisse sind, fördern die moralische Entwicklung und weisen den Weg zu religiösen Erfahrungen. Wanderungen durch den Busch sind bei den **Ngarinyin** ein Mittel der Erziehung, bei dem man direkt aus der Erfahrung lernt und den geheimnisvollen Zeugnissen der Vergangenheit auf dem **dulwan nimindi** (Pfad des Wissens) begegnet. Aber ohne Einladung sollten wir niemals vordringen. So warten wir auf ihre Aufforderung, gehen hinter ihnen her, geführt von diesen vier **munnumburra**. **Nyawarra** bestätigt:

Mit dem Gesetz darf man nicht scherzen
geheimnisvolle Dinge ... unterwegs auf dem Pfad ...
auf dem Pfad
Nyawarra

Le Pathway Project est né de la suggestion des quatre **munnumburra** quand ils m'ont emmené voir une peinture ancienne à **Alyaguma**. C'est une remarquable image de l'arbre de connaissance **guloi** qu'ils décrivent comme étant un **dulwan** ou « chemin ». Leur but était de relever assez de preuves de leur « chemin » dans le bush pour relier leur connaissance de l'art **Gwion** à la loi **Wunan** et à la terre. Ce projet a un double objectif : conserver la connaissance des aînés et transmettre un témoignage substantiel – écrit et photographique – pour la génération suivante. Il y a aussi le besoin immédiat pour les **munnumburra** de faire connaître au monde extérieur la culture intrinsèque à leur pays. Utiliser un nouveau médium pour présenter leur message les amène également sur le chemin des nouvelles technologies. Toutes les différentes formes sous lesquelles le message est présenté, servent de base à un nouveau chemin pour l'éducation et la connaissance **Ngarinyin** d'aujourd'hui. Par le choix du mot « chemin », ils invitent ceux qui sont étrangers à leur culture à y rentrer et à découvrir les aspects multidimensionnels de la cosmologie **Ngarinyin**, mais ce terme « chemin » implique aussi une direction morale personnelle. **Nyawarra** insiste sur les exigences de la culture :

« Une voie bien dégagée ... une route
on va sur cette route unique »
c'est ce que veut dire le chant
Nyawarra

La connaissance doit voyager. Lorsque les **munnumburra** du conseil aborigène **Ngarinyin** ont décidé de révéler leurs liens ancestraux avec l'art **Gwion** et ont posé les bases du Pathway Project en 1992, ils ont par là dévoilé un peu leurs chemins sacrés **(dulwan mamaa)** qui sont à l'origine de leur histoire. Il en résulta une exposition photographique au Musée National d'Histoire Naturelle et un forum sur leur témoignage culturel à l'UNESCO. Les deux événements eurent lieu à Paris en 1997.

Comme les lois commencent dès la naissance, les secrets jouent le rôle de « graines » de connaissance à chaque étape de l'apprentissage. Les lois **Wunan,** imprégnées de secrets, stimulent le développement moral et mettent l'accent sur les pratiques religieuses. L'éducation des **Ngarinyin** exige de marcher dans le bush, l'acquisition de l'expérience et le respect des preuves tangibles des secrets situés sur leur **dulwan nimindi,** leur chemin du savoir. Mais nous ne devons jamais nous imposer là où nous ne sommes pas invités. Donc nous ne les suivons que lorsque nous y sommes invités, marchant derrière eux, guidés et informés par les quatre **munnumburra** comme **Nyawarra** le confirme :

Tout est très dangereux dans la Loi
il y a des choses secrètes ...
des secrets sur ce chemin ... sur ce chemin
Nyawarra

That was really strict law before
We still the bosses!

Someone break the law in that area
he only got short life to live

But now if they want this law
where it can stand up strong again
we like to bring it back today
make it more stronger

Früher, da war das Gesetz wirklich streng
Wir sind aber immer noch die Herren!

Wenn einer hier in der Gegend das Gesetz brach
der hatte nicht mehr lange zu leben

Aber wenn sie heute ein Gesetz haben wollen
das wieder richtig stark ist
dann würden wir gern das alte zurückholen
und es noch stärker machen

La Loi était vraiment plus dure autrefois
Mais c'est toujours nous les patrons !

Si quelqu'un transgressa la Loi par ici
il lui resta pas longtemps à vivre

Mais maintenant si vous voulez que cette Loi
soit forte à nouveau
on peut la faire renaître aujourd'hui
la rendre encore plus forte

Ngarjno

We only gotta little time us older people
and when older people go
we got it already in a book or in a film
it will be translated and documented
that's what we want to see happen
before we die... gone older people
and that's why we anxious to see it done
soon as possible
Nyawarra

So we want to try
and show it to the white Australian
and that's why this very important for us
we want to satisfy before we die
that we did something
for everybody in the country
to learn and understand
who we are in this country

Wunan munnumburra
... really full Aborigine Law people

And this wasn't done long time ago
and this only time left
we want to do it now
very short time we have
We want it done sooner
because we have reason
we only got... ah older people
we only got little time
and we want to try and
get this done properly
because only **Ngarinyin**...
it been done in the **Ngarinyin** tribe
Banggal

Wir haben nur wenig Zeit, wir Alten
und wenn die Alten gehen
dann haben wir es in einem Buch oder Film
es wird übersetzt und festgehalten
das wollen wir noch erleben
bevor wir sterben ... bevor die Alten alle fort sind
deshalb liegt uns so viel daran
dass es so schnell wie möglich geschieht
Nyawarra

Deshalb wollen wir
dass die weißen Australier es sehen
deshalb ist das so wichtig für uns
wir wollen mit dem Gefühl sterben
dass wir etwas getan haben
für alle im Land
damit sie lernen und verstehen können
wer wir in diesem Lande sind

Wunan munnumburra
... richtige Gesetzeshüter

Das haben wir früher versäumt
und jetzt ist die letzte Gelegenheit
wir wollen es jetzt tun
es bleibt nur noch wenig Zeit
So schnell wie möglich müssen wir es tun
dafür gibt es gute Gründe
wir haben nur noch ... ach alte Leute
die Zeit wird knapp
und wir wollen sehen,
dass wir dies richtig machen
denn nur die **Ngarinyin** ...
die **Ngarinyin** müssen es tun
Banggal

On a plus beaucoup de temps, nous, les vieux
et quand les plus vieux s'en iront
ce sera déjà dans un livre ou un film
traduit et documenté
c'est ce qu'on voudrait voir arriver
avant notre mort ...
avant qu'ils soient partis les vieux
et c'est pour ça qu'on veut vraiment
que ça se fasse le plus vite possible
Nyawarra

Donc on va essayer
et on va montrer tout ça aux Australien blancs
c'est pour cela que c'est si important pour nous
on veut pouvoir se féliciter avant de mourir
qu'on aura fait quelque chose
pour tous dans le pays
tout le monde pourra apprendre et comprendre
qui on est dans ce pays

Wunan munnumburra
... les gardiens de la Loi aborigène

Et ça c'était pas fait avant
et avec le peu de temps qui reste
on doit le faire maintenant
il nous reste très peu de temps
On veut que ça soit fait au plus vite
parce qu'on a des raisons
on a plus... ah les vieux
il nous reste peu de temps
alors on veut essayer
et faire ça bien
car seuls les **Ngarinyin** peuvent...
ça doit être fait par la tribu des **Ngarinyin**
Banggal

We here in this gorge
ganda wanyedna nilu Yandama
*place called **Alyaguma***
We very frighten this country
rain... every year rain

*This where **wanjina** walked through*
*this place here **Alyaguma***
he went through here...
through the gorge
that the path we follow

dulwan nimindi... *that is the pathway*
Banggal

Hier in dieser Schlucht
ganda wanyedna nilu Yandama
*der Ort heißt **Alyaguma***
Wir sorgen uns um dieses Land
Regen ... jedes Jahr Regen

*Hier ist der **wanjina** durchgekommen*
*das hier, das ist **Alyaguma***
hier ist er gegangen ...
durch diese Schlucht
das ist der Pfad dem wir folgen

dulwan nimindi ... *das ist der Pfad*
Banggal

Nous sommes ici dans cette gorge
ganda wanyedna nilu Yandama
*un endroit qui s'appelle **Alyaguma***
On a très peur pour ce pays
il pleut... tous les ans il pleut

*C'est par ici que le **wanjina** est passé*
*à cet endroit là **Alyaguma***
ils sont passés par ici ...
à travers cette gorge
sur ce chemin qu'on suit

dulwan nimindi ... *c'est le chemin*
Banggal

Every fruit grow... **mangarri...** food
ganmangu... jalgud... yam
fish... turtle... all belong to this water
tucker belong to here
Ungudman

But that is the **dulwan...** road
now **dulwan** follow up that river
when they said

"We'll stop here!
this is the place we can put all our painting"
Banggal

Alle Früchte wachsen hier ... **mangarri ...** Essen
ganmangu ... jalgud ... Jamswurzeln
Fische ... Schildkröten ...
alles gehört zu dem Wasser hier
alles was man essen kann
Ungudman

Aber das ist der **dulwan ...** der Pfad
von hier folgt der **dulwan** den Fluss hinauf
bis da wo sie gesagt haben

„Hier bleiben wir!
hier können wir unsere Bilder malen"
Banggal

Tous les fruits poussent ici ...
mangarri, c'est la nourriture
ganmangu ... jalgud ... ignames
poissons ... tortues ... tout vient de cette eau
toute la nourriture vient de là
Ungudman

Voilà ça c'est le **dulwan ...** le chemin
maintenant le **dulwan** longe cette rivière
jusqu'à l'endroit où ils ont dit

« On s'arrête ici !
voilà l'endroit où nous pourrons nous exprimer
à travers nos peintures »
Banggal

And we wanted to record in here some songs *some songs belong to **Ngarinyin** tribe* *So this is how they belong to this area* ***Ngarinyin** tribe... ceremonies... lawsongs*	*Und wir wollten hier ein paar Lieder festhalten* *ein paar Lieder des **Ngarinyin**-Stammes* *Denn so gehören sie zu dieser Gegend* ***Ngarinyin**-Stamm … Feste … Gesetzeslieder*	*Nous voulons enregistrer ici des chants* *des chants qui appartiennent à la tribu **Ngarinyin*** *Voilà pourquoi ils appartiennent à cet endroit* *la tribu **Ngarinyin** … cérémonies … chants de la Loi*
*That one there **Munggundu wanjina*** *everything is come from **Munggundu*** *from "soft" and that is the **Munggundu*** *very very important* *It's a gum... **Munggundu** gum* *proper **Munggundu** when we was formed* *when this land was formed like a jelly*	*Das da ist der **Munggundu wanjina*** *alles kommt von **Munggundu*** *„weich" das bedeutet **Munggundu*** *das ist sehr sehr wichtig* *Es ist wie Gummi … **Munggundu** weich wie* ***Munggundu** als wir gemacht wurden* *als dieses Land gemacht wurde, weich wie Pudding*	*Ça, là, c'est **Munggundu wanjina*** *tout vient du **Munggundu*** *du « mou », c'est ça le **Munggundu*** *c'est très très important* *c'est une gomme … **Munggundu**, la gomme* *on était en **Munggundu** quand on a été créé* *ce pays s'est formé c'était comme de la gelée*
And that it is yellow one there ***gumbaru**... yellow painting* *represent real power that **gumbaru*** *and that painting now is the life in water* Banggal	*Und das da drüben das gelbe* ***gumbaru** gelbe Farbe* *die bedeutet Kraft, **gumbaru*** *und das Bild hier das ist Leben im Wasser* Banggal	*Et cette chose qui est jaune là* *c'est de la peinture jaune **gumbaru*** *cette **gumbaru** représente le grand pouvoir* *et cette peinture là c'est comme la vie dans l'eau* Banggal

Joi iri jina budmenu-yo! *"Big" name man they are doing it yo!*	***Joi iri jina budmenu-yo!*** *Mann mit großem Namen sie tun es, jawohl!*	***Joi iri jina budmenu-yo !*** *nom de « grand » homme ils le font oui !*
wali nyangalugun joi iri *wait your name "big" name*	***wali nyangalugun joi iri*** *warte auf deinen Namen „großen" Namen*	***wali nyangalugun joi iri*** *attends ton nom « grand » nom*
Galeru.ngarri malyangga *Galeru.ngarri tribe saying it*	***Galeru.ngarri malyangga*** *Galeru.ngarri Stamm sagt ihn*	***Galeru.ngarri malyangga*** *la tribu Galeru.ngarri en le disant*
warrawarran nyayin.geri brugu nyndu manga *longtime we were going away from you*	***warrawarran nyayin.geri brugu nyndu manga*** *vor langer Zeit gingen wir von dir fort*	***warrawarran nyayin.geri brugu nyndu manga*** *il y a longtemps nous nous éloignons de toi*
ganagan ju joli nyindaran *today coming towards you*	***ganagan ju joli nyindaran*** *heute kommen wir zu dir*	***ganagan ju joli nyindaran*** *venant vers toi aujourd'hui*
ngulmud li ongo budmenu *strangers see you they do it*	***ngulmud li ongo budmenu*** *Fremde sehen dich sie tun es*	***ngulmud li ongo budmenu*** *étrangers te voient ils le font*

JILLINYA   MAMAA

The Sacred Great Mother
She is the Great Mother... **Jillinya** *the mother of all*   Nyawarra

Die Heilige Urmutter
Das ist die Große Mutter... **Jillinya** *die Mutter von allen*   Nyawarra

La Grande Matriarche Sacrée
Elle est la Grande Mère... **Jillinya** *la mère de tous*   Nyawarra

All these the bosses here
munnumburra wongai
law women belong this country
Ungudman

That what they're telling us
all that lot hand there... all that lot hand
hand is up there in that painting
there saying stop!
All this lot hand where they holding up
"you gotta listen"
Understand what they're telling us
all that lot hand there
They facing where they come from
they follow 'em this creek
they chosen this place... they say
"We stop here we no go further"
Banggal

Die hier die haben das Sagen
munnumburra wongai
die Hüterinnen des Gesetzes hier für das Land
Ungudman

Das wollen sie uns sagen
die Hände da ... die Hände auf dem Bild
die hochgehaltenen Hände
die sagen Halt!
Die Hände die sie hochhalten sagen
„Hör mir zu"
Verstehst du was sie uns sagen wollen
die vielen Hände
Sie zeigen nach da wo sie herkommen
sie sind dem Bach hier gefolgt
sie haben den Platz hier ausgesucht ... und gesagt
„Hier bleiben wir und gehen nicht weiter"
Banggal

Celles qui commandent
c'est les **munnumburra wongai,**
les gardiennes de la Loi, elles sont d'ici
Ungudman

C'est ce qu'elles nous disent
toutes ces mains là... toutes ces mains
les mains levées sur ces peintures
elles disent stop !
toutes ces mains qui se dressent
« tu dois écouter »
Essaies de comprendre ce qu'elles nous disent
toutes ces mains là
Elles font face à l'endroit d'où elles viennent
elles ont suivi ce cours d'eau
elles ont choisi cet endroit... et dit
« Arrêtons-nous ici, nous n'irons pas plus loin »
Banggal

They have names belong to them
Jalmi… Romul
we gotta call that name of that woman
yeah… this one name **Njumillibulli**

and this next one…
this next one is **Jumbowulla**
Jumbowulla… *you get 'em?*
Ungudman

Sie haben ihre eigenen Namen
Jalmi… Romul
man muss den Namen der Frau rufen
ja… die da heißt **Njumillibulli**

und die da…
die heißt **Jumbowulla**
Jumbowulla… *hast du das?*
Ungudman

Elles ont chacune un nom
Jalmi… Romul
il faut que je dise le nom de cette femme
oui… ce nom-là, **Njumillibulli**

et la suivante là…
la suivante c'est **Jumbowulla**
Jumbowulla… *tu les as enregistrées?*
Ungudman

Nad gudi. Jallala li unon ngarri
Nad gudi emeri yali
jirri jallala
Baing unun go irir.
Mowuriyal wa modor modor
gugayirri emeri yali yirri jirin
jallala jirri

Stop! Stop! don't trespass
Stop! listen to us
And this is the hand sign saying stop

Nad gudi emeri
yali jirri jallala jirri
Nad gudi bumiru budagangarri biri
emeri yali jirri jallala bumay

Gotta listen... gotta understand me
I'm talking to you!
you come and see me
but I'm the one telling you!
You have to listen
Banggal

Nad gudi. Jallala li unon ngarri
Nad gudi emeri yali
jirri jallala
Baing unun go irir.
Mowuriyal wa modor modor
gugayirri emeri yali yirri jirin
jallala jirri

Halt! Halt! geh nicht weiter
Halt! hör uns an
Und die Hand hier, die sagt Halt

Nad gudi emeri
yali jirri jallala jirri
Nad gudi bumiru budagangarri biri
emeri yali jirri jallala bumay

Du musst zuhören … musst mich verstehen
ich spreche zu dir!
du bist zu mir gekommen
aber ich bin die, die zu dir spricht!
Hör mir zu
Banggal

Nad gudi. Jallala li unon ngarri
Nad gudi emeri yali
jirri jallala
Baing unun go irir.
Mowuriyal wa modor modor
gugayirri emeri yali yirri jirin
jallala jirri

Stop ! Stop ! pas plus loin
Stop ! écoutes-nous
C'est ce signe de main qui dit stop

Nad gudi emeri
yali jirri jallala jirri
Nad gudi bumiru budagangarri biri
emeri yali jirri jallala bumay

Tu dois m'écouter… faut que tu comprennes
je te parle !
c'est toi qui viens me voir
mais c'est moi qui parle !
Tu dois m'écouter
Banggal

Algi... this one name **Algi**
Ungudman

Yeah now in my area Rowe River
where **Jillinya** is a big painting
mamaa... sacred
all these **mob** they giving her present
all these spear all these sorta spear
Jillinya... they knew her
and they were happy
so they had good things
that would make her happy
we call that **lulwa... lulwa** it's a gift!
So they brought all these gift to her
these spear and this one **woomera**
and it's still painted out there
all round there in the caves
Banggal

Algi ... die da heißt **Algi**
Ungudman

Also in meiner Gegend am Rowe River
wo es ein großes Bild von **Jillinya** gibt
mamaa ist das ... heilig
da kommen die Leute und bringen ihr Geschenke
lauter Speere, alle möglichen Speere
Jillinya ... sie wussten, wer sie war
und sie waren glücklich
sie haben ihr schöne Sachen gebracht
und das hat **Jillinya** glücklich gemacht
wir nennen es **lulwa ... lulwa**
das heißt Geschenk!
Und sie haben ihr also Geschenke gebracht
die Speere hier und die Speerschleudern
und das ist alles noch auf den Bildern
überall hier in den Höhlen
Banggal

Algi ... ce nom-là, **Algi**
Ungudman

Oui aujourd'hui dans ma région à Rowe River
où **Jillinya** apparaît
sous la forme d'une grande peinture
mamaa ... c'est sacré
tous les gens lui font des cadeaux
toutes ces lances, toutes sortes de lances
Jillinya ... ils la connaissaient
et ils étaient heureux
ils avaient de bonnes choses
pour la rendre heureuse
on appelle ça **lulwa ... lulwa** c'est un cadeau !
Donc ils lui apportaient tous ces cadeaux
ces lances et aussi des propulseurs
et c'est toujours peint là-bas
tout autour des grottes là-bas
Banggal

All the gifts they bring to her *Jillinya*
everyone been bringing from say...
*that **Gwion***
and all sorts of animals bring it over

*That **Wanjina wungud***
they brought it over
*and they give it to that **Jillinya***
*what we say **Wunan lulwa***

***lulwa** they will give her*
like present you take to someone else
give present to her... don't pay money
*well that **lulwa** means her present*
... everything
Nyawarra

*All die Geschenke, die bringen sie **Jillinya***
alle brachten etwas, zum Beispiel aus ...
*die **Gwion** da*
alle bringen etwas, Tiere und Menschen

*Das ist **Wanjina wungud***
sie haben es hergebracht
*und der **Jillinya** geschenkt*
*wir nennen das **Wunan lulwa***

***lulwa** bringen sie ihr*
wie ein Geschenk, das man jemandem mitbringt
sie schenken ihr etwas ... aber kein Geld
***lulwa,** das ist das Geschenk für sie*
... alles
Nyawarra

*Tous ces présents qu'ils apportaient à **Jillinya***
tout le monde en amenait depuis disons ...
*les **Gwion***
tous amenaient quelque chose
hommes et animaux

*amenaient le **wungud,** l'essence du **Wanjina***
Ils l'amenaient
*et le donnaient à cette **Jillinya***
*on appelle ça **Wunan lulwa***

*Ils lui donnent le **lulwa***
comme un présent
qui vient de quelqu'un d'autre
et qu'on lui donne ... mais pas de l'argent
*eh bien **lulwa** c'est un cadeau pour elle*
... n'importe quelle chose
Nyawarra

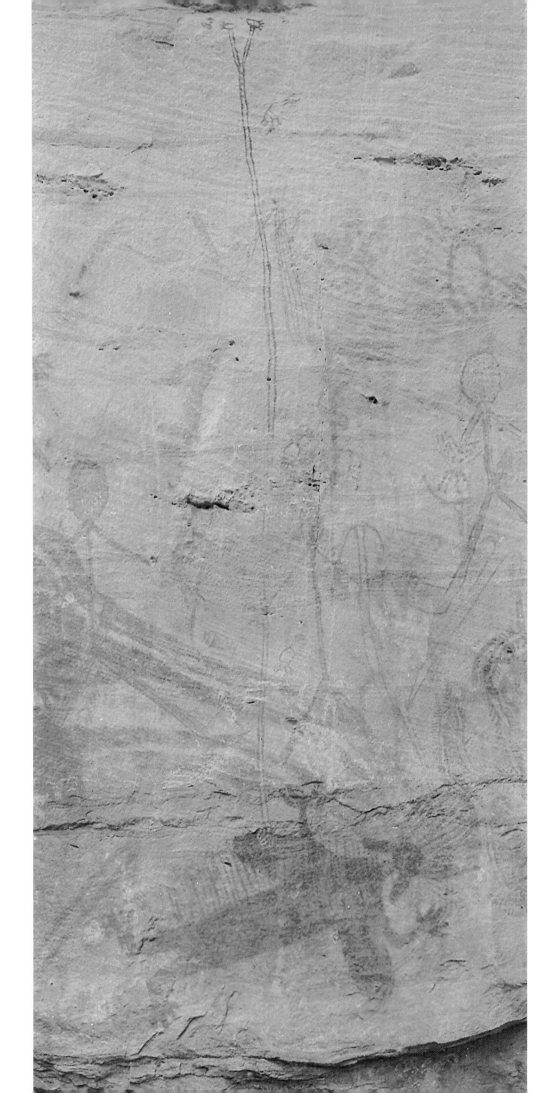

This is her place...
Jillinya** is **wungud
She was like a mother of all...
and all nations...
she's a Great Mother
Nyawarra

Jillinya... she was a great woman
belong to this north west area
*this coastal area **Guringi***
*near **garramarra**... saltwater*
and she painted there
*it called **mamaa** that place*

She painted in yellow ochre
and she painted naked
she sitting on a rock
sitting down in the wall of a cave
She was the biggest woman in this coastline
Banggal

Das ist ihr Ort...
Jillinya** ist **wungud
Sie ist die Mutter von allen...
von allen Stämmen
die Große Mutter
Nyawarra

Jillinya... eine große Frau war das
für uns hier im Nordwesten
*hier an der Küste bei **Guringi***
*nicht weit vom **garramarra**... Salzwasser*
da ist das Bild von ihr
***mamaa** ist der Ort*

Sie ist in gelbem Ocker gemalt
und sie ist nackt
sie sitzt auf einem Felsen
sitzt da an der Wand in der Höhle
Sie war die mächtigste Frau an der Küste
Banggal

Ici c'est sa place...
Jillinya** est **wungud
Elle était comme la mère de tous...
et de tous les peuples...
C'est la Mère originelle
Nyawarra

Jillinya... c'était une grande femme
elle est de cette région du nord-ouest
*cette région côtière appelée **Guringi***
*près de **garramarra**... la mer*
et elle est peinte à cet endroit
*dont on dit qu'il est **mamaa***

Elle est peinte avec de l'ocre jaune
et elle est peinte nue
elle est assise sur un rocher
assise au bas du mur d'une grotte
Elle est la femme la plus importante
sur ce littoral
Banggal

No young people go there teenagers no!
only elder people only married people
they have to go through initiation ceremony
When they old enough
then they can go and see her
Very important in place called **mamaa**
because it **mamaa** means
"really top one, holy woman"
and that's her place now
Banggal

So she was a Great Mother
and all the kids would go straight to her
like these **Wunan** people now
these ones painted here
came from all over the place
south... east... north... west...
all these things
Nyawarra

Junge Leute gehen da nicht hin, keine Teenager!
nur die Älteren nur Verheiratete
erst müssen sie die Initiation hinter sich haben
Wenn sie alt genug sind
dann können sie hingehen und sie ansehen
Das ist sehr wichtig an diesem Ort
der heißt **mamaa**
denn **mamaa** das heißt
„oberste von den Frauen, heilige Frau"
und das hier das ist ihr Ort
Banggal

Sie war also eine Große Mutter
und die Kinder, die kamen alle gleich zu ihr
wie die **Wunan** hier
die hier gemalt sind
die kamen von überall her
Süden… Osten… Norden… Westen…
von überall
Nyawarra

Les jeunes ne vont pas là-bas,
c'est interdit aux adolescents !
seulement pour les plus vieux, les gens mariés
il faut qu'ils soient initiés
Quand ils sont assez grands
alors ils peuvent aller et la voir
Elle est très importante à cet endroit
qui est **mamaa**
parce que **mamaa** ça veut dire
« vraiment la plus grande,
la plus sacrée des femmes »
et c'est son endroit maintenant
Banggal

C'était donc une Grande Matriarche
et tous les enfants allaient droit vers elle
comme ces gens du **Wunan** maintenant
ceux qui ont peint ici toutes ces choses-là
sud… est… nord… ouest…
toutes ces choses-là
Nyawarra

amurangga… man

Gwion Gwion *it's his name…*
Gwion Gwion *they're flash people*
they been dress well this **mob**
beautiful!
woman and man

all these all in here dressed up
we do it too here they told us what to do
and that's all this dressing here
People can see it when they do it in ceremony
properly painted up… really flash!
Banggal

amurangga … ein Mann

Gwion Gwion *ist sein Name…*
Die **Gwion Gwion** *das sind schicke Leute*
die waren immer gut angezogen, diese Leute
richtig schön … Frau und Mann

alle hier haben sich fein gemacht
wir tun das auch wie sie es uns gezeigt haben
die ganzen Kostüme kann man hier sehen
Man kann sehen
was sie bei den Zeremonien anhaben
hier auf dem Bild … wirklich schick!
Banggal

amurangga … homme

Gwion Gwion *c'est son nom…*
Les **Gwion Gwion**
ce sont des gens qui ont la classe
ils étaient toujours bien vêtus ces gens-là
beaux… les femmes comme les hommes

ils sont tous là, bien habillés
nous aussi on le fait ici,
ils nous ont dit quoi faire
et c'est tous ces habits-là
Les gens peuvent les voir
quand ils le font dans des cérémonies
proprement peints… vraiment remarquables!
Banggal

numurangga... *woman*
Ngarjno

mambi... *waist girdle*
When she don't want this "sex" thing
to be covered up in the front
she put in the back way...

I used to see that thing happening
The mother hand it over to her
and then this mother to her child girl
little girl... daughter... he keep travelling down
Nyawarra

birrina... *joining dance...* **wudu...** *around*
amurangga... *man and* **numurangga...** *woman*
nambud burlwin... *joining*
Ngarjno

numurangga ... *eine Frau*
Ngarjno

mambi ... *Lendenschurz*
Wenn sie vorne ihr Geschlecht
nicht bedecken will
trägt sie ihn andersherum ...

Das habe ich oft gesehen
Die Mutter gibt ihn an die Tochter weiter
und die gibt ihn ihrem eigenen Mädchen
wenn sie noch ganz klein ist ...
von Mutter zu Tochter, immer weiter
Nyawarra

birrina ... *zusammen tanzen ...* **wudu ...** *im Kreis*
amurangga ... *Mann und* **numurangga ...** *Frau*
nambud burlwin ... *zusammen*
Ngarjno

numurangga ... *femme*
Ngarjno

mambi ... *tournure sur la taille*
quand elle veut pas que cette « chose sexuelle »
sur le devant soit couverte
elle la met à l'envers ...
J'ai vu ça arriver déjà
La mère la transmet à sa fille
et cette mère à sa propre fille
petite fille, fille et ça continue à voyager ainsi
Nyawarra

birrina ... *entrer dans la danse ...* **wudu ...** *autour*
amurangga ... *homme et* **numurangga ...** *femme*
nambud burlwin ... *rejoindre*
Ngarjno

That's all their dressing
we exactly dress too in here in bush
in this area old people used to tell me
*These the **mob** now*
*before **wanjina** have give them law*
*these the ones **Gwion***

They have tools
before they have dancing ceremonies
and these were the dancing
for initiation ceremony
and those songs they still here today...
we use 'em
Banggal

So waren sie gekleidet
genau wie wir hier im Busch
so wie die Alten es mir erzählt haben
Das da sind die Menschen
*bevor die **wanjina** ihnen das Gesetz gaben*
*das sind die **Gwion***

Erst hatten sie Werkzeuge
dann kamen die Tänze
und das war der Tanz
für die Initiation
die Lieder sind immer noch da ...
und wir singen sie
Banggal

Ce sont leurs habits
on s'habillait pareil ici dans le bush
dans cette région les vieux me disaient
Eux, tous ceux-là aujourd'hui
*avant que les **wanjina** leur aient donné la Loi*
*eux c'étaient donc les **Gwion***

Ils avaient des outils
avant d'avoir des danses cérémonielles
et ces danses, c'étaient les danses
pour les cérémonies d'initiation
et ces chants-là,
ils sont toujours là aujourd'hui...
on s'en sert
Banggal

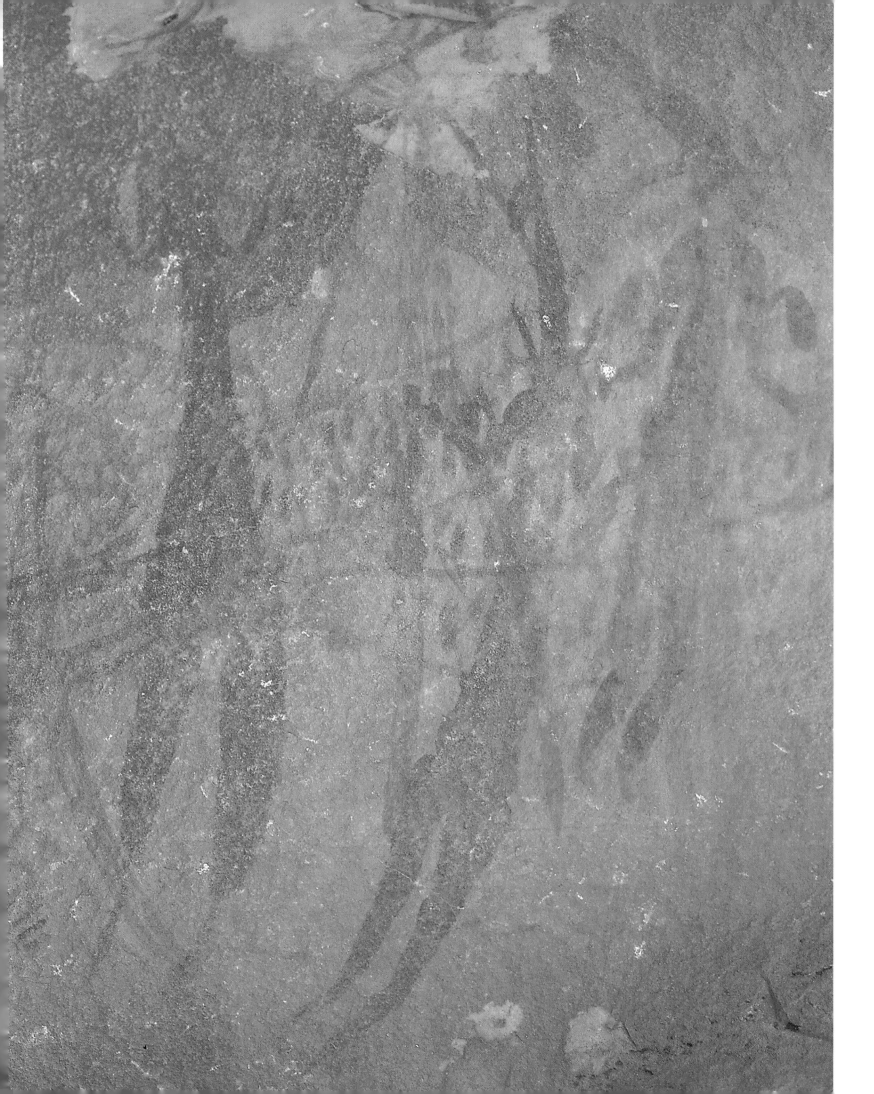

wandagi... white arm band
skin of kangaroo and they paint it up
white one narrow one like belt
make a small one on their arm
and up the side a cowrie shell... **binja winja**
tie it up with a string
mudurra tie it up and make it sharp point
or make it square **mudurra** wig
put it gum **gumaa** to smooth
and tighter like glue
it will hold it **galwadi**...
gumbaru... yellow one
like clay colour

When we moved away
from **Kunmunya** and **Munja** mission
40s I think...
just before the end of War II
some were still using wigs... **mudurra**
They put a white feather...
I still been see that happening

Wangalu... Laundi...
another old man is **Yullamaiya**
those **mob** still using it
one from **Wila Wila** side or **Wunambul**
old man **Badjayei** in that **Jillinya** area
that traditional owner
of that country **Gumbayeei**

Nyawarra

---

wandagi... ein weißes Armband
aus Känguruleder hier auf dem Bild sieht man es
ein weißer Riemen wie ein Gürtel
ein schmaler Riemen um den Arm
an der Seite eine Kaurimuschel... **binja winja**
mit einem Band befestigt
oder sie binden ihn um die **mudurra**, Perücke
machen die **mudurra** spitz oder quadratisch
reiben sie ein mit **gumaa**, Gummi das macht sie glatt
und fest, wie Klebstoff ist das
hält sie zusammen wie **galwadi**...
gumbaru... gelbe Farbe
wie Lehmfarbe

Als wir fortgingen
von den **Kunmunya**- und **Munja**-Missionsstationen
in den vierziger Jahren glaube ich...
kurz vor dem Ende des zweiten Kriegs
trugen einige noch immer Perücken... **mudurra**
Damals steckten sie eine weiße Feder an...
Ich habe das noch gesehen

Wangalu... Laundi...
einer von den Alten hieß **Yullamaiya**
die tragen sie noch
einer von den **Wila Wila** oder von den **Wunambul**
der alte **Badjayei** im Land der **Jillinya**
der Besitzer von dem Land hier
von dem Land **Gumbayeei**

Nyawarra

---

wandagi... un brassard blanc
en peau de kangourou qu'ils peignaient
une fine bande blanche, comme une ceinture
ils en font une petite qu'ils attachent
avec un cordon en haut de leur bras
et en haut sur le côté maintenu par un cordon
un coquillage-porcelaine... **binja winja**
mudurra, tu l'attaches et la rends pointue
ou alors tu la fais carrée, la coiffe **mudurra**
tu mets de la gomme, **gumaa**, pour la lisser
et la durcir comme avec de la glue
cela la maintiendra, **galwadi**...
la couleur... c'est **gumbaru**, jaune
comme la glaise

Quand on est parti
de la mission de **Kunmunya** et de **Munja**
dans les années quarante je pense...
juste avant la fin de la deuxième guerre
il y en avait encore avec les coiffes... **mudurra**
et ils utilisaient des plumes blanches...
J'ai vu ça arriver encore

Wangalu... Laundi...
un autre vieil homme c'est **Yullamaiya**
tous ces hommes les portent encore
un du côté des **Wila Wila** ou des **Wunambul**
le vieux **Badjayei** dans cette région de **Jillinya**
le propriétaire coutumier
de ce pays **Gumbayeei**

Nyawarra

That **mandzu**... praying mantis
is wind one... big wind one
belong to **Jillinya**

She is the Greatest Mother
the mother of all

Nyawarra

Das ist eine **mandzu**... Gottesanbeterin
sie ist der Wind... der Geist des Windes
sie gehört zu **Jillinya**

Sie ist die größte unter den Müttern
die Mutter von allen

Nyawarra

Cette **mandzu**... cette mante religieuse
c'est un souffle... un grand souffle
qui appartient à **Jillinya**

Elle est la Grande Matriarche
la mère de tous

Nyawarra

All this lot happy now
it's time for ceremony and offerings their life
and it was that dressings they put on
for big celebrations for big dance
for initiation to make man
out of this knife... **gimbu** stone knife
and that's what they did
So they don't use **banad** when
they're are going into the law
but they use them when they finished
after **wir.nganyen**... after smoking them

Nyawarra

Alle sind fröhlich hier
es ist Zeit für das Ritual Zeit ihr Leben zu schenken
so waren sie gekleidet
für große Feste und Tänze
für die Initiation die macht sie zum Mann
mit diesem Messer... Messer aus **gimbu**-Stein
so haben sie das gemacht
Sie tragen keine **banad**
wenn sie Teil des Gesetzes werden
aber sie benutzen sie später
wir.nganyen... wenn der Rauch weg ist

Nyawarra

Tous ceux-là ils sont heureux là
c'est le moment pour faire les cérémonies
et pour offrir sa vie
et ils mettaient ces habits-là
pour les grandes célébrations et la grande danse
de l'initiation qui fait devenir homme
par ce couteau, un couteau fait avec la pierre
gimbu et c'est ce qu'ils faisaient
Donc ils n'utilisaient pas le **banad**
quand ils commençaient à entrer dans la Loi
mais ils l'utilisaient après
quand ils avaient fini... après **wir.nganyen**...

Nyawarra

wongai munnumburra... law woman
She the one that's in the centre

Mother she's got two names
Jillinya* or *Mumuu

***Jillinya*... all the kids go to her...**
never forgotten mother
Always will be gifts to her

***Jillinya* is the Great Mother**
All the kids can go to her
say like all the families father and mother
They bring all the presents to her
They might have seven or eight sons
or nine daughters
they'll bring all the presents to her
***Jillinya*... they will give it to her**
she's the Great Mother... mother of all
***Jillinya* was the Greatest Mother**

Nyawarra

wongai munnumburra ... die Hüterin des Gesetzes
Das ist die Frau in der Mitte

Die Mutter hat zwei Namen
Jillinya* oder *Mumuu

***Jillinya* ... zu der gehen alle Kinder ...**
zu der Mutter, die man nie vergisst
Bringen ihr immer Geschenke

***Jillinya* ist die Große Mutter**
Alle Kinder können zu ihr gehen
und die Familien auch Väter und Mütter
Alle bringen ihr Geschenke
Und wenn sie sieben oder acht Söhne haben
oder neun Töchter
dann bringen alle Geschenke
***Jillinya* ... sie geben ihr Geschenke**
sie ist die Große Mutter ... die Mutter von allen
***Jillinya* war die größte Mutter**

Nyawarra

wongai munnumburra ... la gardienne de la Loi
Elle est celle qui est au centre

La Matriarche a deux noms
Jillinya* ou *Mumuu

***Jillinya* ... tous les enfants vont vers elle ...**
on n'oublie jamais la Matriarche
Il y aura toujours des présents pour elle

***Jillinya* est la Grande Matriarche**
Tous les enfants peuvent aller vers elle
disons que c'est comme n'importe quelle famille
père et mère lui apportent tous les présents
Ils peuvent avoir sept ou huit fils
ou neuf filles
ils lui apporteront tous les présents à elle
***Jillinya* ... ils les donneront à elle**
elle est la Grande Matriarche ... la mère de tous
***Jillinya* était la Mère originelle**

Nyawarra

All these women
who are in the new generation
*they are **Jillinya***

Nyawarra

All die Frauen
der neuen Generation
*die sind alle **Jillinya***

Nyawarra

Toutes ces femmes
qui sont de la nouvelle génération
*elles sont **Jillinya***

Nyawarra

It's like a pattern this land...
what I was just talking about
that all this food here
this lot here is like all their food
yam... also some water lily

they travel around the **Wunan**
any little thing never go without **Wunan**
they all in that **Wunan**
Nyawarra

Wunan is created
from beginning
to share everything in life
It's a total care of life that **Wunan**
Banggal

Das ist wie ein Muster, das Land…
wovon ich eben geredet habe
das hier, das ist das Essen
das Muster hier, das ist wie ihr Essen
Jamswurzeln … und auch ein paar Seerosen

sie wandern auf den **Wunan**-Pfaden
auch das Allerkleinste gehört zum **Wunan**
alles gehört zum **Wunan**
Nyawarra

Das **Wunan** war da
von Anfang an
es gehört zum ganzen Leben dazu
Wunan schließt das ganze Leben ein
Banggal

C'est comme un canevas, un réseau ce pays…
c'est ce que je disais juste à l'instant
que toute cette nourriture là
l'igname… le nénuphar aussi

ils circulent par le **Wunan**
la moindre petite chose
ne va jamais sans le **Wunan**
ils sont tous dans le **Wunan**
Nyawarra

Le **Wunan** fut créé
dès le début
pour partager toutes les choses de la vie
Ce **Wunan** prend soin de toute la vie
Banggal

Gwion Gwion...
they found out what is good... eatable
and they given it name
*this one **ganmangu**... yams*
***jarrgun**... potato*
All sorts of food that we eat
like vegetables
*but they still in the **Wunan***
because everybody been share tucker
it's the living spirit
*this is the **mangarri**... food*

It means tucker...
***mangarri** means everything what we eat*

***mangarri** can be anything... can be flour*
it can be damper... it can be bread
could be anything or bush tucker
*that's all **mangarri** what we eat*

Long as people eat that or animal eat it
*that the **mangarri** that the word*
the name of the whole thing
*what we eat... that **mangarri***
Nyawarra

Gwion Gwion...
die haben herausgefunden was gut ist... essbar
und haben ihm einen Namen gegeben
*das sind **ganmangu**... Jamswurzeln*
***jarrgun**... Kartoffeln*
Alles was wir essen
zum Beispiel Gemüse
*die gehören auch zum **Wunan***
weil die Nahrung allen gehört
das ist das Wesen des Lebens
*das ist **mangarri**... Nahrung*

Es bedeutet Essen...
***mangarri** ist alles was wir essen*

***mangarri** kann alles sein...*
Mehl oder Brotfladen... oder Brot
alles Mögliche die Sachen die wir im Busch finden
*alles ist **mangarri** alles was wir essen*

Ob Menschen es essen oder Tiere
*es ist **mangarri** das ist das Wort*
der Name für das Ganze
*für das was wir essen... **mangarri***
Nyawarra

*Les **Gwion Gwion**...*
ils trouvèrent ce qui est bon... comestible
et ils donnèrent un nom
*ça, c'est **ganmangu**... les ignames*
***jarrgun**... la patate*
toutes sortes de choses qu'on mange
comme les légumes
*elles sont toujours dans le **Wunan***
parce que tout le monde a partagé la nourriture
c'est l'esprit vivant
*c'est **mangarri**... la nourriture*

Ça veut dire la nourriture...
***mangarri** ça veut dire tout ce qui se mange*

***mangarri** ça peut être n'importe quoi...*
de la farine
ça peut être damper [un pain non levé]...
ça peut être du pain
ça peut être tout de la nourriture du bush
*tout ce qui se mange c'est **mangarri***

À partir du moment où on mange une chose
ou qu'un animal en mange
*c'est **mangarri**, c'est le mot*
le nom pour tout ça
*tout ce qu'on mange... c'est **mangarri***
Nyawarra

*All this lot **Gwion** now*

Everything that they had they carried
where they settle down to put their painting
and their food and gear that they had

Banggal

*Das da, das sind die **Gwion***

Alles, was sie hatten, trugen sie bei sich
als sie sich hier niederließen und ihre Bilder malten
ihr Essen und alles was sie an Sachen hatten

Banggal

*Tous ces **Gwion***

Tout ce qu'ils avaient ils l'ont emmené
où ils se sont posés pour mettre leurs peintures
et la nourriture et les affaires qu'ils avaient

Banggal

He look like all the vegetables
and everything when they throw it out
you know... when they was real happy
when they give the celebration
and everybody was happy throw it up
give a party and everything

Nyawarra

Das da sieht aus wie das Gemüse
und die anderen Sachen die sie hochwarfen
weißt du ... wenn sie wirklich fröhlich waren
wenn sie ein Fest gefeiert haben
und alle waren so richtig glücklich
da haben sie Sachen hochgeworfen
eine richtige Party

Nyawarra

Ça ressemble à des légumes
qu'on a jeté en l'air
tu vois... quand ils étaient vraiment contents
quand ils célébraient
tout le monde était heureux, de le lancer
de faire la fête, tout ça

Nyawarra

They share it out with the people

maybe **Wodoi** people... **Jungun** people
they all share it out
all this tucker all these things here
What are in this cave here
they all share it out
whole lot in this **Wunan**
even little kid can't miss out
even the dog must have the skin of kangaroo
they throw it to him
still have that share with these people
Nyawarra

Sie haben alles mit den anderen geteilt

Wodoi-Leute vielleicht ... und **Jungun**-Leute
die haben alles geteilt
das ganze Essen die ganzen Sachen hier
Alles was man hier in der Höhle sieht
das haben sie alles geteilt
das alles gehört zum **Wunan**
selbst kleine Kinder bekommen etwas
sogar der Hund bekommt die Känguru-Haut
die werfen sie ihm hin
selbst mit dem teilen sie
Nyawarra

Ils partageaient tout entre tous

les **Wodoi**... les **Jungun**
ils partagent tout
toute cette nourriture, toutes ces choses
qui sont dans cette grotte là
ils partagent tous tout dans le **Wunan**
même un petit enfant ne peut pas y échapper
même le chien doit avoir la peau du kangourou
ils la lui lancent
ils partagent toujours entre tous
Nyawarra

a

b

c

All **Ngarinyin** acknowledge the pre-eminence of **Jillinya** as the Great Mother of everyone. It was **Jillinya** who gave women their genitals and the gift of motherhood. Most people imagine that the mystery of birth would have been the first big question facing humankind. All humans appear from women. Men must have been in awe and truly have wondered at the magic that women demonstrated in creating life from inside their bodies. Women make everyone as flesh and blood; the fecund and procreative power of women promotes many myths and religious beliefs. For the **Ngarinyin,** the origins of the first people – those with the independent power of human birth – grow from one eternal mother **Jillinya**.

Jillinya is revered as the proto-female, the mother of all the **Gwion** ancestors. The **Ngarinyin** firmly believe that the first animals and humans were put on earth by **Wanjina**. But it was **Jillinya,** also known by the sacred name **Mumuu,** who gave women their womb and va- ginas and the power of reproduction (as **Ngarjno** and **Nyawarra** reveal with the greatest discretion and mod- esty). That women had great authority among **Gwion** people from the earliest days is demonstrated by the strong and imposing matriarchal icons at **Alyaguma** waterhole. Beneath the dominating presence of these female leaders proclaiming their authority with raised hands, any visitor, feels humble. **Ungudman** came before this group of great mothers spreading out across the gal- lery wall, and reverently, reached up to touch and name each one. Then he approached the icon of **Algi,** one ancient reincarnation of **Jillinya,** the Great Mother her- self. **Algi** rests horizontally; she is painted with large breasts, and many faded spears are superimposed all over her large reclining body. It was her multitude of children, the **Gwion,** who gathered and presented all these spears to the Mother as tribute, a **lulwa** (gift) of respect.

The **Algi** icon reclines at the base of the **Alyaguma** wall, with a long **dulwan** (pathway) coming from her abdomen. Several small birds form part of the track of this pathway as it ascends high up the rock face. It culminates in two feet that divide the very top, one for each of the pair of **skin** groups forming the **moiety** kinship system originated by **Wodoi** and **Jungun**. **Algi** is positioned immediately above a narrow, dark cavity that extends back under the wall of numerous paintings. In this shady crevice of striped yellow and grey layers of stone, is a shallow bed of damp sand holding an array of mossy herbs known for the potent healing powers attributed to **Jillinya**.

Alle **Ngarinyin** sehen in **Jillinya** die Große Mutter, die Mut- ter allen Lebens. **Jillinya** schenkte den Frauen ihr Geschlecht und die Gabe, Kinder zu gebären. Für die meisten ist das Geheimnis der Geburt das erste große Rätsel der Mensch- heit. Alle Menschen sind von Frauen geboren. Es muss die Männer mit Ehrfurcht und Staunen erfüllt haben, als sie sahen, wie die Frauen auf wundersame Weise im Inneren ihres Körpers neues Leben erschaffen konnten. Frauen geben jedem einen Körper aus Fleisch und Blut, und die Fruchtbarkeit der Frauen ist der Ursprung zahlloser Mythen und religiöser Vorstellungen. Für die **Ngarinyin** stammen die ersten Menschen, die selbst Kinder gebären konnten, von einer einzigen ewigen Mutter ab – **Jillinya**.

Jillinya wird verehrt als der Inbegriff des Weiblichen, die Mutter aller **Gwion**-Ahnen. Die **Ngarinyin** glauben, dass die ersten Tiere und Menschen von der **Wanjina** auf die Erde gebracht wurden. Doch erst **Jillinya** – auch bekannt unter dem heiligen Namen **Mumuu** – schenkte den Frauen die Gebärmutter und die Vagina und die Gabe der Fort- pflanzung (wie **Ngarjno** und **Nyawarra** mit viel Takt und Diskretion zu berichten wissen). Dass Frauen bei den **Gwion** von Anfang an hohes Ansehen genossen, zeigen die eindrucksvollen Frauendarstellungen an der Wasser- stelle von **Alyaguma**. Im Angesicht dieser imposanten weiblichen Gestalten, deren erhobene Hände von Autorität künden, beugt sich jeder Besucher in Demut. Als **Ungudman** vor diese in einer langen Reihe auf der Felswand abgebildeten Muttergestalten hintrat, erhob er voller Ehrfurcht die Hand, berührte sie eine nach der anderen und nannte sie beim Namen. Dann näherte er sich dem Bild von **Algi,** einer uralten Inkarnation der **Jillinya,** der Großen Mutter selbst. **Algi** ist liegend und mit großen Brüsten dargestellt; und auf den riesigen Körper sind viele, kaum noch sichtbare Speere aufgemalt. Es waren ihre zahllosen Kinder, die **Gwion,** die sich ver- sammelten und der Mutter all diese Speere als Tribut darbrachten; als **lulwa** (Geschenk) das als Zeichen der Ehrfurcht gilt.

Das Bild der liegenden **Algi** findet sich am Fuß der Fels- wand von **Alyaguma,** und an ihrem Unterleib beginnt ein langer Pfad **(dulwan)**. Einige kleine Vögel sind Teil dieses Pfades, der über die Felswand nach oben führt. Ganz oben mündet er in zwei Füße, einer für jede der beiden von **Wodoi** und **Jungun** geschaffenen **moieties** oder **skins**. **Algi** ruht unmittelbar oberhalb einer engen, dunklen Höhle, die sich längs unter der mit zahlreichen Figuren be- malten Felswand erstreckt. In diesem schattigen Spalt aus gelbem und grauem Schichtgestein wachsen auf einer feuchten Sandfläche allerlei Moose und Kräuter, deren heilkräftige Wirkung **Jillinya** zugeschrieben wird.

Tous les **Ngarinyin** admettent la prééminence de **Jillinya,** la Mère de tous. C'est **Jillinya** qui a donné aux femmes leurs organes génitaux et le don de maternité. La plupart des gens pensent que le mystère de la naissance est la première grande question que l'humanité se soit posée. Tous les humains sortent du corps des femmes. Les hommes ont dû rester pensifs et émerveillés devant la magie des femmes créant la vie à l'intérieur de leur corps. Les femmes font le monde de chair et de sang ; la fécondité et le pouvoir de procréation des femmes sont à l'origine de nombreux mythes et croyances religieuses. Pour les **Ngarinyin,** à l'origine, les premiers êtres vivants, ceux qui n'ont pas eu besoin de naître d'un être humain, sont venus d'une mère éternelle – **Jillinya**.

Jillinya est vénérée en tant que proto-femme, en tant que mère de tous les ancêtres **Gwion**. Les **Ngarinyin** croient fermement que les premiers animaux et humains ont été placés sur terre par les **Wanjina**. Mais c'est **Jillinya,** également connue sous le nom de **Mumuu** qui a donné aux femmes leur utérus, leur vagin et le pouvoir de la reproduction (**Ngarjno** et **Nyawarra** révèlent cela avec discrétion et humilité). On peut en avoir pour preuve que les femmes avaient une grande autorité parmi les **Gwion** depuis les temps les plus reculés, en voyant les fortes et imposantes figures matriarcales du point d'eau d'**Alyaguma**. Devant la présence dominatrice de ces repré- sentations féminines proclamant leur autorité par leurs mains levées, tout visiteur se sent humble. **Ungudman** vint près de ce groupe d'images de mères s'étendant sur tout le mur de la galerie, et, avec respect, leva le bras pour toucher et nommer chacune d'elles. Ensuite, il s'approcha de l'image d'**Algi,** une ancienne réincarnation de **Jillinya,** la Mère originelle. **Algi** repose horizontale- ment, elle est représentée avec de gros seins et de nom- breuses lances aux couleurs passées qui sont dessinées en surimpression sur tout son corps majestueux. C'est la mul- titude de ses enfants, les **Gwion,** qui ont rassemblé et donné ces lances à la Mère comme tribut, un **lulwa** (don) de respect.

L'image d'**Algi** en position allongée s'étale à la base du mur d'**Alyaguma,** avec un long chemin **(dulwan)** sortant de son abdomen. Plusieurs petits oiseaux forment des éléments de ce chemin qui monte sur la roche. Il culmine par deux pieds qui divisent le sommet, un pour chaque paire de **skin** (« peaux ») des **moitiés** créées par **Wodoi** et **Jungun**. **Algi** se trouve juste au-dessous d'une étroite et sombre cavité qui se prolonge, couverte de nombreuses peintures. Dans cette crevasse où l'on voit des couches de pierres rayées jaune et grise, il y a un lit creux de sable humide abritant un ensemble d'herbes moussues connues pour leurs puissants pouvoirs de guérison attribués à **Jillinya**.

Alyaguma

a

b

c

There are numerous **Gwion** paintings with a female association. These may represent **Gwion** as **Jillinya's** children during that matriarchal period when women constituted the dominant authority. When they talk about the practice of **Gwion** bringing **lulwa**, for her, the belief is clearly expressed that **Gwion** worshipped her, as children worship their mother. When **munnumburra** men talk of **Jillinya** and her influence today, they always show deep respect for **munnumburra** women, "law women", who carry their authority from the Great Mother with great vitality.

While male authority increased with the establishment of patrilineal clan estates, there is one **dambun** permanently named after **Jillinya** at **Anaut.ngarri;** this is a coastal territory associated with **mandzu** (mantis) and sacred wind totems belonging to the **Jungun moiety.** Virtually all **Gwion** images are considered to be **Jillinya's** children and all modern **Ngarinyin** women to be living reincarnations of **Jillinya** herself. Groups of small figures portrayed with breasts in **Jillinya's** sanctuary portray young women developing milk for the first time; they also have haloed heads that hint at later **wanjina** imagery (a).

Jillinya icons are streaked with red brush-strokes that flow rhythmically over a painted white ground. Red, the universal colour of blood, can represent the substance of life flowing from the Great Mother. Some early **Gwion** images, painted in blood, would have been appropriate for the children of **Jillinya.** Blood was probably the first paint used as sacred art in **Jillinya's bunja** (rock-shelter). This concurs with the traditional accounts of how the first paintings appeared, when the "cave-bird" **Gwion** used its beak to wipe blood across the surface of stone.

Gender is not obviously marked in most **Gwion** human figures. There are numerous elaborately dressed humans without either obvious male genitals or female breasts. These may represent **Gwion** as **Jillinya's** children living around sacred female places associated with the dominant authority of the Great Mother. **Numurangga** (females) may be portrayed with fuller shape of thigh, stomach and hip, but are best distinguished through differences in clothing, like the **mambi** (triangular waist girdles) of possum or kangaroo hide (b).

Es gibt zahlreiche **Gwion**-Malereien mit weiblichen Motiven. Sie dürften die **Gwion** als Kinder der **Jillinya** in der Zeit des Matriarchats zeigen, als die Herrschaft des Stammes in den Händen der Frauen lag. Wenn davon die Rede ist, dass die **Gwion** ihr **lulwa** bringen, spricht daraus deutlich, dass die **Gwion** sie verehrten, so wie Kinder ihre Mutter verehren. Wenn die männlichen **munnumburra** von **Jillinya** und ihrem heutigen Einfluss sprechen, zeigen sie immer große Achtung vor weiblichen **munnumburra,** den Hüterinnen des Gesetzes, die mit viel Elan die von der Großen Mutter verliehene Autorität ausüben.

Mit dem Entstehen von patrilinearen Clangebieten nahm auch die Macht der Männer zu; doch im **Anaut.ngarri** hat sich auch ein **dambun** erhalten, das den Namen der **Jillinya** trägt; dieses Küstengebiet wird assoziiert mit der **mandzu** (Gottesanbeterin) und mit den heiligen Wind-Totems, die der **Jungun moiety** zugeordnet sind. Im Grunde gelten sämtliche Bilder der **Gwion** als Darstellungen der Kinder **Jillinyas** und alle heutigen **Ngarinyin**-Frauen als lebende Reinkarnationen der **Jillinya.** Die Gruppen von kleinen Figuren, die im Heiligtum der **Jillinya** mit Brüsten dargestellt sind, lassen sich als junge Frauen deuten, die zum ersten Mal Milch produzieren; sie tragen eine Art Heiligenschein, der schon an spätere **wanjina**-Bilder denken lässt (a).

Typisch für die **Jillinya**-Darstellungen sind die rhythmisch fließenden roten Pinselstriche auf einem weißen Malgrund. Das Rot, die allgegenwärtige Farbe des Blutes, ist als Inbegriff der Substanz des Lebens zu verstehen, die von der Großen Mutter ausströmt. Für einige frühe **Gwion**-Darstellungen der Kinder **Jillinyas** wäre es durchaus angemessen gewesen, wenn man sie mit Blut gemalt hätte. Blut dürfte der erste Farbstoff gewesen sein, mit der die heiligen Bilder in der **bunja** (Felsengrotte) des **Jillinya**-Heiligtums gemalt wurden. Das entspräche auch den traditionellen Berichten, nach denen die ersten Bilder entstanden, als der „Höhlenvogel" **Gwion** seinen blutigen Schnabel an dem Felsen abwischte.

Bei den meisten Menschendarstellungen der **Gwion** ist das Geschlecht nicht eindeutig bestimmbar. Es gibt viele reich geschmückte Figuren, die weder sichtbare männliche Genitalien noch Frauenbrüste haben. Sie dürften die **Gwion** als Kinder der **Jillinya** in der Zeit des Matriarchats zeigen, als die Herrschaft nach den Überlieferungen des Stammes noch in den Händen der Frauen lag. Bisweilen sind die Frauen **(numurangga)** mit runderen Formen an Schenkeln, Bauch und Hüfte dargestellt, doch am besten erkennt man sie an Unterschieden in der Kleidung, etwa am **mambi** (dreieckiger Lendenschurz) aus Possum- oder Känguruleder (b).

De nombreuses peintures **Gwion** sont associées à l'image de la femme. Elles peuvent représenter des **Gwion** en enfants de **Jillinya** pendant la période matriarcale quand les femmes étaient l'autorité dominante. Quand elles représentent la pratique des **Gwion** consistant à apporter des **lulwa** pour **Jillinya,** on y voit la croyance que les **Gwion** l'adoraient comme les enfants adorent leur mère. Quand les hommes **munnumburra** parlent de **Jillinya** et de son influence aujourd'hui, ils montrent toujours beaucoup de respect pour les femmes **munnumburra,** « les femmes gardiennes de la Loi » qui tiennent toujours de façon très vivante leur autorité de la Mère originelle.

Alors que l'autorité masculine a augmenté avec l'établissement des domaines claniques patrilinéaires, il y a cependant un **dambun** qui tient son nom de **Jillinya** à **Anaut.ngarri.** C'est un territoire côtier associé à **mandzu** (la mante) et aux totems sacrés des vents appartenant à la **moitié Jungun.** Quasiment toutes les représentations **Gwion** sont considérées comme étant des enfants de **Jillinya** et toutes les femmes **Ngarinyin** contemporaines comme étant des réincarnations vivantes de **Jillinya.** Des groupes de petites figures avec des seins dans le sanctuaire de **Jillinya** montrent les jeunes femmes ayant leurs premières montées de lait. Elles ont également des têtes auréolées qui sont une allusion à l'imagerie **wanjina** plus tardive (a).

Les images de **Jillinya** sont striées de raies rouges obtenues par des mouvements rythmés du pinceau, ondulant en rythme sur un fond peint en blanc. Le rouge, symbole universel du sang, peut être la représentation de la substance de vie provenant de la Grande Matriarche. Certaines images **Gwion** anciennes, peintes avec du sang, sont bien appropriées pour les enfants de **Jillinya.** Le sang a probablement été la première peinture utilisée pour l'art sacré, dans l'abri sous roche **(bunja)** de **Jillinya.** Cela concorde avec les récits traditionnels qui racontent que les premières peintures sont apparues quand « l'oiseau des cavernes » **Gwion** a utilisé son bec pour étaler du sang sur la pierre.

Le sexe n'est pas indiqué de façon précise dans la plupart des représentations humaines **Gwion.** Il y a de nombreux êtres humains soigneusement habillés mais sur lesquels n'apparaissent pas clairement des organes génitaux masculins ou des poitrines féminines. Ils représentent peut-être les **Gwion** en enfants de **Jillinya** pendant la période matriarcale, lorsque les femmes étaient l'autorité dominante. Les femmes **(numurangga)** peuvent être représentées avec des cuisses, estomacs et hanches plus rondes mais se reconnaissent le plus par leurs différences dans l'habillement, comme par exemple avec leurs ceintures triangulaires **(mambi)** faites en peau d'opossum ou de kangourou (b).

numurangga

d

e

f

Feathers consistently ornament heads and wigs, limbs and bodies; there is some elaborate off-the-shoulder plumage. All generations of images show utilitarian **garagi** (bags) being carried by both sexes. The **garagi** indicate the nomadic way of life of the people at that time. Women should wear flat **mambi** (triangular hide skirts) that hang behind from the waist, but they are often pictured with shorter aprons (c) called **wuduwan**. They also wear **wa.ngara** (string or hide skirts with tassels) which are especially common. Because breasts generally are not shown on female forms, gender distinctions may be mistaken by an observer confusing a rounded belly or bulbous waist on a female with the **jangun** (belt) on a male.

Only **amurangga** (males) should wear the bulky **jangun** of rope made from kangaroo-hair and wrapped around the waist. They alone should wear the **walbud** (girdles that are made of possum-hide); these are painted as a bulbous shape with three distinct peaks, and often distinguish **amurangga** apparel (d).

Gwion figures of both sexes are depicted wearing many kinds of **yururu.mal,** necklaces of feather and string. Also depicted are **jalim.baran** (dancing wands) a flexible branch often ending with a feather stripped along the spine except at the tip (e).

Boomerangs held in the hand prevail as a motif throughout all generations of **Gwion** images whereas spears are often absent. **Munnumburra** evidence consistently supports other oral history from central desert to northern coast, identifying the beaked forms as the prototype boomerang. This form, known as **lung.gudengari** or "Number 7", exploited the natural "elbow" shape found in a branch of hardwood. Its shape, similar to the erect head of the bush turkey (Kori Bustard), gives this boomerang its everyday name, the **banad.**

The other, more recent type of boomerang is the crescent shaped **mandi** (f). This is normally carved from lighter wood, and is most often shown being held in one hand. This pose is typical of participants in dance, implying that the dancers are singing to the sound of clapping; **mandi** are instruments of rhythm for the long sequences of **Wunan** songs.

Federn sind ein beliebter Kopfschmuck und zieren Perücken, Gliedmaßen und Körper, und ein weiterer kunstvoller Federschmuck wird auf der Schulter getragen. Unabhängig von ihrer Entstehungszeit sieht man auf den Bildern Männer wie Frauen mit den vielseitig einsetzbaren Taschen, den so genannten **garagi.** Diese **garagi** sind ein Indiz für die nomadische Lebensweise der damaligen Aborigine-Bevölkerung. Die Frauen tragen in der Regel einen flachen **mambi** (dreieckiger Lendenschurz) der auf der Rückseite von der Taille herunterhängt, aber man sieht sie auch oft mit einem kürzeren Schurz, dem **wuduwan** (c). Vielfach tragen sie auch als **wa.ngara** bezeichnete Röcke aus Schnüren oder Leder mit Quasten. Da die weiblichen Figuren in der Regel ohne Brüste dargestellt werden, sind Geschlechtsunterschiede nur schwer zu erkennen, und es kann leicht vorkommen, dass der Betrachter den gerundeten Bauch einer Frau für den **jangun** (Gürtel) eines Mannes hält.

Die sperrigen **jangun** aus einer um die Taille gewickelten Schnur aus Känguru-Haaren sind Männern **(amurangga)** vorbehalten. Sie sind auch die einzigen, die den **walbud** (Lendenschurz aus Opossumleder) tragen; auf den Bildern erscheint er als rundliche Form mit drei deutlich erkennbaren Spitzen und ist oft ein Anzeichen dafür, dass es sich bei dem Dargestellten um einen Mann handelt (d).

Männer wie Frauen werden mit einer Vielzahl von Halsketten aus Federn und Schnüren dargestellt, den **yururu.mal.** Außerdem tragen sie jalim.baran (Tanzstäbe) – biegsame Zweige, oft mit einer bis auf die Spitze gerupften Feder am Vorderende (e).

Vielfach halten die Figuren auf den Felsbildern der **Gwion,** gleich aus welcher Epoche, einen Bumerang in der Hand; Speere finden sich dagegen nur selten. Die Aussagen der **munnumburra** decken sich genau mit anderen mündlichen Überlieferungen aus der Wüstenregion Zentralaustraliens bis hin zur Nordküste: Alle nennen den Hakenbumerang als älteste Form. Diese **lung.gudengari** oder „Nummer sieben" genannte Form machte sich den natürlichen, ellenbogenartigen Knick eines Hartholzastes zunutze. Da die Silhouette an den hoch aufgereckten Kopf einer Buschtrappe erinnert, trägt dieser Bumerang auch den Namen **banad.**

Die neueren Bumerangs **(mandi)** sind eher sichelförmig und in der Regel aus leichterem Holz geschnitzt (f); auf den Bildern werden sie meist in einer Hand gehalten. Diese Haltung ist typisch für Tänzer und zeigt, dass sie singen und ihren Gesang durch Aneinanderschlagen der Bumerangs untermalen. **Mandi** sind rhythmische Begleitinstrumente für die langen Sequenzen der **Wunan**-Lieder.

Des plumes ornent souvent les têtes, les coiffes, les membres et le corps; il existe aussi des plumages complexes qui partent des épaules. Des images de différentes époques montrent que les **garagi** (sacs utilitaires) étaient portés par les deux sexes. Les **garagi** indiquent que ces gens étaient des nomades à l'époque. Les femmes devraient porter des **mambi** (jupes plates triangulaires en peau) qui pendent sur le derrière depuis la taille, mais elles sont souvent représentées portant des tabliers plus courts (c) qu'on appelle **wuduwan.** Elles portent également des **wa.ngara,** jupes faites en cordons ou en peau, ornées de pompons, éléments particulièrement courants. Parce que les seins ne sont généralement pas représentés sur les formes féminines, distinguer le sexe d'une figure est parfois difficile, et on peut se méprendre et confondre un ventre rond ou une grosse taille sur une image féminine avec une **jangun** (ceinture) sur un personnage masculin.

Seuls les hommes **(amurangga)** peuvent porter la volumineuse **jangun** faite en corde de poils de kangourou et qui s'enroule autour de la taille. Eux seuls également peuvent porter les **walbud** (ceintures en peau d'opossum); celles-ci sont peintes sous une forme volumineuse avec trois protubérances distinctes et marquent souvent l'habillement masculin (d).

Les figures **Gwion** des deux sexes portent différentes sortes de **yururu.mal,** colliers en plume et cordons. On y retrouve également les **jalim.baran** (bâtons de danse) faits d'une branche souple se terminant souvent par une plume, dénudée autour de la hampe sauf à l'extrémité (e).

Dans les images **Gwion** de toutes périodes les boomerangs tenus à la main sont très courants alors que les lances sont souvent absentes. Le témoignage des **munnumburra** corrobore une autre histoire orale, véhiculée du désert central à la côte nord, qui établit que les formes dites « à bec » sont le prototype du boomerang. Ce type de boomerang, connu sous le nom de **lung.gudengari** ou « numéro 7 », tire parti de la forme naturelle en « coude » d'une branche de bois dur. Sa forme, similaire au profil d'une tête d'outarde australienne (Kori Bustard, appelé aussi dindon sauvage) est à l'origine du nom usuel de ce boomerang, **banad.**

L'autre type, plus récent, de boomerang est le **mandi** (f), en forme de croissant; il est normalement taillé dans un bois plus léger et est le plus souvent représenté tenu dans une main. Cette posture est typique des participants à des danses, ce qui implique que les danseurs chantent accompagnés au son du claquement des boomerangs **mandi** qui rythment les longues périodes des chants **Wunan.**

amurangga

a
b
c

Most original cultures prevailing throughout the tropical regions of northern Australia and southern Papua preserve traditions of the origin of the human family that begin with humans as the children of one great eternal mother. She is known by many names, but the common symbol of this enormous and generous proto-female is the praying mantis.

The praying mantis, which significantly releases and stands guard over a multitude of fully formed but miniature offspring, is revered as a natural manifestation of the primordial mother's power and prolific fecundity. The **Ngarinyin** eternal mother **Jillinya** as mother of the first real humans also has the praying mantis or **mandzu** as her living symbol and totemic sign. Ancient graphic evidence of the metaphoric association between the Great Mother and the insect **mandzu** is preserved in one of her sanctuaries at **Guringi**. Two aspects of the mother-mantis relationship are preserved here in neighbouring, but quite different paintings. The residue of two bold black figures wearing **mandzu mudurra** remain on the same high wall as the sacred icon of **Jillinya** herself. Nearby on a slab of stone on the floor is a delicately painted scene of a **birrina** dance that is surely ancient.

The taller of the two black residual images is a particularly enigmatic mantis-human figure partially submerged beneath layers of surface stains and other superimposed images (these more recent additions include a red kangaroo, probably the ancestor **Binbin** whose name originated in this region, and two trailing infant-like anthropomorphic figures).This impressive black **mandzu** dancer has several female features found in **Gwion** representations of women; rounded legs and thighs and the typical women's **wa.ngara** (girdle made from fibre or hide string) that hangs to make a long skirt. The most significant feature is the unique triangular **mudurra** representing the head of the praying mantis (a). The bulbous eyes of a mantis round out the base of the triangle and a pointed beak shapes the apex of this uniquely formed wig. Also extending upwards from this **mandzu mudurra** are two very long **yululun** (feathers) representing the two insect antennae of the living mantis. The pair of **yululun** sweep away as if swaying in unison to the dancer's movement. This **mandzu mudurra** virtually replaces the human head of the figure as befits a trance dancer revealing **Jillinya** the Great Mother herself. Holding two **mandi** in one hand implies songs associating **Jillinya** with **mandzu.** They were performed when this artist worked here in **Jillinya's** sanctuary.

Bei den meisten alten Kulturen der tropischen Regionen von Nordaustralien und Süd-Papua gibt es Mythen über den Ursprung der Menschen, die von diesen als den Kindern einer großen Urmutter sprechen. Man kennt sie unter vielen Namen, doch das allen gemeinsame Symbol dieses gewaltigen, unendlich fruchtbaren Urtyps des Weiblichen ist die Gottesanbeterin.

Die Larven der Gottesanbeterin, die sie wachsam behütet, schlüpfen in großer Zahl als vollständig ausgebildete Miniaturausgaben der Mutter, und deswegen wird sie verehrt als das lebendige Abbild der Kraft und Fruchtbarkeit der Urmutter. Den **Ngarinyin** gilt die Urmutter **Jillinya** als Mutter der ersten eigentlichen Menschen, und die Gottesanbeterin **(mandzu)** ist ihr lebendes Symbol und Totemzeichen. Alte Bildbelege für die Verbindung zwischen der Großen Mutter und der Gottesanbeterin sind in ihrem Heiligtum in **Guringi** erhalten. Dort sehen wir zwei Aspekte der Mutter-**mandzu**-Beziehung in benachbarten und dennoch völlig verschiedenartigen Malereien. Die Überreste zweier in kräftigem Schwarz gemalter Figuren mit **mandzu mudurra** sind auf derselben hohen Wand zu erkennen wie das heilige Bild der **Jillinya.** Nicht weit davon entfernt, auf einer Steinplatte am Boden, findet sich die mit feinen Linien gemalte uralte Darstellung eines **birrina**-Tanzes.

Die größere der beiden nur teilweise erhaltenen schwarzen Figuren zeigt eine ausgesprochen rätselhafte Verbindung aus Mensch und Gottesanbeterin, teils unter Oberflächenschäden und mehreren Schichten von Übermalungen verschwunden (zu diesen späteren Hinzufügungen gehört das Bild eines roten Kängurus, vermutlich das Ahnenwesen **Binbin,** dessen Name in dieser Gegend seinen Ursprung hat, gefolgt von zwei anthropomorphen Figuren, bei denen es sich um Kinder handeln könnte). Diese faszinierende schwarze **mandzu**-Tänzergestalt hat eine Reihe von weiblichen Zügen, wie sie typisch für die Frauendarstellungen der **Gwion** sind: gerundete Beine und Oberschenkel und den typischen **wa.ngara** (Gürtel aus Schnüren oder Lederstreifen), die zusammen einen langen Rock ergeben. Der auffälligste Zug ist die unverwechselbare dreieckige Perücke, die für den Kopf der Gottesanbeterin steht (a). An der Basis des Dreiecks sieht man die typischen gewölbten Insektenaugen, und die Krönung dieser einzigartigen Perücke bildet eine Art spitzer Schnabel. Überragt wird die **mandzu mudurra** von zwei extrem langen **yululun** (Federn), die für die Fühler der Gottesanbeterin stehen. Die beiden **yululun** bilden einen schwungvollen Bogen, als wiegten sie sich im Takt zur Bewegung der Tänzerin. Auf diesem Bild verdeckt die Perücke den Menschenkopf der Figur fast vollständig, wie es für eine Tänzerin in Trance, die **Jillinya** verkörpert, die Große Mutter, nur angemessen ist. Die zwei **mandi** in ihrer Hand lassen darauf schließen, dass die Arbeit des Künstlers hier im Heiligtum der **Jillinya** begleitet wurde von Gesängen, die **Jillinya** mit der **mandzu** in Verbindung brachten.

La plupart des cultures, dans les régions tropicales d'Australie du nord et de la Papouasie, conservent dans leurs traditions une Grande Matriarche qui a pour enfants toute l'espèce humaine. Elle porte différents noms, mais le symbole de cette énorme et généreuse proto-femme est généralement la mante religieuse.

La mante religieuse donne la vie et protège une multitude d'êtres semblables en miniature. Elle est adorée comme la représentation dans la nature du pouvoir de fécondité. La mère éternelle des **Ngarinyin, Jillinya,** qui est la mère des premiers êtres humains, a aussi comme symbole vivant et totémique la mante religieuse ou **mandzu.** Un témoignage peint, ancien, de l'association symbolique entre la Grande Matriarche et la **mandzu** est conservé dans l'un de ces sanctuaires à **Guringi.** Là, deux représentations de la mère-mante sont présentes sur des peintures voisines quoique différentes. Ce qui est encore visible de deux puissantes figures noires portant des **mandzu mudurra** se trouve sur la même paroi que l'image sacrée de **Jillinya.** Au sol, non loin de là, sur une dalle de pierre, se trouve une peinture d'une scène de la danse **birrina** qui est vraisemblablement très ancienne.

La plus grande des deux figures noires dont il ne reste plus que des vestiges est une figure mi-femme mi-mante particulièrement énigmatique, partiellement cachée sous une superposition de couches de couleurs et d'images (dans les ajouts plus récents, le kangourou roux est probablement l'ancêtre **Binbin** dont le nom est originaire de cette région et les deux figures anthropomorphiques rampantes ressemblant à deux enfants en bas âge). Cette impressionnante danseuse noire **mandzu** présente plusieurs caractéristiques féminines qu'on trouve dans les représentations **Gwion** de femmes : jambes et cuisses rondes et la **wa.ngara** (ceinture féminine typique faite de cordons en fibre ou de peau) qui pend et donne l'aspect d'une jupe. La caractéristique la plus significative est la très particulière **mudurra** triangulaire représentant la tête de la mante religieuse (a). Les yeux globuleux de la mante arrondissent la base du triangle et son bec pointu à l'extrémité rend cette coiffe exceptionnelle par sa forme. Il y a aussi, s'étendant au-dessus de cette **mandzu mudurra,** deux très longues plumes **(yululun)** représentant les deux antennes de la mante. Les deux plumes se courbent comme si elles se balançaient avec le mouvement du danseur. Cette **mandzu mudurra** remplace la tête humaine de cette figure, comme on suppose que cela se passe lorsqu'un danseur en transe révèle **Jillinya,** la Mère originelle. La tenue de deux boomerangs **(mandi)** dans une main laisse supposer que les chants associant **Jillinya** à la **mandzu** furent joués quand l'artiste a travaillé dans ce sanctuaire de **Jillinya.**

mandzu

a

b

c

The second black figure (see p. 54) is much smaller and is almost lost to view, but it appears to be contemporary with the larger image. The head is nearly obliterated by dark brown and white seepage and weathering, but with close examination it is possible to perceive a mantis-shaped head and outstretched arms. When viewing these two mantis figures, preserved on the same wall as the huge **Jillinya** icon, they combine to create an overpowering sense of their matriarchal origin. When your eyes take in their dark intensity, they seem to reach towards you.

In another part of **Jillinya's** sacred **bunja** is an animated scene of people dancing, almost as if their bodies are floating in a space inside the stone. The composition beautifully preserves the connection between mantis and women by illustrating the dance known by **Ngarinyin** as the **birrina.** The **birrina** is for the public joining of women and men, an occasion for both sexes to wear long **mudurra** in a kind of ritual parade. Generations of **Gwion** artists have expertly painted layers of fully-wigged women dancing with opened arms.

In front of them, also dancing, is a man wearing an elongated **mudurra** that ends in a ball of trimmed feathers. Wearing **yidmunggul** (emu-hide epaulets) on his shoulders, he carries a pair of song boomerangs in one hand and trails a long **jalim.baran** (a). This male dancer has two small figures near his feet. As interpreted by **munnumburra,** the larger of these two figures appears recently to have undergone a ritual initiation into adulthood. One male youth, in a seated position and clearly of slight body in scale to his long hanging wig, appears to be watching the women. Wearing a distinctly male tri-pointed **walbud** (girdle), he is holding a pair of small boomerangs and a **garagi** (carry bag). After the conclusion of the **birrina** they would journey widely for a special "untouchable" period of considerable freedom, and would travel equipped with stone knives, ochres and any magic objects safely kept in a small **garagi** worn under the arm.

Die zweite schwarze Figur ist wesentlich kleiner und kaum mehr sichtbar, scheint aber aus der gleichen Zeit zu stammen wie das größere Bild (s. Seite 54). Der Kopf ist durch dunkelbraune und weiße Sickerwasserspuren und Verwitterung fast verschwunden, doch bei genauem Hinsehen kann man die Umrisse einer Gottesanbeterin und die ausgestreckten Arme noch erkennen. Die beiden kleinen Figuren finden sich an derselben Felswand wie das große Bild der **Jillinya,** und zusammen erzeugen sie einen überwältigenden Eindruck von der Urkraft des Mütterlichen. Wenn man sie in ihrer dunklen Intensität betrachtet, dann ist es gerade so, als streckten sie die Arme nach dem Betrachter aus.

An anderer Stelle der heiligen Höhle **(bunja)** der **Jillinya** ist eine beschwingte Tanzszene dargestellt, fast als schwebten die Körper der Tänzer im Inneren des Steins. Die Komposition bewahrt aufs Schönste die Verbindung zwischen den Frauen und der Gottesanbeterin in einer Illustration des Tanzes, den die **Ngarinyin birrina** nennen. Der **birrina** ist ein Tanz, bei dem Männer und Frauen zusammenkommen, und beide Geschlechter tragen dazu lange **mudurra** in einer Art rituellen Parade. Generationen von **Gwion**-Künstlern haben mit großem Geschick lange Reihen von Perücken tragenden Frauen gemalt, die mit ausgebreiteten Armen tanzen.

Vor ihnen, ebenfalls tanzend, steht ein Mann mit einer besonders hohen **mudurra,** die in einer Kugel aus beschnittenen Federn endet. Auf den Schultern trägt er **yidmunggul** (Epauletten aus Emuleder), in einer Hand ein Paar sichelförmige Bumerangs, die als Rhythmusinstrumente dienen, und er zieht einen langen Taktstock hinter sich her, den **jalim.baran** (a). Zu Füßen dieses Tanzenden finden sich noch zwei kleinere Figuren. Nach Deutung der **munnumburra** hat der Größere von beiden kurz zuvor seine rituelle Initiation ins Erwachsenenleben vollzogen. Ein sitzend dargestellter Junge, dessen schmächtiger Körper unter der Perücke mit lang herabhängendem Haar fast verschwindet, schaut offenbar den Frauen zu. Er trägt einen **walbud** (dreieckiger Lendenschurz der Männer), und hat zwei kleine Bumerangs und einen Beutel **(garagi)** in der Hand. Nach dem Ende des **birrina** zogen die frisch Initiierten noch einige Zeit, in der sie als „unberührbar" galten, relativ frei durchs Land, ausgerüstet mit steinernen Messern, Ockerfarbe und allerlei magischen Gegenständen, die sie in einem kleinen **garagi** unter dem Arm sicher verwahrten.

La seconde figure noire est beaucoup plus petite, presque invisible, mais elle semble être contemporaine de la plus grande (cf. p. 54). La tête est presque effacée par une coulure brune et blanche et par les intempéries mais, en l'examinant de près, il est possible d'apercevoir la forme d'une tête de mante et des bras ouverts. En regardant ces deux images de mante visibles sur le même mur que l'imposante **Jillinya,** on voit qu'elles se combinent pour accentuer l'aspect matriarcal; quand on les regarde intensément, elles semblent se mouvoir vers le spectateur.

Dans une autre partie du **bunja** sacré de **Jillinya,** il y a une scène animée où des gens dansent presque comme si leurs corps flottaient dans un espace à l'intérieur de la pierre. Illustration de la danse des **Ngarinyin** connue sous le nom de **birrina,** cette composition entretient d'une très belle manière le lien entre les femmes et les mantes. La **birrina** se danse comme une parade d'accouplement rituelle, en public; c'est une occasion pour les deux sexes de porter les longues **mudurra.** Des générations d'artistes **Gwion** ont peint de manière experte des couches d'images de femmes portant des coiffes et dansant les bras ouverts.

Devant elles, dansant aussi, il y a un homme portant une **mudurra** allongée qui se termine en une boule ornée de plumes. Portant sur ses épaules des **yidmunggul** (épaulettes en peau d'émeu), il a dans une main une paire de boomerangs qui servent lors des chants et traîne une longue baguette de danse, la **jalim.baran** (a). Ce danseur a deux petites figures près de ses pieds. Suivant l'interprétation donnée par les **munnumburra,** la plus grande de ces deux figures aurait récemment subi un rituel d'initiation pour l'entrée dans l'âge adulte. Un jeune homme en position assise, le corps visiblement menu par rapport à sa longue coiffe, semble regarder les femmes. Portant une ceinture masculine à trois pointes **(walbud),** il tient une paire de petits boomerangs et un sac **(garagi).** Une fois la danse **birrina** terminée, l'initié est momentanément intouchable et il part le temps que dure cette période d'intense liberté, équipé de couteaux en pierre, d'ocres et de nombreux objets magiques conservés soigneusement dans un **garagi** qui se porte sous le bras.

mandzu

d

e

f

Various forms of **jalim.baran** are used by dance leaders but can be presented later to new initiates as a kind of passport for safe travel through other people's lands. These items can symbolise that a recently initiated youth in full adult attire is now **bunun.guli** literally "blood free to go".

Just like the praying mantis guarding her offspring, **Jillinya** vigilantly watches over her children and monitors their births. The **birrina**, as painted so long ago in **Jillinya's** sanctuary, was an event for the proclamation of marriages in her presence. Seen rising and dancing, with graceful fluidity, these **Gwion** people appear well aware of their own beauty.

The central female dancer (a) wears a long tapering **mudurra** and is carefully painted. She displays exceptionally jointed arms in gestures epitomising the classical pose of a praying mantis. With arms bent at the elbow and hands extended, she gracefully arches her back while rising on her toes, ready to mime the swaying movement of the **mandzu** (b). With an expert eye, the artist has composed firmly shaped spaces between each part of her body, thus creating a perfect balance between solid and space. Her strong, rounded thighs taper down the sensual form of the leg to small feet, superbly drawn, as if seen from the dancer's own perspective. When one's eye follows these details, they increase the suggestion of self-control and flexibility of this **mandzu** dancer. The arms-out poses of other dancers are further graphic evidence of the enduring symbolic association between mother and mantis – **Jillinya** and **mandzu**.

Während der Tänze tragen die Anführer **jalim.baran** in verschiedenen Formen; später gehen diese Stäbe oft als Geschenk an die frisch Initiierten und sind eine Art Pass für die sichere Reise durch das Land anderer Stämme. Sie bringen symbolisch zum Ausdruck, dass ein initiierter junger Mann im vollen Erwachsenengewand nun **bunun.guli** ist, was wörtlich etwa heißt, dass das Blut ihm die Erlaubnis erteilt hat, zu gehen.

So wie die Gottesanbeterin ihre Brut beschützt, wacht **Jillinya** aufmerksam über ihre Kinder und ist bei jeder Geburt zugegen. Der **birrina,** wie er vor so langer Zeit im Jillinya-Heiligtum gemalt wurde, war ein Ritual, durch das in ihrer Gegenwart eine Heirat bekannt gemacht wurde. Die **Gwion,** die man auf den Gemälden hüpfen und tanzen sieht, scheinen sich ihrer eigenen Schönheit durchaus bewusst.

Die Tänzerin in der Mitte (a) trägt eine lange, spitz zulaufende **mudurra** und ist besonders kunstvoll ausgeführt. Sie zeigt außergewöhnlich gelenkige Arme in einer Bewegung, die die klassische Haltung der Gottesanbeterin nachahmt. Die Arme angewinkelt, die Hände ausgestreckt, den Rücken elegant gebogen, tanzt sie auf Zehenspitzen, als ob sie jeden Moment in die schaukelnde Bewegung der Gottesanbeterin verfallen wolle (b). Mit gutem Blick hat der Künstler klar umrissene Flächen zwischen den einzelnen Körperpartien geschaffen, die für die perfekte Balance zwischen Masse und Raum sorgen. Die kräftigen, gerundeten Schenkel verjüngen sich zu zierlichen Füßen, und das ganze Bein hat etwas Sinnliches, perfekt gezeichnet, als sei es aus der Perspektive der Tänzerin selbst gesehen. Wenn man das Auge an diesen Details entlangwandern lässt, sieht man erst, wie sehr Selbstbeherrschung und Flexibilität dieser **mandzu**-Tänzerin darin zum Ausdruck kommen. Die Haltung der anderen Tänzer mit weit ausgebreiteten Armen ist sichtbarer Beweis für die bis heute gültige symbolische Verbindung zwischen Mutter und Gottesanbeterin – **Jillinya** und **mandzu**.

Des **jalim.baran** de diverses formes sont utilisés par les meneurs de la danse, mais ils peuvent être offerts plus tard aux nouveaux initiés comme une sorte de passeport pour voyager en toute sécurité à travers les terres d'autres groupes. Ces objets peuvent symboliser qu'un jeune récemment initié vêtu en adulte est maintenant **bunun.guli** traduit littéralement par « un sang libre de s'en aller ».

Comme les mantes religieuses gardant leur progéniture, **Jillinya** surveille avec vigilance ses enfants et contrôle leur naissance. La **birrina,** comme celle peinte il y a si longtemps dans le sanctuaire de **Jillinya,** était un événement pour proclamer des mariages en sa présence. Représentés en élévation, dansant avec grâce et fluidité, ces êtres **Gwion** semblent être bien conscients de leur beauté.

La danseuse au centre (a) porte une longue **mudurra** fuselée et est peinte avec soin. Elle arbore des bras joints dans une position similaire à la pose classique d'une mante religieuse. Avec ses coudes repliés et ses mains en extension, elle cambre son dos avec grâce tout en s'élevant sur la pointe des pieds, prête à mimer les mouvements oscillants d'une **mandzu** (b). Avec un œil expérimenté, l'artiste a composé des espaces fermement façonnés entre chaque partie de son corps, créant ainsi un parfait équilibre entre les pleins et les espaces vides. Ses fortes et rondes cuisses s'effilent pour donner une forme sensuelle à sa jambe jusqu'à ses petits pieds, superbement dessinés comme s'ils étaient vus dans la propre perspective du danseur. Quand un œil suit ces détails, ils augmentent la sensation de maîtrise et de flexibilité de cette danseuse **mandzu**. Les poses bras écartés des autres danseurs sont d'autres preuves picturales de l'association symbolique entre mère et mante – **Jillinya** et **mandzu**.

mandzu

a

b

c

Jillinya is also known as a provider for all her children. She gave them plenty of vegetables to eat, and she taught them to share food. On a small boulder beneath her massive sacred figure is a polychrome painting enshrining the concept of sharing through exchange. The sharing icon consists of two elements: a border of edible yams and water-lilies surrounds a panel of red lines on a white ground forming a grid. The interwoven lines of the grid symbolise the multi-directional exchange of the vegetables, a graphic model for the larger network of **Wunan** trading routes. This abstraction of the social principle of sharing demonstrates the fundamental influence of **Jillinya**.

Many imprints of string girdles and yam vines mark the high ceiling of **Jillinyas bunja mamaa,** her sacred sanctuary (c). On its weathered walls and ceiling, a kind of ritual graffiti has been created by throwing objects dipped in blood or dark paint. This kind of graffiti is widespread and is thought to be some of the oldest marking made by humans (b).

The original perspective of **Gwion,** as a nomadic people spreading out across a land without boundaries, was first shaped and socially centred by **Jillinya's** authority as the Great Mother. Evidence of her influence still speaks at this and other sites preserving icons of homage to her. The imposing figure of **Jillinya** that dominates the large wall of her sanctuary is not for reproduction or public display. Like much mysterious art, this icon is believed by **Ngarinyin** to dissolve our normal sense of time and "capture" the mind. **Munnumburra** warn that the mind of any man can be influenced and temporarily controlled by **Jillinya** in dramatic and profound ways. **Ngarjno** insisted that any uninitiated man looking directly at her sacred icon (a, detail) will inexplicably lose his memory for a few days.

Jillinya ist auch dafür bekannt, dass sie für all ihre Kinder sorgte. Sie gab ihnen reichlich Gemüse und lehrte sie, das Essen miteinander zu teilen. Auf einem kleinen Stein unterhalb der imposanten heiligen Figur ist ein mehrfarbiges Gemälde zu sehen, ein Sinnbild des Teilens durch Tausch miteinander. Dieses Bild des Teilens ist selbst zweigeteilt; eine Einfassung mit Darstellungen essbarer Jamswurzeln und Seerosen umgibt ein Mittelfeld aus schraffierten roten Linien auf weißem Grund. Die miteinander verflochtenen Linien symbolisieren den Austausch der Nahrungsmittel in alle Richtungen, eine Abstraktion des größeren Netzwerks der **Wunan-**Handelswege. Diese abstrakte Darstellung des sozialen Grundsatzes des Teilens führt vor Augen, wie weitreichend der Einfluss **Jillinyas** ist.

Zahlreiche Abdrücke von Frauenröcken und rankenden Jamswurzelpflanzen markieren die hohe Decke in **Jillinyas** heiliger Höhle, der **bunja mamaa** (c). Entstanden sind diese rituellen Graffiti an den verwitterten Wänden und Decken, indem man mit Blut oder dunkler Farbe getränkte Gegenstände dagegenschleuderte. Solche Graffiti finden sich häufig und zählen vermutlich zu den ältesten Zeugnissen der Menschheit (b).

Die ursprüngliche Weltsicht der **Gwion,** eines Nomadenvolkes, das sich in einem Land ohne Grenzen bewegte, erhielt seine Prägung und seinen sozialen Mittelpunkt durch die Autorität der Großen Mutter **Jillinya.** Hier und an anderen Orten, wo heilige Bilder von ihr erhalten sind, ist ihr Einfluss nach wie vor spürbar. Die imposante Jillinya-Figur, die die große Wand ihres Heiligtums beherrscht, ist nicht der Öffentlichkeit zugänglich und darf auch nicht reproduziert werden. Wie viele Kunstwerke, die einem Kreis von Eingeweihten vorbehalten sind, setzt auch dieses Bild unser Zeitempfinden außer Kraft und nimmt uns ganz gefangen. Die **munnumburra** warnen davor, dass der Verstand jedes Betrachters von **Jillinya** beeinflusst werden kann und er vorübergehend sogar völlig in ihren Bann geraten kann. **Ngarjno** versicherte mir, dass jeder Uninitiierte, der dieses heilige Bild (a, Detail) direkt ansieht, für ein paar Tage das Gedächtnis verliert.

C'est également **Jillinya** qui fournit des vivres à tous ses enfants. Elle leur a donné beaucoup de légumes à manger et leur a appris à partager la nourriture. Sur une petite pierre au-dessous de sa grande image sacrée se trouve une peinture polychrome qui relate le concept du partage à travers l'échange. Cette image de l'échange consiste en deux éléments : une bordure de différentes ignames comestibles et de nénuphars entoure un panneau de lignes rouges sur une surface blanche formant une grille. Les lignes entrelacées de la grille symbolisent l'échange multidirectionnel des légumes ; c'est un exemple graphique du réseau plus étendu des routes d'échanges **Wunan.** Cette représentation abstraite du principe social de l'échange démontre l'influence fondamentale de **Jillinya.**

Beaucoup de traces de ceintures en cordelettes et de pieds d'ignames marquent le haut plafond élevé du **bunja mamaa,** le sanctuaire sacré de **Jillinya** (c). Sur ses murs et son plafond, qui ont subi des intempéries, des sortes de graffiti rituels ont été faits en lançant des objets trempés dans du sang ou de la peinture de couleur sombre. Ce type de graffiti est très répandu et on pense que c'est une des formes les plus anciennes de marques faites par l'homme (b).

L'horizon premier des **Gwion,** peuple nomade se déplaçant sur une terre sans bornes, a été défini et a trouvé une première base sociale par l'autorité de **Jillinya,** la Grande Matriarche. La preuve de son influence se trouve dans ce site et dans d'autres qui conservent son image. La figure imposante de **Jillinya** qui domine le grand mur de son sanctuaire ne peut être reproduite ou montrée au public. Comme tout art mystérieux, cette image a la réputation de nous faire perdre notre sens du temps et de « capturer » l'esprit. Les **munnumburra** avertissent que l'esprit de tout homme peut être influencé ou temporairement mis sous le contrôle de **Jillinya,** et ce de manière spectaculaire et profonde. **Ngarjno** insista que tout homme non initié qui regarde directement son image sacrée (a, détail) perd inexplicablement la mémoire pendant quelques jours.

mangarri

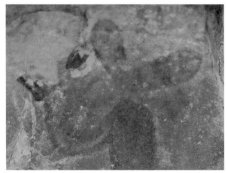

a

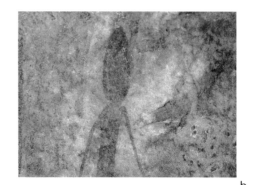

b

c

From their appearance in numerous paintings, we can recognise wigs as one graphic motif that distinguishes **Gwion** culture. The diverse form and types of **mudurra** (structured wigs made from human hair) are crucial to appreciation of their resonance in **Ngarinyin** and neighbouring cultures. Although distinctive linguistically and geographically, many northern Australian peoples share the cosmology of the Great Mother. Wigs are a defining motif of the ancient cultural environment that embraces northern Australia with Papua on the southern side of the island of New Guinea. In **Gwion** paintings, **mudurra** can be seen as an extension of the human form (c), symbolising the totemic human body and creating links with the wider cultural region.

Munnumburra recognise **mudurra** as emblems with a variety of totemic and ancestral links. Various **Gwion** figures are depicted as wearing various elongated, conical and tubular, squat and bulbous forms with fine **jowul** (skewers) or plumes attached. Some **mudurra** are sculptures of hair flattened into flanged or divided forms, such as those wigs representing the listening ears (a) of the red kangaroo **wanjina, Walambaa**. The salient shapes of those **mudurra** worn during ceremonies give graphic clues for **munnumburra** to provide insight into the motives of the **Gwion** artist. Some Kimberley paintings show solitary **Gwion** wearing **mudurra**; the **munnumburra** interpret these as signifying that the figures portrayed are in a private state of being with their ancestors. When a solitary image is intact at a local **wungud** place, and definitely not painted as if participating in public rituals, it is seen as representing its role as a spiritual custodian of the site. From the **Ngarinyin** perspective, much **Gwion** art is a form of legal document, a native title written on stone, establishing beyond doubt their tenure over the land of paintings.

Mudurra have a crucial presence in **Gwion** paintings as links to sacred creative identities and to identities such as **Jillinya**. Their existence in every generation of imagery in **Jillinya's** sanctuary at **Guringi** clearly demonstrates the association of the **mudurra** with the Great Mother, and represent her connection with **mandzu**. As well as the triangular, mantis-head form, there is a flat-topped helmet form representing the conical egg-case of the mother mantis. This squat cocoon-type normally only appears on figures with a curved belly symbolic of the achievement of motherhood. Other pointed **mudurra** are distinguished by beak shapes (b) and characteristics of various birds emblematic of families of the era preceding the **Wunan**.

Daraus, dass sie auf zahlreichen Bildern zu sehen sind, können wir schließen, dass Perücken in der **Gwion**-Kultur eine zentrale Rolle spielen. Die verschiedenen Formen und Typen von **mudurra** (kunstvollen Perücken aus Menschenhaar) sind geradezu ein Erkennungsmerkmal der Kultur der **Ngarinyin** und ihrer Nachbarn. Auch wenn sie sprachlich und geografisch klar geschieden sind, ist die kosmologische Vorstellung einer Großen Mutter doch vielen nordaustralischen Stämmen gemeinsam. Perücken sind ein charakteristisches Sinnbild des uralten Kulturraumes, der Nordaustralien mit Papua auf der Südseite der Insel Neuguinea verbindet. Bei den Felsbildern der **Gwion** lassen sich die **mudurra** als Erweiterung des menschlichen Körpers auffassen (c), als Symbol der totemistischen Identität des Menschen, und sie binden die Darstellungen in den Kontext der weiteren Kulturregion ein.

Die **munnumburra** deuten die **mudurra** als Embleme, die auf vielfältige Weise auf totemistische Bezüge und Verbindungen zu den Ahnenwesen hinweisen. Eine Vielzahl von **Gwion**-Figuren ist mit den verschiedensten länglichen, kegel- oder röhrenförmigen, gedrungenen oder zwiebelförmigen Perücken dargestellt, geschmückt mit feinen **jowul** (Speeren) oder Federn. Manche **mudurra** sind wahre Haar-Skulpturen, ausgearbeitet zu vorspringenden oder gehörnten Formen wie etwa bei den Exemplaren, die die horchend aufgerichteten Ohren des Känguru-**wanjina Walamba** darstellen sollen (a). Die auffälligen Formen der bei den Zeremonien getragenen **mudurra** sind für die **munnumburra** bildliche Anhaltspunkte, die ihnen etwas von den Motiven der **Gwion**-Künstler verraten. Einige Malereien aus der Kimberley-Region zeigen einzelne **Gwion**-Figuren mit **mudurra**; die **munnumburra** deuten es so, dass diese Figuren stille Zwiesprache mit ihren Ahnen halten. Wenn an einem Ort des **wungud** ein solches einzelnes Bild erhalten und eindeutig nicht in die Darstellung eines allgemeinen Rituals einbezogen ist, dann gilt es als Abbild des spirituellen Wächters dieses Ortes. Für die **Ngarinyin** ist vieles an der Kunst der **Gwion** eine Art Urkunde, ein auf Stein geschriebener Rechtstitel, ein Native Title der Aborigines, der zweifelsfrei ihr Besitzrecht auf das Land belegt, in dem sich die Malereien befinden.

Die **mudurra** sind von zentraler Bedeutung für die Bilder der **Gwion**, denn sie stellen Verbindungen zu den sakralen und übernatürlichen Wesen wie **Jillinya** her. In jeder Generation von Bildern im **Jillinya**-Heiligtum von **Guringi** sind sie zu sehen. Dies beweist, dass die **mudurra** mit der Großen Mutter assoziiert werden, und es dokumentiert ihre Verbindung zu der **mandzu**. Neben der dreieckigen Form, die für den Kopf der Gottesanbeterin steht, gibt es eine Art Helm mit flacher Oberseite als Symbol der Eikapsel der Mantis-Mutter. Diese kokonartige Form tritt in der Regel nur bei Figuren mit gerundetem Bauch auf, die Mutterschaft symbolisieren. Andere spitze **mudurra** sehen aus wie Schnäbel (b) und haben weitere Charakteristika einer Reihe von Vögeln, die symbolisch für die Familien vor der Zeit des **Wunan** stehen.

Les coiffes apparaissent dans de nombreuses peintures; on peut admettre qu'elles sont un motif graphique caractérisant la culture **Gwion**. Les diverses formes et types de **mudurra** (coiffes faites à partir de cheveux humains) sont un élément fondamental pour apprécier leur impact dans les cultures **Ngarinyin** et avoisinantes. Bien que distincts linguistiquement et géographiquement, beaucoup de peuples australiens ont en commun la cosmologie de la Grande Matriarche. Les coiffes sont un élément de l'ancien continuum culturel qui relie le nord australien à la Papouasie située au sud de l'île de la Nouvelle Guinée. Dans les peintures **Gwion**, les **mudurra** peuvent être interprétées comme une extension de la forme humaine (c), un symbole totémique du corps humain et un lien à l'aire culturelle régionale étendue.

Les **munnumburra** reconnaissent les **mudurra** comme étant des emblèmes ayant une variété de liens totémiques et ancestraux. Plusieurs figures **Gwion** sont représentées portant des **mudurra** de différentes formes: allongées, coniques, tubulaires, bulbaires ou rondes ornées de **jowul** ou de plumes. Certaines **mudurra** sont des sculptures en cheveux aplatis pour leur donner une forme plate ou en éléments séparés, comme par exemple ces coiffes représentant les oreilles (a) du kangourou roux **wanjina Walamba**. Les formes saillantes de ces **mudurra** portées pendant les cérémonies donnent des indications graphiques aux **munnumburra** pour interpréter le travail des artistes **Gwion**. Certaines peintures des Kimberley montrent un seul **Gwion** portant une **mudurra**; les **munnumburra** donnent comme interprétation que ces représentations ont une relation privilégiée avec leurs ancêtres. Quand une image est seule et intacte dans un lieu **wungud** et n'a pas été peinte comme si elle participait à des rituels publics, elle est perçue comme étant la gardienne spirituelle du site. Du point de vue des **Ngarinyin**, la majorité des représentations de l'art **Gwion** doit être considérée comme une forme de document légal, un « Native Title » écrit sur pierre qui prouve leur droit à la jouissance de la terre où sont ces peintures.

Les **mudurra** tiennent une place fondamentale dans les peintures **Gwion** car elles constituent un lien aux divinités et aux personnages tels que **Jillinya**. Leur présence dans chacune des générations d'images peintes dans le sanctuaire de **Jillinya** à **Guringi** prouve l'association des coiffes **mudurra** avec la Mère originelle et représentent clairement son lien avec **mandzu**. En plus de la forme triangulaire semblable à celle de la tête, il existe une coiffe aplatie semblable à l'enveloppe protectrice des œufs de la mante. Cette forme d'épais cocon n'apparaît que sur les figures qui ont un ventre arrondi, symbole de maternité. D'autres **mudurra** en pointe sont caractérisées par leur forme en bec (b) et présentent les caractéristiques de divers oiseaux, emblèmes des familles de l'époque précédent le **Wunan**.

mudurra

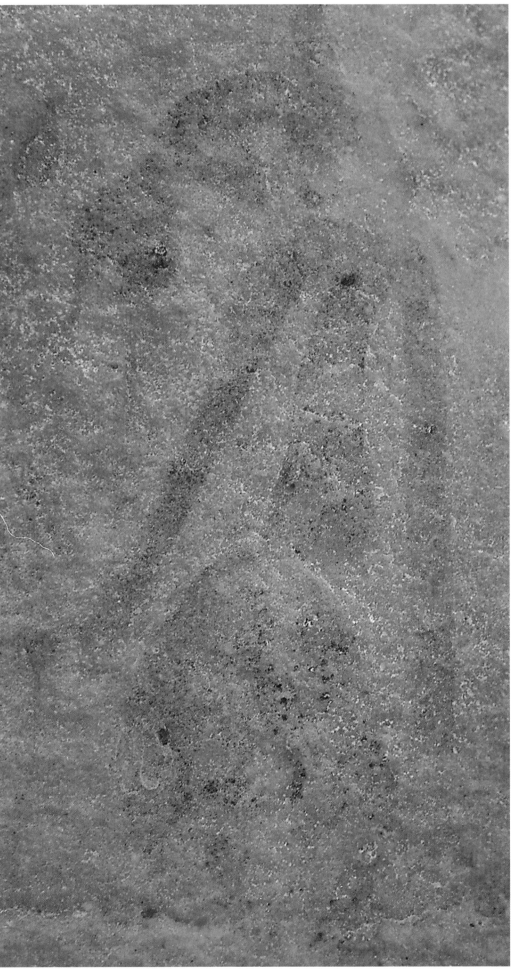

Gwion... all these oldest people
beginning of this country... land

this mob Gwion Gwion *now*
they're the beginning of long long time
Banggal

Gwion... das waren die ersten Menschen
der Anfang dieses ganzen Landes

aber die **Gwion Gwion**
die stehen am Anfang einer langen langen Zeit
Banggal

Gwion... tous ces gens très anciens
au commencement de ce pays...

tous ceux qu'on appelle **Gwion Gwion**
ils étaient là au commencement
il y a très très longtemps
Banggal

*Gwion Gwion... paintings they go right across
spreading right over wall here...*
Ungudman

*They got very long story
we got all this one's song
... this **Gwion**
all the songs belong 'em*
Ngarjno

*Gwion Gwion ... sie reichen bis dort drüben
über die ganze Wand hier*
Ungudman

*Sie haben eine sehr lange Geschichte
von diesen hier haben wir all die Lieder
von den **Gwion** hier ... ihre Lieder sind das*
Ngarjno

*Gwion Gwion ... leurs peintures sont sur
tout le mur tout le long du mur*
Ungudman

*Ils ont une très longue et riche histoire
tous nos chants viennent d'eux
ces **Gwion** ... tous les chants leur appartiennent*
Ngarjno

Artists and Inventors

Gwion *was a secret to protect man... blood... law*

Ngarjno, Ungudman, Banggal, Nyawarra

Künstler und Erfinder

Gwion *war ein Geheimnis, um Mensch ... Blut ... Gesetz ... zu schützen*

Ngarjno, Ungudman, Banggál, Nyawarra

Artistes et Inventeurs

Gwion *c'était un secret pour protéger... l'homme ... le sang ... la Loi*

Ngarjno, Ungudman, Banggal, Nyawarra

GWION

The first man **Gwion Gwion**
created by the **Wanjina** from the grass
making the limbs and body
by tying the grass together
then the **Wanjina** make the grass figure alive
by putting it in the black soil mud
around the spring water country

When this figure came alive
he became the **Munga.nunga**
looking for tools to use
then he made tools... **gallid**
and the **woomera nyarndu**
he then went hunting

After hunting he looked
for a way to cook his meat
so he found fire... **nabun** or **gunan**
by finding dry grass and fire sticks
to rub together to make fire
and cooked his meat
Nyawarra

Der erste Mensch der erste **Gwion Gwion**
von dem **Wanjina** aus Gras geformt
er hat den Körper und die Glieder gemacht
hat das Gras zusammengebunden
und dann hat der **Wanjina**
den Grasmenschen zum Leben erweckt
hat ihn in die Erde gesteckt
in den schwarzen Schlamm da wo die Quellen sind

Als die Figur dann lebendig war
da war er **Munga.nunga**
sah sich nach Werkzeugen um
mit denen er arbeiten konnte
dann machte er seine Werkzeuge... Speere, **gallid**
und Speerschleudern, **woomera nyarndu**
damit ging er auf die Jagd

Nach der Jagd überlegte er
wie er sein Fleisch braten sollte
und suchte sich das Feuer... **nabun** oder **gunan**
er suchte sich trockenes Gras und Reibhölzer
die rieb er aneinander und machte Feuer
und briet sich sein Fleisch
Nyawarra

Le premier homme **Gwion Gwion**
a été créé par **Wanjina** avec de l'herbe
il a fait les membres et le corps
en attachant des brins d'herbe ensemble
puis **Wanjina** rendit la figure d'herbe vivante
en le mettant dans la boue de terre noire
dans le pays des sources

Quand cette figure devint vivante
elle devint le **Munga.nunga**
cherchant des outils
alors il fabriqua des outils... les lances,
gallid et le **woomera nyarndu**
alors il partit chasser

Après la chasse il chercha
un moyen de cuire sa viande
alors il trouva le feu... **nabun** ou **gunan**
avec de l'herbe sèche et des bouts de bois
à frotter pour faire du feu
et cuire sa viande
Nyawarra

Gwion Gwion who spun ropes from **boab**
making **jirrgal...** string
so they can make sort of a fence
to catch animal for their feed
These are the sort of people who started law
we call them **Munga.nunga**
they're the **Jenagi**
who started spear stone chipping
Banggal

Die **Gwion Gwion** die haben Seile aus **boab** gedreht
haben Stricke daraus gemacht
Stricke für so eine Art Zaun
damit fangen sie die Tiere und essen sie dann
Das sind die Leute die haben die Gesetze gemacht
wir nennen sie **Munga.nunga**
das sind die **Jenagi**
die haben die Speerspitzen erfunden
Banggal

Les **Gwion Gwion** faisaient des cordes avec le **baobab**
pour fabriquer ensuite une sorte de filet
pour attraper des animaux pour se nourrir
Ce sont des gens comme eux qui ont crée la Loi
on les appelle **Munga.nunga**
Ce sont les **Jenagi**
qui commencèrent la taille des lances
Banggal

He very dangerous in the Law
secret things... **mamaa**
he on that path

Hey! they couldn't talk about it
in Aborigine ways in Aborigine Law
it is evil bloke who speak "Jenagi"
If anybody been talk "Jenagi"
in that time... in those early days
they get killed! right there
Nyawarra

That was Jenagi people
who started this law... long time
that the Jenagi we painting in cave
Because from that time
it became a Wunan system
from that time

These are Munga.nunga...
beginning of in this area here

They carry their belongings because they travel
that's why they called Jenagi Jenagi
everything they had they carried
That Jenagi Jenagi people
they just traveller in this sandstone country
and they painting all around
Banggal

Mit dem Gesetz darf man nicht scherzen
geheimnisvolle Dinge... **mamaa**
unterwegs auf dem Pfad

He! die konnten nicht darüber reden
nach unserem Gesetz nach Aborigine-Gesetz
spricht man nicht über die „Jenagi"
Wenn jemand „Jenagi" gesagt hätte
damals... in der alten Zeit
den hätten sie umgebracht! auf der Stelle
Nyawarra

Das waren die Jenagi
die haben das Gesetz gemacht... vor langer Zeit
und die Jenagi die sind in den Höhlen gemalt
Denn von da an
gehörte alles zum Wunan
von da an

Das sind Munga.nunga...
hier in der Gegend hat das angefangen

Sie haben ihre Sachen dabei denn sie sind unterwegs
deswegen heißen sie Jenagi Jenagi
alles was sie besaßen trugen sie mit sich herum
Diese Jenagi Jenagi
die waren unterwegs hier in der Sandsteingegend
und überall haben sie gemalt
Banggal

Des objets très dangereux dans la Loi
il y a des choses secrètes... **mamaa**
des secrets sur ce chemin...

Hé ! Ils pouvaient pas en parler
chez les Aborigènes, dans la Loi aborigène
c'est un type diabolique celui qui parle des « Jenagi »
Si quelqu'un parlait des « Jenagi »
à cette époque... dans ces temps anciens
il était tué ! Sur le champ !
Nyawarra

Et les Jenagi
qui créèrent cette Loi... il y a longtemps
c'est les Jenagi qui sont peints dans la grotte
parce que depuis ce moment
c'est devenu un système le Wunan
depuis ce temps

Ceux-là sont les Munga.nunga...
ils sont nés près d'ici

Ils emportent leurs affaires avec eux
parce qu'ils voyagent
c'est pour ça qu'on les appelle Jenagi Jenagi
ils portaient tout ce qu'ils avaient
Ces Jenagi Jenagi
sont simplement des nomades dans ce pays de grès
et leurs peintures sont partout
Banggal

They didn't have spear this **Jenagi mob**
no they the beginning of long long time
They made spin some ropes from **boab** tree
and made traps
They lived with the meat and with the water lily
killing fish you know... black breams

These are **gallid**...
hook ones they used for what you call it?
we call „min min min min"
ripple in the water for breams to come
and they poke 'em to catch 'em bream
like that **jumubumuru**... black bream
that what they was made for yeah?
and we been doing that

My father I seen 'im...
"What 're you doing Dad?"
"I want to kill this fish!"
"What... with that **gallid**?"
"Yeah with a **gallid**"

And a ripple ripple...
and all the fish come for the ripple
... that was the calling of the fish
an "we poke" 'em
then lift them up from the water
an' that what they did yeah!
and this **Gwion Gwion mob**
who started all this from that time
that **gallid** and what they made
that's where the law started

Banggal

Sie hatten keine Speere die **Jenagi**
das war alles vor langer Zeit
sie haben sich Seile gedreht aus Fasern vom **boab**
und Fallen gestellt
Sie haben Fleisch gegessen und Seerosen
und Fische gefangen ... schwarze Brassen

Das sind **gallid**...
Speere mit Haken wie nennt man das
wir rufen „min min min min"
der Speer macht Wellen im Wasser
die Fische kommen
dann stechen wir zu und fangen sie die Brassen
jumubumuru sagen wir schwarze Brasse
dafür sind die Speere hier da verstehst du?
so fangen wir Fische

Bei meinem Vater habe ich das gesehen
„Was machst du da, Dad?"
„Ich will einen Fisch fangen!"
„Was ... mit dem **gallid** da?"
„Genau, mit dem **gallid**"

Man dreht ihn und macht Wellen
und das lockt die Fische an
... damit werden die Fische gerufen
und dann stechen wir zu
und holen sie aus dem Wasser
genau wie damals oh ja!
und die **Gwion Gwion**
die haben damit angefangen
mit dem **gallid** haben sie das gemacht
da fing das Gesetz an

Banggal

Ils n'avaient pas de lances ces **Jenagi**
ils étaient là au début des temps
Ils tressaient des cordes avec des lianes
de **baobab** et fabriquaient des pièges
Ils vivaient de la viande et du nénuphar
ils attrapaient des poissons tu vois...
des brèmes noires

Ça c'est des lances, **gallid**...
les crochues servaient à comment tu dis ?
nous on dit « min min min min »
faire des rides sur l'eau et les brèmes viennent
et ils piquaient les brèmes pour les attraper
comme ça là **jumubumuru** ... la brème noire
c'était fait pour ça tu vois ?
et on faisait ça

Mon père je l'ai vu faire...
« Qu'est-ce tu fais, Papa ? »
« Je veux attraper ce poisson ! »
« Quoi... avec cette **gallid** ? »
« Oui avec une **gallid** »

Et on faisait des rides sur l'eau
et tous les poissons venaient
à cause de l'ondulation...
c'était l'appel du poisson
et on piquait le poisson
puis on le sortait de l'eau
et c'est ce qu'ils faisaient oui !
et c'est les **Gwion Gwion**
qui ont créé tout ça depuis ce temps-là
cette lance **gallid** et ce qu'ils faisaient
c'est là que la Loi a commencé

Banggal

Before **woomera** that we use today
it was invented after this hook one
this is a **nyarndu**... we call it **nyarndu**
because it's a forked tree... young one
they cut a tree to make a **woomera**
and this name is **nyarndu**
that's how they use the sharp spear
And that's why it painted here
it's the same sort
that's how they use the sharp spear
They had to find a **woomera** tree
... it's a corkwood tree

I used this once too
when I was training to be hunter
My uncle showed me so he says...
"I'm going to make a spear"

And he made a shovelnose spear
... put a **gimbu** on it and wax it
Then ah he cut this young Leichardt pine
he showed me young one... very solid one
And he killed a kangaroo front of me
with that **gimbu**! he killed it
that river wallaby... **gundilli** yeah!
he showed me in mustering camp
I never forget...
he showed me If you got no **woomera**
if you're walking around...
you know if your **woomera** break...
just cut one of these trees wherever you see it
So we can use them any time this one
if we got no **woomera** use this **nyarndu**
I never forget this **nyarndu**

Banggal

Die **woomera** die wir heute haben
die kam erst nach denen hier mit den Haken
das ist ein **nyarndu** … **nyarndu** heißt das bei uns
weil der nämlich aus einem Baum geschnitten ist
sie nahmen eine Astgabel für die **woomera**
und das heißt **nyarndu**
damit haben sie den scharfen Speer geschleudert
Und deshalb ist die hier gemalt
diese Art von Schleuder
die haben sie für den scharfen Speer genommen
Sie mussten den richtigen Baum finden
… ein Korkholzbaum ist das

Ich habe so etwas auch einmal genommen
als ich gelernt habe wie man jagt
Mein Onkel hat es mir gezeigt und er hat gesagt
„Zuerst mache ich einen Speer"

Und er hat einen Speer mit breiter Spitze gemacht
… mit Wachs eine **gimbu** drangesteckt
Dann hat er eine junge Leichardt-Kiefer gefällt
er hat mir eine junge gezeigt … eine sehr kräftige
Und er hat vor meinen Augen ein Känguru erlegt
mit dem **gimbu**! damit hat er es getötet
Oh ja! ein **gundilli**, Flinkwallaby
er hat es mir beigebracht im Viehlager
das vergesse ich nie …
er zeigte mir wie man ohne **woomera** auskommt
wenn man unterwegs ist …
du weißt wenn deine Speerschleuder zerbricht …
dann muss man nur einen dieser Bäume suchen
und kann sich eine Schleuder machen
haben wir keine **woomera** nehmen wir den **nyarndu**
den **nyarndu**, den vergesse ich nie

Banggal

Le **woomera** qu'on utilise aujourd'hui
il a été inventé après celui-là qui est crochu
c'est un **nyarndu** … **nyarndu** on l'appelle
parce que c'est un arbre crochu … un petit arbre
ils coupent un arbre pour faire un **woomera**
et son nom est **nyarndu**
c'est comme ça qu'ils utilisent la lance acérée
Et c'est pourquoi c'est peint là
c'est la même chose
c'est comme ça qu'ils utilisent la lance acérée
Il fallait qu'ils trouvent un arbre à **woomera**
… c'est du bois de liège cet arbre

Je m'en suis servi aussi
quand j'apprenais à être un chasseur
Mon oncle m'a montré et il a dit …
« Je vais fabriquer une lance »

Et il a fabriqué une lance à bout plat
… mis une **gimbu** dessus et l'a fixée
Après voilà il a coupé ce petit pin
il m'a montré, un petit … un très solide
Et il a tué un kangourou juste devant moi
avec cette **gimbu** ! il l'a tué !
Ce wallaby de rivière, ce **gundilli** oui !
il m'a montré … J'oublierai jamais
il m'a montré que si t'as pas de **woomera**
si tu es à la chasse …
et si ton **woomera** se casse …
t'as qu'à couper un de ces arbres si t'en vois un
On peut vraiment les utiliser n'importe quand
si t'as pas de **woomera** donc prend ça, le **nyarndu**
Je n'oublie jamais qu'il y a le **nyarndu**

Banggal

It is a fat kangaroo... this we call it **wudma**
name belong to it... **wudma**
and that kangaroo she very soft
You got three names there
gundilli... walmarro... arririn
the mother woman **wudma** that his wife
the husband is **arririn... walmarro... gundilli**
We don't eat baby kangaroo from this **wudma**
because this ankle here we get weak
he can't walk that baby get ah crippled up
that's why all these type of meat **mamaa**
Young people have to listen and understand
It very untouchable...
that river wallaby baby we never touch 'em
even mother and father never eat 'em
for till that child crawl an' grow and walk
they never eat 'em 'till they get big
only that time they can eat this kangaroo
because they killed it
and that was their meat... kangaroo
and because that kangaroo is the chosen one
belong to that lord **wungud**
that lord **wanjina**

Banggal

Die dicken Kängurus hier die nennen wir **wudma**
so heißt das... **wudma**
und das Känguru da das ist sehr zart
Das hat drei Namen
gundilli... walmarro... arririn
wudma die Mutter das ist seine Frau
der Mann heißt **arririn... walmarro... gundilli**
Die Kängurubabys der **wudma** essen wir nicht
das Sprungbein macht uns schwach
dann kann man nicht mehr laufen
und die Babys verkrüppeln
darum ist dieses Fleisch **mamaa**
Junge Leute müssen zuhören und verstehen
Das ist unberührbar...
das Flusswallaby-Baby würden wir nicht anrühren
nicht mal die Mutter und den Vater von ihm
die würden wir nicht essen
bis das Kleine da kriechen kann bis es laufen kann
erst dann essen wir sie erst wenn sie groß sind nur
dann darf man ein Känguru essen
denn sie haben sie ja gejagt
damit sie etwas zu essen hatten... die Kängurus
und weil das Känguru etwas Besonderes ist
gehört es dem **wungud** dem Herrn des Lebens
... gehört es dem **wanjina**

Banggal

Ça c'est un kangourou gras, on dit **wudma**
c'est son nom... **wudma**
et ce kangourou est très tendre
il a trois noms
gundilli... walmarro... arririn
wudma c'est sa femme
le mari c'est **arririn... walmarro... gundilli...**
On ne mange pas le bébé de cette **wudma**
à cause de sa cheville-là... on devient faible
on ne peut plus marcher
on le donne pas au bébé ou il devient handicapé
voilà pourquoi ces viandes sont **mamaa**
les jeunes gens doivent écouter et comprendre
Lui il est vraiment intouchable...
ce petit de wallaby de rivière on n'y touche jamais
même le père et la mère on ne les mange jamais
jusqu'à ce que ce petit rampe et marche
ils ne les mangent pas tant qu'ils sont pas grands
seulement à ce moment ils peuvent les manger
parce qu'ils l'ont tué
et c'était leur viande... kangourou
et parce que ce kangourou est l'élu
il appartient à ce seigneur **wungud**
... ce seigneur **wanjina**

Banggal

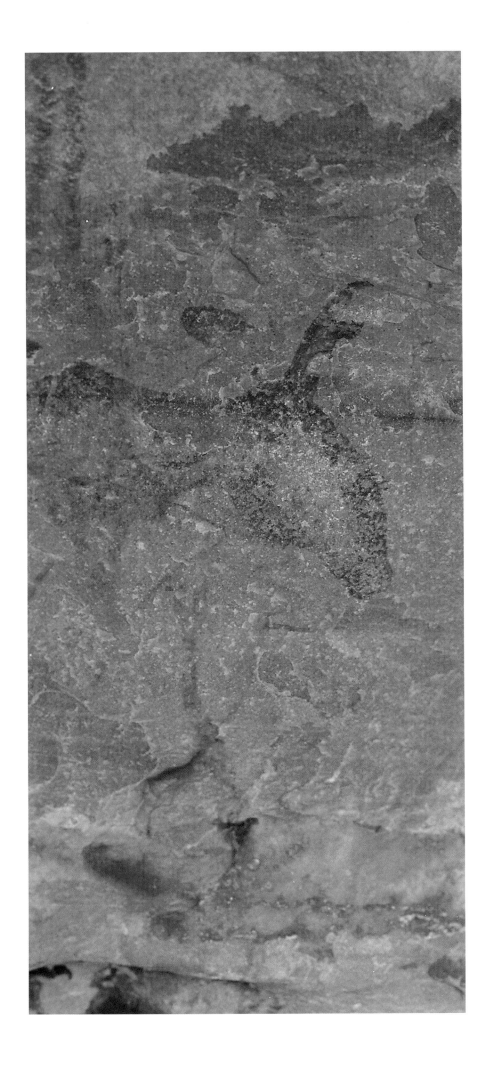

Because those days animals
everybody was living really close
really family
and that's why they give 'em
those animal names
and we use that name today
Those animals wasn't wild like today
in early days everything
really was close by
everybody lived together
like snakes and lizards... **goanna**
and you know... bird
that was really living together
after many... many centuries
Nyawarra

Damals in den alten Zeiten
haben alle eng zusammengelebt
auch die Tiere wie eine Familie
deshalb verwenden wir Tiernamen
und wir nehmen diese Namen bis heute
Früher waren die nicht wild
nicht so wie heute
in den alten Zeiten
da waren wirklich alle ganz nah beieinander
alle lebten miteinander
Schlangen und Eidechsen... Warane
ja... und Vögel auch
ganz eng haben sie zusammengelebt
viele... viele Jahrhunderte lang
Nyawarra

Parce qu'en ces temps les animaux,
tout le monde, on vivait très rapproché
comme une famille et c'est pourquoi
on a pris ces noms d'animaux
et on utilise ces noms aujourd'hui
Ces animaux étaient pas sauvages
comme aujourd'hui
dans les premiers temps, tout
tout le monde vivait ensemble,
les serpents et les lézards... **goanna**
et tu sais... les oiseaux
ils vivaient vraiment ensemble,
pendant des siècles... de nombreux siècles
Nyawarra

They told me that his name is called
Munga.nunga
means people who started working things
and stone... the **gimbu** *that they invented*
for using it for knives and for killing
We call those ah... Munga.nunga
who started the stone knives
and that stone tommyhawk
that stone axe **menda**

Banggal

Soviel ich weiß, heißen sie
Munga.nunga
die Leute die die Werkzeuge erfunden haben
auch die aus Stein ... die **gimbu**
die haben sie erfunden als Messer und für die Jagd
Und wir nennen sie ... Munga.nunga
die haben die Steinmesser erfunden
und die Steinaxt
das steinerne Beil **menda**

Banggal

Ils m'ont dit que son nom est prononcé
Munga.nunga
qui veut dire les gens qui commencèrent
à faire marcher les choses
et la pierre ... la **gimbu** *qu'ils ont inventée*
pour faire des couteaux et pour chasser
On les appelle ah ... Munga.nunga
ceux qui ont commencé à faire
des lames en pierre
et cette pierre de tomahawk
cette hache de pierre, **menda**

Banggal

So this **Yandama** painting
this kangaroo that **Yandama** he kill 'em there
He got 'em spear here... hook spear
gallid... what that hook spear
where man killed that kangaroo
Ungudman

This one called **nyarndu**
They looked at this hook here... **bunji** we call it
now this long spear they put a hook on it
made it more longer... tough
it called **gallid...** name belong to it this one here
so they can throw it more longer then
Nyawarra

Alyaguma... name they put here
because they said "we got no good knee"
Alyaguma is this knee...!
Yandama he broken his knee
Yeah... he couldn't walk any more
Ungudman

Also dieses **Yandama**-Bild hier
dieses Känguru wie **Yandama** es erlegt
Hier steckt der Speer... der Speer mit Zacken
gallid... der Speer mit Zacken
damit hat er das Känguru erlegt
Ungudman

Das hier das ist ein **nyarndu**
Sie haben sich den Haken hier angesehen...
bunji nennen wir den
und den langen Speer haben sie vorne eingehakt
dadurch wird er noch länger... der hält was aus
er heißt **gallid...** das ist der Name für diesen Speer
damit fliegt er noch viel viel weiter
Nyawarra

Alyaguma... so heißt der Ort hier
hier haben sie gesagt „Uns tut das Knie weh"
Alyaguma heißt nämlich Knie...!
Yandama hatte sich das Knie gebrochen
Ja... er konnte nicht mehr weiter
Ungudman

Dans cette peinture de **Yandama,**
ce kangourou, **Yandama** il le tue là
il l'a eu avec sa lance là... lance au crochet
gallid... la lance avec des dents au bout
c'est là où il a tué ce kangourou
Ungudman

Celui là on l'appelle **nyarndu**
Ils cherchaient un crochet comme ça...
on appelle ça **bunji**
ils prenaient cette longue lance
et mettaient un crochet dessus
pour qu'il soit plus long... plus fort
on appelle ça **gallid...** c'est le nom de cette chose
comme ça ils pouvaient le lancer plus loin
Nyawarra

Alyaguma... c'est le nom de cet endroit
parce qu'il disait « je n'ai pas un bon genou »
Alyaguma c'est ce genou...!
Yandama il a cassé son genou
Oui... il ne pouvait plus marcher
Ungudman

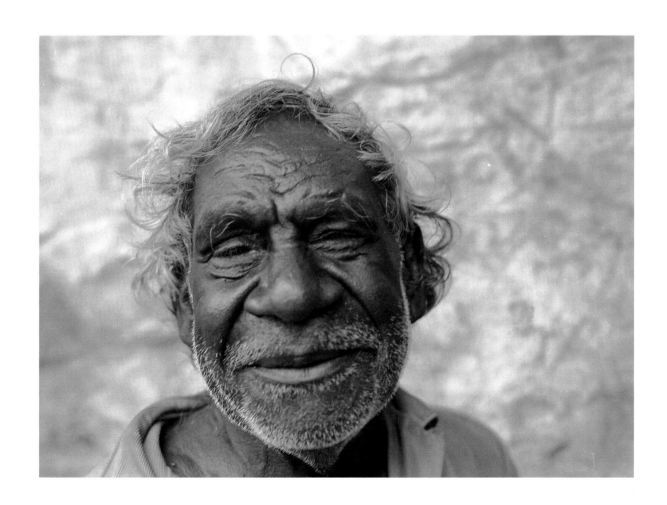

mamaa means holy place... It's a blood place
We call them **yalmalnyu malngud**
... means boggy area
mamaa means no good
Anybody don't believe us?

They gotta stone there... you'll see 'em
They bring that cooked one
kangaroo here from **Bimbidora**
where **Yandama** killed that kangaroo

an' they cooked it there
they got a firestick we call it **gunan**
they spin **gunan**... and they made fire
because it was raining
he had rain then they made these stones hot
an' when it was hot they put that kangaroo
and put all the hot stones on top of it
for there wasn't any earth... it was all mud
and they cleared up a flat table stone
and they cooked it there

All those signal stone **jallala**
where they all standing up
that's them sitting down waiting till it cook
all those stone... **jallala**
stone arrangement and in the middle
that's where that kangaroo was cooking

And they waiting like half and hour
or maybe two hours because it was rain time
and they cook it there...
an same way rain time
we kill kangaroo we cook it in hot rock
because we can't bury him in the mud
because there is two ways of cooking kangaroo
what they did... and we do it today
and that place become **mamaa**
nobody come there

anybody just don't walk around there
or banging otherwise rain will fall
rain come to fill up that place
it kill all the fire
and that's why we always be careful
no it very important
and **Yandama** look after it
and do it the right way
what he did... we do it
and that's why it's so important
where **Yandama** cook that kangaroo
Alyaguma... Yandama
Banggal

---

mamaa heißt heiliger Ort... Ort des Blutes
Wir nennen ihn **yalmalnyu malngud**
... das heißt sumpfige Gegend
mamaa bedeutet Vorsicht
Und wehe wenn uns jemand nicht glaubt

Hier gibt es Steine... ich zeige sie gleich noch
Sie haben das Känguru zum Braten
von **Bimbidora** hergebracht
wo **Yandama** es erlegt hatte

und sie haben es hier gebraten
sie hatten Reibhölzer, wir nennen sie **gunan**
die rieben sie aneinander... und machten Feuer
es regnete nämlich, es war Regenzeit, und sie
machten die Steine heiß
und als sie heiß waren, nahmen sie das Känguru
und deckten es mit den heißen Steinen zu
denn sie hatten keine Erde... alles war Schlamm
deswegen machten sie einen flachen Stein sauber
und da legten sie es drauf und brieten es

Diese aufrechten Steine da, **jallala**
da wo die heute stehen
da haben sie gesessen und gewartet
dass es gar wurde
die Steine da... das sind **jallala**
die stehen zur Erinnerung an der Stelle
wo sie das Känguru gebraten haben

Und sie haben anderthalb Stunden gewartet
oder vielleicht auch zwei, denn es war Regenzeit
und da haben sie es gebraten...
und wenn wir heute in der Regenzeit
ein Känguru jagen
dann braten wir es so unter heißen Steinen
weil man es nicht im Schlamm vergraben kann
es gibt nämlich zwei Arten,
ein Känguru zu braten
so wie sie das damals gemacht haben...
so machen wir es noch heute
und der Ort wurde **mamaa**, ein heiliger Ort
und niemand geht hierhin

hier geht man nicht einfach spazieren oder treibt
sich herum, sonst ruft man den Regen herbei
dann kommt der Regen und überschwemmt alles
löscht das Feuer und deshalb sind wir
immer besonders vorsichtig
das ist sehr wichtig
und **Yandama** wacht über diesen Ort
und verlangt, dass wir es richtig machen
so wie er es getan hat... und das machen wir
deshalb ist es ein so wichtiger Ort
wo **Yandama** sein Känguru gebraten hat
Alyaguma... Yandama
Banggal

---

mamaa ça veut dire : endroit sacré...
c'est un lieu où du sang a été versé
On l'appelle **yalmalnyu malngud**
... ça veut dire un lieu marécageux
mamaa ça veut dire dangereux aussi
quelqu'un ne nous croit pas ?

Il y a un signal en pierre là-bas... tu verras
ils ont amené celui-là qui est cuit
ce kangourou de **Bimbidora**
là où **Yandama** a tué ce kangourou

et ils le cuirent là avec un bâton pour faire du
feu, on l'appelle **gunan**
qu'ils tournent et frottent, le **gunan**...
ils firent du feu, parce qu'il pleuvait
il pleuvait et après ils firent chauffer les pierres
et quand c'était chaud ils ont mis le kangourou
après ils mettent les pierres chaudes dessus
parce qu'il n'y avait pas de terre... c'était que de
la boue alors ils ont nettoyé une dalle
de pierre plate et ils l'ont cuit dessus

Tout ça ce sont des pierres dressées, des **jallala**
là où ils se tiennent tous debout
c'est eux qui sont assis attendant que ça soit cuit
toutes ces pierres... ces **jallala** en cercle
il y a cette disposition de pierres
et un four au milieu
c'est là qu'ils cuisent le kangourou

Ils attendirent près d'une heure et demi
ou plutôt deux heures comme il pleuvait
et ils le cuirent ici...
c'est pareil quand il pleut on tue le kangourou
et on le cuit sur des pierres chaudes
parce qu'on ne peut pas le mettre dans la boue
en fait il y a deux façons de cuire le kangourou
comme ils faisaient... et comme on fait aujourd'hui
et cet endroit est devenu **mamaa**
personne ne vient là

personne ne marche autour d'ici
on ne fait pas de bruit ou alors il pleuvra
la pluie viendra et recouvrira l'endroit
éteindra tout le feu
et c'est pour ça qu'on fait toujours attention
c'est un lieu vraiment important
et **Yandama** en est le gardien
il a bien fait ce qu'il a fait... on le fait
et c'est pourquoi c'est un endroit si important
là où Yandama a cuit ce kangourou
Alyaguma... Yandama
Banggal

*The fire we call it **winjangun***
***winjangun** to make in camp*
***winjangun** in hunting when we go out*
when your cooking something
*that's all **winjangun***

*When you make big **winjangun***
*we call it **malgara***
***malgara** for kangaroo*
when you go hunting
and to make big fire for kangaroo
*then you call him **malgara***
Nyawarra

*The **Jenagi** mob*
when they been doing their hunting
they catch these kangaroo
Banggal

*Das Feuer nennen wir **winjangun***
***winjangun** wenn wir es im Lager machen*
***winjangun** machen wir auf der Jagd im Busch*
wenn man sich da was brät
*das heißt **winjangun***

*Wenn man ein großes **winjangun** macht*
*das heißt **malgara***
***malgara** braucht man für ein Känguru*
wenn man auf der Jagd ist
und ein großes Feuer für ein Känguru braucht
*dann nennt man das **malgara***
Nyawarra

*Die **Jenagi***
wenn die auf der Jagd waren
haben sie immer Kängurus gejagt
Banggal

*Le feu de camp on l'appelle **winjangun***
*le **winjangun** on le fait dans un campement*
*quand on part chasser on fait un **winjangun***
pour faire cuire quelque chose
*tout ça c'est **winjangun***

*Quand on fait un grand **winjangun***
*on dit **malgara***
*on fait un **malgara** pour le kangourou*
quand on part à la chasse
on fait un grand feu pour le kangourou
*on appelle ça **malgara***
Nyawarra

*Les **Jenagi***
quand ils chassaient ils attrapaient
des kangourous comme ceux-là
Banggal

Ngarinyin attribute the discovery of the practical use of fire to the **Gwion** and credit them with the invention of much hunting technology, in particular advances in pressure flake stone tools. **Ngarinyin** consistently acclaim **Gwion** as the inventors of a variety of notched or denticulated stone blades and axes.

They invented the bulky hand and hafted axes **borr** with **menda/jirriwal** blades. They crafted much smaller stone blades as sharp tips to improve wooden spears. When **Gwion** invented the first stone points for fastening to shafted spears they exploited local mineral resources to manufacture six distinct types of stone blade speartips, normally known by **Ngarinyin** by two or more names but a basic list of distinct types includes:

jimbila, common tapering bi-facial blade, (some
  denticulated) worked from translucent white chert
guruwal, common tapering bi-facial blade from
  red/yellow stone
windja.lalan, ruby-like blade used for sacred men's
  speartips etc
murru.minji, a long blade made from a black stone
jad.ngar, transparent glass like ngallad (a) flake
  stone spearpoint
gimbu, denticulated tri-facial blade struck from
  yellow-red-brown jasper-like stone; originally and
  primarily used for speartips but also valuable as a
  scalpel and later employed as a woomera-tip burin.

During the manufacturing process of stone tools, any practical edges on fragments can be exploited for stone knives (**gandad**). Various deposits of stone tools remain in the bush today wherever hunters worked, and can even be found collected by **juiban** (the bower-bird) which uses bright objects to decorate his display ground or **yanad wulurru,** built of branches.

In der Vorstellung der **Ngarinyin** waren die **Gwion** die ersten, die den praktischen Nutzen des Feuers erkannten, und sie waren auch die Urheber einer Reihe von technischen Neuerungen für die Jagd, vor allem bei der Herstellung von Steinklingen nach dem Absplitterungsverfahren. Deshalb gelten die **Gwion** als die Erfinder einer Vielzahl von gezahnten oder mit Kerben versehenen Steinklingen und -beilen.

Sie entwickelten die **menda-** oder **jirriwal**-Klingen für die groben Beile (**borr**), die man entweder in der Hand halten oder an einem Stiel befestigen konnte. Aber sie stellten auch weitaus kleinere Steinklingen her, die als Speerspitzen die hölzernen Speere zu einer wirkungsvollen Waffe machten. Als die **Gwion** ihre ersten steinernen Speerspitzen anfertigten, nahmen sie die Steine, die sie vor Ort fanden, und so entwickelten sich sechs verschiedene Typen von Speerspitzen, für die es bei den **Ngarinyin** in der Regel zwei oder mehr Namen gibt, die sich jedoch zu den folgenden Grundtypen zusammenfassen lassen:

jimbila, eine häufig vorkommende, spitz zulaufende,
  zweiseitige Klinge (teilweise gezahnt) aus durch-
  scheinendem weißem Feuerstein
guruwal, eine häufig vorkommende, spitz zulaufende
  zweiflächige Klinge aus rotem oder gelbem Stein
windja.lalan, eine Klinge aus einem rubinartigen
  Stein für Speere, die die Männer bei bestimmten
  Ritualen tragen
murru.minji, eine lange Klinge aus einem schwarzen
  Stein
jad.ngar, eine Speerspitze aus einem transparenten,
  glasartigen Stein namens ngallad (a)
gimbu, eine gezahnte dreiflächige Klinge aus
  einem gelb-rot-braunen, jaspisartigen Stein; sie
  wurde ursprünglich überwiegend für Speerspitzen
  verwendet, diente aber auch als Skalpell und
  später als Spitze (burin) für die Speerschleuder.

Die bei der Herstellung von Steinwerkzeugen abfallenden Splitter konnten als Steinmesser (**gandad**) verwendet werden. Noch heute findet man Depots solcher Werkzeuge im Busch, die von Jägern dort zurückgelassen wurden, oder in den aus Ästen gebauten Lauben (**yanad wulurru**) des Großen Bowervogels (**juiban**) der darin gern schimmernde Gegenstände zur Schau stellt.

Les **Ngarinyin** attribuent la découverte de l'usage du feu aux **Gwion**, tout comme ils leur attribuent également l'invention de la plupart des techniques de chasse, en particulier les progrès apportés aux outils de taille et de percussion. Les **Ngarinyin** rappellent souvent que les **Gwion** sont les inventeurs d'une grande variété de lames en pierre crantées ou dentées ainsi que de hâches.

Ils inventèrent des hâches avec et sans manches **(borr)** constituées de lames **jirriwal** et **menda.** Ils fabriquaient aussi des lames beaucoup plus petites et à bout pointu pour leurs lances en bois. Quand les **Gwion** inventèrent les premières pointes de pierre pour accroître la vitesse de leurs lances, ils se servirent des resources minérales locales pour fabriquer six différentes pointes de lance en pierre. Elles sont connues sous deux noms ou plus par les **Ngarinyin**; voici leurs principales caractéristiques:

jimbila, lame effilée à deux faces assez commune
  (certaines sont dentées) faites avec une pierre très
  dure constituée de silicate blanche et transparente
guruwal, lame effilée à deux faces assez commune,
  en pierre rouge/jaune
windja.lalan, lame ressemblant à du rubis, utilisée
  pour les pointes de lances rituelles
murru.minji, longue lame de pierre noire
jad.ngar, pointe de lance en éclat de pierre,
  ngallad (a) ressemblant à du verre transparent
gimbu, lame trièdre et dentée, éclat d'une pierre
  jaune/rouge/marron, le jaspe; utilisée originellement
  comme pointe de lance, mais également efficace
  comme scalpel et employée plus tard comme burin
  pour les pointes de woomera.

Durant la fabrication des outils de pierre, n'importe quel tranchant d'éclat de pierre peut-être utilisé pour les couteaux de pierre, **gandad.** On trouve les différentes variétés d'outils dans le bush aujourd'hui, là où des chasseurs ont travaillé, et peuvent même être trouvées rassemblées par **juiban,** un passereau qui se sert d'objets brilants pour décorer son nid (**yanad wulurru**) fait de branches.

a

jimbila

Gwion they invented all these spear points
rock from different rocks
and they namin' these rocks
They got many colour that stone... **ngallad**
they seen it from a distance
shining you know
It got many colour
it was shining and they said
"what that shining? oh! it's a stone"

Because **ngallad** means...
what do you say in English?
... errr like a shining but **ngallad**
more like different word
because it been like err...
it sort of vibration ah light!
you know? it been flickering light
and that what **ngallad** mean

Banggal

Die **Gwion** die haben die Speerspitzen erfunden
Stein aus anderen Steinen
und sie gaben ihnen Namen
Sie haben viele Farben die Steine ... **ngallad**
sie sahen sie schon von weitem
sie glänzten verstehst du
Es hatte viele Farben
es schimmerte und sie sagten
„was glänzt denn da? Oh! das ist ein Stein"

Denn **ngallad** heißt so viel wie ...
wie sagt man das?
... so ein Schimmern aber **ngallad**
heißt noch mehr
das ist wie ...
so eine Art flirrendes Licht!
verstehst du? es flackert und blitzt
und das heißt **ngallad**

Banggal

Les **Gwion** ont inventé toutes ces pointes
de lance avec différentes sortes de pierres
et ils donnent un nom à tous ces cailloux
Cette sorte de pierre a plein de couleurs ...
c'est **ngallad**
ils la voyaient de loin, ça brille tu vois
Y' a plein de couleurs
et quand ça brillait ils disaient
« Qu'est-ce qui brille là ? Oh ! C'est une pierre ! »

Parce que **ngallad** ça veut dire ...
comment tu dis ça?
mmm ... comme briller mais **ngallad**
c'est un peu différent
parce que c'était comme ...
comme si ça bougeait, comme de la lumière
tu vois ? ça scintillait
voilà **ngallad** ça veut dire ça

Banggal

*Before they put stone **gimbu** on that*
they had to find that wax
where we weld it with the wax
on the point of the spear
The way we blend it with the wax
on the point of the spearstone
*the **gimbu** that they invented*
for using it for knives and for killing

*this spear is sharp with the **gimbu***
and they threw it and it worked it speared!
speared something that they wanted to catch

***gimbu**... that is the **gimbu** they call it*
we followed all the spear stones
what they chosen and name 'em
Those names we still use it today
Banggal

*Bevor sie den **gimbu**-Stein aufsetzen konnten*
mussten sie das Wachs finden
weil wir ihn mit dem Wachs festmachen
vorne auf dem Speer
Wir befestigen ihn mit dem Wachs
die Spitze aus Speerstein
*den **gimbu** den sie erfunden haben*
und als Messer und zum Jagen nehmen

*das ist ein scharfer **gimbu**-Speer*
sie warfen ihn und er traf gut!
er spießte auf was sie fangen wollten

***gimbu**... so haben sie es genannt*
wir haben die gleichen Steine genommen
die gleichen wie sie
Und die Namen verwenden wir noch heute
Banggal

*Avant de mettre la pierre **gimbu** dessus*
il fallait qu'ils trouvent de la cire
Ensuite on soude la pierre avec la cire
sur la pointe de la lance
Cette manière de mettre la cire
sur la pointe de la lance
*c'est la **gimbu** qu'ils ont inventée*
pour faire des couteaux et pour tuer

*Cette lance est bien coupante avec la **gimbu***
Ils le lançaient et ça marchait, ça transperçait!
ça transperçait ce qu'ils voulaient attraper

gimbu**... ils appellent ça la **gimbu
nous faisons toutes les pierres de lance pareil
comme ils les ont choisies et nommées
Ces noms on les utilise toujours aujourd'hui
Banggal

*pulling kangaroo roo sinew... **julwungi***
Ungudman

*So wird die Kängurusehne gezogen... **julwungi***
Ungudman

*tirer le tendon du kangourou... **julwungi***
Ungudman

*... holding spear bamboo... **gingu***
*on hot anvil stone... **warid wani mumal***
*binding kangaroo roo sinew... **julwungi***
Ungudman

*... Bambus für den Speer... **gingu***
*auf heißem Amboss-Stein... **warid wani mumal***
*wird die Kängurusehne aufgewickelt... **julwungi***
Ungudman

*... tenir la lance de bambou ... **gingu***
*une enclume de pierre chaude ... **warid wani mumal***
*lien en tendon de kangourou ... **julwungi***
Ungudman

*They belong to **gimbu** tribe*
*who started the spear **gimbu***
*and we call them **Jenagi Jenagi***
because they travellers and spear chippers
Banggal

*Sie gehörten zum **gimbu**-Stamm*
*die haben den **gimbuu**-Speer erfunden*
*und wir nennen sie **Jenagi Jenagi***
weil sie Wanderer und Speermacher waren
Banggal

*Ils appartiennent à la tribu de la **gimbu***
*ceux qui ont inventé la lance à **gimbu***
*et on les appelle **Jenagi Jenagi***
parce que ce sont des voyageurs
et des tailleurs de lances
Banggal

a

b

c

The raw material for the sharpest spear point, the lustrous, deep-brown **gimbu**, is found protruding from sandstone matrix deposits. Chunks of **gimbu** are fire-treated so that they can be broken into pieces and knapped into tools. The core material is first tapped with a wooden flaking tool (it has three names: **garrinjal, mad.da, ngariwanji**), to produce blanks for blades.

Smaller blades of suitable weight for spear-points are selected and both edges (**re.al, mogga**) reworked by pressure-flaking towards the apex – known as the **ambul** "eye" – to form a denticulated blade that is called **gurin** or **umralu** (a). The pressure-flaking is done with the leverage of the wrist towards the body using the pointed kangaroo **ayaal** (ulna), made into a **ngaal, lindith** pressure-flaking tool. The kangaroo **jun.bii** (tibia) is good for the same job.

The **gimbu** blade has a trihedron form; it is light but exceptionally durable, and serves well as a spear point. The cutting-edge remains sharper than bottle-glass; it rarely fractures or becomes blunt with use. Contemporary **Ngarinyin** evidence of this vital **Gwion** invention is a **gimbu** (b) crafted by **Ngarjno**; its dual shafts of hollow bamboo and solid hardwood are firmly bound together with cord made from kangaroo tail sinew, **julwungi** (also called **julai** and **gambul**).

Banggal prepared the **julwungi** by stripping the sinew along the length of the tail, and cleaning away any excess flesh by pulling it between his teeth. Then he bound the round white sinew cord around a substitute shaft, whittled smooth by **Ungudman**, so that it flattened into a tight coil as it half dried. This ensured that the binding cord could be overlapped for maximum grip. Wood and bamboo shafts can be painted with a toxic yellow clay that has the effect of confusing the prey; it is also daubed over the spinifex resin mount that fixes the exact alignment of the **gimbu** spear-point.

The technological advantages of a spear tipped with a razor-sharp **gimbu** spear-point, along with the extra impetus and directional thrust gained from a **nyarndu** (spear-thrower) allowed hunters to pierce the thick hides of emu and kangaroo. They could abandon their reliance on **boab**-fibre rope and nets to trap large prey. The **Gwion** hunter also had a ready knife to butcher fresh meat and a fine scalpel for **brilgi** (symbolic body scars) and for surgical operations such as circumcision and genital subincision and for cleaning ulcers.

Das Ausgangsmaterial für die schärfsten Speerspitzen, der glänzend-dunkelbraune **gimbu** findet sich als Einlagerung in Sandsteinsedimenten. Die **gimbu** werden im Feuer gehärtet, sodass sich Splitter abschlagen und weiter behauen lassen, als Rohlinge für die Klingen. Dies geschieht mit Hilfe eines hölzernen Werkzeugs, das drei Namen hat – **garrinjal, mad.da** oder **ngariwanji**.

Kleinere Klingen, die das richtige Gewicht für Speerspitzen haben, werden durch Druck an beiden Seiten (**re.al, mogga**) zur als **ambul** oder „Auge" bezeichneten Spitze hin abgesprengt, bis eine gezahnte Klinge (**gurin** oder **umralu**) entsteht (a). Dabei arbeitet man zum Körper hin, und als Werkzeuge (**ngaal, lindith**) dienen der spitz zulaufende Ellenknochen (**ayaal**) oder das Schienbein (**jun.bii**) eines Kängurus.

Die dreiseitigen **gimbu** sind leicht, aber außerordentlich widerstandsfähig und bleiben auf Dauer schärfer als Glasscherben, weil sie nur selten zerbrechen oder durch Gebrauch stumpf werden. Ein modernes, von den **Ngarinyin** stammendes Beispiel für diese bahnbrechende Erfindung der **Gwion** ist ein von **Ngarjno** angefertigter **gimbu**-Speer (b) mit einem Doppelschaft aus hohlem Bambus und massivem Hartholz, die mittels der Schwanzsehne **julwungi** (auch **julai** oder **gambul**) eines Kängurus fest miteinander verbunden sind.

Banggal bereitete diese **julwungi** vor, indem er die Sehne aus dem Känguruschwanz herauslöste und anschließend mit den Zähnen von Fleischresten befreite. Dann wickelte er sie um einen von **Ungudman** geschnitzten Ersatzschaft, bis eine flache, elastische Spirale entstanden war. Diese Sehne kann später überlappend um den Schaft gewunden werden und sorgt für einen sehr guten Halt. Speerschäfte aus Holz oder Bambus sind bisweilen mit einer giftigen gelben Lehmfarbe bestrichen, die die Beute betäubt. Mit dieser Farbe behandelt man auch die Befestigungsmasse aus dem klebrigen Saft des Spinifex-Grases, mit der die **gimbu**-Spitze genau in Position gebracht wird.

Dank der technischen Überlegenheit eines solchen Speers mit seiner rasiermesserscharfen Spitze aus **gimbu**-Stein und der zusätzlichen Schubkraft und Zielgenauigkeit, die man durch die Verwendung einer Speerschleuder (**nyarndu**) gewann, konnten die Jäger auch dickhäutiges Wild wie Emus und Kängurus erlegen. Die Seile und Fangnetze aus den Fasern des **boab**-Baums, mit denen sie bis dahin größere Beutetiere fingen, hatten ausgedient. Der **Gwion**-Jäger trug außerdem ein Messer zum Zerlegen der Jagdbeute und eine kleine, skalpellartige Klinge bei sich. Mit Letzterer wurden Ziernarben (**brilgi**) in die Haut geritzt, vereiterte Wunden gereinigt und chirurgische Eingriffe wie die Beschneidung der Vorhaut und das Aufschneiden der Harnröhre an der Penis-Unterseite (Subinzision) vorgenommen.

La matière première pour obtenir la pointe de lance la plus acérée, **gimbu**, d'un ton brun foncé lustré, est trouvée en affleurement des bancs de grès délités. Ces morceaux sont chauffés pour que des fragments puissent être éclatés et taillés. Le nodule est d'abord frappé doucement à l'aide d'un percuteur en bois qui porte trois noms – **garrinjal, mad.da, ngariwanji** – pour obtenir des ébauches de lames.

Ensuite, les plus petites lames, d'un poids qui convient aux pointes de lances, sont sélectionnées et les deux bords (**re.al, mogga**) sont retravaillés par pression dans la direction de la pointe – connue sous le nom d'**ambul** (« œil ») –, formant ainsi une lame dentée appelée **gurin** ou **umralu** (a). On fait sauter les éclats par pression en faisant levier par un mouvement du poignet vers le corps, en utilisant un os pointu, le cubitus du kangourou (**ayaal**) transformé en percuteur (**ngaal, lindith**). Le tibia (**jun.bii**) du kangourou convient pour le même travail.

La lame trièdre **gimbu** est légère mais exceptionnellement solide et s'utilise bien comme pointe de lance. Les bords tranchants restent plus aiguisés que du verre car ceux-ci se fracturent ou s'émoussent rarement à l'usage. Une preuve contemporaine de ce savoir faire **Gwion** transmis aux **Ngarinyin** est une lance (**gimbu**) réalisée par **Ngarjno** (b); elle a un étui en bambou creux, fermement attaché à un manche de bois dur par un lien en tendon de queue de kangourou appelé **julwungi** (ou encore **julai** ou **gambul**).

Banggal a préparé le lien – **julwungi** – en enlevant le tendon sur toute la longueur de la queue, puis il a ôté la chair qui y adhérait en faisant glisser le tendon blanc entre ses dents. Il l'a ensuite enroulé autour d'un manche de travail et après avoir été lissé et aplati par **Ungudman** le tendon est devenu un rouleau très serré et à moitié séché. Ceci permet un enroulement très serré et donc une excellente tenue. Le bois et l'étui de bambou peuvent être recouverts d'une glaise jaune toxique qui affecte le système nerveux des proies. On en passe également sur la résine extraite du spinifex qui sert à attacher la pointe (**gimbu**) parfaitement dans l'axe du manche.

Les bénéfices, sur le plan technologique, d'une lance terminée par une pointe (**gimbu**) aussi coupante qu'un rasoir, à laquelle on ajoute la force et la précision d'un propulseur (**nyarndu**), ont permis aux chasseurs de réussir à percer l'épaisse peau d'un émeu ou d'un kangourou. Ainsi, grâce à cette invention, ils ont pu s'affranchir de la nécessité d'utiliser la corde en fibre de **boab** et les filets pour attraper les larges proies. Le chasseur **Gwion** avait également toujours sous la main un couteau pour dépecer les proies et un scalpel qui pouvait lui servir pour les scarifications corporelles (**brilgi**) et pour des opérations chirurgicales telles que la circoncision, la subincision du pénis ou pour débrider un abcès.

gimbu

That's **mamandu** that tree
where I'm holding that's **mamandu**
and they smack that bark off that tree
… that **mamandu**
they use those for paintings
It is sticking like a glue
this tree **mamandu**
it's in a finger here… sticky!
You stick on that stone there
because it's got glue already… **mamandu**

Banggal

Der Baum da der heißt **mamandu**
das ist **mamandu**-Rinde die ich da habe
sie schlagen die Rinde vom Baum ab
… **mamandu**
die nimmt man zum Malen
Der ist klebrig wie Leim
der **mamandu**-Baum
hier habe ich sie am Finger… so klebrig ist die!
Man bleibt an dem Stein da kleben
denn da ist der Leim schon mit drin… **mamandu**

Banggal

C'est **mamandu** cet arbre
ce que je tiens là c'est **mamandu**
et ils décollent l'écorce en tapant sur cet arbre
… ce **mamandu**
ils l'utilisent pour les peintures
ça tient comme de la colle
cet arbre **mamandu**
c'est sur mon doigt… c'est collant !
ça colle sur cette pierre
parce qu'il y a déjà de la colle, **mamandu**

Banggal

*Yeah this stone **norgun***
*stone palettes... **wungurrurun mamandu***
Got a hollow in there to...
maybe you want to crush some paint
*or red ochre... **jimbri** or anything*

*We call that the **norgun***
and then they put it there
and crush all those things
make 'em really fine then they use it
paint somebody with that thing
now they just have to put water in there
*paint it up... that's the **norgun***

Nyawarra

*Da, dieser Stein, den nennen wir **norgun***
*eine Palette aus Stein ... **wungurrurun mamandu***
Da hat er eine Vertiefung ...
wenn man Farbe zerreiben will
*oder roten Ocker ... **jimbri** oder so etwas*

*Wir nennen ihn **norgun***
die Farbe wird da hineingelegt
und dann zermahlen
die muss fein sein ehe man sie gebrauchen kann
ehe man damit malen kann
dann muss man nur noch Wasser hineintun
*dann kann's losgehen ... so funktioniert der **norgun***

Nyawarra

*Oui cette pierre, **norgun***
*des palettes de pierre ... **wungurrurun mamandu***
Il y a un creux ici ...
si tu veux tu peux écraser du pigment
*ou de l'ocre rouge ... **jimbri** ou n'importe quoi*

*on appelle ça le **norgun***
et après ils le mettent là
et écrasent toutes ces choses
on fait ça très fin et après on peut l'utiliser
quelqu'un peut peindre avec cette chose
il faut juste mettre de l'eau dedans
*et peindre ... c'est le **norgun***

Nyawarra

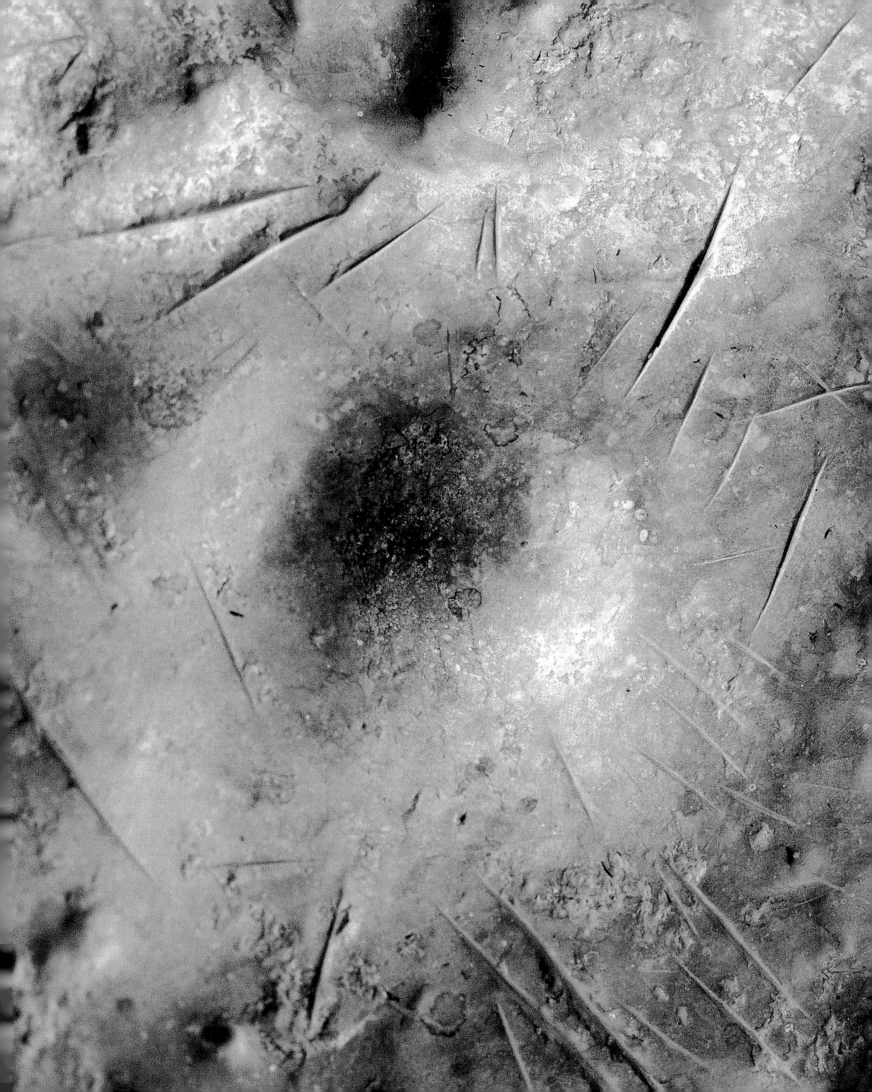

These wise people
Jenagi *people who started this*
find out what is better for painting
mamandu *it's got glue already*
Banggal

These ones... that mark left behind
*that **darrawani** mark never be moved*
forever not be changed
these ones here what painted in the caves
*they all in the **Wunan***
*this one **dal.gnana**... fan of palm*
Nyawarra

mudurra *that is **dal.gnana***
dal.gnana *is palm*
Ngarjno

Die weisen Männer
*die **Jenagi** von denen wir alles haben*
die fanden raus was das Beste zum Malen ist
mamandu *da ist der Leim schon mit drin*
Banggal

Das da ... dieser Abdruck
*der **darrawani** der darf nie verwischt werden*
nie verändert für alle Zeiten
alles was hier in den Höhlen gemalt ist
*das ist alles **Wunan***
*das hier ist eine **dal.gnana**... Fächerpalme*
Nyawarra

*Die **mudurra** da heißt auch **dal.gnana***
***dal.gnana** heißt Palme*
Ngarjno

C'étaient des sages des personnes avisées
*ces **Jenagi** qui créèrent tout ça*
et trouvèrent ce qui était le mieux pour peindre
mamandu *avec de la colle déjà*
Banggal

Là... cette marque laissée derrière eux
*cette marque **darrawani** ne sera jamais déplacée*
elle ne changera jamais
celles qui sont peintes dans les grottes
*elles sont toutes dans le **Wunan***
*celle-là c'est **dal.gnana**... le palmier-éventail*
Nyawarra

mudurra *c'est comme un **dal.gnana***
***dal.gnana** c'est le palmier*
Ngarjno

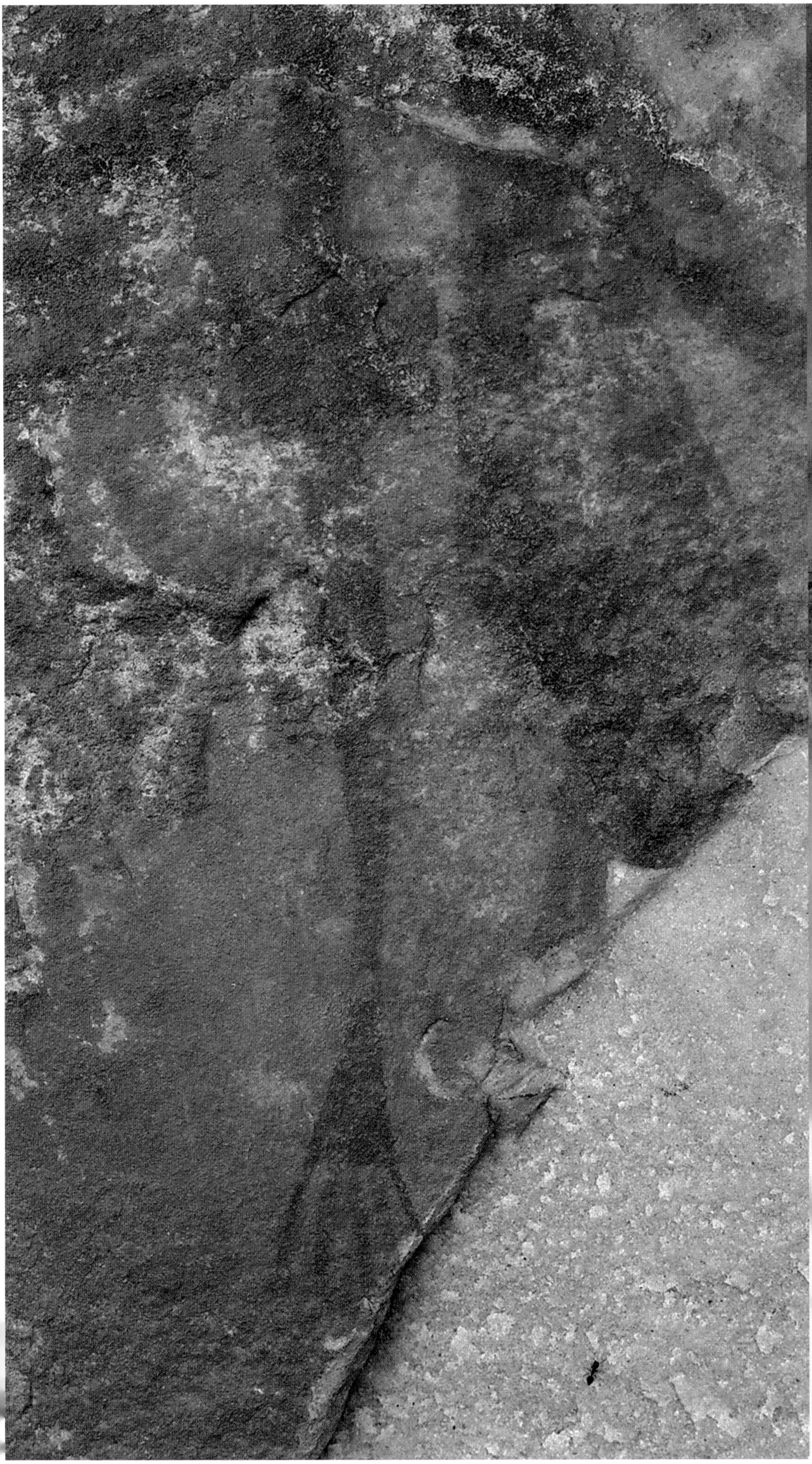

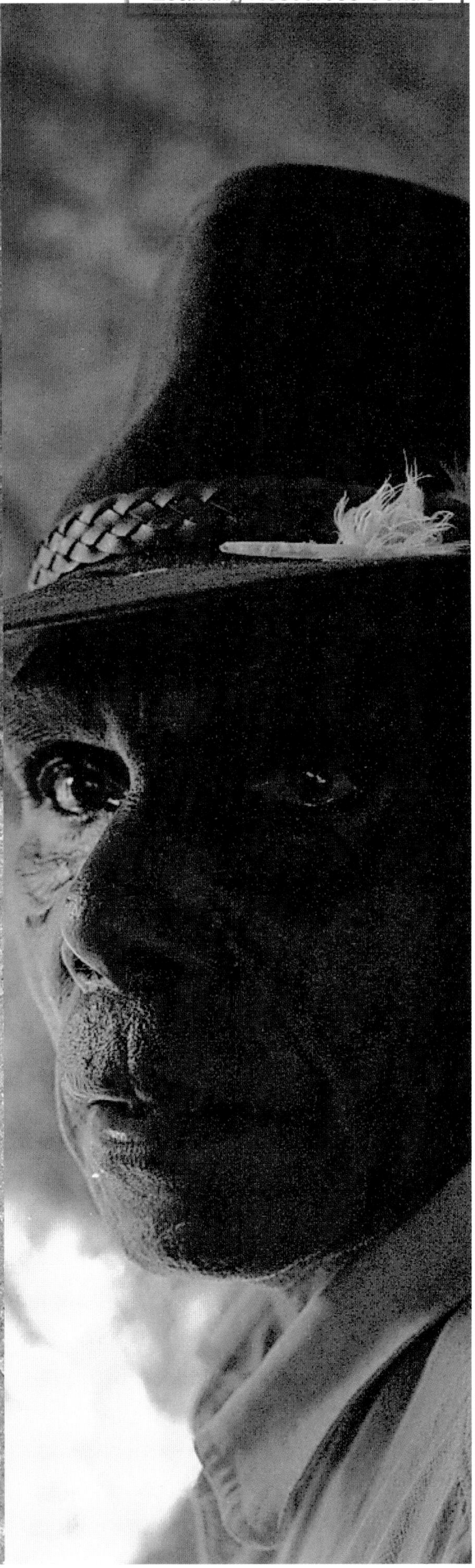

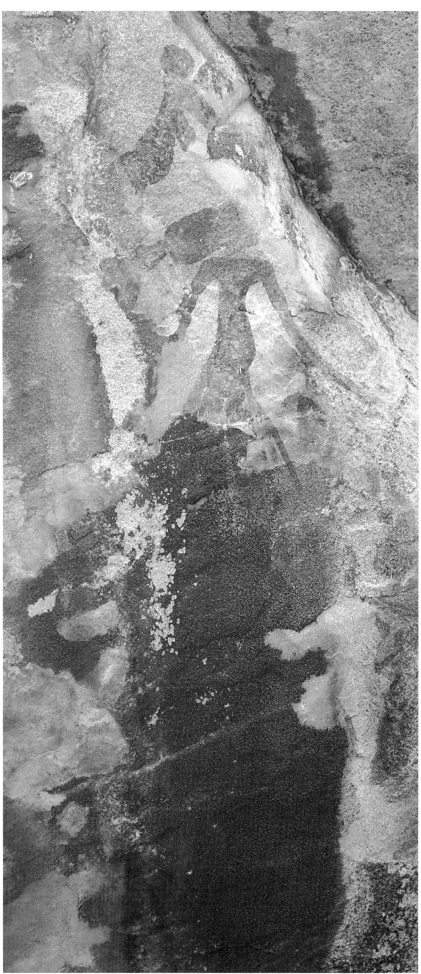

Well they was a human being in the first place
this **mob** bird... they was yeah!
they was a human being and after... birds
when they have the other secret ceremony
on this man **Argad**

There was two **Argad**
and one took his brother's wife
Probably they was making a string
up in that **boab** tree y'know?
And **Argad** went up there
one bloke went up there...
the eldest brother **Argad**
He went up on top tree making string

y'know young **Argad** was picking up
all these **boab** nuts
to make a big hole there
and cook it all and have a feed
And he went up there
and the young bloke said
"I'm going to take my brother's wife"

Where he was climbing it like a ladder
that **biyu** we call it... he took it
to pull that thing down
and then throw it down and he took off
That two wife of these two crows
Wang.gura... run away with it
and they come out in the other **mob** there
when they have this big **corroboree**
... this Boomerang ceremony

And this **Argad** bloke was still up there
he was trying to make some string
to get down there at the bottom

He stayed there for a coupla days
making this rope from that **boab** tree
He keep on skinning it up... making it long
he just throw it down 'til it was half way
to make more... to make it down again
make it right down to the bottom
... touch the bottom

Argad he was right
So he had to go down with that rope
follow his brother... follow him up
right up in that place
where they had the big dance
and his brother was in there now dancing

And when **Argad** came up there slowly
he didn't come up to the other people
he just came up and checking y'know
he just quiet down and sneaking up there
looking at the people... and they tell him
"ohh your brother gonna be the last man"
in the Boomerang dance

Y'know the Boomerang dance?
young **Argad**
had the Boomerang behind him
y'know straight across here!
another Boomerang
and another Boomerang was here

And then they start to sing that corroboree
and he was waiting with that spear
when they called this last corroboree
and he was angry when he see that
aaah!...

**Juwi i barrgoni Juwi i barrgoni
gulungulu
Wanggara yabu yabu wanggara
Juwi i barrgoni o Juwi i barrgoni**

(Lying on his side he was attached
to the guilty one **Wang.gura** Crow,
moving side to side)

And this Boomerang **corroboree**
they had that **Juwi barrgoni**
very bad in that time
So he break the law...
take his own brother's wife

Like this time they didn't break law
everybody married anyway
but that was **Wunan** y'know really good
like **Wodoi**'s wife... **Jungun**'s wife
nobody been break the law

But that's only young **Argad**
... break the law
about the wife business

The other **mob** came dancing first
and break up and go out
and he was the last bloke
and **Argad** got the spear
and but it been hit im
spear got his brother

So when his brother spear him
his young brother... young **Argad**
everybody turn into birds now in that time
Everybody been turn into birds
"Garrd garrd garrd garrd"

Another **mob** bird...
another one been say
"gri gri gri gri gri gri"
another one been say
"wahg wahg wahg wahg wahg wahg"
another one go
"gog gog grrog grrog grrog"

Everybody they all been turn
... into birds at that time

Nyawarra

Also am Anfang, da waren sie Menschen
die ganzen Vögel... ehrlich!
sie waren Menschen, und dann... Vögel
da gab es die andere geheime Zeremonie
mit einem Mann, der hieß **Argad**

Es gab zwei namens **Argad**
und der eine nahm seines Bruders Frau
Wahrscheinlich haben sie sich ein Seil gemacht
für den **boab**-Baum, verstehst du?
Und **Argad** kletterte hinauf auf den Baum
der eine kletterte da hinauf...
der ältere von den beiden
Er kletterte hoch auf den Baum, mit einem Seil

und der jüngere Argad pflückte die Brotfrüchte
er wollte ein Loch machen und sie kochen
sich ordentlich den Bauch voll schlagen
Also kletterte er nach oben
und da sagte der Jüngere
„Ich werde meinem Bruder die Frau wegnehmen"

Der andere kletterte hoch, wie auf einer Leiter
biyu nennen wir sie... aber der Jüngere packte sie
und riss sie ab und sie zogen sie nach unten
und machten sich aus dem Staub
Die beiden Frauen gehörten zum Krähen-Clan
Wang.gura... die sind damit fortgelaufen
und sind rüber zu den anderen
die gerade ihr großes **corroboree** hatten
... die Bumerang-Zeremonie

Aber der andere **Argad** saß immer noch da oben
versuchte, sich einen neuen Strick zu machen
damit er wieder nach unten konnte

Ein paar Tage hat der da oben gesessen
hat die Rinde von dem **boab**-Baum abgeschält
und sich ein Seil daraus gedreht... ein richtig
langes
hat's runtergelassen bis in die Mitte und
musste noch mehr machen
bis er wieder nach unten konnte... so lang
bis es ganz auf den Boden reichte

Argad hatte Recht
Ohne Seil wäre er da nicht runtergekommen
und dann musste er seinem Bruder nach
... immer hinterher bis zu der Stelle
wo sie den großen Tanz hatten
und sein Bruder war dabei und tanzte
zwischen den anderen

Und als **Argad** dort anlangte
ging er nicht zu den anderen
er schlich sich nur hin und sah sich alles an
ganz leise schlich er sich an
sah sich die Leute an... und die sagen zu ihm
„oh, dein Bruder, der wird der letzte sein"
der letzte im Bumerangtanz

Kennst du den Bumerangtanz?
der jüngere **Argad**
der hatte seinen Bumerang hinter dem Rücken
hier, so hinter dem Rücken!
und noch einen zweiten
einen zweiten Bumerang hatte er hier

Und als sie anfingen zu singen bei ihrem
corroboree da wartete der Ältere schon mit
seinem Speer und
als der Letzte an die Reihe kam
oooh!... was war er wütend, als er das sah!

Juwi i barrgoni Juwi i barrgoni gulungulu
Wanggarra yabu yabu wanggarra
Juwi i barrgoni o Juwi i barrgoni

(Da lag er auf der Seite, direkt
neben der Schuldigen, der **Wang.gura**-Krähe
und wälzte sich hin und her)

Und bei diesem Bumerang-**corroboree**
da sangen sie das **Juwi barrgoni** damals,
da war das eine schlimme Sache, er hatte
das Gesetz gebrochen... und dem eigenen
Bruder die Frau weggenommen

Nicht wie heute, wo alle so was machen
jedenfalls die, die verheiratet sind
aber das war **Wunan**, eine heilige Sache
er hätte ebenso gut **Wodois** Frau nehmen
können oder **Junguns**
das waren Gesetze, die hatte noch nie jemand
gebrochen

Aber das war nur der junge **Argad**
... der hat das Gesetz gebrochen, das Ehegesetz

Die anderen tanzten zuerst
und als sie ausgetanzt hatten, gingen sie zur
Seite und er war der Letzte
und **Argad** nahm seinen Speer
und schleuderte ihn nach seinem Bruder

Und als sein Bruder den Speer nach ihm warf
nach dem Jüngeren... dem jungen **Argad**
da verwandelten sich plötzlich alle in Vögel
Alle waren nun Vögel... und sie krächzten
„**Garrd garrd garrd garrd**"

Das waren die einen... andere riefen
„**gri gri gri gri gri gri**" und wieder andere
„**wahg wahg wahg wahg wahg wahg**"
und noch andere
„**gog gog grrog grrog grrog**"

Alle wurden sie in Vögel verwandelt
... alle zur selben Zeit
Nyawarra

En fait, ils étaient des êtres humains tout début
tous ces oiseaux... vraiment oui !
des êtres humains et après... des oiseaux
quand ils ont fait cette cérémonie sacrée
sur cet homme **Argad**

Il y avait deux **Argad**
et l'un a pris la femme de son frère
Sûrement qu'il faisait une corde
en haut de ce **baobab** tu vois ?
Et **Argad** est monté là haut
un des deux est monté là haut...
le plus vieux des frères **Argad**
Il monta en haut de l'arbre et fit une corde

Le jeune **Argad** cueillait
des noix de **baobab**
puis faisait un gros trou là
et les faisait cuire pour faire un repas
Il était monté là haut
et le jeune s'est dit
« Je vais prendre la femme de mon frère »

Il avait grimpé sur une sorte d'échelle
c'est **biyu** qu'on appelle ça... il l'a prise
pour la jeter à terre et il la jeta et partit
les deux femmes de ces deux corbeaux
Wang.gura... elles se sauvèrent avec lui
Et ils arrivent là où sont tous les autres
au moment où ils font ce grand **corroboree**
... cette cérémonie du boomerang

Et cet **Argad** était toujours là-haut
il essayait de faire une corde
pour aller jusqu'en bas

Il est resté quelques jours
fabriquant cette corde avec l'arbre **baobab**
Il continue à la tresser... il allonge cette corde
il la jette en bas jusqu'à que ça
arrive à mi-hauteur
pour aller plus bas... pour aller jusqu'en bas
encore aller jusque tout en bas
... toucher le sol

Argad avait raison
Il fallait qu'il descende avec la corde
qu'il suive son frère... qu'il le poursuive
précisément là où a lieu la grande danse
et son frère était justement là
en train de danser

Et quand **Argad** est arrivé là-haut lentement
il ne s'est pas approché des gens
il est juste monté pour bien regarder tu vois
il s'est calmé et s'est fait discret
observant les gens... et ils lui disent
« ohh ton frère sera le dernier homme »
dans la danse du boomerang

Tu sais la danse du boomerang ?
le jeune **Argad**
avait un boomerang derrière lui
tu vois juste de l'autre côté là

et un autre boomerang
un autre boomerang devant, là
Alors ils ont commencé à chanter ce **corroboree**
et il attendait avec sa lance
alors qu'ils ont commencé
le dernier **corroboree**
et il s'est mis en colère quand il a vu ça aaah !...

Juwi i barrgoni Juwi i barrgoni
gulungu
Wanggara yabu yabu wanggara
Juwi i barrgoni o Juwi i barrgoni

(couché sur le côté il était attaché
à la coupable, **Wang.gura**,
bougeant d'un côté à l'autre)

Et ce **corroboree** du boomerang
ils avaient ce **Juwi barrgoni**
c'était pas très bien en ce temps
ainsi il a violé la Loi...
en prenant la femme de son propre frère

Comme maintenant on n'allait pas contre la Loi
tout le monde se mariait de toute façon
c'était le **Wunan** tu vois c'était vraiment bien
c'était une femme **Wodoi**... ou **Jungun**
personne n'allait contre la Loi

Mais c'est seulement le jeune **Argad**
... qui a violé la Loi
pour une histoire de femme

Les autres sont venus danser en premier
puis se sont dispersés et sont partis
et il était seul
Argad avec sa lance
alors il a frappé son frère
la lance a touché son frère

Donc quand son frère l'a eu avec sa lance
son jeune frère... le jeune **Argad**
tous se sont changés en oiseau à ce moment
Tout le monde est devenu oiseau
« **Garrd garrd garrd garrd** »

Un autre groupe d'oiseaux
un autre a dit
« **gri gri gri gri gri gri** »
et un autre
« **wahg wahg wahg wahg wahg wahg** »
et un autre encore a fait
« **gog gog grrog grrog grrog** »

Tous ils se sont transformés
... en oiseaux à ce moment
Nyawarra

That was really sad story anyway
Everybody they all been turn into birds

They was the human being in those times
And **Argad** went and killed his brother
everybody been ended up birds

So when his brother spear him
his young brother... young **Argad**
everybody turn into birds now in that time
they still in the law
Nyawarra

mandi... wallagari or **karabri** boomerang
boomerang he got three name
Ngarjno

They carry their belongings because they travel
that's why they called **Jenagi Jenagi**
everything they had they carried
That **Jenagi Jenagi** people
they this traveler in this sandstone country
and they painting all along
Banggal

Das war wirklich eine traurige Geschichte
Alle sind sie in Vögel verwandelt worden

Zuerst waren sie Menschen
Dann ging **Argad** hin und tötete seinen Bruder
und alle wurden zu Vögeln

Als der Bruder den Speer nach ihm warf
nach dem jüngeren Bruder... dem jungen **Argad**
da wurden sie alle zu Vögeln
denn damals herrschte noch das Gesetz
Nyawarra

mandi... wallagari oder **karabri**
drei Namen für den Bumerang
Ngarjno

Sie haben ihre Sachen dabei denn sie sind unterwegs
deswegen heißen sie **Jenagi Jenagi**
alles was sie besaßen trugen sie mit sich herum
Diese **Jenagi Jenagi** die waren immer hier
in der Sandsteingegend unterwegs
und überall haben sie gemalt
Banggal

C'était une triste histoire cependant
Tout le monde s'est changé en oiseau

C'était les hommes de ce temps
Et **Argad** est venu et a tué son frère
et tout le monde a fini en oiseau

Quand son frère l'a tué avec sa lance
son jeune frère... le jeune **Argad**
tout le monde a été changé
en oiseau à ce moment
et les oiseaux sont toujours dans la Loi
Nyawarra

mandi... wallagari ou **karabri**
le boomerang a trois noms
Ngarjno

Ils emportent leurs biens parce qu'ils voyagent
c'est pourquoi on les appelle **Jenagi Jenagi**
tout ce qu'ils possédaient ils l'avaient avec eux
Ces **Jenagi Jenagi**
ce sont des voyageurs dans ce pays de grès
et ils peignaient un peu partout
Banggal

wura.wura... Partridge Pigeon in the grass
gumba.lawal... White-quilled Rock-Pigeon
all got their name written there
in that **maya.ngarri**
all still in this **Wunan**

The **gri gri** secret places...
wanjina place... **wungud** places
they still own it this bird
That's why we say
"don't play with the birds...
don't kill **dumbi!**"
or something like that
don't play with the birds
They very good y'know... they still in the law
today they still in the law

Nyawarra

wura.wura... heißt die Taube im Gras
die auf den Felsen das ist **gumba.lawal...**
die Namen sind alle aufgeschrieben
da auf den **maya.ngarri**
das gehört alles zum **Wunan**

Die heiligen Orte der **gri gri**...
wanjina... **wungud**
die gehören bis heute den Vögeln
Deshalb sagen wir
„Lass die Vögel in Ruhe...
bring die **dumbi** nicht um!"
oder so etwas was bedeutet
dass man die Vögel in Ruhe lassen soll
Die Vögel sind nämlich gut... die halten das Gesetz
das alte Gesetz bis heute

Nyawarra

wura.wura... le pigeon dans l'herbe
gumba.lawal... le pigeon à plumes blanches
tous ont leur nom écrit là
dans ce **maya.ngarri**
tous sont encore dans le **Wunan**

Les endroits sacrés de **gri gri**...
les lieux des *wanjina...* les endroits **wungud**
ça appartient toujours aux oiseaux
C'est pour ça qu'on dit
« ne joue pas avec les oiseaux...
ne tue pas **dumbi !** »
ou quelque chose comme ça
ne joue pas avec les oiseaux
Ils sont bien... sont toujours dans la Loi
toujours dans la Loi

Nyawarra

Even this **wir.nganyen** ceremony too
this **wir.nganyen songs** all in the birds
Ngarjno

yooo! mister **gri gri**
goro.goro... Blue-winged Kookaburra
marririn... Red-winged Parrot
borror... Frogmouth Owl
they all in the song too this **maya.ngarri**
warrana... like eaglehawk
burrin.burrin... Rainbow Bee-eater
gorrodoo... Magpie... **margi**... honeyeater
belnged... Sulphur-crested Cockatoo
durran... Black Cockatoo
that crow **wang.gura**
and **dindiwal**... Peregrine Falcon
argad... Brown Falcon

but they still own the tribes all these birds
they still in the **Wunan**
and everybody's name of that country
they still own everything
Nyawarra

Selbst die **wir.nganyen**-Zeremonie
das **wir.nganyen**-Ritual kommt von den Vögeln
Ngarjno

Oh ja! Mister **gri gri**
goro.goro... Blauflügel-Kookaburra
marririn... Rotflügelsittich
borror... Eulenschwalm
die sind alle auch in den Liedern in den **maya.ngarri**
warrana... der große Keilschwanzadler
burrin.burrin... Bienenfresser
gorrodoo... Elstern... **margi**... Honigfresser
belnged... der Gelbhaubenkakadu
durran... der Rabenkakadu
die Krähe **wang.gura**
und **dindiwal**... Wanderfalke
argad... Gabelweihe

aber die Stämme gehören immer den Vögeln
alle gehören sie noch dazu
zum **Wunan** und alle Namen hier im Land
die gehören alle ihnen
Nyawarra

Même cette cérémonie **wir.nganyen** aussi
ces chants **wir.nganyen** tout est aux oiseaux
Ngarjno

Hé ! monsieur **gri gri**
goro.goro... le kookaburra à ailes bleues
marririn... le perroquet à ailes rouges
borror... la chouette à bouche de grenouille
ils sont tous dans le chant aussi **maya.ngarri**
warrana... comme un aigle-faucon
burrin.burrin... l'oiseau guêpier arc-en-ciel
gorrodoo... la pie...
margi... oiseau mangeur de miel
belnged... le cacatoès blanc à huppe jaune
durran... le cacatoès de Banks
ce corbeau c'est **wang.gura**
et **dindiwal**... le faucon pèlerin
argad... le milan à queue fourchue

mais ils possèdent toujours les tribus
tous ces oiseaux
ils sont toujours dans le **Wunan**
et tous les noms de tout le monde dans ce pays
ils possèdent encore tout
Nyawarra

*And them birds all them **yululun**... feathers*
that's why they got 'em up in their heads
they dressed themselves
These real people who really flashing themselves
to start off in life

*Whatever **Gwion** did we do and this*
*all this dressing **yululun***
We will dress up in white cockatoo feather
an' black cockatoo feather
turkey feather... emu feather
Banggal

*Alle Vögel haben **yululun**... Federn*
darum machten sie früher Kopfschmuck daraus
wenn sie sich schmücken wollten
wenn sich die Leute groß herausgeputzt haben
für die Zeremonie
für den Eintritt ins Erwachsenenleben

*Wir machen es genau wie die **Gwion***
*wir schmücken uns mit **yululun***
Wir schmücken uns mit weißen Kakadufedern
und mit schwarzen Kakadufedern
mit Truthahnfedern... Emufedern
Banggal

*Et ces oiseaux ont des plumes, des **yululun**...*
c'est pourquoi ils les ont mis sur leur tête
ils se sont habillés
ces gens purs qui se sont vraiment embellis
pour entrer dans la vie

*Tout ce que les **Gwion** faisaient nous le faisons*
*et tout ces vêtements avec des **yululun***
On s'habille avec des plumes
de cacatoès blancs à huppe jaune
et de cacatoès de Banks
plumes d'outarde... plumes d'émeu
Banggal

And in their shoulder
yidmunggul... *emu hide epaulets*
*Where they have ah bag... we call them **garagi***
where they have their stone knives
and whatever they collect
and they carry them home

Nyawarra

*Und auf der Schulter haben sie **yidmunggul***
das sind Schulterklappen aus Emuleder
*Und darüber die Tasche... **garagi** nennen wir die*
da wo sie ihre steinernen Messer drinhaben
und alles was sie sonst noch sammeln
das tragen sie darin nach Hause

Nyawarra

Et sur leurs épaules
ils ont des épaulettes en peau d'émeus
yidmunggul
*Et ils ont une sorte de sac... qu'on appelle **garagi***
là ils mettent leurs couteaux de pierre
et tout ce qu'ils cueillent
et ils ramènent tout à la maison

Nyawarra

*Here **yululun...** feathers*

We call those in their arms
*up here... **urilimul***
they have those little bands
*we call them **urilimul** round their neck*

Banggal

*Das hier, das sind **yululun**... Federn*

Die Armbinde hier
*die heißt **urilimul***
und die Bänder die sie um den Hals haben
*die nennen wir auch **urilimul***

Banggal

*Ce sont des **yululun**... des plumes*

Celles sur leurs bras
*là en haut... on les appelle **urilimul***
ils ont ces petites bandes
*autour du cou qu'on appelle **urilimul***

Banggal

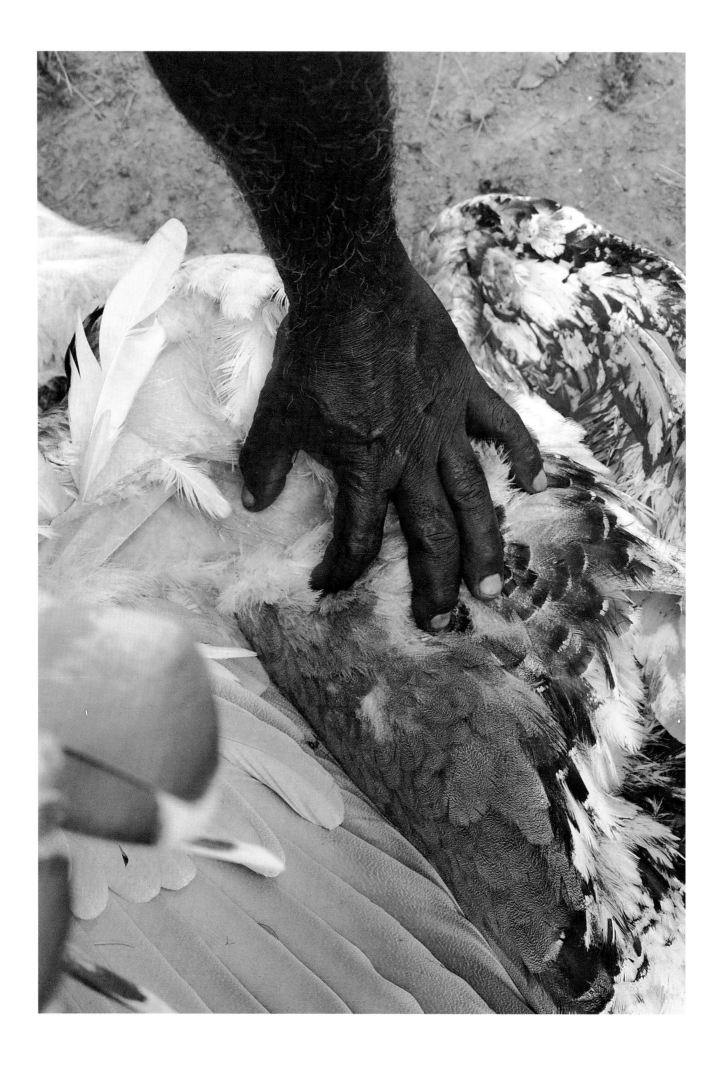

Banad... bush turkey
Fat... we call them **wurd.ngun**
Now they had to use fats for anointing objects
things that they made... wood objects
To make and polish them up

Gwion *he stretching lying down... he lies down*
See all these birds along side them
banad... *bush turkey...* **jebera**... *emu*
That's why they got painting here
that **modeden**... *footprint belong to bird*
turkey and emu **modeden**

Banggal

Banad... ein Busch-Truthahn
Die geben Fett... wir nennen das **wurd.ngun**
Mit Fett haben sie Sachen eingerieben
Sachen die sie gemacht hatten... aus Holz
Die haben sie damit poliert

Der **Gwion** *da liegt ganz ausgestreckt... hier*
Sieh dir die ganzen Vögel da an, an seiner Seite
banad... *Truthahn...* **jebera**... *Emu*
Das bedeuten die Zeichen hier
Das sind **modeden**... *Fußspuren von Vögeln*
modeden *von Truthahn und Emu*

Banggal

Banad... l'outarde
la graisse... on l'appelle **wurd.ngun**
Ils avaient besoin
de graisse pour des choses des choses qu'ils
fabriquaient... des objets en bois
Pour les fabriquer et les enduire

Ce **Gwion** *est allongé et s'étire*
Regarde tous ces oiseaux à côté de lui
banad... *l'outarde...* **jebera**... *l'émeu*
C'est pourquoi elles sont peintes
ces empreintes de pied, **modeden**...
qui appartiennent aux oiseaux
modeden *d'outarde et d'émeu*

Banggal

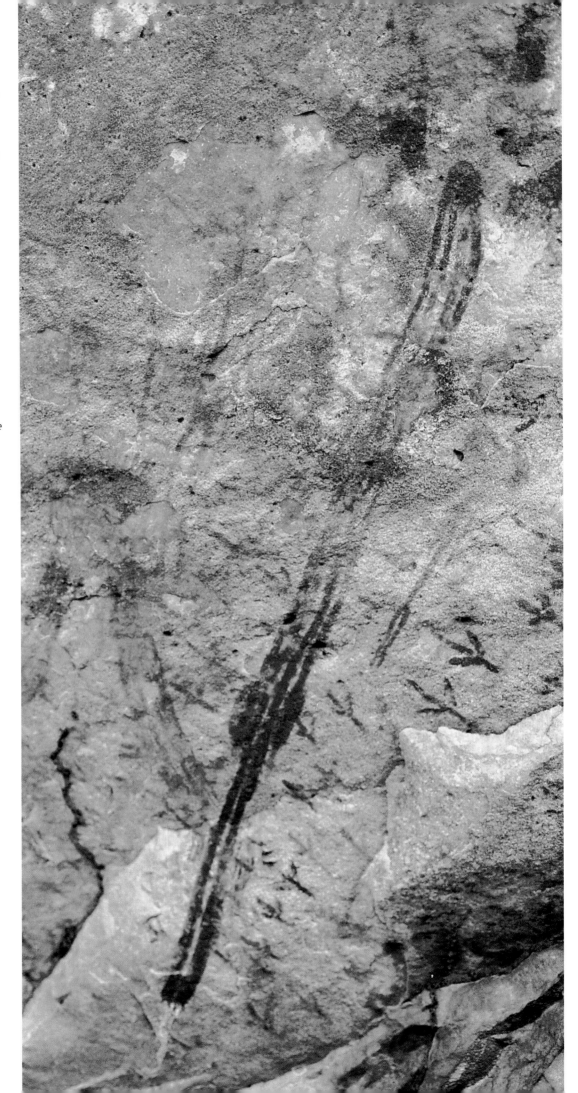

Now this *bird here*
that the one who painted
*the **Jenagi Jenagi***
he put painting down in that cave

Jenagi Jenagi they call 'em
but that bird...
that bird he got long nose
he got long nose like this!
only bendier in front
but pretty hard to find 'em
that bird only walk around at night

no... we can see him!

Also dieser *-Vogel hier*
*das ist der, der die **Jenagi Jenagi***
gemalt hat, da in der Höhle

Jenagi Jenagi ... heißen sie
aber dieser Vogel ...
der hat einen langen Schnabel
hier, so lang ist der Schnabel!
nur vorne beweglicher
aber die sind nicht leicht zu finden
diese Vögel, die sind nur
nachts unterwegs

nein ... wir können ihn sehen!

Maintenant cet oiseau
c'est celui qui a peint
*les **Jenagi Jenagi***
les peintures qu'il a mis dans
cette grotte

Jenagi Jenagi ils les appellent
mais cet oiseau ...
cet oiseau a un long nez
il a un nez long comme ça !
seulement plus courbé devant
mais c'est plutôt dur de le trouver
cet oiseau ne se déplace que la nuit

non ... on peut le voir !

Banggal

Nyawarra

Ngarjno

a

b

c

Gwion art began with the charismatic bird called Gwion Gwion. Explanations of the origin of the dark red paintings tell of a magic bird wiping fresh blood from the tip of its curved beak onto the walls of rock-shelters. The Gwion Gwion bird made the very first painting marks. Narratives of the Ngarinyin and their Kimberley neighbours describe the Gwion bird as a cave-dweller, one imbued with exceptional magical influence.

The Gwion Gwion bird is known by munnumburra as an extremely alert and crafty creature. It not only flies around the rock-shelters containing ancient paintings, it has the power to influence the minds of people today. When viewing the paintings, visitors can be distracted and have strange or fearful encounters with a Gwion Gwion bird. Strangers may experience visions and deceptive ideas for which they cannot account. The proper pronunciation of "Gwion Gwion" is a phonetic approximation of a descending nasal shriek from the bird, similar to but not to be confused with that of juiban, the Great Bower Bird.

Gwion Gwion remains a hereditary name currently carried by young women of the Brrejirad dambun, whose Hibiscus Clan territory adjoins the northern side of the Prince Regent River. This indicates the significance of the area as the location of the source of the Gwion Gwion bird. Human artists of this delicate fine art, while also called Jenagi Jenagi and Munga.nunga are now known in public by the formal title Gwion Gwion. This ancient and still sacred name embraces the artists and the distinct society that they portrayed.

Die Kunst der Gwion begann mit einem geheimnisvollen Vogel namens Gwion Gwion. Geschichten über die Herkunft der dunkelroten Malereien berichten von einem magischen Vogel, der sich an den Wänden von Felsunterständen frisches Blut von der Spitze seines geschwungenen Schnabels wischte. Die Erzählungen der Ngarinyin und ihrer Nachbarn in der Kimberley-Region beschreiben den Vogel Gwion als Höhlenbewohner mit außerordentlichen magischen Kräften.

Den munnumburra gilt der Gwion als ausgesprochen wachsames und listiges Geschöpf. Man sieht ihn nicht nur in den Felsunterständen fliegen, an deren Wänden sich die alten Höhlenmalereien finden, sondern er hat zudem die Macht, das Denken heutiger Menschen zu beeinflussen. Ein Besucher, der die Bilder betrachtet, sollte auf seltsame oder Angst einflößende Begegnungen mit einem Gwion-Vogel gefasst sein. Fremde haben Visionen oder erliegen unerklärlichen Täuschungen. Die richtige Aussprache von „Gwion Gwion" ahmt den eigentümlichen nasalen Schrei des Vogels nach; er erinnert an den Schrei des juiban, des Großen Bowervogels, mit dem er jedoch nicht verwechselt werden sollte.

Gwion Gwion bleibt ein vererbter Name, dessen heutige Trägerinnen junge Frauen aus dem Brrejirad dambun sind, ein Mitglied des am Nordufer des Prince Regent River beheimateten Hibiskus-Clans. Das deutet schon darauf hin, dass in dieser Region der Ursprung des Gwion-Vogels zu suchen ist. Die Künstler der Vorzeit, von denen die feinen Felszeichnungen stammen und für die auch die Bezeichnungen Jenagi Jenagi und Munga.nunga gebräuchlich sind, tragen heute offiziell den Namen Gwion Gwion. Dieser uralte und bis heute heilige Name umfasst neben den Künstlern auch die Gesellschaft, die sie im Bild festhielten.

La première manifestation religieuse de l'art Gwion est l'oiseau remarquable appelé Gwion Gwion. Les explications sur l'origine des peintures rouge sombre disent qu'un oiseau magique a essuyé le sang frais qu'il avait sur le bout de son bec recourbé sur les parois des abris sous roche. C'est l'oiseau Gwion qui a laissé les toutes premières traces peintes. Le récit des Ngarinyin et de leurs voisins du Kimberley décrivent l'oiseau Gwion vivant dans des cavernes et disposant d'un pouvoir magique exceptionnel.

Les munnumburra reconnaissent en l'oiseau Gwion Gwion une créature extrêmement alerte et habile. Il ne se contente pas seulement de voler autour des abris sous roche où sont peintes d'anciennes images, mais il a encore le pouvoir d'influencer nos pensées. Quand les visiteurs regardent les peintures, ils peuvent avoir l'esprit troublé et avoir d'étranges ou effrayantes rencontres avec un oiseau Gwion Gwion. Même des non-initiés peuvent avoir des apparitions et des hallucinations qu'ils ne peuvent expliquer. La prononciation correcte du terme « Gwion Gwion » est une imitation du cri perçant et nasal de l'oiseau ; ce cri est similaire mais ne doit pas être confondu avec celui de juiban, le grand oiseau de paradis australien.

Gwion Gwion reste un nom héréditaire porté de façon courante par les jeunes femmes du Brrejirad dambun, dont le territoire clanique qu'on appelle l'hibiscus jouxte la rive nord de la rivière Prince Regent. Cela démontre que c'est de cette région que « provient » l'oiseau Gwion Gwion. Les artistes qui ont réalisé cet art délicat sont appelés Jenagi Jenagi et Munga.nunga ; ils sont connus aujourd'hui du public sous la dénomination classique de Gwion Gwion. Ce terme ancien et toujours sacré désigne à la fois les artistes et la société particulière qu'ils ont représentée.

Gwion Gwion

That one I just painted there
he connected...

you know that one we see
*in that **Jillinya** place*
on that north west coast
he connected
long way from this creek here
Nyawarra

Der, den ich da gerade gemalt habe
der gehört zu dem anderen ...

dem großen den wir gesehen haben
*da wo **Jillinya** ist*
an der Küste im Nordwesten
zu dem gehört er
weit weg von dem Fluss hier
Nyawarra

Celui-là que je viens de peindre
il est lié ...

Tu sais celui qu'on a vu là-bas
*à l'endroit de **Jillinya***
sur cette côte nord-ouest
il est lié
bien loin de ce ruisseau ici
Nyawarra

a

b

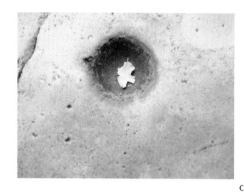

c

The peculiar red colour of **Gwion jegabi** images comes from an indelible paint prepared from mulberry-like trees, the rough-barked **mamandu**. In the scorched sandstone escarpment country where crests and gorges are strewn with sun-baked rocks, and around boulders where **bunja** (rock-shelters and overhangs) often contain paintings, **mamandu** invariably grow nearby.

When **Banggal** selected a flat stone from loose cave-fill, he deftly knapped one thin edge until it was sharp and suitable for use as a chopper. Then, using it as a **menda** (hand-axe) he cut and exposed the bloody inner bark of a nearby **mamandu**. In a concave **norgun** (stone palette) he broke the bark into pieces and easily ground it to a bright paste that exuded red fluid until a glistening liquid residue was ready for use. Red ochres and oxides (b) can be ground on any flat surface with water, but fixatives such as orchid sap or wattle gum must be added to the blend. **Mamandu** needs only time for the colour to seep out and settle, which makes a concave **norgun** invaluable to the **Gwion** artist. The deep red **mamandu** sap provides both fixative and dye; its rich colour still stains many ancient **norgun** (c) worn deep into boulders at the base of walls of **Gwion** paintings. Thick **mamandu** paint is used today to coat wooden spears like **wadba** and **gallid** because its deep colour is so penetrating and durable, particularly when the spear is first rubbed with grass made wet with fluid from kangaroo intestine.

Some stone outcrops, fragmented into groups of large boulders and separated by narrow passages and crevices, offer well-protected painting surfaces. Boulders that, over time, have opened up along a crack, can leave a smooth surface perfect for a fine brush. Early painters are said to have copied the **Gwion** bird by applying blood. Their use of a feather brush could be instrumental in producing the fine, flowing outlines and minute details that give such life to the small **Gwion** silhouettes.

Charakteristisch für die **jejabi**-Felsbilder der **Gwion** ist die unverwüstliche rote Farbe, die aus der rauen Rinde des **mamandu**, einer Art Maulbeerbaum, gewonnen wird. In dem schroffen, glutheißen Sandsteinmassiv, wo Bergkämme und Schluchten übersät sind mit sonnenverbrannten Felsen und wo sich im Schutz von Höhlen und Felsüberhängen (**bunja**) zahlreiche Felsmalereien erhalten haben, ist der **mamandu** allgegenwärtig.

Banggal suchte sich im Geröll einer Höhle einen flachen Stein und bearbeitete ihn mit wohl platzierten Schlägen, bis eine dünne, scharfe Klinge entstand. Mit diesem Handbeil (**menda**) schälte er nun die auf der Innenseite blutrot gefärbte Rinde eines **mamandu**-Baums ab, zerkleinerte sie in der Vertiefung einer steinernen Palette (**norgun**) und zerstieß sie zu einer Paste, bis eine leuchtend rote Flüssigkeit austrat, die sich zu einem glänzenden roten Bodensatz verdickte. Roter Ocker und farbige Oxide lassen sich auf jeder beliebigen flachen Oberfläche zermahlen und mit Wasser anrühren, aber man muss der Mischung ein Fixiermittel wie Orchideensaft oder Akaziengummi zusetzen. Bei der Rinde des **mamandu**-Baums dauert es zwar einige Zeit, bis die Farbe austritt und dick wird, was die konkave **norgun** zu einem unschätzbaren Utensil für den **Gwion**-Künstler werden ließ, aber der tiefrote Saft des **mamandu** ist Fixiermittel und Farbstoff zugleich. In vielen alten, tief in den Felsen gegrabenen **norgun** (c) am Fuß der **Gwion**-Felsbilder finden sich noch immer Reste dieser leuchtenden roten Farbe. Heute dient die dicke **mamandu**-Farbe zum Bemalen von hölzernen Speeren wie zum Beispiel **wadba** und **gallid**, weil die kräftige Farbe tief eindringt und dauerhaft ist, insbesondere wenn der Speer zunächst mit Gras abgerieben wird, das man zuvor mit der Flüssigkeit von Känguruinnereien getränkt hat.

Manche größeren Felsen sind auseinander gebrochen und bestehen aus einzelnen großen Felsblöcken mit schmalen Durchgängen und Ritzen. Hier finden sich gut geschützte Malflächen. Und wenn sich im Laufe der Zeit Risse in einem Felsen gebildet haben, entstehen oft glatte Flächen, die sich hervorragend für die Arbeit mit einem feinen Pinsel eignen. Die ersten Maler haben der Legende nach den **Gwion**-Vogel nachgeahmt und mit Blut gemalt. Die zarten, fließenden Konturen und der Detailreichtum, die den kleinen **Gwion**-Bildern so viel Leben einhauchen, lassen sich vielleicht damit erklären, dass die Künstler mit Federpinseln malten.

La couleur rouge particulière des images **Gwion** de jejabi est une peinture indélébile obtenue à partir d'une espèce de mûrier, le **mamandu** à l'écorce rugueuse. Les arbres **mamandu** poussent toujours non loin des escarpements gréseux, là où les sommets et les gorges sont jonchés de pierres brûlées par le soleil, et autour des rochers où des abris sous roche (**bunja**) et des surplombs abritent souvent des peintures.

Quand **Banggal** a sélectionné une pierre plate détachée des parois de la caverne, il taille habilement son côté mince jusqu'à ce qu'il devienne aiguisé et bon pour être utilisé comme hachoir. Ensuite, en l'utilisant comme une **menda** (petite hache sans manche) il a découpé et mis à nu l'écorce intérieure sanguine d'un arbre **mamandu** qui se trouvait non loin de là. Sur une palette de pierre concave (**norgun**) il a cassé l'écorce en plusieurs morceaux et les a ainsi facilement broyés, obtenant ainsi une pâte brillante qui laisse s'écouler un fluide rouge jusqu'à ce qu'il n'y ait plus qu'un résidu brillant encore liquide, prêt à être employé. Les ocres rouges et les oxydes peuvent être broyés sur n'importe quelle surface plate avec de l'eau, mais des fixatifs comme la sève d'orchidée ou la colle tirée d'un acacia arbustif doivent être ajoutés au mélange. Il faut du temps au **mamandu** pour que la couleur suinte et se stabilise, ce qui rend le **norgun** concave absolument nécessaire à l'artiste **Gwion**. La sève rouge foncé du **mamandu** fournit à la fois le fixatif et le colorant; sa magnifique teinte colore encore beaucoup d'anciennes **norgun** (c) creusées et abandonnées sous la pierraille au pied des murs de peintures **Gwion**. La peinture épaisse **mamandu** est aujourd'hui utilisée pour enduire les lances en bois comme les **wadba** ou **gallid**, car sa couleur foncée est très pénétrante et résistante, particulièrement quand la lance a d'abord été frottée avec de l'herbe humidifiée par du liquide intestinal de kangourou.

Certains affleurements de pierres, fragmentés en groupes de gros rochers et séparés par des passages étroits et des crevasses, offrent des surfaces à peindre bien à l'abri. Des rochers qui, au fil du temps, se sont ouverts en fissure peuvent présenter une surface lisse parfaite pour un artiste travaillant finement. On dit que les premiers peintres ont copié l'oiseau **Gwion** qui était du sang. Les silhouettes **Gwion**, si pleines de vie, si fines ont peut-être été réalisées grâce à un pinceau de plume.

mamandu

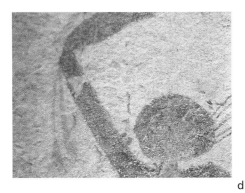

d

e

f

After the feather is moistened between the lips, it is dipped into sticky **mamandu** paint. Then the feather brush must be held over the palette with one hand, so that the thumb and forefinger of the other hand can be slipped over the stem of the quill and dragged down to the feather tip to drain off any extra paint until none shows on the outside of the feather. In this way, the artist knows that the barbules that keep the feather in tension are holding an even amount of paint along the brush. As a result, a fine, steady line can be drawn with consistent thickness on the stone surface. The elastic sap of the **mamandu** has just the right consistency for fine, even brushwork. Its deep and luminous red hue closely matches the colour of many **Gwion** paintings such as the solitary skirted figure watching the ring-dancers in action during a **walu.ngarri**.

All **Gwion** paintings were not monochromatic. Red oxides and haematite can deteriorate or change their original colour over time, and some motifs have sections missing where a white or yellow pigment, or perhaps blood, has eroded away without staining the rock. Where other paint has perished, "negatives" – shapes of absent tools or apparel – can be discerned against the discoloured rock. The space of a particular shape, an **urilimul** (armlet or girdle) easily can be distinguished from eroded gaps in the painted human form (d, f).

Certain negative images show where body paint would have been worn on appropriate parts of the body during formal public rituals. One probable example of missing **onmal** (white pigment) is the figure holding a yam beside a coiled **ngunari** hair noose (f) that is painted near a large **andarri** (possum). The spaces in his body clearly matched similar white body-marking worn by **Banggal** when singing the powerful **gulbrungi** (e) that announces and compels everyone to attend a ceremony. Important performers of these **Wunan** signal songs were likely to have been recorded in paint.

Black pigment readily is found wherever fires have left charcoal on the ground. Deposits of **jimbri** and **gagul** (red) and **gumbaru** (yellow) pigments are often exposed in the floor or banks of creek-beds. **Onmal**, a white pigment, can have various sources, but one favoured deposit is known as the fossilised excrement of **Gubu.ngarri**, the ancestral king brown snake.

Die Feder wird mit den Lippen angefeuchtet und dann in die klebrige **mamandu**-Farbe getaucht. Danach hält man den Federpinsel mit einer Hand über die Palette und fährt mit Daumen und Zeigefinger der anderen Hand am Kiel entlang bis zur Spitze der Feder, um die überschüssige Farbe so weit abzustreifen, bis an den äußeren Rändern der Feder keine Farbe mehr sichtbar ist. Auf diese Weise stellt der Künstler sicher, dass die feinen Federäste, die dafür sorgen, dass die Feder elastisch bleibt, über die ganze Länge des Pinsels gleichmäßig mit Farbe getränkt sind, und er kann nun eine feine, durchgängige und überall gleich breite Linie über die ganze Malfläche ziehen. Der zähe Saft des **mamandu** hat genau die richtige Konsistenz für solche feinen, gleichmäßigen Pinselstriche. Die leuchtend tiefrote Farbe ist charakteristisch für viele Felsbilder der **Gwion**, wie etwa diese einzelne, mit einer Art Rock bekleidete Figur, die über die Tänzer bei einem **walu.ngarri**-Ritual beobachtet.

Die **Gwion**-Gemälde waren ursprünglich nicht alle einfarbig. Rote Oxide und Hämatit können im Laufe der Zeit verblassen oder ihre ursprüngliche Farbe verändern, und so fehlen bei manchen Darstellungen die Teile, die ursprünglich mit weißen oder gelben Pigmenten oder mit Blut ausgeführt waren und verwittert sind, ohne Spuren auf dem Felsen zu hinterlassen. Da, wo andere Farben verschwunden sind, bleiben bisweilen „Negativbilder" der dargestellten Gegenstände – Werkzeuge oder Kleidungsstücke zum Beispiel – auf dem Fels zurück. An der Lücke, die eine solche verwitterte Farbfläche hinterlassen hat, erkennt man zum Beispiel ohne Schwierigkeiten die Umrisse des **urilimul** (Armband oder Gürtel), den die dargestellte Person am Arm trägt (d, f).

Andere Negativbilder lassen erkennen, wo die für bestimmte feierliche Rituale vorgeschriebene Körperbemalung angebracht war. Ein Beispiel für eine Stelle, wo im Laufe der Zeit vermutlich die weiße **onmal**-Farbe verschwunden ist, ist eine Gestalt mit einer Jamswurzel in der Hand, die neben einer zusammengerollten **ngunari**-Schnur (f) und einem großen **andarri** (Opossum) abgebildet ist. Die Lücken in der Darstellung entsprechen genau der weißen Körperbemalung, die **Banggal** trug, als er den feierlichen **gulbrungi**-Gesang vortrug (e), der eine Zeremonie ankündigt und alle zur Teilnahme auffordert. Wahrscheinlich wurden bedeutende Sänger solcher **Wunan**-Gesänge im Bild festgehalten.

Die schwarzen Pigmente stammen natürlich von den Holzkohleresten der Lagerfeuer. Die Pigmente **jimbri** (rot) und **gumbaru** (gelb) finden sich oft in Ablagerungen auf dem Boden oder an den Uferböschungen von Bachbetten. **Onmal**, ein weißes Pigment, hat verschiedene Ursprünge; eine beliebte Quelle sind die fossilen Exkremente von **Gubu.ngarri**, dem braunen Königsnatter-Ahn.

Après que la plume ait été humidifiée entre les lèvres, elle est plongée dans la peinture collante **(mamandu)**. Ensuite, le pinceau de plume doit être tenu au dessus de la palette d'une main et en se servant du pouce et de l'index de l'autre main, en glissant le long de la tige on fait s'écouler l'excédent de peinture. Il ne restera ainsi aucune trace extérieurement à la plume. De cette manière, l'artiste sait que les barbules qui maintiennent la plume-pinceau bien raide ont une quantité égale de peinture. C'est ainsi que l'on peut dessiner sur la pierre un trait délicat et régulier, d'épaisseur constante. La sève élastique de l'arbre **mamandu** a exactement la bonne consistance pour un travail fin et régulier au pinceau. Sa teinte rouge profonde et lumineuse s'accorde avec celle de beaucoup de peintures **Gwion**, comme par exemple celle du personnage solitaire en jupe regardant les danseurs d'un **walu.ngarri**.

Toutes les peintures **Gwion** n'étaient pas monochromes. Les oxydes rouges et l'hématite peuvent se détériorer ou changer de couleur avec le temps et certains motifs ont des parties manquantes où du pigment blanc, jaune ou peut-être du sang se sont désagrégés sans laisser de traces sur la pierre. À l'endroit où d'autres types de peinture ont disparu, on peut discerner des « négatifs » – restes des contours d'outils ou d'habits – sur la pierre qui a perdu sa couleur. Un espace d'une forme particulière, un **urilimul** (d, f) ou une ceinture peuvent se distinguer facilement sur des parties manquantes d'une représentation de forme humaine.

Certaines images en négatif montrent où les décorations corporelles ont du être faites pendant les rituels communs. Le personnage tenant une igname à côté d'un nœud coulant de crin enroulé, **ngunari** (f), lui-même peint à côté d'un grand **andarri** (opossum) est très certainement un exemple de peinture où du pigment **onmal** a disparu. Les espaces sur son corps correspondent clairement aux marques corporelles que **Banggal** porte lorsqu'il chante le puissant chant **gulbrungi** (e) qui annonce une cérémonie et où tout le monde doit assister. Ce sont les interprètes importants de ces chants **Wunan** qui ont probablement été peints.

Le pigment noir se trouve aisément partout où il reste du charbon de bois brûlé. Des dépôts de **jimbri** et les pigments **gagul** (rouges) et **gumbaru** (jaunes) affleurent sur le fond ou les parois des ruisseaux. **Onmal**, un pigment blanc, peut avoir diverses origines mais un des gisements tout particulièrement appréciés a la réputation d'être fait des excréments fossilisés du **Gubu.ngarri**, le serpent brun ancestral.

onmal

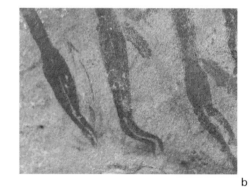

a

b

c

Early **Gwion** figures – those underlying a series of super-impositions (d) – appear more basic in shape, with stiff limbs described with an even, thick line (p. 123, f). **Gwion** artists learned how to conduct a curve, as rough outlines of human forms developed into delicate, sinuous figures. The body became fully profiled, with legs shown from different angles and appearing to turn in motion (b). To convey the human body as a fluid form during a dance, the drawing must suggest both substance and space. Painting the human body requires the artist to have clarity of vision before putting paint on rock. The basic profiles of the **jegabi** (image of the human body) require a minimum of twenty lines. Closer examination of later figures reveals that those with very fine profiles were firmly outlined first, then evenly blocked or filled in to complete the silhouette (c). **Gwion jegabi** show well-observed body shapes with thigh, knee and calves curving down and straightening with long shins to thin ankles (e). Larger figures can display a greater detail of ritual apparel and adornment. Obvious male and female genitals or breasts are absent from most **Gwion** art.

Hands depicted with five fine lines radiating from a triangular palm can suggest the slender wrists of a woman, as on one long, elegant arm wearing a bold, square armlet covering the elbow. Now lacking any surface pigment, the complete arm is preserved within the patina of the surface. It has become **darrawani**, a mark resistant to change. Some images are painted with such even outlines that only a paint of smooth consistency like **mamandu** and brushes as thin as feathers could achieve such fine results. Exceptional skill in realising anatomical detail can be seen in the accurate definition of elbow bone structure displayed in the painting of a long arm holding a curved **mandi** (c). Many small silhouette figures appear to be well protected by a glaze over the rock. Generations of **Gwion** images are layered beneath a clear or milky silicate encrustation. Some were possibly once red but have darkened with age, even to verge on black. Some could have had charcoal added to deepen the hue for crispness, but this appears restricted to taller figures with a tell-tale uneven saturation of gritty colour. Exposed paintings are often marked by water seeping down the rock-face, becoming dissected or submerged under rust and speckled black stains (g).

Die älteren, mehrfach übermalten **Gwion**-Figuren (d) waren stark stilisiert und hatten starre Gliedmaßen, die durch gleichmäßig breite und dicke Linien angedeutet wurden (S. 123, f). Später benutzten die Künstler der **Gwion** geschwungene Linien, und die grob umrissenen menschlichen Gestalten entwickelten sich zu zarten, geschmeidigen Figuren. Die Körper gewannen Kontur, und die Beine wurden aus verschiedenen Blickwinkeln gezeigt, sodass es aussah, als seien sie in Bewegung (b). Um die Bewegungen eines tanzenden Menschen darzustellen, muss das Abbild sowohl ein Gefühl von Masse als auch von Bewegung im Raum vermitteln. Ein Künstler, der einen Menschenkörper darstellen will, muss wissen, was er malt, bevor er anfängt, die Farbe aufzutragen. Das Grundgerüst für ein **jegabi** (Abbild des menschlichen Körpers) besteht aus mindestens 20 Strichen. Bei späteren Malereien stellt man fest, dass bei den Figuren mit besonders zarten Konturen zunächst die Umrisse gezeichnet und sie anschließend ausgemalt wurden (c). Die **jegabi** der **Gwion** mit ihren gewölbten Oberschenkeln, Knien und Waden, den langen Schienbeinen und schmalen Fesseln lassen erkennen, dass die Künstler den menschlichen Körper sehr genau beobachtet haben (e). Bei größeren Figuren erkennt man zum Teil rituelle Kleidungsstücke und Körperschmuck. Auffällig ist, dass männliche oder weibliche Genitalien oder Brüste auf den meisten **Gwion**-Felsbildern fehlen.

Die Hände, bei denen fünf feine Linien strahlenförmig um eine dreieckige Handfläche angeordnet sind, können wegen der schlanken Handgelenke und wegen des langen, anmutigen Arms, bei dem der Ellenbogen unter einer auffällig breiten Armbinde verschwindet, als Frauenhände verstanden werden. Obwohl auf der Felsoberfläche keine Farbpigmente mehr erhalten sind, ist die Farbe so tief in den Fels eingedrungen, dass der Arm zu einem unauslöschlichen Zeichen (**darrawani**) geworden ist. Manche Bilder haben so gleichmäßige Konturen, wie man sie nur mit einer Farbe mit sehr glatter Konsistenz wie **mamandu** und einem Pinsel, der so fein ist wie eine Feder, zustande bringt. Die präzise Knochenstruktur des Ellenbogens, wie man sie bei dem Bild eines Arms sieht, der einen halbmondförmigen **mandi** hält (c), zeugt vom Geschick bei der Wiedergabe anatomischer Details. Viele kleine Figuren sind offenbar deswegen so gut erhalten, weil sie durch eine Art Glasur fixiert sind. Mehrere Schichten von **Gwion**-Bildern liegen unter einer durchsichtigen oder milchig-trüben Silikatschicht. Manche von ihnen waren vielleicht ursprünglich rot, sind aber im Laufe der Zeit so weit nachgedunkelt, dass sie jetzt fast schwarz erscheinen. Bei manchen könnte Holzkohle beigemischt sein, um den Farbton zu vertiefen und den Kontrast zu erhöhen, doch scheint dieses Mittel, das an ungleichmäßiger Sättigung und körnigem Farbauftrag zu erkennen ist, auf größere Figuren beschränkt zu sein. Weniger geschützt liegende Bilder sind oft durch Sickerwasser geschädigt, das über die Felswände läuft und die Malereien teilweise auflöst oder unter Rostspuren und schwarzgesprenkelten Flecken verschwinden lässt (g).

Les premières figures **Gwion** (d), celles sous-jacentes aux surimpositions successives, paraissent de forme moins élaborée, avec des membres raides représentés par un trait régulier et épais (p. 123, f). Les artistes **Gwion** ont appris à faire des courbes, transformant ces approximations de formes humaines en de délicates et sinueuses silhouettes. Le corps devint alors bien dessiné, avec les jambes vues sous différents angles et semblant tourner lors des mouvements (b). Pour donner l'impression qu'un corps humain est une forme fluide pendant une danse, le dessin doit suggérer à la fois l'idée de substance et l'idée d'espace. Peindre le corps humain exige de l'artiste une vision globale avant de mettre la couleur sur la pierre. L'image de base **jegabi** d'un corps humain requiert un minimum de vingt traits. En examinant de près des silhouettes plus récentes on voit que celles qui ont des contours très fins en ont eu à l'origine d'autres plus appuyés, peu à peu améliorés par ajouts ou suppressions (c). Les images **jegabi Gwion** témoignent d'une bonne observation des formes du corps avec cuisse, genou et mollets se galbant puis devenant droits avec de longs tibias se terminant par de minces chevilles (e). Des images plus grandes peuvent montrer de façon plus détaillée l'habillement rituel et les ornements. Les appareils génitaux masculins et féminins ou les seins sont pratiquement toujours absents de l'art **Gwion**.

Des mains représentées par cinq traits fins irradiant d'une paume triangulaire peuvent faire penser aux minces poignets d'une femme comme par exemple sur une image où un long bras élégant porte un brassard épais et carré couvrant le coude. Maintenant qu'il a perdu son pigment, le bras entier se voit au milieu de la patine de cette surface. Elle est devenue **darrawani,** marque opposée à tout changement. Certaines images sont peintes avec des contours si réguliers que seule l'utilisation d'une peinture d'une consistance uniforme comme le **mamandu** et de pinceaux aussi fins que des plumes peuvent donner d'aussi bons résultats. Un savoir-faire exceptionnel pour réaliser les détails anatomiques transparaît dans la réalisation précise de la structure osseuse du coude qu'on voit dans cette peinture du long bras tenant un **mandi** recourbé (c). Beaucoup de petites images de silhouettes paraissent bien protégées par un glacis. Des générations de peintures **Gwion** sont conservées sous une couche de silicate transparente ou laiteuse. Certaines étaient probablement rouges à l'origine mais se sont assombries avec le temps, virant au noir. On a pu ajouter du charbon pour foncer le fond afin que la peinture ressorte mieux mais cela est réservé aux grandes représentations où on trouve l'indication d'une irrégularité dans l'apport de couleurs grumeleuses. Les peintures exposées aux intempéries ont souvent des marques laissées par l'eau s'écoulant le long de la roche ; elles se morcellent ou sont recouvertes par des oxydations et des taches noires (g).

jegabi

d

e

f

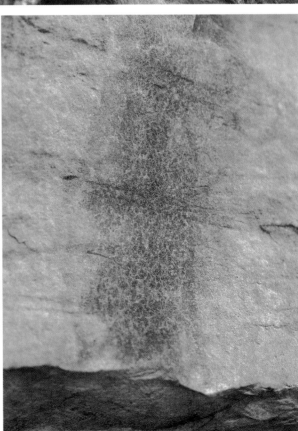

g

125

a

b

c

Always needing to camp close to fresh water, the nomadic **Gwion** employed throwing-sticks to hunt numerous wetland birds in easy range. Slow-moving birds, such as **galambi** were the most convenient source of meat before spears and spear-throwers were invented and used to secure kangaroo and emu (a, b, c) that can outrun humans. **Gwion** carved heavy hardwood boomerangs and throwing-sticks to knock down the plentiful duck and geese that frequent freshwater swamps and streams. Large striding birds of the drier woodland and grassy savannah, such as **banad** (bush turkey), **burrunba** (brolga), and **jebera** (emu) have always been prized for their **wurd.ngun** (body fat). Bird fat can be used to preserve wooden weapons and utensils, and is an excellent lineament for healing wounds and soothing a songman's throat.

Humans and animals are often indicated in rock-paintings by **ambalaru** (footprints), and **modeden** (tracks). One example of a **Gwion** artist using an aerial view of **modeden** shows birds gathering alongside a basic human figure wearing large bracelets. This bare, elongated figure is stretched out, suggesting that it is sleeping or reclining on the ground.

Gwion paintings are almost exclusively human, yet they consistently show bird characteristics. A **Gwion** self-portrait may appear human in all respects, except for the three digits on its hands and feet. As in the icon of the famed hunter, **Yandama** at **Alyaguma**, three, not five, fingers on hands can symbolise ancestral links between human and bird, through bird clans that carry important names in the "law".

The avian association with the **Gwion** identity is more flamboyantly expressed in rock-paintings by their decorative use of elaborate plumage. This can extend to a complete pair of wings attached to the head. **Gwion** males might be portrayed wearing bulky **yidmunggul** (shoulder epaulets of emu hide), and females pictured wearing **jalgun** (bustles of emu down). Heads and limbs of each sex are often decorated with broad wing-feathers from eagle, hawk, cockatoo and brolga; **yululun** (feathers) might be shown fastened with string in rows along arms and legs. Other avian attributes may also represent magical states of dance and trance, or be the visible evidence of transformations between ancestors of human and bird.

Da die umherwandernden **Gwion** ihr Lager immer in der Nähe einer Wasserstelle aufschlugen, lag es nahe, dass sie mit ihren Wurfhölzern Jagd auf die zahlreichen Wasservögel in ihrer unmittelbaren Umgebung machten. Langsame Vögel wie der Silberreiher **(galambi)** ließen sich damit ohne große Schwierigkeiten erlegen, noch bevor man Speere und Speerschleudern erfunden hatte, die die Jagd auf schnelleres Wild wie Kängurus und Emus (a, b, c) ermöglichten. Die **Gwion** schnitzten schwere Bumerangs und Wurfhölzer aus Hartholz und stellten damit den reichen Enten- und Gänsebeständen in Süßwassersümpfen und an Wasserläufen nach. Die größeren Laufvögel der trockeneren Waldgebiete und Grassavannen wie Wammentrappen **(banad)**, Brolgakraniche **(burrunba)** und Emus **(jebera)** sind seit jeher beliebt wegen ihres Fetts **(wurd.ngun)**. Es dient zur Imprägnierung von hölzernen Waffen und Werkzeugen und liefert eine ausgezeichnete Wundsalbe, die auch hilft, wenn ein Sänger Halsschmerzen hat.

Menschen und Tiere werden auf den Felsbildern oft mittels ihrer Fußabdrücke **(ambalaru)** oder Fährten **(modeden)** dargestellt. Ein Beispiel für die Verwendung solcher aus der Vogelperspektive gesehener **modeden** durch einen **Gwion**-Künstler zeigt eine Gruppe von Vögeln, die sich um eine stark stilisierte menschliche Gestalt mit auffälligen Armbändern scharen. Die nackte, lang gestreckte Figur ist in der Horizontale dargestellt, was darauf schließen lässt, dass sie schläft oder am Boden liegt.

Die Felsbilder der **Gwion** zeigen fast ausnahmslos menschliche Gestalten, die jedoch durchweg Vogelmerkmale tragen. Das Selbstporträt eines **Gwion**-Künstlers kann in jeder Hinsicht menschlich erscheinen, bis auf die Anzahl der Finger und Zehen. Wie auf dem Bild des berühmten Jägers **Yandama** in **Alyaguma** können drei anstelle von fünf Fingern auf uralte Verbindungen zwischen Menschen und Vögeln hindeuten, die in den Vogel-Clans, deren Namen im System des Gesetzes großes Gewicht haben, fortbestehen.

Noch auffälliger zeigen die Felsbilder die Verbindung der **Gwion** zur Vogelwelt durch die Darstellung von kunstvollem Federschmuck – manchmal ziert gar ein vollständiges Flügelpaar den Kopf der Figur. Männliche **Gwion** tragen zum Beispiel ausladende Epauletten aus Emuleder **(yidmunggul)**, und auf Frauendarstellungen sieht man die **jalgun** (üppige Tournüren aus Emudaunen). Unabhängig vom Geschlecht sind Köpfe und Gliedmaßen oft mit breiten Federn aus den Flügeln von Adlern, Falken, Kakadus oder Kranichen geschmückt. Auf den Bildern sieht man, dass solche Flügelfedern **(yululun)** manchmal mit Hilfe einer Schnur in einer Reihe an Armen und Beinen befestigt waren. Darüber hinaus können Vogelattribute auch das Wirken magischer Kräfte während des Tanzens oder in der Trance versinnbildlichen, und sie sind der sichtbare Beweis für Verwandlungen, die zwischen den Ahnen von Menschen und Vögeln stattgefunden haben.

Les nomades **Gwion** avaient toujours besoin de camper près des points d'eau potable ; ils utilisaient des petites javelines pour chasser de nombreux oiseaux des zones humides qui étaient à une portée facile. Les animaux se déplaçant lentement, comme par exemple la **galambi** (aigrette blanche), étaient la source la plus facile d'approvisionnement en viande avant que les lances et propulseurs soient inventés et utilisés et que l'on puisse compter sur les kangourous et les émeus qui courent plus vite que les hommes (a, b, c). Les **Gwion** ont taillé des boomerangs dans des bois durs et lourds et des javelines pour assommer canards et oies qui fréquentent les marécages d'eau douce et les cours d'eau. Les gros oiseaux marcheurs des régions boisées plus sèches et des savanes comme par exemple la **banad** (l'outarde), la **burrunba** (grue) et le **jebera** (émeu) ont toujours été prisés pour leur **wurd.ngun** (graisse). La graisse d'oiseau peut être utilisée pour conserver les armes et ustensiles en bois et a aussi d'excellentes propriétés pour la cicatrisation des blessures et elle est calmante pour les maux de gorge d'un chanteur.

Les humains et les animaux sont souvent indiqués par des **ambalaru** (empreintes de pieds) et des **modeden** (traces) dans les peintures rupestres. Un exemple fait par un **Gwion** qui a utilisé un point de vue aérien de **modeden** montre des oiseaux groupés aux côtés d'une figure humaine portant de gros bracelets. Ce personnage dénudé et tout en longueur est étendu suggérant le sommeil ou le repos sur le sol.

Les peintures **Gwion** représentent presque toujours des humains mais elles comportent régulièrement des caractéristiques propres aux oiseaux. Un autoportrait **Gwion** peut paraître humain sous tous les rapports sauf pour les doigts des mains et des pieds. Comme dans l'image du célèbre chasseur **Yandama** à **Alyaguma,** trois et non cinq doigts aux mains peuvent symboliser les liens ancestraux entre les humains et les oiseaux ; par les oiseaux, les clans ont aussi des noms représentatifs importants dans la Loi.

L'association entre les oiseaux et l'identité **Gwion** est exprimée de façon encore plus éclatante dans les peintures rupestres par l'utilisation décorative de plumages très raffinés. Cela peut même aller jusqu'à une paire complète d'ailes sur la tête. Les personnages **Gwion** masculins peuvent être représentés portant de volumineuses **yidmunggul** (épaulettes en peau d'émeu) et les figures féminines des **jalgun** (tournures en duvet d'émeu). Les têtes et les membres de chaque sexe sont souvent décorés de larges plumes provenant d'ailes de faucon, d'aigle, de cacatoès et de grue ; des **yululun** (des plumes d'ailes) peuvent être attachées en rang avec des cordons le long des bras et des jambes. D'autres attributs d'oiseaux peuvent aussi représenter les phases magiques d'une danse et d'une transe ou être la preuve visible des transformations réalisées entre les ancêtres des humains et les oiseaux.

jebera

d

e

f

Perhaps the greatest influence of birds has been their voice; their original role in the evolution of human speech and song probably influenced the form of early human languages everywhere. In the **Argad** narrative, humans once turned into birds and, ever since, the two have been closely linked in **Ngarinyin** thought. Many bird species are protected from hunters by laws preserving ancestral connections, and today their ancient identities remain rich with symbolism. Around the camp-fire, the **munnumburra** often discuss the role of each bird species in forming laws. They retain a remarkably large repertoire of ancient law songs about specific birds, and these form the core verses of ritual music.

Most daily encounters with birds prompt happy greetings, as if they too are human. **Munnumburra** will respond by giving out each bird's ancient name. Often the law song of that bird will follow, sung in its intimate company. Bird names in **Ngarinyin** often echo the sound of their voices. "Wura.wura" is the sound of the Partridge Pigeon; "goro.goro" mimics the raucous talk of the Blue-winged Kookaburra; "gumba.lawal" a pronunciation of the rhythmic murmur from the chest of the rare White-quilled Rock-Pigeon, endemic to the isolated rocky gorges of the Kimberley and the indirect ancestor of the common cosmopolitan pigeons. But the distinctive rhythm and sound of each bird's voice and call can only be fully appreciated when heard live in the dense ambience of the bush.

Local birds give many prominent signs in the bush, and their typical habits or different behaviours can signify the seasonal availability of food on the ground or in water. Cormorants always indicate the presence of fish. White cockatoos and corellas often broadcast their sighting of humans with shrieks in alarm or, by their soft, distinctive murmurs of satisfaction, they might signify a ripening bush-apple tree. Honeyeaters busy in a flowering gum, dipping long tongues into blossoms, lead people to fresh nectar. **Burrunba** (brolgas), are famous for agile dancing, (d, f); pairs move in unison with fluid movements and display outspread wings in a fan of feathers or stand in graceful dancing poses balanced on long legs.

Der wohl nachhaltigste Einfluss, den die Vögel seit jeher auf die Menschen ausüben, sind ihre Lautäußerungen, denn als die Menschen anfingen zu sprechen und zu singen, müssen die Vogellaute überall die Frühformen menschlicher Sprache mit geprägt haben. In der Geschichte der **Argad**-Brüder wird erzählt, wie sich die Menschen einst in Vögel verwandelten, und seither sind diese beiden in der Vorstellungswelt der **Ngarinyin** eng miteinander verknüpft. Viele Vogelarten sind durch Gesetze, in denen die Verbindung zu den Ahnen lebendig bleibt, vor Jägern geschützt, und ihre uralte symbolische Bedeutung ist unvergessen. Wenn die **munnumburra** am Lagerfeuer zusammensitzen, sprechen sie oft über die Rolle der verschiedenen Vögel bei der Entstehung der Gesetze. Ein beträchtlicher Teil ihres Repertoires an alten Gesetzesgesängen handelt von bestimmten Vögeln, und diese Gesänge machen einen wichtigen Teil der rituellen Musik aus.

Wenn man im täglichen Leben einem Vogel begegnet, wird er meist freundlich begrüßt, als sei er ebenfalls ein menschliches Wesen. Die **munnumburra** nennen jeden Vogel bei seinem alten Namen. Nicht selten schließt sich daran in einer Art vertrautem Zwiegespräch zwischen Sänger und Vogel der traditionelle Gesang über diesen Vogel an. Die Vogelnamen in der Sprache der **Ngarinyin** ahmen oft die Vogellaute nach. So ist „wura.wura" der Ruf der Schuppenbrusttaube und „goro.goro" imitiert den heiseren Schrei des Blauflügel-Kookaburra. „Gumba.lawal" imitiert das rhythmische Gurren der in den Felsschluchten der Kimberley-Region beheimateten seltenen Weißspiegeltaube, der indirekten Ahnherrin der heute weltweit verbreiteten Taube. Aber dem unverwechselbaren Rhythmus und Klang jeder Vogelstimme und jedes Vogelrufs weiß nur der wirklich zu schätzen, der ihn draußen im dichten Buschland hört.

Die Vögel des Buschs geben viele wichtige Signale, und ihre typischen Gewohnheiten und Verhaltensweisen liefern Hinweise auf die jahreszeitlich bedingte Verfügbarkeit von Nahrung auf dem Boden oder im Wasser. Kormorane sind ein untrügliches Zeichen für Fischvorkommen. Weiße Kakadus und Nacktaugenkakadus warnen mit durchdringenden Schreien vor herannahenden Menschen, und oft ist ihr unverkennbares zufriedenes Murmeln ein Indiz, dass irgendwo ein wilder Apfelbaum reife Äpfel trägt. Honigfresser, die ihre langen Zungen in die Blüten des Eukalyptus tauchen, zeigen dem Menschen den Weg zu frischem Nektar. Die Brolgakraniche **(burrunba)** sind berühmt für ihre eleganten Tänze (d, f); die Paare tanzen mit harmonischen, fließenden Bewegungen und weiten, fächerförmig gespreizten Flügeln, oder sie stehen graziös wie eine Ballerina auf einem Bein.

Il est possible que la plus grande influence des oiseaux ait été leur voix; leur rôle dans l'évolution du langage humain et dans les chants doit avoir influencé la forme des premières langues partout dans le monde. Dans le récit **Argad,** les humains, à un moment, se sont transformés en oiseaux et depuis humains et oiseaux ont toujours été étroitement liés dans la pensée **Ngarinyin.** Des lois préservant ces liens ancestraux interdisent la chasse de nombre d'espèces d'oiseaux et leurs anciennes identités demeurent aujourd'hui riches en symbolisme. Autour du feu de camp, les **munnumburra** discutent souvent du rôle de chaque espèce d'oiseau dans l'élaboration des lois. Ils gardent un répertoire remarquablement vaste d'anciens chants de la Loi qui ont pour sujet certains oiseaux et ceux-ci constituent la base des couplets dans la musique rituelle.

La plupart des rencontres quotidiennes avec les oiseaux provoquent des saluts joyeux comme s'il s'agissait d'humains. Les **munnumburra** donnent aux oiseaux leurs anciens noms. Souvent, on chantera le chant de la Loi concernant l'oiseau près de celui-ci. Dans la langue **Ngarinyin** les noms d'oiseaux rappellent souvent leur chant. « Wura.wura » est le son de la perdrix ; « goro.goro » imite le bruit rauque du kookaburra à ailes bleues ; « gumba.lawal » est une prononciation du murmure rythmé provenant de la poitrine du rare pigeon des roches à plumes blanches, oiseau originaire des gorges rocheuses isolées du Kimberley et qui est l'ancêtre indirect des pigeons du monde entier. Mais on n'apprécie vraiment le rythme distinct et le son de chaque cri et chant d'appel d'oiseau que lorsqu'on l'entend dans la forte atmosphère du bush.

Les oiseaux locaux donnent beaucoup d'indications importantes dans le bush, et leurs habitudes caractéristiques et comportementales peuvent indiquer la présence, selon la saison, de nourriture sur le sol ou dans l'eau. Les cormorans indiquent toujours la présence de poissons. Les cacatoès blancs à huppe jaune et les corellas (nom australien du cacatoès nasique) annoncent les humains par des cris d'alarme perçants et, par leurs doux et caractéristiques murmures de satisfaction, ils peuvent indiquer la présence d'un pommier du bush dont les fruits sont mûrs. Les mangeurs de miel, affairés dans les gommiers en fleur, plongeant leur longue langue dans les fleurs, guident les humains vers le nectar frais. Les **burranba** (brolgas) sont connues pour leurs danses agiles ; elles se déplacent par paires, à l'unisson dans des mouvements fluides, et montrent leurs ailes déployées en un éventail de plumes ou se prennent des poses gracieuses en équilibre sur leurs longues jambes (d, f).

argad

Artists and Visionaries

Why they call **Munga.nunga** is "mun"... You know when we look
what we plan and what we see to make things
that word is called **Munga.nunga**... the long long time of language
that **Munga.nunga** beginning of in this area here   Banggal

Name is **Munga.nunga** mean when you looking
you know looking out when you walking
and you looking out...
that **Munga.nunga**   Nyawarra

Künstler und Visionäre

Munga.nunga kommt von „mun"... Das ist, wenn man sich vorstellt,
was man machen will – wenn man es vor sich sieht
das heißt dann **Munga.nunga**... ein uraltes Wort ist das
Munga.nunga, damit hat hier alles angefangen   Banggal

Munga.nunga heißt Ausschau halten
man muss schauen, wenn man geht
und wenn man schaut...
das ist **Munga.nunga**   Nyawarra

Artistes et Visionnaires

La raison pour laquelle ils s'appellent **Munga.nunga**
c'est « mun »... Tu sais quand on regarde ce qu'on prévoit et ce qu'on voit
pour faire des choses ce mot se dit **Munga.nunga**... c'est un mot très ancien
ces **Munga.nunga** sont là depuis le début ici   Banggal

ce nom **Munga.nunga**
ça veut dire quand tu regardes tu sais tu guettes
et si on regarde...
c'est **Munga.nunga**   Nyawarra

MUNGA.NUNGA

It's out over here **Wodoi.ngarri** tribe
Manirri country just down here
not too far he cross over Moran River
We cross over Roe River and then
we'll come out to Prince Regent
and then you'll find that **Wodoi** area

Nyawarra

Da drüben ist der **Wodoi.ngarri**-Stamm
und da unten liegt das **Manirri**-Land
das geht da hinten über den Moran River
Auf der anderen Seite vom Roe River
da kommen wir zum Prince Regent River
und da ist das **Wodoi**-Gebiet

Nyawarra

C'est juste là, la tribu **Wodoi.ngarri**
le pays **Manirri** se trouve juste là
pas très loin on croise la rivière Moran
On traverse la rivière Roe et là
on arrive à la rivière Prince Regent
et là on trouve le pays **Wodoi**

Nyawarra

Wodoi and **Jungun**
these two men made this song
beginning of law... **Wunan**

Man called **Wibalma**
in this ranges country... at **Gelngu**
he had a wife **Nyamanbiligi**
blind woman... couldn't see

He told her
"I'll be making law... sacred objects"
and she said
"Yeah! why not... you make 'em"
So he made all these sacred objects
sacred objects... **maya.ngarri**
and he had a workshop there
bunja we call them
and he had **jallala** too... secret signal stone

That old man **Wibalma**
he didn't want to show everybody
he was keeping it for himself
maya.ngarri... sacred things

But these two didn't want it that way
they wanted to put it in the **Wunan**
... in the law

Banggal

Wodoi und **Jungun**
die zwei Männer haben das Lied hier gemacht
den Anfang des Gesetzes ... **Wunan**

Ein Mann namens **Wibalma**
in diesem Bergland ... in **Gelngu**
der hatte eine Frau, die hieß **Nyamanbiligi**
sie war blind ... konnte nichts sehen

„Ich mache Gesetze"
hat er ihr gesagt, „heilige Sachen"
und sie hat gesagt
„Aber ja ... geh nur!"
Und so hat er all die heiligen Sachen gemacht
heilige Gegenstände ... **maya.ngarri**
er hatte eine Werkstatt da draußen
bunja nennen wir das
und **jallala** hatte er auch ... Steine geheime Zeichen

Wibalma war ein alter Mann
er wollte niemandem zeigen, was er da hatte
er wollte sie für sich behalten
die **maya.ngarri** ... die heiligen Sachen

Aber die anderen beiden wollten es anders
sie fanden, dass sie zum **Wunan** gehören sollten
... zum Gesetz

Banggal

Wodoi et **Jungun**
ces deux hommes ont écrit ce chant
au commencement de la Loi ... du **Wunan**

Il y a un homme appelé **Wibalma**
dans ce pays de montagnes... à **Gelngu**
il avait une femme, **Nyamanbiligi**
cette femme était aveugle ... elle ne voyait pas

Il lui dit
« Je vais faire la Loi... des objets sacrés »
et elle dit
« Oui ! pourquoi pas... fais-le »
Alors il fabriqua tous ces objets sacrés
objets sacrés... **maya.ngarri**
et il avait un atelier là-bas
bunja on appelle ça
et il avait une **jallala** aussi ...
une pierre dressée qui sert de signal

Ce vieil homme, **Wibalma**
il ne voulait pas les montrer à tout le monde
il les gardait pour lui
ces choses sacrées... **maya.ngarri**

Mais ces deux-là n'étaient pas d'accord
ils voulaient que ça fasse partie du **Wunan**
... que ce soit dans la Loi

Banggal

131

Wibalma... he went hunting now
"I've gotta have fat to anoint them objects
grease 'em up with fat!"
so he go for emu fat... ***wurd.ngun***
then he went hunting
And these two ***Wodoi*** and ***Jungun***
knew where he was camping... stopping

Wibalma ... der ging auf die Jagd
„Ich brauche Fett
damit ich meine Sachen einreiben kann!"
also ging er auf die Emujagd
damit er ***wurd.ngun*** bekam, das Fett
Und die beiden ***Wodoi*** und ***Jungun***
die wussten wo er war ... wo sein Lager war

Wibalma ... il est parti chasser
« J'ai besoin de graisse pour huiler ces objets
pour les graisser ! »
alors il est parti chercher
de la graisse d'émeu, ***wurd.ngun***
il est parti chasser
Et ces deux-là ***Wodoi*** et ***Jungun***

so these two fella went there
they see only his blind wife there
"Hey old woman where your husband?"
"No... he go hunting for emu...
but in there he got his workshop...
mamaa... I not allowed to go"
Banggal

und da sind die zwei Burschen hingegangen
aber sie sehen, da ist nur seine blinde Frau
„He, Alte, wo steckt dein Mann?"
„Der ist nicht da … der jagt Emus…
aber hier hat er seine Werkstatt…
mamaa … ich darf da nicht rein"
Banggal

savaient où il campait… où il s'était arrêté
alors les deux sont allés là-bas
ils y ont juste trouvé sa femme aveugle
« Hé ! vieille femme, où est ton mari ? »
« Pas là… il est allé chassé l'émeu…
mais là-bas il a son atelier…
c'est *mamaa*… j'ai pas le droit d'y aller »
Banggal

Wodoi and *Jungun*
they just wanted to know... then two fellas say

"OK well we'll have a look"
she give them permission,
"Yes you two can go there"

And when they went there they see
all these sacred objects... so two fella look

ngowrun...
of the sacred wind or inside breath of food...
plants and animals

manjilarri...
of running without help
because the law is after you

nyamun-buna...
of hanging on by your oath
not going against the law
because it means trouble and punishment

Wodoi and *Jungun* they take them out one
manjilarri... and run away

Wodoi und *Jungun* die waren einfach neugierig...
und deswegen sagen sie

"Na, wir sehen uns das mal an"
und sie hat es ihnen erlaubt
"Ja ihr zwei, ihr dürft da hinein"

Und sie sind da hineingegangen
all die heiligen Sachen... haben sie sich angesehen

ngowrun...
der geheime Atem von allem was essbar ist
... Tiere und Pflanzen

manjilarri...
wenn man flieht aber ohne Hoffnung
weil das Gesetz einem auf den Fersen ist

nyamun-buna...
wenn man einen Schwur hält
nicht gegen das Gesetz verstößt
denn das bedeutet Kummer und Strafe

Wodoi und *Jungun* eins haben sie mitgenommen
manjilarri... damit sind sie davongelaufen

Wodoi et *Jungun* ils voulaient juste
savoir... alors les deux ont dit

« D'accord, on va jeter un œil »
elle leur donna la permission
« C'est bon vous deux pouvez aller là-bas »

Et quand ils sont allés là-bas ils ont vu
tous ces objets sacrés... alors les deux ont regardé

ngowrun...
c'est le vent sacré ou le souffle qui habite
la nourriture... les plantes et les animaux

manjilarri...
c'est fuir sans espoir
parce que la Loi est après toi

nyamun-buna...
c'est tenir son serment
ne pas violer la Loi
ça signifie des problèmes et un châtiment

Wodoi et *Jungun* ont pris un des objets
manjilarri... et ils se sont sauvés

Wibalma... that man in hunting
he got feeling like a telephone ting! ting!
inside here...
he stop hunting he let 'em go emu
he go straight back to his home
to his wife and he say
"Hey you! old woman...
somebody been come round here?"

"Yes! she said..."
"Two... Wodoi and Jungun come here"
"Hey what they been doing?"
"Well I just told them that er... you got
a workshop there and they went over there
I heard them rattling... rattling... rattling
and from that time they never come back to me
two fella been go straight on"

So he got upset
he knew that because they didn't come back
he look... he seen this main one gone
manjilarri... manjilarri

Banggal

Wibalma auf seiner Jagd
der hat das gespürt als hätt' er ein Telefon
hier drin „drring-drring"
er hat die Emus laufen lassen
und nichts wie ab zurück nach Hause
und er sagt zu seiner Frau „He, Alte...
ist einer hier gewesen?"

„Ja", sagt sie...
„Zwei... Wodoi und Jungun waren hier"
„Was haben sie gemacht?"
„Na, ich habe ihnen nur gesagt dass du...
tja dass du da deine Werkstatt hast
und dann sind sie reingegangen
Ich hab gehört wie sie gewühlt haben
wie es geklappert hat
zu mir sind die gar nicht mehr zurückgekommen
die sind direkt nach draußen"

Und er war wütend
er konnte sich denken was das hieß
er sieht nach... und das Wichtigste fehlt
das manjilarri... ausgerechnet das manjilarri

Banggal

Wibalma... cet homme parti à la chasse
c'est comme si il avait entendu
le téléphone dring! dring!... en lui-même...
il s'arrêta de chasser laissant partir les émeus
il est rentré tout droit chez lui
et il dit à sa femme « Hé toi! vieille femme...
quelqu'un est venu par ici? »

« Oui! elle a dit...
« Deux... Wodoi et Jungun sont venus ici »
« Ha! et qu'est-ce qu'ils ont fait? »
« Hé bien, je leur ai juste dit que... tu avais
un atelier là et ils y sont allés
Je les ai entendus qui faisaient du bruit
qui cherchaient...
et depuis ce moment ils ne sont pas revenus ici
les deux gars sont partis directement »

Alors il se mit en colère
il savait pourquoi ils n'étaient pas revenus
il regarde... il voit que l'objet le plus important
a disparu... manjilarri... manjilarri

Banggal

Wibalma... he get wild!
*he get that **banad**... turkey head boomerang*
he split 'em, ironwood tree
Sacred object been changed... stand up
*the object turn into that **manjilarri mamul***
*now **maya.ngarri** once he split it*
and he said to his wife
"I'm going"

Banggal

He go straight for the ironwood... split 'em!
he didn't share it out with with the people
the mean bloke that keeping it to yourself
and he got this boomerang
and he throw straight for that ironwood
***wungarun** we call it*
***wungarun** that the ironwood tree*
Hit! that ironwood
*and that **maya.ngarri** been "stand up"*
***Wibalma**... he been keeping those things*
secret for himself
he didn't want to give out to anybody
*Anyway the mean bloke... **Wibalma***
he didn't want to share it out with the people

Nyawarra

Wibalma... der tobt vor Wut!
*er holt den **banad**... seinen Truthahn-Bumerang*
und spaltet den Eisenbaum
da erwachen die heiligen Sachen zum Leben
*und da werden die Sachen zu **manjilarri mamul***
*die **maya.ngarri** als er auf den Baum schlägt*
und er sagt zu seiner Frau
„Ich muss los"

Banggal

Der hat auf den Eisenbaum eingedroschen!
aber er wollte nicht mit den anderen teilen
er war ein Geizkragen er wollte alles für sich
und er nahm seinen Bumerang
und ging auf den Baum los
***wungarun** nennen wir ihn*
***wungarun** das heißt Eisenbaum*
Er ging auf den Eisenbaum los
*und das hat die **maya.ngarri** zum Leben erweckt*
***Wibalma**... der hatte das alles für sich behalten*
der wollte es als Geheimnis
er wollte die Sachen niemandem zeigen
*Ein Geizkragen war das... **Wibalma***
er wollte mit niemandem teilen

Nyawarra

Wibalma... il devient fou!
*il prend ce **banad**... ce boomerang à tête*
d'outarde et fend cet arbre de bois de fer
et les objets sacrés sont transformés,
*ils s'animent, **manjilarri mamul***
*maintenant qu'il a fendu ce **maya.ngarri***
il se lève et dit à sa femme
« Je m'en vais »

Banggal

Il va droit vers le bois de fer... il le fend!
il n'avait pas partagé avec les gens
ce type avare qui gardait tout pour lui
et il prit ce boomerang
et le lança sur le bois de fer
*on l'appelle **wungarun***
***wungarun** c'est l'arbre à bois de fer*
Cogne! ce bois de fer
*et ces **maya.ngarri** se sont « levés »*
***Wibalma**... il gardait toutes ces choses*
secrètes pour lui-même
il ne voulait rien donner à qui que ce soit
*Oui le méchant type... **Wibalma***
il ne voulait pas partager avec les gens

Nyawarra

The story goes this way... he followed them track
when they came to plain like that ground
... he look for the track
***ambalaru**... footprints can't find 'em*
*... can't find 'em **mamalan** in sand ground*
he look "oh might be in that stone place"
***Wibalma**... he look 'em stone track there*
he follow 'em...
two different stories... that open space in sand
he never seen that track he seen them in the rock

Banggal

*Anyway the mean bloke **Wibalma***
he didn't want to share it out with the people
*that **Wibalma** follow their track*
and he went back there
*and follow these two bloke **Wodoi** and **Jungun***
when they been walking in the flat ground
like this kind of ground he didn't see their track!
but in the rock he see their track
He follow them... follow them right up
*where they had the big **Wunan** meeting*

Nyawarra

So geht es weiter... er folgte ihren Spuren
und als sie in die Ebene kamen so wie hier...
da sieht er sich nach ihren Spuren um
***ambalaru**... Fußspuren aber er findet keine*
*findet keine **mamalan** im Sand und er überlegt*
„Oh, vielleicht eher bei den Steinen"
***Wibalma**... jetzt sucht er bei den Steinen*
da folgt er den Spuren...
zwei verschiedene Geschichten... da auf dem Sand
da hat er keine Spuren gefunden
aber auf den Felsen da schon

Banggal

Jedenfalls wollte dieser Geizkragen
*dieser **Wibalma** nicht mit den anderen teilen*
und deshalb ist er den Spuren nachgegangen
und ist wieder dahin gekommen
*und folgte **Wodoi** und **Jungun***
als sie auf dem flachen Land unterwegs waren
so wie hier da hat er ihre Spuren nicht gefunden!
aber auf den Felsen da waren sie zu sehen
Und da ist er ihnen nach... bis er sie einholte
und dann gab es ein großes Wunan-Treffen

Nyawarra

L'histoire suit son chemin... il suivit leur piste
quand ils arrivèrent à une plaine
comme celle-là... il cherche la piste
***ambalaru**... il n'arrive pas à trouver les empreintes*
*il peut pas trouver leur **mamalan** sur le sable*
il regarde « oh! ça pourrait être sur ces rochers »
***Wibalma**... il voit leur piste sur les pierres*
là il les suit... là c'est une autre histoire...
sur cet espace de sable dégagé
il n'a pas trouvé leur piste il les a vus sur les rochers

Banggal

*Bref **Wibalma**, cet avare*
qui ne voulait pas partager avec les gens
*ce **Wibalma** suivait leur piste*
et il revint chez lui et il les poursuivit
*ces deux gars, **Wodoi** et **Jungun***
quand ils marchaient sur le sol plat
comme cette sorte de sol-là,
il ne voyait pas leur piste!
mais sur les rochers il voyait leur piste
Il les suivit... les suivit jusqu'à l'endroit
*où ils avaient leur grande réunion du **Wunan***

Nyawarra

The first people who put their foot tracks...
their footprints still in the stone
hardened up from long long time... **darrawani**
Wibalma... *then he come out... he said*
"I'm happy and let's do it...
*let this **Wunan** lay down forever!"*

And they been put it that way...
"We didn't have law
we want to make law now... new law
we can share and really marry one another"
Banggal

Die Ersten die ihre Spuren hinterlassen haben...
ihre Fußabdrücke die sind heute noch zu sehen
versteinert in langer langer Zeit... **darrawani**
Wibalma... *er kam hervor... und sagte*
"Lasst es uns so machen, ich bin zufrieden...
*lasst uns das **Wunan**-Gesetz festlegen für alle Zeit!"*

Und so haben sie es gemacht...
"Wir hatten kein Gesetz
aber jetzt wollen wir eines machen... ein neues
ein Gesetz über das Teilen und das Heiraten"
Banggal

Les premiers à laisser leurs
empreintes de pieds...
leurs empreintes sont encore dans la pierre
durcies depuis tout ce temps... **darrawani**
Wibalma... *alors il sort... et il dit*
« Je suis heureux et allons-y...
*installons le **Wunan** pour toujours ! »*

Et ils l'ont fait...
« on n'avait pas de loi
on veut en faire une... une nouvelle Loi
pour partager et se marier vraiment »
Banggal

They done their job in the first place
*when **Wodoi** and **Jungun** they steal that...*
*when they took that **maya.ngarri***
*sacred object from that **Wibalma***
*and put it in the **Wunan**...*
*And that **maya.ngarri** thing*
was already made out of that tree

*and **Wibalma** said*
"Bring it over and
hand it over to the people eh?
You can put it through you two bloke
*can put it through the **Wunan** law"*

*And they did put it through the **Wunan***
that their job they done
*And they done it and today the **Wunan***
still running... **maya.ngarri**

***Jungun** and **Wodoi** right then*
been make the big party see
like a parliament
or something that they do like that
and when they had that party over there
*... put in this **Wunan***
they wasn't there... these two wasn't there
*that **Wodoi** and **Jungun** you know?*

when we name all the stones around the table
they wasn't there...
those two wasn't there in that area
*It's only all the **Wunan** people...*
*the other **mob** that make the **Wunan***
Nyawarra

Die beiden hatten ihre Arbeit ja schon getan
***Wodoi** und **Jungun** als sie es stahlen...*
*als sie **Wibalma** das **maya.ngarri** wegnahmen*
den heiligen Gegenstand
*und damit fing es an das **Wunan**...*
*und das **maya.ngarri***
das war ja auch aus diesem Baum

*und **Wibalma** sagte*
"So, ihr wollt es herbringen
damit alle es haben, hm?"
"Also gut, ihr zwei, ihr könnt es haben
*für das **Wunan**-Gesetz"*

*Und sie machten das **Wunan**-Gesetz*
das war ihre Aufgabe
*das haben sie fertig gebracht und das **Wunan***
das gibt es bis heute... **maya.ngarri**

*Und da haben **Jungun** und **Wodoi***
gleich ein großes Fest gefeiert
so eine Art Parlament
oder so etwas in der Art
und da bei diesem Treffen
*da haben sie das **Wunan** beschlossen*
aber die waren nicht dabei... die zwei
***Wodoi** und **Jungun** die waren nicht dabei*

als wir den Steinen am Tisch Namen gaben
da waren sie nicht dabei...
die zwei waren anderswo
*Nur all die **Wunan**-Leute...*
*die anderen, die haben das **Wunan** gemacht*
Nyawarra

Ils ont été les premiers à faire çà
*quand **Wodoi** et **Jungun** ont volé ça...*
*quand ils ont pris ce **maya.ngarri***
*cet objet sacré qui était à **Wibalma***
*et l'ont mis dans le **Wunan**...*
*Et ce **maya.ngarri***
était déjà fait de ce bois

*et **Wibalma** dit*
« Amène-le
et donnes-le aux gens, d'accord ?
Vous pouvez y arriver vous deux
*vous faites aboutir la Loi, le **Wunan** »*

*Et ils l'ont mis dans le **Wunan***
ils ont fait leur boulot
*Ils l'ont fait et aujourd'hui encore le **Wunan***
*marche toujours... et les **maya.ngarri** aussi*

*Alors **Jungun** et **Wodoi***
ont organisé le grand rassemblement
comme un parlement
ou quelque chose comme ça
et il y a eu ce rassemblement là
*... on a mis en place le **Wunan***
ils n'étaient pas là... ces deux là n'étaient pas là
***Wodoi** et **Jungun**, tu vois ?*

quand nous avons nommé toutes les pierres
autour de la table... ils n'étaient pas là...
ces deux n'étaient pas là à cet endroit
*C'est seulement les gens du **Wunan**...*
*les autres qui ont fait le **Wunan***
Nyawarra

Jungun said to **Wodoi**...
"And you can be my brother-in-law...
you can be my father-in-law...
You marry my daughter or my sister"

and **Wodoi** said...
"Okay! You marry my daughter
*and my sister", to the **Jungun***
*and **Jungun** said "Okay!"*

Jungun take 'em **Wodoi**
and **Wodoi** take 'em **Jungun** wives
Nyawarra

Jungun sagte zu **Wodoi**...
„Und du kannst jetzt mein Schwager sein ...
du kannst mein Schwiegervater sein ...
Heirate meine Tochter oder meine Schwester"

und **Wodoi** sagte ...
„Gut! Dann heiratest du meine Tochter
*und meine Schwester", sagte er zu **Jungun***
*und **Jungun** sagte „Abgemacht!"*

Jungun nahm Frauen von **Wodoi**
und **Wodoi** nahm Frauen von **Jungun**
Nyawarra

Jungun a dit à **Wodoi**...
« Et tu peux être mon beau-frère ...
tu peux être mon beau-père ...
Tu n'as qu'à te marier avec ma fille ou ma sœur »

et **Wodoi** dit...
« Okay ! Tu te maries avec ma fille
*et ma sœur, avec **Jungun** »*
*et **Jungun** dit « d'accord ! »*

*les **Jungun*** prennent des femmes **Wodoi**
et les **Wodoi** prennent des femmes **Jungun**
Nyawarra

From that time all this **Gwion mob** now
that bird **mob** what been start 'em off
what we been calling them from that time
They put it through the rule
so everybody marry
Wodoi's daughter to **Jungun's** son
Wodoi's son then marry **Jungun's** daughter

Like today still going marrying
some people break it... don't obey the law
most people they'll want to marry the right **skin**
Wodoi and **Jungun**

So everybody marry straight line...
sharing system everything
Wodoi and **Jungun**
one **Wunan**
Nyawarra

Und so halten sie es seither, die **Gwion**-Leute
die Leute aus den Vogel-Clans
seither nennen wir sie so
Und sie haben es zum Gesetz gemacht
so heiraten wir
Wodoi-Töchter heiraten **Jungun**-Söhne
Wodoi-Söhne heiraten **Jungun**-Töchter

So ist das immer noch mit dem Heiraten
nicht alle halten sich dran... brechen das Gesetz
die meisten schon
Wodoi und **Jungun**

Deshalb heiraten alle wie es sich gehört...
alles wird geteilt
Wodoi und **Jungun**
aber nur das eine **Wunan**
Nyawarra

Depuis ce temps tous ces **Gwion** maintenant
tous ces oiseaux qui ont commencé ça
on les appelle comme ça depuis ce temps
Ils ont réussi à faire la Loi
pour que tout le monde se marie
la fille de **Wodoi** au fils de **Jungun**
et le fils de **Wodoi** à la fille de **Jungun**

Aujourd'hui le mariage existe toujours
il y en a qui le font pas, qui suivent pas la Loi
la plupart des gens épousent la bonne « peau »
Wodoi et **Jungun**

Donc tout le monde se marie comme il faut
le système de partage c'est pour tout
Wodoi et **Jungun**
un seul **Wunan**
Nyawarra

This is ah, we call 'em **ornad** my **skin**
not Paddy's **skin**... not Paddy's tribe
he **Jungun**... that one **amalar**
not this **skin**... I marry his sister or daughter
doesn't matter... promise wife he give me
Paddy he keep 'em straight in the land

This my skin... that **Wodoi** nightjar tribe
Wodoi tribe this one now
all that what was in cave
that the **ornad**...
this **brrornad** that's all the **Wodoi** tribe
Banggal

Wir nennen sie **ornad** meine Leute
nicht Paddys... Paddy ist einer der anderen
er ist **Jungun**... **amalar**
er gehört zur anderen Hälfte...
ich heirate seine Schwester oder Tochter
egal welche... er hat mir eine Frau versprochen
Paddy sorgt dafür dass sie sich daran halten

Das ist meine Hälfte... **Wodoi**
der Clan des Gefleckten Nachtfalken
Das hier gehört zum **Wodoi**-Stamm
alles was da in der Höhle war
das ist **ornad**...
das ist **brrornad** der **Wodoi**-Stamm
Banggal

On appelle ça **ornad**... c'est ma « peau »
c'est pas la peau de Paddy... pas la tribu de Paddy
lui il est **Jungun**... lui, **amalar**
pas ma peau... Je peux marier sa sœur ou sa fille
peu importe... elle m'est promise
Paddy respecte la Loi ici

C'est ma peau... la tribu de l'Engoulevent, **Wodoi**
La tribu **Wodoi** c'est celle-là
tout ce qui est dans cette grotte
c'est **ornad**...
brrornad c'est à la tribu **Wodoi**
Banggal

And the **Gwion** put it that way
Wunan... from that time
Wunan... we still hold it today

And here we are...
that symbol we look at it there
we don't talk about it...
without looking at the symbol

Because its controlling us...
that **Wunan** symbol
you know... that table... **angga**...
you know that **jallala?**

If we died that thing **angga**
would still lay there
Wunan would be still there
and the land itself still here yet

The **Wunan** is there now
this is where all the sacred places are
for us to look after 'em
you know every man and woman
got their responsibility

Banggal

So haben die **Gwion** es gemacht
Wunan... von jener Zeit an
Wunan... bis heute halten wir uns daran

Und hier sind wir an der Stelle...
das ist das Zeichen das wir hier sehen
wir reden nur darüber...
wenn wir das Zeichen vor uns haben

Denn es hat Macht über uns...
das **Wunan**-Zeichen
und der Tisch hier... **angga**...
und das hier sind **jallala** weißt du?

Wenn wir sterben, dann ist der **angga**
der ist dann immer noch da
das **Wunan** ist immer noch da
und das Land selber das ist auch immer noch da

Das **Wunan,** das ist jetzt da
und dazu gehören die heiligen Orte
um die müssen wir uns kümmern
jeder Mann jede Frau
wir haben eine große Verantwortung

Banggal

Et les **Gwion** l'ont créé comme ça
c'est le **Wunan**... depuis ce temps là
le **Wunan**... c'est toujours là aujourd'hui

Et nous voilà...
ce symbole qu'on regarde là
on n'en parle pas...
sans le voir ce symbole

Parce qu'il nous contrôle...
ce symbole du **Wunan**
tu sais... cette table... **angga**...
tu sais ce **jallala?**

Si on meurt, cette chose **angga**
restera posée là
le **Wunan** restera
et cette terre même elle est encore là

Le **Wunan** est là maintenant
c'est là où sont tous les endroits sacrés
nous devons les surveiller
chaque homme, chaque femme tu vois
a sa part de responsabilité

Banggal

Kamali jallala... lawmaker stones
*That's why all these **jallala** here*

that's where the conversation was
agreements and all the title...
everything... land right and all that

*But the **Wunan** system*
we all been created from here
Nobody is forgotten... nobody outside
... that the land
but we not outside... we inside
we inside here
and once and for all we got that song

Kamali jallala ... Steine der Gesetzesmacher
*Deswegen stehen so viele **jallala** hier*

hier haben sie ihre Versammlung gehalten
Vereinbarungen getroffen das Land aufgeteilt ...
alles ... Landrechte und alles

*In dem **Wunan***
sind wir alle entstanden
Niemand ist vergessen ... niemand ausgeschlossen
... hier im Land
aber wir stehen nicht abseits ...
wir gehören dazu
und das Lied das bleibt uns für alle Zeiten

Kamali jallala ... les pierres des créateurs de Loi
*S'il y a tous ces **jallala** ici*

c'est parce qu'ici a eu lieu la discussion
les arrangements et tous les titres ...
tout... les droits fonciers et tout ça

*Dans ce système **Wunan***
on a tous été créés ici
personne n'est oublié ... personne n'est en dehors
... du pays
nous on n'est pas en dehors ... on est dedans
on est là dedans
et une fois pour toutes on a ce chant

angga... table first a bed of stringy bark tree
***golani muna...** big plum dish*
turned into stone

Humans turned into birds
and then into stone

Where we own land...
where our symbols are... it started from here
We all in different areas
the nature that we look after
That's why it was formed here
Banggal

angga ... der Tisch, zuerst aus Rinde
***golani muna ...** ein großes Pflaumengericht*
eine große Schale, in Stein verwandelt

Menschen, in Vögel verwandelt
und dann in Stein

Hier auf unserem Land ...
wo unsere Zeichen sind ... hat alles angefangen
Jeder hat sein Gebiet
sein Stück Natur um das er sich kümmert
Das haben sie hier ausgehandelt
Banggal

angga ... la table
d'abord faite une grande feuille d'écorce
***golani muna ...** un grand plat de prunes*
qui s'est transformé en pierre

Les hommes sont devenus des oiseaux
et puis cette pierre

C'est là qu'est notre pays ...
là où nos symboles sont ... ça a commencé ici
Nous avons chacun un endroit différent
et nous en sommes les gardiens
Tout ça a été créé ici
Banggal

That table **angga** the everlasting life
he stand there and he stays there
You know he gotta roots in this
and he stays really permanent

He stay that way he got the roots inside him
... this stone here never can move it
it stays inside so that's how it is...
the man have to be err... strong
to stand up you know

He's pretty strong... he got the **wungud** inside
we say that **Wunan** never break

Dieser Tisch **angga** der ist ewig
der hat schon immer da gestanden
und er wird immer da stehen
Er hat nämlich Wurzeln hier in der Erde
und der steht hier felsenfest

Der bleibt wo er ist der hat Wurzeln tief drinnen
... der Stein hier der bleibt an seinem Platz
der bleibt in der Erde und das steht fest...
der Mann der muss ganz schön Kräfte haben
der den hochstemmt

Der Stein hat Macht... **wungud** hat er in sich
wir sagen er ist wie das **Wunan** er wird nie vergehen

La table **angga** est éternelle
elle se tient là, et demeure là
Tu sais que tu es enraciné en elle
et que c'est vraiment pour toujours

La table reste comme ça
avec les racines en dedans
... cette pierre là on ne peut pas la bouger
ça reste en nous c'est comme ça...
il faut que l'homme soit... fort
pour faire face tu vois

Il se sent vraiment fort... il a le **wungud** en lui
on dit que le **Wunan** ne se rompt jamais

wunbanburan anybody can't change him
he stays that way he stay that way
that's the **wunbanburan**
wunbanburan means just like...
they stay in the one place forever

that's **wunbanburan**
he stay that way least you can't blow it up
no you can't change him
and that **Wunan** they will never stop

He had to obey the law... that's the way it is
Nyawarra

wunbanburan das heißt unveränderlich
er bleibt wie er ist für alle Zeit
er ist **wunbanburan**
wunbanburan das heißt so viel wie ...
etwas bleibt immer am gleichen Ort

das heißt **wunbanburan**
der bleibt so den kriegt keiner hier weg
den kann keiner verändern
und das **Wunan** wird immer so bleiben

Er musste das Gesetz befolgen
... so war es ihm bestimmt
Nyawarra

wunbanburan, personne ne peut le changer
ça reste comme ça, ça reste comme ça
c'est **wunbanburan**
wunbanburan ça veut dire en fait...
il reste à cet endroit précis pour toujours

c'est **wunbanburan**
il reste comme ça tu peux pas le détruire
non tu ne peux pas le changer
ce **Wunan** ça ne s'arrêtera jamais

Il faut suivre la Loi... c'est comme ça
Nyawarra

143

And they been put that **Wunan** there see
like a parliament or something
that they do like that and they said
"We have to make a rule and a law"

But the main roots of it is here
the picture of that system is here
in this area now this where design is
and we going to represent this
because we know this is all the southern area
and that one going sunrise...
that one sundown

Wunan.gu... calling for the **Wunan**
All this lot here all this **mob** here waited
See that dotted line there!
that's where all walked like
that name was called... that man
and they were all pushing one another
all along like that
they all come in one by one here
Then everyman like that fella over there
he can't interfere unless this one
give him permission to come here

Nyawarra

Und so haben sie das **Wunan** beschlossen
wie ein Parlament oder so etwas
das haben sie getan und haben gesagt
„Wir brauchen Regeln und Gesetze"

Aber die wichtigste Wurzel ist hier
das Abbild der ganzen Ordnung ist hier
an dieser Stelle hier da ist es aufgezeichnet
wir zeigen dir was da geschrieben steht
denn hier am Erdboden kann man es sehen
da geht es zum Sonnenaufgang hin...
und da zum Sonnenuntergang

Wunan.gu... sie rufen nach dem **Wunan**
Hier standen sie alle Schlange
hier an der gestrichelten Linie!
da rückten sie vor einer nach dem anderen
bis ihr Name gerufen wurde
alle haben geschubst und gedrängelt
bis sie drankamen einer nach dem anderen
alle müssen warten wie der Bursche da drüben
keiner kann sich vordrängen
jeder muss warten bis der hier vorn
ihm die Erlaubnis gibt

Nyawarra

Et ils ont mis le **Wunan** là tu vois
comme un parlement ou quoi
quelque chose comme ça et ils ont dit
« Il faut qu'on fasse des règles, une loi »

Mais ses racines principales sont là
l'image de ce système est visible là
dans cet endroit là où c'est dessiné
et on va te représenter tout ça
on sait qu'ici c'est tout le côté sud
et là le lever du soleil...
et là le coucher du soleil

Wunan.gu... l'appel pour réunir le **Wunan**
Tout ce groupe là, toute cette bande là attendait
Regardes cette ligne en pointillés là !
c'est là que tous s'avançaient
on appelait un nom... cet homme
et ils se poussaient tous les uns les autres
tout du long comme ça
ils sont tous entrés un par un, là
Puis chaque homme comme celui-là là-bas
il peut pas interférer à moins que celui-là
lui donne la permission de venir ici

Nyawarra

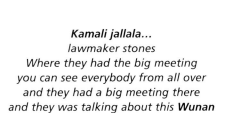

Burroi
Banbangi
Jurull
Margi
Goro.goro
Borror
Dadall
Belnged
Nudu.nudu
Yowinjella
Dumbi
Wo.wa
Garan.garan
Gorrodoo
Gumba.lawal
Ganjal
Wowarra

Kamali jallala…
lawmaker stones
Where they had the big meeting
you can see everybody from all over
and they had a big meeting there
and they was talking about this **Wunan**
Nyawarra

Kamali jallala …
Steine der Gesetzesmacher
Hier hatten sie die große Versammlung
man kann noch sehen
wie sie von überall her kamen
eine große Versammlung war das
und sie haben über das **Wunan** geredet
Nyawarra

Kamali jallala …
les pierres des créateurs de Loi
Là où ils ont fait le grand rassemblement
tu peux voir du monde venu de partout
le rassemblement a eu lieu ici
et ils parlèrent du **Wunan**
Nyawarra

*nyarra – **Wunambul** saying "us **Wunambul**"*
people from the north west coast

***Wulamu** saying "sunrise **mob**"*
main group from the desert to the east
*yeh yeh **nyarrama** all talking in meeting*

*he sundown **mob**... **Wororra** come this way*
*We all in different areas... **dambun***
the nature that we look after
That's why it was formed here
Banggal

*nyarra – **Wunambul**, sie sagen*
*„wir sind **Wunambul"***
die Leute von der Nordwestküste

*Die **Wulamu** sagen, wir kommen vom*
Sonnenaufgang
der größte Stamm aus der Wüste, aus dem Osten
*ja, **nyarrama**, alle reden bei der Versammlung*

Die Leute vom Sonnenuntergang
*... die **Wororra**, die kamen von da*
*Jeder hat sein eigenes Land... sein **dambun***
das Land, um das wir uns kümmern
Das haben sie hier beschlossen
Banggal

*nyarra – **Wunambul**, disant « nous, les **Wunambul** »*
les gens de la côte nord-ouest

*Les **Wulamu**, ça veut dire les gens du levant*
le principal groupe du désert à l'est
*yeh yeh **nyarrama** ils parlent tous au*
rassemblement

*Tous ceux du couchant... les **Wororra**,*
viennent par là
*On est tous dans des endroits différents... **dambun***
on s'occupe de la nature
C'est pourquoi ça a été créé ici
Banggal

Golani... sweet plum
not really sweet it's not like jam or sugar
it bit different from those two
*When **jebera** want to change his body*
when he get too fat
if he want to change his body
he eat that fruit and he get skinny
... change his body
ooh well maybe a couple of months time
he get fat again
Nyawarra

jebera... that their tucker
people used to go hunting
they see a track of emu
*and they look at that **golani***
*they heap up all that **golani** in the ground*
*and they climb up on top of that **golani** tree*
and they wait there...
they go there about 6 o'clock in the morning
*and the **jebera** come up*
and then when he eat... they just spear him
Ngarjno

And this is the life tree
that they minced this fruit up
*like a big mince **golani**...*
like a football and they said
„We have to make a rule and a law
this is our life... the tree we stand up"

Golani ... die süße Pflaume
aber sie ist nicht so süß wie Zucker oder Marmelade
sie schmeckt schon anders
*Wenn **jebera** zu fett wird*
wenn er gerne mal anders aussehen will
eine Schlankheitskur machen
dann isst er die Früchte da und wird ganz mager
... sieht ganz anders aus
aber das dauert vielleicht zwei Monate
dann ist er wieder fett
Nyawarra

jebera, der Emu ... die essen die früher
als die Leute auf die Jagd gegangen sind
und sie haben Spuren von einem Emu gesehen
*dann haben sie gesucht ob sie **golani** finden*
*und haben die **golani** auf ein Häufchen gelegt*
*und sie sind auf den **golani**-Baum geklettert*
und haben gewartet ...
sie gehen so gegen sechs Uhr morgens hin
*und dann kommt der **jebera***
und wenn er isst ... dann werfen sie den Speer
Ngarjno

Das ist der Baum des Lebens
die Früchte, die haben sie zerdrückt
*zu einem großen **golani**-Teig ...*
wie ein Fußball sah das aus und sie haben gesagt
„Wir müssen Regeln machen und Gesetze
das ist unser Leben ... der Baum, der uns hält"

Golani ... c'est une prune sucrée
pas aussi sucrée que de la confiture ou du sucre
c'est un peu différent de ces deux-là
*Quand **jebera** veut transformer son corps*
quand il devient trop gros
s'il veut transformer son corps
il mange ce fruit et il devient maigre
... ça change son corps
ooh ça dure peut-être deux mois
et il redevient gros
Nyawarra

jebera, l'émeu ... c'est ça qu'il mange
quand les gens allaient à la chasse
si ils voyaient une piste d'émeu
*ils cherchaient ça, des **golani***
ils en faisaient un petit tas sur le sol
*et ils montaient en haut de ce prunier **golani***
et ils attendaient là ...
ils viennent là à six heures du matin à peu près
*et le **jebera** apparaît et là quand il mange ...*
ils le transpercent d'un coup de lance
Ngarjno

Et ça c'est l'arbre de la vie
dont ils hachèrent les fruits
*c'est comme un hachis de **golani** ...*
gros comme un ballon de football et ils disaient
« Il faut qu'on fasse une règle et une loi
c'est notre vie ... l'arbre qui nous maintient »

It must be in the heart of our guts here!
yes its in here in the centre!
*Thats why that true **golani** was here*
in the centre... middle of the table

*This one **jallala**... significant stone*
represent the way they cooked it
*over this way that **golani***
*here this is the fire stone... **nabun***
you know all that lot stone we been looking at

*This eye pupil is a **golani**...*
that black one there... that little one
*that little one that's the **golani** too*
this fruit here he connected in our eye
*this little fruit that's called **golani***
Banggal

Der steckt hier in unseren Eingeweiden!
hier mittendrin!
*Deshalb waren die **golani** auch da*
in der Mitte ... in der Mitte von dem Tisch

*Der **jallala** hier das ist ein wichtiger Stein*
der steht dafür wie sie das Brot gebacken haben
*das **golani**-Brot hier drüben*
*hier ist die Feuerstelle, **nabun***
die ganzen Steine die man hier sieht

*Die Pupille im Auge das ist eine **golani** ...*
das Schwarze da ... das Kleine
*das Schwarze im Auge heißt auch **golani***
die Früchte hier stehen für unsere Augen
*die kleine Frucht die wir **golani** nennen*
Banggal

Ça doit être dans le cœur de nos tripes ici !
oui c'est là au centre !
*C'est pour ça que cette vraie **golani** était ici*
au centre ... au milieu de la table

*Cette **jallala** est une pierre importante*
c'est là qu'ils l'ont cuite
*par là, ces **golani***
*là c'est la pierre pour **nabun**, le feu*
tu vois toutes ces pierres dont on parle

*La pupille de l'œil c'est aussi comme une **golani** ...*
la noire là ... la petite
*cette petite-là c'est une **golani** aussi*
ce fruit-là il a un lien avec notre œil
*ce petit fruit qui s'appelle **golani***
Banggal

Every **Gwion** people from there...
Wunan mob... all the people
all what been belong to this country
all mixed there whole lot
everybody been come line 'emself
for that **golani** now in that table
that **golani** been sit down there
Gwion they all been waiting there
these three **Jebera...** emu tribe
Jebera lot from desert been outside
they been all waiting there

Somebody was named... **"Ganjal"**
Jebera called out "me?"
"no no... you sit down!"
they been tell him all th'way this fella

Right... he come little more close up
close up... close up... close up

Nyawarra

This is the one was saying
"Who me?... **niyan.gawa?**"
"No! they said... you will wait
you belong to sunrise
long way before you ever get any food!"

Telling them... "you blokes have to wait!
you blokes still under the sunrise"

Banggal

Von überall her kamen die **Gwion**...
die Schöpfer des **Wunan**... alle Stämme
alle die zu diesem Land gehört hatten
alle kamen sie da zusammen
in einer langen Reihe standen sie
damit sie ihren Anteil vom **golani**-Brot bekamen
hier in der Mitte liegt das
und die **Gwion** stehen und warten
auch die drei **Jebera**... aus dem Emu-Stamm
die **Jebera** draußen aus der Wüste
und alle stehen und warten

Einer wurde gerufen... „Ganjal"
und der **Jebera** rief „ich?"
„nein, nicht du... bleib, wo du bist!"
immer wieder mussten sie ihm das sagen

Also... dann rückte er ein Stückchen weiter vor
näher... und näher... und näher

Nyawarra

„Wer, ich?" hat er gefragt „niyan.gawa?"
„Nein!" antworteten sie... „warte
du gehörst zu den Sonnenaufgangs-Leuten
du bist noch lange nicht dran mit dem Essen!"

„Wartet, bis ihr an der Reihe seid"
haben sie ihnen gesagt
„ihr vom Sonnenaufgang"

Banggal

Tous les **Gwion** étaient ici...
ceux du **Wunan**... tous les gens
tout ce qui a jamais appartenu à ce pays
tous mélangés ici, tous ensemble
tout le monde se met en ligne
pour ce pain **golani** sur la table
ce **golani** était là
les **Gwion** attendaient tous là
ces trois **Jebera**... de la tribu de l'émeu
tous ces **Jebera** du désert étaient en dehors
ils attendaient tous là

Quelqu'un a été appelé... « Ganjal »
Jebera prend la parole et dit « moi ? »
« non non... tu restes assis ! »
ils lui ont dit tout du long à celui-là

Voilà... il vient un petit peu plus près
plus près... plus près... plus près

Nyawarra

C'est lui qui disait « qui moi ?... **niyan.gawa** ? »
« Non ! » ils ont dit... « tu attendras
tu appartiens au levant
il y a longtemps avant que tu reçoives
quelque nourriture ! »

Ils leur disent... « Vous les gars devez attendre !
Vous en êtes toujours au lever du soleil »

Banggal

But he came from a long way **"niyan.gawa"**
it's because he coming from another place
"niyan.gawa" it could be **Unggumi...**
that language or **Bunaba**
"niyan.gawa"... nothing in **Ngarinyin**
or **Wororra** or **Wunambul**
that's what he said... yeah **"niyan.gawa"**
and this word is the last he said... okay?

Alright this one **Jebera** been coming
he come down from on top hill now
he come all the way
Now these fellows been waiting too long
broke the law, yeh!
that three there standing up on top that hill
that three standing up there

Nyawarra

Aber er kam von weit her, sagte „niyan.gawa"
weil er von weit her kam
„niyan.gawa" das könnte **Unggumi** sein
diese Sprache, oder **Bunaba**
„niyan.gawa"... das gibt es nicht auf **Ngarinyin**
oder den **Wororra** oder den **Wunambul**
das hat er gesagt... ja, „niyan.gawa"
und das war sein letztes Wort... verstehst du?

Also dieser **Jebera** war von weit her gekommen
von oben aus den Bergen
den weiten Weg kam er hierher
die Burschen haben zu lange warten müssen
tja, und da haben sie das Gesetz gebrochen
die drei standen da oben auf dem Hügel
da oben standen sie

Nyawarra

Il venait de loin, « **niyan.gawa** »
il venait d'un autre endroit
« **niyan.gawa** » ça pourrait être du **Unggumi**
ce langage ou du **Bunaba**
« **niyan.gaw** ... » ça veut rien dire en **Ngarinyin**
ou en **Wororra** ou en **Wunambul**
c'est ce qu'il a dit... oui « **niyan.gawa** »
et ce mot c'est le dernier qu'il a dit... tu vois ?

Oui donc celui-là **Jebera** est venu
il descend du haut de la colline
maintenant il vient il vient
Maintenant ces gars ont attendu trop longtemps
et ils ont violé la Loi, oui !
ces trois-là debout en haut de cette colline
ces trois debout là

Nyawarra

Jebera thought
"I'd better make a dash into that table"
He came here... move closer here...
he stand up here now here... this is where
he made a dash
He got angry... he dance here dance here
around country dance here... keep going
keep going... he look back... he dance here...
he put his foot here... so he was confused
this one stones now... this one see the foot?
and here this is a emu foot
see how it's a real foot?

"No! I'm not going to take them back" he said
He didn't change his mind...
they tried to make him change his mind
to bring it back

"No!" he said "I'm not gonna do that
Not going to change my mind!"

Jebera said
"No... I've decided I'm not gonna listen to you!"
He said "no way... I've already done it
... I'm gonna do it"
Banggal

Jebera dachte
„Lieber jetzt gleich nach vorn"
Hier kam er ...und dann näher ...
hier hat er gestanden ...
und von hier aus ist er dann nach vorn gesprintet
Er wurde ungeduldig ... wippte hin und her
hier überall ist er herumgetanzt ... immer weiter
immer weiter ... dreht sich um ... hier tanzt er
hier hat er den Fuß hingesetzt ... er war wirr
hier die Steine ... siehst du da den Fuß?
hier das ist ein Emufuß
das ist ein richtiger Fuß siehst du?

„Nein!", hat er gesagt, „das gebe ich nicht zurück"
Er war fest entschlossen ...
sie wollten ihn überreden
er sollte das Brot zurücklegen

„Nein!", sagte er, „es bleibt dabei
ich will es und ich behalte es!"

Jebera sagte
„Nein ... ich will das das könnt ihr vergessen!"
„Gebt's auf", hat er gesagt, „ich hab's getan
... und jetzt bleibt es auch dabei"
Banggal

Jebera pensa...
« Je ferais mieux de me jeter sur cette table »
Il vient là ... il s'approche là ...
Il est debout là maintenant ici ...
c'est là qu'il sauta dessus
Il s'énerve ... il danse là il danse
tout autour il danse là ... il continue
il continue ... il se retourne ... il danse ici ...
il met son pied là ... donc il était énervé
ces pierres là ... celles-là, tu vois le pied ?
là, c'est un pied d'émeu
tu vois que c'est un vrai pied ?

« Non ! Je ne vais pas le ramener » il a dit
Il n'a pas changé d'idée ...
ils ont essayé de lui faire changer d'idée
de lui faire ramener le pain

« Non ! » il a dit « Je ne vais pas faire ça
Je vais pas changer d'idée ! »

Jebera dit
« Non ... J'ai décidé que je vous écouterai pas ! »
Il a dit « pas question ... Je l'ai fait
... J'irais au bout »
Banggal

Yeh well, that's how he broke the law
Ngarjno

*When this **Jebera** went to pick up*
*that black plum **golani**...*
*before him pick up that **golani***
he was just walking slowly
y'know moving in slowly
They cut this plum and give it to somebody
*and **Jebera** say*
*"what time I'm gonna get that **mangarri?**"*
"No!" they said "You gotta wait!
*you **Wari.ngarri** sunrise man"*

But before they even finish
this fellow been make a trouble
take one and leave one behind
and he went up there
*and he had to just pick up that **golani***
Nyawarra

Tja, so hat er das Gesetz gebrochen
Ngarjno

*Als dieser **Jebera** hinging*
*und sich das schwarze Pflaumen-**golani** holte*
*... bevor er hinging und das **golani**-Brot stahl*
da ist er ganz langsam vorgerückt
verstehst du, Stückchen für Stückchen
Sie haben ein Stück Pflaumenbrot abgeschnitten
*und der **Jebera** sagt*
*„wann bin ich endlich dran mit dem **mangarri?**"*
„Nein", sagen sie, „du wartest!
*du **Wari.ngarri** aus dem Land des Sonnenaufgangs"*

Aber bevor sie das zu Ende gesprochen haben
da sprintet dieser Bursche nach vorne
schnappt sich eins und eines lässt er da
hier ist er hingelaufen
*musste sich das **golani**-Brot nur noch schnappen*
Nyawarra

Oui voilà, c'est comme ça qu'il a brisé la Loi
Ngarjno

*Quand ce **Jebera** est venu ramasser*
*cette prune noire, cette **golani** ...*
*avant qu'il ramasse ce pain **golani***
il marchait tout doucement
tu sais très lentement
Ils en coupent et donnent à quelqu'un
*et **Jebera** dit*
*« quand est-ce que j'aurai cette **mangarri?** »*
« Non ! » ils disaient « Tu dois attendre
*toi **Wari.ngarri** l'homme du levant »*

Mais avant même qu'ils aient fini
ce gars a causé des problèmes
il en a pris un et en a laissée un autre
et il est monté là-haut
*il avait juste ramassé ce pain **golani***
Nyawarra

They telling them...
"you bloke have to wait!
you bloke still under the sunrise more top
you gotta wait longer!"
And then this **mob** been getting angry
and the bloke had to go over there
and pick it up! break the law
and just keep going with it
This **mob** been waiting too long
and they... one said
"I'm going to go and pick it up eh!
so we'll have one
and they can share one
we'll take that one! grab that
grab that **golani!**"

He took that full one... untouched one
So they wanted that untouched one back again
to put 'em back there and share it properly
golani made the **Wunan**
And these two meet him here half way
and they all took off... three of them
and the song goes...

rorrij amanbalu jina golani
steal bring here that **golani** back
Banggal

Sie haben ihm gesagt
„Mann, du musst warten!
ihr vom Sonnenaufgang seid noch nicht dran
du musst noch eine ganze Weile warten!"
Und da sind diese Burschen wütend geworden
und der eine konnte nicht anders er ist nach vorne
und hat es genommen! das Gesetz gebrochen
und sich damit davongemacht
Diese Burschen haben zu lange warten müssen
und dann… hat einer von ihnen gesagt
„Ich geh' jetzt nach vorn und hol' es mir einfach!
dann haben wir eines
und sie können sich das andere teilen
eines nehmen wir uns!
nimm das **golani,** nimm es dir!"

Er nahm das eine Brot, das ganze
und das wollten sie wieder auf dem Tisch haben
und teilen, wie es sich gehört
die **golani** teilen wie es das **Wunan** befiehlt
die anderen zwei kommen auf halbem Wege dazu
… und dann auf und davon, alle drei…
und das Lied heißt…

rorrij amanbalu jina golani
du Dieb bring die **golani** zurück
Banggal

Ils leur disent…
« Vous les gars devez attendre !
vous êtes toujours sous le soleil levant
… vous devez attendre plus longtemps ! »
Et alors cette bande ils se sont énervés
et le gars a du aller là
et la ramasser ! violer la Loi
et continuer comme ça
ils ont attendu trop longtemps
et ils… l'un d'eux a dit
« Je vais y aller et en ramasser eh !
comme ça on en aura un
et ils peuvent partager l'autre
on va prendre celle-là ! l'attraper
attraper ce pain **golani** »

Il a pris celui qui était entier... pas entamé
Et ils ont voulu le récupérer
pour le remettre et le partager correctement
la **golani** faisait le **Wunan**
Et les deux autres l'ont rencontré là à mi-chemin
et ils partirent tous... tous les trois
et le chant continue…

rorrij amanbalu jina golani
voleur amène ici cette **golani**
Banggal

When he been pick it up from there
he didn't have that plum dish **angga**
he just pick up the **mangarri**... food
that **golani** itself

But this bloke went in there
and just pick one up from there
and he keep on yelling
"wow! wow wow wow!"
he was dancing round there in that **mob**
running round with it

And he took off with that **mangarri golani**
When he put his foot down
he took off with it... take it for good!
He looked back here he caught this one
he dance here he put his foot here
"No! I'm not going to take them back!" he said
Nyawarra

Als er es wegnahm von da
da hatte er nichts zum Tragen, keine **angga**
er schnappte sich nur das Essen… **mangarri**
das **golani**

Der ist tatsächlich da hingegangen
und hat sich eins von den Broten genommen
und er hat immer wieder gebrüllt
„wow! wow wow wow!"
und ist rund um den Tisch getanzt
und die anderen immer hinterher

Dann ist er auf und davon mit dem **mangarri golani**
Stampfte mit dem Fuß auf
und schon war er weg … mit dem **golani**-Brot!
Als er zurückblickte, ist er hier stehen geblieben
hier hat er getanzt und seinen Fuß hingesetzt
„Nein!" rief er „ich bringe das nicht zurück!"
Nyawarra

Quand il l'a pris là-bas
il n'avait pas pris le plat, ce coolamon, cet **angga**
il a juste ramassé la nourriture… **mangarri**
la **golani** elle-même

Ce gars est entré ici
et en a pris juste un là
et il arrêtait pas de crier
« wow ! wow wow wow ! »
et il dansait là avec cette bande
courant tout autour avec eux

Et il partit avec cette **mangarri golani**
il arrête de bouger
et il se sauve avec… il l'a prise pour de bon !
Il regarde en arrière ici et la prend
il danse ici, il met son pied là
« Non ! Je ne vais pas la ramener ! » il a dit
Nyawarra

And those two run down with the **golani**
and he been put it inside that **jirrgal jalba** bag
and he put it in their shoulder
jirrgal is that string in that **jalba**
and then they took off

Jalbanuma they call it
and those two blokes have that **angga**
they put it on their shoulder
and just carry on run with it... **jaljalbi**
where that hill called **Jalbanuma**

And **Dududu.ngarri...** what we saying
that's when he was running...
you can hear his echo
And when they was running
they made that big noise y'know with their foot
and they call that place **Dududu** and this fella
Jebera got took off with that **golani**
he was carrying that thing **jalba** in arm
bottom of the arm and they call uh **Jalbanuma**
that picture of that **golani** it's ah...
is in that mountain now... **Jalbanuma**
So she **Jalbanuma**... this mountain here

Nyawarra

Die beiden anderen laufen runter mit ihrem **golani**
und tun das Brot in den **jirrgal jalba**... ihr Netz
sie hängen es sich über die Schulter
jirrgal ist das Netz für den **jalba**
und dann nichts wie weg

Jalbanuma heißt der Berg da
und die zwei Burschen tragen die **angga**
die haben sie sich über die Schulter gehängt
und sie laufen und laufen... **jaljalbi**
da an dem Berg **Jalbanuma**

Dududu.ngarri... so nennen wir das
wenn einer läuft...
dann hört man das Echo
Und beim Laufen da haben sie
fürchterlichen Krach gemacht mit ihren Füßen
deshalb heißt dieser Ort **Dududu** und dieser
Jebera der den **golani** hatte
der hatte die Tasche **jalba** im Arm
unter dem Arm und das heißt jetzt **Jalbanuma**
das ist ein Bild von dem **golani**
und... das ist der Berg hier **Jalbanuma**
deshalb heißt der **Jalbanuma**... der Berg hier

Nyawarra

Et ces deux descendent en courant avec le **golani**
avec ce **jirrgal jalba**... leur sac
et il l'ont mis dans ce **jirrgal**
dans ce jalba et après ils sont partis avec
et il l'ont mis sur leur épaule

Jalbanuma ils l'appellent
et ces deux gars ont cet **angga**
ils le mettent sur leur épaule
et ils le portent et courent avec... **jaljalbi**
Là où il y a cette colline appelée **Jalbanuma**

Et **Dududu.ngarri**... ce qu'on disait
c'est quand il courait...
tu pouvais entendre son écho
Et quand ils couraient
ils faisaient du bruit avec leurs pieds tu vois
et on appelle cet endroit **Dududu** et ce gars
ce **Jebera** est parti avec ce **golani**
il portait ce **jalba,** ce sac de corde dans ses bras,
en bas de son bras ça s'appelle... **Jalbanuma**
l'image de cette **golani** c'est ah...
c'est cette montagne maintenant... **Jalbanuma**
Elle est **Jalbanuma**... cette montagne ici

Nyawarra

152

And when they was running
they made those big noise
y'know when um put their foot
and they call that place **Dududu.ngarri**
When he was running they made lot of noise
you know **dudu… dudu… dudu**
Yeah through the gap… he make that gap

Banggal

They made lot of noise
du du du du du… all the way up
and it called **dududu** he stamped
he shaked the earth… **Dududu.ngarri**

Ngarjno

Und beim Laufen
da haben sie fürchterlichen Krach gemacht
mit ihren Füßen weißt du
deshalb heißt der Ort jetzt **Dududu.ngarri**
Beim Laufen da haben sie viel Krach gemacht
verstehst du, das Stampfen **dudu… dudu… dudu**
durch die Schlucht… die Schlucht machten sie

Banggal

Einen Haufen Krach
du du du du du… die ganze Strecke
wir sagen **dududu,** von dem Stampfen
da hat die ganze Erde gebebt… **Dududu.ngarri**

Ngarjno

Et quand ils couraient
ils faisaient tout ce bruit
tu sais quand ils mmm… posent leur pied
et on appelle cet endroit **Dududu.ngarri**
Ils faisaient beaucoup de bruit en courant
tu vois **dudu… dudu… dudu**
Oui à travers la trouée, il a fait une trouée

Banggal

Ils faisaient beaucoup de bruit
du du du du du… tout le long du chemin
et ça s'appelle **dududu** là ou il piétinait
il secouait la terre… **Dududu.ngarri**

Ngarjno

So they wanted that untouched one back again
and they put it back there and share it properly
So if we have any trouble... we get punished
... judgement come upon us

Banggal

Sie wollten das ganze, frische Brot zurück
sie wollten es zurück und richtig aufteilen
Wenn wir Ärger machen ... werden wir bestraft
... Strafe ereilt uns

Banggal

Ils voulaient que ce pain pas entamée revienne
qu'on le remette là, qu'on le partage correctement
Donc si on a un problème avec la Loi ... on est puni
... le jugement s'abat sur nous

Banggal

*When they go up in that place near **Barilamma***
and three all stand up there
*and the other two **Jebera** told him*
"No! you take it out that a way
and we'll run down this way"
split up where they wanted to go
*and he went to **Barilamma** he stop there in cave*

***Jebera** took that **golani** thing away*
and caused a lot of trouble he had broke the law
and I think they been mean to kill him for that
So all the birds first tried to get him back
till him half way no!... they couldn't catch up
*he was too fast... the **Wunan** song goes...*

***Wowarra**... Bronzewing Pigeon*
***numanda**... wake up*
***nyirri gunduba**... you curled up*
***barrij**... get up*
***buren**... they took off*

*Two **Wowarra** fella making that spear point*
*spear points **naling jimbila** we call it*
***gimbu**... making that spear point*
and they was just sitting quiet there
ah just sitting over there waiting
Maybe they knew that thing could happen
or something could happen?
Law people said to them
"You two the fast runner to catch up to it."

*two **Wowarra** said "Oh alright, we'll try"*

Nyawarra

*Dann sind sie da hinaufgestiegen nach **Barilamma***
alle drei haben sie da oben gestanden
*und die anderen beiden **Jebera** sagten*
„Nein! du gehst da lang
und wir laufen hier rüber"
sie haben verhandelt wer welche Richtung nimmt
*und er ist dann nach **Barilamma** und hat sich in*
der Höhle ausgeruht

***Jebera** hat das **golani**-Brot gestohlen*
hat viel Ärger gemacht hat das Gesetz gebrochen
dafür sollte er nun wohl sterben
Deshalb sind sie ihm zuerst alle Vögel nach
bald merkten sie ... sie holten ihn nicht mehr ein
*er war zu schnell ... im **Wunan**-Lied heißt es ...*

***Wowarra** ... Bronzeflügeltaube*
***numanda** ... erwache*
***nyirri gunduba** ... du liegst und schläfst*
***barrij** ... steh auf*
***buren** ... sie sind entflohen*

*Zwei **Wowarra**-Burschen machten ihre Speere fertig*
***naling jimbila** nennen wir die Speerspitzen*
***gimbu** ... die scharfe Speerspitze*
und sie haben einfach nur still dagesessen
haben da gesessen und gewartet
Vielleicht haben sie sich schon gedacht
wie es kommen würde
dass es so kommen würde
Die Hüter des Gesetzes haben zu ihnen gesagt
„Ihr zwei, ihr seid die Schnellsten ihr holt sie ein"

*und die beiden **Wowarra** haben gesagt*
„Na gut, wir probieren's"

Nyawarra

*Ils montent à cet endroit près de **Barilamma***
et les trois sont debout là-haut
*et les deux autres **Jebera** lui disent*
« Non ! tu pars d'un côté
et nous allons descendre de ce côté »
ils se séparent pour aller là où ils veulent aller
*il alla à **Barilamma**, s'arrêta là dans cette grotte*

***Jebera** emmena cette chose, ce **golani** ailleurs*
et causa beaucoup de problèmes, il avait violé la Loi
et je crois qu'ils voulaient vraiment le tuer pour ça
Donc tous les oiseaux essayèrent d'abord
de le faire revenir
jusqu'à ce qu'il soit à mi-chemin ... non ! ...
ils ne pouvaient pas l'attraper
il était trop rapide ...
*le chant du **Wunan** continue ...*

***Wowarra** ... pigeon à aile de bronze*
***numanda** ... réveille-toi*
***nyirri gunduba** ... recroquevillé dans son sommeil*
***barrij** ... lève-toi*
***buren** ... ils sont partis*

*Il y avait deux types **Wowarra***
qui fabriquaient cette pointe de lance
*pointes de lances, **naling jimbila** on appelle ça*
***gimbu** ... ils fabriquaient cette pointe de lance*
et ils étaient simplement assis là tranquillement
ah juste assis là à attendre
Peut-être qu'ils savaient que ça pouvait arriver
ou que quelque chose pouvait arriver ?
Les gens de la Loi leur ont dit
« Vous les deux qui courez vite, attrapez-le »

*les deux **Wowarra** ont dit « D'accord on va essayer »*

Nyawarra

Brrrrr!... they get up and get those two spear
gallid *we call that spear... and they got the* ***gallid***
well they had one each... they both had one
Right! ***Wowarra*** *took off... follow that* ***Jebera***
right up through the gap
Nyawarra

Brrrr! ... sie springen auf und greifen zwei Speere
gallid *nennen wir die ... sie nahmen ihre* ***gallid***
sie hatten jeder einen ... jeder einen
nun waren die ***Wowarra*** *unterwegs ... folgten* ***Jebera***
hoch durch die Schlucht
Nyawarra

Brrrrr ! ... ils se lèvent et prennent leurs deux lances
gallid *on les appelle ... et ils prennent les* ***gallid***
bon ils en avaient une chacun ...
ils en avaient une tous les deux
Bon ! ***Wowarra*** *partit ... suivit ce* ***Jebera***
justque là-haut à travers la trouée
Nyawarra

And they had to send out these two ***Wowarra***
some of those King... y'know the law men?
"We gotta go and ask these two over here
they ***Wowarra*** *the fast runners*
they might catch up to that ***Jebera***"
The law men went over there and ask them,
"You two can try and catch up to that Emu"
Banggal

They look in the gap where he was running
right till they been see these track
they been run again other side
and they look in the gap
"Nah! ***Jebera*** *still going..."*

They run more further up... they look again
they come across this road
where he was running
and they look ahhh! they seen the fresh one
little bit fresh and they run again

They look in the road
"Ahh! there the fresh one now!"
where he been run through the water
and the water lying in the rock
"ahh! that's the last... we'll run more further up"
they run right up... they look... no track
And they wait there they look... shhhh
there he coming along
he keep on looking back
eating half of that ***golani***
Nyawarra

Und sie mussten zwei ***Wowarra*** *nachschicken*
zwei der Anführer ... den Gesetzgebern, weißt du?
„Hier, die zwei, die müssen wir fragen
die ***Wowarra,*** *das sind gute Läufer*
die können diesen ***Jebera*** *vielleicht noch einholen"*
Die Hüter des Gesetzes gingen hin und fragten
"Ihr zwei, könnt ihr versuchen, den Emu zu fangen?"
Banggal

Sie sahen sich in der Schlucht um
in die er gelaufen war bis sie die Spuren fanden
und dann sind sie zur anderen Seite gelaufen
und haben von da in die Schlucht geschaut
„Kein ***Jebera*** *hier der ist schon weiter vorn ..."*

Sie laufen vor ... schauen sich wieder um
sie kommen über den Weg
wo er gelaufen ist
und aaah! da sehen sie eine frische Spur
noch ziemlich frisch und sie laufen weiter

Sie sehen sich um auf dem Weg
„Ahh, da sind jetzt die ganz frischen!"
wo er durchs Wasser gelaufen war
und das Wasser ließ Spuren auf dem Fels zurück
„aaah, die sind ganz frisch ... komm weiter"
sie laufen weiter ... sie sehen sich um ... keine Spur
Und sie warten und halten Ausschau ... psssst
da kommt er
blickt sich immer über die Schulter
und isst gerade die Hälfte von dem ***golani****-Brot*
Nyawarra

Et ils devaient envoyer ces deux ***Wowarra***
certains d'entre eux sont comme des rois ...
tu sais les gardiens de la Loi ?
« Nous devons demander à ces deux là-bas
Eux les ***Wowarra*** *les bons coureurs*
ils peuvent attraper ce ***Jebera*** »
Les gardiens de la Loi y allèrent et leur demandèrent
« Vous deux pouvez essayer de l'attraper
cet homme du clan de l'Émeu »
Banggal

Ils regardent dans la trouée à travers
laquelle il courait
jusqu'à ce qu'ils aient vu sa trace
ils coururent encore de l'autre côté
et regardèrent par la trouée
« Nah ! ***Jebera*** *court toujours ... »*

Ils courent encore, plus haut ... ils regardent
encore ils trouvent cette route où il courait
et ils regardent ahhh ! ils voient la piste fraîche
assez fraîche et ils courent encore

Ils regardent sur la route
« Ahh ! voilà la piste fraîche ! »
là il a traversé l'eau
il y a de l'eau sur le rocher
« Ahh ! c'est la piste ... on va courir plus loin »
ils courent droit devant ... ils regardent ...
... pas de piste
Et ils attendent et là ils le voient ... shhhh
là, le voilà qui vient
il n'arrête pas de regarder derrière
mangeant la moitié de cette ***golani***
Nyawarra

And this **Jebera** bloke where got the spear
it right in the back
and drop all that **golani** in there
somewhere up in this **Brregural**
And they took it back right back to those people
they showed them the feather... *yululun*
They took some of those *yululun* back
blood with that *yululun* and spear
and they took it back there
and show those people and they all been happy
they'd been rid of that thing... that **Jebera**
and then they had a big party...
everybody been happy

Nyawarra

Und da hat dieser **Jebera** den Speer
mitten in den Hintern gekriegt
hat die **golani** allesamt fallen lassen
irgendwo da oben auf dem **Brregural**
Sie haben sie zu den Leuten gebracht
haben die Federn gezeigt ... *yululun*
ein paar von den *yululun* haben sie genommen
da war Blut an den *yululun* und dazu am Speer
den haben sie mit zurückgenommen
und den Leuten gezeigt und alle waren froh
dass sie ihn endlich los waren ... diesen **Jebera**
und da haben sie ein großes Fest gefeiert...
und alle waren glücklich

Nyawarra

Et ce **Jebera** a reçu la lance en plein dans le dos
et il laisse tomber là le **golani**
quelque part là-haut à **Brregural**
Et ils ramenèrent ça directement à ces gens
et ils leur montrèrent les plumes... *yululun*
Ils ramenèrent une partie de ces *yululun*
il y avait du sang sur ces *yululun* et sur la lance
et ils les ramenèrent là-bas
et ils les montrèrent aux gens qui étaient heureux
ils étaient débarrassés de ce type... ce **Jebera**
et alors ils firent une grande fête...
tout le monde était heureux

Nyawarra

And they picked up and took that spear off
leaving stone spear point... *jimbila* we call it
behind his back... y'know in that tail part
they took that *jowul* back to those people
and carry that spear back what has his blood
and the *jimbila* what he been spear him
stayed in his back

Nyawarra

Jebera they got nothing here
they got no fat in here
that **Wowarra** been kill'em here
only one part part of emu
that's one he got no fat

Ngarjno

Und sie hoben ihn auf und zogen den Speer raus
die steinerne Speerspitze... *jimbila* heißt die
die blieb drin... in seinem Hinterteil
den *jowul* den haben sie mit zurückgenommen
den Speer an dem sein Blut dran war
aber die *jimbila* mit der sie ihn getötet hatten
die ließen sie stecken

Nyawarra

Die **Jebera** die haben hier nichts
die haben kein Fett hier hinten
hier haben die **Wowarra** ihn erwischt
es gibt nur eine Stelle beim Emu
wo er kein Fett hat

Ngarjno

Et ils retirèrent cette lance
laissant la pointe de lance en pierre...
jimbila on l'appelle
derrière dans son dos... tu sais dans la queue
et après ils ramenèrent ce *jimbila* à ces gens
ils ramenèrent la lance avec son sang dessus
et la *jimbila* qui l'avait touché
resta dans son dos

Nyawarra

Les **Jebera** n'ont rien ici
ils n'ont pas de graisse à cet endroit
ce **Wowarra** l'a tué là
c'est la seule partie, la seule partie de l'émeu
qui n'a pas de graisse

Ngarjno

They made a big sharing system for **dambun** for land
people had all different totems of land
they shared the land… **dambun**
to become caretaker of the nature

So all this was named up here at **Dududu.ngarri**
All those men got all the land from that time
so we become the servants of the nature
looking after the country

And we didn't trespass one another
It was done rightly you know because of identifying
every man had to identify his own block of land
land rights and all that

And that's what this **Wunan** was formed for
in those early stage long long time ago
Banggal

Sie haben das ganze Land aufgeteilt in **dambun**
jedes Stück Land gehörte zu einem anderen Totem
das Land haben sie aufgeteilt… **dambun**
damit sie die Natur bewahren können

So haben sie es festgelegt in **Dududu.ngarri**
Und von da an hatten alle ihr Land
und wir wurden zu Dienern der Natur
wir haben das Land gehütet

Keiner hat vom Land des anderen genommen
nichts war unrechtmäßig, es war alles geregelt
denn jeder musste beweisen,
dass er Anrecht auf ein Stück Land hatte
Landrechte und das alles

Dafür haben wir das **Wunan** gemacht
damals vor langer, langer Zeit
Banggal

Ils créèrent un grand système de partage
des **dambun**, des terres
les gens avaient tous un totem différent
pour leur terre ils partageaient la terre… **dambun**
et ils sont devenus les gardiens de la nature

Donc tout ça a été attribué à **Dududu.ngarri**
Tous les hommes ont leur terre depuis ce temps
on est devenu les serviteurs de la nature
on prend soin du pays

Et on n'a pas empiété l'un sur l'autre
ça a été fait correctement tu vois à cause de l'identification
chaque homme devait s'identifier à sa terre
les droits fonciers et tout ça

Et c'est pour ça que ce **Wunan** a été créé
dans ces premiers temps, il y a longtemps longtemps
Banggal

This one **Jebera** brought a reason to do that
manjilarri because he get punished
anybody make wrong in this life...
now we get punished
and that is what he is saying... this emu here
the story belong to emu... **Jebera**
to make a judgement
Don't do anything wrong...
law always be there
That is what he is representing... this emu here
... it's a hard hard law

that Southern Cross... that bottom star
that's where he bending down now
this emu... **Jebera** he got punished!
there in that **Wallagunda** where the pool is
and emu he bend down here
with the spear stuck on 'im
he got punish for trying to break the law

Wallagunda he lay down right across
white man call him Milky Way...
we call him **Wallagunda**
His head on the south that **wanjina**
and his leg on the north
it cover the whole land
he tie it up like a belt the whole Australia
that Milky Way that's that water there now
that's called **Wallagunda** that water there now
and then **golani** because it's the dark water
and that's where we get sweet water from
every year from supply... from there
rainwater... rain he from there now
Milky Way give us the water all year round

It along side of pool
where they say Southern Cross there?
see that's a **golani** that's the **wunginunna**
it's a pool of water there dark one
golani... that the pool
Banggal

So when he broke the **Wunan** law
he went up into the Milky Way
and he stayed there and you can see
that the spear sticking out in his back
when he bending over y' know
You can see his neck bending over
and he couldn't hardly take it off
he got no long arm to reach over his back
to pull that spear out
but he had to just stay that way
and they stay up there in the Milky Way
Nyawarra

Dieser **Jebera**, der ist schuld daran
wegen dem **manjilarri**, deswegen musste er
bestraft werden
wenn wir jetzt etwas falsch machen im Leben
werden wir bestraft
und das sagt er hier... dieser Emu
die Geschichte handelt von dem Emu
... von **Jebera** wie er bestraft wird
Verstoße nicht gegen das Gesetz...
das Gesetz ist immer da
Das bedeutet das Bild... dieser Emu hier
... das Gesetz ist sehr sehr hart

das Kreuz des Südens... der unterste Stern
da beugt er sich herunter
der Emu... der **Jebera** bekam seine Strafe!
da in der **Wallagunda**, da wo das Wasserloch ist
da beugt der Emu sich vor
mit dem Speer im Rücken
er wurde bestraft, weil er das Gesetz brechen wollte

Wallagunda, da liegt er ausgestreckt
bei den Weißen heißt es Milchstraße
wir nennen es **Wallagunda**
Den Kopf hat er im Süden, der **wanjina**
und die Beine im Norden
er liegt über dem ganzen Land
er hält es zusammen wie ein Gürtel
ganz Australien
die Milchstraße, das ist das Wasser
das heißt **Wallagunda**, das Wasser da oben
und **golani**, weil das Wasser dunkel ist
und von da kommt unser Süßwasser
Jahr für Jahr aus dieser Quelle... von da
Regenwasser... von da kommt der Regen
die Milchstraße schenkt uns Wasser
das ganze Jahr

Siehst du da neben dem Wasserloch
neben dem Kreuz des Südens, wie ihr es nennt?
das ist ein **golani**, das ist **wunginunna**
ein Wasserloch mit dunklem Wasser
golani... so heißt das Wasserloch
Banggal

Und als er das **Wunan**-Gesetz brach
kam er hinauf an die Milchstraße
da blieb er, und man kann ihn heute noch sehen
das ist der Speer, der steckt noch in seinem
Rücken, da wo er sich zusammengekrümmt hat
Man kann sehen, wie er den Kopf eingezogen hat
und er konnte den Speer nicht herausziehen
sein Arm war nicht lang genug
bis an den Rücken, aber er musste es zulassen
und da oben in der Milchstraße bleiben
Nyawarra

Ce **Jebera** il méritait qu'on lui fasse ça
Il a été puni à cause du **manjilarri**
si quelqu'un agit mal dans la vie...
maintenant il est puni
et c'est ce qu'on a dit... cet émeu là
c'est l'histoire de l'émeu... **Jebera**
on en a fait un exemple
Ne fais rien de mal
la Loi sera toujours derrière toi
C'est ce qu'il représente... cet émeu, là
... c'est une loi dure, très dure

Cette Croix du Sud... cette étoile en bas
c'est là qu'on le voit penché en avant là
cet émeu... **Jebera**, il a été puni!
là dans cette **Wallagunda** où il y a le puits
l'émeu il est plié là
avec la lance plantée sur lui
il a été puni pour avoir tenté de violer la Loi

Wallagunda est allongé juste au travers
l'homme blanc l'appelle la Voie lactée
nous on l'appelle **Wallagunda**
il a sa tête au sud, ce **wanjina**
et sa jambe au nord
ça couvre tout le pays
il entoure l'Australie comme une ceinture
cette Voie lactée c'est cette eau là maintenant
ça s'appelle **Wallagunda** cette eau là
et aussi **golani** parce que c'est l'eau sombre
et c'est de là qu'on a de l'eau douce
tous les ans depuis on se fournit... de là
l'eau de pluie... la pluie vient de là maintenant
la Voie lactée nous donne notre eau toute l'année

C'est sur le côté du puits
que vous appelez Croix du Sud, là?
tu vois c'est une **golani**, c'est le **wunginunna**
c'est un bassin d'eau là, sombre
golani... c'est la mare
Banggal

Donc quand il a enfreint la Loi
il est parti dans la Voie lactée
et il est resté là et tu peux voir
la lance qui dépasse de son dos
il est penché en avant tu vois
Tu peux voir son cou se plier en avant
il pouvait pas l'enlever
il n'avait pas un bras assez long
pour atteindre son dos, pour enlever cette lance
Il fallait qu'il reste comme ça
et il reste comme ça là haut dans la Voie lactée
Nyawarra

a b c

When the **Wunan** is discussed by **munnumburra** in daily conversation, diagrams are drawn into the earth to illustrate the layout of events and to map the country where the law originated. This version of the story incorporates the voices of **Nyawarra** and **Banggal** as recorded on location and in the presence of **Ngarjno** and **Ungudman** who, apart from prompting and checking the accuracy of the dialogue, enriched it with many **Wunan** songs. Ancient narratives only produce their full power when expressed in situ and punctuated by the voice in song. Themes and details that suffer from translation and abbreviation when told in a language foreign to the land, may be clarified by this summary.

Wunan law originated with a path taken by **Wodoi** of the Spotted Nightjar clan and his friend and cohort **Jungun** of the Owlet Nightjar clan. The two **Gwion** nomads resolved many disputes between each other. Then they went on a secret quest for knowledge to the region of **Gelngu** (b), where a famous **banman** mystic, **Wibalma**, was known to make **maya.ngarri** (sacred objects). Because **Wibalma** was absent on a hunt for emu fat with which to anoint a new wooden **maya.ngarri**, they instead encountered his blind wife, **Nyamanbiligi**. Although unable to watch him work, she had often heard **Wibalma's** activities, and she innocently gave them directions to visit him at the **bunja** where he worked. Entering the deserted workshop, they saw the many sacred objects that **Wibalma** had stored there. **Maya.ngarri** retain dormant sources of various powers of meaning, such as **ngoru** of the sacred wind or inside breath of food-plants and animals, **nyamun-buna** of taking your oath and not going against the law because it means trouble and punishment, and **manjilarri** of running away without hope of escape because the law is after you.

Wodoi and **Jungun** were impressed by what they saw, and realized that all this sacred power was too much for one man to possess. Deciding to take one object to share with all people, they removed the **maya.ngarri** known as **manjilarri**. Although he was far away hunting, **Wibalma** sensed the theft and rushed back to his workshop.

Wenn sich die **munnumburra** im Alltag über das **Wunan** unterhalten, zeichnen sie dazu oft Illustrationen des Geschehens in den Sand oder Landkarten der Orte, an denen die Gesetze ihren Ursprung haben. Die Geschichte basiert auf Erzählungen von **Nyawarra** und **Banggal**, aufgenommen vor Ort und in Gegenwart von **Ngarjno** und **Ungudman**, die Stichworte lieferten, die die Richtigkeit des Gesagten bestätigten und es durch zahlreiche **Wunan**-Gesänge bereicherten. Die überlieferten Berichte entfalten ihre volle Wirkung nur, wenn sie am Ort des Geschehens erzählt werden und wenn die dazugehörigen Gesänge dabei erklingen. Motive und Einzelheiten, die bei der Übersetzung in eine fremde Sprache verloren gehen, können vielleicht in dieser Zusammenfassung noch geklärt werden.

Das **Wunan**-Gesetz hat seinen Ursprung in einem Pfad, den **Wodoi** aus dem Clan des Gefleckten Nachtfalken und sein Freund und Gefährte **Jungun** aus dem Baumschwalm-Clan nahmen. Die beiden umherschweifenden **Gwion** fochten manchen Disput miteinander aus. Dann brachen sie auf der Suche nach Weisheit heimlich in die Region **Gelngu** (b) auf, wo der berühmte **banman** oder Mystiker **Wibalma** seine **maya.ngarri** (heilige Gegenstände) fertigte. **Wibalma** war aber gerade auf der Emujagd, weil er das Fett zum Einreiben neuer hölzerner **maya.ngarri** brauchte, und sie trafen nur seine blinde Frau **Nyamanbiligi** an. Sie konnte **Wibalma** zwar nicht bei der Arbeit zusehen, aber sie hatte doch vieles mit angehört und dachte sich nichts dabei, als sie die beiden zu der **bunja** schickte, wo er arbeitete. Sie kamen an die verlassene Werkstatt und sahen die vielen heiligen Gegenstände, die **Wibalma** dort aufbewahrte. In den **maya.ngarri** schlummern bestimmte Mächte, etwa **ngoru**, der innere Atem von essbaren Pflanzen und Tieren, **nyamun-buna**, die Verpflichtung zum rechtmäßigen Leben, ein Schwur, dessen Bruch Kummer und Strafe heraufbeschwört, und **manjilarri**, die Flucht ohne Hoffnung, wenn die erbarmungslose Kraft des Gesetzes einen verfolgt.

Wodoi und **Jungun** waren beeindruckt von dem, was sie da sahen, und sie fanden, dass so viel geheime Macht zu viel für einen einzigen Mann war. Sie beschlossen, einen der heiligen Gegenstände mitzunehmen, damit sie ihn mit aller Welt teilen konnten, und wählten den **maya.ngarri** namens **manjilarri**. Auch wenn er noch so weit fort auf der Jagd war, spürte **Wibalma** den Diebstahl und eilte zurück zu seiner Werkstatt.

En évoquant les **Wunan,** les **munnumburra** font des croquis sur le sol pour illustrer le déroulement des événements et pour faire les plans de la région où est née la Loi. Cette version de l'histoire incorpore les voix de **Nyawarra** et **Banggal** enregistrées sur place en la présence de **Ngarjno** et **Ungudman** qui, au-delà d'interventions et de vérifications du dialogue, l'ont également enrichi de nombreux chants **Wunan**. Les anciens récits n'ont vraiment toute leur puissance que lorsqu'ils sont dits sur place et qu'ils sont ponctués par des chants. Les thèmes et détails (qui perdent de leur sens à cause des abréviations et de la nécessité pour les munnumburra d'utiliser une langue étrangère à leur terre) peuvent être clarifiés par le résumé suivant :

La loi **Wunan** est née avec le chemin qu'ont pris **Wodoi,** du clan de l'engoulevent tacheté, et son ami et compagnon **Jungun,** du clan de la chouette. Les deux nomades **Gwion** résolurent de nombreux conflits qui existaient entre eux deux. Ensuite, ils partirent pour une quête secrète du savoir dans la région de **Gelngu** (b) où un fameux **banman** – un mystique, **Wibalma,** était connu pour fabriquer des **maya.ngarri**, des objets sacrés. **Wibalma** était absent, car il était parti à la chasse pour se procurer de la graisse d'émeu pour oindre un nouveau **maya.ngarri** en bois. Ils trouvèrent à la place sa femme aveugle, **Nyamanbiligi**. Bien que ne pouvant le regarder travailler, elle avait souvent entendu ce que faisait **Wibalma** et, innocemment, elle leur indiqua la direction pour aller le voir au **bunja** où il travaillait. En entrant dans l'atelier désert, ils virent de nombreux objets sacrés que **Wibalma** y avait entreposés. Les **maya.ngarri** conservent différents pouvoirs en sommeil, comme par exemple **ngoru** (vent sacré ou souffle intérieur des plantes comestibles et des animaux), **nyamun-buna** (faire un serment et ne pas enfreindre la loi parce que cela induit des désordres et entraîne une punition) ou encore **manjilarri** qui signifie s'enfuir sans espoir de s'échapper car la Loi vous poursuit.

Wodoi et **Jungun** furent impressionnés par ce qu'ils virent et se rendirent compte que tout ce pouvoir sacré était beaucoup trop important pour être possédé par un seul homme. Décidant de prendre un objet pour le partager avec tout le monde, ils enlevèrent le **maya.ngarri manjilarri**. Bien qu'il fut loin, en train de chasser, il retourna précipitamment à son atelier.

Wibalma

d

e

f

On arrival, he asked his wife if she had seen anyone. **Nyamanbiligi** mentioned **Wodoi** and **Jungun,** and how she had told them where to look for him. **Wibalma's** anger erupted at his discovery of the theft of the sacred object. Enraged, he used his **banad** (hooked boomerang) to cleave a **wungarun** (ironwood tree) of the hardest timber, thus bringing to life all the sacred objects, including the **maya.ngarri** with the name **manjilarri** then being carried away by **Wodoi** and **Jungun.**

Wibalma immediately went after them but had trouble finding their tracks. The great spiritual energy in the **manjilarri maya.ngarri** empowered **Wodoi** and **Jungun,** so that they magically left no footprints in sand. **Wibalma** detected them only after crossing a large river near the coast, and noticing that their **ambalaru** (tracks) were appearing in stone. With this visible **junjun** (evidence of their spirit power) to follow, he carefully tracked their **dulwan mamaa** (secret pathway) south until he encountered them with the **manjilarri maya.ngarri**. **Wibalma** agreed with **Wodoi** and **Jungun** that sharing knowledge as law was a good idea, and so the **Wunan** was born.

Wodoi and **Jungun** celebrated their partnership by the intermarriage of each other's daughters and sons. All the other nomadic **Gwion** adopted their example of publicly sharing their blood as law to unite all people. Thus, a far-reaching social revolution began here, but similar common laws are active across much of Australia. The **Wunan angga** (law table) remains as evidence of one source of law to share blood this way. **Wunan** moiety laws are preserved not only throughout the Kimberley but also across the plateau to the north-western coast, and north-east to **Arnhem Land,** directly east past **Balgo,** across the Tanami desert and out into Central Australia, across deserts to the south east and north again, passing along the Larapinta River through Central Australia and north to the Gulf of Carpentaria. Over time, particularly among desert groups, the duality of the **moiety** system has been subdivided into four or eight subsections. Even more complex relationships evolved through numerous local totemic connections, but the basic elements of the binary sub-division remain as social foundations in law.

Als er zu Hause ankam, fragte er seine Frau, ob jemand vorbeigekommen sei. **Nyamanbiligi** berichtete von **Wodoi** und **Jungun** und davon, dass sie ihnen verraten hatte, wo sie ihn finden konnten. **Wibalma** sah sogleich, dass einer der heiligen Gegenstände gestohlen war, und tobte vor Wut. Er nahm seinen **banad** (Hakenbumerang), spaltete damit einen **wungarun** (Eisenbaum), und erweckte so all die heiligen Gegenstände zum Leben, darunter auch den **maya.ngarri** namens **manjilarri,** den **Wodoi** und **Jungun** gerade davontrugen.

Wibalma nahm sofort die Verfolgung auf, doch anfangs fand er ihre Spuren nicht. Die große spirituelle Kraft, die dem **manjilarri maya.ngarri** innewohnte, gab **Wodoi** und **Jungun** Macht, sodass sie wie durch Zauberkraft keine Fußspuren im Sand hinterließen. **Wibalma** entdeckte sie erst, als sie schon einen großen Fluss nahe der Küste überquert hatten und er sah, wie dort ihre **ambalaru** (Fährte) im Stein Gestalt annahm. Nun wo er die sichtbaren **junjun,** den Beleg ihrer spirituellen Macht, vor Augen hatte, konnte er ihnen auf ihrem **dulwan mamaa** (geheimer Pfad) nach Süden folgen, bis er die Diebe schließlich eingeholt hatte. **Wibalma** ließ sich von **Wodoi** und **Jungun** überzeugen, dass es gut wäre, Wissen zu teilen und ein Gesetz daraus zu machen, und so kam das **Wunan** in die Welt.

Wodoi und **Jungun** besiegelten die Übereinkunft damit, dass sie ihre Kinder miteinander vermählten. Alle anderen umherwandernden **Gwion** folgten ihrem Beispiel, und die Verbindung des Blutes wurde zum Gesetz, das alles Volk einigen sollte. Dies führte zu einem tief greifenden sozialen Wandel. Ähnliche Gesetze sind in fast ganz Australien in Gebrauch. Der **Wunan angga** (Tisch, an dem man sich über das Gesetz verständigt hatte) bleibt als Beleg dafür, dass das Mischen des Blutes die Quelle des Gesetzes ist. Die **moiety**-Gesetze des **Wunan** haben sich nicht nur in der Kimberley-Region erhalten, sondern auch über das Plateau hinaus zur Nordwestküste und im Nordosten bis nach **Arnhem Land** ausgebreitet, ostwärts über **Balgo** hinaus durch die Tanami-Wüste und bis hinein nach Zentralaustralien, bis jenseits der Wüsten im Südwesten und im Norden, entlang des Larapinta River durch das Landesinnere und nördlich zum Golf von Carpentaria. Im Laufe der Zeit haben sich, vor allem bei den Wüstenbewohnern, die zwei ursprünglichen **moieties** in eine Vierer- oder Achtereinteilung aufgespalten. Noch komplexer wurden die Beziehungen durch zahlreiche lokale Totemverbindungen, doch das binäre Prinzip bleibt das soziale Fundament ihres Gesetzes.

À son arrivée, il demanda à sa femme si quelqu'un était venu ; **Nyamanbiligi** mentionna **Wodoi** et **Jungun** et comment elle leur avait dit où ils pouvaient le trouver. La colère de **Wibalma** éclata à la découverte du vol de l'objet sacré. Enragé, il utilisa son **banad** (boomerang à bec) pour fendre un **wungarun** (l'arbre de bois de fer), le plus dur qu'on puisse trouver, donnant ainsi vie à tous les objets sacrés, y compris le **maya.ngarri** portant le nom de **manjilarri** que **Wodoi** et **Jungun** étaient en train d'emporter.

Wibalma se mit immédiatement à leur poursuite, mais il eut du mal à trouver leurs traces. L'énergie spirituelle du **manjilarri maya.ngarri** donna à **Wodoi** et **Jungun** le pouvoir magique de ne pas laisser d'empreintes dans le sable. **Wibalma** trouva leur piste seulement après qu'ils eurent traversée une grosse rivière près de la côte et qu'il eut remarqué leurs **ambalaru** (leurs empreintes de pieds) visibles sur la pierre. Après avoir vu cette **junjun,** cette preuve tangible de leur pouvoir, il suivit prudemment le **dulwan mamaa** (chemin secret) vers le sud jusqu'à ce qu'il les rencontre avec le **manjilarri maya.ngarri**. **Wibalma** accepta les arguments de **Wodoi** et **Jungun** qui insistaient sur le fait que le partage de la connaissance comme principe de loi était une bonne idée ; et c'est ainsi que le **Wunan** est né.

Wodoi et **Jungun** célébrèrent leur association par le mariage croisé de leurs filles et de leurs garçons. Tous les autres nomades **Gwion** suivirent leur exemple et partagèrent publiquement leur sang, créant ainsi une loi unificatrice, une véritable révolution sociologique. Des lois semblables sont en vigueur à travers presque tout le continent. La **Wunan angga** (table de la Loi) demeure une preuve de l'origine de la Loi qui consiste à partager ainsi son sang. Le système des **moitiés** matrimoniales instauré par les lois du **Wunan** est toujours observé non seulement dans l'ensemble du Kimberley mais aussi au-delà de ce plateau, sur la côte nord-ouest ; vers le Nord-Est, à **Arnhem Land** ; plein est, au-delà de **Balgo,** par-delà tout le désert de Tanami ; et vers le sud-est, jusqu'en Australie centrale ; remontant de là vers le nord, par la rivière Larapinta, jusqu'au golfe de Carpentaria. Avec le temps, le système dualiste des **moitiés** s'est subdivisé en quatre ou huit sous-sections, particulièrement parmi les groupes du désert. Des associations encore plus complexes ont été élaborées avec les nombreux liens totémiques locaux, mais les éléments fondamentaux de la subdivision binaire demeurent la base sociale de la Loi.

Wibalma

a

b

c

Ngarinyin kinship connections were extended to embrace every living thing, so that individuals became categorised as being either **amalar** when connected to **Jungun,** or **ornad** if associated with **Wodoi.** Being of one or the other **skin** meant language also divided; for example, the large foraging crane or **Brolga** is known as both **burrunba** and **guranguli. Ngarinyin** language reflects this division of meaning and association by using separate names and **moiety** titles for virtually everything alive.

Wodoi and **Jungun** are enshrined in the cosmos as the pair of Large and Small Magellanic clouds near the Milky Way, forever side-by-side. The actions of **Wodoi** and **Jungun** in taking the **manjilarri maya.ngarri** culminated in formation of the great **Wunan angga** (law table) at **Dududu.ngarri.** Here, the nomadic **Gwion** tribes met to agree on the sharing law of blood and land. The first table – a symbol of sharing – was made of stringybark timber, laid out, round and flat, for all the **Gwion** clans to share **golani** from the centre or "guts" of the **angga.**

Today, the **manjilarri maya.ngarri** is a massive flat stone resting in soft earth and surrounded by a circle of twenty upright stones. Two of these tall stones are named for the **golani** (fruit) and the **nabun** (fire) used to cook it (b). The rest signify **Gwion** tribes represented by their leaders. Eighteen central stones, as named by **munnumburra,** identify original **Kamali** clans with the names of birds. Other arrangements of stones mark the positions of different language groups, including the **Ngarinyin's** close neighbours, the **Wororra** from the coastal region to the west (a) and **Bunaba,** from the south. These language groups are marked by rings of stones where leaders from the western "sunset" clans gathered; opposite are the eastern sunrise **mob** from inland. The northern coastal groups, including **Wila Wila,** are marked by pairs and clusters of stones positioned around the central table. A long straight row of **jallala** (stones), reaching to the table, marks where distant **Gwion** clan leaders approached from the east and north. Another disjointed line of stones represents the actions of a greedy **Jebera** Emu clan member from **Balgo,** who stole sacred **golani** from the table before running to the desert.

Die Verwandtschaftsbeziehungen der **Ngarinyin** umfassten alles, was lebte, und jeder wurde als **amalar** betrachtet, wenn er zu **Jungun-moiety** oder als **ornard,** wenn er zu **Wodoi-moiety** gehörte. Die zu einer **moiety,** einer **skin** (Haut) spiegelt sich auch in der Sprache wider; zum Beispiel ist der große Wander- oder Brolgakranich unter den Namen **burrunba** und **guranguli** bekannt. Die **Ngarinyin**-Sprache bringt diese Zweiteilung in Wortbedeutung und Zugehörigkeit dadurch zum Ausdruck, dass es im Grunde für alles Lebende verschiedene Namen und Bezeichnungen bei den **moieties** gibt.

Wodoi und **Jungun** haben ihren Platz am Firmament als Große und Kleine Magellansche Wolke in der Nähe der Milchstraße, Seite an Seite für alle Ewigkeit. Die Abenteuer von **Wodoi** und **Jungun,** als sie den **maya.ngarri manjilarri** raubten, gipfelten im Entstehen des großen steinernen **Wunan**-Tisches, **angga,** in **Dududu.ngarri.** Hier kamen die umherschweifenden nomadischen **Gwion**-Stämme zusammen und einigten sich auf gemeinsame Land- und Blutgesetze. Der Erste dieser Tische – ein Symbol des Teilens – bestand aus dem Holz eines Eukalyptusbaums; es war ein langer, flacher Tisch, in dessen Mitte die **golani** lagen, die alle **Gwion**-Clans miteinander aßen.

Heute ist der **manjilarri maya.ngarri** ein schwerer, flacher Stein, der im weichen Erdboden ruht und von einem Kreis von zwanzig aufrecht stehenden Steinen umgeben ist. Zwei dieser großen Steine sind nach den Früchten, **golani,** und nach der Feuerstelle zum Kochen, **nabun,** benannt (b); der Rest steht für **Gwion**-Stämme, vertreten von ihren Anführern. Achtzehn innere Steine, von den **munnumburra** mit Namen belegt, bezeichnen die ursprünglichen **Kamali**-Clans, die sämtlich nach Vögeln benannt sind. Weitere Steine markieren den Platz verschiedener Sprachgruppen, darunter die nächsten Nachbarn der **Ngarinyin,** die **Wororra** aus der Küstenregion im Westen (a) und die **Bunaba** aus dem Süden. Diese Sprachgruppen sind durch eigene Steinkreise an der Stelle bezeichnet, an der sich die Anführer der westlichen „Sonnenuntergangs"-Clans versammelten; auf der anderen Seiten stehen die Steine der „Sonnenaufgangs"-Clans aus dem Landesinneren. Die Stämme der nördlichen Küstenregion, darunter die **Wila Wila,** sind durch Paare und Gruppen von Steinen rund um den zentralen Tisch bezeichnet. Eine lange gerade Reihe von **jallala** (Steine) die bis an die Tafel heranreichen, bezeichnen die **Gwion**-Anführer, die aus fernen Gegenden im Osten und Norden kamen. Eine zweite unzusammenhängende Steinreihe steht für die Taten eines gierigen Angehörigen des **Jebera**-Emu-Clans aus **Balgo,** der heiliges **golani** vom Tisch stahl, bevor er in die Wüste flüchtete.

La notion de groupe ancestral s'est élargie chez les **Ngarinyin** pour englober toutes les choses vivantes ; ainsi les individus ont été classés soit comme **amalar,** quand ils sont en rapport avec **Jungun,** soit comme **ornard** s'ils le sont avec **Wodoi.** Être de l'une ou de l'autre de ces « peaux » implique également une distinction dans la langue ; par exemple, pour nommer la grosse grue fouisseuse (grue antigone) ou Brolga, on dit soit **burrunba** soit **guranguli.** La langue **Ngarinyin** reflète cette division de sens et d'association en utilisant des noms et des titres différents pour chaque **moitié** de tout ce qui est vivant.

On dit que **Wodoi** et **Jungun** sont enchâssés à jamais l'un à l'autre dans le cosmos, ce sont les Grand et Petit nuages de Magellan, près de la Voie lactée. L'action commune de **Wodoi** et **Jungun** dans la prise du **manjilarri maya.ngarri** a culminé dans la création de la **angga** (table de pierre) **Wunan** à **Dududu.ngarri.** Là, les tribus nomades **Gwion** se rencontrèrent pour inventer la loi du partage du sang et de la terre. La première table en bois, symbole du partage, était ronde pour que tous les clans **Gwion** puissent partager des **golani** placées au centre considéré comme les « entrailles » de la table **angga.**

Aujourd'hui, le **manjilarri maya.ngarri** est une énorme pierre plate reposant sur la terre et entourée par un cercle de vingt pierres levées. Deux de ces hautes pierres portent le nom du fruit **golani** et du feu, **nabun,** utilisé pour le cuire (b) ; les autres représentent les tribus **Gwion,** qui sont nommées d'après leurs chefs. Les dix-huit pierres appelées « centrales » par les **munnumburra** sont les images des clans **Kamali** originaux et portent des noms d'oiseaux. D'autres agencements de pierres indiquent les positions des différents groupes linguistiques, comprenant les voisins des **Ngarinyin,** les **Wororra** de la région côtière occidentale (a) et les **Bunaba** du sud. Ces groupes linguistiques sont indiqués par des cercles de pierres où se rassemblent les chefs des clans de l'ouest du « coucher du soleil » ; à l'opposé se trouvent les clans du groupe du « lever du soleil » des terres de l'intérieur. Les groupes des zones côtières du nord, auxquelles s'ajoutent les **Wila Wila,** sont indiqués deux par deux ou en groupes dans des empilements de pierres placés autour de la table centrale. Un long alignement de pierres **jallala,** aboutissant à la table, indique le chemin des chefs des clans **Gwion** éloignés arrivant de l'est et du nord. Un autre alignement discontinu de pierres symbolise les actes d'un membre cupide du clan **Jebera** (Émeu) de **Balgo,** qui vola un pain **golani** sacré de la table avant de s'enfuir dans le désert.

Kamali

a   b   c

The influence of the original events lives on in the stones, and in the **munnumburra** constantly "talking the land" of **Guru.ngongo dambun.** During our initial recording, **Banggal** approached the table and mimed the theft with agility energised by the character of the selfish **Jebera** man. **Nyawarra** animatedly narrated the drama while drawing in sand a diagram of the action. The passionate involvement of **Ngarinyin munnumburra** during law songs and the narration of history is convincing through its integrity and their passion to educate.

The dark **golani** (native plum) is a favourite food of emus; a pile of ripe fruit serves to lure emus to within easy range of a hunter hidden in tree branches. **Banggal** described the similarity in shape and colour of the cooked **golani** and the black pupil of his eye. This visual metaphor for what is part of everyone symbolises the common law of **Wunan.** To confirm their mutual allegiance by public demonstration, all the **Gwion** clan leaders gathered to share the **golani** growing in the vicinity of the stone table. **Golani** fruit was collected and beaten to a paste, and a fire made to bake it in two football-sized loaves. These loaves of **golani** were placed in the centre of the table for everyone to share as **mangarri** (public food).

As clan leaders queued for their shares, a long line led up to the table, now marked by numerous **jallala** (signal stones). After some leaders had taken their sacramental portion from one **golani** loaf, one of three representatives of the **Jebera** Emu clan was impatient and greedily took the law into his own hands. The **Jebera** leader did not respect the queue, and kept pretending they were calling him; taking steps forward, he asked **"niyan.gawa?"** – "who me?" During his mime, **Banggal** included this non-**Ngarinyin** term, apparently preserved from an old **Tanami** desert language. **Jebera** edged closer to the table until the hawk name **ganjal** was called, when he dashed forward to snatch the untouched loaf. During the uproar at this outrageous act, **Jebera** defiantly stamped his foot in protest, and where this action occurred is now marked by three stones embedded together in the earth (b) like the imprint of the three toes of the emu.

Der Einfluss dieser Ereignisse bleibt in den Steinen lebendig, und die **munnumburra** erhalten die Beziehung zum Land des **Guru.ngongo dambun** dadurch aufrecht, dass sie immer wieder die zum Land gehörigen Mythen erzählen und die Lieder singen (singen, „talking the land"). Als wir unsere ersten Aufnahmen machten, näherte sich **Banggal** dem Tisch und spielte die Abläufe des Diebstahls nach, und der Charakter des selbstsüchtigen **Jebera** beflügelte ihn regelrecht. **Nyawarra** erzählte mit Begeisterung die Geschichte dazu und zeichnete eine Skizze der Geschehnisse in den Sand. Die lebendige Art, mit der die **munnumburra** der **Ngarinyin** solche Lieder und Geschichten vortragen, überzeugt durch die Integrität der Erzähler und die eindeutig erzieherische Absicht.

Die dunkle einheimische **golani** (Pflaume) ist eine Lieblingsspeise der Emus; ein Häufchen reifer Früchte wird als Köder ausgelegt und lockt die Tiere in die Reichweite des Jägers, der sich auf einem Baum versteckt. **Banggal** sprach von der Ähnlichkeit in Form und Farbe, die eine gekochte **golani** mit der schwarzen Pupille eines Auges hat. Diese Bildmetapher für das, was allen gemeinsam ist, ist ein Symbol für das allumfassende Gesetz des **Wunan.** Alle Anführer der **Gwion** waren zusammengekommen, um sich gegenseitig der Treue zu versichern, und das äußere Zeichen dafür war das gemeinschaftliche Mahl, bei dem sie die **golani** aßen, die in der Gegend des steinernen Tisches wuchsen. Die **golani** wurden gesammelt und zu einer Paste zerdrückt, und dann entfachten sie ein Feuer und buken zwei fußballgroße Brote daraus. Diese **golani**-Brote kamen in die Mitte des Tisches, und jeder bekam etwas – **mangarri** (gemeinschaftliches Essen).

Die Clanführer standen in einer langen Reihe an, um ihren Anteil zu erhalten, so wie es heute durch die **jallala** (Steine) festgehalten ist. Nachdem eine Reihe von Anführern ihren rituellen Anteil an dem **golani**-Brot erhalten hatte, verlor plötzlich einer der drei Vertreter des **Jebera**-Clans, des Emu-Clans, die Geduld und nahm aus Gier die Sache selbst in die Hand. Der **Jebera**-Anführer missachtete die Wartenden und tat immer wieder so, als sei er schon aufgerufen; er trat vor uns, sagte: „niyan.gawa" – „wer, ich?" **Banggal** spielte es uns vor und sagte dabei diese Worte, die nicht zur **Ngarinyin**-Sprache gehören und sich offenbar aus einer alten Sprache der **Tanami**-Wüste erhalten haben. **Jebera** arbeitete sich immer weiter an den Tisch vor, bis der Name des Schwarzmilans, **ganjal,** aufgerufen wurde, da sprang er vor und raubte das noch unangeschnittene Brot. In dem Tumult, der daraufhin losbrach, stampfte **Jebera** zornig mit dem Fuß auf den Boden, und die Stelle, an der er das tat, ist heute mit drei Steinen markiert, die gemeinsam in der Erde stecken wie der Abdruck der drei Zehen eines Emus (b).

L'influence qu'ont eu ces premiers événements reste présente dans ces pierres et dans l'esprit des **munnumburra** qui constamment « parlent la terre » du **dambun** de **Guru.ngongo.** Lors de notre premier enregistrement, **Banggal** s'est approché de la table et a mimé le vol avec l'agilité qu'avait eu l'égoïste du clan **Jebera. Nyawarra** raconta avec animation le drame tout en faisant dans le sable un dessin de l'événement. La participation passionnée des **munnumburra Ngarinyin** pendant les chants de la Loi et le récit rigoureux de l'histoire est frappante par son désir d'éduquer le spectateur.

La **golani** (prune du bush de couleur foncée) est la nourriture favorite des émeus; un tas de fruits mûrs, qui se trouve à portée pour le chasseur caché dans les branches d'arbre, sert à piéger les émeus. **Banggal** a décrit la similarité de forme et de couleur entre la prune **golani** cuite et la pupille noire de son œil. Cette métaphore visuelle d'une chose que tout le monde possède symbolise la Loi commune du **Wunan.** Pour confirmer leur fidélité mutuelle lors d'une manifestation publique, tous les chefs des clans **Gwion** se rassemblent pour partager les **golani** poussant aux abords de la table de pierre. Les fruits **golani** sont ramassés puis réduits en pâte; un feu est agencé pour les cuire entre deux feuilles, comme un pain ou un gâteau de la taille d'un ballon de football. Des tranches de **golani** sont placées au centre de la table pour un échange de **mangarri** (nourriture commune) pour tous.

Autrefois, les chefs des clans ont fait la queue pour obtenir leur part à la table. Cette longue ligne est aujourd'hui indiquée par de nombreuses **jallala** (pierres). Après que certains chefs aient pris leur portion sacrée de **golani,** un des trois représentants du clan Émeu, **Jebera,** impatient, prit cupidement ce symbole de la Loi entre ses mains. Le chef **Jebera** ne respecta pas l'ordre et fit comme si on l'appelait et tout en s'avançant il disait « niyan.gawa? » – « Qui, moi ? ». Pendant qu'il mimait cela, **Banggal** prononça ce terme non-**Ngarinyin,** vraisemblablement hérité d'une ancienne langue du désert de **Tanami. Jebera** força son chemin encore plus près de la table et, au moment où on appela le nom du faucon **ganjal,** il se précipita soudain pour s'emparer de la portion restante. Pendant le tumulte causé par cet acte scandaleux, **Jebera** tapait du pied d'un air de défi en signe d'opposition, et l'emplacement où cet événement eut lieu est aujourd'hui indiqué par trois pierres fichées en terre (b), comme le serait une empreinte de trois doigts de pattes d'émeu.

manjilarri

d

e

f

Declaring nothing would change his mind, **Jebera** fled eastwards accompanied by two other Emu clan members. While clutching the **golani** with his short arms, he dropped some, so forming a mountain that preserves the name **Jalbanuma.** As they fled eastward past the mountain, a gap now known as **Dududu.ngarri** was formed (e). **"Dududu"** mimics the sound of stamping feet, and **"ngarri"** is a suffix for "the people and the place belonging to". The name identifies the location where the **Wunan** began.

The brazen theft tested the newly-formed authority of the **Gwion** lawmakers. The **Kamali** council of leaders unanimously decided to execute the intransigents, and they ordered the fittest men to chase the **Jebera** to spear them to death. But nobody could catch up with the elusive lawbreakers who, once out of range, separated, and many pursuers returned exhausted. The **Gwion** leaders then selected two men of the **Wowarra** (Bronzewing Pigeon) clan to punish the lawbreakers. Where these two men were sitting and crafting **jimbila** stone spear points, is represented by two **jallala** (signal stones) inserted in a cracked boulder overlooking the table. With freshly-made spears ready, they followed **Jebera** to the fossillised reef of the Napier Range. Here at **Barilamma,** where he had rested in a high shelter in the limestone cliffs, the **Jebera** is immortalised in a large icon painted in partial relief within the stone formation. Continually repainted across the generations, **Jebera** has become an emu hoarding **golani.**

From here, **Jebera** decided not to take the predictable route due east to his homeland; instead, he turned north in a long winding arc to avoid his pursuers. But the fast **Wowarra** men following his tracks hunted down the lawbreaker when he left wet footprints after crossing a creek near **Gananinjal,** south of **Warmun. Jebera** was executed with a single spear thrust deep into the small of the back. The **Wowarra** collected the bloodied spear and returned to the table to present this evidence to the lawmakers. So the **Wunan** was consolidated through the installation of capital punishment by agreement of the **Kamali** lawmakers at **Dududu.ngarri.** The influence of the original sacred object made by **Wibalma,** that was taken and given to the people by **Wodoi** and **Jungun,** now became enshrined as law. The meaning of the **maya.ngarri manjilarri** – "the law will always catch up with you" – lives on in the **Wunan.** The shape of **Jebera,** bent over as the spear hits his spine, is signified by the dark cloud known as the Coalsack and located at the base of the Southern Cross.

Nichts, erklärte **Jebera,** könne ihn umstimmen, und er floh, begleitet von zwei weiteren Mitgliedern des Emu-Clans, in Richtung Osten. Er umklammerte das Brot mit seinen kurzen Armen und ließ dabei einige Krümel fallen, und daraus entstand ein Berg, der noch immer den Namen **Jalbanuma** trägt. Sie flohen weiter gen Osten, und jenseits des Berges entstand eine Schlucht, die heute unter dem Namen **Dududu.ngarri** bekannt ist (e). Das „Dududu" ahmt den Klang der aufstampfenden Füße nach, die Silbe „ngarri" bedeutet „die Leute und das Land, das ihnen gehört". Der Name bezeichnet die Stelle, an der das **Wunan** seinen Ursprung hatte.

Der unverfrorene Diebstahl war eine Probe für die neue Autorität der **Gwion**-Gesetzgeber. Der **Kamali,** der Rat der Stammesältesten, beschloss einstimmig den Tod der Gesetzesbrecher, und die kräftigsten Männer erhielten den Auftrag, den **Jebera** nachzusetzen und sie mit Speeren zu töten. Doch keiner konnte die Übeltäter einholen, die getrennter Wege gingen, als sie erst einmal außer Sichtweite waren, und viele Verfolger kehrten erschöpft zurück. Als Nächstes bestimmten die **Gwion** zwei Männer aus dem **Wowarra**-Clan, dem Clan der Bronzeflügel-Taube, dazu, die Gesetzesbrecher zu bestrafen. Die Stelle, an der diese beiden saßen und ihre **jimbila,** die steinernen Speerspitzen, vorbereiteten, ist ebenfalls durch zwei **jallala** markiert, die in einen Felsspalt oberhalb des Tisches gesteckt sind. Die frischen Speere bereit, folgten sie **Jebera** zu dem versteinerten Riff des Napier Range. Hier in **Barilamma,** wo er in einem Unterschlupf hoch oben in den Kalksteinfelsen geruht hatte, ist **Jebera** in einem großen Bild festgehalten, das, teils im Relief, in den Stein hineingemalt ist. Das Bild, das über die Generationen immer wieder nachgemalt wurde, zeigt **Jebera** heute als einen Emu, der die **golani** hortet.

Jebera beschloss, von hier nicht die nahe liegende Route geradewegs nach Osten zurück in sein Stammesland zu nehmen; stattdessen wandte er sich nordwärts, um in einem großen, geschlängelten Bogen seinen Verfolgern zu entkommen. Aber die flinken **Wowarra** kamen dem Übeltäter auf die Spur, und nahe **Gananinjal,** südlich von **Warmun,** fanden sie feuchte Fußabdrücke, wo er eben einen Bach durchquert hatte. Mit einem einzigen Speerwurf in den Rücken wurde **Jebera** hingerichtet. Die **Wowarra** holten den blutigen Speer und kehrten an die Tafel zurück, wo sie den Gesetzesmachern die Spitze als Beweis der Vollstreckung übergaben. So wurde dem **Wunan** durch die Einführung der Todesstrafe Macht verliehen, durch gemeinschaftlichen Beschluss der **Kamali**-Gesetzgeber von **Dududu.ngarri.** Der Einfluss jenes heiligen Gegenstandes, den **Wibalma** geschaffen und **Wodoi** und **Jungun** geraubt und dem Volk übergeben hatten, wurde nun Gesetz. Die Bedeutung des **maya.ngarri manjilarri** – „keiner entgeht seiner gerechten Strafe" – besteht im **Wunan** fort. Die Umrisse des **Jebera,** gekrümmt mit dem Speer im Rücken, zeigen sich am Sternenhimmel in Gestalt des „Coalsack", des dunklen Schattens unter dem Kreuz des Südens.

Déclarant que rien ne le ferait changer d'avis, **Jebera** s'enfuit vers l'est accompagné de deux autres représentants du clan Émeu. Tout en serrant le **golani** dans ses bras trop courts, il en perdit un peu, ce qui forma une montagne portant le nom de **Jalbanuma.** Et comme ils s'enfuyaient toujours plus à l'est au-delà de cette montagne, il se dessina un ravin que l'on appelle aujourd'hui **Dududu.ngarri** (e). « Dududu » évoque le son de battements de pieds et « ngarri » est un suffixe signifiant « peuple » et « lieu appartenant à ». Le nom indique le lieu d'origine des **Wunan.**

L'impudent voleur mit à l'épreuve l'autorité nouvelle des créateurs des lois **Gwion.** Le conseil **Kamali** composé des chefs décida unanimement d'exécuter ceux qui ne voulaient pas se plier aux lois et ordonna aux meilleurs hommes de poursuivre **Jebera** et ses deux amis pour les tuer à coups de lance. Mais personne ne réussit à rattraper ces fugitifs hors la loi qui, une fois hors d'atteinte, se séparèrent, et bien des poursuivants revinrent exténués. Les chefs **Gwion** choisirent alors deux hommes du clan **Wowarra** (pigeon brun) pour punir les hors la loi. L'endroit où ces deux hommes s'assirent et fabriquèrent les pointes de lance en pierre **jimbila** est représenté par deux pierres **jallala** insérées dans un rocher fendu surplombant la table. Avec les lances qu'ils venaient de confectionner, ils suivirent **Jebera** jusqu'au récif fossilisé du Napier Range. À **Barilamma,** là où il s'est reposé dans un abri en hauteur dans les escarpements de calcaire, **Jebera** est immortalisé par une image partiellement en relief peinte à l'intérieur de la formation rocheuse. Repeint génération après génération, **Jebera** est devenu un émeu amassant des **golani.**

De là, **Jebera** décida de ne pas prendre un chemin évident pour ses poursuivants, c'est-à-dire allant vers l'est, sa région d'origine ; à la place, il tourna vers le nord en faisant un long arc de cercle pour éviter ses poursuivants. Mais les rapides hommes **Wowarra,** suivant ses traces, le repérèrent à ses empreintes humides après le passage d'une crique près de **Gananinjal,** au sud de **Warmun.** C'est là que **Jebera** fut tué par un seul coup d'une lance enfoncée profondément dans le creux de ses reins. Les **Wowarra** prirent la lance en pierre **(jimbila)** ensanglantée et retournèrent à la table pour présenter cette preuve aux créateurs des lois. Le **Wunan** fut ainsi renforcé par l'adoption de la peine capitale par un accord entre les créateurs des lois **Kamali** à **Dududu.ngarri.** L'influence du premier objet sacré fait par **Wibalma,** pris puis donné aux hommes par **Wodoi** et **Jungun** fut alors conservée pieusement comme Loi. Le sens du **maya.ngarri manjilarri** – « la Loi vous rattrapera toujours » – se perpétue dans le **Wunan.** La forme cosmologique de **Jebera,** penché au moment où la lance touche sa colonne vertébrale, est représentée par un nuage sombre connu sous le nom de « sac à charbon », qui se situe à la base de la Croix du Sud.

manjilarri

Whenever this **Wunan** was created
then everybody had their own symbols
own blocks for land
representing different symbols
like ah... my hibiscus... *jirad*
is my **dambun** name **Brrejirad**
So every man had his own place and symbols
and symbol is the one... is different tribes
Only those ones who got symbols
can tell his own story
because he the manager
he the servant of that place
because he look after the whole area

Banggal

Damals als das **Wunan** geschaffen wurde
hatten alle ihre eigenen Symbole
für jedes Stück Land
ein anderes Symbol
wie ... mein Hibiskus hier ... *jirad*
mein **dambun** heißt **Brrejirad**
Alle hatten ihre eigenen Orte und Symbole
jedes Symbol ... steht für verschiedene Stämme
Nur wer ein Symbol hat
kann seine Geschichte erzählen
denn er ist der Verwalter
der Diener dieses Ortes
denn er kümmert sich um die ganze Gegend

Banggal

Au moment où ce **Wunan** a été créé
alors tout le monde avait son propre symbole
sa propre parcelle de terre
avec chacune un symbole
comme moi... moi c'est l'hibiscus... *jirad*
mon **dambun,** c'est **Brrejirad**
Donc chaque homme avait sa propre terre
et son propre symbole
et un symbole à lui... différent des autres tribus
Chacun a un symbole
et il peut dire seulement sa propre histoire
parce qu'il est le gardien, le serviteur du lieu
parce qu'il est responsable de tout un endroit

Banggal

That's why we say this land is like a pattern
see those marks there they are like that
no place not clear... they all covered in the land
wunbanburan... old time... fixed

That's how the **Wunan** works under tribal people
Wodoi people and **Jungun** people
any little thing... that always be shared out
with the people are in the **Wunan**
it run to **Wodoi** people
and to the **Jungun** people

Nyawarra

Deshalb sagen wir das Land ist wie ein Muster
hier ist ein Zeichen und da
alles eindeutig ... überall im Land sind Zeichen
wunbanburan ... unveränderlich
... seit uralter Zeit

So ist das alle stehen unter dem Gesetz des **Wunan**
die **Wodoi** und die **Jungun**
bis in die kleinste Kleinigkeit
... alles ist eingeteilt
für alle die unter dem **Wunan** stehen
und das gilt für die **Wodoi**
und auch für die **Jungun**

Nyawarra

C'est pour ça qu'on dit que ce pays
c'est comme un patchwork
tu vois ces marques là elles sont toutes égales
pas d'endroit qui soit sans nom ...
tous le pays est couvert
wunbanburan ... depuis longtemps ... immuable

C'est comme ça que le **Wunan** marche
avec les tribus, les **Wodoi** et les **Jungun**
chaque petite chose était toujours partagée
avec les gens qui sont dans le **Wunan**
ça va des **Wodoi**
jusqu'aux **Jungun**

Nyawarra

That one there... the way his head facing
Everyone must all head facing east
because they people who see the sunrise first
Before our time... always facing east

This place is **bunja**... this cave named **bunja**
We have ceremony
when we bring them down to our platform
and they're all painted up
anointed with kangaroo fat
Put in wallet... paperbark wallet

Big dance for bringing them back... big dance
to the families where they all cry... everybody
We do it just before the sun get behind the world
While the sun is up...
that means darkness is not hiding anymore
It's back to the family again

When that ceremony finished
he lives there with his community
maybe twelve months
then we bring them back here
We open the wallet all the paperbark wallet
they no longer locked up...
they free to end up where they belong

Banggal

Dieser hier... die Art wie sein Kopf liegt
Der Kopf muss immer nach Osten blicken
das sind die Ersten die den Sonnenaufgang sehen
Früher als wir... immer nach Osten blickten

Das ist eine **bunja**... solche Höhlen heißen **bunja**
Wir haben eine Zeremonie
da holen wir sie zu uns herunter
und dann werden sie angemalt
und mit Kängurufett eingerieben
Dann kommen sie in eine Hülle Papierbaumrinde

Wenn wir sie zurückholen...
gibt es einen großen Tanz
zurück zu den Familien wo alle weinen... jeder
Wir machen das kurz bevor die Sonne
hinter der Welt verschwindet
Solange die Sonne am Himmel steht...
wenn die Dunkelheit nichts mehr verbirgt
Dann geht es zurück zur Familie

Wenn die Zeremonie vorbei ist
dann bleibt er bei seinen Leuten
zwölf Monate vielleicht
dann bringen wir ihn hierher zurück
Wir öffnen die Hülle die Hülle aus Rinde
und dann ist sie nicht mehr verschlossen...
sie sind frei und können da enden
wohin sie gehören

Banggal

Celui-là... la manière dont sa tête fait face
Tout le monde doit avoir la tête tournée vers l'est
parce que c'est eux, qui voient le soleil en premier
Avant notre époque... toujours tournés vers l'est

Là c'est une **bunja**... cette grotte est appelée **bunja**
On a une cérémonie
quand on les descend de la plate-forme
et que tous les os sont peints
huilés avec de la graisse de kangourou
On les met dans une valise... en paperbark

Il y a une grande danse quand on les ramène...
une grande danse pour les familles...
où tout le monde pleure
On le fait juste avant que le soleil
passe derrière le monde
Tant que le soleil est haut... ça veut dire
que la pénombre ne cache pas encore tout
C'est de nouveau dans la famille

Quand cette cérémonie est finie
il vit là avec sa communauté
pour douze mois peut-être puis on le ramène ici
On ouvre la valise, toute la valise en paperbark
son esprit n'est plus enfermé...
il peut retourner au lieu d'où il vient

Banggal

Yeah put 'em back this bone
now they get 'em they take 'em wash 'em
paint 'em gotta red ochre
Ngarjno

Kangaroo fat
Banggal

And come **yarrad**... bone everything
and put 'em on **gagul**... red paint
and I take 'em... put 'em in the sun
make 'em dried up

Where they get 'em paperbark now
they get 'em nice one they cut 'em paperbark
look after them properly
and big one for all the bone
everything... head
and all that big one... he's a big one
Ngarjno

Genau die Knochen kommen zurück
sie holen sie und waschen sie
sie bemalen sie mit rotem Ocker
Ngarjno

Kängurufett
Banggal

Und dann kommen die **yarrad**... alles Knochen
und sie bemalen sie mit **gagul**... roter Farbe
und dann nehme ich sie... lege sie in die Sonne
bis sie ausgetrocknet sind

Dann kommt die Rinde vom Papierrindenbaum
sie suchen einen schönen aus und schälen sie ab
da werden sie eingewickelt wie es sich gehört
ein großes Stück Rinde für sämtliche Knochen
alles... der Kopf
und der große hier... das ist ein großer
Ngarjno

Oui, on les remet chez eux ces os
maintenant on peut les prendre, les laver
les peindre avec de l'ocre rouge
Ngarjno

Graisse de kangourou
Banggal

Alors arrive **yarrad**... tous les os
on les recouvre de **gagul**... de peinture rouge
et on le prend... on les met au soleil
pour bien les faire sécher

Après on va chercher du paperbark pour les os
on en prend de jolis morceaux, on coupe l'écorce
on fait ça bien proprement
on prend une plus grande pour tous les os
pour tout... la tête une grande
Ngarjno

These the people that are looking after that
Jenagi painting... that is their painting
this **mob** here... they cared for it

We honourable people... we were honoured
We die away...
another honourable man take over
That is the system this **Wunan** here

they turn around
and face the place where they went from
they guiding it from there...
that the history of it

They only travellers
they put their figures all over the place
their name called **Jenagi Jenagi**
Banggal

Das sind die Leute, die das hier versorgen
die **Jenagi** haben das gemalt … das ist von denen
den Leuten hier … die haben dafür gesorgt

Wir sind achtbare Leute … werden geehrt
Und wenn wir sterben …
dann übernimmt ein anderer geachteter Mann
So ist das geordnet … so ist das **Wunan**

sie drehen sich um
und schauen dahin wo sie herkommen
sie führen uns von dort …
das ist die Geschichte

Sie sind durchs Land gereist
und haben überall ihre Bilder gemalt
Jenagi Jenagi hießen sie
Banggal

Ce sont les gens qui s'occupent de ça
cette peinture **Jenagi** … c'est leur peinture
ceux-là … ils s'en sont occupé

Nous sommes des hommes d'honneur... et honorés
Quand on vieillit qu'on se meurt
un autre homme honorable prend la suite
C'est comme ça le **Wunan**

ils se retournent
et regardent vers l'endroit d'où ils sont venus
ils se guident depuis là-bas…
c'est ça l'histoire

C'est juste des voyageurs
ils ont laissé leurs peintures un peu partout
leur nom est **Jenagi Jenagi**
Banggal

a b c

It takes us time to imagine what the wide horizon of the land meant to the first nomadic people spread out across north-western Australia. **Munnumburra** say that some laws move through the **Wunan** in a long arc south, before connecting with western **Arnhem Land**. **Munnumburra** believe this was because people at that time in the near north were separated from the Kimberley by saltwater seas spreading down towards the centre of the continent at the time the laws originated. It was probably many years after the initial settlement of Australia, with increasing population, that competition for resources and armed conflict over land had to be controlled.

When all the wandering **Gwion** gathered to form the **Wunan** council around the stone table, they established the first permanent regional boundaries for each family group or clan. This secured the status of each clan, at that time known only by the names of birds that moved nomadically as they did. As everyone now inherited rights to land and permanent water, one of the basic causes of conflict was removed. The clan estates are called **dambun**; half are associated with **Wodoi** and half with **Jungun**, thus forming two interrelated **skin** groups in a patchwork of shared territory. The **moiety** system operates to regulate marriage across the two **skins**, and the network of **dambun** effectively creates two integrated groups sharing the same landscape and environment (see basic list opposite).

As the original wandering **Gwion** identity shifted from nomadism to seasonal movement, and to continuous custodianship of **dambun** (homelands), the powerful doctrine of **wunbanburan** (unchanging law), resulted in families occupying the same **dambun** throughout generations of **Gwion** art up to the present. One deeply stained and faint red image of over thirty realms, outlined as shapes with some strong common lines, appears to be an ancient diagram or map of more than thirty **dambun** estates connected to the lines of major rivers (f). Once people spent most of their lives within these permanent **dambun**, geographical orientation became more significant as their country grew in meaning. We can imagine how somebody would be looking in the direction of home. Finding a suitably smooth surface under an overhang of sandstone, they marked, in proper alignment on the rock wall, their figure wearing a wig symbolic of their **dambun** and facing where they came from.

Wir brauchen eine Weile, bis wir uns vorstellen können, was der unendliche Horizont für die ersten nomadisierenden Völker bedeutete, als sie sich über den Nordwesten Australiens ausbreiteten. Die **munnumburra** sagen, dass manche Gesetze des **Wunan** sich in einem lang gestreckten Bogen südwärts ausdehnen und dann im Westen die Verbindung zum **Arnhem Land** herstellen, denn die unmittelbar benachbarten Stämme im Norden waren von der Kimberley-Region durch einen Meeresarm getrennt, der sich in der Entstehungszeit der Gesetze von der Küste landeinwärts bis zur Mitte des Kontinents erstreckte. Wahrscheinlich waren nach der ersten Besiedlung Australiens viele Jahre vergangen, ehe die Zunahme der Bevölkerung es notwendig machte, den Wettbewerb um die Nahrungsvorräte und die kriegerischen Auseinandersetzungen um Landbesitz gesetzlich zu regeln.

Als die umherschweifenden **Gwion** zusammenkamen, um am steinernen Tisch ihren **Wunan**-Rat abzuhalten, legten sie die ersten permanenten Grenzen fest, die jeder Familiengruppe, jedem Clan, ein fest umrissenes Gebiet zuwies. Das sicherte die Rechte jedes Clans, die bis dahin nur nach Vögeln benannt gewesen waren, die ebenso wenig sesshaft waren wie sie selbst. Da das Anrecht auf ein bestimmtes Gebiet und die permanenten Wasserquellen damit erblich wurden, fiel einer der Hauptgründe für Streitigkeiten untereinander weg. Die den einzelnen Clans zugewiesenen Landesteile heißen **dambun**; sie gehören entweder zur **Wodoi**- oder zur **Jungun-moiety**, sodass sie zwei vielfach miteinander verflochtene **skins** in einen Flickenteppich aus gemeinschaftlichem Landbesitz bilden. Das **moiety**-System regelt Heiraten zwischen den beiden **skins**, und das **dambun**-Netzwerk (siehe Karte gegenüber) schafft letzten Endes zwei integrierte Gruppen, die sich dieselbe Landschaft und dieselbe Umwelt teilen.

Als sich die Lebensform der **Gwion** vom reinen Nomadentum zu jahreszeitlich bedingten Wanderzügen und der permanenten Bewirtschaftung des **dambun** (Stammesland) wandelte, führte das mächtige Prinzip des **wunbanburan** (unveränderliches Gesetz) dazu, dass eine Familie über Generationen hinweg dasselbe **dambun** bewohnte, sodass sich dort **Gwion**-Malereien aus jenen ersten Tagen bis in die heutige Zeit erhalten haben. Ein mit dunklen Flecken übersätes und stark verwittertes Felsbild umreißt mit kräftigen verbindenden Linien über dreißig Landstriche, offenbar eine uralte Landkarte oder Skizze, die über 30 **dambun** mitsamt den verbindenden Flussläufen zeigt (f). Als die Stämme erst einmal den Großteil ihrer Zeit in den festen **dambun**-Gebieten verbrachten, wuchs der Stellenwert von Grund und Boden. Wir können uns vorstellen, wie sich allmählich das Gefühl eines Zuhauses entwickelte. Die Menschen suchten sich einen möglichst glatten Grund unter einem überhängenden Sandstein und malten säuberlich an die Felswand ihre Figuren, deren Perücken symbolisch für ihr **dambun** standen und die ihren Blick in die Richtung gewandt hatten, aus der ihre Maler gekommen waren.

Il est difficile d'imaginer d'emblée ce que ce vaste horizon de terre qui s'étend d'un bout à l'autre du Nord-Ouest de l'Australie pouvait signifier pour les premiers peuples nomades. Les **munnumburra** disent que certaines lois se sont déplacées à travers les **Wunan** sur un long arc de cercle au sud avant de se relier à **Arnhem Land** de l'ouest; à l'époque où les lois furent créées, les gens qui vivaient au nord étaient séparés du Kimberley par des mers qui s'étendaient jusqu'au centre de l'Australie. Cela s'est probablement passé bien des années après le peuplement initial de l'Australie; à cause de l'accroissement de la population, la rivalité pour les ressources naturelles et les conflits armés pour les territoires nécessitaient une réglementation.

Les nomades **Gwion** se rassemblèrent donc pour créer le conseil **Wunan** autour de la table de pierre et établirent les premières frontières régionales pour chaque groupe familial ou clan. Cela fixa le statut de chacun des clans connus à cette époque seulement sous des noms d'oiseaux nomades comme eux. Une des causes fondamentales de conflit fut ainsi écartée, puisque désormais tout le monde avait des droits héréditaires, tant sur la terre que sur les points d'eau. Les domaines claniques sont appelés **dambun**; la moitié de ces territoires est associée à **Wodoi** et l'autre à **Jungun**, formant ainsi deux groupes de skin (« peaux ») aux relations imbriquées dans un patchwork de territoires partagés. Le système des **moitiés** fonctionne pour réguler les mariages entre les deux « peaux » et le réseau de **dambun** crée deux groupes bien intégrés qui se partagent la même région (voir carte ci-contre).

À mesure que la société **Gwion** passait du nomadisme aux migrations saisonnières et à la continuité dans la garde des terres **dambun**, la puissante doctrine de **wunbanburan** (la loi définitive) aboutit à ce que des familles occupent le même **dambun** de génération en génération, de l'époque de l'art **Gwion** jusqu'à aujourd'hui. Une image effacée de couleur rouge, très tachée et divisée en plus de trente formes entourées par quelques lignes aux lignes communes plus accentuées, semble être un diagramme ou une carte de plus de trente territoires **dambun** et de leur relation avec des rivières importantes (f). Une fois que les gens se mirent à passer la majorité de leur vie dans ces **dambun** permanents, l'orientation devint plus importante avec la notion d'appartenir à une terre. Nous pouvons imaginer comment les individus pouvaient regarder leur pays. Trouvant une surface adéquate et lisse dans un abri sous roche, ils ont peint sur la paroi des personnages portant des coiffes symboliques de leurs **dambun** et faisant face à la direction de leurs territoires.

dambun

d

e

f

WODOI DAMBUN

BRREMIDJI YAWALAW.NGARRI BRREWARRGU DAWUNJI.NGONGO

LANGARRIGONA GUNJA.NGONGO GALARU.NGARRI AWUL.NGAARRI

LARLAN.NGARRI JIBILI.NGARRRI BRREJALNGA BANGUNDU MAN.GARADIGONA AGULA.NGONGO

WAJAWAJ.NGARRI MINIRR.NGARRI BARARU.NGARRI YAWARL.NGONGO UMBORRAYIGONA

GURU.NGONGO LANDAD.NGARRI BRREGURAL BRREJIRAD WARRGALI.NGONGO DILA.NGARRI

WUNBA.NGUWA GUNJA.NGONGO WODOI.NGARRI GARNJI.NGARRI MANYAR.NGARRI

DIWA MORRONGO MORRONGO WAYAN.NGARRI WAJIN.NGO GURUGONA

GALERU.NGARRI MANJILWA JANUN.NGARRI BIYARR.NGONGO MANANGURR.NGARRI

ANAWURR.NGARRI NGARA.NGARRI NGORUNGORU BALALA.NGARRI MARNDA.NGARRI

BRREMARARRA GUPUNGARRI GANBU.NGARRI GUMLORURU NGUNG GANJAL.NGARRI

WAMARN WINARRAGUDA BRRELANDARR GAMALUWA GALIYAMBA BANGURR DUNA

JUNGUN DAMBUN

dambun

JENAGI

Artists and Messengers
Jenagi *people who started this law...*
long time belong to Ngarinyin country   Ngarjno

Künstler und Botschafter
Jenagi *die haben das Gesetz gemacht...*
das uralte Gesetz der Ngarinyin   Ngarjno

Artistes et Messagers
Jenagi *ceux qui ont crée la Loi...*
depuis bien longtemps celle du pays Ngarinyin   Ngarjno

*A man belonging to this country with different sacred **gi***
he holds it... but this is shared by everyone
*sacred objects travel in all our various **dambun***
*One big group goes down this way... the **Wunan** mob*
We all travel sacred objects...
*coming with the East **mob** they brought it down here*
*climbing up... the Southern **mob** go up*
***wulari**... sacred objects are coming down the South-east*
Those in their country hold every object in their hand
This law indeed they make... they do it here
*everyone in camp holding sacred **gi** belonging to people*
*holding everything in **Bararru.ngarri** country*

Banggal

*Ein Mann der zu diesem Land gehört, der hat verschiedene **gi***
er hat sie... aber das wird mit jedem geteilt
*heilige Gegenstände gehen durch verschiedene **dambun***
*eine große Gruppe geht diesen Weg... die **Wunan**-Leute*
wir reisen alle mit heiligen Gegenständen
Leute aus dem Osten brachten es herunter
***wulari**... heilige Objekte kommen aus dem Südosten*
Die in ihrem Land halten jedes Objekt in ihren Händen
Das Gesetz was sie gemacht haben... das haben sie hier gemacht
*jeder hier der das geheiligte **gi** hat*
*gehört zum Land **Bararru.ngarri***

Banggal

*Un homme de ce pays, avec son propre **gi** sacré*
il le possède... mais c'est partagé par tout le monde
*les **maya.ngarri** voyagent dans tous nos **dambun***
*Un groupe important descend par là... ceux du **Wunan***
On voyage tous avec nos objets sacrés...
en venant avec ceux de l'est ils descendent ici
ils grimpent... ceux du sud montent
***wulari**... les objets sacrés descendent depuis le sud-est*
Ceux qui sont dans leur pays
tiennent tous les objets dans leur main
Cette loi en fait, ils la font... ils la créent ici
*tout le monde dans le camp possède son **gi** sacré,*
qui appartient à tout le monde
*tout se tient dans le pays **Bararru.ngarri***

Banggal

Andu   jinda dambun ngarri   gi   ama
duna   biji wilingindi dambun nadaga bunda yora
gulerr   biya Wunan gyra   dambun   di ngarrnulin
wulari biyerri Warin.ngarri   walu yarrig burwan balu
gullal   walu   baj bidinga   arawarri ngarri
walu bi.alu   wulari bi enya arawadi
dambun di duna   biji warrwun
ganda yali juman wudmanga
ngarilla mindi gi biji marun ngarri
bunda duna Barurrangarri   dambun

Banggal

178

mangiwarunga...
that is the first time to get together
the starting off point... the point of starting
*that tells you to begin sharing... **maya.ngarri***
to put a point onto the sacred object and
the whole team of everybody that gather round
Banggal

*All got their **dambun** name written*
*there in that **maya.ngarri***
***Gwion** all been put their name in that area*
This law been given to us... it stays that way
we can't change to another way of thinking
the way it was written... the law was written
Everything was written in this painting thing here
thats how it was written
and it stays that way... we can't change it
Nyawarra

*Sometimes somebody might be from **wunindid***
coming into from that area
and they want to
*put something through the **Wunan***
*well that's the **wunindid** pathway*
*we call it **wunindid***
when he bring it into the line
*and he put it in that **dulwan** now*
*that **Wunan** he follow it now*
Nyawarra

*I still got to see that one **maya.ngarri***
what is in Mt Barnet now and I'll be right
Ngarjno

Might be this rain time now we'll have a look
you can see it... we'll go and visit it
Too many main road coming in
tourists and all that
they might find it and take em
Nyawarra

Ohh I'm careful about that thing
we ought to move it now!
Now bushfire I'm thinking
he not in a cave place
Ngarjno

mangiwarunga...
da kommt man zum ersten Mal zusammen
da fängt alles an... von da geht es aus
*das zeigt einem das Teilen... **maya.ngarri***
da sieht man den heiligen Gegenstand
überhaupt alle die da zusammenkommen
Banggal

*Die Namen aller **dambun** stehen da geschrieben*
*auf dem **maya.ngarri***
*Die **Gwion** haben ihre Namen hier aufgeschrieben*
Das ist unser Gesetz... es bleibt wie es war
wir können nicht plötzlich anders denken
so wie es geschrieben steht... so ist das Gesetz
Und geschrieben steht es alles hier auf dem Bild
so steht es geschrieben
und es bleibt wie es ist... unveränderbar
Nyawarra

*Manchmal kommt einer vielleicht aus dem **wunindid***
der kommt von da
und will etwas weitergeben
*auf den Weg durch das **Wunan***
*ja das ist das **wunindid***
***wunindid** nennen wir das*
er bringt es auf den Weg
*er bringt es auf den **dulwan**, den Pfad*
*den Weg durch das **Wunan***
Nyawarra

*Das eine **maya.ngarri** da, am Mount Barnet*
muss ich noch sehen, dann habe ich alle beisammen
Ngarjno

Wir können es uns ja in der Regenzeit ansehen...
dann weißt du Bescheid... wir sehen es uns an
Da sind zu viele Straßen
Touristen und so weiter
irgendwann finden die das und nehmen es mit
Nyawarra

Das macht mir wirklich Sorgen
wir sollten es lieber anderswohin bringen!
Mir machen die Buschfeuer Sorgen
es ist schließlich nicht in einer Höhle
Ngarjno

mangiwarunga...
c'est le premier moment du rassemblement
le point de départ... le moment
*qui montre le partage... **maya.ngarri***
qu'il faut choisir un lieu pour l'objet sacré
et pour tout le monde rassemblé autour
Banggal

*Tous les noms des **dambun** sont inscrits là*
*dans ce **maya.ngarri***
*Les **Gwion** ont mis leur nom partout dans ce pays*
Cette Loi nous a été donnée... et reste comme ça
on ne peut pas la changer
pour une autre façon de penser
la manière dont la Loi a été écrite...
Tout a été écrit dans cette peinture là
c'est comme ça que ça a été écrit
et ça reste comme ça... on ne peut pas le changer
Nyawarra

Un jour il se peut que quelqu'un
*qui soit **wunindid**, quelqu'un de la Loi*
vienne dans cet endroit
*et veuille mettre quelque chose dans le **Wunan***
*eh bien c'est le **wunindid***
*on l'appelle **wunindid***
il le met dans le réseau
*il met l'objet sacré dans ce chemin, ce **dulwan***
*il suit le **Wunan** maintenant*
Nyawarra

*Je dois aller voir ce **maya.ngarri***
celui qui est à Mont Barnet maintenant
et j'aurai plus de soucis
Ngarjno

Peut-être pendant
le temps des pluies, on va regarder
tu pourras le voir... on va aller le visiter
Il y a trop de grandes routes qui arrivent là
les touristes et tout ça
ils pourraient le trouver et le prendre
Nyawarra

Ohh je fais attention avec cet objet
il faut le déplacer maintenant
Maintenant je pense au feu il est pas
dans une grotte
Ngarjno

amurangga... man
holding **ganmangu**... *long yam*
And he get paid for that sugar bag
or kangaroo or anything
So they put 'em in that law
and it stay on that **Wunan** *now*
wunindid naga *we call it*
wunindid naga
he put it in that **Wunan** *now*
he bring it into the **Wunan**
it go straight through
Nyawarra

mudurra... *hair stuffed wig*
mudurra... *he stuck everything in his hair*
and make it real flat
and put all the stuff inside
to make it strong tie him up with string
mudurra *that's the one*
Ngarjno

People in **Wunan** *now they...*
holding yam... **ganmangu**
everybody will come through here
must donate a present
and never go past without putting anything
he saying "Hi! I'm here to look after you"
doesn't matter what blackfella
he can't go through that
without giving him a present
woman... kid... everybody

This is the life of being loyal to the **Wunan**
donating the gifts... it is our life of gift that
he look after us we look after him...
and nobody can't just go past
without giving him present
and that is the law... **Wunan**... *it's the* **Wunan**
Banggal

amurangga... Mann
mit **ganmangu**... *Jamswurzel*
Er bekommt etwas für den Honig
oder für das Känguru oder sonst etwas
So ist das Gesetz
und es bleibt das **Wunan** *bis heute*
wunindid naga *sagen wir*
wunindid naga
jetzt gehört das zum **Wunan**
er bringt es in das **Wunan**
... und dann geht es immer so weiter
Nyawarra

mudurra... *ausgestopfte Perücke aus Haar*
mudurra... *er schmiert alles Mögliche in die Haare*
und macht sie ganz flach
und stopft das ganze Zeug hinein
wenn sie ganz fest ist bindet er eine Schnur darum
mudurra *nennt man das*
Ngarjno

Die Leute gehören zum **Wunan**...
sie halten eine Jamswurzel... **ganmangu**
jeder der hier vorbeikommt
muss ein Geschenk geben
keiner geht hier vorbei ohne eine Gabe
er sagt „Hallo! Ich bin hier und sorge für dich"
ganz gleich wer es ist
er kann nicht vorbeigehen
ohne dass er ihm etwas schenkt
Frauen... Kinder... alle

So muss man leben wenn man das **Wunan** *achtet*
mit Geschenken... wir schenken unser Leben
er sorgt für uns wir sorgen für ihn...
und niemand geht einfach vorbei
ohne ihm etwas zu schenken
das ist das Gesetz... **Wunan**... *so ist das* **Wunan**
Banggal

amurangga ... un homme
tenant une **ganmangu** ... une igname longue
Et il est payé avec ce sac de sucre
ou un kangourou ou n'importe quoi
Comme ça il se met dans la Loi
et il reste dans le **Wunan**
wunindid naga on l'appelle
wunindid naga
il se met dans le **Wunan** maintenant
il l'apporte au **Wunan**
... directement dedans

Nyawarra

mudurra ... coiffe en cheveux
mudurra ... il coince ce qu'il veut dans ses cheveux
et les rend très plats
et il met des choses dedans
il attache avec de la ficelle pour que ça tienne
... c'est ça une **mudurra**

Ngarjno

Les gens du **Wunan** maintenant ...
ils tiennent une igname ... **ganmangu**
tout le monde va passer par là
et doit donner un présent
on ne doit jamais passer sans poser quelque chose
il dit « Salut ! Je suis là pour vous protéger »
tous les Noirs comme nous
ne peuvent passer par là
sans donner un présent
femme ... enfant ... tout le monde

C'est comme ça qu'on est fidèle au **Wunan**
en donnant des choses ... c'est notre vie par le don
il nous protège et on le protège ...
et personne ne peut passer comme ça
sans lui remettre un présent
c'est la Loi ... le **Wunan** ... c'est le **Wunan**

Banggal

181

Nobody living outside the sharing system *Kids... wives... husbands* *All inside... everything all inside* *Bird... every animal... dog* *no one outside the line* *they always be inside this* **Wunan** *everybody... even animals* *they all inside this inside this* **Wunan** *every living creature it is all in the* **Wunan** Nyawarra	*Alle teilen alles miteinander* *Kinder ... Frauen ... Männer* *Keiner ist ausgeschlossen ... alle gehören dazu* *Vögel ... alle Tiere ... Hunde* *niemand bleibt draußen* *alle gehören immer zum* **Wunan** *dazu* *jeder ... auch die Tiere* *die gehören alle zum* **Wunan** *jedes lebendige Geschöpf gehört zum* **Wunan** Nyawarra	*Personne ne vit en dehors du système de partage* *les gosses ... les femmes ... les maris* *Tous dedans ... tout est dedans* *l'oiseau ... tous les animaux ... le chien* *personne n'est au-delà de la ligne* *ils ont toujours été dans ce* **Wunan** *tout le monde ... même les animaux* *ils sont tous là-dedans, dans ce* **Wunan** *toutes les créatures vivantes sont dans le* **Wunan** Nyawarra

*That's all in the **Wunan** system*	*All das umfasst das **Wunan***	*Tout est dans le système **Wunan***
*doesn't matter what **dambun***	*ganz gleich zu welchem **dambun** man gehört*	*peu importe le **dambun***
*always be in the **Wunan***	*alle gehören zum **Wunan***	*c'est toujours dans le **Wunan***
doesn't matter what language	*egal welche Sprache*	*peu importe leur langue*
*they always be inside the **Wunan***	*keiner bleibt draußen beim **Wunan***	*ils sont toujours dans le **Wunan***
*they share it out... in the **Wunan***	*es ist allen gemeinsam ... das ist das **Wunan***	*ils partagent... dans le **Wunan***
***Wunan** sharing system for everything*	*Nach dem **Wunan** wird alles geteilt*	*Le système de partage du **Wunan** ça vaut pour tout*
Give right channel... nobody outside the channel	*alles hat seine Ordnung ... keiner bleibt draußen*	*Il montre la bonne voie... personne n'est en dehors*
*all... everybody family in one **Wunan***	*alle ... das **Wunan** ist eine einzige große Familie*	*tous... toutes les familles dans un seul **Wunan***
*Yeah! one **Wunan***	*Oh ja! Ein **Wunan** für alle*	*Oui ! un seul **Wunan** pour tous*
Nyawarra	Nyawarra	Nyawarra

*From... **Binjirri** this thing important*
*important song... **Yara** law*

Yeah that's for us all round the place
its for the Kimberley right up to Ayers Rock
*we kept the **Wunan** thing from Kimberley*
that which go all around travel round
*thats in the **Wunan** you know*
line all the time

All animal that belong us all here
*and these people belong to **Uluru** people*
***Warlpiri** and **Arrernte** they know this for us too*
*And **Arrernte... Pijantjatjara... Warlpiri***
these people know here for this country

But they know what we got there
from this way here
this part things go round like that
right round 'til they stay here now
these people remember
what language we put'im
for they got it
when they want to send it back to us

It not long from our place Kimberley
it go right 'round
we got short way from here
*to Ayers Rock... **Uluru***
this is the one now and it from there
*right up from this place... **Binjirri***
*right up to **Arnhem Land** all round there*
everything they send from there...
*here we got it... here... all in the **Wunan***

Ngarjno

*Aus ... **Binjirri,** das ist wichtig*
*ein wichtiges Lied ... **Yara**-Gesetz*

Ja das haben wir alle gemeinsam
von hier im Kimberley bis zum Ayers Rock
*wir haben das **Wunan** des Kimberley bewahrt*
überall macht es die Runde
*das ist Teil des **Wunan** verstehst du*
immer vom einen zum anderen

Alles was hier lebt gehört mit dazu
*und die Leute da auch die vom **Uluru***
*die **Warlpiri** und **Arrernte** die wissen das auch*
Arrernte ... Pijantjatjara ... Warlpiri
die kennen das Land hier

sie wissen was wir hier haben
durch diesen Pfad hier
auf dem die Dinge herumgehen
die Runde machen bis sie wieder hier sind
diese Leute erinnern sich
wie wir es genannt haben
sie wissen Bescheid
wenn sie es zu uns zurückschicken wollen

Es ist nicht lange weg von hier vom Kimberley
es macht die Runde
es ist nicht weit von hier
*bis zum Ayers Rock ... zum **Uluru***
das da das kommt von dort
*von diesem Ort ... von **Binjirri***
*bis rauf nach **Arnhem Land** ganz herum*
alles was sie von da schicken ...
*haben wir hier ... hier ... alles gehört zum **Wunan***

Ngarjno

*Elle est de ... **Binjirri** cette loi*
*c'est un chant important ... la loi **Yara***

Oui elle est à nous tout autour d'ici
des Kimberley jusqu'à Ayers Rock
*on a gardé le **Wunan** du Kimberley*
et ça fait tout le tour
*Elle est dans le **Wunan** tu vois*
sur ce chemin tout le temps

Tous les animaux qui sont à nous sont ici
*et ces gens font partie des gens d'**Uluru***
*les **Warlpiri** et les **Arrernte** les connaissent*
*et les **Arrernte** ... les **Pijantjatjara** ... les **Warlpiri***
ces gens savent que c'est d'ici, de ce pays

mais ils savent ce qu'on a ici
pas ce chemin-là
ça part en cercle comme ça ... en cercle
jusqu' à ce qu'elle revienne ici
ces gens connaissent
les mots que nous avons mis dedans
parce qu'ils les utilisent
quand ils veulent nous la renvoyer

Il y a pas long de chez nous, le Kimberley
ça a fait le tour
*il y a un raccourci d'ici à Ayers Rock ... **Uluru***
c'est cette loi maintenant et elle est d'ici
*de cet endroit exactement ... **Binjirri***
*tout autour jusqu'à **Arnhem Land***
tout ce qu'ils nous envoient depuis là-bas ...
*ici on le reçoit ... ici ... on le met dans le **Wunan***

Ngarjno

Yara place called **Binjirri**... big mountain there
All the young people living today
and this their country... in **Binjirri** they from there
they belong to there where this law started
this **Yara**... gray kangaroo started it

What they been doing these **Gwion** people
they heaped up all the kangaroo bone
heaped it up and they sung that song
Burn that big area for kangaroo
so when them heaped up
that was many many kangaroo was killed
all the bone was collected

That the song for those kangaroo
so when they sing that **mamaa** song
he sort of numb them with that song
they don't go anywhere... far away
That song bring all the kangaroo together
this bones here been heaped up that's ah...
it's a casting a spell onto the kangaroo
to quieten 'em down... that's the song now

Nyawarra

Der Ort gehört **Yara** er heißt **Binjirri**... großer Berg
Alle jungen Leute die heute leben
das ist ihr Land... **Binjirri** von da sind sie
da gehören sie hin wo dieses Gesetz herkommt
Yara... das graue Känguru hat es angefangen

Die **Gwion**-Leute, die haben hier
die ganzen Känguruknochen zusammengetragen
auf einen Haufen und dann haben sie gesungen
Die haben alles hier angesteckt
damit die Kängurus rauskamen
und dann war hier ein großer Haufen
so viele Kängurus haben die gejagt
und alle Knochen hier zusammengetragen

Das ist das Lied für die Kängurus
mamaa ist das Lied und wenn sie das singen
dann sind die wie betäubt
die bleiben einfach sitzen... ganz in Gedanken
Das Lied das ruft die Kängurus alle zusammen
und hier der Haufen mit den Knochen, das ist... äh
das ist ein Zauber die Kängurus werden verzaubert
dann sind sie ganz ruhig... das kommt von dem Lied

Nyawarra

L'endroit de **Yara** s'appelle **Binjirri**...
il y a une grande montagne là-bas
Tous les jeunes d'aujourd'hui...
c'est leur pays... **Binjirri** ils sont de là
ils sont de cet endroit, là où cette loi a commencé
ce kangourou gris **Yara** il a tout commencé

Ce qu'ils ont fait ces gens les **Gwion**
ils ont entassé tous les os de kangourous
ils les ont entassés et ils ont chanté ce chant
ils ont brûlé toute l'herbe de cet endroit
pour chasser le kangourou
donc quand ils les ont entassés c'est que
plein plein de kangourous avaient été tués
tous les os ont été rassemblés

C'est le chant pour ces kangourous
quand ils chantent ce chant **mamaa**
ça les engourdit ce chant
ils peuvent plus aller nulle part... loin
Ce chant fait venir tous les kangourous
quand ces os ont été entassés
c'est un piège comme un sort qu'on jette
pour endormir le kangourou... c'est ça le chant

Nyawarra

*But this one **Yara***
this song what I been singing
that for that whole lot of kangaroo
right! we kill that kangaroo
proper fat one belong to that boss man
because he invited everybody proper
right way... you know

*Aber das hier das ist **Yara***
das Lied das ich gerade gesungen habe
das ist für all die Kängurus
also wir jagen die Kängurus
ein richtig fettes bekommt immer der Älteste
weil er alle eingeladen hat
das gehört sich so … du weißt schon

*Mais ce **Yara***
ce chant que je chantais
c'est pour tous les kangourous
oui ! on tue le kangourou
celui qui est bien, le gras, il est pour le boss
parce qu'il a invité tout le monde
selon les règles, tu vois

We don't go burning grass
trespassing other parcels of the land
Then we give 'em nice nice juicy kangaroo
with plenty of fat... cook it for 'im
and we give him thanking 'im for inviting us
Everybody going to their own home
go to their own rock shelter for rain

Wir gehen da nicht hin und verbrennen das Gras
wir gehen nicht einfach auf anderer Leute Land
Wir geben ihnen ein schönes saftiges Känguru
mit viel Fett dran … wir braten es für ihn
und schenken es ihm, als Dank, für die Einladung
Und dann gehen alle wieder nach Hause
jeder in seinen eigenen Felsunterstand
wenn der Regen kommt

On ne va pas brûler l'herbe
empiéter sur les autres parcelles de terre
On lui donne un beau kangourou bien fondant
avec plein de graisse… on le cuit pour lui
et on le remercie de nous avoir invités
Tout le monde rentre à son endroit à lui
à son propre abri sous roche pour la pluie

But white people don't know
***Wunan...** this is a big thing*
from animal it been come... dog...
snake... ah this important snake
***malu...** that kangaroo hill kangaroo*
*and that plains kangaroo… **Yara***

Aber die Weißen die kennen sich nicht aus
*mit dem **Wunan** … eine wichtige Sache ist das*
es kommt von den Tieren … vom Hund …
von der Schlange … ja die Schlange ist wichtig
***malu** … das Känguru ist ein Bergkänguru*
*und das lebt im Flachland … **Yara***

Les Blancs ne savent pas
*le **Wunan** … c'est quelque chose de puissant*
il vient des animaux … du chien…
du serpent … c'est important le serpent
***malu** … le kangourou des collines*
*et le kangourou des plaines … **Yara***

*going right round to **Balgo***
to come this way and he go that way
and the main business come like that
*right round to run **Wunan** out there*
but how do they explain that?
But people have to understand that thing
just man business going from here...

*der geht rüber nach **Balgo***
und dann hier herum und dann geht er da
und das Wichtigste das kommt von hier
*das da ist der Weg den das **Wunan** nimmt*
aber wie erklären sie das?
Die Leute müssen das verstehen
das ist die Sache der Menschen …

*ça va jusque vers **Balgo***
pour revenir par ici et repartir par là
et le plus important vient comme ça
*en cercle pour amener le **Wunan** par ici*
mais comment on explique ça ?
Les gens doivent comprendre cette chose
qui est l'affaire des hommes ici …

animal which moved law
he got red kangaroo... **Walamba**
grey plains kangaroo **Yara**
We got no place much opened this way
open place... saltwater right round
but animal have to come this way to here
go right here right around **Balgo**

das Tier das das Gesetz gemacht hat
aus dem wurde das rote Känguru ... Walamba
das graue Flachlandkänguru das ist **Yara**
wir haben nicht viele Stellen die so offen sind wie
hier offenes Land... ringsherum Salzwasser
aber die Tiere müssen hier durch
die kommen hier entlang, rüber nach **Balgo**

les animaux qui ont fait bougé la loi
le Kangourou roux... Walamba
le Kangourou gris des plaines... **Yara**
Il n'y a pas d'endroit bien dégagé par là...
la mer tout autour
les animaux ont du venir par là, jusqu'ici
par là et jusqu'à **Balgo**

from **Balgo** he go down to this way
now this running all **Wunan** thing
all the man's business all there
This **mob** they're sending track
right up to **Balgo**
right round Christmas Creek
Nookanbah... Looma... Mowanjum

von **Balgo** geht er dann hier herunter
der ganze Weg das ist alles **Wunan**
das ist die Sache der Menschen
Die Leute, die schicken es auf den Weg
bis hoch nach **Balgo**
vorbei am Christmas Creek
Noonkanbah... Looma... Mowanjum

depuis **Balgo** il descend dans cette direction
maintenant ça parcourt tout le sytème du **Wunan**
toutes les affaires des hommes c'est là
tous ces gens ils envoient des signent
jusqu'à **Balgo**
jusqu'à Christmas Creek
Nookanbah... Looma... Mowanjum

come right back to Kimberley
some people dont understand now... I do!
this **Yara** law that start in **Binjirri**
this really connect each other
right up to Maningrida and all round
he get up right round to Warbuton Ranges
thats the hill brother **Yara**

und dann wieder zurück nach Kimberley
manche Leute verstehen das nicht... ich schon!
dieses **Yara**-Gesetz, das hat in **Yara** angefangen
das hängt alles zusammen
bis hoch nach Maningrida und überall
das geht bis oben zu den Warbuton Ranges
das ist der Bergbruder **Yara**

puis ça revient jusqu'au Kimberley
il y a des gens qui ne comprennent plus...
moi je comprends !
cette loi **Yara** qui a commencé à **Yara**
elle nous relie vraiment les uns aux autres
jusqu'à Maningrida et autour
jusqu'aux montagnes de Warbuton
c'est **Yara**, le frère des collines

well he go round there
he connect with this **mob Warlpiri**
from **Balgo** he go straight on now
up to in this place here Warlpiri
Pijantjatjara... all those peoples in the law
we making **Wunan**!
Well thats our **Wunan** now

Ngarjno

also hier ist er rumgegangen
und zu den Leuten gekommen, den **Warlpiri**
von **Balgo** aus ist er weitergezogen
bis rauf zu den **Warlpiri**
Pijantjatjara ... die gehören alle dazu
mit denen haben wir das **Wunan** gemacht!
Und das **Wunan** das haben wir noch immer

Ngarjno

après il va par là
il est en relation avec ce groupe, les **Warlpiri**
depuis **Balgo** il va tout droit maintenant
jusqu'à cet endroit là, **Warlpiri**
Pijantjatjara ... tous ceux-là sont dans la loi
ensemble nous constituons le **Wunan**
Voilà, c'est ça notre **Wunan**

Ngarjno

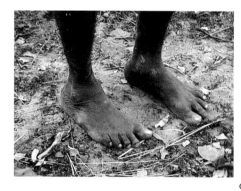

a b c

The free translation of **Jenagi Jenagi** is the "wandering nomads". This is commonly extended to mean the "messengers", particularly when talking about **maya.ngarri,** the sacred message-boards and other objects exchanged through the **Wunan.**

In any discussion of the **Wunan** and **maya.ngarri,** it is necessary to recognise that many **maya.ngarri** objects have secret sacred meanings that may be deliberately obscured. Cryptic messages were required for the communication of sacred information. It remains improper to publish any detailed description or reproduction of these **maya.ngarri,** particularly in relation to their activation as totemic conduits. This is because they are alive with sacred meaning that must be conserved and protected. Any violation should result in either execution or excommunication by **Wunan** members.

Problems are caused by publication of photographs and detailed descriptions of **maya.ngarri** and their use in ceremonies by naked men. Too often, **Wunan** custodians have been denied any right of veto or due respect for what belongs to them in the most personal way imaginable. Outsiders respecting their secrets are shown respect in turn. It is not the intention of the **munnumburra** who inform this book to insult their ancestors. However, to educate the public about the significance of **maya.ngarri** within the cultural stream connecting **Gwion** art and **Ngarinyin munnumburra,** it became necessary to outline their influential role in **Wunan** exchange. What follows, then, is a compromise between the pragmatic need to educate outsiders, and the necessity to protect secret sacred meaning.

Practical messages are needed for the organisation of ceremonies. With many people coming from different directions, it was vital to nominate landmarks and locations (g) in the vast landscape. By cryptic coding, distant ritual experts involved in organising ceremonies could be informed of an exact location. **Mamaa** (secret sacred messages), using **nguniri,** are vital to many rituals (d, e, f). Ceremonies, which can be held to resolve conflict or initiate a law, are also forums for exchanges of general information, but paramount is the influential "message" of law contained by **maya.ngarri.**

Frei übersetzt heißt **Jenagi Jenagi** so viel wie „umherziehende Nomaden". Dies ist auch die Bezeichnung für die „Botschafter", vor allem für jene, die **maya.ngarri** überbringen, die rituellen Holzbretter oder flachen Steine und andere kultische Objekte, die innerhalb des Gültigkeitsbereichs des **Wunan** ausgetauscht werden.

Für die Beschäftigung mit dem **Wunan** und den **maya.ngarri** muss man wissen, dass die **maya.ngarri** geheime, heilige Bedeutungen haben, die oft absichtlich verschleiert werden. Um die heiligen Inhalte weiterzugeben, brauchte man solche verschlüsselten Botschaften. Es wäre ungehörig, **maya.ngarri** abzubilden oder im Detail zu beschreiben, gerade in ihrer Funktion als Mittel, mit dem Totem in Verbindung zu treten, denn sie sind ganz und gar durchdrungen von ihren geheimen Bedeutungen, die bewahrt und geschützt werden müssen. Jeder, der innerhalb des **Wunan** gegen diese Regel verstößt, riskiert es, getötet oder aus der Gemeinschaft ausgeschlossen zu werden.

Bilder oder Beschreibungen der **maya.ngarri** und ihrer Rolle bei den Ritualen der unbekleideten Männer zu veröffentlichen erfordert Takt. Allzu oft wird den Hütern des **Wunan** in solchen Fällen keinerlei Mitspracherecht eingeräumt, und es fehlt jeglicher Respekt gegenüber solchen außerordentlich privaten Dingen. Wer als Außenstehender das Geheimnis respektiert, wird auch zuvorkommend behandelt werden. Die **munnumburra,** die sich bereit erklärt haben, Informationen für dieses Buch zu liefern, wollen damit nicht das Andenken ihrer Ahnen entehren. Es hat sich jedoch als notwendig erwiesen, der Öffentlichkeit einen besseren Begriff von dem Stellenwert der **maya.ngarri** in jenem kulturellen Kontinuum zu geben, das die **Gwion**-Kunst und die **munnumburra** der **Ngarinyin** verbindet, und die wichtige Rolle, die sie im System des **Wunan** spielen, zumindest anzudeuten. Die folgenden Passagen sind ein Kompromiss zwischen dem praktischen Erfordernis, Außenstehenden Informationen zu geben, und der Notwendigkeit, die geheimen, heiligen Inhalte vor Unbefugten zu schützen.

Zur Durchführung der Zeremonien müssen bestimmte Nachrichten übermittelt werden. Bei der Vielzahl von Beteiligten, die aus allen erdenklichen Richtungen zusammenkamen, war es entscheidend, dass man in der Weite der Landschaft Orientierungspunkte schuf (g). Durch geheime Zeichen konnten den Eingeweihten in der Ferne der exakte Ort einer Zeremonie bekannt gegeben werden. Die **mamaa** (geheime, heilige Botschaften), bei deren Übermittlung **nguniri** zum Einsatz kamen, sind für viele Rituale von entscheidender Bedeutung (d, e, f). Zeremonien, die zum Beispiel dazu dienen, einen Streit beizulegen oder ein Gesetz in Kraft zu setzen, geben auch Gelegenheit zum allgemeinen Meinungsaustausch, aber das ist nicht mit den eigentlichen Gesetzesbotschaften zu verwechseln, die auf den **maya.ngarri** festgehalten sind.

Une traduction libre de **Jenagi Jenagi** est « nomades errants », entendu au sens de « messagers », particulièrement lorsque l'on parle des **maya.ngarri,** planches-messages secrètes et d'autres objets échangés à travers le **Wunan.**

Dans toute discussion sur le **Wunan** et les **maya.ngarri,** il est nécessaire de se rendre compte que beaucoup d'objets **maya.ngarri** ont des sens secrets et sacrés pouvant être délibérément masqués. Il était exigé d'utiliser des messages énigmatiques pour communiquer une information sacrée. Il serait donc déplacé de publier une quelconque description détaillée ou une reproduction de ces **maya.ngarri,** particulièrement dans leur rôle totémique. C'est parce qu'ils sont vivants et ont des significations sacrées qui doivent être conservés et protégés. Toute violation de ces secrets aboutirait à une exécution ou à une excommunication par les membres du **Wunan.**

La publication de photographies et de descriptions précises des **maya.ngarri** et de leur utilisation pendant les cérémonies par les hommes nus posent problème. Trop souvent, les gardiens du **Wunan** se sont vus nier tout droit de contrôle sur ce qui leur appartient le plus intimement. Les étrangers qui respectent leurs secrets sont estimés pour cela en retour. Les **munnumburra** qui nous informent dans ce livre n'ont pas l'intention d'insulter leurs ancêtres. Mais, pour faire connaître au public la signification des **maya.ngarri** et le lien culturel qui relie l'art **Gwion** aux **munnumburra Ngarinyin,** il devient nécessaire d'exposer brièvement leur rôle influent dans les échanges **Wunan.** Ainsi, ce qui suit est un compromis entre le besoin pragmatique d'éduquer les étrangers et la nécessité de protéger les significations sacrées et secrètes.

Des indications pratiques sont nécessaires pour l'organisation des cérémonies. Comme beaucoup de personnes viennent de différents endroits, il s'est avéré indispensable de désigner des points de repères et des lieux dans ces vastes régions (g). Éloignés les uns des autres, les experts en rituels peuvent être avisés de l'endroit exact où elles se produisent par un système de codes secrets. Les **mamaa** (messages secrets et sacrés) faisant usage du **nguniri** sont essentiels dans beaucoup de rituels (d, e, f). Les cérémonies qui peuvent avoir lieu pour résoudre des conflits ou instaurer une loi sont aussi des forums d'échanges d'informations générales ; mais cela ne doit pas être confondu avec les « messages » de la loi transmis par les **maya.ngarri.**

Jenagi Jenagi

d

e

f

g

a

b

c

Forms of **maya.ngarri** evolved that contained ideas that "had to be sent around as messages". To fulfil their potential social value, they exist as both object and idea, holding both totemic and legal force. But they are only for circulation and exchange between experts who are intimate with **dulwan** (pathways) of the **Wunan**. Anyone violating the sacred aspect of **maya.ngarri** could be executed with wooden **wadba** spears (c). **Jimbila** (stone spear points) were left next to **maya.ngarri** to guard them with magical powers of retribution, and to protect them safely in storage places.

What are called **maya.ngarri** or **mamul** take many forms depending on their essential power. Marked flat boards of wood, and shaped stones vary in meaning from magical pools of water to musical "bull-roarers" (b); many crafted objects are incised and painted, or bound with coloured string, to conform with designs, diagrams and maps. Elements of sacred designs sometimes notate actions of ancestors to be mimed by ritual experts or novices during initiation events (e).

As the decisive historical events that created **Wunan** laws were honoured with ceremony, the relationships and positions of people during the events, or actions of performers also formed part of the language of "law" songs and message designs. Portable **mamul** associated with ancestral events and spiritual sources were circulated throughout the **Wunan** network; they came to be re-painted over time and inscribed with a visual language read only by **munnumburra**. Today, such visionary **Munga.nunga** designs still stimulate the imagination and activate songs and narratives.

Maya.ngarri only exist in relation to the specific narrative and song that belongs to them; in that sense, it is carried as a "message stick". That is why the **Gwion** are also called **Jenagi Jenagi** – messengers. By their constant circulation and handling, **maya.ngarri** bring responsibility to **munnumburra** for the education in **Wunan** law. Individuals cannot be dictatorial or selfish when they act as a conduit for law and the narratives that express it. The **Gwion** invented a way of balancing both knowledge and authority. As the **Jenagi Jenagi** (messengers) and the **Munga.nunga** (visionaries), the **Gwion** were responsible as artists for the far-ranging transmission of ideas communicated with **maya.ngarri** across the **Wunan** network.

Im Laufe der Zeit entwickelten sich **maya.ngarri,** die Ideen enthielten, die „als Botschaften die Runde machen mussten". Um ihre gesellschaftliche Funktion zu erfüllen, existieren sie sowohl als Objekt wie als Idee, und ihre Kräfte erstreckten sich auf den totemistischen Bereich ebenso wie auf den des Gesetzes. Aber sie sind nur zum Austausch zwischen Eingeweihten bestimmt, die mit den **dulwan** (Pfad) des **Wunan** vertraut sind. Jeder, der ein solches **maya.ngarri** entweihte, konnte mit hölzernen **wadba** (Speeren) hingerichtet werden (c). **Jimbila** (steinerne Speerspitzen) ließ man als Wächter bei den **maya.ngarri** zurück; sie sollten Übeltäter bestrafen und verhindern, dass die Objekte von ihrem Aufbewahrungsort entfernt wurden.

Maya.ngarri oder **mamul,** wie sie auch genannt werden, gibt es in vielerlei Gestalt, je nach den Kräften, die ihnen innewohnen. Geschnitzte flache Holzbretter oder behauene Steine können z. B. ein mythisches Wasserloch symbolisieren oder als Schwirrholz dienen (b). Viele von ihnen sind mit Schnitzereien oder Bemalungen versehen oder mit farbiger Schnur umwickelt und zeigen Muster, Zeichnungen oder Karten. Solche sakralen Darstellungen halten oft die Taten von Ahnen fest, die von erfahrenen Tänzern oder Novizen bei den Initiationsritualen nachgestellt werden (e).

Die mythologischen Ereignisse, die zur Schaffung der **Wunan**-Gesetze führten, sind in Ritualen verewigt, und die Stellung, die alle Beteiligten während dieser Ereignisse innehatten, ihre Beziehungen zueinander und die Rollen des Einzelnen sind in den „Gesetzesliedern" festgehalten. Die **mamul,** die mit diesen Erlebnissen der Ahnen und den Quellen spiritueller Kraft assoziiert wurden, kursierten im gesamten **Wunan**-Bereich; sie wurden im Laufe der Zeit immer wieder neu bemalt und mit Aufschriften in einer Bildsprache versehen, die nur die **munnumburra** lesen können. Bis heute stimulieren die visionären Zeichnungen der **Munga.nunga** die Phantasie und regen dazu an, die zugehörigen Geschichten zu erzählen oder Gesänge anzustimmen.

Die **maya.ngarri** sind stets mit einem Lied oder einer Erzählung verknüpft und dienen damit zugleich als Gedächtnisstütze. Deswegen werden die **Gwion** auch **Jenagi Jenagi** (Botschafter) genannt. Die **maya.ngarri** sind ständig im Umlauf, ein Mittel der Unterweisung in den **Wunan**-Gesetzen. Ein Einzelner hat keinen persönlichen Einfluss auf die Gesetze und deren Anwendung und dient lediglich als Gefäß für die Gesetze und Erzählungen. Die **Gwion** fanden einen Ausgleich zwischen Wissen und Autorität. Wie die **Jenagi Jenagi** (Botschafter) und die **Munga.nunga** (Visionäre), waren die **Gwion** für die künstlerische Übermittlung der Ideen der **maya.ngarri** im gesamten **Wunan**-Bereich verantwortlich.

Certains aspects des **maya.ngarri** ont évolué, renfermant des idées qui « devaient être envoyées sous forme de messages ». Pour remplir leur fonction sociale, ils existent à la fois en tant qu'objet et idée, car c'est une puissance qui procède à la fois du totem et de la loi. Mais seuls les initiés ayant une connaissance approfondie des **dulwan** (chemin) du **Wunan** y ont accès. Toute personne dévoilant l'aspect secret des **maya.ngarri** peut être exécutée avec une lance **wadba** (c). Des **jimbila** (pointes de lance) chargées de pouvoirs magiques sont laissées à côté des **maya.ngarri** pour les garder et pour les protéger dans des lieux sûrs.

Ce qu'on appelle **maya.ngarri** ou **mamul** peut se présenter sous beaucoup de formes suivant leur pouvoir. Les planches de bois qui portent des marques et les pierres taillées ont des significations variées qui peuvent aller de points d'eau magiques à des rhombes (b). Beaucoup d'objets sont incisés et peints ou entourés de cordons colorés pour s'adapter aux dessins et aux cartes. Des éléments de ces dessins sacrés sont parfois la transcription des actes d'ancêtres qui seront mimés par les spécialistes des rituels ou les novices lors des initiations (e).

De la même manière que l'on honorait dans les cérémonies la mémoire des événements marquants qui ont créé les lois **Wunan,** les relations et rapports aux événements qu'avaient les participants ou les interprètes constituaient aussi une partie de ce qui est dit dans les chants de la Loi et exprimé dans les dessins. Les **mamul** transportables associés aux événements ancestraux et aux sources spirituelles circulaient à travers le réseau **Wunan** ; ils furent repeints périodiquement et représentaient un langage visuel lisible seulement par les **munnumburra**. Aujourd'hui de tels dessins **Munga.nunga** stimulent toujours l'imagination et génèrent chants et récits.

Les **maya.ngarri** n'existent qu'en relation avec les récits et les chants qui leur correspondent ; en ce sens, ils sont portés comme des « bâtons-messages ». C'est pourquoi les **Gwion** s'appellent également **Jenagi Jenagi** (messagers). C'est par leur circulation et leur maniement constant que les **maya.ngarri** ont du pouvoir dans les lois **Wunan**. Les personnes qui manient les objets ayant pour rôle de montrer la Loi et de raconter les récits qui vont avec ne peuvent pas avoir un comportement autoritaire ou égoïste. Les **Gwion** ont inventé une façon d'équilibrer savoir et autorité. Tout comme les **Jenagi Jenagi** (messagers) et les **Munga.nunga** (visionnaires), les **Gwion** étaient responsables en tant qu'artistes de la transmission d'idées de toutes sortes communiquées par les **maya.ngarri** à travers le réseau **Wunan**.

Jenagi Jenagi

d

e

f

Living in such an open, expansive landscape places a great emphasis on knowing numerous landmarks to pinpoint the location of cultural evidence – **junjun.** The exact locations of the **junjun** justifying the narrative of ancient songs might be mapped by verbal diagrams at the start of songs. Preambles naming nearby landmarks or referring to the local terrain with explicit descriptions preserve knowledge of the exact location of a **wungud** source. Histories may be recalled with the fluency and emotional power of myth, but experience of the location and the living substance of the source, combined with reference to the stars, join as **junjun** to make narratives unforgettable.

When ceremonial life revolves around these narratives, ritual language and **mamul** (essential forms) are recognised as the manifestation of the **wungud** (living essence) residing in its place. But **maya.ngarri** are neither metaphor nor object. As the sculptor Constantin Brancusi said, "They are imbeciles who call my work abstract; that which they call abstract is the most realist, because what is real is not the exterior form but the idea, the essence of things." To understand how to engage with some inside power, ritual experts use the essential form of **maya.ngarri** for intimate physical communion with the source.

The essence of inside power could be communicated through layered codes and symbolic colour; e.g. **guli wodoi** (fine red ochre) precious residual blood of **Wunan** ancestor **Wodoi** (d). Some **maya.ngarri** are marked with red ochre to signify the blood of the individuals who are in touch with them at each ceremony. Others, when associated with a certain frog ancestor, are coated with **gumbaru** (yellow pigment ground to a powder); and **gumbaru** might later be sprinkled over the ground where such an object is stored.

As visionaries, the ancient **Munga.nunga** recognised that law had to move when people travelled. Revered **wulari** (ritual objects) became mobile sources of powerful ethics. Gradually, the **Munga.nunga** refined a range of **mamul** (sacred objects) in a variety of finely carved and sculptured forms, that enshrine the essence of law and ideas contained in **maya.ngarri.**

Wer in einer so weiten, offenen Landschaft lebt, der braucht möglichst viele Orientierungspunkte, sichtbare Zeichen seiner Kultur – die **junjun.** Die genaue Lage der **junjun,** die jeweils das Rezitieren alter Lieder und Erzählungen auslösen, kann zu Beginn der Lieder durch eine Art verbale „Landkarte" skizziert werden. Vorbemerkungen, die auf Orientierungspunkte in der unmittelbaren Umgebung verweisen oder eine ausführlichere Beschreibung der Landschaft geben, bewahren das Wissen über den genauen Ort einer **wungud**-Quelle. Vergangene Ereignisse lassen sich mit der Leichtigkeit und emotionalen Kraft eines Mythos in Erinnerung rufen, aber erst durch die **junjun,** die Erfahrung eines Ortes und der lebendigen Kraft einer solchen Quelle, verbunden mit Hinweisen auf den Sternenhimmel, wird eine solche Erzählung unvergesslich.

Bei den Zeremonien, die um diese Erzählungen kreisen, gelten die Sprache des Rituals und die Grundformen der **mamul** als Manifestationen der **wungud** (Essenz des Lebens), die einem bestimmten Ort innewohnt. Doch die **maya.ngarri** sind weder Metapher noch Objekt. Wie der Bildhauer Constantin Brancusi einmal sagte: „Wer meine Werke abstrakt nennt, ist ein Schwachkopf, denn die Realität ist nicht die äußere Gestalt, sondern die Idee, die Essenz der Dinge." Wenn sie mit einer inneren Kraft in Verbindung treten wollen, benutzen Ritualkundige die **maya.ngarri** als greifbares Mittel, um den Kontakt zu der Quelle dieser Kraft herzustellen.

Das Wesen der inneren Kraft kann durch verschiedene Grade der Verschlüsselung und durch symbolische Farben ausgedrückt werden wie z.B. **guli wodoi** (feiner, rötlicher Ocker), der als Überrest des **Wunan**-Ahnens **Wodoi** gilt (d). Manche **maya.ngarri** zeigen Spuren von rotem Ocker, die für das Blut derjenigen stehen, die bei den Zeremonien mit ihnen in Berührung kommen. Andere, die mit einem bestimmten Frosch-Ahnen in Verbindung gebracht werden, sind mit **gumbaru** (zu Pulver zerstoßenes gelbes Pigment) bemalt, und **gumbaru** wird manchmal auch an dem Ort verstreut, am dem ein solches Objekt aufbewahrt wird.

Als Visionäre erkannten die alten **Munga.nunga,** dass Gesetze mitwandern mussten, wenn ein Volk auf Wanderschaft war. Aus den verehrten **wulari** (kultische Objekte) wurden bewegliche Quellen ethischer Kraft. Nach und nach entwickelten die **Munga.nunga** das Spektrum der **mamul** zu einer Vielzahl von fein geschnitzten und gestalteten Formen; sie sind der sichtbare Ausdruck der Gesetze und Vorstellungen, die sich in den **maya.ngarri** manifestieren.

Vivre dans un paysage découvert et vaste nécessite la connaissance de nombreux points de repères afin de pouvoir localiser avec précision les lieux qui sont des **junjun** (témoignages culturels). Les emplacements exacts des **junjun** peuvent être indiqués oralement au début des chants. Des préambules nommant les points de repères proches ou faisant référence à l'aspect du terrain et comportant des descriptions circonstanciées permettent de conserver la connaissance de l'endroit précis où se trouve une source de **wungud.** Les gens peuvent se souvenir de l'histoire grâce à une narration claire et grâce au pouvoir émotionnel des mythes, mais connaître par une expérience directe le lieu d'origine – encore vivant – et le mettre en relation avec les étoiles devient par là une **junjun** et les récits deviennent inoubliables.

Quand la vie cérémonielle se fait autour de ces récits, la langue rituelle et les formes élémentaires de **mamul** sont vues comme la manifestation du **wungud** (l'essence vivante qui habite un lieu). Mais les **maya.ngarri** ne sont ni des métaphores ni des objets. On peut dire, comme le sculpteur Constantin Brancusi : « Il y a des gens de peu d'esprit qui appellent mon travail abstrait ; ce qu'ils appellent abstrait est en fait ce qu'il y a de plus réaliste parce que ce qui est réel n'est pas la forme extérieure mais l'idée, l'essence des choses. » C'est ainsi qu'on peut comprendre comment, pour pouvoir accéder à certains pouvoirs intérieurs, les experts des rituels utilisent la forme des **maya.ngarri** pour entrer en communion intime et physique avec l'origine de cette force.

La nature du pouvoir intérieur peut être montrée par des codes et des couleurs symboliques appliquées sur les **maya.ngarri** ; par exemple, **guli wodoi** (ocre rouge et fin) résidu précieux du sang de l'ancêtre **Wodoi** (d). Certains **maya.ngarri** sont marqués d'ocre rouge pour indiquer le sang des personnes qui les manipulent à chaque cérémonie. D'autres, associés à un ancêtre grenouille, sont recouverts de **gumbaru** (pigment jaune réduit en poudre) qui peut être saupoudré ultérieurement sur le sol à l'endroit où sont conservés ces objets.

Les anciens **Munga.nunga** eurent l'intuition que la Loi devait se déplacer avec les gens. Vénérés, les **wulari** (objets rituels) devinrent les bases mobiles du pouvoir moral. Peu à peu, les **Munga.nunga** mirent au point une variété de **mamul** (objets sacrés) de diverses formes sculptés avec finesse et qui conservent l'essence de la loi et des idées contenues dans les **maya.ngarri.**

Jenagi Jenagi

a

b

c

It was **Wodoi** and **Jungun** who first publicly distributed profound knowledge. Their revealing of **maya.ngarri** and their seminal example of sharing knowledge is embodied in the function of the stone table at **Dududu.ngarri**. The table, a site where everyone meets and shares, is also imbued with the power of inescapable justice. It was originally a crafted object, then a wood and bark platform that later metamorphosed into an **angga** (stone table).

The **Dududu.ngarri** table became the source of a defining moral principle of the **Wunan** that has endured for millennia: any receiver of sacred knowledge automatically becomes a giver. Being a member of the **Wunan** means that one is a link in a chain; as such, an individual is unable to achieve supremacy over others. Every clan is a connecting link along a complex chain of branching relationships so that everything is passed down the line. Each individual is always in the middle of a line, taking from one end and handing on to the other. This process of give-and-take is known as **molu**. The leader of one **dambun** takes a middle position as **molu ijirinari**; this means to "wait with hands ready" (recorded by **Ngarjno** and **Banggal** at the **Wunan** table).

The **Wunan** in action has been represented in a painting recording the formal transfer of **maya.ngarri** (b). The artist has focused attention on two people passing on a **maya.ngarri** that each is "holding". Neither person touching the object is in possession of it; rather, they are linked by their proximity to the object. In this long composition, these two figures appear to be backed by a line of future recipients of the **wulari** law object who are standing along the rock wall (e).

The painting epitomises the role of the **molu** in **Wunan** relationships, where all members connect with each other according to their original positions as fixed at the **Dududu.ngarri** table. Here, a **maya.ngarri** is exchanged as legal power, through the formal presentation of a gift of law, **lulwa wunandi.**

Die Ersten, die die **maya.ngarri** enthüllten und das geheime Wissen mit anderen teilten, waren **Wodoi** und **Jungun**. Das Symbol für ihre Tat ist der steinerne Tisch von **Dududu.ngarri**. Dieser Tisch, ein Ort, an dem alle zusammenkommen und alles miteinander teilen, ist überdies ein Sinnbild für die unausweichliche Macht der Gerechtigkeit. Ursprünglich war er ein geschnitztes Objekt, dann eine Art Plattform aus Holz und Rinde, die sich schließlich in einen **angga** (Tisch aus Stein) verwandelte.

Der Tisch von **Dududu.ngarri** wurde zum Quell eines grundlegenden Moralprinzips, des **Wunan,** das die Jahrtausende überdauert hat: Jeder, der heiliges Wissen erwirbt, hat die Verpflichtung, es mit den anderen zu teilen. Wer in das **Wunan** eingeweiht ist, ist ein Glied in der Kette, und deshalb kann der Einzelne niemals einem anderen überlegen sein. Jeder Clan ist ein Bindeglied in einer komplexen Kette von Beziehungen, entlang derer alles Wissen immer weitergegeben wird. Jeder steht immer in einer solchen Kette, bekommt etwas vom einen Ende und gibt es zum anderen weiter. Dieser Prozess des Weitergebens wird **molu** genannt. Das Oberhaupt eines **dambun** nimmt eine Mittelstellung als **molu ijirinari** ein, was so viel heißt wie „warten, die Hände bereit" (wie **Ngarjno** und **Banggal** am **Wunan**-Tisch erklärten).

Die Funktionsweise des **Wunan** ist auf einem Bild dargestellt, das die formelle Übergabe eines **maya.ngarri** festhält (b). Dabei konzentriert sich der Künstler auf zwei Gestalten, die ein **maya.ngarri** von Hand zu Hand weiterreichen. Keiner von beiden hat es in diesem Augenblick allein in seinem Besitz; eher könnte man sagen, dass das Objekt ein Bindeglied zwischen beiden ist. Auf dem lang gestreckten Bild erscheint hinter den beiden Figuren, an der Felswand stehend, eine lange Reihe zukünftiger Empfänger des **wulari** (e).

Das Gemälde verdeutlicht die Rolle des **molu** innerhalb des **Wunan**-Beziehungsgeflechts, in dem alle Mitglieder entsprechend den Positionen, die sie ursprünglich am Steintisch von **Dududu.ngarri** einnahmen, miteinander in Verbindung treten. Hier wird ein **maya.ngarri** als Sinnbild des Gesetzes ausgetauscht, und zwar durch die förmliche Übergabe eines „Gesetzesgeschenks", eines **lulwa wunandi.**

Ce sont **Wodoi** et **Jungun** qui ont les premiers fait connaître les savoirs fondamentaux. Leur révélation des **maya.ngarri** et leur exemple du partage de la connaissance sont mis en œuvre dans le rôle inhérent à la table en pierre de **Dududu.ngarri**. La table, lieu de rencontre et de partage pour tous, possède en elle un subtil pouvoir de justice auquel personne ne peut se dérober. Elle était à l'origine un objet fabriqué, ensuite ce fut une plate-forme en bois et en écorce, métamorphosée plus tard en une **angga** (table de pierre).

La table de **Dududu.ngarri** devint la source du principe moral du **Wunan** qui a perduré pendant des millénaires ; tout récipiendaire des connaissances sacrées devient en même temps un donateur. Être un membre du **Wunan** signifie qu'on est un maillon de la chaîne ; de ce fait, un individu ne peut dominer les autres. Chaque clan est un lien dans la série complexe des relations de parenté ramifiées. Chaque individu est toujours au milieu d'une ligne d'informations qu'il reçoit et passe ensuite à quelqu'un d'autre. Ce processus qui consiste à donner et à recevoir est connu sous le terme de **molu**. Le chef d'un **dambun** prend une position d'intermédiaire appelée **molu ijirinari** qui veut dire « attendre tout en ayant les mains prêtes à agir » (comme l'on décrit **Ngarjno** et **Banggal** à la table du **Wunan**).

Le **Wunan** en action a été représenté dans une peinture décrivant la cérémonie de transfert des **maya.ngarri** (b). L'artiste a montré deux individus se transmettant un **maya.ngarri** qu'ils « ont en main » tous les deux. Aucun des deux personnages qui touchent cet objet n'en a la possession ; on peut plutôt dire qu'ils sont reliés par cet objet qui les rapproche. Dans cette composition très étendue (e), ces deux personnages semblent être accompagnés d'une longue file de personnes qui recevront ultérieurement l'objet de loi **(wulari).**

La peinture incarne le rôle de **molu** dans les relations **Wunan** où tous les membres sont associés entre eux suivant leurs places originelles définies à la table de pierre de **Dududu.ngarri**. Ici, un **maya.ngarri** est échangé comme symbole de pouvoir légal par la remise solennelle d'un cadeau de loi, le **lulwa wunandi.**

maya.ngarri

d   e   f

The ancient **Gwion** image records the action of **wunindid naga** – putting it through the **Wunan** (b).

The **maya.ngarri** object portrayed has a specific form with a base of three parts: a solid triangle, an oblong, and a smaller triangle fringed like a fan. This distinctive **maya.ngarri**, painted at the very moment of its exchange, preserves a legal power that is recognised by **Ngarinyin** as being in circulation through the north-eastern **Wunan** network at the present time. Its name and song are known by **munnumburra**, but such **mamaa** (secret sacred information) cannot be made public.

Other **maya.ngarri** remain as reservoirs of civic morality and result in social cohesion. **Wunan** membership demands the transfer of **maya.ngarri** from one to another group or place, but only according to strict patterns of **moiety** distribution. The network of **dulwan** (pathways) throughout the **Wunan** are a common theme of conversation among **munnumburra**. They often recite lists of **dambun** names along paths of distribution. They regularly discuss each stage of the localised exchanges policed by them, and decide on the time, place and the correct group of people for **wunindid naga**. People in mourning must first conclude funeral obligations such as smoking rituals that "cleanse" and liberate the grieving before the next exchange can begin.

When **munnumburra** leave camp to visit a **maya.ngarri** where it has been safely deposited, they must take every care, using only a "clear path" to approach the sacred object. They will wear fresh **onmal**, as the white paint of law, when exposing and viewing a **maya.ngarri** or performing songs that belong to it.

Das alte **Gwion**-Felsbild hält den Akt des **wunindid naga** fest – das Weiterreichen innerhalb des **Wunan** (b).

Das abgebildete **maya.ngarri** hat eine spezifische Form mit dreiteiliger Basis: ein großes Dreieck, ein langes Oval und ein kleineres Dreieck mit einem Rand wie bei einem Fächer. Dieses außergewöhnliche **maya.ngarri**, das genau im Augenblick der Übergabe abgebildet ist, verkörpert ein Gesetz, von dem die **Ngarinyin** sagen, dass es heute überall im **Wunan**-Netzwerk des Nordostens zirkuliert. Die **munnumburra** kennen seinen Namen und das dazugehörige Lied, doch mehr darf von diesem **mamaa** (geheimes heiliges Wissen) nicht publik gemacht werden.

Andere **maya.ngarri** sind Sinnbilder von moralischen und zivilen Grundsätzen, die für den Zusammenhalt der Menschen untereinander sorgen. Die Zugehörigkeit zum **Wunan** fordert die Weitergabe von **maya.ngarri** von einer Gruppe oder einem Ort zum nächsten, doch nur gemäß einem genau festgelegten Muster innerhalb der **moieties**. Das Netz von **dulwan** (Pfaden) im Bereich des **Wunan** ist ein beliebtes Gesprächsthema bei den **munnumburra**. Oft zählen sie die Namen der **dambun**-Gebiete auf, die an bestimmten Verbreitungsrouten liegen. Regelmäßig diskutieren sie jede Stufe des Austausches, den sie überwachen, und beschließen dann, welches die richtige Zeit, der richtige Ort und die richtigen Leute für **wunindid naga** sind. Wenn jemand in Trauer ist, müssen zuerst die Bestattungszeremonien abgeschlossen werden, etwa die rituelle Reinigung mittels Rauch, die den Trauernden „befreit", bevor der nächste Austausch beginnen kann.

Wenn die **munnumburra** das Lager verlassen, um ein **maya.ngarri** an seinem sicheren Aufbewahrungsort aufzusuchen, müssen sie sehr vorsichtig sein und dürfen sich nur auf einem „sauberen Pfad" nähern. Sie tragen die frische **onmal**-Bemalung (die weiße Farbe des Gesetzes), wenn sie ein **maya.ngarri** hervorholen und betrachten oder die zugehörigen Lieder singen.

Cette ancienne peinture **Gwion** raconte l'acte de **wunindid naga**, la transmission au sein du **Wunan** (b).

L'objet **maya.ngarri** représenté à une forme particulière avec une base en trois parties: un triangle parfait, un rectangle déformé et un triangle plus petit en forme d'éventail. Ce **maya.ngarri**, peint lors de son échange, conserve en lui un pouvoir légal, qui est reconnu par les **Ngarinyin** comme étant encore actuellement en circulation dans le réseau **Wunan** du nord-ouest. Son nom et le chant qui l'accompagne sont connus des **munnumburra** mais une telle **mamaa** (information secrète et sacrée) ne peut être dévoilée.

D'autres **maya.ngarri** engrangent l'éthique morale et civique qui unissent les hommes entre eux. L'adhésion au **Wunan** exige le transfert des **maya.ngarri** d'un groupe ou d'un endroit à un autre, mais uniquement en suivant les modèles précis de répartition des **moitiés**. Le réseau des **dulwan** (chemins) à travers le **Wunan** est un sujet de conversation courant parmi les **munnumburra**. Ils récitent souvent les listes des noms des **dambun** suivant ces répartitions. Ils discutent régulièrement de chaque étape des échanges qui sont de leur ressort et décident de l'heure, du lieu et du groupe de personnes pour le **wunindid naga**. Les gens en deuil doivent d'abord finir leurs obligations funéraires, comme par exemple exécuter les rituels de fumigation qui « nettoient » et libèrent le chagrin, avant que l'échange suivant puisse commencer.

Quand les **munnumburra** quittent le camp pour aller voir un **maya.ngarri** à l'endroit où il est caché, ils doivent faire très attention, utilisant seulement un « chemin sans obstacles » pour s'approcher de l'objet sacré. Ils portent de l'**onmal** (la couleur blanche de la Loi) quand ils dévoilent et regardent un **maya.ngarri** ou lorsqu'ils interprètent des chants qui lui appartiennent.

maya.ngarri

That's what it tells ya... to grow it up
People give everyone **mangarri**
everywhere as they coming they sing along there
because they sing... **balbrangi balbri**
are waiting in the serving system to reach us
as they come along they singing

that song right?... that's the **balbrangi**
I'm standing on it you know
on the ground to reach my foot
and all the **Wunan** men
we line 'em up that's **balbrangi**...
I stand up waiting patiently for it to come

This one hair here is **nguniri**
this is for mustering up people
when this one they singing
for this one to catch them up
this one here this is a hair **nguniri**
this one hair belong to them
that's how they put in picture... dreamtime
that's their hair... we never draw this lot

This hair noose is **nguniri**
then the messenger go
he must run everybody, everybody
This one for mustering... it's a message
messenger take 'em
and then they come round
because this one has reached them already
and they don't have to wait any longer
they all move this one... **nguniri**

this move 'em to the actual dancing place
where everybody unite and dance and worship
Those the ones where they come
priestess woman and priest man
this is for that all in the **Wunan**
it's the education place for law

Banggal

nguniri...
is pretty important thing the **nguniri**
Everybody need that **nguniri** for law
... secret law
secret probably when they use that **nguniri**
they know that sacred thing
into that bloke
when he got that **nguniri** in his neck

neck... he got it over there
and they give it to him
or sometimes he hand it over to other people
he still got that **nguniri** on his neck
He can't go without the **nguniri**
Sometimes they call it **nguniri** or **galwal**

Nyawarra

Das ist es was es dir sagt... es zu stärken
Alle bekommen **mangarri**
sie kommen von überall her und singen
und sie singen... **balbrangi balbri**
die warten darauf zu uns zu kommen
wenn sie kommen dann singen sie

das Lied hier?... das ist **balbrangi**
das kommt hier aus der Erde
aus der Erde auf der ich stehe
und alle Männer die zum **Wunan** gehören
die stehen in einer Reihe das ist **balbrangi**...
Ich stehe und warte dass es zu mir kommt

Das da sind Haare **nguniri** nennen wir die
damit werden die Leute zusammengerufen
die ruft sie zum Singen
die fängt sie ein
die **nguniri** aus Haaren
die Haare sind von denen
da auf den Bildern... aus der Traumzeit
das sind ihre Haare... wir malen so was nie

Die Schlinge aus Haaren heißt **nguniri**
damit macht sich der Bote auf den Weg
er muss überall hinlaufen, überall
Damit ruft er die Leute herbei... eine Botschaft
der Botschafter überbringt sie
und dann kommen sie zusammen
weil er sie schon erreicht hat
und sie müssen nicht länger warten
sie folgen ihr alle... der **nguniri**

die ruft sie auf den Tanzplatz
wo alle sich treffen und tanzen und beten
Zu denen da kommen sie hin
zu der Priesterin und dem Priester
das ist für alle die schon zum **Wunan** gehören
hier werden sie ins Gesetz eingeweiht

Banggal

nguniri...
die ist ziemlich wichtig, die **nguniri**
Alle brauchen die **nguniri** für das Gesetz
... das geheime Gesetz
geheim wird es wenn die **nguniri** im Spiel ist
alle wissen es ist was Heiliges
der bringt etwas Heiliges
wenn er die **nguniri** um den Hals hat

um den Hals... er bindet sie sich um den Hals
und sie geben ihm die Botschaft
oder er gibt sie weiter an andere
aber immer mit der **nguniri** um den Hals
Ohne die **nguniri** kann er nicht gehen
Manchmal heißt sie **nguniri** manchmal **galwal**

Nyawarra

C'est ce qu'il te dit... de faire que cela arrive
Les gens donnent du **mangarri** à tous
quand ils arrivent de partout, ils chantent là
ils chantent... **balbrangi balbri**
ils attendent de nous rejoindre
quand ils arrivent ils chantent

ce chant, là ?... c'est le **balbrangi**
Je me tiens debout là tu vois
et fait venir les gens jusqu'à mes pieds
et tous les hommes du **Wunan**
on s'aligne, c'est le **balbrangi**...
Je me tiens là attendant patiemment sa venue

Ces cheveux là c'est le **nguniri**
c'est pour rassembler les gens
avec ça ils chantent
pour qu'il les attrape
ceux-là, ces cheveux c'est un **nguniri**
ces cheveux leur appartiennent
c'est comme ça qu'ils se représentent
dans l'image... dans le rêve
c'est leurs cheveux... on ne dessine jamais ça nous

Ce lasso en cheveux c'est **nguniri**
puis le messager part
il doit courir voir tout le monde, tout le monde
le **nguniri** c'est pour rassembler... c'est un message
le messager le prend
et puis ils viennent autour
parce que le **nguniri** les a déjà atteints
et ils n'ont pas à attendre plus longtemps
ils suivent tous ce **nguniri**

cela les amène au lieu de danse en fait
où chacun se réunit et danse et prie
C'est là qu'ils vont
la prêtresse et le prêtre
c'est pour ceux qui sont dans le **Wunan**
le lieu où on enseigne la Loi

Banggal

nguniri...
c'est vraiment important le **nguniri**
Tout le monde a besoin de ce **nguniri** pour la Loi
... la loi secrète
lorsqu'ils utilisent ce **nguniri**
ils savent que cette chose sacrée
est dans le corps de cet homme
quand il a ce **nguniri** autour de son cou

autour du cou... il l'avait là
et les hommes de la Loi le lui ont donné
ou parfois ils le transmettent à d'autres
il a toujours ce **nguniri** sur son cou
Il ne peut partir sans le **nguniri**
Parfois ils l'appellent **nguniri** ou **galwal**

Nyawarra

Wiji.ngarri... native cat they call him
uh on the **Kuri Kuri** side... *Wiji.ngarri*

Well we call him *Wiji.ngarri*
he's the composer for the *walu.ngarri*
When they ring dancing you know
that's the beginning of everything in the place
the *Wudmangu* songs
Nyawarra

gulowa... sister-in-law hitting brother-in-law
winya... for this we must do it
dudu-narawi... stamping around
and fighting in play
wutminji... moving in a strong
and smart formal rush
Wudmangu... where *walu.ngarri* began
Wiji.ngarri... composer the Spotted Quoll man
Ngarjno

Wiji.ngarri... eine einheimische Katze ist das
aus **Kuri Kuri** ... *Wiji.ngarri*

Wir nennen ihn *Wiji.ngarri*
von dem stammen die Lieder für den *walu.ngarri*
wenn sie im Kreis tanzen
damit fängt alles an
mit den Liedern aus *Wudmangu*
Nyawarra

gulowa... die Schwägerin haut den Schwager
winya... deshalb müssen wir das tun
dudu-narawi... wir stampfen auf den Boden
... tun so als ob wir kämpfen
wutminji... mit einem Ruck nach vorn
das ist geübt
Wudmangu... wo das *walu.ngarri* angefangen hat
Wiji.ngarri... der Komponist
der Tüpfelbeutelmarder-Mann
Ngarjno

Wiji.ngarri... la « martre » tâchetée ils l'appellent
du côté des **Kuri Kuri** ... *Wiji.ngarri*

Oui on l'appelle *Wiji.ngarri*
C'est lui qui a composé le *walu.ngarri*
Quand ils dansent en cercle tu sais
c'est le commencement de tout
les chants *Wudmangu*
Nyawarra

gulowa... la belle-sœur frappe son beau-frère
winya... on doit le faire, on doit danser
dudu-narawi... piétiner le sol ... jouer à se battre
wutminji... mouvement de bousculade violent
mais très étudié et formalisé
Wudmangu... là où le *walu.ngarri* a été créé
Wiji.ngarri... c'est le compositeur
l'homme « martre » tâchetée
Ngarjno

Place called **Wudmangu**
where **Wiji.ngarri** started the law`

the **walu.ngarri** law to circumcise everybody
everybody... all the birds... everybody
nobody can go without that law
you bring everybody in there

and they all been circumcised right?
there all the young people and...
that's the **walu.ngarri** they call it
started here at **Wudmangu**

That old **Wiji.ngarri** started it
he put that law and it stay there
and that law is still there... **Wudmangu**
spread everywhere the **walu.ngarri**
Wiji.ngarri started

Nyawarra

Der Ort heißt **Wudmangu**
da hat **Wiji.ngarri** das Gesetz begründet

walu.ngarri das Gesetz der Beschneidung
alle ... jeder Clan ... keine Ausnahme
keiner kommt um das Gesetz herum
da gehört jeder dazu

alle werden beschnitten, verstehst du?
alle jungen Leute und ...
das ist **walu.ngarri** so heißt das
hier in **Wudmangu** hat das angefangen

Der alte **Wiji.ngarri** war der Erste
er hat das Gesetz begründet und so ist es geblieben
und das Gesetz haben wir bis heute ... **Wudmangu**
walu.ngarri gibt es überall
Wiji.ngarri, der war der Erste

Nyawarra

Un endroit appelé **Wudmangu**
où **Wiji.ngarri** a créé la Loi

la loi **walu.ngarri**, pour circoncire tout le monde
tout le monde ... les oiseaux ... tout le monde
personne ne peut échapper à cette Loi
tout le monde doit passer par là

et alors ils ont tous été circoncis, n'est-ce pas ?
là, tous les jeunes gens et ...
le **walu.ngarri**, on l'appelle
ça a commencé ici à **Wudmangu**

Ce vieux **Wiji.ngarri** l'a créée
il a fait la Loi et c'est resté
et cette Loi est toujours là ... **Wudmangu**
elle répand partout le **walu.ngarri**
que **Wiji.ngarri** a initié

Nyawarra

*In **Wudmangu** this song start there*
*place called **Wudmangu***
let's dance ah... ring dance they been say
dreamtime... you know?
when they been start law
for initiating young people
*place called **Wudmangu***
Banggal

*In **Wudmangu**, da hat das Lied angefangen*
***Wudmangu** heißt der Ort*
lass uns tanzen... Kreistanz nannten sie das
du weißt schon... in der Traumzeit
als das mit den Gesetzen angefangen hat
mit der Initiation für die jungen Leute
***Wudmangu** heißt der Ort*
Banggal

*À **Wudmangu** ce chant commence ici*
*à un endroit appelé **Wudmangu***
dansons ah... une danse circulaire ils disaient
le rêve... tu sais?
quand ils ont créé la Loi
pour initier les jeunes gens
*à un endroit appelé **Wudmangu***
Banggal

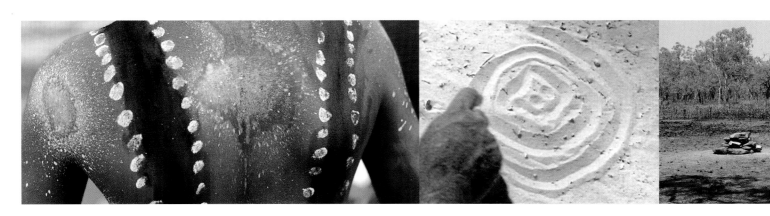

We come back here to make history
Now we we come here and teach the law
anybody can understand what the law was
now that's why they got to learn
young people
***Duduk.ngunga** we call'im this new ring*
*new ground for **walu.ngarri** at **Marranba.bidi***
Ungudman

Wir kommen hierher zurück
wir schreiben Geschichte
Wenn wir herkommen und die Gesetze weitergeben
dann versteht jeder was das Gesetz einmal war
deshalb müssen sie das lernen
die jungen Leute
***Duduk.ngunga** nennen wir den neuen Tanzplatz*
*den neuen Ort für den **walu.ngarri***
*in **Marranba.bidi***
Ungudman

On revient ici pour écrire notre histoire
Maintenant on revient ici et on enseigne la Loi
tout le monde peut comprendre
ce qu'était la Loi
c'est pour ça qu'ils doivent apprendre
les jeunes
***Duduk.ngunga** on l'appelle*
ce nouveau cercle
*cercle pour le **walu.ngarri***
*cet espace à **Marranba.bidi***
Ungudman

Now people come from everywhere
to do this **Wunan** initiation ceremony
Because **Jenagi** started it
then it became a new law
from that time... and we still do it today
once we get here... all our spear... **woomera**
they take 'em all the elders and store 'em up
we stop here everyone all naked
you going there to the creation time
in that ceremony... **walu.ngarri**
Only that elders do all the hunting
they not a woman... anybody no go out hunting
they be locked up yeah
all the elders watching them
they have a like ah watchmen it's a guard
like a policeman watching everybody yeah?

And all the committee men and women
have meeting and that's why
that song have to be danced
for the young people because of that
every young people... every Aborigine
he not allowed to have foreskin
he must be cut 'em because he'll be law man
when he not cut with a foreskin
he not a law man... he outsider
it's important because he have to carry on
when he older man when he got wife and kids
he have to look after the song and country
he **munnumburra** full initiated man
we call him **munnumburra** when he elder

Banggal

Zu der **Wunan**-Initiation
da kommen die Leute von überall her
Die **Jenagi** die haben damit angefangen
und dann wurde ein neues Gesetz daraus
von da an ... wir halten uns heute noch daran
wenn wir ankommen ... unsere Speere ... **woomera**
die Ältesten ... sie nehmen sie und legen sie weg
hier lagern wir und alle sind nackt
wie in der Zeit als die Welt geschaffen wurde
bei dieser Zeremonie ... dem **walu.ngarri**
Nur die Ältesten gehen auf die Jagd
keine Frauen ... niemand geht auf die Jagd
die werden sogar eingesperrt
alle Ältesten passen auf sie auf
jemand wird als Wächter davor gestellt
wirklich wie ein Polizist behält der sie im Auge

Und alle aus dem Rat Männer und Frauen
die kommen zusammen und darum
wird gesungen und getanzt
für die jungen Leute, deswegen
keiner von den jungen Leuten ... kein Aborigine
darf eine Vorhaut haben
er muss beschnitten werden
sonst gehört er nicht zum Gesetz
wenn seine Vorhaut nicht beschnitten ist
dann gehört er nicht dazu ... ein Außenseiter
das ist wichtig denn er soll ja alles weiterführen
wenn er älter ist und Frau und Kinder hat
muss er die Lieder hüten und das Land
dann ist er ein vollständig Initiierter
ein **munnumburra**
munnumburra das heißt Ältester

Banggal

Maintenant les gens viennent de partout
pour cette cérémonie d'initiation du **Wunan**
Les **Jenagi** l'ont créée
et c'est devenu une nouvelle loi
depuis ce temps ... et on le fait encore aujourd'hui
une fois qu'on est là ... nos lances ... nos **woomera**
les anciens les prennent et les rangent
on s'arrête là tout le monde est nu
on revient là au temps de la création
dans cette cérémonie ... **walu.ngarri**
Seuls les Anciens font la chasse
pas de femmes ... personne ne sort chasser
ils sont enfermés oui
les anciens les surveillent
ils ont comme des gardiens, un garde
comme un policier qui surveille tout le monde oui ?

Et tout le conseil, les hommes et les femmes
se réunissent et c'est pourquoi
ce chant doit être dansé
pour les jeunes, c'est à cause de ça
et pour tous les jeunes ... aucun Aborigène
n'est autorisé à garder son prépuce
il doit être coupé car il sera un homme dans la Loi
s'il est pas coupé, qu'il a gardé son prépuce
c'est pas un homme dans la Loi, c'est un étranger
c'est important parce qu'il est là pour transmettre
quand il sera vieux qu'il aura femme et enfants
il aura à s'occuper du chant et du pays
il sera un homme complètement initié
un **munnumburra** quand il devient ancien
un Ancien ça se dit **munnumburra**

Banggal

I will follow that **walu.ngarri**
from that old people
and I gotta hold that thing today
Take this **walu.ngarri** now
I gotta put my grandson there
Nyawarra come second after me
he belong this place now
he gotta make a big place now
They gotta make proper ring dance
walu.ngarri for this **Marranba.bidi** place

Ngarjno

Ich werde zum **walu.ngarri** gehen
wie unsere Väter
und ich werde ihn heute abhalten
Der **walu.ngarri** zum Beispiel
da muss ich mit meinem Enkel hin
Nyawarra kommt als Zweiter
der wohnt jetzt dort
der macht einen wichtigen Ort daraus
Da werden jetzt echte Kreistänze getanzt
walu.ngarri da in **Marranba.bidi**

Ngarjno

Je suivrai ce **walu.ngarri**
comme ces vieux
et je maintiendrai cette chose aujourd'hui
Dans ce **walu.ngarri** maintenant
je dois mettre mon petit-fils
Nyawarra vient en second après moi
il est de cet endroit maintenant
il doit avoir une bonne place
Ils doivent bien faire la danse circulaire
dans ce **walu.ngarri** à cet endroit **Marranba.bidi**

Ngarjno

They bring us in another law now...
out bush... we stop there
they been put us out in bush

Your mother dead... you got no mother now
these people been telling... frightening us
when go out bush
We thought it was true... we nearly cry!
they giving us signal... "dont cry"
Banggal

Little boy you know?
he climb in that **Jaawa** rainbird home
that little boy get in that cave
where that woman live
he get down in little cave
he diggin' down in cave
nice place where she live
Jaawa she walkin' there

righto... she get that round rock
little round stone you know?
it round that one
and she grab him here
she hold that little boy here
smash him head !
eat 'im up... eat up all the brain
she eat 'im up all the brain
shut 'im up that young man

Sie stellen uns jetzt unter ein anderes Gesetz
draußen im Busch... suchen wir uns einen Platz
sie haben uns raus in den Busch geschickt

Deine Mutter ist tot... du hast keine Mutter mehr
das haben sie gesagt... haben uns Angst gemacht
da draußen im Busch
Wir haben das geglaubt... hätten fast geheult!
aber sie haben signalisiert... „weint nicht"
Banggal

Ein kleiner Junge, weißt du?
stieg hinauf wo **Jaawa** die Regenvogelfrau wohnt
der Junge kam rein in die Höhle
die Höhle von der Frau
da ist er reingeschlüpft in die kleine Höhle
ganz tief reingekrochen
schön war es da in der kleinen Höhle
doch dann kommt **Jaawa** reinspaziert

oh je... und sie packt sich einen Stein
einen kleinen runden Stein
so einen kleinen runden
und schnappt sich den Jungen
und schlägt dem Kleinen mit dem Stein
den Schädel ein!
und fängt an zu picken... das Hirn rauszupicken
das ganze Hirn hat sie rausgepickt
und da war's vorbei mit dem jungen Mann

that boy died
that **Jaawa** she do that
she judge him
she singing out here all around now
that rainbird **Jaawa**

I tell these two young boys
never make toilet near her nest
don't make a noise

all right he gone now that **Jaawa**
they can make a noise now
Ungudman

der Junge war tot
das war **Jaawa** die Regenvogelfrau
und dann hat sie ihn noch verspottet
überall hier draußen kann man sie singen hören
Jaawa die Regenvogelfrau

Den beiden Jungs hier, denen sage ich
geht nicht mal zum Pinkeln in die Nähe
von so einem Nest
die machen keinen Mucks

aber jetzt ist **Jaawa** erstmal weg
da können sie wieder Radau machen
Ungudman

Ils nous amènent vers la loi maintenant...
dans le bush... on s'arrête là
ils nous ont sortis dans le bush

Ta mère est morte maintenant... t'as plus de mère
ces gens disaient ça... pour nous faire peur
quand on est parti dans le bush
Nous on pensait que c'était vrai...
on pleurait presque !
on nous disait... « ne pleurez pas »
Banggal

Le petit gosse tu sais ?
il monte chez ce Jaawa
dans la maison de cet « oiseau de pluie »
ce gosse il va dans la grotte où cette femme vit
il descend dans la petite grotte
il creuse dans la grotte
dans le joli endroit où elle vit
et Jaawa arrive à ce moment

bon... elle prend ce caillou rond
un petit caillou rond, tu vois ?
celui-là il est rond et elle l'attrape là
elle tient le petit gosse ici
et lui fracasse la tête !
elle le mange... elle mange tout le cerveau
elle lui mange tout le cerveau
elle le fait taire ce jeune garçon

ce garçon meurt
c'est Jaawa qui a fait ça
elle l'a jugé
elle chante tout autour là maintenant
cet « oiseau de pluie », Jaawa

J'ai dit à ces deux jeunes garçons
ne faites jamais votre toilette près de son nid
fais pas de bruit

c'est bon il est parti ce Jaawa
ils peuvent faire du bruit maintenant
Ungudman

This place belong man
painting ground here this place now
This one man up there where they painting
and the different **mamaa...** secrets
This one here tribal place for all the man here
They the **Jungun** tribe
this where they paint up two **Wodoi** boys
and we walk that way
Banggal

Wodoi got to have white **onmal**
this **walu.ngarri...** can't play up with 'em
'e know thats his culture
he must understand...
he come back to that old time
everybody gotta come back
all the young boys
Ngarjno

Der Ort hier ist nur für die Männer
hier werden die Jungen bemalt
Der Mann da oben der bemalt sie
das ist alles geheim... **mamaa**
Der Ort hier ist für alle Männer im Stamm
Die Männer sind **Jungun**
da bemalen sie die beiden **Wodoi**-Jungen
da gehen wir hin
Banggal

Die **Wodoi** werden mit weißer **onmal** bemalt
für den **walu.ngarri...** damit ist nicht zu spaßen
er weiß das gehört zu seiner Kultur
das muss er lernen...
er kehrt zurück in die alte Zeit
alle müssen zurück
alle Jungen
Ngarjno

Cet endroit appartient aux hommes
c'est là qu'on les peint
Cet homme là-haut à l'endroit où on peint
et les différents secrets... **mamaa**
C'est un endroit pour tous les hommes de la tribu
Eux c'est la tribu **Jungun**
là ils ont peint ces deux garçons **Wodoi**
et on va y aller
Banggal

Les **Wodoi** doivent porter de l'**onmal** blanc
à ce **walu.ngarri...** on peut pas tricher
ils sait que c'est dans sa culture
il doit le savoir...
il revient à ces temps anciens
tout le monde doit y revenir
tous les jeunes garçons
Ngarjno

202

Wodoi ngangurr warra
Wodoi boy for initiation

I take 'em and paint 'em up
*paint 'em up because this is **Jungun** song...*
They got to know you... anybody got to know
When they find you anywhere
they know that man been in law
People got to know... that bloke there
*that **ngangurr warra**... boy for initiation*
Ungudman

*onmal... The white paint we call it **onmal***
***munilla**... when we put it straight down here*
and he put it just straight down forehead here
*and round you round face here... **mondollo***
*that's the **mondollo***
When we get down to the body
*paint up down here we call it **yalungarri***
yalungarri** that white **onmal
***onmal** is good for using culture or ceremony*
everything what you have it or spear
***onmal** he made outa King Brown snake*
*snake... **Gubu.ngarri***
when snake go to toilet
and you see that white line...
*that the **onmal** we call it*
Nyawarra

Wodoi ngangurr warra
*ein **Wodoi**-Junge für die Initiation*

Ich nehme sie und bemale sie
*das mache ich weil es ein **Jungun**-Lied ist...*
Man muss es sehen... jeder muss es sehen
Ganz egal wo sie einem begegnen
die wissen dann der gehört zum Gesetz
Die Leute müssen wissen... der Junge da
*der **ngangurr warra**... der kommt zur Initiation*
Ungudman

*onmal... so heißt die weiße Farbe **onmal***
***munilla**... hier kommt sie hin*
so quer über die Stirn
*und rings um das Gesicht... **mondollo***
*das heißt **mondollo***
Dann kommt der Körper
*die Flecken hier die heißen **yalungarri***
***yalungarri** so heißt das Weiße hier*
***onmal** das ist gut für Zeremonien oder Ritual*
das kann man für alles nehmen auch für den Speer
***onmal** das kommt von der braunen Königsnatter*
*der Schlange... **Gubu.ngarri***
wenn die Schlange kackt
siehst du die weiße Linie da...
***onmal** nennen wir das*
Nyawarra

Wodoi ngangurrwarra
*garçon **Wodoi** prêt pour l'initiation*

Je le prends et je le peins
*je le peins parce que c'est un chant des **Jungun**...*
Ils doivent te reconnaître... tous doivent le savoir
Quand ils te voient n'importe où
ils savent que tu es dans la loi
Les gens doivent savoir... ce type là
*ce **ngangurr warra**... ce garçon est prêt*
pour l'initiation
Ungudman

*onmal... la peinture blanche on l'appelle **onmal***
***munilla**... on la met juste là ici*
et ici juste en dessous du front
*et tout autour autour du visage là... **mondollo***
*c'est le **mondollo***
Quand on descend le long du corps
*et qu'on peint jusque-là on appelle ça **yalungarri***
***yalungarri** c'est cet **onmal** blanc*
*on dit **onmal** pour la culture ou la cérémonie*
tout ce que tu portes ou que tu tues avec ta lance
*l'**onmal** est fait avec le serpent roi brun*
*le serpent... **Gubu.ngarri***
quand le serpent va aux toilettes
là tu vois cette ligne blanche...
***onmal** on l'appelle*
Nyawarra

You talking about my son
and where he's married from

*My son he's married to that **Jungun's** daughter*
*but that **Jungun's** daughter?*
*mother of that girl? she's **Wodoi***
she go by the father that daughter one...
*she's **Jungun** and he's **Jungun** too*

*But the mother... that **Jungun** father's wife*
*... she's **Wodoi***
Nyawarra

Du sprichst von meinem Sohn
und mit wem er verheiratet ist

*Mein Sohn heiratete die Tochter eines **Jungun***
*und die Tochter von diesem **Jungun?***
*die Mutter von dem Mädchen? die ist eine **Wodoi***
aber die Tochter kommt nach dem Vater...
*deswegen ist sie eine **Jungun** genau wie er*

*Aber die Mutter... die Frau vom Vater des **Jungun***
*... die ist eine **Wodoi***
Nyawarra

Tu parles de mon fils
et de où est-ce qu'il s'est marié

*Mon fils est marié à la fille de ce **Jungun***
*mais la fille de ce **Jungun** ?*
*la mère de cette fille ? elle est **Wodoi***
ça passe par le père pour la fille...
*elle est **Jungun** et il est **Jungun** aussi*

Mais la mère... la femme de ce père qui est
Jungun**... elle est **Wodoi
Nyawarra

*We **Wunan** with this **Wodoi mob***
*with these **Nyawarra** boys*

*in the area we **Jungun***
***Jungun** man have to dance*
Ungudman

*Das **Wunan** verbindet uns mit diesen **Wodoi***
*den Jungen der **Nyawarra***

*wir hier in der Gegend sind **Jungun***
*die **Jungun**-Männer müssen tanzen*
Ungudman

*Nous sommes **Wunan** avec ce groupe **Wodoi***
*avec les garçons de **Nyawarra***

*dans cette région ici on est **Jungun***
*l'homme **Jungun** il doit danser*
Ungudman

Wiji.ngarri** started **walu.ngarri** at **Wudmangu
*yeah we started in **Wudmangu** near that **Binjirri***
*and when **Wiji.ngarri***
went to the other ceremony they had down here
*what's that place here?... **Brrunjini***
it got all mixed up
where he started it was another one possum
***andarri**... Ring-tailed possum*
they all been mixed there... blind folks
Wiji.ngarri** and possum **andarri
*and **degulan**... Frilled Lizard*
*that **degulan** they all been there right*
*he died right there **Wiji.ngarri***
*he handed **walu.ngarri** to blind folks*
*But he still carry on that **andarri***
*and this other one **degulan***
*when **Wiji.ngarri** died*
he tell blind folk to take over
*probably to warn them... **munya***
Nyawarra

***Wiji.ngarri** hat mit dem **walu.ngarri** angefangen*
*in **Wudmangu***
*ja, in **Wudmangu** da haben wir angefangen*
*nicht weit von **Binjirri***
*und als **Wiji.ngarri***
zu der anderen Zeremonie ging die hier unten war
*wie heißt das?... bei **Brrunjini***
da kam alles durcheinander
als er anfing war da noch eine andere Beutelratte
***andarri** der Gleitbeutler*
alles kam durcheinander... die Leute waren blind
Wiji.ngarri** und die Beutelratte **andarri
*und **degulan**... die Kragenechse*
*und **degulan** alle waren sie da*
*er ist da unten gestorben der **Wiji.ngarri***
*und überließ den **walu.ngarri** den Blinden*
*Aber sie haben weitergemacht, **andarri***
*und der andere, **degulan***
*als **Wiji.ngarri** starb*
er sagte den Blinden sie müssen weitermachen
*vielleicht als Warnung... **munya***
Nyawarra

Wiji.ngarri** a commencé le **walu.ngarri
*à **Wudmangu***
*oui on a commencé à **Wudmangu** près de **Binjirri***
*et quand **Wiji.ngarri***
est allé à la cérémonie qu'ils ont fait plus bas
*quel est cet endroit ?... **Brrunjini***
tout s'est complètement mélangé
quand ça a commencé
il y avait là un autre opossum
***andarri**, l'opossum à queue annelée*
ils se sont tous mélangés ici... c'était des aveugles
Wiji.ngarri** et l'opossum **andarri
*et **degulan**... l'iguane australien*
*avec ce **degulan**, ils étaient tous là*
*il est mort juste là **Wiji.ngarri***
*il a donné le **walu.ngarri** aux aveugles*
*Mais il a continué cet **andarri***
*et cet autre là **degulan***
*quand **Wiji.ngarri** est mort*
il a dit à ces aveugles de prendre la suite
*sûrement pour les avertir... **munya***
Nyawarra

*munnumburra... woman... law woman... **wongai***

*young girls there... **yangudi**
they been taught how to cook tucker
how to catch water...
how to get wood and all that preparation
because her brother being initiated*

*And that young woman gotta work and learn
before she ever get married*
Ngarjno

*munnumburra... Frau...
Hüterin des Gesetzes... **wongai***

*die jungen Mädchen... **yangudi**
die lernen wie man Essen kocht
wie man Wasser findet...
Holz sammelt und für alles vorsorgt
denn ihr Bruder kommt zur Initiation*

*Und die junge Frau muss arbeiten und alles lernen
sonst kann sie nicht heiraten*
Ngarjno

*la femme... **munnumburra**...
la femme de la Loi... **wongai***

*les jeunes femmes là... **yangudi**
on leur a appris comment cuire la bouffe
comment trouver de l'eau...
comment trouver du bois et tout préparer
parce que son frère va être initié*

*Et cette jeune femme doit travailler et apprendre
avant qu'elle soit mariée*
Ngarjno

*That blue tongue ancestor... **Waluwi**
in long burrow where Blue-tongued Lizard*

*big flood... they been swimming
this mother one been swimming with them
only those children safe... she save them
they in **Luma** on top standing up in the line
like that lot stone up there
that these stones three... four standing up*

*But mother one got drowned...
People might think it's ah anthill standing up
standing up like **jungi**... termite mound
but it's a stone like a **jungi**
there where she got drowned
But she saved her children
they standing up there now*

*And that what all this initiation ceremony
is all about
to save lives of young people
and that's why she saved her children*
Banggal

*Blu-tongued Lizard – we call it **waluwi**
waluwi... she got two names
duma... they call her **duma** or **waluwi***
Nyawarra

*Da war die Ahnin mit der blauen Zunge... **Waluwi**
die saß in ihrem langen Bau die Blauzungenechse*

*es kam eine große Flut... sie mussten schwimmen
die Mutter und die Kleinen mussten schwimmen
die Kinder waren in Sicherheit... sie hat sie gerettet
oben in **Luma** da kann man sie sehen
da stehen sie in einer Reihe
die drei vier Steine die da aufrecht stehen*

*Aber die Mutter die ist ertrunken...
Leute glauben vielleicht das ist ein Ameisenhügel
der da steht wie ein **jungi**... Termitenhügel
aber es ist ein Stein wie ein **jungi**
da an der Stelle wo sie ertrunken ist
Aber ihre Kinder hat sie gerettet
und die stehen jetzt da oben*

*Und darum geht es bei der ganzen Initiation
um das Leben der jungen Leute
deshalb hat sie ihre Kinder gerettet*
Banggal

*Die Blauzungenechse – wir nennen sie **waluwi**
waluwi... sie hat zwei Namen
duma... sie heißt **duma** oder **waluwi***
Nyawarra

*C'est l'ancêtre à la langue bleue... **Waluwi**
dans un profond terrier
le lézard [scinque] à langue bleue*

*il y a eu une grosse inondation... ils ont nagé
cette mère elle nageait avec eux
seuls les enfants ont été sauvés, elle les a sauvés
ils sont à **Luma** en haut de ce rocher
debout alignés comme toutes ces pierres là-haut
les trois... ou quatre qui sont debout*

*Mais la mère elle s'est noyée
Les gens peut-être ils pensent
que c'est une fourmilière ce bloc vertical
ou bien que c'est une termitière... **jungi**
mais c'est une pierre comme une **jungi**
là où elle s'est noyée
Mais elle a sauvé ses enfants
ils se tiennent debout là-haut maintenant*

*Et toute cette cérémonie d'initiation
c'est à propos de ça
sauver la vie des jeunes gens
et c'est pourquoi elle a sauvé ses enfants*
Banggal

*Le lézard à langue bleue...
on l'appelle **waluwi**
waluwi... elle a deux noms
duma... ils l'appellent **duma** ou **waluwi***
Nyawarra

breb-brenya... everyone get up	*breb-brenya...* alle stehen auf	*breb-brenya...* tout le monde se lève
wade... don't wait... don't miss a second all together... come on quick!	*wade...* nicht warten keine Sekunde verpassen alle zusammen... auf geht's	*wade...* n'attends pas, ne perds pas une seconde... tous ensemble... allez
numbila... everyone come to the **Wunan**	*numbila...* schnell alle kommen zum **Wunan**	*numbila...* vite, tout le monde vient au **Wunan**
ngawarra wanggi wunandi... So they play together all in the right **skin**	*ngawarra wanggi wunandi...* Sie tanzen zusammen jeder da wo er hingehört	*ngawarra wanggi wunandi...* et ils jouent ensemble, au sein de leur peau
bulba biji nyina ngunda... Let them women come along woman gotta be one side and man gotta be one side again	*bulba biji nyina ngunda* Lasst die Frauen herkommen Die Frauen müssen auf die eine Seite und die Männer auf die andere	*bulba biji nyina ngunda* Laissez les femmes venir ici les femmes doivent se mettre d'un côté et les hommes de l'autre côté
Ngarinyin songs goes...	und das Lied der **Ngarinyin** das geht...	et le chant **Ngarinyin** continue...
bulba biji nyina ngunda	*bulba biji nyina ngunda*	*bulba biji nyina ngunda*
Gagan.ba biya nginda ngunda	*Gagan.ba biya nginda ngunda*	*Gagan.ba biya nginda ngunda*
Biriwudi adman nalli ganangan	*Biriwudi adman nalli ganangan*	*Biriwudi adman nalli ganangan*
walwinya barruru wa nyanga.	*walwinya barruru wa nyanga.*	*walwinya barruru wa nyanga.*
walwinya gulambari nyanga	*walwinya gulambari nyanga*	*walwinya gulambari nyanga*
ngangurr warra Ngarjno	*ngangurr warra* Ngarjno	*ngangurr warra* Ngarjno

All man here line up and they in a ring dance...
all this lot in a ring dance

Banggal

Alle Männer stellen sich in eine Reihe ...
und tanzen im Kreis
zusammen tanzen sie den Kreistanz

Banggal

Tous les hommes s'alignent
et font la danse circulaire...
tous sont dans la danse circulaire

Banggal

Two lines of people all coming
in that afternoon show...
when all these women decide to come in too
that's the coming to the ring...
that the **walu.ngarri** ground

Banggal

Das sind zwei Reihen von Leuten
die tanzen am Nachmittag ...
wenn die Frauen auch dazukommen
dann beginnt der Kreistanz ...
das ist der Platz für den **walu.ngarri**

Banggal

Deux rangées de personnes arrivent
à ce spectacle qui a lieu l'après-midi ...
quand toutes ces femmes décident de venir aussi
elles entrent dans le cercle ...
c'est l'endroit pour le **walu.ngarri**

Banggal

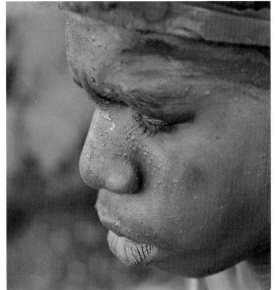

bararu.ru nollabiallu
walking up to dance ground
when we playing we get sweaty
you know all our sweat running
we rub... you can smell the man's odour
you can smell the song **walbo gudina**
that's why people put odour under armpits
ngolo ngolo!... come up, walk along
let's dance ah ring dance
they been say dreamtime... you know
when they been start law
for initiating young people
place called **Wudmangu**

Banggal

bararu.ru nollabiallu
der Weg zum Tanzplatz
wenn wir tanzen kommt der Schweiß
der Schweiß kommt aus allen Poren
den verreiben wir... man riecht die Männer
man riecht das Lied **walbo gudina**
deshalb reiben sich die Leute unter den Achseln ein
ngolo ngolo!... los komm lass uns gehen
lass uns tanzen im Kreis
das sagen wir seit der Traumzeit... du weißt
schon als sie die Gesetze gemacht haben
die Initiation für die jungen Leute
an einem Ort namens **Wudmangu**

Banggal

bararu.ru nollabiallu
marcher jusqu'au terrain de danse
quand on joue on transpire
tu sais toute la sueur qui coule
on se frotte... tu peux sentir l'odeur de l'homme
tu peux sentir le chant, **walbo gudina**
c'est pourquoi les gens mettent du parfum
sous les aisselles
ngolo ngolo!... viens là, marche avec nous
dansons ah la danse circulaire
ils disaient que c'était le rêve... tu sais
quand ils ont créé la Loi
pour initier les jeunes gens
à un endroit qui s'appelle **Wudmangu**

Banggal

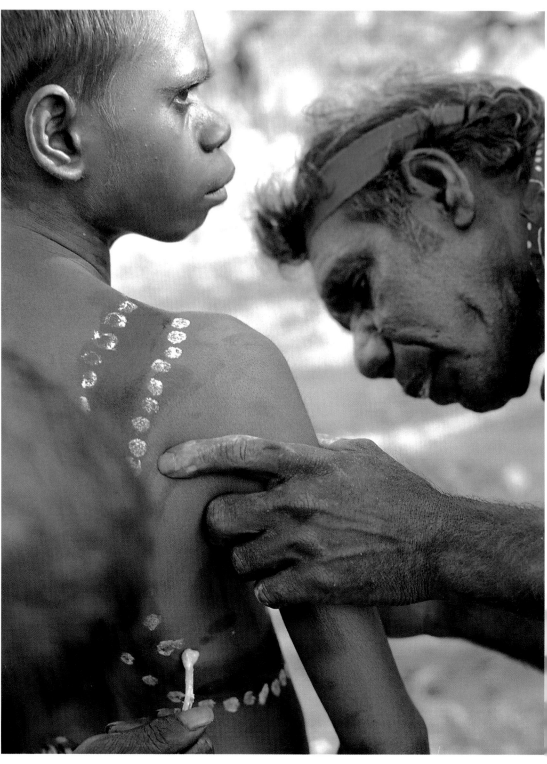

He gotta be green all the way in this life
that's the long life
... not breaking the law or he get punished
you gotta educate him all the way
anybody you gotta be green all the time
... not dry up

Nyawarra

Sein Leben lang muss er bleiben wie ein grüner Ast
dann lebt er lange
... nicht die Gesetze brechen sonst gibt es Strafe
sein Leben lang muss er lernen
jeder muss bleiben wie ein grüner Ast
... sonst vertrocknet man

Nyawarra

Il doit rester toujours vert tout le long sa vie
ainsi il vivra longtemps
... sans violer la Loi ou sinon il sera puni
tu dois l'éduquer tout le temps
tout le monde doit être vert, naïf tout le temps
... pas aride et dur

Nyawarra

Paint those two with that oil
and get red ochre put 'em on
Yeah you know that song
that sweat from arm... under our arm
we rub these young people with this sweat
... sweat everyone

Banggal

Die zwei werden mit diesem Öl bemalt
und dann kommt roter Ocker dazu
Na du kennst ja das Lied
der Schweiß aus der Achselhöhle ... unserer Achsel
wir reiben die jungen Leute ein mit dem Schweiß
... Schweiß von allen

Banggal

Peins ces deux avec cette huile
et prend de l'ocre rouge que tu leur mets dessus
Oui tu connais ce chant
cette sueur du bras... sous nos bras
on frictionne ces jeunes gens avec cette sueur
... on met de la sueur sur chacun d'eux

Banggal

*wir.nganyen... **Gwion** teaching songs...*
*that's why they got 'em **yululun***
up in their heads too
*them **yululun**... feather*
they dressed themselves
Nyawarra

wir.nganyen ... die Lieder
*die haben wir von den **Gwion***
deshalb haben sie die Federn auf dem Kopf
*haben sich geschmückt mit **yululun***
Nyawarra

*wir.nganyen ... les chants d'enseignement **Gwion**...*
c'est pourquoi ils en ont sur la tête aussi
*des plumes, des **yululun**,*
avec lesquelles ils s'habillent
Nyawarra

This is spear... it remind us too
*because this woman **wongai** now*
*when they given their present... to **Jillinya***
this is spear and because she boss woman

*And this **munnumburra** woman*
leading the way in for dance
while this lot of young people dancing
'cause of boss woman there

Banggal

Cette lance nous rappelle quelque chose
*... parce que cette femme est **wongai***
*quand ils donnent leur présent... à **Jillinya***
ils donnent une lance
parce que c'est la patronne

*Et cette femme **munnumburra***
elle montre la voie pour la danse
pendant que tous ces jeunes ils dansent
car elle qui commande

Banggal

Der Speer hier der ist auch zur Erinnerung
*... wegen dieser Frau dieser **wongai***
*wenn sie ihr Geschenke brachten... der **Jillinya***
den Speer weil sie die Oberste der Frauen ist

*Und die **munnumburra**-Frau*
die führt die anderen zum Tanz
und die jungen Leute hier die tanzen schon
weil die Oberste von den Frauen da ist

Banggal

bararu.ru   dance ground

Guliran.gun   white trees

Wodoi Jungun   mixed group

Gunya jerr wudma narnar?   where's the women?

ngolo ngolo! gwiallu   come up walk along

bararu.ru nollabiallu   walking up to dance ground

gungelle bana   echo travelling over hills

beng.ba beng.ba   Yay! Yay!

bararu.ru   Tanzplatz

Guliran.gun   weiße Bäume

Wodoi Jungun   gemischte Gruppe

Gunya jerr wudma narnar?   wo bleiben die Frauen?

ngolo ngolo! gwiallu   los komm! lass uns gehen

bararu.ru nollabiallu   auf zum Tanzplatz

gungelle bana   das Echo schallt über die Berge

beng.ba beng.ba   Hey! Hey!

bararu.ru   piste de danse

Guliran.gun   arbres blancs

Wodoi Jungun   groupe mélangé

Gunya jerr wudma narnar?   où sont les femmes ?

ngolo ngolo! gwiallu   viens ! marche avec nous

bararu.ru nollabiallu   terrain de danse

gungelle bana   écho se répandant au-delà des collines

beng.ba beng.ba   Yay ! Yay !

gudmerrermeri…
grab one another direction to dancers

This is where the boy is lifted here
The boy will be carried from here
this is where the dancing ground
is this lot will go round and this behind man
this man come right around this ring
and join up and catch the last man's hand
Ngarjno

Yeah when they bring 'em then
birrawudi *dance*
birrawudi… *that big ring dance*
he sit down on the man's back

Those boys sit down
and they carry him round the ring dance
then they have a large supper… ***mangarri***
Banggal

gudmerrermeri…
die Tänzer fassen sich alle in einer Richtung

Da wird der Junge hochgehoben
Von hier wird er getragen
das hier das ist der Tanzplatz
alle machen einen Kreis und der Letzte
der Erste kommt zum Letzten
legt ihm die Hand auf die Schulter
Ngarjno

Ja und wenn sie die Jungen herbringen
zum ***birrawudi****-Tanz*
birrawudi… *das ist der große Kreistanz*
dann sitzen sie auf den Rücken der Männer

Da sitzen die Jungen
und die Männer tragen sie herum beim Kreistanz
und dann gibt es ein großes Essen… ***mangarri***
Banggal

gudmerrermeri…
montrer une autre direction aux danseurs

C'est là que le garçon est soulevé
Le garçon sera porté depuis là
c'est là qu'est le terrain de danse
ils iront tourner là autour derrière l'homme
cet homme fait le tour du cercle
et rejoint et attrape la main du dernier
Ngarjno

Oui quand ils l'amènent alors
c'est la danse ***birrawudi***
birrawudi… *cette grande danse circulaire*
il s'assoit sur le dos de l'homme

Le garçons s'assoit
et ils le portent tout autour de la danse circulaire
après ils font un grand repas… ***mangarri***
Banggal

*It's the ring dance... **walu.ngarri**
and that's what going to happen
Wodoi woman... **Jungun** woman
Jungun man... **Wodoi** man*

*This is the woman **Wodoi**
and this is the man **Jungun***

*That's the right marriage
and the right way of doing it
There's no confusions*

*And then ah **Wodoi** woman
do marry that **Jungun** man*

*Marriage business we married in the law
and in this ground here
we married in everything... that's the law*
Banggal

*Das ist der Kreistanz ... **walu.ngarri**
und so geht das jetzt
Wodoi-Frau ... **Jungun**-Frau
Jungun-Mann ... **Wodoi**-Mann*

*Das ist die **Wodoi**-Frau
und das ist der **Jungun**-Mann*

*So wird geheiratet
so gehört sich das
Da kommt nichts durcheinander*

*Und dann heiratet die **Wodoi**-Frau
einen **Jungun**-Mann*

*Wie man heiratet das gehört zum Gesetz
das steckt hier in der Erde
mit allem sind wir verheiratet ... das ist das Gesetz*
Banggal

*C'est la danse circulaire ... **walu.ngarri**
et c'est ce qui va arriver
la femme **Wodoi** ... la femme **Jungun**
l'homme **Jungun** ... l'homme **Wodoi***

*Ça c'est la femme **Wodoi**
et ça c'est l'homme **Jungun***

*C'est le bon mariage
la bonne façon de le faire
Il n'y a pas de confusion possible*

*Et cette femme **Wodoi**
épouse cet homme **Jungun***

*La question du mariage ça se fait dans la Loi
et à cet endroit
on se marie tous dans la Loi*
Banggal

221

This lot **Gwion**... see their knees bend
they dance now all in a line
all these woman wear... man wear
for cover their pubic areas... **walbud... jalgun**
and that's why they here and they stuck out long
when they play in the **walu.ngarri**...
beautiful people... you know when they dancing
yeah it like ah following
you know float in the air
and that's why this lot they invented for
us to use today
We make little sticks... very sharp, sharp one
We spear woman in the bottom here
... and she bleed blood
And she spear us too... we bleed blood
... this is bleeding time
we take the pain
before the young people get initiated
see we... we spill the blood before them

That's why these little ah little **jowul** spears
ones what we use in the **walu.ngarri**
where they started it all
Banggal

Das da sind **Gwion**... siehst du
wie sie die Knie beugen?
die tanzen alle in einer Reihe
und die Frauen... die Männer auch
die bedecken ihre Scham mit **walbud... jalgun**
deswegen haben sie die an... die Schurze fliegen
wenn sie sich drehen beim **walu.ngarri**
schöne Menschen sind das... wenn sie tanzen
als ob die Röcke hinter ihnen herfliegen
als ob sie in der Luft schweben
die haben die damals für uns erfunden
und wir tragen sie noch heute
Wir nehmen kleine Stöcke... spitze, sehr spitze
und stechen den Frauen in den Hintern
... bis das Blut kommt
Und sie stechen uns auch... wir bluten auch
... alle müssen bluten
wir nehmen den jungen Leuten die Schmerzen
bevor die Initiation beginnt
verstehst du... wir bluten für sie

Deshalb diese kleinen **jowul**-Spieße
die wir beim **walu.ngarri** nehmen
wo das alles angefangen hat
Banggal

Tous ces **Gwion**... regarde leurs genoux pliés
ils dansent tous en rang maintenant
tous ces habits de femmes... ces habits d'hommes
c'est pour couvrir leur pubis... **walbud... jalgun**
c'est pour ça qu'ils sont là et qu'ils dépassent bien
quand ils font le **walu.ngarri**...
ils sont beaux... tu sais quand ils dansent
oui c'est comme... ça pend
tu sais ça flotte dans l'air
et c'est pour ça que eux ils ont inventé ça
pour que nous on s'en serve aujourd'hui
On fait des petits bâtons... très très pointus
On transperce la femme dans le derrière là
... et elle saigne du sang
Et elle nous pique aussi... et on saigne du sang
... c'est le moment où on saigne
on doit souffrir nous aussi
avant que les jeunes soient initiés
tu vois... on répand le sang avant eux

C'est pour ça qu'on a ces petites lances,
ces petites **jowul**
celles qu'on utilise dans le **walu.ngarri**
depuis qu'il a été créé
Banggal

And we carry this sticks here... *jowul*
this here see *jowul* that's for ceremony
We poke them in that ceremony
and we make little sticks very sharp... sharp one!
we spear women in the bum here

And that what that ceremony is...
spearing ourselves and everybody
for big big laugh... this lot big laugh now

We really dance happily
and they enjoying that dance
we kill all his nerves and we kill all his fear
we make 'em happy
and it's like a putting anaesthetic to a boy
then he doesn't frighten he just happy
and he don't know what coming
and we we cut his foreskin then
because he still happy
he never forget that dancing it's like anaesthetic
putting it through that young fella
and this song is like that
That's the last one... they go in bush then
in the morning six... five o'clock
in the morning they cut 'em then...
foreskin... that's the *gaybo gerd*

Because when he get cut
he know where he is
he realise what been happening in the night
in the night dance
that's in *walu.ngarri* and *wir.nganyen*

The same thing will take place this year
and next year belong to our ceremony
belong to this country
and this same thing is going to take place
We going to spear ourselves
spear a woman... blood bleeding
man bleeding... before young people bleed
it's the young people they enjoy this fun
it's like anaesthetic... it doesn't have that fear
for early morning for when they being initiated
While it is dark... when it's red
that's the time we cut those boys
because it represent their blood
If that man got foreskin he outside the law
Banggal

That little boys who is going to get cut
his name is... *ngawarra*
Everybody been crying for their two boys
all the family... mother auntie sister
they all been crying for their two boys
Ngarjno

Wir haben diese kleinen Stöcke hier … *jowul*
das ist ein *jowul* der ist für die Zeremonie
Damit pieksen wir sie bei der Zeremonie
wir machen die kleinen Spieße sehr, sehr spitz
und stechen die Frauen in den Hintern

Das gehört zu der Zeremonie
jeder piekst jeden und alle lachen dabei …
alle haben ihren Spaß

Richtig fröhlich sind wir beim Tanzen
und die Jungen haben ihren Spaß
wir nehmen ihnen die Angst
wir bringen sie zum Lachen
das ist wie ein Betäubungsmittel
dann haben sie keine Angst und feuen sich
sie vergessen was kommt
und dann schneiden wir ihm die Vorhaut ab
solange er noch so glücklich ist
den Tanz wird er nie vergessen
wie eine Betäubung ist das
bevor wir den Jungen beschneiden
und das Lied das geht so
Das kommt zuletzt … danach gehen sie in den Busch
um sechs Uhr morgens … oder um fünf
am Morgen werden sie beschnitten …
die Vorhaut … *gaybo gerd* heißt die

Denn wenn der Schnitt kommt
dann weiß er wo er ist
er versteht was in der Nacht geschehen ist
bei dem Tanz in der Nacht
das sind *walu.ngarri* und *wir.nganyen*

So wird es dieses Jahr auch wieder sein
und nächstes Jahr das ist eben die Zeremonie
die gehört zu diesem Land
und alles wird wieder genauso sein
Wir stechen uns mit dem Speer
stechen eine Frau … bis das Blut kommt
ein Mann blutet … bevor die Jungen bluten
und die jungen Leute haben ihren Spaß daran
es betäubt … vertreibt die Angst
vor dem frühen Morgen bei der Beschneidung
Wenn es noch dunkel ist … der Himmel rot wird
das ist die Zeit da beschneiden wir die Jungen
die Morgenröte die steht für ihr Blut
Ein Mann mit Vorhaut gehört nicht zum Gesetz
Banggal

Die kleinen Jungs die beschnitten werden
die heißen … *ngawarra*
Alle haben um die zwei Jungen geweint
die ganze Familie … Mutter Tante Schwester
die haben um ihre zwei Jungen geweint
Ngarjno

Et on apporte ces bâtons ici … ces *jowul*
tu vois ça ces *jowul* c'est pour la cérémonie
on les pique avec dans cette cérémonie
on fait des petits bâtons très très pointus …
on les plante dans les fesses des femmes là

Et c'est pour ça que cette cérémonie c'est…
nous transpercer les uns les autres
pour bien rigoler… on se marre tous maintenant

On danse en étant vraiment joyeux
et il apprécie cette danse
on calme ses nerfs et on tue sa peur
on le rend heureux
et c'est comme un anesthésiant pour le garçon
après il a pas peur et il est juste content
et il ne sait pas ce qui va arriver
et nous on lui coupe le prépuce
tandis il est toujours joyeux
il oubliera jamais cette danse
qui est comme un anésthésiant
qu'on injecte à ce jeune gars
et ce chant c'est ça
C'est le dernier… ils vont dans le bush après
le matin à six… cinq heures
au matin ils le coupent à ce moment…
le prépuce… c'est le *gaybo gerd*

Parce que quand il est coupé
il sait où il est
il réalise ce qu'il s'est passé pendant la nuit
dans la danse la nuit
c'est dans le *walu.ngarri* et le *wir.nganyen*

La même chose va se faire cette année
et l'année prochaine aussi
ça fait partie de notre pays, cette cérémonie
et la même chose va se faire cette année
On va se transpercer avec les lances
transpercer les femmes… le sang va couler
les hommes vont saigner…
avant que les jeunes saignent
c'est les jeunes ils aiment ce jeu
c'est comme un anésthésiant…
il n'y a pas cette peur
parce qu'au petit matin quand ils vont être initiés
Pendant qu'il fait encore sombre…
quand c'est rouge
c'est le moment où on coupe ces garçons
parce que ça représente leur sang… si un homme
a encore son prépuce il n'est pas dans la Loi
Banggal

Ces petits garçons qui vont être coupés
on les appelle… *ngawarra*
Tout le monde a pleuré pour les deux garçons
toute la famille… la mère, la tante, la sœur
elles ont toutes pleuré pour leurs deux garçons
Ngarjno

Daybreak **brad** when it's still red in colour
brad it connected with the blood... **guli**
brad that red colour
because when daybreak red colour come...
his blood must drip
and that's why it's very important
This is blood coming up... **guli**
and blood is spreading with the **brad**
dawn red colour is **brad**
before flies come around... we initiate that boy

He wait for that song when we make ready
all the men kneel down like a table
And then that boy lay down on top man
... it's a table top

brad das ist die Morgendämmerung
wenn der Himmel noch rot ist
brad gehört zum Blut... **guli**
brad ist die rote Farbe
denn wenn der Tag kommt der Himmel rot wird...
dann muss sein Blut fließen
deshalb ist das so wichtig
Das ist sein Blut da am Himmel... **guli**
und mit **brad** fließt das Blut
die Morgenröte die heißt **brad**
bevor die Fliegen kommen... da machen wir
die Beschneidung

Er wartet auf das Lied
während wir uns bereitmachen
alle Männer knien sich hin wie ein Tisch
Und dann legt sich der Junge oben drauf
... es ist wie eine Tischplatte

Au lever du jour, **brad,** quand tout est
encore rouge **brad** c'est lié au sang... **guli**
le **brad** c'est cette couleur rouge
au moment où le jour pointe,
où tout devient rouge... son sang doit couler
et c'est pour ça c'est important
C'est le sang qui monte... **guli**
et le sang se répand en même temps que le **brad**
la couleur rouge de l'aurore c'est **brad**
avant que les mouches arrivent
on initie le garçon

Il attend le chant pendant qu'on se prépare
tous les hommes s'agenouillent
et font comme une table
... un dessus de table

All the man laying down on ground in bushes
on top the bushes and that boy right on top
and when they hear this song
we telling them to get up this song
telling them to come with your **gimbu**
and cut 'em foreskin

This is the song belong to that doctor man
with the **gimbu** to cut him
They just cut the foreskin off
and bury him in a hole
we put a stone there like signal stone

If you see this rock standing up there
that's your warning
that's the one we call **jallala** the way he standing
If anybody break the law to go in there
he get into a lot of problem
That's **jallala**... **jallala** is a warning

Banggal

Alle Männer legen sich im Busch auf den Boden
über die Büsche und der Junge kommt obendrauf
und wenn sie das Lied hier hören
mit dem Lied sagen wir dass alle bereit sind
dass sie kommen können mit ihrer **gimbu**-Klinge
und sie beschneiden

Das ist das Lied für den Medizinmann
der kommt mit der **gimbu** und beschneidet ihn
er schneidet ihm die Vorhaut ab
und die begräbt er in einem Loch
und wir stellen einen Stein drauf zum Zeichen

Wenn man einen Stein wie den da drüben sieht
dann heißt das Vorsicht
jallala nennen wir die Steine
Wenn jemand das Gesetz bricht ihm zu nahe kommt
der wird es bereuen
Das ist **jallala**... **jallala** ist eine Warnung

Banggal

Tous les hommes s'allongent par terre
dans les herbes
sur les herbes et le garçon est au-dessus
et quand ils entendent le chant
on lui dit de se lever
le chant lui dit de venir avec leur **gimbu**
et de lui couper le prépuce

Ce chant appartient au docteur
avec sa **gimbu** pour le couper
Il enlève juste le prépuce
et l'enterre dans un trou
on met une pierre là pour le signaler

Si tu vois ce caillou dressé là-haut
c'est pour te prévenir
c'est ça qu'on appelle **jallala** quand c'est debout
Quiconque viole la Loi en venant ici
il s'expose à avoir des problèmes
Ce **jallala**... ce **jallala** c'est un avertissement

Banggal

banman... medicine man there
who straight away put that charcoal
to stop the bleeding
Banggal

Bring them back here put them in smoke
Keep that *juruma* ash medicine
with that *guli...* blood... make it better

when he get better... when blood stopped
them get that boy now chuck them in water

after get dry bring 'em fat... kangaroo fat
rub 'em now... rub 'em up

banman... der Medizinmann
der tut sofort Asche drauf
dann hört es auf zu bluten
Banggal

Bringt sie hierher zurück dann kommt der Rauch
Die *juruma*-Asche und das *guli...* Blut
die hebt er auf... und dann tut es nicht mehr weh

wenn es ihm besser geht... es nicht mehr blutet
dann stecken sie die Jungen ins Wasser

wenn sie trocken sind reiben sie sie ein
mit Kängurufett... reiben sie ein mit Fett

banman... c'est comme un médecin
c'est lui qui met tout de suite un bout de charbon
pour arrêter le sang
Banggal

On les ramène ici et on les met dans la fumée
On garde cette cendre médicinale, *juruma*
avec le sang, *guli...* c'est mieux

quand il va mieux... quand le sang ne coule plus
ils prennent le garçon et le
balancent dans l'eau

après qu'il ait séché on amène
de la graisse... de la graisse de kangourou
et on le frotte avec...

then when their blood away now clean
then they get 'em that red paint...
now they paint them face
they paint 'em face... body

get that paperbark like that
you know them got that *garagi...* bush-bucket

garagi properly all paint 'em that red ochre
got 'em there paint on *garagi* for *juruma*
mark 'im *Gulingi* rain *wanjina*
... kangaroo... bird in that *garagi* mark 'im
get 'em ready before they give 'em young people

they hide 'em this one now
that *ngoru...* that water belong *Gulingi* now
young people don't want to find 'em
Ngarjno

und wenn das Blut weg ist wenn sie sauber sind
dann kommt die rote Farbe...
ihr Gesicht wird bemalt
erst das Gesicht... dann der Körper

dann nehmen sie ein Stück Papierbaum
so wie hier aus der man *garagi* macht

garagi ganz und gar mit rotem Ocker bemalt
da hat er sie bemalte *garagi* für *juruma*-Asche
mit dem Zeichen von *Gulingi* dem Regenbringer
... Känguru... Vögel auf den *garagi*
sie werden bemalt
und die Jungen bekommen sie

das hier das verstecken sie jetzt
das *ngoru...* das Wasser das gehört *Gulingi*
die jungen Leute sollen das nicht finden
Ngarjno

ensuite, quand le sang est parti, que c'est propre
ils prennent cette peinture rouge...
et ils lui peignent le visage
d'abord le visage... puis le corps

on prend de l'écorce comme ça
tu sais ils ont ces sacs du bush, ces *garagi*

les *garagi* on les peint bien avec l'ocre rouge
on peint les *garagi* pour le *juruma*
on les marque du signe de *Gulingi*
wanjina de la pluie
le kangourou... l'oiseau
sont marqués sur les *garagi*
on les prépare avant de les donner aux jeunes

ils les cachent après
c'est *ngoru...* cette eau est à *Gulingi* maintenant
les jeunes ne doivent pas les trouver
Ngarjno

*Singing **"yumungonday bolgay"***
that grandmother or auntie
she sing out in the morning
for that young fella... she gotta say
"Where you are?
what you still digging boabnut?
or what you doing?... where are you?"

For morning she sing out
she sing out for him
and he don't answer her... nothing
because he long way away... with man business
that song... because that darkness
hiding that young man belong to her
because he in bush there with the men

He go for good
after he stopped in the bush initiation
after they cut him
Banggal

*Sie singt **„yumungonday bolgay"***
die Großmutter oder Tante
das singt sie am Morgen
für den jungen Burschen... sie muss sagen
„Wo bist du?
warum suchst du noch nach Boabfrüchten?
oder was machst du da?... wo steckst du?"

Am Morgen singt sie das
sie singt für ihn
aber er antwortet nicht mehr... kein Wort
er ist weit fort... er ist jetzt bei den Männern
dieses Lied... weil die Dunkelheit
den jungen Mann verbirgt ihren jungen Mann
denn der ist jetzt im Busch mit den anderen

Der kommt nicht mehr zu ihr zurück
wenn sie ihn beschnitten haben
wenn er im Busch war
Banggal

*Elle chante « **yumungonday bolgay** »*
cette grand-mère ou cette tante
elle chante au petit matin
pour ce petit gars... elle dit
« Où es-tu ?
*tu creuses toujours une noix de **baobab** ?*
ou sinon tu fais quoi ?... Où es-tu ? »

Le matin elle chante
elle chante pour lui
et il lui répond pas... rien
parce qu'il est loin loin... à faire un truc d'hommes
ce chant... à cause de la pénombre
qui cache ce jeune homme qui est à elle
il est dans le bush là-bas avec les hommes

Il est parti pour de bon
il s'est arrêté à la cérémonie d'initiation
dans le bush... après qu'ils l'aient coupé
Banggal

And man when they cutting them
man ís singing out *"ijai jai jaî"* making noise!
So if any boy cry he ís covered...
his cry is covered
And when they all finished...
one man um when they say *"ijai"*
and then the signal go to the women

And they cry when the *"ijai"* stopped
That's the signal
when the *"ijai"* is stopped in that place
and lot women they know and they cry
they happy because everything done very good
They know then... that ís the signal
when the *"ijai"* stopped
Nyawarra

"didiyii" when they call 'em...
"didiyii" then all finished
Ngarjno

Und die Männer wenn die Beschneidung kommt
die singen *„ijai jai jaî"* und ein Krach ist das!
Wenn da ein Junge schreit...
dann hört man das nicht
Und wenn alle fertig sind...
wenn dann ein Mann *„ijai"* sagt
dann ist das ein Zeichen für die Frauen

Sie weinen wenn das *„ijai"* aufhört
Das ist ihr Zeichen
wenn wir mit dem *„ijai"* fertig sind
dann wissen die Frauen Bescheid und sie weinen
sie sind glücklich weil alles vorbei ist
Dann wissen sie es... das ist ihr Zeichen
wenn das *„ijai"* aufhört
Nyawarra

„didiyii" wenn sie das schreien...
„didiyii" dann ist alles vorbei
Ngarjno

Et les hommes quand il le coupent
les hommes ils chantent *« ijai jai jaî »* très fort!
Comme ça si un garçon pleure ça couvre ses pleurs
Et quand ils ont tout fini...
un homme dit *« ijai »*
et le signal arrive aux femmes

Et elles pleurent quand le *« ijai »* s'arrête
C'est le signal
quand le *« ijai »* s'arrête à cet endroit
toutes les femmes savent, elles pleurent
elles sont contentes
ça veut dire que tout est bien fait
Elles savent à ce moment... c'est le signal
quand le *« ijai »* s'arrête
Nyawarra

« didiyii » quand ils les appellent...
« didiyii » quand tout est fini
Ngarjno

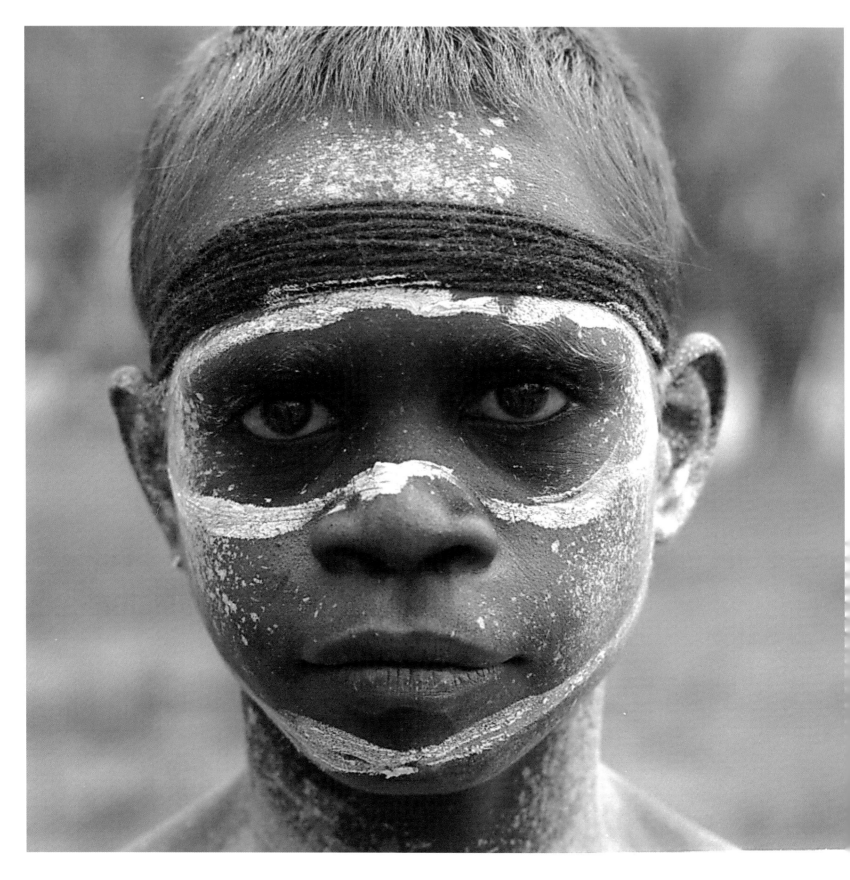

Jenagi people who started this law...
long time belong to **Ngarinyin** country
Old people and I got to hold that thing today
Ngarjno

Die *Jenagi* die haben dieses Gesetz begründet
seit ewiger Zeit gehört das zum Land der **Ngarinyin**
Alte Leute wie ich die halten das heute am Leben
Ngarjno

Les *Jenagi* ont créé cette Loi ... depuis longtemps
elle fait partie du pays **Ngarinyin**
Les vieux et moi, on doit maintenir ça aujourd'hui
Ngarjno

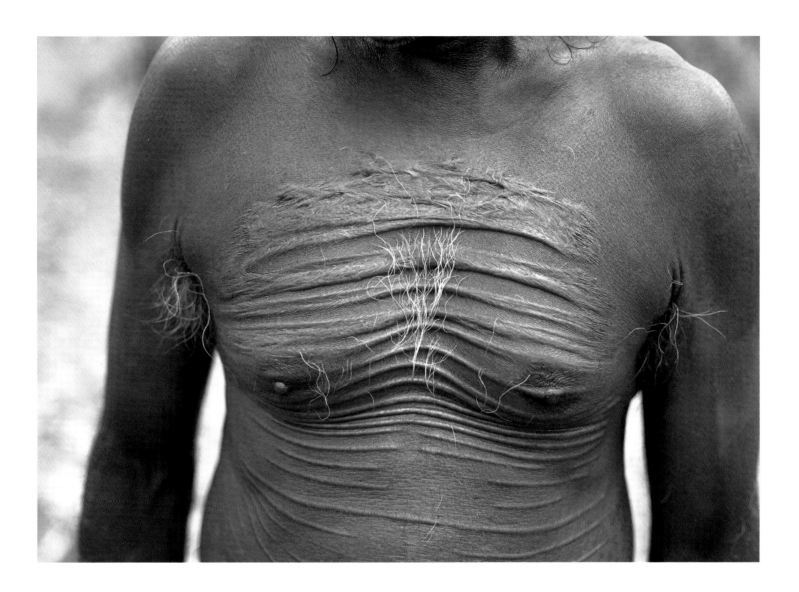

*Now this mark **munnumburra**
and man himself **munnumburra**
because the end of the cut... is right across
that's the land... belonging... he home
and that's what this **munnumburra** means*

***munnumburra** forever... y'know till he die
Spills his blood on the earth
on earth to look after the whole country
that's the **munnumburra***

*That's why it's important
because he have to carry on
when he older man when he got wife and kids
he have to look after the song
and the country*

*He fully initiated man...
we call him **munnumburra** when he elder
elder man is **munnumburra**
Like me and Paddy now we are **munnumburra***
Banggal

*Das hier das sind die Zeichen der **munnumburra**
wer das hat der ist **munnumburra**
da wird ein Schnitt gemacht ... hier quer rüber
das ist das Land ... hier gehört er hin ... sein Zuhause
das hat das **munnumburra**-Zeichen zu bedeuten*

***munnumburra** ist man für immer ... bis man stirbt
Er vergießt sein Blut auf die Erde
er sorgt für das Land
dafür gibt es die **munnumburra***

*Deshalb ist das so wichtig
weil er es weitertragen muss
wenn er älter ist wenn er Frau und Kinder hat
dann muss er das Lied bewahren
und das Land*

*Ein initiierter Mann ...
wenn er älter wird nennen wir ihn **munnumburra**
die Stammesältesten das sind **munnumburra**
Wie ich und Paddy hier wir sind **munnumburra***
Banggal

*Voilà cette marque c'est **munnumburra**
et l'homme lui-même est **munnumburra**
parce que la fin de l'incision ... c'est l'horizon
c'est la terre ... il est d'ici ... il est chez lui
et c'est ce que ce **munnumburra** veut dire*

*Il est **munnumburra** pour toujours ...
jusqu'à sa mort
Il a versé son sang sur la terre
sur la terre pour veiller sur tout le pays
c'est le **munnumburra***

*C'est important parce qu'il est là pour transmettre
il aura à s'occuper des chants et du pays
quand il sera vieux
quand il aura femme et enfants
il faudra qu'il s'occupe du chant et du pays*

*ce sera un homme complètement initié
on l'appelle **munnumburra** quand il devient un
ancien un ancien ça se dit **munnumburra**
comme Paddy et moi maintenant
on est **munnumburra***
Banggal

maba… mabajiri… old man maba
*he's a **munnumburra***
but he's getting older Yep!
*old **munnumburra** man gettin' older and older*
you want to hand it over to someone else
*well we call him **maba**… that old man **maba***

he some time out from the law now that old man
I'm not meaning really out but it's just ahhh…
finished from having the responsibility
*for that country… or the **Wunan** law*
or something he handing it over to somebody

maba … mabajiri … maba das ist ein Alter
*wenn einer **munnumburra** ist*
und noch älter wird oh ja!
*ein alter **munnumburra**-Mann wenn er ganz alt ist*
wenn es Zeit ist es an einen anderen weiterzugeben
*den nennen wir **maba** … den alten Mann, **maba***

Der ist kein Gesetzeshüter mehr weil er so alt ist
nicht dass er sich nicht mehr dran halten muss
ich meine … er trägt keine Verantwortung mehr
*Verantwortung für das Land … das **Wunan**-Gesetz*
das gibt er jetzt an jemand anderen weiter

maba … mabajiri … un vieil homme, maba
*c'est un **munnumburra***
mais il devient vieux, hein !
*un vieux **munnumburra** mais qui vieillit,*
qui vieillit il veut transmettre à quelqu'un
*on l'appelle **maba** … ce vieil homme c'est **maba***

il est parfois un peu en dehors
de la Loi ce vieil homme
pas vraiment hors de la Loi mais juste un peu …
il a plus la responsabilité
*de ce pays … ou de la Loi du **Wunan***
ou de n'importe quoi,
il le transmet à quelqu'un

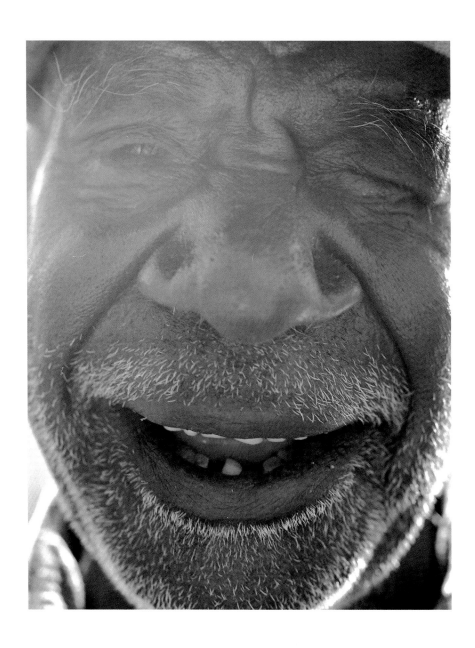

*and he be **maba** now and he been **ambiliji***
*what you call it getting blind… that's a **maba***
he finished from his time now
Nyawarra

*und dann ist er ein **maba** … ein **ambiliji***
*wie nennt ihr das, er wird blind … deswegen **maba***
seine Zeit ist um
Nyawarra

*et maintenant il est **maba**, il est **ambiliji***
*comment tu dis, il devient aveugle … c'est un **maba***
il a fait son temps quoi
Nyawarra

*He is in the **Wunan***
He spilled his blood now on the earth
that young fella
*That's why the **Wunan** is like that*
*nobody outside the **Wunan***
but he spilled his blood...
he's in for the rest of his life
that young fella he can't change his life
... he's initiated forever

Nyawarra

*Er ist jetzt im **Wunan***
Er hat sein Blut auf die Erde vergossen
der junge Bursche
*So ist das **Wunan***
*niemand steht außerhalb des **Wunan***
wenn er sein Blut vergossen hat...
dann gehört er für den Rest seines Lebens dazu
der junge Bursche kann das nicht mehr ändern
... die Initiation die gilt für immer

Nyawarra

*Il est dans le **Wunan***
Il a fait couler son sang sur la terre
ce jeune gars
*C'est pourquoi c'est comme ça le **Wunan***
*personne est en dehors du **Wunan***
il a fait couler son sang...
il y est pour le restant de sa vie
ce jeune gars ne peut plus changer sa vie
... il est initié pour toujours

Nyawarra

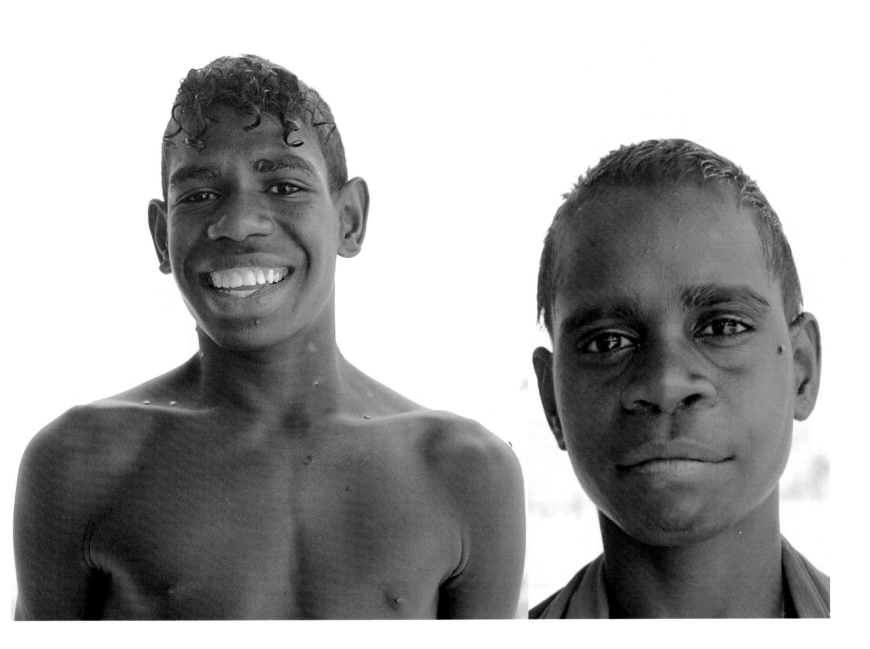

And that's why initiation ceremony
always save young life
... to understand culture

Banggal

Darum geht es bei der Initiation
die rettet das junge Leben
... damit es die Kultur versteht

Banggal

Et c'est pourquoi la cérémonie d'initiation
elle protège toujours les jeunes
... elle leur fait comprendre leur culture

Banggal

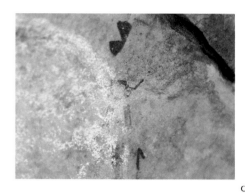

a

b

c

Cultural connections exist between a recent **Ngarinyin** **walu.ngarri** initiation ceremony and a **Gwion** painting on a single large sandstone boulder. The painting represents men and women commencing a ring-dance (b). The participants are painted one above the other and the scene is composed to simulate the perspective of animated male and female dancers converging.

Women in the foreground start the inner ring while male dancers opposite form a line to start the outer ring; some separate figures are placed at the edge of the action. Led by a female **munnumburra** wearing a tall conical wig outlined in white, the line of women dance with knees bent, rising and falling on their toes as they approach a central individual. **Banggal** identified this tall figure as the singer who is always in the middle of the ring-dance (but he observed that both ritual novice and expert song-man could occupy this position during the **walu.ngarri**). Because the painting of the head is now severely eroded, the residual image created some confusion as to the exact identity of this now androgynous figure; the outline also suggested the maternal presence of **Jillinya**. Restored sections of exfoliated surface have been re-painted in the past with very fine lines of different scale to the original. The re-painting does confirm **Banggal's** assertion, made at the site, that generations of local ancestors treasured this cultural icon of **walu.ngarri** origins.

At the top right is a solitary figure, faint of body but clearly holding a **nyarndu** (spear-thrower). Little red paint remains, suggesting that it had a mainly white-painted body typical of a **munnumburra** painted with **onmal**. Most clay-based white pigments easily erode away. What red residue remains is significant, providing a stark silhouette of the angular **mudurra** (wig) with two sharply pointed ears (c). This motif represents **Wiji.ngarri**, the celebrated composer of the songs originating the **walu.ngarri** ring-dancing.

Facing them from the opposite direction is a more formal grouping of four male figures forming a line (a). The four men are represented holding **gallid** (barbed spears) and being led by a man wearing a bending **mudurra**. The odd trouser-like appearance of their dark legs is a result of the erosion of their painted torsos.

Die Wurzeln des heutigen Initiationsrituals der **Ngarinyin**, des **walu.ngarri**, sind auf einem **Gwion**-Felsbild auf einem großen Sandsteinfindling zu sehen. Das Bild zeigt Männer und Frauen, die eben einen Kreistanz beginnen (b). Die Teilnehmer sind übereinander dargestellt, und die Komposition soll die Perspektive der aufeinander zukommenden Tänzer und Tänzerinnen zum Ausdruck bringen.

Die Frauen im Vordergrund setzen zum inneren Kreis an, die Männer gegenüber bilden eine Reihe für den äußeren Kreis; einige einzelne Figuren stehen noch am Rande des Geschehens. Angeführt von einer weiblichen **munnumburra** mit einer in weißen Umrissen gezeichneten hohen konischen Perücke, tanzen die Frauen in einer langen Reihe, die Knie gebeugt erheben sie sich auf die Zehenspitzen und lassen sich wieder herab und bewegen sich dabei auf eine Gestalt in der Mitte zu. **Banggal** identifizierte diese statt-liche Gestalt als den Sänger, der stets in der Mitte des Kreis-tanzes bleibt (fügte jedoch hinzu, dass beim **walu.ngarri** sowohl der Initiand als auch der Vorsänger diese Position einnehmen könne). Der Kopf der dargestellten Figur ist stark verwittert, und aus den spärlichen Überresten ist die Identität der heute androgynen Figur nicht leicht zu deuten; die Umrisse lassen einen Bezug auf die Urmutter **Jillinya** vermuten. Manche Partien der abgeblätterten Oberfläche sind mit sehr feinen Linien in einem anderen Maßstab als bei dem Original nachgemalt worden. Diese Übermalungen bestätigen die von **Banggal** vor Ort gege-bene Versicherung, dass Generationen von Vorfahren dieses **walu.ngarri**-Bild als heilig verehrten.

Oben rechts ist eine einzelne Figur zu erkennen, von schmächtiger Gestalt, doch eindeutig mit einer **nyarndu** (Speerschleuder) in der Hand. Da nur wenig rote Farbe erhalten ist, kann man vermuten, dass der Körper ursprüng-lich weitgehend weiß gemalt war, typisch für einen **mun-numburra** mit seiner **onmal**-Körperbemalung. Die meisten weißen Pigmente auf Lehmbasis verwittern sehr schnell. Doch auch die Überreste roter Farbe sind aufschlussreich und zeigen noch die kräftigen Umrisse einer eckigen **mudurra** (Perücke) mit zwei ausgeprägt spitzen Ohren (c). Dieses Motiv steht für **Wiji.ngarri**, den gefeierten Schöpfer der Lieder, die bei den **walu.ngarri**-Kreistänzen gesungen werden.

Auf der gegenüberliegenden Seite steht eine formellere Gruppierung von vier Männerfiguren in einer Reihe (a). Die Männer halten Speere mit Widerhaken (**gallid**) und werden angeführt von einem Mann mit einer geschwun-genen **mudurra**. Das merkwürdige Aussehen der schwarzen Beine, die wie Hosen wirken, ist eine Folge der Erosion, bei der die Oberkörper der Figuren verblasst sind.

Des liens culturels existent entre la cérémonie récente des **Ngarinyin**, le **walu.ngarri** et une peinture **Gwion** qui se trouve sur un gros rocher de grès isolé. La peinture représente des hommes et des femmes commençant une danse circulaire (b). Les participants sont peints les uns au-dessus des autres et la scène est composée de façon à simuler l'idée de danseurs hommes et femmes en train de converger.

Les femmes au premier plan commencent à former le cer-cle intérieur pendant que les danseurs à l'opposé sont en ligne pour amorcer le début du cercle extérieur ; certains personnages indépendants sont placés en bordure de la scène. Menée par une femme **munnumburra** portant une haute coiffe de forme conique aux contours blancs, la rangée de femmes danse avec les genoux pliés, se levant et retombant sur leurs doigts de pieds tandis qu'elle s'approche d'un individu au centre. **Banggal** identifia cette figure comme étant le chanteur qui se trouve toujours au centre de la danse circulaire (mais il fit remarquer qu'à la fois le novice du rituel et le chanteur qui est un spécia-liste pouvaient occuper cette même place pendant le **walu.ngarri**). Étant donné que la tête est aujourd'hui très effacée, ce qu'il reste de l'image prête à confusion pour pouvoir identifier cette figure désormais androgyne ; le contour laissait également supposer la présence mater-nelle de **Jillinya**. Des parties restaurées de la surface qui a perdu son revêtement ont été repeintes dans le passé avec des traits très fins, à une échelle différente de l'original. Les retouches confirment l'affirmation qu'a faite **Banggal** sur le site en disant que des générations d'ancêtres lo-caux attachaient beaucoup d'importance à cette image montrant les origines de **walu.ngarri**.

Il y a un personnage tout seul en haut à droite dont les couleurs du corps ont pâli mais qui tient clairement un **nyarndu** (propulseur). Il reste peu de peinture rouge, ce qui suggère que son corps était principalement peint en blanc à la manière d'un **munnumburra** peint avec de l'**onmal** (pigment blanc). La plupart des pigments blancs à base d'argile se désagrègent. Ce qu'il reste de rouge est significatif, donnant une allure raide à la **mudurra** (coiffe) en cheveux tout en angles avec deux oreilles en pointe (c). Ce motif est une représentation de **Wiji.ngarri**, le célèbre compositeur de chants qui est à l'origine de **walu.ngarri**, la danse circulaire.

Leur faisant face depuis l'autre côté, il y a un groupe de quatre hommes en rang (a). Les quatre hommes sont représentés portant des **gallid** (lances à picots) et sont menés par un homme portant une **mudurra** recourbée. L'aspect étrange de ces jambes foncées qui ont l'air d'être des pantalons est dû en fait à l'érosion de la peinture de leurs torses.

walu.ngarri

d

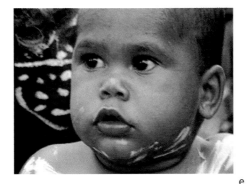
e

f

Two dancers in the approaching women's line are each wearing a small **jalgun** (apron made of fluffy emu down), and here the **jalgun** are painted clearly, floating as bustles light enough to be lifted by the dancer's rising and falling movements.

Another nearby painting records a moment later in the ceremony, when a man reaches for thin skewers of sharpened wood hidden in his hair. These **jowul** were worn there ready to surprise and jab each woman dancer in the backside to draw a drop of blood. Mock fighting between women and men develops in sight of the initiates sitting on the ground in the centre of the ring-dancing. As the boisterous noise gets louder, with more people screaming in theatrical pain, the initiates become distracted and emotionally conditioned to accept a ritual flow of their own blood.

During this stage at a recent **walu.ngarri,** men and women harmlessly threw water at each other, but with the same distracting effect on the initiates. This **walu.ngarri** ring-dance was held at **Marranba.bidi** over several days in 1995; it concluded with the circumcision of two **Wodoi** boys, overseen by all the **Jungun munnumburra** (f). The final **wir.nganyen** (blood rituals) were enacted in the seclusion of the men's bush camp. The ritual encounters with totemic animals were incorporated with a sequence of law songs under the leadership of the senior songman, **Ngarjno.**

While everyone else returned by truck to their communities along the Gibb River road, the two boys just circumcised remained to recuperate in the care of **Nyawarra,** their father. On the second morning of their healing, **Nyawarra** and his two newly initiated sons observed a group of emus arrive at the **walu.ngarri** ground clearly marked with bare earth from the dance-ring of flattened grass after four days of ceremony. Several younger emus soon reclined next to the **Duduk.ngunga** (stone seat of the songmen), exactly where the boys had sat just two nights before. **Nyawarra,** with Clinton and Kane, witnessed the adult emus group and shuffle majestically, as they moved around the **walu.ngarri** circle for some time, dancing in front of their young people.

Zwei Tänzerinnen in der Frauengruppe, die sich den Männern nähert, tragen den **jalgun** (kurzer Federbausch aus Emudaunen), und in diesem Falle sind die **jalgun** sorgfältig gemalt und schweben wie Tournüren, die im Takt des Tanzes auf und ab wippen.

Ein weiteres Bild in der Nähe zeigt einen etwas späteren Zeitpunkt der Zeremonie, wo ein Mann nach den angespitzten Stäben greift, die er im Haar verborgen hat. Diese **jowul** hält er dort bereit, um sie den Tänzerinnen ins Hinterteil zu stechen, bis ein Tröpfchen Blut hervorkommt. Männer und Frauen liefern sich vor den Augen der Initianden, die im Mittelpunkt des Tanzringes auf dem Boden sitzen, solche Scheingefechte. Der Lärm wird immer lauter, alle stoßen theatralische Schmerzensschreie aus. Dieser lenkt die Initianden ab und bereitet sie innerlich auf das Ritual vor, bei dem ihr eigenes Blut fließen wird.

Bei einem **walu.ngarri** in jüngerer Zeit bespritzten sich die Männer und Frauen gegenseitig mit Wasser, und die Ablenkungswirkung war die Gleiche. Dieser Kreistanz fand 1995 bei einer mehrtägigen **walu.ngarri**-Zeremonie in **Marranba.bidi** statt, die mit der Beschneidung zweier **Wodoi**-Jungen unter der Aufsicht sämtlicher **Jungun munnumburra** endete (f). Die abschließenden **wir.nganyen** (Blutrituale) fanden in der Abgeschiedenheit des Männercamps im Busch statt. Für die rituelle Begegnung mit Totemtieren sorgte eine Folge von Gesetzesliedern, die unter der Leitung des ältesten Sängers, **Ngarjno,** gesungen wurde.

Der Großteil der Teilnehmer kehrte per Lastwagen zu den Siedlungen entlang der Gibb-River-Straße zurück, doch die beiden frisch beschnittenen Jungen blieben in der Obhut ihres Vaters **Nyawarra** zurück, damit ihre Wunden heilen konnten. Am zweiten Morgen dieser Ruhezeit sahen **Nyawarra** und seine beiden nun initiierten Söhne, Clinton und Kane, eine Gruppe von Emus, die auf den Platz des **walu.ngarri** gekommen waren, der nach den vier Festtagen an der blanken Erde und dem zertretenen Gras deutlich zu erkennen war. Schon bald fanden sich mehrere junge Emus am **Duduk.ngunga** (steinerner Sitz für die Sänger) ein, genau da, wo die Jungen noch zwei Abende zuvor gesessen hatten. **Nyawarra,** Clinton und Kane sahen zu, wie die erwachsenen Emus sich formierten, majestätisch auf- und abstolzierten und eine ganze Weile rund um den **walu.ngarri**-Kreis für ihre Kinder tanzten.

Deux danseuses dans la rangée des femmes qui s'approche portent chacune un **jalgun** (petit tablier fait en duvet soyeux d'émeu) représenté très clairement, flottant comme une tournure assez légère pour pouvoir être soulevée dans les mouvements verticaux de la danse.

Une autre peinture non loin de là décrit un passage ultérieur de la cérémonie, lorsqu'un homme attrape les fines baguettes de bois taillées cachées dans ses cheveux. Ces **jowul** sont là pour surprendre et piquer chaque danseuse dans le dos afin de faire couler une goutte de sang. Un simulacre d'un combat entre femmes et hommes se déroule devant les initiés assis sur le sol au centre du cercle formé par la danse et, tandis que le vacarme augmente du fait que de plus en plus de gens crient d'une manière théâtrale, les initiés perdent leur contrôle et se trouvent en condition d'accepter la perte rituelle de leur sang.

À cette étape de la cérémonie, lors d'un récent **walu.ngarri,** les hommes et les femmes se sont lancés de l'eau tout en réussissant à obtenir le même effet de diversion sur les initiés. Cette **walu.ngarri** a eu lieu en 1995 à **Marranba.bidi** pendant plusieurs jours et s'est terminée par la circoncision de deux garçons **Wodoi,** cérémonie observée par tous les **Jungun munnumburra** (f). Les **wir.nganyin** (rituel avec le sang) finaux se sont déroulés à l'abri des regards au campement des hommes dans le bush. Les rencontres rituelles avec les animaux totémiques faisaient partie de la cérémonie et de la séquence de chants de la loi dirigée par le chanteur doyen **Ngarjno.**

Alors que tous les autres retournaient en camion dans leurs communautés qui s'étirent le long de la route de Gibb River, les deux garçons qui venaient d'être circoncis restèrent pour se rétablir sous la garde de leur père, **Nyawarra.** Au deuxième matin de leur cicatrisation, **Nyawarra** et ses deux fils virent un groupe d'émeus à l'endroit où avait eu lieu la **walu.ngarri,** clairement reconnaissable à l'herbe qui avait été aplatie lors de la danse circulaire pendant les quatre jours de la cérémonie. Plusieurs jeunes émeus s'allongèrent assez rapidement près du **Duduk.ngunga** (la siège de pierre des chanteurs), à l'emplacement exact où les deux garçons s'étaient assis deux nuits auparavant. **Nyawarra,** Clinton et Kane virent le groupe d'émeus adultes s'avancer majestueusement et se mettre à tourner pendant quelques temps autour du cercle **walu.ngarri,** tout en dansant devant les jeunes émeus.

walu.ngarri

WANJINA

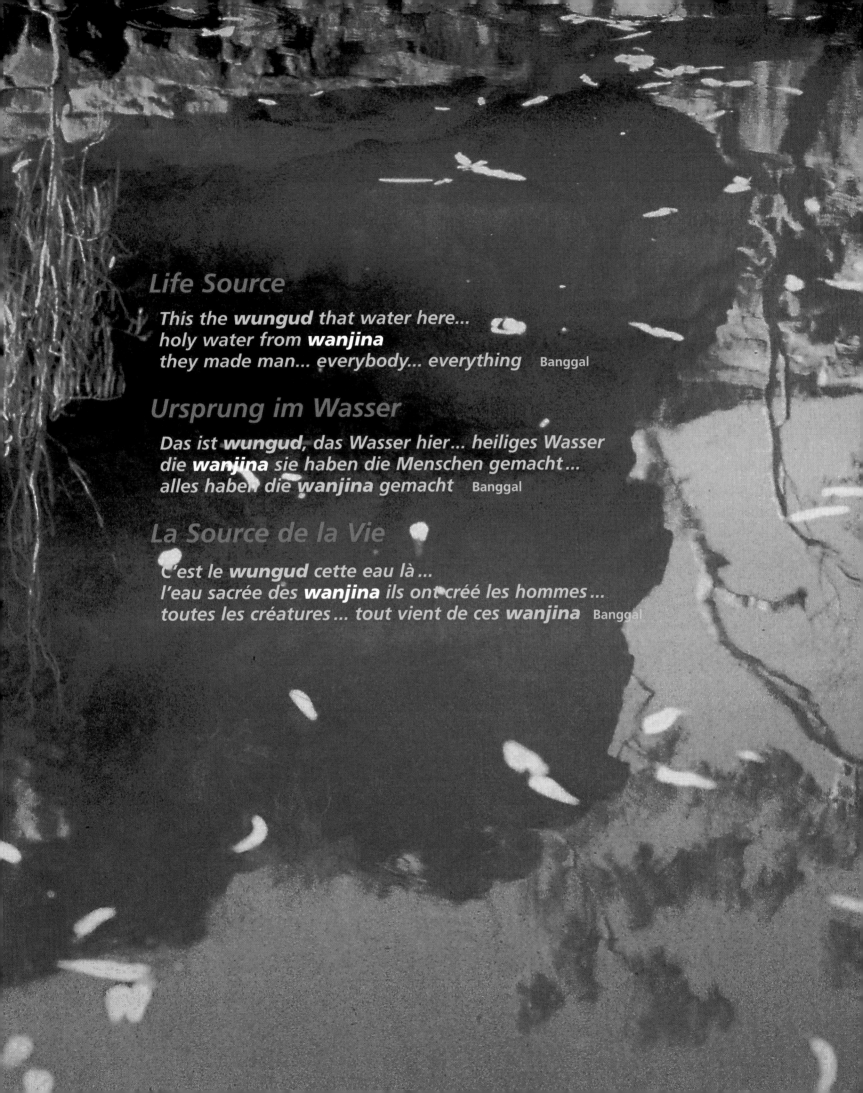

Life Source

This the **wungud** that water here...
holy water from **wanjina**
they made man... everybody... everything   Banggal

Ursprung im Wasser

Das ist **wungud**, das Wasser hier... heiliges Wasser
die **wanjina** sie haben die Menschen gemacht...
alles haben die **wanjina** gemacht   Banggal

La Source de la Vie

C'est le **wungud** cette eau là...
l'eau sacrée des **wanjina** ils ont créé les hommes...
toutes les créatures... tout vient de ces **wanjina**   Banggal

That all the tree and pandanus
all that belong to **wanjina**
They say "Don't touch it!"

When little babies are born
they soft as the jelly
it come from there
from the **wungud** water
that's why it's painted
up there in the caves
Banggal

Die Bäume da, die Pandanus-Palmen
die gehören den **wanjina**
Die sagen „Rühr sie nicht an!"

Wenn kleine Kinder geboren werden
dann sind sie weich wie Gelee
das kommt von hier
aus diesem Wasser das ist **wungud**
das sieht man auch auf den Bildern
da in den Höhlen
Banggal

Tout ça les arbres et les pandanus
tout ça appartient aux **wanjina**
Il est dit : « On ne touche pas ! »

Quand les petits bébés naissent
ils sont mous comme de la gelée
ça vient de là
de l'eau **wungud**
c'est pour ça que c'est peint
là dans ces grottes
Banggal

Wanjina belong to this area... **Marranba.bidi**
place with **wungurrurun**
... deep permanent water... **wuludi**

That rain always be here
wanjina don't go from here
rain only from this cloud
these **wanjina** cloud you see behind
them form here
He not forming from that other way
that another lot forming themselves
He belong here this rain... **Gulingi**
Cloud from this water here
he get up from this water... straight up
Banggal

*Die **wanjina** gehören hierher... **Marranba.bidi***
da ist **wungurrurun**
... tiefes Wasserloch... **wuludi**

Der Regen der ist immer hier
die **wanjina** gehen nicht von hier weg
aus diesen Wolken da kommt der Regen
die Wolken da hinten die **wanjina**-Wolken
die bilden sich hier
Woanders gibt es die nicht
das sind andere die da entstehen
Der Regen gehört hierher... **Gulingi**
Die Wolke kommt aus dem Wasser hier
hier aus dem Wasser steigt sie auf
... direkt nach oben
Banggal

*Les **wanjina** appartiennent à cette région...*
Marranba.bidi
un endroit qui a un **wungurrurun**
... un plan d'eau permanent... **wuludi**

Cette pluie a toujours été là
le **wanjina** ne vient pas de là
la pluie vient seulement de ce nuage
ce nuage **wanjina** que tu vois derrière
il s'est formé là
Ils ne s'est pas formé par là-bas
comme d'autres qui se forment de cette manière
Elle est d'ici cette pluie... **Gulingi**
Le nuage vient de cette eau là
il s'élève de cette eau... tout droit
Banggal

That's the **jalla** and that white one
is the flat water running
that white one that clean water yo!

all this lot **jalla**
That white one is the flat
and rain that dark one underneath
yeah this dark one it is rain water
all this black one that called **jalla**
this front one here is called **jalla**

That's the water sponge in the river... **jalla**
that's where we squeeze him
where he sprinkle there that's **jalla**
that green one that's the **jalla** now... this one

We find children from water
thats why we're water people
We spirits hide in the water
... come out in the open
We all belong water
because **wanjina** belong water

Das ist **jalla** und das Weiße da
da fließt das Wasser da ist es flach
das Weiße da ist klares Wasser, oh ja!

das da, das ist alles **jalla**
Da wo es weiß ist da ist es flach
und drunter das Schwarze ist Regen
ja das Schwarze da ist Regenwasser
das Schwarze da das heißt **jalla**
das hier vorne das ist **jalla**

Das ist wie ein Schwamm im Wasser ... **jalla**
und wenn wir es drücken
dann kommt Wasser heraus das ist **jalla**
das Grüne das ist **jalla** ... dieses hier

Unsere Kinder kommen aus dem Wasser
deshalb sind wir Wassermenschen
Unsere Geister die wohnen im Wasser
... und dann kommen sie heraus
Wir gehören alle dem Wasser
weil das Wasser den **wanjina** gehört

C'est le **jalla** ce qui est blanc là
c'est l'eau qui coule
ce blanc-là c'est de l'eau claire oui !

tout ça c'est **jalla**
Le blanc c'est l'eau de source
et le noir là en dessous c'est de la pluie
oui cette eau noire c'est de l'eau de pluie
tout ce noir s'appelle **jalla**
ça devant s'appelle **jalla**

C'est l'éponge dans la rivière ... **jalla**
c'est là qu'on la presse
là où il coule ce **jalla**
ce vert là c'est le **jalla** aussi ... celui-là

On trouve les enfants dans l'eau
c'est pourquoi on est un peuple de l'eau
On est des esprits cachés dans l'eau
... on est sorti de l'eau
On appartient tous à l'eau
parce que les **wanjina** appartiennent à l'eau

That is why every man or girl
they come out from each **wungud** water
wanjina gives us back...
then we know where that child come from
... everybody know
Our spirit come from water
because we all come from spirit water

Banggal

Deshalb kommt jeder Mann und jedes Mädchen
die kommen alle aus dem **wungud**-Wasser
der **wanjina** gibt uns zurück ...
und dann wissen wir von wo die Kinder kommen
... alle wissen das
Unser Geist kommt aus dem Wasser
weil wir alle aus dem heiligen Wasser kommen

Banggal

C'est pourquoi tout homme
toute femme
tous sortent de l'eau **wungud**
le **wanjina** nous là rend ...
alors on sait d'où vient cet enfant
... tout le monde sait
Notre esprit vient de l'eau
parce qu'on vient tous de l'esprit de l'eau

Banggal

Water is nice... that water he holy water
*belong to **Wanjina Gulingi***
*He not a dry **wanjina**... he belong rain*
*They hold the water all this **mob***
*these are **wanjina**... they **mamaa***
*people know that **wungud** water*
***wungud** means **mamaa**... sacred*
You know not allowed to play around
*in the water when **wungud** is there*
maybe say like a snake or kangaroo or dog
*'long as he's **wungud***

And that's very important place
nobody can play around in that area
in that water he really important
Sometimes someone get accident
*it's very bad... from **wungud***
Yep, it can be life you can find a little baby
*coming from that **wungud***
You dream sometimes you dream that baby
and hand it over to the mother
*he born... he come from that **wungud***
*Yep all sort of animals they all from the **wungud***
*The man is that **wungud***

Wasser ist schön... das Wasser ist heiliges Wasser
*das gehört dem **Wanjina Gulingi***
*Das ist kein trockener **wanjina**...*
dem gehört der Regen
Da ist das Wasser drin
*in den **wanjina**... die sind **mamaa***
*Wasser ist **wungud** das wissen alle*
***wungud** bedeutet **mamaa**... heilig*
Verstehst du man vergreift sich nicht
*an dem Wasser wenn **wungud** da ist*
eine Schlange oder ein Känguru oder ein Hund
*solange er **wungud** ist*

Das ist ein sehr wichtiger Ort
in der Gegend hier da spielt man nicht herum
man spielt nicht mit dem Wasser es ist zu wichtig
*Manchmal wird man bestraft... von dem **wungud***
Denn dort findet man Leben ein kleines Baby
*das aus dem **wungud** kommt*
Manchmal träumt man, man träumt das Baby
und gibt es der Mutter, es kommt zur Welt
*... es kommt aus dem **wungud***
*Ja, alles was lebt, das kommt aus dem **wungud***
*Der Mensch ist das **wungud***

L'eau est belle... cette eau est sacrée
*elle appartient au **Wanjina Gulingi***
*Ce n'est pas un **wanjina** sec... il possède la pluie*
Ils possèdent l'eau tous ceux-là
*ce sont des **wanjina**... ils sont **mamaa***
*les gens savent que c'est de l'eau **wungud***
***wungud** veut dire **mamaa**... sacré*
Tu n'as pas le droit de faire le malin autour
*ou dans l'eau quand le **wungud** est là*
avec un serpent, un kangourou ou un chien
*du moment qu'il est **wungud***

Et c'est un lieu vraiment important
personne ne peut venir jouer là dans ce coin
dans cette eau elle est très sacrée
Parfois quelqu'un a un accident
*c'est très grave... c'est **wungud***
Oui, ça peut être la vie, tu peux voir un petit bébé
*sortir de ce **wungud***
Parfois tu rêves, tu rêves de ce bébé
tu le donnes à sa mère
*il est né... il vient de ce **wungud***
*tous les animaux viennent du **wungud***
*L'être humain, c'est ce **wungud***

***wanjina** water people laying around*
they really reverently take that water
They tell us to get mouthful
and just spray throw it spisssshhhh!
*because he know... that **wanjina** know...*
that you're saying to him
"Don't send rain!"
He listen to the young fella
*and that **wanjina** know that he is being initiated*
*that young fella **ngangurr warra***
Banggal

***wanjina**, die Leute des Wassers, die hier sind*
sie trinken das Wasser ganz andächtig
Sie sagen uns wir sollen einen Mund voll nehmen
und dann versprüht man es – pschhhh!
*weil nämlich... dann weiß der **wanjina**...*
dass man ihm sagt
„Schick' jetzt keinen Regen!"
Er hört dem jungen Burschen zu
*und der **wanjina** weiß, dass er beschnitten wird*
*der junge Bursche **ngangurr warra***
Banggal

*Les **wanjina**, peuple de l'eau, sont tout autour là*
prennent cette eau avec respect
Ils nous disent de nous remplir la bouche d'eau
et de la cracher en l'air spisssshhhh !
*parce qu'il sait... ce **wanjina** il sait...*
que tu lui dis
« N'envoies pas la pluie ! »
Il écoute le jeune homme
*et ce **wanjina** comprend qu'il sera initié*
*... ce jeune homme **ngangurr warra***
Banggal

Always be like initiation in water circle	*Das ist immer wie eine Initiation*	*C'est toujours comme une initiation,*
***jumubumuru…** Black Bream*	*der Kreis im Wasser*	*le cercle dans l'eau*
*young crocodile… **ngerdu***	***jumubumuru** … die Brasse*	***jumubumuru** … la brême noire*
*and that eel… **arru***	*ein junges Krokodil … **ngerdu***	*le jeune crocodile … **ngerdu***
*and that **yemben**… water goanna*	*und der Aal … **arru***	*et cette anguille … **arru***
*and longneck turtle… **wurrumurru***	*und **yemben** … der Wasserwaran*	*et **yemben** … le goanna d'eau*
*all belong to **wanjina***	*und die Schlangenhalsschildkröte … **wurrumurru***	*et la tortue à cou de serpent … **wurrumurru***
	*alle gehören sie den **wanjina***	*tous apartiennent aux **wanjina***

wanjina chose a place
and put there this lot water lily... that *yungulli*
and *manbata* with small oval leaf
and *ungia* with hanging roots
favoured food of *wanjina*

Banggal

*Der **wanjina** hat sich eine Stelle ausgesucht
und lässt da viele Seerosen wachsen ... **yungulli**
und die mit den kleinen ovalen Blättern **manbata**
und **ungia** die mit den langen Wurzeln
die Lieblingsspeise des **wanjina***

Banggal

*le **wanjina** choisit un endroit
et y met tous ces nénuphars... ces **yungulli**
et ces **manbata** qui ont des petites feuilles ovales
et les **ungia**, nénuphars aux racines pendantes
nourriture favorite des **wanjina***

Banggal

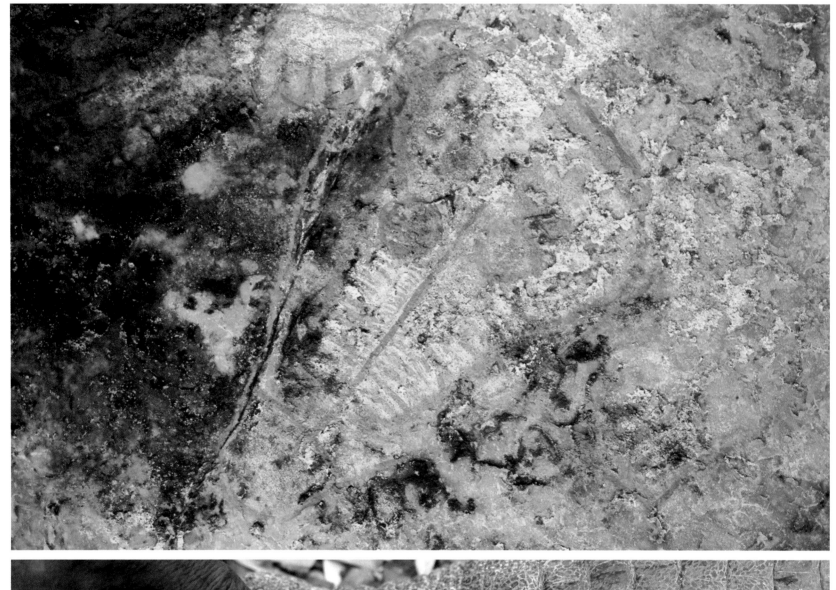

Wunan this one...
skin... you know crocodile skin
brilgi** this one belong **Ngerdu wanjina
Banggal

*Das ist **Wunan** ...*
die Haut ... Krokodilhaut
*die **brilgi** da ... die gehören dem **Ngerdu wanjina***
Banggal

Wunan celui-là ...
la peau, la peau du crocodile
*ce **brilgi** appartient au **Ngerdu wanjina***
Banggal

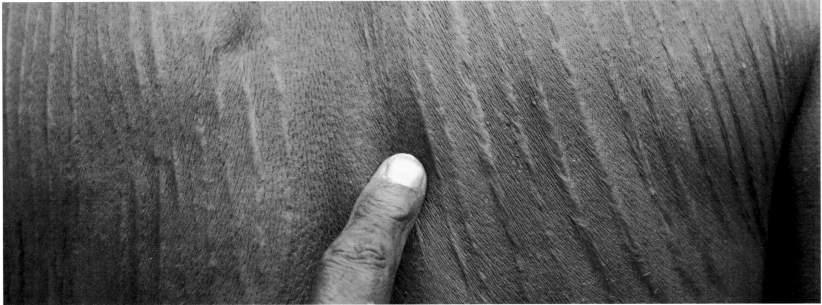

brilgi, *that skin stamp*
see all this skin here
that was yeah... **Ngerdu...** *crocodile* **wanjina**
Banggal

brilgi, *die Narben hier*
siehst du die Haut hier
ja, das war **Ngerdu...** *der Krokodil-***wanjina**
Banggal

brilgi *c'est cette marque sur la peau*
tu vois toute cette peau là
c'est **Ngerdu...** *le* **wanjina** *crocodile*
Banggal

There's the stone he stamp
*all this skin on stone is **brilgi***
*like **brilgi** I got*

Live turtle put on his back
when young fella I was like that too
live turtle been scratch my back
*they been scratching **brilgi***
Banggal

Das ist der Stein mit dem Abdruck
*die Haut auf dem Stein hier das sind **brilgi***
genau wie meine eigenen

Die Schildkröte wird ihm auf den Rücken geritzt
als ich ein junger Bursche war da war ich auch so
da hat mir eine Schildkröte den Rücken zerkratzt
*und das waren **brilgi**, die Zeichen*
Banggal

C'est la pierre où il a laissé son empreinte
*toute cette peau sur la pierre c'est **brilgi***
*comme les **brilgi** que j'ai sur mon corps*

Une tortue vivante posée sur le dos
moi aussi quand j'étais jeune
une tortue vivante m'a griffé le dos
*ces **brilgi** sont ses griffures*
Banggal

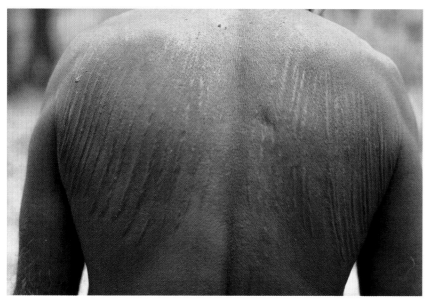

That **ngerdu**... crocodile with the tail...
we talking about the **amad**... kidney
that's **amad-di winjangun**
winjangun... he's the fire
so he got it in his kidney – that crocodile
so – **Garraraji ombudi ombi**
marks showing on her ribs
they got them in their kidney

He was going to take the fire into that water
and ah that blue-mountain parrot eh?
she grab it quick
before he took it to the water
and she bring it outside
then everybody use it outside with the fire stick
The fire we call it **winjangun**

It would have been outside in the land
but they want to put it inside the water
nabun... fire... you can see it in the back
crocodile ... yeah that's the one
those two fellas were arguing over fire

He was going to take it in the water
we don't know what was happen
but the **Marririn** had a good idea
to take it off from there
Marririn... **Guli.ngulindi**
he got two different parrot in there
one is **Guli.ngulindi**
another one is **Marririn**... pretty colour
you can see that fire around her neck
or round the wings everywhere
... that's the **Marririn**

Marririn that one... this **Jungun** tribe
Ungudman he **Jungun** tribe... **amalar** we say
I'm **Wodoi**... ornad

Banggal

Dieses **ngerdu**... das Krokodil mit dem Schwanz...
in der Niere hatte es das
Niere... das heißt **amad-di winjangun**
winjangun... das ist das Feuer
ja, er hatte es in der Niere – das Krokodil
ja – **Garraraji ombudi ombi**
man sieht es auf ihren Rippen
sie hatten es in der Niere

Er wollte das Feuer mit ins Wasser nehmen
und dann kam der Blue-Mountain-Papagei hier
und hat es ihm weggeschnappt
bevor er es unter Wasser nahm
hat er es wieder rausgeholt
seither machen alle draußen Feuer
mit dem Reibholz
Das Feuer nennen wir **winjangun**

Es wäre draußen auf dem Land gewesen
aber sie wollten es im Wasser haben
nabun... Feuer... du siehst es in seinem Rücken
das Krokodil... ja das war es
über das Feuer haben sie sich gestritten

Er wollte es mit ins Wasser nehmen
wir wissen nicht wie das zuging
aber **Marririn** hatte eine gute Idee
und nahm es ihm weg
Marririn... **Guli.ngulindi**
da drin gibt es zwei verschiedene Sittiche
der eine ist **Guli.ngulindi**
der andere **Marririn**... mit bunten Federn
der trägt das Feuer um den Hals
und überall an den Flügeln
... das ist **Marririn**

Das ist **Marririn**... vom **Jungun**-Stamm
Ungudman ist ein **Jungun**... wir sagen **amalar**
ich bin **Wodoi**... ornad

Banggal

---

ngerdu... ce crocodile avec sa queue...
on parle de son rein
le rein... c'est **amad-di winjangun**
winjangun... c'est le feu
et il l'avait dans son rein ce crocodile
et – **Garraraji ombudi ombi**
les marques qu'on voit sur ses côtes
ils les a dans ses reins

Il allait emmener le feu dans cette eau
et ce perroquet des Blue Mountains hein?
il l'attrape vite
avant qu'il l'emmène dans l'eau
et le sort dehors
et maintenant tout le monde
l'utilise avec un bâton de feu
Le feu de camp on l'appelle **winjangun**

Il devait être dehors sur la terre
mais il voulait le mettre à l'intérieur de l'eau
le feu, **nabun**... tu peux le voir dans son dos
le crocodile... oui, c'est celui-là
ces deux types-là se disputaient pour le feu

Au moment où il allait le prendre dans l'eau
on sait pas ce qui s'est passé
mais **Marririn** a eu une bonne idée
il l'a sorti de là
Marririn... **Guli.ngulindi**
il y a deux perroquets différents par ici
l'un est **Guli.ngulindi**
l'autre c'est **Marririn**... il a une jolie couleur
tu peux voir cette couleur feu autour de son cou
ou autour des ailes tout autour
... c'est **Marririn**

Ce **Marririn**... il est de la tribu **Jungun**
Ungudman, c'est un **Jungun**... on dit **amalar**
Je suis un **Wodoi**... ornad

Banggal

*That's right... **wanjina** water*	*Das stimmt... das **wanjina**-Wasser*	*C'est ça... l'eau **wanjina***
*everybody need **wungud***	*jeder braucht **wungud***	*tout le monde a besoin de **wungud***
*even the trees need **wungud***	*sogar die Bäume brauchen **wungud***	*même les arbres ont besoin de **wungud***
when it rains... even the grass needs water	*wenn es regnet... sogar das Gras braucht Wasser*	*quand il pleut... même l'herbe elle a besoin d'eau*
*If we wouldn't have the **wungud** well*	*Wenn wir die **wungud**-Quelle nicht hätten*	*si on n'avait pas le **wungud** eh! bien*
*the **Wanjina Gulingi** and everything*	*würde uns der **Wanjina Gulingi** und die anderen*	*le **Wanjina Gulingi** et les autres*
wouldn't give us any more water	*kein Wasser mehr geben*	*ne nous donneraient plus d'eau*
everything would be dry dead	*alles würde vertrocknen und sterben*	*tout serait sec et mort*
even the human being would be dead	*sogar die Menschen würden sterben*	*même les hommes seraient morts*
It's the life of people and animals	*für Menschen und Tiere ist Wasser das Leben*	*c'est la vie des hommes et des animaux*
Banggal	Banggal	Banggal

Young crocodile... all these chosen animals
*belong to **wanjina***
young people can't eat 'em you know
Ungudman

Ein junges Krokodil ... alle heiligen Tiere
*gehören den **wanjina***
die jungen Leute dürfen sie nicht essen
Ungudman

Un jeune crocodile ... tous ces animaux élus
*appartiennent aux **wanjina***
les jeunes ne peuvent pas les manger tu vois
Ungudman

People used to camp here rain time	In der Regenzeit hatten die Leute hier ihr Lager	Les gens campaient ici quand il pleuvait

People used to camp here rain time
all this lot cave this is their home
*belong to **Ngegamorro** tribe and they stop here*
and people camp here every flood time
*This one **Ngegamorro** chosen this cave*
and he put his picture here
***Ngegamorro** standing up there*

Banggal

In der Regenzeit hatten die Leute hier ihr Lager
die ganzen Höhlen hier waren ihr Zuhause
*Leute vom **Ngegamorro**-Stamm haben hier gelagert*
hatten ihr Lager da wenn alles überschwemmt war
*Die Höhle hat **Ngegamorro** ausgesucht*
und hat sein Bild zurückgelassen
*das ist **Ngegamorro** da oben*

Banggal

Les gens campaient ici quand il pleuvait
toutes ces grottes-là c'est leur maison
*ça appartient à la tribu **Ngegamorro***
et ils s'arrêtaient ici
les gens campaient là à chaque inondation
*Ce **Ngegamorro** il a choisi cette grotte*
et il s'est peint là
***Ngegamorro** se tient là*

Banggal

Ngegamorro is painting here
because his was upset for his turtle
So he looking for her that's right...
and they call him **Ngegamorro**

He was putting his jaw all over the place
to find her... **Wurrumurru**
but she went right underneath
right under the waterlily
we call him **anjum** this waterlily
And she went inside that tunnel there
we call him **gaama**
it's a cave belonga crocodiles and turtles
They go inside there when flood waters running
they safe inside otherwise they get drowned

So this **Ngegamorro** he lost her
half way long this creek here
She went inside this **gulug**
and she keep going inside and he said
"Where are you? where are you?"
He put his jaw out... you know his jaw?
"Where are you... come out to me!"
he was saying this **Ngegamorro**
and that's why he called **Ngegamorro**
because his jaw and his face
were looking all over like this

Banggal

Das Bild das ist **Ngegamorro**
der hat sich Sorgen um seine Schildkröte gemacht
Und hat überall nach ihr gesucht
Ngegamorro hieß er

Er reckte das Kinn in alle Richtungen
weil er Ausschau nach ihr hielt... **Wurrumurru**
aber sie war untergetaucht
unter den Seerosen verschwunden
anjum nennen wir die, die Seerosen
da in den Tunnel ist sie reingekrochen
gaama heißt der Tunnel
eine Höhle für Krokodile und Schildkröten
Die kriechen bei der Überschwemmung rein
dort sind sie in Sicherheit sonst würden sie ertrinken

Ngegamorro hatte sie aus den Augen verloren
irgendwo hier an diesem Bach
Sie ist in den **gulug** gekrochen
immer tiefer hinein und er rief
„Wo bist du? wo bist du?"
Er reckte sein Kinn vor... so wie ich
„Wo bist du?... komm heraus zu mir!"
das rief er der **Ngegamorro**
und deswegen heißt er **Ngegamorro**
wegen dem Kinn
weil er das immer so vorgereckt hat

Banggal

Ngegamorro s'est peint là
parce qu'il était énervé avec sa tortue
Donc il la cherche en fait
et il l'appelle **Ngegamorro**

Il mettait sa mâchoire un peu partout
pour la trouver... **Wurrumurru**
mais elle s'était mise juste en dessous
juste en dessous du nénuphar
on l'appelle **anjum** ce nénuphar
Et elle rentrée dans ce tunnel-là
on l'appelle **gaama**
c'est une grotte aux crocodiles et aux tortues
Ils vont là-dedans quand il y a des inondations
ils sont en sécurité dedans
sinon ils sont noyés

Donc **Ngegamorro** il l'a perdue
à mi-chemin le long de ce ruisseau là
Elle est allée dans ce **gulug**
et elle continue à s'enfoncer et il dit
« Où es-tu ? où es-tu ? »
Il avance sa mâchoire... tu connais sa mâchoire ?
« Où es-tu ? Viens me voir ! »
il disait ce **Ngegamorro**
et c'est pour ça il s'appelle **Ngegamorro**
parce que sa mâchoire et son visage
regardaient partout comme ça

Banggal

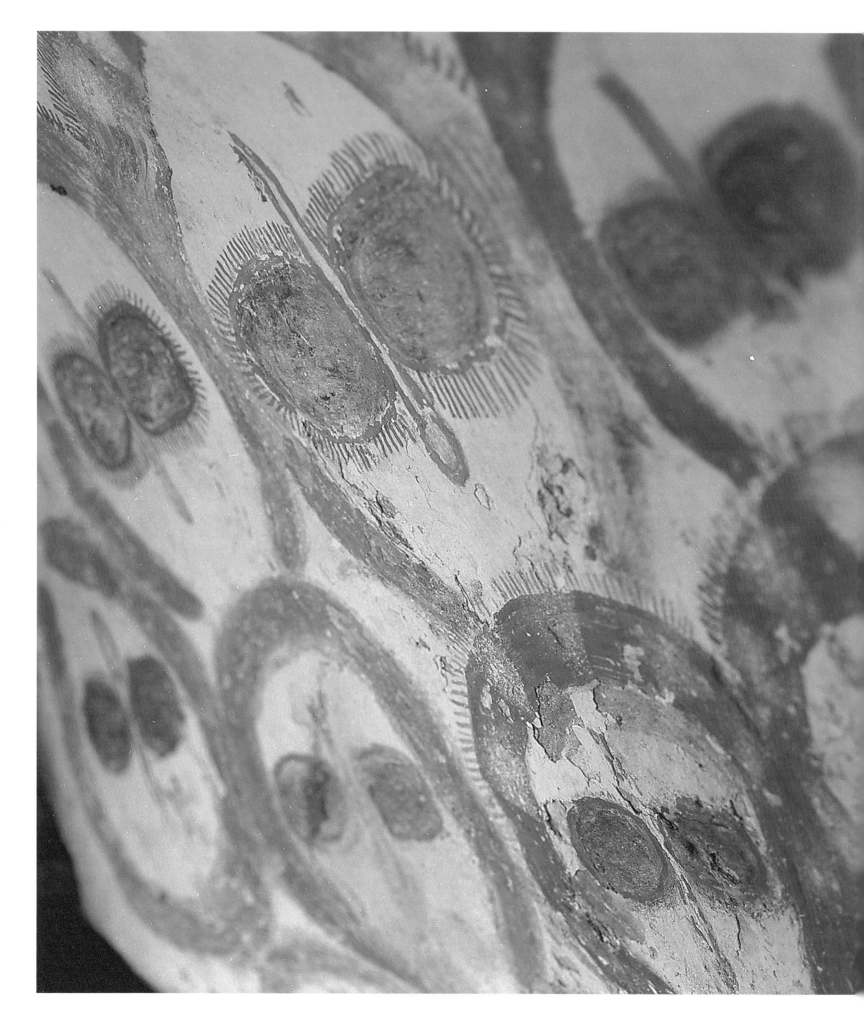

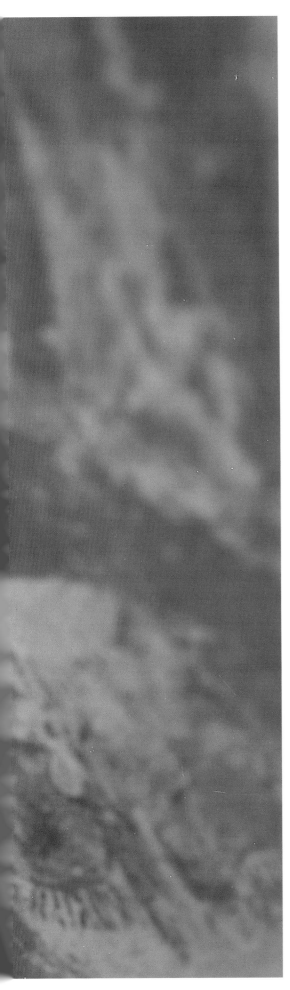

This one **Ngegamorro**

Ngegamorro chose **Wurrumurru**
this is the long-neck turtle **Wurrumurru**
She end up here in this little pool here
she was jammed up here
that long-neck turtle... **Wurrumurru**

He got hold of her there
... and she slipped out of his hand
and she took off and he was upset about it
because he loved her **Wurrumurru** properly
Banggal

Das ist **Ngegamorro**

Ngegamorro hatte sich in **Wurrumurru** verliebt
Wurrumurru die Schlangenhalsschildkröte
Schließlich kam sie hier in diesen kleinen Tümpel
da steckte sie fest
die Schildkröte ... **Wurrumurru**

Er hat sie gepackt
... aber sie glitschte ihm aus der Hand
und war verschwunden und er furchtbar unglücklich
denn er hat die **Wurrumurru** wirklich geliebt
Banggal

Lui c'est **Ngegamorro**

Ngegamorro a choisi **Wurrumurru**
c'est la tortue à cou de serpent **Wurrumurru**
Elle arriva là dans cette petite mare là
elle s'est retrouvée coincée sous l'eau
la tortue à cou de serpent... **Wurrumurru**

Il l'attrapa ici
... mais elle glissa de sa main
et elle s'échappa et lui ça l'a énervé
parce qu'il l'aimait vraiment sa **Wurrumurru**
Banggal

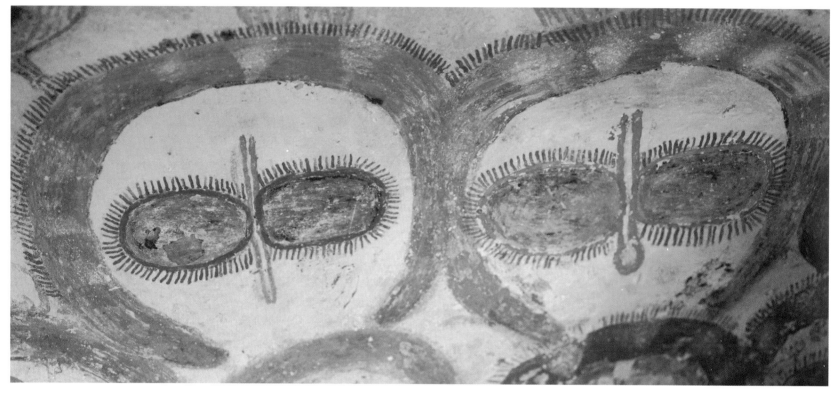

Ngegamorro really loved that **Wurrumurru**
he put his jaw out...
Ngegamorro he was saying this

"Where are you? where are you?
Where are you... come out to me!"

"Where are you?
even if you blow your bubbles up
I still love your bubbles too"

then he found her... he was happy then
and he painted with her there
in that **Ngegamorro** painting

Banggal

Ngegamorro liebte die **Wurrumurru** wirklich
er hat sein Kinn vorgereckt…
und **Ngegamorro** rief

„Wo bist du? wo bist du?
Wo bist du … komm heraus zu mir!"

„Wo bist du?
sogar wenn ich nur noch Luftblasen von dir habe
dann liebe ich noch die Luftblasen"

dann fand er sie … und da war er glücklich
und deswegen ist er hier mit ihr gemalt
da auf dem **Ngegamorro**-Bild

Banggal

Ngegamorro aimait vraiment cette **Wurrumurru**
il sortit sa mâchoire…
Ngegamorro il disait ça

« Où es-tu ? où es-tu ?
Où es-tu ? Viens me voir ! »

« Où es-tu ?
même quand tu m'envoies que des bulles,
j'aime aussi tes bulles »

enfin il l'a trouvée… il était content alors
et il s'est peint avec elle là
c'est cette peinture de **Ngegamorro**

Banggal

Ngegamorro... blood father of **Yemben**
and adopting father of **Yirrbal**

Wurrumalu... son of **Yemben**
Muni yalla... daughter of **Yemben**
Bangmorro... son of **Wurrumalu**
Ngarjno

Ngegamorro... der leibliche Vater von **Yemben**
und der Adoptivvater von **Yirrbal**

Wurrumalu... Sohn des **Yemben**
Muni yalla... Tochter des **Yemben**
Bangmorro... Sohn des **Wurrumalu**
Ngarjno

Ngegamorro... le père de sang de **Yemben**
et le père d'adoption de **Yirrbal**

Wurrumalu... le fils de **Yemben**
Muni yalla... la fille de **Yemben**
Bangmorro... le fils de **Wurrumalu**
Ngarjno

You can see he has no mouth
you can see all this white thing
... it's beyond our knowledge
it's very taboo...
that's why we call them **mamaa**

Banggal

Er hat keinen Mund, siehst du
und siehst du das Weiße da
... das geht über unser Wissen hinaus
das ist alles tabu ...
deshalb nennen wir das **mamaa**

Banggal

Tu peux voir il n'a pas de bouche
tu peux voir tout cette chose blanche
... ça dépasse les limites de notre savoir
c'est très tabou...
c'est pour ça qu'on les dit **mamaa**

Banggal

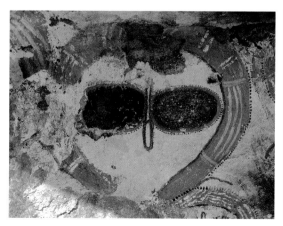
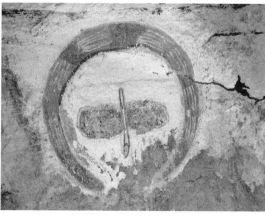

This **goanna...** water **goanna** called **yemben yemben...** blood son of **Ngegamorro wanjina yemben...** that water **goanna** special one
and they all belong to here
everything belong to water
... all belong to water **wanjina**
Banggal

Der **goanna** da ... der Wasserwaran, **yemben yemben ...** leiblicher Sohn des **Ngegamorro wanjina yemben ...** der Wasserwaran ist etwas besonderes ...
die gehören alle hierher
alles gehört dem Wasser
... alle gehören dem Wasser-**wanjina**
Banggal

Ce **goanna** ... ce **goanna** d'eau appelé **yemben yemben ...** le fils de sang du **Ngegamorro wanjina yemben ...** c'est un **goanna** spécial ...
et ils sont tous d'ici
tout appartient à l'eau
... tout appartient aux **wanjina** de l'eau
Banggal

... it's beyond our knowledge

Banggal

... das geht über unser Wissen hinaus

Banggal

... ça dépasse les limites de notre savoir

Banggal

257

Binjiraregu... place going
walamba... red kangaroo
wamba... nervous
briyal... arm
kane-kane... looking down

Red kangaroo is nervous
going to **Binjirri**
He looks at his arm
Licking the sweat coming down
because he must get to **Binjirri**
for **walu.ngarri**

Ngarjno

Binjiraregu... unterwegs
walamba... rotes Känguru
wamba... nervös
briyal... Arm
kane-kane... blickt nach unten

Das rote Känguru ist nervös
es will nach **Binjirri**
schaut seinen Arm an
leckt den Schweiß der da herunterläuft
weil es nach **Binjirri** muss
zum **walu.ngarri**

Ngarjno

Binjiraregu... aller quelque part
walamba... le kangourou roux
wamba... nerveux
briyal... le bras
kane-kane... regarder en bas

Le kangourou roux est nerveux
il va à **Binjirri**
Il regarde son bras
Il lèche la sueur qui coule
parce qu'il doit aller à **Binjirri**
pour le **walu.ngarri**

Ngarjno

ambalaru... footprint
modu anyi... travelling footprints
oru liwarad... kangaroo ears
mudurra... big hair wig
nu meri... doing it... growing up... listening
Ngarjno

ambalaru ... Fußspuren
modu anyi ... Fährte
oru liwarad ... Känguruohren
mudurra ... große Perücke
nu meri ... richtet sich auf ... horcht
Ngarjno

ambalaru ... l'empreinte de pied
modu anyi ... l'empreinte de pied en déplacement
oru liwarad ... l'oreille de kangourou
mudurra ... la grande coiffe en cheveux
nu meri ... faisant, grandissant ... écoutant
Ngarjno

If you see this rock standing up there
that's your warning!
jallala the way he standing
… that's the one we call *jallala*

If anybody break the law to go in there
He get into a lot of problem... that's *jallala*

He can be secret place *mamaa*
he can be *wungud* place that's still *mamaa*
He can be what they call this ummm *Maraja* area
he's still *mamaa* everything is *mamaa*

Nyawarra

Wenn du den Stein da oben stehen siehst
das ist eine Warnung!
jallala, so wie der da steht
… solche Steine nennen wir *jallala*

Wenn jemand das Gesetz bricht
und da reingeht
das wird er bereuen … das ist *jallala*

Das kann ein heiliger Ort sein, *mamaa*
oder ein *wungud*-Ort, auch der ist *mamaa*
Der kann in, mmh wie sagt man, *Maraja* sein
dann ist er immer noch *mamaa*
alles ist *mamaa*

Nyawarra

Quand tu vois ce rocher dressé là-bas
c'est un avertissement!
c'est *jallala*, on le voit à manière
dont c'est dressé… c'est un *jallala*

Si quelqu'un viole la loi en entrant ici
il va avoir de sérieux problèmes… c'est *jallala*

Un endroit secret c'est *mamaa*
un lieu qui est *wungud* c'est toujours *mamaa*
Ce qu'on appelle heu… un lieu *Maraja*
c'est encore *mamaa*, tout est *mamaa*

Nyawarra

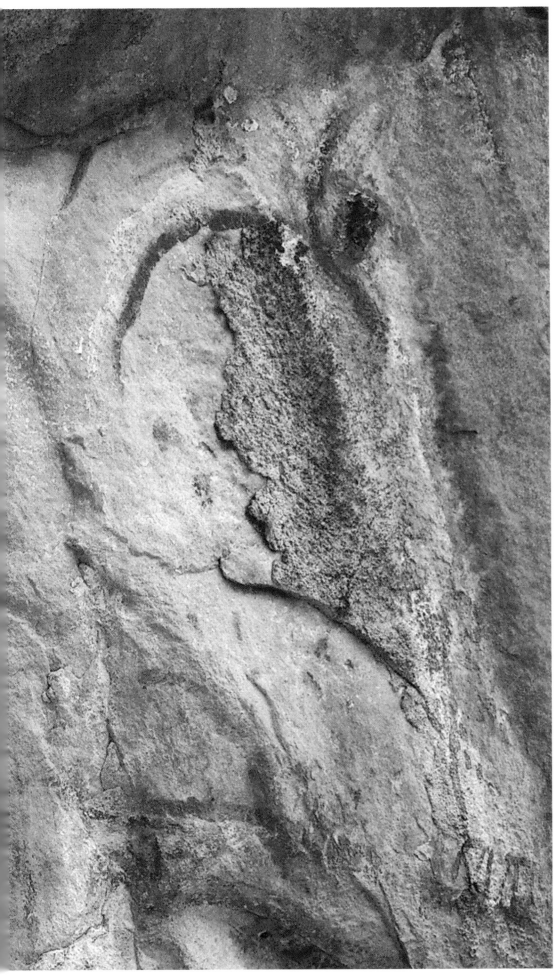

You are talking about the **walgunu**
the secret thing which travel round
and put it in the caves
Where people coming
droving that thing down to other tribes
that's the **walgunu**... we call it **walgunu**

mamaa... everything is **mamaa**
not to break the law
or not to break anything or do something wrong
that's the **mamaa** that's why we say **mamaa**
If someone go steal something
or robbing something y'know?
it's very bad for them getting into lot of problem
They breaking the rules and all that
they'll have to say...
that's what we call **mamaa**

Nyawarra

Man spricht vom **walgunu**
dem heiligen Gegenstand, der herumgereicht
und in Höhlen aufbewahrt wird
Wo die Leute hinkommen
und ihn weitergeben an die anderen Stämme
der heißt **walgunu**... **walgunu** nennen wir den

mamaa... alles ist **mamaa**
das Gesetz darf man nicht brechen
nichts zerstören und nichts Böses tun
das heißt **mamaa**... deshalb sagen wir **mamaa**
wenn jemand etwas stiehlt verstehst du?
oder jemanden beraubt
dann kriegt der eine Menge Ärger
Leute brechen die Regeln und alles
aber es kommt doch heraus...
das nennen wir **mamaa**

Nyawarra

Tu parles du **walgunu**
cet objet secret qui circule
et qu'on cache dans les grottes
Les gens viennent
et le conduisent vers les autres tribus
c'est le **walgunu**... on l'appelle **walgunu**

mamaa... tout est **mamaa**
pour pas violer la Loi
ou faire quelque chose de mal
c'est pour ça qu'on dit que c'est **mamaa**
Si quelqu'un va voler quelque chose
c'est grave pour lui
il va avoir de sérieux problèmes
Il viole les lois et tout ça
il faudra qu'il dise...
c'est pour ça qu'on dit **mamaa**

Nyawarra

Binbin – Ballmirriya – Jadgud.gude – Walamba – Biyad.ngerri – Wudmi.mulimuli

*Sometime we call 'em **Walamba***
that's the red kangaroo
*and **Walamba** means he's an important bloke*

*Very **mamaa** very important bloke*
sometimes they kill 'im
and finish it off by themselves... all the men
y'know in the bush... secret place
they don't bring it into camp

sometimes they take it into the public
for everyone to have a feed
but only thing... they don't call his name
*They don't say **Walamba**...*
*they say **Balmirriya** or **Jadgud.gude***

Nyawarra

*Manchmal nennen wir ihn **Walamba***
das Rote Riesenkänguru
*und **Walamba** ist ein mächtiger Bursche*

*Sehr **mamaa**, sehr sehr mächtiger Bursche*
manchmal töten sie ihn
und essen ihn ganz alleine auf … alle Männer
im Busch, weißt du … am geheimen Ort
das bringen sie nicht mit ins Lager

manchmal bringen sie ihn aber auch mit
damit alle etwas zu essen haben
aber eins ist wichtig … man sagt nicht seinen Namen
*Man sagt nicht **Walamba**…*
*man sagt **Balmirriya** oder **Jadgud.gude***

Nyawarra

*Des fois on l'appelle **Walamba***
c'est le Kangourou roux
*et **Walamba** ça veut dire*
que c'est un type important

*Très **mamaa**, très important ce type*
des fois ils le tuent
et ils le mangent entre eux … tous les hommes
tu sais dans le bush … à un endroit secret
ils l'amènent pas au camp

des fois ils le montrent aux autres
pour que tout le monde en mange
mais la seule chose … on ne dit pas son nom
*Ils disent pas **Walamba**…*
*ils disent **Balmirriya** ou **Jadgud.gude***

Nyawarra

Walamba means that *Jadgud.gude*
mean he got the red ochre in his hair
Balmirriya is his name
and the *Walamba* his name
he's really an important bloke

Nyawarra

Walamba der heißt *Jadgud.gude*
weil er roten Ocker im Haar hat
Balmirriya heißt er
und *Walamba* heißt er
der ist wirklich mächtig der Bursche

Nyawarra

Walamba ça veut dire aussi *Jadgud.gude*
ça veut dire il a de l'ocre rouge dans ses cheveux
Balmirriya est son nom
et c'est un *Walamba*
c'est vraiment un type important

Nyawarra

This place where I'm sitting now
its **Wallagari Merrbini**
wallagari means that **mandi**... boomerang
So when you lookin' at this creek
you say it's like boomerangs
yeah **Walamba** he threw it down
throw that boomerang that **wallagari**
put it this name down in the ground
and he made this water
And the **Walamba wanjina** came along
and he stayed there... **Walamba** said

"No I'll stay here...
in the head of the **Wallagari**"

And he stays here on that creek
where he going down that way like boomerang
and this country called **Wallagari**

Nyawarra

Der Ort wo ich jetzt sitze
das ist **Wallagari Merrbini**
wallagari nennt man den **mandi**... Bumerang
Und wenn man dieses Wasser hier ansieht
dann sieht das aus wie ein Bumerang
ja, **Walamba**, der hat ihn geworfen
der hat den Bumerang geworfen, den **wallagari**
der hat seine Spuren da im Boden hinterlassen
und das Wasser hier gemacht
und der **Walamba wanjina** kam vorbei
und blieb hier... **Walamba** sagte

„Nein, ich bleibe hier...
hier am Bogen des **Wallagari**"

Und da bleibt er, hier an dem Bach
da wo er eine Biegung macht wie ein Bumerang
und die Gegend hier, die heißt **Wallagari**

Nyawarra

Cet endroit où je suis assis là
c'est **Wallagari Merrbini**
wallagari veut dire **mandi**... boomerang
Donc quand tu regardes ce cours d'eau
tu vois c'est comme un boomerang
oui c'est **Walamba** qui l'a lancé
qui a lancé ce **wallagari**
qui a mis ce nom sur ce sol
et il a fait cette eau
Et le **Walamba wanjina** est venu là
et il est resté là... a dit **Walamba**

« Non je resterai là...
dans la tête du **Wallagari** »

Et il reste là sur ce cours d'eau
là où il s'écoule comme un boomerang
et ce pays s'appelle **Wallagari**

Nyawarra

*this is in **Barraru.ngarri dambun** area*

And say like when all the mothers
maybe have too many kids
so when she touch
*that **mandi**... boomerang*
she won't have any more kids
that's what we say when
we put it long side her
straight down her stomach here
so you won't get any more babies
And she can only have seven
or eight that's good enough

*That's the **wallagari**... boomerang... **mandi***

*It's **mamaa**... **wungud**... **maya.ngarri**...*
*we call it **mandi***
Nyawarra

*Das ist im **Barraru.ngarri dambun***

Und wenn die ganzen Frauen
mal zu viele Kinder kriegen
dann fassen sie den Bumerang an
*den **mandi**... Bumerang*
und dann werden sie nicht mehr schwanger
das sagt man jedenfalls
wenn wir ihn neben sie legen
hier vorne am Bauch
dann bekommt sie keine Babys mehr
Sie bekommt nur sieben oder acht
das ist genug

*Das ist der **wallagari**... Bumerang... **mandi***

***Mamaa** ist der... **wungud**... **maya.ngarri**...*
*wir nennen ihn **mandi***
Nyawarra

*C'est la région du **Barraru.ngarri dambun***

Et par exemple quand les mères
elles ont trop d'enfants
elles touchent ce boomerang
*ce **mandi**... le boomerang*
et elles n'auront plus d'enfants
c'est ce qu'on dit
quand on le met là
juste en-dessous de son estomac là
comme ça t'auras plus de bébés
Et elle peut en avoir que sept ou huit
ça suffit

*C'est le **wallagari**... boomerang... **mandi***

*C'est **mamaa**... **wungud**... **maya.ngarri**...*
*on l'appelle **mandi***
Nyawarra

271

Walamba means this is **wungud**
*He got **wungud** in there...*
that mountain over there
*that woman kangaroo... **Guroni***
*wife partner of **Walamba***

Sometimes them old ladies
*don't call him **Walamba***
*they just say **Balmirriya** or **Jadgud.gude***
that means red kangaroo
they just say it like that...
*they don't call his name **Walamba***
Nyawarra

*Walamba, das heißt, das hier ist **wungud***
*Da drin ist **wungud**...*
da drüben in dem Berg
***Guroni**... die Kängurufrau*
*Frau und Gefährtin von **Walamba***

Die alten Frauen
*nennen ihn manchmal nicht **Walamba***
*sie sagen nur **Balmirriya** oder **Jadgud.gude***
das heißt rotes Känguru
sie sagen das einfach so...
*sie nennen ihn nicht bei seinem Namen **Walamba***
Nyawarra

*Walamba ça veut dire que c'est **wungud***
*Elle est **wungud**...*
cette montagne là-bas
*cette femme kangourou... c'est **Guroni***
*c'est la femme de **Walamba***

Des fois les vieilles femmes
*elles l'appellent pas **Walamba***
*elles disent juste **Balmirriya** ou **Jadgud.gude***
ça veut dire le Kangourou roux
elles disent juste ça c'est tout...
*elles prononcent pas son nom, **Walamba***
Nyawarra

This one we sit on now...	*Der Stein hier auf dem wir hier sitzen*	*Là où on est assis là*
*that's what it is **Walamba***	*das ist **Walamba***	*c'est **Walamba***
He have to look after the song and the country	*Der muss für das Lied sorgen und für das Land*	*Il protège le chant et le pays*
In the bush... secret place	*Im Busch ... geheimer Ort*	*dans le bush ... endroit secet*
Nyawarra	Nyawarra	Nyawarra

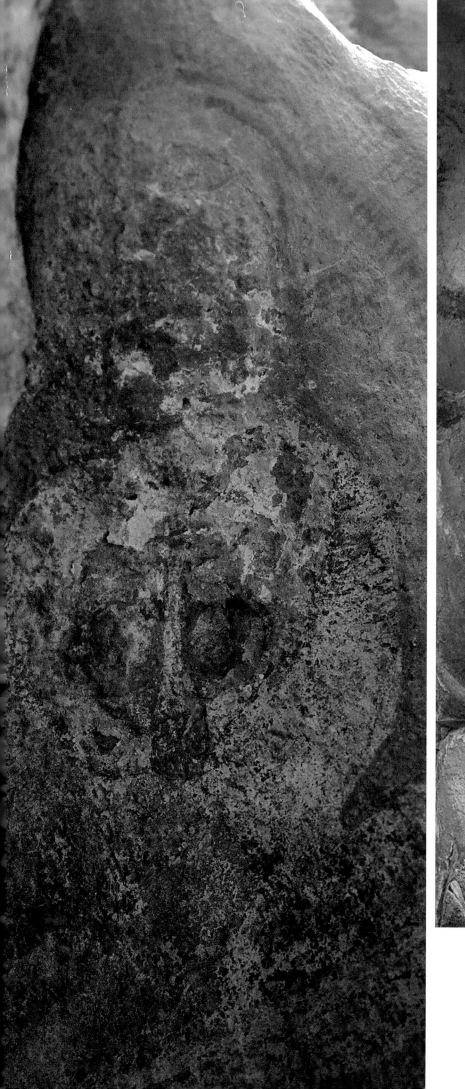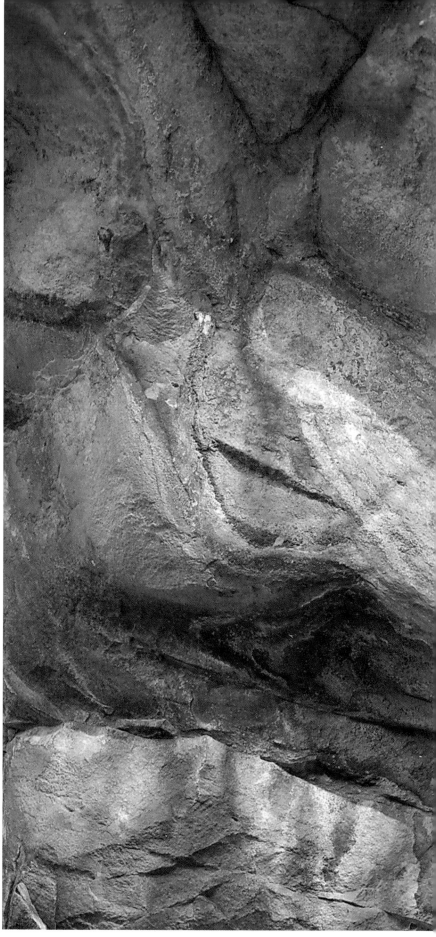

This one now **Gulingi**
He lightning **wanjina**
He **mamaa**

Ungudman

Und das ist **Gulingi**
*der Blitz-***wanjina**
Der ist **mamaa**

Ungudman

Celui-là ici c'est **Gulingi**
C'est le **wanjina** *de la foudre*
Il est **mamaa**

Ungudman

a

b

c

Anyone walking across **Ngarinyin** country may become transfixed by reflections in the many rock-pools and billabongs along the freshwater streams. Water not only initiates and supports life in its fluid mass, it creates almost cinematic images on the skin of its fluid surface. At dawn, tall spirals of **wilmi** (mist), evidence of the spirits of children to be born, glide along enigmatically (a).

Around the deep pool below the paintings at **Alyaguma** is a shallow margin of wet black rock. A startling stripe of intense green instantly captures one's attention.The luminous band of deep emerald-green is **jalla** (freshwater alga). Soon after a baby is born, moist handfuls of fresh **jalla** are collected carefully and dried in the sun (b). Then, small bundles of dried **jalla** are fired to smolder, and the smoke blown by its mother into the eyes of the newborn to stimulate its **mun** (imagination). **Jalla** given as incense to a newborn baby, also is a power in the storm clouds – its sulphurous green appearance in clouds heralds lightning strikes from **Wanjina Gulingi**. **Munnumburra** call out *"Jalla!"* at the approach of dark-gray clouds suspended like heavy bars across the white nimbus of an approaching storm. This reflection of energy and meaning from the realms below to those above is carried over into many aspects of **Ngarinyin** cosmology. Rain demonstrates the permeation of **wungud** throughout the living world. All this life, all form and structure and "spirit", originates in water.

Five water animals are all **wanjina** and are central to the origin and formation of human beings: **arru** – eel, **jumubumuru** – Black Bream, **ngerdu** – crocodile, **yemben** – water goanna, and **wurrumurru** – long-neck turtle. As much as brothers and cousins are closely related, so are people to the five special water animals of **wanjina**. Each may be encountered during significant initiation rituals and education leading to **munnumburra** status. Secret sacred songs belonging to them are taught in seclusion during **wir.nganyen** (circumcision rituals). Some songs only contain perhaps four old, extremely precious words from the source of the **Wunan**. During these and continuing initiations, the human skin is marked with **brilgi**, fine cicatrice patterns associated with the living animal. Adult initiates meet live animals face-to-face to learn their laws. **Brilgi** (scars) result from rituals when the living animal is placed on the human body, bonding people with **wanjina** and animal.

Jeder, der im Land der **Ngarinyin** unterwegs ist, wird fasziniert sein von den Spiegelbildern in den zahllosen Felstümpeln und Billabongs, die entlang der stillen Seitenarme der Flüsse liegen. Das Wasser ist nicht nur Ursprung und Erhalter des Lebens, sondern schafft auch die spektakulärsten Bilder des Himmels auf seiner stets wandelbaren Oberfläche. Im Morgengrauen steigen rätselhafte **wilmi** (Nebelspiralen) auf, Symbole für die Seelen der noch Ungeborenen (a).

Die tiefe Wasserstelle unterhalb der Felsbilder von **Alyaguma** umfasst ein schmaler Rand aus feuchtem schwarzem Stein. Ein leuchtend grüner Streifen zieht sofort die Aufmerksamkeit auf sich, ein smaragdgrünes Band der **jalla** (Süßwasseralge). Wenn ein Kind auf die Welt kommt, holt man einige Hände voll **jalla** und trocknet sie sorgfältig in der Sonne (b). Diese kleinen **jalla**-Bündel werden entzündet, bis sie kokeln, und dann bläst die Mutter dem Neugeborenen den Rauch in die Augen, um seine **mun** (Phantasie) zu beflügeln. **Jalla**, die den Babys als Weihrauch dargebracht wird, findet sich auch in den Gewitterwolken – die schwefelgrüne Erscheinung an der Oberseite der Wolken kündigt die Blitze an, die der **Wanjina Gulingi** bald hinabschleudern wird. Die **munnumburra** rufen „Jalla!", wenn die dunkelgrauen Wolken zu sehen sind, die wie schwere Balken vor den Nimbuswolken eines aufziehenden Unwetters stehen. Diese Projektion von Energie und Deutung vom Erdboden an den Himmel findet sich in vielen Aspekten der **Ngarinyin**-Kosmologie. Die Dualität zeigt, dass alles Lebendige vom **wungud** durchdrungen ist. Alles Leben, alle Form und Struktur, aller „Geist", hat seinen Ursprung im Wasser.

Fünf Wassertiere gelten als **wanjina** und sind von entscheidender Bedeutung für Ursprung und Entwicklung eines Menschen: **arru**, der Aal; **jumubumuru**, die Brasse; **ngerdu**, das Krokodil; **yemben**, der Wasserwaran, und **wurrumurru**, die Schlangenhalsschildkröte. So wie Brüder und Vettern eng miteinander verwandt sind, so sind Menschen mit den fünf Wassertieren der **wanjina** verwandt. Mit jedem von ihnen kann es bei den Initiationsritualen zu bedeutsamen Begegnungen kommen, zu Wissen, das zum Status des **munnumburra** führt. Geheime heilige Lieder, die zu diesen Tieren gehören, werden in der Abgeschiedenheit der **wir.nganyen** (Beschneidungsrituale) weitergegeben. Manche Lieder enthalten vielleicht nur vier heilige Worte, die besonders alt und wertvoll sind, weil sie dem Ursprung des **Wunan** entstammen. Während dieser und weiterer Initiationen werden in die Haut **brilgi** eingeritzt, feine Narbenmuster, die mit dem entsprechenden Tier assoziiert werden. Initiierte Erwachsene treten den Tieren von Angesicht zu Angesicht gegenüber, damit sie deren Gesetze erlernen können. Auch bei diesen Ritualen, bei denen das lebendige Tier mit dem menschlichen Körper in Berührung gebracht wird, entstehen **brilgi** (Narben), die den Menschen mit dem Tier und dem **wanjina** verbinden.

Toute personne qui traverse le pays des **Ngarinyin** peut être pénétrée par les images reflétées dans l'eau des nombreux bassins formés au creux des rochers ou des mares stagnant après la saison des pluies le long des cours d'eau. L'eau n'est pas seulement à l'origine la vie et permet de la garder, elle crée aussi des images mouvantes à sa surface. Au lever du jour, de grandes **wilmi** (spirales de brume) liées aux esprits des enfants à naître, glissent sur l'eau de manière énigmatique (a).

Au dessous des peintures à **Alyaguma** existe une mare profonde dont les bords rocheux sont noirs et humides. Là, une étonnante bande verte intense capture immédiatement l'attention. Cette bande lumineuse vert émeraude est du **jalla** (algue d'eau douce). Peu de temps après la naissance d'un bébé, des poignées de **jalla** fraîches et humides sont ramassées avec soin et séchées au soleil (b). Ensuite, des petits paquets de **jalla** séchées sont allumés et la flamme est étouffée. La fumée ainsi obtenue est envoyée par la mère dans les yeux de son nouveau-né pour stimuler son **mun**. La **jalla** utilisée comme de l'encens a un pouvoir de protection contre l'orage pour le nouveau-né. Elle a la couleur verte sulfureuse des nuages annonciateurs de la foudre du **Wanjina Gulingi**. Les **munnumburra** crient « jalla ! » à l'approche des nuages sombres suspendus comme de lourdes barres au milieu du nimbus. Ce reflet de l'énergie et des significations de la terre dans le ciel se retrouve dans beaucoup d'aspects de la cosmologie **Ngarinyin**. Cette dualité prouve la présence de **wungud** dans tout ce qui est vivant. Toute vie, toute forme ou « esprit » a pour origine l'eau.

Cinq animaux aquatiques sont **wanjina** et ont une place centrale dans l'origine et la création des êtres humains : l'**arru**, l'anguille, la **jumubumuru**, brème noire, le **ngerdu**, crocodile, le **yemben**, **goanna** d'eau et la **wurrumurru**, tortue à cou de serpent. Les gens qui sont apparentés à ces cinq animaux aquatiques totémiques des **wanjina** doivent être considérés d'une même proximité que le sont frères ou cousins. On peut rencontrer chacun d'eux lors des importants rituels d'initiation et au cours de l'apprentissage aboutissant au statut de **munnumburra**. Des chants sacrés et secrets les concernant sont appris à l'écart pendant les **wir.nganyen** (rituels de circoncision). Certains chants ne possèdent peut-être que quatre anciens mots extrêmement précieux qui datent de l'origine du **Wunan**. Pendant ces initiations, la peau des hommes est marquée de **brilgi** (fines cicatrices) dont les motifs sont associés à l'animal vivant. Les initiés adultes doivent se retrouver nez-à-nez avec les animaux vivants pour apprendre leurs lois. Les **brilgi** sont faites pendant les rituels où l'animal vivant est placé sur le corps et cela dans le but de lier les hommes aux **wanjina** et à l'animal.

wungud

d

e

f

Ngarinyin believe that the primary creator of all life is **Wanjina Gulingi** who invigorates the cosmos and gives water to everything on earth. **Wanjina** manifest creative power coming from the earth, the water and the sky. Lightning demonstrates the power and the flow of energy from **Gulingi** who ensures the constant circulation of life with rain and water.

Wungud is the essence of **wanjina**. All living things have **wungud** (life essence) given by **wanjina**. Named places of **wanjina** water are sources of **wungud**, both of animals and of humans that share the bush together. Water is the source of **wungud** that gives both body and soul to the newborn. As you cannot separate a child from its mother, you cannot separate each human and animal from its source of **wungud**.

As a child first grows in its mother's belly, **wungud** is influential as body and spirit take form. Whenever the mother carries the unborn baby anywhere near **wungud** water the father, even if elsewhere at that moment, should imagine a sign of the baby's **gi** (spiritual connection) to its **wungud** place of spiritual origin. His intuitive vision will define the identity and locality of the baby's totemic **wungud** spirit source, now responsible for forming the spiritual person to be. This private aspect of the individual personality is forged through lifelong experiences of the **gi**, with spiritual pathways leading back to their **wungud** place. The child acquires a social identity always inherited from the father who represents his ancestral **moiety skin** and **dambun** (family estate) of land with associated responsibilities.

Ngarinyin maintain family descent from local **wanjina**. **Wanjina** deposit **wungud** everywhere and form their images through living animals and imposing icons in rock shelters near permanent waterholes; consequently, the personal identity of children has its origin in local **wanjina** water. These local waters, as sources of **wungud**, are central to the landscape of each **dambun**. They are revered deeply as places of origin for many generations of **Ngarinyin** people who carry their name from **wanjina**. For example, Simone **Bangmorro** (e) traces her family descent to the patriarch **Ngegamorro wanjina** (f).

Die **Ngarinyin** verehren den **Wanjina Gulingi** als Schöpfer des Lebens; er schenkt allem auf Erden das Wasser und bringt dem ganzen Kosmos Fruchtbarkeit. Die **wanjina** stehen für die schöpferische Kraft, die aus der Erde, dem Wasser und dem Himmel kommt. Blitze symbolisieren die Macht und Energie von **Gulingi**, der mit Regen und Wasser für den ständigen Kreislauf des Lebens sorgt.

Wungud ist die Essenz der **wanjina**. Allen lebendigen Dingen wohnt **wungud** (Lebensessenz) inne, die ihnen von den **wanjina** verliehen wird. Die **wanjina**-Wasserlöcher sind Quellen des **wungud**, für Tiere wie Menschen gleichermaßen, denn sie leben gemeinschaftlich im Busch. Wasser ist der Quell des **wungud** und verleiht dem Neugeborenen den Körper wie die Seele. So wie man ein Kind nicht von seiner Mutter trennen kann, so lassen sich Mensch und Tier nicht von der Quelle ihres **wungud** trennen.

Wenn ein Kind im Mutterleib heranwächst, gibt das **wungud** Körper und Geist Gestalt. Sobald die Mutter mit dem Ungeborenen in die Nähe einer **wungud**-Quelle (einer heiligen Wasserstelle) kommt, sollte der Vater, selbst wenn er anderswo ist, ein Bild des **gi** sehen, der spirituellen Verbindung des Babys mit seinem **wungud**, dem Ursprungsort seiner Seele. Diese Vision, die sich von selbst einstellt, entscheidet über die spirituelle Heimat des Babys, sein Totem, das von nun an seine Persönlichkeit formt. Diese private Seite, die individuelle Persönlichkeit, entwickelt sich durch lebenslangen Kontakt mit den **gi**, die sie mit der Quelle ihres **wungud** verbinden. Die soziale Identität des Kindes wird stets geprägt durch den Vater und dessen Zugehörigkeit zu einer **skin** oder **moiety** und dem **dambun** (Familienland) mit allen sich daraus ergebenden Pflichten.

Die **Ngarinyin** leiten die Herkunft der Familien von den lokalen **wanjina** her. Die **wanjina** hinterlassen überall **wungud** und erscheinen in Gestalt von lebenden Tieren und imposanten Wandbildern in Felsunterständen in der Nähe der permanenten Wasserlöcher; entsprechend hat die persönliche Identität von Kindern ihren Ursprung in lokalem **wanjina**-Wasser. Diese Wasserstellen, Quellen des **wungud**, bilden den Mittelpunkt eines jeden **dambun**. Sie werden von den **Ngarinyin**, die die Namen der **wanjina** tragen, über viele Generationen hinweg als Orte des Ursprungs verehrt. So führt zum Beispiel Simone **Bangmorro** (e) den Ursprung ihrer Familie auf den Patriarchen **Ngegamorro wanjina** (f) zurück.

Les **Ngarinyin** croient que le premier créateur de toute vie est **Wanjina Gulingi** qui donne sa vigueur au cosmos et donne de l'eau à tout ce qu'il y a sur terre. Les **wanjina** montrent le pouvoir créateur venant de la terre, de l'eau et du ciel. La foudre est la preuve du pouvoir et du flux d'énergie émanant de **Gulingi** qui garantit la circulation constante de la vie par la pluie et l'eau.

Wungud est l'essence des **wanjina**. Toute chose vivante possède **wungud** (l'essence de vie) donnée par les **wanjina**. Les endroits où il y a des eaux **wanjina** sont la source de **wungud**, à la fois pour les animaux et pour les humains qui se partagent le bush. L'eau est la source de **wungud** qui donne corps et âme aux nouveau-nés. De la même manière qu'on ne peut pas séparer un enfant de sa mère, on ne peut pas séparer hommes et animaux de leur source de **wungud**.

Pendant le développement de l'enfant dans le ventre de sa mère, le **wungud** a une influence sur la formation du corps et de l'esprit. Lorsque la mère est enceinte et se trouve près d'eaux **wungud**, le père, même s'il est ailleurs à ce moment-là, doit sentir un signe des **gi** (liens spirituels) de son bébé qui l'unissent à l'endroit de son origine spirituelle **wungud**. Sa vision intuitive déterminera l'identité et le lieu de la source de l'esprit totémique **wungud** de son bébé, esprit qui sera désormais responsable de la formation spirituelle. Cet aspect intime de la personnalité est forgé par les expériences acquises tout au long d'une vie à travers ses **gi** et les chemins spirituels qui renvoient au lieu de son **wungud**. L'enfant acquiert une identité sociale toujours héritée de son père qui représente sa **skin** ancestrale en rapport avec sa **moitié** et par le **dambun** familial avec les responsabilités qui y sont associées.

Les **Ngarinyin** ont conscience de leur généalogie par les **wanjina** locaux. Les **wanjina** déposent partout du **wungud** et créent leur image sous la forme d'animaux vivants et de grandes images peintes dans les abris sous roche situées près des bassins d'eau permanente ; en conséquence, l'identité personnelle des enfants trouva son origine dans les eaux locales **wanjina**. Ces points d'eau, en tant que sources **wungud**, ont une place centrale dans le paysage de chaque **dambun**. Ils sont vénérés en tant que lieu d'origine de beaucoup de générations de **Ngarinyin** dont les noms viennent des **wanjina**. Par exemple Simone **Bangmorro** (e) retrace sa généalogie jusqu'au patriarche **Ngegamorro wanjina** (f).

wungud

a

b

c

High on a winding ridge in **Galeru.ngarri dambun,** an immense boulder rests among piles of sun-shattered sandstone. Elevated on the ridge crest, this huge rock has shade only where fragrant **malarra** trees grow at the base of the northern cliff-face. High up this steep and undulating, red-stained wall are several **wanjina** faces in a richly painted frieze protected from the weather under a deep ledge. From here they look out over the spread of savannah woodlands that merge horizon into horizon, until everything becomes "as far as you can see". Three hazy profiles of distant hills rise out there in the north-west.

Past those three hills is **Guringi,** where the history of the red kangaroo ancestor **Binbin** originates. He first appeared albino white before being eaten alive by native cat men until only some bones and skin were left. But **Binbin** reconstructed his whole body and survived, changing his name before travelling east. He was eaten again but again regrew his body and renamed himself, this time painting himself charcoal black as **Balmirriya wanjina.** With his wife **Guroni,** he created mountains along his ancestral pathway; the travelling red kangaroo ancestor formed many other landmarks to link several **dambun** before arriving at **Wallagari Merrbini.** Sitting down in red ochre as **Walamba,** he formed the billabong of permanent water near the present **Ngarinyin** camp at **Marranba.bidi,** where he threw down his **banad** (boomerang). Later, he underwent the same experience of being consumed, followed by his reconstruction as **Biyad.ngerri,** Finally, he was reincarnated with the sacred name **Wudmi.mulimuli.**

The names of **Walamba,** as well as that of his wife, are held today by the **Nenowatt** family, as custodians of the **bunja** (rock shelter) in **Barraru.ngarri.** Songs of the life of the great red kangaroo ancestor are always heard in **Ngarinyin** land.

Auf einem geschwungenen Bergkamm im **dambun** des **Galeru.ngarri**-Stamms erhebt sich ein gewaltiger Fels inmitten von Bergen aus sonnendurchglühtem Sandsteingeröll. An seinem erhöhten Standort bekommt er nur da etwas Schatten, wo am Fuß der nördlichen Felswand duftende **malarra**-Sträucher wachsen. Hoch oben auf dieser sanft gewellten, mit roten Flecken übersäten Steilwand befindet sich im Schutz eines tiefen Felsüberhangs ein reich ausgeschmückter Fries mit **wanjina**-Gesichtern. Von dort blicken sie über die weite, baumbestandene Savanne, die sich ringsum bis zum Horizont erstreckt. Weit im Nordwesten erheben sich verschwommen die Umrisse von drei Hügeln.

Hinter diesen drei Hügeln liegt **Guringi,** wo die Geschichte des Känguru-Ahnen **Binbin** ihren Anfang nimmt. Er war anfangs weiß wie ein Albino, bevor er von den Wildkatzen-Menschen bei lebendigem Leibe gefressen wurde, sodass nur noch die Haut und ein paar Knochen übrig blieben. Doch **Binbin** überlebte, regenerierte aus diesen Überresten seinen gesamten Körper und nahm einen neuen Namen an, bevor er nach Osten wanderte. Er wurde erneut gefressen, und wieder ließ er seinen Körper nachwachsen und gab sich einen neuen Namen. Diesmal malte er sich mit kohlschwarzer Farbe als **Balmirriya wanjina** an. Zusammen mit seiner Frau **Guroni** erschuf er Berge entlang seines Pfades; auf dem Weg nach **Wallagari Merrbini** hinterließ er viele Spuren in der Landschaft und schuf so Verbindungen zwischen den verschiedenen **dambun.** Schließlich ließ er sich als **Walamba** in rotem Ocker nieder, und als er seinen **banad** (Bumerang) auf den Boden warf, entstand der Billabong in der Nähe des heutigen **Ngarinyin**-Camps von **Marranba.bidi.** Später wurde er nochmals gefressen und erlebte eine neue Wiedergeburt, diesmal unter dem Namen **Biyad.ngerri;** in seiner letzten Reinkarnation trägt er den heiligen Namen **Wudmi.mulimuli.**

Die Namen von **Walamba** und seiner Frau tragen heute Mitglieder der **Nenowatt**-Familie; sie sind die Hüter der **bunja** (Höhle) von **Barraru.ngarri.** Die Lieder über das Leben des Roten Riesenkängurus hört man allenthalben im Land der **Ngarinyin.**

En hauteur, sur une corniche sinueuse dans le **dambun Galeru.ngarri,** il y a un immense rocher parmi les piles de grès fendus par le soleil. En élévation sur la crête, cet énorme rocher n'a de l'ombre que par les arbres odorants **malarra** qui poussent à la base de la face nord de la falaise. Très haut, sur ce mur ocre et ondulé, on trouve plusieurs têtes **wanjina** magnifiquement peintes en frise sous un profond rebord qui les protègent des intempéries. De là, ces têtes font face à l'étendue des forêts de savane qui fusionnent à l'horizon « à perte de vue ». Trois silhouettes floues de collines éloignées s'élèvent quelque part au nord-ouest.

Au delà de ces trois collines, il y a **Guringi** d'où est originaire l'histoire de **Binbin** (l'ancêtre Kangourou roux). Tout d'abord, apparu sous la forme d'un kangourou blanc albinos il fut mangé par des hommes-chat et il n'en resta plus que les os et la peau. Mais **Binbin** reforma son corps en entier et survécut ; il changea son nom avant de se mettre en route vers l'est. À nouveau mangé, il refit une fois de plus son corps et changea de nom ; cette fois, il se peignit avec du charbon noir comme **Balmirriya wanjina.** Avec sa femme, **Guroni,** il créa des montagnes le long de son chemin ancestral et beaucoup de points de repères dans le paysage afin de relier plusieurs **dambun,** avant d'atteindre **Wallagari Merrbini.** S'étant assis dans de l'ocre rouge comme **Walamba,** il créa un plan d'eau permanente remplie à chaque saison des pluies près de l'actuel camp **Ngarinyin** de **Marranba.bidi** où il a jeté à terre son **banad** (boomerang). Ultérieurement, il fut à nouveau mangé et se reforma en **Biyad.ngerri,** et se réincarne finalement sous le nom sacré de **Wudmi.mulimuli.**

Les noms de **Walamba,** tout comme celui de sa femme sont aujourd'hui gardés par la famille **Nenowatt** qui sont les gardiens de **bunja** (abris sous roche) à **Barraru.ngarri.** On entend toujours dans le territoire **Ngarinyin** des chants racontant la vie de l'ancêtre Kangourou roux.

Walamba

a

b

c

A **munnumburra** may sense spiritual influences while he is within the realm of a painting, especially when repainting the **wanjina** icon. While in the sanctuary of a **bunja,** he may sit quietly beside the icon and be intimate with the spirit source of the place, or be visited by the living animal associated with them. The influential totemic relationship of the **wanjina** can determine personal health and vitality. A person's **gi** (their individual spiritual connections) are best not discussed in public. Daily actions can be influenced by the **wanjina** in profound and prosaic ways.

In a stone alcove beneath the **Walamba** are icons of **warrana** the Wedge-tailed Eagle and the one-armed image of **Laajmorro** a **wanjina** form of the Milky Way **Wallagunda.** Along the ridge a short distance is another shelter beneath a boulder, with imposing images of **Jundiwan** and **Bundiwin,** a pair of lightning deities, who carry names for the lightning heralding a cyclonic storm. **Mul.ngirri** follows next, with **Naiya** "the wife" and **Olgi,** the infant and smallest form of lightning.

Near these images, many split and fractured rocks have tumbled down the steep slope and come to rest on the flat savanna plain. Here, the "Old People" collected loose rocks to construct permanent gardens of the **ganmangu** (long yam). These plantings survive for many years protected by waist-high wells of stone. Circles of piled stones are built to catch dew and funnel any nocturnal moisture to the vine roots in the center. They also retain heavy **winjin** (rain), keeping the shaded ground moist long after the monsoon season has passed. Observing the heart-shaped leaves on the wandering vines, **Ngarinyin** come to dig for the mature **ganmangu,** and replant some vine for it to grow into the next season.

Nähert sich ein **munnumburra** einem Felsbild, so kann es vorkommen, dass er das Wirken der spirituellen Kräfte spürt, insbesondere dann, wenn er das Bild des **wanjina** erneuert. Wenn er sich in einem solchen **bunja** (Felsheiligtum) befindet, kann es sein, dass er neben dem Bild verharrt, in stillem Zwiegespräch mit der geistigen Quelle des Ortes, oder er erhält tatsächlich Besuch von dem Tier, dem dieser Ort geweiht ist. Die totemistische Verbindung zu dem **wanjina** kann entscheidenden Einfluss auf die persönliche Gesundheit und Lebenskraft haben. Über das **gi** (die individuelle Beziehung eines Menschen zur Geisterwelt) spricht man besser nicht in der Öffentlichkeit. Die **wanjina** können das alltägliche Leben sowohl auf konkrete als auch auf übertragene Weise beeinflussen.

In einer Felsnische unterhalb der Darstellung des Känguru-Ahnen **Walamba** sieht man **warrana,** den Keilschwanzadler, und ein Bild des einarmigen **Laajmorro,** einer **wanjina-**Form von **Wallagunda,** der die Milchstraße bildet. Ein Stück weiter, unter einem Felsvorsprung, findet sich eine weitere Höhle mit imposanten Darstellungen von **Jundiwan** und **Bundiwin,** zwei Blitzgottheiten, deren Namen die Blitze bezeichnen, die einem Wirbelsturm vorausgehen. Auf sie folgt **Mul.ngirri** mit „der Ehefrau" **Naiya** und dem kindlichen **Olgi,** der schwächsten Form des Blitzes.

In der Umgebung dieser Bilder sind große Mengen von Steinen und Geröll den steilen Abhang hinab auf die ebene Savanne gestürzt. Hier sammelten die „Alten" die Steine für die dauerhaften Gärten, in denen die **ganmangu** (längliche Jamswurzeln), wuchsen. Geschützt durch taillenhohe Steinmauern überdauern solche Pflanzenarten viele Jahre. In Mauerkreisen aus aufgeschichteten Steinen sammeln sich Tau und Nachtfeuchtigkeit und werden den Wurzeln der Kletterpflanzen zugeleitet. Darüber hinaus speichern die Mauern auch den heftigen Monsunregen **(winjin),** sodass der Boden in ihrem Schatten auch nach der Regenzeit noch lange feucht bleibt. Wenn die Pflanze herzförmige Blätter an den langen Ranken bekommt, dann ist die Frucht reif für die Ernte. Die **Ngarinyin** kommen und graben die nächste reife **ganmangu** aus und pflanzen für die nächste Erntezeit gleich wieder einen Teil der Ranken ein.

Un **munnumburra** peut sentir des influences spirituelles lorsqu'il se trouve auprès d'une peinture et particulièrement quand il est en train de repeindre une image de **wanjina.** Lorsqu'il est dans le sanctuaire d'un **bunja,** il peut s'asseoir, silencieusement à côté d'une image et entrer en relation avec les esprits du lieu ou être « visité » par l'animal vivant associé à eux. La relation totémique aux **wanjina** peut déterminer la santé et la vitalité d'une personne. Il est préférable de ne pas discuter des **gi** (liens spirituels personnels) d'un individu en public. Les activités quotidiennes peuvent être influencées par les **wanjina** que ce soit de manière profonde ou prosaïque.

Dans une niche en pierre sous le **Walamba,** il y a des peintures : une de **warrana** (l'aigle audacieux) et une autre à un bras représentant **Laajmorro, wanjina** représentée dans la Voie lactée **Wallagunda.** Non loin de là, le long de la corniche, il y a un autre abri sous un rocher avec d'imposantes images de **Jundiwan** et **Bundiwin,** deux divinités liées à la foudre portant les noms qu'on utilise pour désigner les éclairs annonçant un cyclone. On trouve ensuite **Mul.ngirri** avec **Naiya** « l'épouse » et **Olgi** qui est à la fois l'enfant et la plus petite forme d'éclair.

À côté de ces peintures, beaucoup de roches fendues et cassées se sont éboulées, arrêtées sur la plaine après avoir dévalé la pente raide. C'est là que les « ancêtres » ont ramassé des pierres pour construire les jardins où se plantent les **ganmangu** (longs ignames). Ces plantations durent de nombreuses années, protégées par des margelles en pierre à hauteur de poitrine. Des cercles de pierres empilées retiennent la rosée et canalisent l'humidité nocturne vers les racines de ces plantes grimpantes. Elles retiennent également les **winjin** (fortes pluies) en gardant le sol humide protégé de l'évaporation par les pierres longtemps après la fin de la mousson. Quand ils voient les feuilles en forme de cœur des plantes, ce qui est un signe de maturité, les **Ngarinyin** creusent pour récolter les **ganmangu** et en replantent en vue de la prochaine saison.

Walamba

Bundiwin his name I see him now

Bundiwin those that Lightning brothers
everytime always look at the lightnings

When the rain come
First in the front you'll see that lightning
always flash... flash hit the front first
where the rain travelling towards the...
might be west... north... east
he just travelling like that
always put his lightning in the front

And you can see little lightning sometime
just hit the top trees
*that what we call **Mul.ngirri***
***Mul.ngirri** always put it in the front*
*That the man **Mul.ngirri***
*and this his wife **Naiya***

***Naiya** second... she is the wife*
She not really strong enough
to hit big tree or something
That woman she always hit hollow tree
or small tree
Sometimes she don't knock the tree down
*she just split it... that's that woman **Naiya***

*Even with that little boy **Olgi***
He go for the soft one trees...
Sometimes he don't knock the tree down
he just split 'em small one
*for the little one **Olgi** they call him*
***Algala.olgi** they call'im*
***Olgi** he's the one that hit'em **galwa**...*
He don't hit the hard tree yet
*He go for that little one there that **galwa***
***galwa**... got a yellow flower*
See it down there standing up?
*He hit that one **galwa**... and that **jalla***
*he hit **jalla** when it raining*

Well used to be
Aborigine people training like that too
Father one stand behind the back
and little boy in front
Always hold his head and he just struggling
and then he hit the tree
Big tree the father
and the little boy hit the young one tree
*Like the **jalla** and **galwa** those soft tree*
He don't hit the hard tree yet

*Well I know **Bundiwin***
I got a story from my old people
Nyawarra

Bundiwin heißen die, die ich da sehe

Bundiwin das sind die Blitzbrüder
Wir achten immer auf die Blitze

Wenn der Regen kommt
Dann sieht man immer als Erstes den Blitz
den Blitz sieht man als Erstes... er geht voraus
wenn der Regen heranzieht
Richtung... Westen... Norden... Osten vielleicht
er zieht einfach so heran
immer mit den Blitzen vorneweg

Manchmal sieht man auch einen kleinen Blitz
der nur oben in die größten Bäume einschlägt
*der heißt **Mul.ngirri***
***Mul.ngirri** der kommt immer zuerst*
*Das ist der Mann **Mul.ngirri***
*und seine Frau heißt **Naiya***

***Naiya** kommt als Zweite... das ist die Frau*
Die hat nicht die Kraft für einen
großen Baum oder so was
Diese Frau, sie schlägt nur in hohle Stämme ein
oder kleine Bäume
Manchmal bleibt ein Baum stehen
*wird nur gespalten... das macht **Naiya** die Frau*

*Und **Olgi** der kleine Junge*
Der nimmt sich die jungen Bäume vor...
Manchmal wirft er den Baum nicht um
er spaltet ihn nur, einen kleinen Baum
*für den kleinen Blitz, **Olgi** wird er genannt*
***Algala.olgi** nennen sie ihn*
***Olgi**, das ist der, der in die **galwa** einschlägt...*
Für die großen Bäume ist er noch zu klein
*Die kleinen da, die nimmt er sich vor, die **galwa***
***galwa**... die mit den gelben Blüten*
Siehst du da hinten? da steht einer
*Die **galwa** nimmt er sich vor... und die **jalla***
*Bei den **jalla** schlägt er in der Regenzeit zu*

Bei uns
die Aborigines haben das früher genauso gemacht
Der Vater hat hinten gestanden
der kleine Junge davor
hielt dem Jungen den Kopf weil es schwer ist
und dann haben sie auf die Bäume geschlagen
der Vater auf den großen Baum
und der Kleine auf die kleinen
*Die **jalla** und **galwa**, die sind weich*
Für die harten Bäume da ist er noch zu klein

*Ich kenne **Bundiwin***
ja, so haben es mir die Alten erzählt
Nyawarra

Bundiwin est son nom, je le vois maintenant

Bundiwin c'est eux les frères de l'Eclair
Regardes bien les éclairs

Quand il pleut
D'abord c'est devant, tu verras que cet éclair
il flashe toujours
il frappe d'abord devant, là où va la pluie
vers le... peut-être l'ouest... le nord... l'est
il se déplace comme ça
et il flashe toujours sur le devant

Et tu peux voir des petits éclairs des fois
qui frappent juste les arbres les plus hauts
*on les appelle **Mul.ngirri***
***Mul.ngirri** tape toujours sur le devant*
*C'est l'homme **Mul.ngirri***
*et c'est sa femme **Naiya***

***Naiya** est deuxième... c'est la femme*
elle n'est pas assez forte pour avoir
les grands arbres ou quoi
cette femme elle atteint toujours
un arbre creux ou un petit arbre
Des fois elle ne descend pas vraiment l'arbre
*elle le déchire c'est tout... c'est la femme **Naiya***

*Pareil pour ce petit gosse, **Olgi**, le garçon-éclair*
il s'attaque aux arbres tendres
Des fois il le descend pas
il le déchire seulement le petit
*On l'appelle **Olgi**...*
***Algala.olgi**, c'est son nom*
***Olgi** c'est celui qui frappe le **galwa**...*
il ne frappe pas encore les arbres forts
*il choisit le petit **galwa***
***galwa**... celui qui a une fleur jaune*
Tu le vois debout là-bas dressé ?
*Il frappe celui-là, le **galwa**... et ce **jalla***
*Il frappe le **jalla** quand il pleut*

Autrefois aussi
les Aborigènes s'entraînaient comme ça aussi
le père se tient derrière
et le petit garçon devant
Il tient tête et il se bat
et il frappe l'arbre... un gros arbre pour le père
et le petit garçon un jeune arbre
*des arbres tendres comme le **jalla** et le **galwa***
il ne frappe pas encore les gros arbres

*Oui je connais **Bundiwin***
je tiens cette histoire de mes vieux
Nyawarra

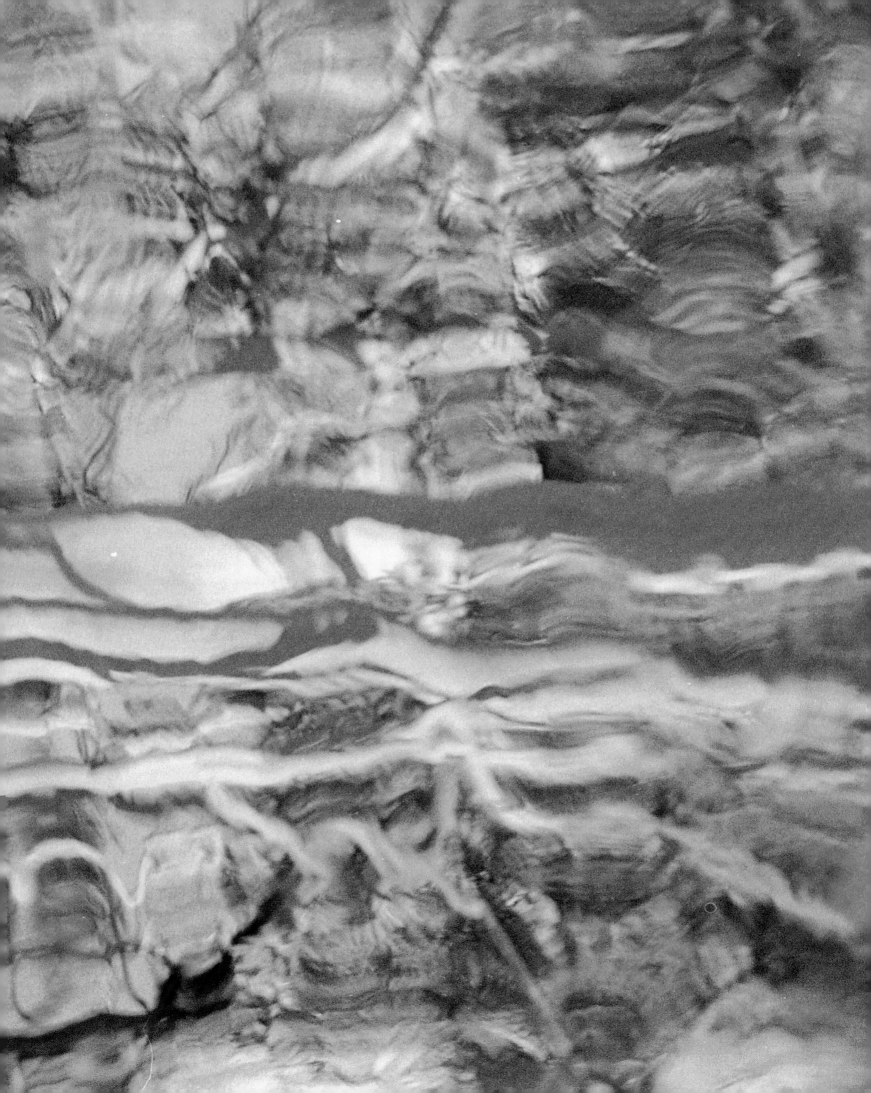

Wanjina Gulingi is all

They can't go without it

Creator of all

*its the **wungud**... he's the water*

Nyawarra

*Der **Wanjina Gulingi** ist alles...*

Ohne ihn kann nichts entstehen

Der Schöpfer von allem...

*ist **wungud**... er ist das Wasser*

Nyawarra

*Le **Wanjina Gulingi** est tout*

on ne peut rien faire sans lui

il est le créateur de tout...

*c'est le **wungud**... il est l'eau*

Nyawarra

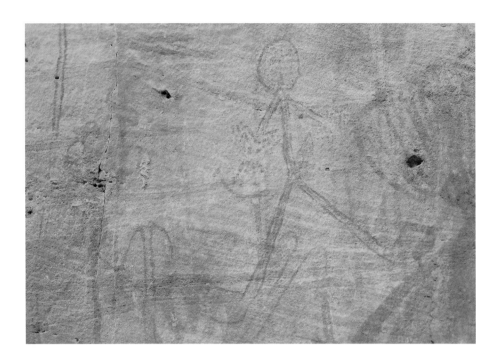

Laisse-nous te dire
L'éclair vient de partout
mullawundin *est partout !*
le voilà ce type
il fait bang ! il a un grand pouvoir
Ungudman

Il les fait éclater comme une fourche
éclair en forme de fourche … ***mullawundin***
parce qu'il a ses jambes écartées tu vois
Celle-là est écartée de l'autre côté
et cette jambe là tu vois … son pied est dans ce sens
et là main là vient toucher la fourche
cet éclair s'appelle ***mullawundin***
mullawundin, *quand il a ses jambes écartées*
Banggal

Les éclairs … tu sais les éclairs ?
Ungudman

Partout … ***mullawundin***
c'est le type là qui fait bang !
mullawundin *a vraiment un grand pouvoir*
Banggal

Et il va partout
Ungudman

une fourche, ***mullawundin*** *est fourchu*
parce qu'il ses jambes déployées
Banggal

mullawundin *est son nom*
Ungudman

C'est lui là, maintenant
Banggal

l'éclair qui brille …
Ungudman

Let us tell you
Lightning from everywhere here
mullawundin *everywhere!*
that's the fella now
and he go bang! from a big power
Ungudman

And he go everywhere bust 'em fork
fork one... ***mullawundin***
because he got his leg spread see
This one is spread right across
like leg see leg here… foot this way
and hand there will touch that fork
lightning called ***mullawundin***
mullawundin *where he got his leg spread*
Banggal

Lightning... you know lightning?
Ungudman

Everywhere... ***mullawundin***
that's the fella now and he go bang!
mullawundin *proper big power*
Banggal

And he go everyway
Ungudman

Fork... forked one ***mullawundin***
because he got his leg spread see
Banggal

mullawundin *his name*
Ungudman

This one now
Banggal

Lightning one... lightning one
Ungudman

Hier blitzt es von überall her
das kannst du uns glauben
mullawundin *überall!*
der Bursche da ist das
und der macht wumm! solche Kraft hat der
Ungudman

Der fährt überall rein und macht alles kaputt
der gespaltene Blitz … ***mullawundin***
der hat nämlich die Beine gespreizt siehst du, so
Der steht da mit breiten Beinen
hier ist ein Bein und … da ist der Fuß
und die Hand da berührt
den gespaltenen Blitz ***mullawundin***
mullawundin *ist der mit den gespreizten Beinen*
Banggal

Blitz … verstehst du, Blitze?
Ungudman

mullawundin *… überall*
der Bursche da ist das und der macht wumm!
mullawundin *der ist unheimlich stark*
Banggal

Der fährt überall rein
Ungudman

Gespalten … der gespaltene Blitz ***mullawundin***
der hat nämlich die Beine gespreizt … siehst du
Banggal

mullawundin *heißt der*
Ungudman

Hier dieser
Banggal

Der Blitz … da, siehst du
Ungudman

288

Only that old man he control
munnumburra he say
"You must listen to animal!"
that **arru**… eel he belong to **wanjina**
young people don't eat them
That **arru** is **wanjina** fish

We follow him from his back
wanjina… we not front of them
we living creatures that follow
yeah! and that's the pathway

We don't come from front side y'know
we come from behind side

Banggal

Nur der alte Mann lenkt das
der **munnumburra** sagt
„Ihr müsst auf die Tiere hören!"
dieser **arru**… der Aal, der gehört den **wanjina**
junge Leute essen ihn nicht
Der **arru** ist ein **wanjina**-Fisch

Wir treten von hinten an ihn heran
wanjina… man stellt sich nicht vor ihn hin
wir lebendigen Geschöpfe gehen hinter ihm
oh ja! und das ist der Pfad

Verstehst du wir kommen nicht von vorne
wir kommen von hinten, von der Seite

Banggal

Il n'y a que ce vieil homme qui contrôle
c'est un **munnumburra**, il dit
« Tu dois écouter les animaux ! »
cette **arru**… l'anguille, elle appartient aux **wanjina**
les jeunes ne la mangent pas
Cette **arru** est un poisson **wanjina**

On le suit de derrière
le **wanjina**… on n'est jamais devant lui
nous les êtres vivants on le suit
oui ! sur ce chemin

On ne vient pas avant lui tu vois
on vient après lui

Banggal

Jundiwan… Bundiwin
lightning brothers one
all this lot… all got lightning

And that's what the land is…
because all the power connected

lightning painting… **wanjina** painting
… snake painting
all that power is outside looking after the land
Banggal

Jundiwan … Bundiwin
Blitzbrüder sind das, die alle hier
die haben Macht über den Blitz

Und das hier das ist das Land
denn alles ist eine Kraft

Blitzbild … **wanjina**-Bild
… Schlangenbild
die ganze Kraft ist da draußen, sorgt für das Land
Banggal

Jundiwan … Bundiwin
les frères éclairs
tous … ils ont tous des éclairs

Et c'est comme ça que cette terre est faite …
à cause de tous ces pouvoirs connectés

les peintures des éclairs … les peintures de **wanjina**
… les peintures de serpents
tout cette puissance déployée protège le pays
Banggal

*agula... his name is **agula***
he like a devil man

Or say like a spirit of the person
*that's what we call **emmalen***
***emmalen**... he just like a ghost*
He travel anyway
and he paint up anyway too
*he go with the **Gwion***
*... **emmalen***
Nyawarra

agula**... der da heißt **agula
der ist eine Art Teufel, Mann

Oder wie der Geist eines Menschen
*den nennen wir **emmalen***
***emmalen**... der ist wie ein Gespenst*
Er ist immer unterwegs
und überall findet man Bilder von ihm
*er ist mit den **Gwion** unterwegs*
*... **emmalen***
Nyawarra

agula**... son nom est **agula
c'est comme un diable ce homme

Ou disons comme un esprit de la personne
*c'est pour ça qu'on l'appelle **emmalen***
***emmalen**... il est comme un fantôme*
Il voyage partout
et il s'est peint partout aussi
*il suit les **Gwion***
*... **emmalen***
Nyawarra

*All this lot **banman** got lightning*
everyone of them woman and man
all got lightning... everyone
Banggal

*Die **banman** haben Macht über den Blitz*
alle von denen, Frauen und Männer
die wissen wie man mit dem Blitz umgeht
Banggal

*Tous ces **banman** ils ont des éclairs*
tous, les hommes et les femmes
ils ont tous des éclairs... tous
Banggal

That tree only special tree
to remind 'em to dig it
cut those tree where where he grow
because only one here to remind everybody
you must cut those stick to dig these yam
that's why it's standing right in middle
this **dinjid** here... it's the main one
he don't grow anywhere in the basalt country
only in sandstone country where the food grow
this only the reminder
telling us to take the action

This **Dinjid** we call him... his name **Dinjid**
that lord **wanjina** now and ah, we tell him
we bring you present stone or bushes
And we give 'em and we tell him
"this is your present from me"
everyone of them
then we don't catch that **dinjid**
you know that sniffing sickness thing?
we don't catch it then
that's why that **Dinjid** is there
and we offer him gift... **lulwa**
we give him and he all in **Wunan**
we gotta give him present all the time...
Dinjid wanjina

Banggal

Der Baum da ist etwas Besonderes
der ist zur Erinnerung, dass wir Grabstöcke
abschneiden sollen, da wo er wächst
hier steht nur der eine und der erinnert daran
man muss Stöcke schneiden und nach Jams graben
deswegen steht er direkt in der Mitte
dieser **dinjid** da ... der ist der Wichtigste
der wächst nirgendwo im Basaltland
nur im Sandsteinland wo auch Essen wächst
dieser hier ist nur zur Erinnerung
damit wir nicht vergessen was wir tun müssen

Dieser heißt **Dinjid** ... **Dinjid** das ist der Name
dem **Dinjid wanjina** dem sagen wir hier
wir bringen dir Geschenke, die Steine und Zweige
die bringen wir ihm und sagen
„Das ist mein Geschenk für dich"
jedes Mal sagen wir das
und dann bekommen wir keinen **dinjid**
keinen Schnupfen bei dem einem die Nase läuft
den bekommen wir nicht
dafür ist der **Dinjid** gut
deswegen bringt man ihm Geschenke ... **lulwa**
wir geben ihm was und alles gehört zum **Wunan**
man muss ihm immer etwas schenken ...
dem **Dinjid wanjina**

Banggal

Cet arbre-là, c'est un arbre spécial qui rappelle
qu'il faut creuser, on le coupe où il pousse
c'est le seul qui rappelle à tout le monde
qu'on doit couper des bâtons
pour fonir les ignames
c'est pourquoi il se dresse là au milieu
ce **dinjid** là ... c'est le plus grand
il pousse pas dans les régions de basalte
seulement dans les pays de grès,
là où la nourriture pousse
c'est juste ça qui nous rappelle
qui nous dit qu'il faut agir

Ça on l'appelle **Dinjid** ... son nom c'est **Dinjid**
ce seigneur **wanjina,** on lui dit
on t'apporte des pierres ou des herbes en cadeau
et on lui donne et on lui dit
« voilà le cadeau que je te fais »
chacun d'entre eux
après on n'attrape plus le **dinjid**
tu connais cette maladie qui fait renifler ?
on l'attrape plus comme ça
c'est pour ça que le **Dinjid** est là
et on lui fait ce don... **lulwa**
on lui donne et il est dans le **Wunan**
on doit lui donner des présents tout le temps ...
à ce **Dinjid wanjina**

Banggal

Gulilli she can attack your stomach
then this lot outside... what we see
is all the woman this lot jungi... anthill
don't muck around with them jungi
very important... mamaa
and we have to be frightened of them
otherwise they wipe us out
All these Gulilli area because they over here
we don't... not allowed to go there
That's women's business... It's a women's secret

This part this middle is the stomach
that belongs to woman you know?
This one here is the border of her stomach
this area womb side...
this area belong to a woman
they special they don't marry...
nothing this mob here
If we don't treat them well
they get that green stick
and they put a congealed blood in our stomach

Gulilli, die kann einem auf den Magen schlagen
und das da draußen... was wir da sehen
das gehört alles ihr, jungi... Ameisenhaufen
mit einem jungi treibt man keinen Spaß
die sind sehr wichtig... mamaa
und wir müssen sie fürchten
sonst bringen sie uns um
Die ganze Gegend hier, die gehört Gulilli
wir gehen da... wir dürfen da nicht hin
Das ist Frauensache... Das ist ihr Geheimnis

Der Teil hier in der Mitte das ist der Bauch
der gehört den Frauen, verstehst du?
Hier, bis dahin reicht ihr Bauch
das hier ist der Schoß...
der Teil hier, der gehört einer Frau
die sind was Besonderes die heiraten nicht...
die bleiben für sich
Wenn wir die nicht gut behandeln
dann nehmen sie so einen grünen Stock
und lassen uns das Blut im Magen gerinnen

Gulilli, elle peut t'attaquer l'estomac
et puis ça dehors... ce qu'on voit là
c'est aux femmes ça, jungi... la fourmilière
ne traîne pas autour des jungi, des fourmilières
très important... c'est mamaa
et on doit avoir peur d'elles
ou sinon elles nous exterminent
Ces endroits sont réservés à Gulilli
... on ne peut pas... on n'a pas le droit d'aller là
C'est l'affaire des femmes... un secret des femmes

Cette partie là au milieu c'est l'estomac
ça appartient à la femme tu vois ?
ça là c'est le bord de son estomac
cet endroit là c'est l'utérus...
ça appartient à une femme
elle est spéciale elle se marie pas...
ni rien celle-là
Si on la traîte pas bien
elle prend ce bâton vert
et elle met du sang coagulé dans notre estomac

We get sick... we die
so we have to respect all this women
because they powerful women... they Gulilli

That is women's business
its women... is secret all this Gulilli area
All this area is mamaa area
and that we have to be fear
otherwise we'll die
this is all the bad place belonga woman
that woman story you get er... tummy ache
you make blood diarrhea... you dead
he warning that way that woman business
that's a woman's secret
and nobody can cure that one

The teaching knowledge... dulwan nimindi
it's ah building a fear from while you're young
to respect everything in nature
because you... they telling her
you gonna be boss over this area
and that one waterhole
we see the whole basin of that place
where she stop

Banggal

Wir werden krank... wir sterben
deshalb müssen wir diese Frauen respektieren
die sind mächtig diese Frauen... sie sind Gulilli

Das ist Frauensache
geheim, nur für Frauen... die ganze Gulilli-Gegend
Die ganze Gegend hier ist mamaa
und da müssen wir uns vorsehen
sonst sterben wir
das ist ein böser Ort hier, der gehört den Frauen
von der Geschichte bekommst du Bauchschmerzen
Durchfall, bis Blut kommt dann bist du tot
das ist eine Warnung dass das Frauensache ist
Geheimnis der Frauen
die Krankheit kann keiner heilen

Das Wissen das wir lernen... dulwan nimindi
das lehrt uns fürchten von Kindheit an
dass man alles in der Natur respektiert
weil man... die sagen ihr
dass sie über diese Gegend herrschen wird
und über das eine Wasserloch
da sieht man das ganze Becken
da sitzt sie drin

Banggal

On devient malade... et on meurt
donc il faut respecter ces femmes
parce qu'elles sont puissantes ces femmes... Gulilli

C'est une affaire de femmes
de femmes... tout cet endroit de Gulilli
Tout cet endroit est mamaa
et on doit en avoir peur
ou sinon on va mourir
tout cet endroit mauvais il appartient aux femmes
ces histoires de femmes donnent mal au ventre
tu as de la diarrhée avec du sang... tu es mort
tu es prévenu que c'est les affaires de cette femme
c'est un secret de femme
et personne ne peut guérir ça

L'apprentissage du savoir... dulwan nimindi
c'est... apprendre à craindre depuis tout jeune
à respecter les choses de la nature
parce que toi... elles lui disent
tu vas commander cet endroit
et ce trou d'eau
on voit tout ce bassin ici
Là où elle se pose

Banggal

*Gulilli... that woman **Gulilli***
she sit down inside the water... inside
she sit down inside there
that woman one inside in the water
*Well he **wungud** you don't fly over it*
you know he can like a magnet

Banggal

*Gulilli ... die Frau heißt **Gulilli***
und sie sitzt im Wasser ... mittendrin
da sitzt sie drin
da im Wasser da ist sie drin
*das ist **wungud,** da fliegt man nicht drüberweg*
das zieht einen runter wie ein Magnet

Banggal

*Gulilli ... cette femme, **Gulilli***
elle est assise dans l'eau ... dedans
elle est assise dedans là
cette femme là dans l'eau
*Et c'est **wungud,** tu ne voles pas au-dessus*
elle peut t'attirer comme un aimant

Banggal

See this **guli**... blood up here?
this bloodwood tree we call it **guriwin**

and aah this medicine they use it
for when they get cancer in their heart
or weak heart well they use this
put this **guli** in the bucket or in the cup
and they drink it and they very good
and they last longer till they get old
some will live for maybe 90 or 100 years old
pretty long life this thing we call it **guli**

Lot a people I saw them with their sores
and they use this but they pretty good
just like old Aborigine people
been use this medicine
guriwin... bloodwood sap

Nyawarra

Siehst du das Blut hier, **guli?**
das ist der Blutbaum... **guriwin** nennen wir den

und die Medizin da die nehmen sie
wenn jemand Krebs im Herzen bekommt
oder ihr Herz schwach ist dann nehmen sie das
das **guli** tut man in einen Eimer oder einen Becher
und dann trinken sie das und werden gesund
und sie leben lang und werden alt
manche werden 90 oder 100, so lange leben sie
und den Saft den nennen wir **guli**

Ich habe viele kranke Leute gesehen
und sie nehmen das und werden gesund
genau wie die Aborigines früher
die haben auch diese Medizin genommen
guriwin... Saft vom Blutbaum

Nyawarra

Tu vois ce sang-là, **guli ?**
cet arbre dont le bois saigne on l'appelle **guriwin**

et ce médicament ils l'utilisent
pour quand ils ont le cancer du cœur
ou le cœur faible, ils utilisent ça
ils mettent ce **guli** dans un seau ou un bol
ils le boivent et ils vont mieux
ils vivent plus vieux
certains vivront jusqu'à 90 ou 100 ans
ça donne longue vie cette chose, on l'appelle **guli**

Plein de gens que j'ai vus avec des douleurs
ils prennent ça et ils vont mieux
exactement comme les vieux Aborigènes
qui utilisaient ce médicament
guriwin... sève de l'arbre qui saigne

Nyawarra

These are signs...
this tree here is that untouchable tree
everybody know that then we don't touch it
Even old people
when I used to play around long time ago
when I remember my old people
they wouldn't go fiddling around
with a tree or anything
"Hey! what you want to do with that tree
leave it! he want to grow like you too
... you're like it... well he gotta grow"
That was long a sacred thing... tree
Banggal

Yeah when you walkin' through the bush
and you look for this **gurin** here
when you see it like this tree
you just leave it
Nyawarra

Das sind Zeichen...
der Baum hier, der ist unberührbar
jeder weiß das und dann rühren wir ihn nicht an
Sogar die alten Leute
als ich noch jung und leichtsinnig war
vor vielen Jahren wenn ich da an die Alten denke
die haben immer Achtung gehabt
vor Bäumen und solchen Sachen
„He, was hast du da bei dem Baum zu suchen
geh' da weg! der soll genauso wachsen wie du
... der ist wie du ... ihr müsst beide wachsen"
Die Bäume waren heilig ... von alters her
Banggal

Ja wenn man durch den Busch geht
und die **gurin** sucht
und man sieht etwas wie den Baum hier
dann lässt man das in Ruhe
Nyawarra

Ce sont des signes...
cet arbre là est intouchable
tout le monde sait qu'il faut pas le toucher
Même les vieux
quand je jouais là il y a longtemps
quand je me souviens, mes vieux
ils n'allaient pas abîmer un arbre
« Hé ! qu'est-ce que tu fais avec cet arbre
laisse-le ! il veut grandir comme toi
... tu es comme lui ... il doit pouvoir grandir »
Depuis longtemps c'est une chose sacrée ... l'arbre
Banggal

Ouais, quand tu marches au milieu du bush
et que tu cherches ce **gurin** là
quand tu le vois comme tu vois cet arbre
tu le laisses tout simplement
Nyawarra

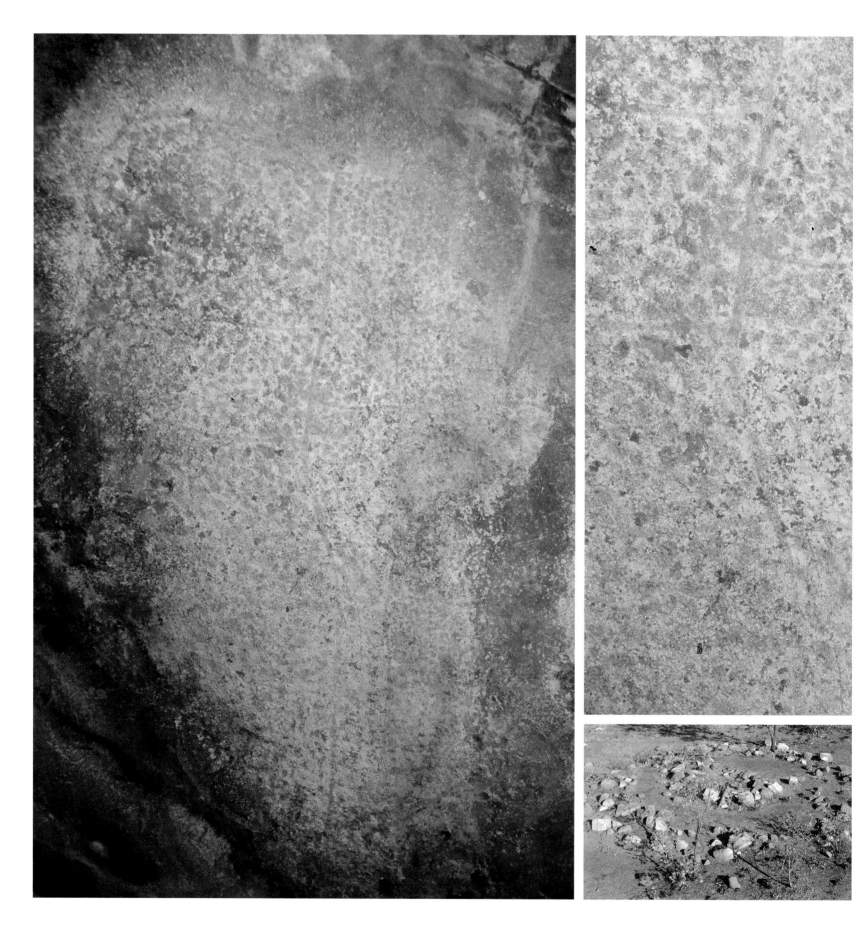

*Camping place of the sugarbag honey **wanjina**...*
Banggal

*Der Honig-**wanjina,** da hat er sein Lager*
Banggal

*C'est le lieu où campe le gourmand **wanjina** du miel*
Banggal

They know which tree is flowering
till they can feed on the wild honey
that honey tree not poor it's all full of honey

There maybe two to three trees
that flower in this month
to keep the honey flowing
and the Aborigines know that
these are signs

The tree itself is **anggurun**...
that orange **maniwan** that's only the flower
red flower he got 'em for sugarbags
And possum he got fat
and the sugarbag gets fat too

Banggal

Die wissen welcher Baum blüht
und dann können sie den wilden Honig holen
der Honigbaum, der ist voll mit Honig

Es gibt vielleicht zwei oder drei Bäume
die um diese Jahreszeit blühen
die sorgen dafür dass immer Honig da ist
und die Aborigines wissen das
hier, daran kann man das erkennen

Der Baum da heißt **anggurun**...
das Orange, **maniwan,** das ist nur die Blüte
in den roten Blüten, da drin ist der Honig
Die Opossums, die werden fett davon
und der Bienenstock auch

Banggal

Ils savent quel arbre fleurit
avec lequel se fait le miel sauvage
cet arbre à miel il est plein de miel

Il y a là peut-être deux ou trois arbres
qui fleurissent ce mois
pour que le miel continue à couler
et les Aborigènes savent ça
ce sont des signes

L'arbre lui-même c'est **anggurun**...
cet orange, **maniwan,** c'est seulement la fleur
une fleur rouge pour le miel
Et l'oppossum il grossit
et le gourmand devient gras aussi

Banggal

Majarumba means the beauty
that grab hold of our eye
when we look at beauty of young people life
and that **majarumba** means it grab hold of us
doesn't matter maybe one woman or girl
walking with the beauty a good looking girl
her eyes shine her hair... everything
her body is so beauty
a young man that is good looking
handsome man in the sharp talk
with the clean teeth shining
and their eye bright that is **majarumba**
what affect us when we admire them
because of the beauty that attract us
that is **majarumba**

Banggal

Majarumba das heißt Schönheit
eine Schönheit die gleich ins Auge springt
wenn wir sehen wie schön die jungen Leute sind
majarumba sagt man wenn uns etwas fesselt
ob es nun eine Frau ist oder ein Mädchen
eine Schönheit, ein Mädchen, das gut aussieht
die Augen leuchten das Haar ... alles
ihr Körper ist schön
oder ein junger Mann der gut aussieht
stattlich sagt man bei euch
mit blitzenden Zähnen
und strahlenden Augen das ist **majarumba**
die packt uns wenn wir sie bewundern
die Schönheit die packt uns
das ist **majarumba**

Banggal

Majarumba veut dire, la beauté
qui saisit le regard
quand on voit la beauté de la vie des jeunes gens
et ce mot **majarumba** veut dire que ça nous saisit
peu importe que ce soit une femme, une fille
qui marche toute belle, une belle fille
ses yeux brillent, ses cheveux... tout
son corps est si beau
un jeune homme beau
un bel homme comme on dit
avec ses belles dents qui brillent
et l'œil vif, c'est **majarumba**
ce qui nous affecte quand on les admire
parce que cette beauté qui nous attire
c'est **majarumba**

Banggal

The name of young people...
children is called **waringi de.de**
How many people in the beginning say

"I'll carry him... I'll carry him baby"
You know everybody love that child
"Let me carry this beautiful little child"

You know? that is this polite little child
good looking... handsome... beautiful
we look at that beauty... we love them
because we love this bush **waringi de.de**
... glowing and shining
it represents young people's life
this special tree

Banggal

Junge Leute, die nennen wir...
Kinder heißen **waringi de.de**
Wenn sie klein sind sagen die Leute immer

„Lass mich es tragen... ich trage das Baby"
Du weißt schon, alle mögen die kleinen Kinder
„Lass mich es tragen das süße Kleine"

Weißt du, was ich meine? alle mögen es
es sieht gut aus... es ist schön... die Schönheit
deswegen haben wir sie gern
denn wir mögen den Busch da, **waringi de.de**
... alles strahlt, alles leuchtet
der steht für das Leben der jungen Menschen
das ist ein ganz besonderer Baum

Banggal

Le nom des jeunes gens...
pour les enfants on dit **waringi de.de**
Combien de gens disent au début

« Je vais le porter... je vais porter ce bébé »
Tu sais tout le monde aime cet enfant
« Laisse-moi porter ce superbe petit enfant »

Tu sais ? c'est ce petit enfant très poli
agréable... mignon... beau
on regarde cette beauté... on les aime
parce qu'on aime ce **waringi de.de** du bush
... qui luit et brille
ça représente la vie, la jeunesse
c'est un arbre spécial

Banggal

a

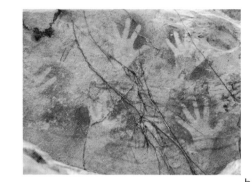

b

c

The meanings of Aboriginal rock imagery vary across the Australian continent and defy ready interpretation. The actual location of a painting or petroglyph is integral to the ideas and values it expresses. Across the Kimberley, **wanjinas** are believed to form themselves as part of the rock. When these icons are repainted under the supervision of **munnumburra,** colours, profiles and contours animate the essential form existing at the exact location of a source of **wungud.** The numerous hand-stencils on rock are not simply personal "signatures". An image of an outstretched hand may signify a request or demand. Some single hand-stencils (a) are read by **munnumburra** as a signal placed there by a local custodian, reminding visitors that they should give a **mangarri** tribute due to the host **dambun** people. Hand-stencils can also be a family mark if grouped liked **wanjina** (b) but may be the cryptic mark of a **banman,** an individual with exceptional ability as a mystic or healer (c).

Separate from the layers of many paintings at **Alyaguma** is a small image on a boulder showing a man becoming a **banman** (d). The simplified body with out-stretched arms and legs – each with three digits – appears to wear a fanned headdress topped with a shape that looks like a feather plume. **Ungudman** and **Banggal** did not read this as either halo or headdress, but instead the head of a **banman** during the moment of revelation. The bulbous shape portrays a bolt of concentrated lightning piercing the **banman's** head while igniting his powers of perception.

There are other small images nearby, stiffened male figures holding jagged clusters of lightning in their hands. The **munnumburra** explained how **mullawundin** (lightning) is closely connected to male potency. Lightning is also rich with secret magical associations that allow the **banman** to travel underground or to "fly around" over considerable distances to perform magic rituals (e). Because **banman** are believed to travel on secret pathways through the earth, any image or evidence marking their activity may be very dangerous to the uninitiated. Most residual paintings of **banman** and the mischevous spirit figures called **agula** are feared and their locations revered as **mamaa** (secret places). Some cryptic images in blood or special ash were probably created without concern for durability and have already faded away (g). Their location may be marked with **jallala** (signal stones) and known through images of prohibition on the killing of special animals (f) or the eating of certain food nearby.

Die Felsmalereien der Aborigines tragen unterschiedliche Bedeutungen in den verschiedenen Regionen des australischen Kontinents und entziehen sich einer einfachen Interpretation. Entscheidend für die Ideen und Werte, die ein Gemälde oder Felsbild zum Ausdruck bringt, ist sein unmittelbarer Standort. Die Bewohner der Kimberley-Region glauben, dass die **wanjina** sich selbst im Felsen abbilden. Wenn diese Malereien unter der Aufsicht der **munnumburra** erneuert werden, erwecken die neuen Farben, Oberflächen und Konturen die zugrunde liegende Form, die am Ort einer **wungud**-Quelle existiert, zu neuem Leben. Die zahlreichen Handabdrücke auf den Felsen sind mehr als nur persönliche „Signaturen". Das Bild einer ausgestreckten Hand kann auch Ausdruck einer Bitte oder Forderung sein. Die **munnumburra** deuten einzelne Handabdrücke (a) bisweilen auch als Signal, das ein Hüter des jeweiligen Ortes dort angebracht hat, um Besucher daran zu erinnern, dass sie die **mangarri** (obligatorisches Geschenk) für die Bewohner des gastgebenden **dambun** nicht vergessen sollen. Handabdrücke, die wie die **wanjina** angeordnet sind, können auch für eine ganze Familie stehen (b), während eine einzelne Hand (c) vielleicht das kryptische Zeichen eines **banman** ist, eines Individuums mit außergewöhnlichen Fähigkeiten als Mystiker oder Heiler.

Abseits von den oft übermalten Felsbildern in **Alyaguma** findet sich auf einem Felsen eine kleine Darstellung eines Mannes, der gerade zum **banman** wird (d). Die stark stilisierte Figur mit ausgestreckten Armen und Beinen – die Hände haben drei Finger, die Füße drei Zehen – trägt allem Anschein nach einen fächerförmigen Kopfschmuck, gekrönt von einem Federbusch. **Ungudman** und **Banggal** sahen darin weder eine Art Heiligenschein noch einen Kopfputz, sondern das Abbild des Kopfes des **banman** im Augenblick der Erleuchtung. Die knollige Form symbolisiert einen konzentrierten Blitz, der in den Kopf des **banman** fährt und seine Wahrnehmung schärft.

In der Nähe gibt es andere kleine Bilder von steifen männlichen Figuren mit gezackten Blitzbündeln in den Händen. Die **munnumburra** weisen auf die enge Verbindung zwischen dem **mullawundin** (Blitz) und der männlichen Potenz hin. Blitze sind auch reich an Zauberkräften, die es dem **banman** gestatten, sich unterirdisch fortzubewegen oder „umherzufliegen", um in beträchtlicher Entfernung magische Rituale auszuführen (e). Da man dem **banman** nachsagt, dass er auf geheimen Pfaden durch die Erde reisen kann, birgt jedes Bild, jedes Zeugnis seines Wirkens, große Gefahren für Uneingeweihte. Erhaltene Felsbilder von **banman** und den trickreichen Geistern **agula** (f) werden gefürchtet und als **mamaa** (geheime Orte) verehrt. Manche kryptischen Darstellungen aus Blut oder spezieller Asche dürften wenig dauerhaft gewesen sein und sind längst verschwunden (g), doch oft künden **jallala** (Signalsteine) oder das Verbot, bestimmte Tiere zu jagen (f) oder bestimmte Nahrungsmittel dieser Gegend zu essen, davon, wo sie sich früher einmal befunden haben.

Les significations des peintures rupestres aborigènes varient d'un bout à l'autre du continent australien et défient les interprétations toutes faites. L'emplacement d'une peinture ou d'un pétroglyphe est intégré dans les idées et les valeurs qu'il exprime. Dans tous le Kimberley on croit que les images **wanjina** se sont créées d'elles-mêmes, comme faisant partie de la roche. Quand ces images sont repeintes sous la direction des **munnumburra,** les couleurs, esquisses et contours donnent vie à la forme déjà existante à l'endroit exact d'une origine de **wungud.** Les nombreuses images de mains en négatif ne sont pas simplement une « signature » personnelle. Une image de main ouverte et tendue peut signifier une requête ou une demande. Certaines mains isolées en négatif (a) sont lues par les **munnumburra** comme étant des messages laissés par un gardien local, rappelant aux visiteurs qu'ils devraient donner un **mangarri** (tribut) à ceux du **dambun** qui abritent la peinture. Les mains en négatif (c) peuvent aussi être la marque d'une famille, si elles sont groupées comme les **wanjina,** ou être la marque secrète d'un **banman,** un individu doté d'une compétence exceptionnelle en tant que mystique ou guérisseur.

Séparée des nombreuses couches de peintures superposées à **Alyaguma,** il y a une petite peinture sur un rocher représentant un homme devenant un **banman** (b). Son corps, dessiné de manière très simplifiée avec bras et jambes tendus – ayant chacun trois doigts à leur extrémité – semble porter une coiffe en éventail surmontée d'une forme qui pourrait être une plume. **Ungudman** et **Banggal** ne l'ont interprétée ni comme une auréole ou une coiffe mais comme étant la tête d'un **banman** au moment d'une révélation. Une forme bulbeuse représente l'éclair transperçant la tête du **banman** au moment où celui-ci met en jeu ses pouvoirs paranormaux.

Il y a d'autres petites peintures non loin de là, représentant des personnages masculins raides tenant des éclairs en zigzag. Les **munnumburra** expliquèrent comment **mullawundin** (l'éclair) est intimement lié à la virilité. L'éclair possède également de nombreuses connections magiques et secrètes qui permettent au **banman** de voyager sous terre ou de « voler » sur de longues distances pour pouvoir exécuter des rituels magiques (e). Comme l'on pense que les **banman** voyagent sur des chemins secrets à travers la terre, toute image ou preuve de leurs activités peut être très dangereuse pour le non-initié. La plupart des peintures qui restent représentant des **banman** et des esprits malveillants appelés **agula** (a) sont craintes et leurs emplacements sont vénérés comme des **mamaa** (lieux secrets). Leurs mystérieuses images faites avec du sang ou de la cendre spéciale ont probablement été crées sans se soucier de leur résistance au temps et se sont déjà effacées (g). Leur emplacement peut être marqué par des **jallala** (pierres) et connu du fait de l'interdiction de tuer certains animaux (f) ou de manger certains types de nourriture aux alentours.

banman

d

e

f

Most **banman** only conduct healing rituals, but on rare occasions they are said to have acted as public executioners, commissioned by **munnumburra.** After such an event, symbolic paintings might have been produced as a precaution against revenge. The reputation of an individual **banman** as an expert interpreter of dreams or healer can vary; but in most bush communities they are widely respected and can achieve a priest-like status, while others are too discrete to be noticed.

Die meisten **banman** sind nur für rituelle Heilungszeremonien zuständig, aber hin und wieder sollen sie im Auftrag von **munnumburra** auch öffentliche Strafvollstreckungen durchgeführt haben. Vielleicht entstanden nach einem solchen Ereignis symbolische Felsbilder zum Schutz vor Racheakten. Manche **banman** genießen als Traumdeuter oder Heiler größeres Ansehen als andere, doch bei den meisten im Busch lebenden Aborigines ist die Achtung groß, und die **banmans** können den Rang eines Priesters erlangen; andere wirken ganz im Verborgenen.

La plupart des **banman** ne dirigent que des rituels de guérison mais on dit qu'en de rares occasions ils ont eu la fonction de bourreau lorsque cela leur a été demandé par des **munnumburra.** Après de tels événements, des peintures ont peut-être été faites comme précaution contre toute vengeance. La réputation des **banman** comme intreprétateurs de songes et guérisseurs peut varier, mais dans la plupart des communautés du bush ils sont très respectés et peuvent arriver à un statut proche de celui de prêtre, alors que d'autres sont trop discrets pour être remarqués.

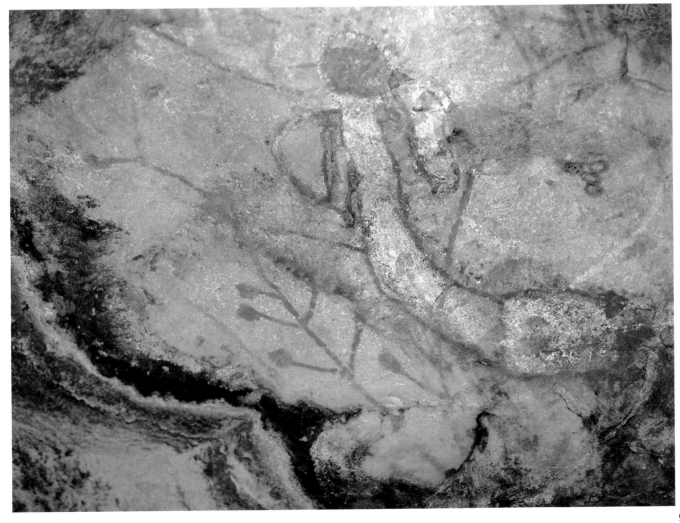

g

banman

a

b

c

Ngarinyin sacred places function as sites to identify the sources of life. Each type of rock, plant, tree, bird and other animal belongs to a certain place that became a source of its **wungud.** Each source may be linked to others through residues of **wungud** essence that form a **dulwan mamaa** (sacred pathway) across the country.

Wungud can be expressed as a kind of radiant energy being released continuously from each sacred realm or "dreaming" place. The exact site of each source of **wungud** is one point in a landscape of many natural features created by the actions of **wanjina.** Known by the **munnumburra** as signs of the power of **wanjina,** such as a landmark or phenomenon could be an egg-shaped stone (a), a nest of burrowing frogs (b), or a billabong. Or a painting. This distribution of **wungud** in its many forms is always linked to the core of fertility that resides at the site of a **wanjina's** icon. **Junjun** (evidence of **wanjina** and ancestors) is found everywhere in the landscape by following signs on the **dulwan** guided by **Ngarinyin** narratives. For example, the kidney stone of the crocodile **ngerdu** may be inspected (f).

Much happens on each path taken in the bush and, later in camp, the spontaneous conversation among **munnumburra** often recalls common experiences and details of paths taken through the bush years before. These meetings provide the opportunity for discreet discussion about the precious **junjun** and the central role it plays in **Wunan** law.

The substance of meaning in **junjun** takes various forms in **Ngarinyin** language through the naming of each plant and animal. Such naming and the direct sighting of human traces act as catalysts for songs. Only through day-to-day experience of the bush can songs acquire their full meaning. Most sacred knowledge is ultimately held in songs, sometimes coded and sometimes overt. There is no pathway without these ancient songs; only through song does the **dulwan** become fully alive, never to be forgotten. Their performance insinuates meanings deep into memories, with the bonding of faces and places. The signs and evidence on the secret and sacred pathways, as interpreted by **munnumburra,** are used as tools for education.

An den heiligen Orte der **Ngarinyin** manifestieren sich die Quellen des Lebens. Jeder Fels, jede Pflanze, jeder Vogel und jedes andere Tier ist einem bestimmten Ort zugeordnet, der die Quelle seines **wungud** ist. Jede dieser Quellen kann durch einen **dulwan mamaa** (heiliger Pfad) durchs Land mit anderen verbunden sein.

Wungud lässt sich beschreiben als eine Art Energie, die ständig von jedem heiligen Ort, der in Verbindung zur Traumzeit steht, ausstrahlt. Die genaue Position jeder **wungud**-Quelle ist nur eines von vielen Elementen einer Landschaft, in der die **wanjina** allenthalben ihre Spuren hinterlassen haben. Die **munnumburra** kennen diese Belege für die Macht und das Wirken der **wanjina,** sei es nun ein eiförmiger Stein (a), ein Erdloch voller Frösche (b) ein Teich oder eben ein Felsbild. Die vielfältigen Erscheinungsformen des **wungud** stehen immer in Verbindung mit der Fruchtbarkeit, die dem Ort innewohnt, an dem ein **wanjina** dargestellt ist. **Junjun** (sichtbare Belege für das Wirken der **wanjina** und der Ahnenwesen) findet man überall in der Landschaft, wenn man den Zeichen auf den **dulwan** folgt, von denen die Erzählungen der **Ngarinyin** berichten. Ein Beispiel hierfür ist die zu Stein gewordene Niere des Krokodils **ngerdu.**

Jeder Pfad durch den Busch birgt viele Geheimnisse, und wenn sich die **munnumburra** nach ihren Streifzügen im Camp über ihre Erlebnisse unterhalten, erinnern sie sich oft an gemeinsame Erfahrungen und Einzelheiten der Pfade, auf denen sie Jahre zuvor durch den Busch gewandert sind. Diese Treffen bieten Gelegenheit für vertraute Gespräche über die heiligen **junjun** und die zentrale Rolle, die sie innerhalb des **Wunan**-Gesetzes spielen.

Die tiefe Bedeutung der **junjun** kommt in der Sprache der **Ngarinyin** durch das vielfältige Benennen der einzelnen Tiere und Pflanzen zum Ausdruck. Wenn man einen solchen Namen ausspricht oder tatsächliche menschliche Spuren entdeckt, wirkt das wie ein Katalysator, eine Art Auslöser für rituelle Gesänge. Nur durch die tägliche Begegnung mit dem Busch können diese Lieder ihre volle Bedeutung erlangen. Der größte Teil des sakralen Wissens steckt letztlich in solchen Liedern, bisweilen verschlüsselt, bisweilen auch offensichtlich. Es gibt keinen heiligen Pfad ohne diese uralten Lieder. Erst durch die Lieder erwacht ein **dulwan** wirklich zum Leben und kann niemals in Vergessenheit geraten. Durch das Singen prägt sich seine Bedeutung tief ins Gedächtnis ein, untrennbar verknüpft mit Gesichtern und Orten. Die Zeichen und Spuren auf den geheimen und heiligen Pfaden und ihre Deutung durch die **munnumburra** sind Instrumente der Erziehung.

Les lieux sacrés **Ngarinyin** servent de sites pour identifier les sources de la vie. Chaque type de pierre, de plante, d'arbre, d'oiseau ou de tout autre animal appartient à un lieu particulier qui devient la source de son **wungud.** Chaque origine peut être liée à d'autres origines par les traces de **wungud** qui forment un **dulwan mamaa** (chemin sacré) d'un bout à l'autre du pays.

Wungud peut se définir comme une sorte d'énergie rayonnante qui émane continuellement de chaque lieu sacré ou « dreaming ». L'endroit exact de chaque source de **wungud** est un point dans le paysage où de nombreuses particularités de la nature ont été créées par les **wanjina.** Connus des **munnumburra** comme étant des signes du pouvoir des **wanjina,** ces points de repères ou phénomènes sont par exemple une pierre en forme d'œuf (a), un élément de grenouilles (b) ou une mare d'eau, ou bien encore une peinture. Cette distribution du **wungud** sous différentes formes est toujours liée à l'élément de fertilité, présent sur tout site d'une image **wanjina. Junjun** (la preuve de l'existence des **wanjina** et des ancêtres) se retrouve partout dans le paysage en suivant les signes sur le **dulwan** tout en étant guidés par les récits **Ngarinyin.** Par exemple, le « caillou du rein » du crocodile **ngerdu** peut être examiné.

Il arrive beaucoup de choses sur chaque chemin qu'on emprunte dans le bush et plus tard, au camp, les **munnumburra** se rappellent souvent dans les conversations ce qu'ils ont fait des années auparavant, les configurations des chemins pris dans le bush. Ces réunions sont une occasion pour discuter discrètement des précieuses **junjun** des ancêtres et du rôle central qu'elles jouent dans la loi du **Wunan.**

La substance même de la notion de **junjun** prend diverses formes dans la langue **Ngarinyin** à travers l'appellation de chaque plante et de chaque animal. De tels noms, comme le fait de voir de façon palpable les souvenirs laissés par les ancêtres, provoque les chants rituelles qui acquièrent leur pleine signification par la fréquentation quotidienne du bush. Une grande partie du savoir sacré est conservé dans les chants, soit sous forme codée soit, parfois, de façon claire. Il n'existe pas de chemin sans ces anciens chants ; c'est seulement par les chants qu'un **dulwan** devient complètement vivant et échappe à l'oubli. Le fait de les chanter fait rentrer des significations importantes dans les mémoires en liant visages et lieux. Les signes et les preuves des chemins secrets et sacrés expliqués par les **munnumburra** sont utilisés pour l'éducation de ceux qui ne sont pas suffisamment initiés.

junjun

a

c

Throughout Aboriginal Australia, there is a sense of "power" within humans and inside the earth itself to the point where they are inseparable. In **Ngarinyin** cosmology, the bonds between humans and animals are so intimate through sacred meaning, that they become united in every realm of the landscape. As the **Walamba** narrative confirms in describing how humans and red kangaroos are related, ancestors shaped the earth and the earth shaped them.

Everything alive is activated by **wungud,** and each life originates in a place that manifests an individual energy and character. The concept of **wungud** also suggests a physical fusion of human with all other life-forms. Australian eucalypts provide many anthropomorphic examples. All the bloodwoods grow with a human-like sinuousness of branch; in the humidity of tropical thunderstorms, their trunks profusely bleed with **guriwin** (pungent red sap) smelling like menstrual blood. Life is known and seen to come from inside the earth; the earth is revered as a reservoir, as a source for each species in turn. Your country is marked with historic places wherever you go. **Ngarinyin** combine recognition of the local **junjun** with observations of the seasonal signs of each fresh day.

Munnumburra continually scan the pathway. Rocks might force a change of direction, so a fringed orchid (b) or a funnel-web spider hole might catch the eye (f). Tracks and traces on the ground indicate insect and animal traffic (d) and different tree barks are examined (e). Intelligent observation both celebrates individual form and evaluates variation with taxonomic clarity. **Ungudman's** eyes fill with a loving appreciation of the bush as he examines the rich botanical diversity of his country.

Allen australischen Aborigines gemeinsam ist der Glaube an eine Kraft, die sowohl dem Menschen als auch der Erde innewohnt, sodass beide untrennbar miteinander verbunden sind. In der Weltvorstellung der **Ngarinyin** sind die als heilig verstandenen Bande zwischen Mensch und Tier so eng, dass sie in jedem Bereich der Landschaft miteinander verschmelzen. Wie man an der Erzählung von **Walamba** sieht, die von der Beziehung zwischen Menschen und Roten Riesenkängurus berichtet, formten Ahnenwesen das Land und das Land formte sie.

Alles was lebt ist durchdrungen von **wungud,** und jedes Leben hat seinen Ursprung an einem Ort, an dem sich seine individuelle Energie und sein individueller Charakter manifestieren. Die Vorstellung von **wungud** geht auch in Richtung einer physischen Verschmelzung des Menschen mit allen anderen Lebensformen. Australische Eukalyptusbäume sind in mancherlei Hinsicht anthropomorph. Die Äste der Bloodwoods (Blutbäume) wirken geschmeidig wie menschliche Gliedmaßen, und in der feuchten Luft tropischer Gewitter fließen aus ihren Stämmen große Mengen von **guriwin** (beißender roter Saft), der wie Menstrualblut riecht. Man weiß und glaubt, dass das Leben aus der Erde kommt; die Erde wird verehrt als ein Reservoir, der Ursprung aller Arten. Auf Schritt und Tritt stößt man auf die Schauplätze wichtiger Ereignisse. Die **Ngarinyin** verbinden die Würdigung der örtlichen **junjun** mit der Beobachtung der jahreszeitlichen Besonderheiten jedes neuen Tages.

Die **munnumburra** haben den Pfad ständig im Sinn. Manchmal zwingt ein Stein sie zu einem Umweg, eine Orchidee (b) oder das Gespinst einer Röhrenspinne (f) erregt ihre Aufmerksamkeit; Fährten und Fußabdrücke auf dem Boden zeugen von der Anwesenheit von Insekten und Tieren (d); die Rinde der Bäume wird sorgsam studiert (e). Der kluge Beobachter erfreut sich an der individuellen Form und ordnet sie in eine klare Systematik ein. Wenn **Ungudman** die vielfältige Flora seines Landes betrachtet, sind seine Augen erfüllt von liebevoller Zuneigung.

Toute l'Australie aborigène a la conscience d'un « pouvoir » inhérent à chaque être humain comme celui inhérent à la terre ; ces pouvoirs sont si puissants qu'ils se combinent et sont inséparables. Dans la cosmologie **Ngarinyin,** les liens entre les humains et les animaux deviennent si intimes par leurs sens sacrés qu'ils sont en symbiose. L'histoire de **Walamba** le confirme en décrivant comment les humains et les kangourous roux sont liés, comment les ancêtres ont donné forme à la terre et comment celle-ci leur a, à son tour, donné forme.

Tout ce qui est vivant est mis en mouvement par le **wungud** et chaque vie prend source à un endroit d'où émane une énergie individuelle et qui a une forme. Le concept de **wungud** laisse entendre aussi une fusion physique de l'être humain avec toutes les autres formes de vie. Les eucalyptus australiens procurent beaucoup d'exemples anthropomorphiques. Tous les arbres à sève rouge poussent avec des branches d'une sinuosité toute humaine ; avec l'humidité des orages tropicaux leurs troncs laissent s'écouler beaucoup de **guriwin** (sève rouge), qui a l'odeur intense du sang menstruel. La vie est connue et vue comme venant de l'intérieur de la terre ; la terre est vénérée comme étant un réservoir, comme l'origine de chacune des espèces. Le pays est marqué de sites historiques, à chacun de vos pas. Les **Ngarinyin** combinent la connaissance de ces **junjun** avec l'observation des changements climatiques quotidiens.

Les **munnumburra** examinent continuellement les chemins. Des pierres peuvent obliger à un changement de direction, ou bien une orchidée à frange (b) ou un trou dans une toile d'araignée peut attirer leur attention (f) ; des traces sur le sol indiquent le passage des insectes et des animaux (d), on regardera soigneusement les écorces d'arbres (e). Une observation intelligente met en valeur la forme individuelle et l'évalue avec une clarté taxinomique. On sent l'amour d'**Ungudman** pour le bush en le voyant regarder la diversité botanique de son pays.

d

e

f

junjun

It's a life form... it's a tree...
we like a tree standing up

This tree **guloi** got the roots
go right down into our foot
right up in here

Banggal

Das ist ein Bild des Lebens ... ein Baum ist das ...
unser Leben das ist wie ein Baum

Der Baum da, der **guloi,** der hat Wurzeln
die reichen hier unten bis in unseren Fuß
und von da ganz nach oben

Banggal

C'est une forme de vie ... c'est un arbre...
on est comme un arbre debout

Cet arbre **guloi** a ses racines
qui vont droit jusque dans nos pieds
et de là jusqu'en haut

Banggal

guloi... guloi dulwan... dulwan mamaa... dulwan nimindi
Nyawarra

And we follow it up everyday living it
that's why this foot here
This foot is a people track
when we young we don't know nothing
We have to be trained or taught
Growing we learn stage by stage all along

Track... **ambalaru**... foot here
this life tree come right down to foot
we don't tell story from that side
we follow 'em from foot side
it's the track... and every life
people like we got foot
... we travel... we follow learning
that's why foot is here on the tree
on the land... that's people... anybody
and this is the country with the life and land
what we see and what we walk to

This fork here... that is the **Wunan**
Wunan sharing system trading root
everything go straight that is the **Wunan** system

Where I been showing you belongs there
that's the **dulwan**... the pathway
We walk to all the dreaming place
and have a look
this is the camping area where these rings are
camping area... people in a tribe... the whole land
where all the **wungud** is they follow **wungud**

and we walk to education place
and this camping places these rings here
that every place is **wungud**
places where is **mamaa**
untouchable places
where they started song
and where people shift camp to camp
for initiation

See these two feet looking down?
There's one for **Jungun** tribe
and another one for **Wodoi** tribe.
And they formed that law of this right marriage
'til we come to older man then we get married
before we ever become an elder of the tribe
this arm here he got foot this way and that way
Wodoi all in line **Jungun** all in line

Banggal

Und wir steigen höher
jeden Tag unseres Lebens deshalb ist der Fuß hier
Der Fuß das ist unsere Spur
wenn wir jung sind wissen wir gar nichts
Wir müssen lernen
Je größer wir werden desto mehr lernen wir

Die Spur... **ambalaru** ist ein Fußabdruck
der Lebensbaum reicht hinunter bis zu dem Fuß
aber wir erzählen die Geschichte nicht von oben
wir erzählen sie von unten, vom Fuß her
das ist der Weg... und alles Leben
Leute wie wir, die sind zu Fuß unterwegs
... wir sind unterwegs... und lernen dabei
deshalb ist der Fuß hier unten am Baum
auf der Erde... das sind wir... alle Menschen
und das hier ist das Land mit allem, was darin lebt
alles was wir sehen und wohin wir gehen

wo die Linien zusammenlaufen... das ist das **Wunan**
Wunan, Teilen und Austauschen ist die Wurzel
alles wie es sich gehört... das ist **Wunan**

Was ich dir gezeigt habe, das gehört da hin
das ist der **dulwan**... der Pfad
Wir gehen zu den Orten aus der Traumzeit
und sehen sie uns an
wo die Kreise sind schlagen sie ihr Lager auf
Lagerplatz... der ganze Stamm... das ganze Land
da wo das **wungud** ist, sie folgen dem **wungud**

und wir gehen an die Orte wo wir lernen
und die Kreise hier das sind die Lagerplätze
jeder von den Orten da ist **wungud**
das sind Orte die sind **mamaa**
unberührbare Orte
wo das Lied angefangen hat
wo Leute von Lager zu Lager ziehen
zur Initiation

Siehst du die beiden Füße, die nach unten zeigen?
Da ist einer für den **Jungun**-Stamm
und der andere für die **Wodoi**
Damals machten sie das Gesetz wie man heiratet
Erst wenn wir Männer älter sind heiraten wir
und später werden wir dann Stammesälteste
Bei dem Arm hier
zeigen die Füße hierhin und dahin
die **Wodoi** und die **Jungun** gehören alle dazu

Banggal

Et on le suit vers le haut
c'est pour ça que ce pied là
Ce pied c'est la piste de chacun
quand on est jeune on ne sait rien
On doit être entraîné ou éduqué
en grandissant on apprend, étape par étape

La piste... **ambalaru,** le pied
l'arbre de vie va jusque dans le pied
on ne peut pas raconter l'histoire depuis le haut
on suit la trace depuis le pied
c'est la piste... et dans toute vie
les gens comme nous ont des pieds
... on voyage... on poursuit notre apprentissage
c'est pourquoi le pied est là sur l'arbre
sur la terre... c'est les gens... tout le monde
et c'est le pays avec la vie et la terre
ce qu'on voit et vers quoi on marche

Cette fourche là... c'est le **Wunan**
le système de partage et d'échange
la racine du **Wunan**
tout va tout droit au **Wunan**

Ce que je t'ai montré ça en fait partie
c'est le **dulwan**... le chemin
On marche vers tous les lieux du rêve
et on regarde
c'est le campement où ces cercles sont
le campement... les gens d'une tribu
... de tout le pays
où se trouve tout le **wungud**, ils suivent le **wungud**

et on marche au lieu d'enseignement
et ces endroits où on campe, ces cercles là
chaque endroit est **wungud**
des endroits **mamaa**
des endroits interdits
là où ils commencèrent les chants
et ou les gens passaient d'un campement à un
autre pour les initiations

Tu vois ces deux pieds dirigés vers le bas ?
Il y en a un pour la tribu **Jungun**
et un autre pour la tribu **Wodoi**
Ils ont créé cette loi pour le mariage
avant qu'on devienne vieux il faut se marier
avant de devenir un ancien de la tribu
un pied de ce coté et un pied de l'autre
les **Wodoi** et les **Jungun** sont tous dans la ligne

Banggal

It is a **winjin**... rain this one here
start watering this tree
And I think middle of November when its raining
December all the fruit start hanging
winjin it make it swell... it make it cook
When lightning start bang! those fruit split

guloi means we cracked open into this world
guloi that's the **guloi** tree when they crack open
So that young life is already cracked open...
from the mother's womb and is out in space now
It's brand new life... very very new and precious
and that tree represent the life of young

guloi it give us sign
every day every year when it flowers
"What are you doing about the young life?"
it's on our shoulder... our responsibility
it telling us that tree "it's your responsibility
if you don't do that it's not worthwhile
I flowerering"

cos' every time it flowers telling us
"you must carry on"
teaching that young fella or her
because she going to have children
just the same as you... so life go on

And that's what **guloi** tree represents our life
that song say its not for one individual person
it is for whole people living in the land

And that is the life tree this is the tree of life
where everybody feed in the story... inside here
without this we wouldn't know anything
you know that what we talking about

Well you understand what I really talkin' about
Life... and that is the pathway
That is from human being and... plant

Banggal

Das hier, das ist **winjin**... Regen
der bringt dem Baum das Wasser
Um die Mitte November, da kommt der Regen
und im Dezember hängen dann Früchte dran
der **winjin** macht sie dick... sie werden reif
Wenn Blitze kommen, bumm! platzen die Früchte

guloi bedeutet, es platzt und wir sind auf der Welt
wie beim **guloi**-Baum wenn die Früchte platzen
Und genauso ist das mit dem jungen Leben
aus dem Mutterleib heraus in die Welt
Das neugeborene Leben... so neu und so kostbar
und der Baum steht für das Leben der Kinder

guloi ist ein Zeichen für uns
jeden Tag und jedes Jahr wenn er blüht
„Wie sorgt ihr für das junge Leben?"
wir tragen die Verantwortung... auf den Schultern
der Baum, der sagt uns „du bist dafür verantwortlich
wenn du das nicht verstehst
dann kann ich mir meine Blüten sparen"

denn jedes Jahr sagen uns die Blüten
„ihr müsst weitermachen"
den Jungen etwas beibringen und den Mädchen
denn sie werden Kinder bekommen
genau wie ihr... damit das Leben weitergeht

Und für unser Leben steht der **guloi**-Baum
das Lied sagt, der ist nicht für einen Einzelnen
der ist für alle die auf diesem Land leben

Und das ist der Baum des Lebens
wo jeder zur Geschichte was dazutut... hier drinnen
ohne das da wüssten wir überhaupt nichts
du weißt schon über das wovon wir gerade reden

Worum es mir wirklich geht, verstehst du
Das ist das Leben... und das hier ist der Weg
Für die Menschen wie für die... Pflanzen

Banggal

Quand la pluie **winjin** vient,
elle commence à cet arbre
vers mi-novembre je crois quand il pleut
en décembre tous les fruits commencent à pendre
le **winjin** les gonfle... ils mûrissent
Et quand il y a la foudre bang ! les fruits éclatent

guloi veut dire éclore en ce monde
guloi c'est l'arbre **guloi** quand ils éclosent
Donc cette nouvelle vie a déjà surgi...
de l'utérus de la mère et est déjà dans l'espace
La toute nouvelle vie... toute nouvelle et précieuse
et cet arbre représente la vie, de l'enfant

le **guloi**, il nous donne un signal
chaque jour, chaque année quand ça refleurit
« Qu'est-ce que tu fais pour cette nouvelle vie ? »
c'est sur nos épaules... c'est notre responsabilité
c'est ce que dit cet arbre
« c'est votre responsabilité, si vous ne faites pas ça
c'est pas la peine que je fleurisse »

parce qu'à chaque fois qu'il refleurit il nous dit
« tu dois continuer, transmettre »
enseigner à ce jeune ou bien à elle
parce qu'elle, elle va avoir des enfants
exactement comme toi... ainsi va la vie

Et ce que l'arbre **guloi** représente notre vie
ce chant dit que ce n'est pas pour une personne
c'est pour tous les gens qui vivent dans ce pays

C'est l'arbre de vie, l'arbre de la vie
où tout le monde se nourrit selon l'histoire
sans ça on ne saurait rien
tu sais de quoi on parle

Oui, tu comprends ce que je dis vraiment en fait
La vie... c'est le chemin
Pour les hommes comme pour les plantes...

Banggal

a

b

c

High on the wall at **Alyaguma** pool, among numerous other revered paintings, is one vital image of a native plum tree with a footprint beside its roots (a). When this **guloi** tree icon is examined and explained by **Ngarinyin munnumburra**, it reveals a unique combination of visual metaphors linking human to plant. The composition is painted from several perspectives to illustrate sequences of education on the **dulwan wunandi** (pathway of law).

The single **ambalaru** (footprint) with ten toes is a mark of the track of the individual ready to journey along the pathway of knowledge. The foot is attached to several roots of the tree that symbolise the family blood that each individual identity begins with, and forever belongs to.

Next is a representation of the wider social identity gained from the **Wunan** law. It is shown as four converging lines forming one strong stem near the base of the tree. Because this painting is on a wall running east to west, the orientation of this root stem matches the actual direction from which the four main groups of people came to the law table at **Dududu.ngarri** to originate **Wunan** law.

Education comes from climbing the trunk of the tree during stages of initiation beginning in youth; these are marked by a series of small rings connected to the lower trunk. Higher up the tree, three long paths lead to larger rings of adult and senior knowledge.

Above these large rings are two straight branches with human feet on their ends. These two feet sharing the tree represent the celebrated **Gwion** heroes, **Wodoi** and **Jungun**, who shared their blood in marriage and split everything into two groups. Equally, the pair of feet signify the binary viewpoint of **munnumburra** of each **moiety.** From their position, facing down the tree, they can look back through all the many complex relationships between every living thing that is connected to people in the two **moieties.** With a full understanding of **Wunan** law, the outlook and role of the fully initiated **munnumburra** changes direction. Now the tree becomes more specific and focused on realistic details of the native plum called **guloi**. A growing branch with two veined leaves ends with a forked stem holding two round **guloi**. Painted lines of vertical rain descend from above the branch, suggesting the arrival of **winjin** (monsoon rains) when lightning triggers the ripe fruit to swell and burst, before cracking open to release new seed.

Hoch oben auf der Felswand der Wasserstelle von **Alyaguma,** inmitten von zahlreichen anderen verehrten Malereien, findet sich die symbolträchtige Darstellung eines einheimischen Pflaumenbaums mit einem Fußabdruck neben der Wurzel (a). Wenn die **munnumburra** der **Ngarinyin** dieses Bild eines **guloi**-Baumes erkunden und deuten, eröffnet sich dem Betrachter eine einzigartige Kombination aus visuellen Metaphern, die Mensch und Pflanze miteinander verbinden, denn die einzelnen Elemente des Bildes versinnbildlichen die verschiedenen Stadien, die der Mensch im Zuge seiner Erziehung auf dem **dulwan wunandi** (Pfad des Gesetzes) durchläuft.

Der **ambalaru** (Fußabdruck) mit den zehn Zehen steht für das Individuum, das bereit ist, seine Reise auf dem Pfad des Wissens anzutreten. Der Fuß ist verbunden mit einigen Wurzeln des Baumes; sie symbolisieren das Blut, die unauflösliche Zugehörigkeit zu einer Familie, mit der jede individuelle Identität ihren Anfang nimmt.

Das nächste Element ist ein Sinnbild der sozialen Identität im weiteren Sinne, die das Individuum aus dem **Wunan**-Gesetz bezieht. Sie wird dargestellt durch vier aufeinander zulaufende Linien, die sich am unteren Ende des Baumstamms zu einem kräftigen Strang vereinen. Da sich das Bild auf einer Felswand befindet, die von Osten nach Westen verläuft, entspricht die Ausrichtung dieses Wurzelstrangs der tatsächlichen Himmelsrichtung, aus der die vier wichtigsten Stammesgruppen an den Steintisch von **Dududu.ngarri** kamen, um dort das **Wunan**-Gesetz ins Leben zu rufen.

Im Zuge der verschiedenen Stufen der Initiation, die mit der Jugend beginnt, erwirbt das Individuum immer größeres Wissen und klettert dabei immer höher empor. Dargestellt werden diese einzelnen Stadien mittels einer Reihe von kleinen Kreisen am Unterende des Stamms. Etwas weiter oben führen drei lange Pfade zu größeren Kreisen, Symbolen für das Wissen der Erwachsenen und Alten.

Oberhalb dieser großen Kreise sieht man zwei gerade Äste mit je einem menschlichen Fuß am Ende. Diese beiden Füße, die sich den Baum gewissermaßen teilen, stehen für die allseits verehrten **Gwion**-Helden **Wodoi** und **Jungun,** die ihr Blut durch Heirat verbanden und alle Welt in zwei Gruppen einteilten. Darüber hinaus stehen die beiden Füße für die binäre Blickrichtung der **munnumburra** beider **moieties.** Baumabwärts, der Wurzel zugewandt. An einem Zweig mit zwei geäderten Blättern sitzt ein gegabelter Stiel mit zwei runden **guloi.** Die vertikalen Linien symbolisieren den heftigen, von Blitzen begleiteten **winjin** (Monsun) der die Früchte auschwellen und platzen lässt. Öffnet sich ihnen der Blick zurück auf die vielen komplexen Beziehungen zwischen allen Lebewesen, die mit den zwei **moieties** verbunden sind. Mit dem Verständnis des **Wunan**-Gesetzes erlangt der vollständig initiierte **munnumburra** eine andere Sicht der Welt und einen neuen Platz in ihr.

En hauteur sur la paroi du bassin d'eau d'**Alyaguma,** parmi les nombreuses autres peintures vénérées, il y a une image fondamentale représentant un prunier avec une empreinte de pied à côté de ses racines. Lorsque cette image de l'arbre **guloi** est examinée et expliquée par les **munnumburra Ngarinyin,** elle se révèle être un ensemble de symboles du lien des humains aux plantes. La composition est peinte sous plusieurs angles de vision pour illustrer des séquences de l'éducation du **dulwan wunandi** (chemin de la loi).

L'**ambalaru** (empreinte de pied) à dix doigts est une marque de l'origine de l'individu prêt à partir sur le chemin de la connaissance. Le pied est attaché à plusieurs racines qui symbolisent le sang familial que tous possèdent au départ et auquel tous appartiennent pour toujours.

Ensuite, il y a une représentation de l'identité sociale élargie que l'on acquiert par la loi Wunan. Elle est représentée par quatre lignes convergentes qui forment une tige solide à côté de la base de l'arbre. Comme cette peinture est sur une paroi orientée est-ouest cette tige est dans la direction des lieux d'origine des quatre groupes principaux qui vinrent à la table de la Loi à **Dududu.ngarri** pour créer les lois.

Symboliquement, l'éducation s'acquiert par l'ascension du tronc de l'arbre pendant les différents stades de l'initiation qui commencent dès l'enfance ; dans cette peinture, ces étapes sont indiquées par des petits cercles reliés au tronc. Plus haut dans l'arbre, trois longs chemins mènent à des cercles plus grands qui symbolisent la connaissance de l'adulte et de l'Ancien.

Au dessus de ces grands anneaux il y a deux branches droites qui ont des pieds humains à leurs extrêmités. Ces deux pieds qui partagent l'arbre représentent les célèbres héros **Gwion Wodoi** et **Jungun** qui ont partagé leur sang à travers le mariage et tout divisé en deux. Ces deux pieds sont la représentation qu'ont les **munnumburra** de la dualité du concept de **moitié.** Par leur position faisant face pour ainsi dire vers la base de l'arbre, ils ont la possibilité de voir tout ce qui fait entrer en relation les êtres vivants depuis l'origine avec chaque part de **moitié.** En ayant une totale connaissance du **Wunan,** les initiés **munnumburra** changent d'aspect, ont de nouveaux devoirs et le but de leur vie change. Les particularités de l'arbre deviennent ensuite plus évidentes avec des détails réalistes caractérisant le prunier appelé **guloi.** Une branche qui pousse avec deux feuilles nervurées se termine par une tige fourchue soutenant deux fruits ronds de **guloi.** Des traits représentant de la pluie qui tombe au dessus de la branche suggèrent l'arrivée de **winjin** (la pluie des moussons), moment où l'orage provoque le gonflement, l'éclatement du fruit et la libération de nouvelles graines.

guloi

And this fruit hanging on the tree
*That the **guloi** tree what we eat*
***guloi mangarri...** what we eat*

*That fruit song... that **marguli** song*
this is the song what belong to that fruit
to fall down because it high up
and they would throw this big rock on it
and all the fruits fall down like rain
Banggal

Und die Früchte da an dem Baum
*an dem **guloi**-Baum, die essen wir*
***guloi mangarri ...** die essen wir*

*Das Lied zu den Früchten ... das **marguli**-Lied*
das ist das Lied das zu den Früchten gehört
damit sie runterfallen weil sie so hoch hängen
deshalb werfen sie einen großen Stein danach
dann kommen die Früchte herunter wie Regen
Banggal

Et ce fruit suspendu à cet arbre
*c'est l'arbre **guloi** dont on mange...*
***guloi mangarri ...** c'est ce qu'on mange*

*Le chant de ce fruit... ce chant **marguli***
c'est le chant qui accompagne ce fruit
pour qu'il tombe parce que ça pousse haut
ils lancent un gros caillou dessus
et tous les fruits tombent comme la pluie
Banggal

Guloi trees demonstrate meanings active to **Ngarinyin** people in country; **guloi** is both a seasonal food and sign of the newborn child, and living evidence of the continuity of knowledge on pathways – **dulwan nimindi.**

Guloi-Bäume sind für die **Ngarinyin** äußere Zeichen der Bedeutung, die das Land in sich birgt; die **guloi**-Früchte dienen zu bestimmten Jahreszeiten als Nahrungsmittel, symbolisieren aber auch das neugeborene Kind und sind ein sichtbarer Beleg für die Kontinuität der Tradition auf den Pfaden des Wissens – den **dulwan nimindi.**

Les arbres **guloi** expriment pour les **Ngarinyin** les significations encore en vigueur dans le pays **guloi**, c'est à la fois un fruit de saison et le signe de l'enfant nouveau-né, et la preuve vivante de la continuité du savoir sur les chemins – **dulwan nimindi.**

guloi

I can't go stealing another man's story... no way!
This story only belong here... one place
All that education belong here to this area
People can respect all different area
when he got his own story

Banggal

Ich kann doch nicht anderen ihre Geschichte stehlen
... das geht nicht!
Diese Geschichte gehört hierher ... hier an diesen Ort
Das was man hier lernen kann
das gehört hier zu dieser Stelle
Jeder respektiert was dem anderen gehört
wenn er seine eigene Geschichte hat

Banggal

Je peux pas aller voler l'histoire d'un autre
c'est pas possible !
Cette histoire c'est celle d'ici ... seulement d'ici
Tout cet enseignement appartient à cet endroit
On peut respecter les autres peuples
quand on connait sa propre histoire

Banggal

NGARINYIN NARRATIVES

Ngarinyin is not a written language. The **Ngarinyin**-English spoken by **munnumburra** and comprising the central narrative of this book includes some culturally ancient **Ngarinyin** words. If we are not **Ngarinyin** speakers, we cannot experience fully the very complex dualism of terminology and meaning that comes from their binary classification of gender and **moiety**. **Ngarinyin** speech employs many subtle sounds impossible to communicate without a detailed phonetic alphabet; scholars have devised and applied such schemes, but they are not appropriate here. We have adopted a simple anglicised form in common usage for spelling and for pronunciation by the reader. Because various European languages use different pronunciation of the same letters, a conservative spelling has been adopted here to simplify phonetic comprehension.

Generally, the consonants c, f, h, p, q, t, v, x, and z are not used in transcribing **Ngarinyin**; there are many vowels and diphthongs, and there are other letter combinations that will be less familiar to the reader. The **"ngarri"** in **Ngarinyin** is strongly pronounced as a soft but fast "nya" by releasing the tongue from the palate so that the sound rolls out as an extended "n". We may use one stop to divide words like **walu.ngarri** into two clear components. This also isolates the very common suffix **"ngarri"**, which means "belonging to the land or region and people of a place".

Ngarinyin speech and song connects and combines ancestors and living animals with names preserved in the language as evidence of ancient laws. Here, the names of people, places and ancestral titles in the law are spelt with capitals – **Wodoi**, whereas the common living animal is in lower case – **wodoi**. **Ngarinyin** words in bold are usually followed by their translated equivalent: e.g. "the female figure wears a **mambi** (triangular apron)".

The **Ngarinyin** have been the subject of some scholarly studies. A major account has been the linguistic work of Coate and Elkin (1974); one aspect of **Ngarinyin** rock-painting was brought to the attention of a wider audience by Crawford (1968); the considerable antiquity of some rock-paintings in the region has been documented by Roberts and others (1997).

Some **Ngarinyin munnumburra,** such as the late David Mowaljarlai **(Banggal)**, have made considerable contributions to scholarly research (Ward 1997). Mowaljarlai's wide reputation is due to his influential involvement with the many outside researchers that he introduced to his people, by taking them inside the country of their ancestors. It is not until now, however, that **Ngarinyin** scholars have had the opportunity to speak for themselves in such an integrated presentation of important aspects of their culture. The **Ngarinyin munnumburra** whose narratives inform this work hope that their relationships to their country, of which their paintings are an essential and central part, will become known to the reader.

NGARINYIN SONGS

Ngarinyin speech provides keys to meaning through metaphors composed as a sequence, or through ideas suspended in the linguistic context of a **Wunan** song. Each song is phrased to be understood as a message, more than a sentence with a familiar structure. Ancient words in **Wunan** song versions can be repeated to vary emphasis of a consistent **Wunan** influence. These **Ngarinyin** key words also engage the listener with rhythmic repetition as part of the musical experience. Key **Ngarinyin** words have local regional significance, and also connect ideas rich with meaning through various cultural uses and daily experience of country. Timeographic phrases from songs are also chanted during gatherings, and become effective as common aphorisms and popular maxims, or may achieve the significance of liturgy. Key phrases of such songs, can also carry core meanings across generations, in a song form not unlike poetry. Original lyrics of **Wunan** songs, such as the few examples roughly translated here, employ very different forms of syntax and grammar to trans-European languages, and defy literal translation.

Because **Ngarinyin** language exists as **Ngarinyin** law, some sacred words are best not put into text form. The oldest **Wunan** songs are often only a cluster of a few words, but resonate with knowledge.

Juwi i barrgoni Juwi i barrgoni gulungulu
Wang.gura yabu yabu wang.gura
Juwi i barrgoni o Juwi i barrgoni

These song words belong to the narrative of the **Argad** brothers, responsible for the metamorphosis of humans into birds during a ceremonial event. At the stage alluded to in the above lyric, a group of men are laying on the earth clutching boomerangs to their chest, and under their arms against their ribs. The powerful sacred words of law songs sung over them penetrate **Argad** and the other men on the ground. They are huddled together in positions like babies being born in the bush. The sacred sweat from under their arms is rubbed into the wooden boomerangs.

This fragment of the **Argad** song only refers to **Argad's** position alongside a man of the **wang.gura** crow clan, but to a **munnumburra** these few words conjure up the whole scene of this intimate stage of the events. It is at this threshold of what is **mamaa** (secret and sacred) that we outsiders must remain. This is in contrast to the "open" lyrics of popular non-sacred songs, composed for musical pleasure and entertainment, such as **gulowada** songs coloured with gossip and romance, Wunan songs must never be changed, or have their deep significance diminished. This explains our reluctance to provide more detailed translations of **Wunan** song lyrics as included in the **Argad** narrative on pages 106 and 107, and other fragments in this book.

The words of **Wunan** lyrics, preserved throughout a very long tradition of music, reflect the sensuality and clarity of **Gwion** ideas. Their music is inseparable from the people at the heart of their country today.

NGARINYIN-GESÄNGE

Die Sprache der **Ngarinyin** vermittelt ihre Aussagen in Ketten von Metaphern oder durch Ideen, die in den Kontext eines **Wunan**-Liedes eingebettet sind. Jedes Lied enthält eine Botschaft, doch nicht in Gestalt einer Aussage mit eindeutiger Satzstruktur. Uralte Worte werden in manchen Fassungen der **Wunan**-Lieder immer wieder wiederholt, um die Allgegenwart des **Wunan** zu unterstreichen. Diese Schlüsselwörter ziehen den Zuhörer zudem durch den gleichmäßigen Rhythmus der Wiederholungen musikalisch in ihren Bann. Rhythmisch wiederholte Phrasen aus Liedern werden auch bei den Versammlungen skandiert und werden als Aphorismen oder Sprichwörter zum Allgemeingut oder wirken wie eine Liturgie. Manche Begriffe gewinnen regional eine besondere Bedeutung und verbinden bestimmte Rituale mit der täglichen Erfahrung des Landes. Die zentralen Elemente solcher Lieder können wichtige Grundvorstellungen über Generationen hinweg bewahren, in einer Form, die der Poesie näher ist als der Prosa. Die Originaltexte der **Wunan**-Lieder, von denen wir einige Beispiele hier grob übersetzt haben, arbeiten mit ganz anderen Formen von Syntax und Grammatik als die europäischen Sprachen und lassen sich nicht ohne weiteres übertragen.

Da die Sprache der **Ngarinyin** zugleich das Gesetz der **Ngarinyin** ist, schreibt man manche heiligen Worte besser nicht nieder. Die ältesten **Wunan**-Lieder sind oft nur eine Ansammlung weniger Worte, doch es sind Worte voller Weisheit.

Juwi i barrgoni Juwi i barrgoni gulungulu
Wang.gura yabu yabu wang.gura
Juwi i barrgoni o Juwi i barrgoni

Diese Zeilen gehören zu der Erzählung über die **Argad**-Brüder, die dafür verantwortlich waren, dass sich die Menschen bei einer Zeremonie in Vögel verwandelten. An dem Punkt, auf den sich der obige Vers bezieht, liegt eine Gruppe von Männern am Boden, und sie drücken sich Bumerangs an die Brust und unter den Armen an die Rippen. Die mächtigen heiligen Worte der Gesetzeslieder, die dabei gesungen werden, durchdringen **Argad** und die anderen Männer am Boden. Sie liegen gekrümmt in einer Haltung wie Babys, die im Busch zur Welt kommen. Der Schweiß unter ihren Achseln gilt als heilig und wird in das Holz der Bumerangs gerieben.

Dieser Auszug aus dem **Argad**-Lied beschreibt nur wie **Argad** neben einem Mann aus dem **wang.gura**-Clan (dem Krähen-Clan) am Boden liegt. Für einen **munnumburra** jedoch erweckt dieser Auszug sofort ein detailreiches Bild der Begebenheit. Die Schwelle dessen, was **mamaa**, was heilig und geheim ist, dürfen wir Außenstehenden nicht überschreiten. Im Gegensatz zu profaner Musik, wie zum Beispiel die **gulowada**, die eher Schlagern ähnlich sind und zum Vergnügen entstehen, dürfen die **Wunan**-Gesänge nie verändert werden, um ihre tiefe Bedeutung nicht zu verändern. Das ist auch der Grund, weshalb die **munnumburra** keine genauere Übersetzung der auf Seite 106 und 107 zitierten Liedtexte geben wollten.

Die Texte der **Wunan**-Gesänge, die durch eine lange musikalische Tradition bewahrt wurden, reflektieren die Sinnlichkeit und die Klarheit der Gedanken der **Gwion.** Ihre Musik ist untrennbar mit den Menschen des Landes verbunden.

LES CHANTS NGARINYIN

Ce qui est dit dans le discours **Ngarinyin** donne la clé qui permet de comprendre ce que signifient les métaphores situées entre les couplets ou dans les idées sous-jacentes au contexte linguistique utilisé dans un chant **Wunan.** Chaque chant est rédigé pour être compris comme un message plus que comme une simple phrase du langage courant. Des mots anciens dans les chants **Wunan** peuvent être répétés pour modifier l'accent donné à la continuité de l'influence du **Wunan.** Les mots-clés **Ngarinyin** font participer l'auditeur à une répétition rythmée qui lui fait ressentir profondément la musique. Ils ont une portée régionale et relient des idées riches de significations qui s'expriment au cours des diverses pratiques culturelles et de la vie quotidienne dans le pays. Certaines parties des chants, à caractère historique, sont également chantées lors des rassemblements et deviennent des proverbes ou des aphorismes; elles peuvent aussi contribuer à donner sa pleine signification à une cérémonie liturgique. Des expressions clés de ces chants peuvent également véhiculer des significations fondamentales à travers les générations sous une forme chantée qui n'est pas sans rapport avec la poésie. Les paroles d'origine des chants **Wunan,** comme les quelques exemples rapportés ici, emploient des formes de syntaxe et de grammaire très différentes de celles des langues européennes, défiant ainsi toute tentative de traduction littérale.

Comme la langue **Ngarinyin** existe en tant que loi **Ngarinyin,** il est préférable de ne pas mettre sous la forme de texte certains mots sacrés. Les plus anciens chants **Wunan** ne sont souvent qu'un agrégat de quelques mots, mais ils sont imprégnés des accents de la connaissance.

Juwi i barrgoni Juwi i barrgoni gulungulu
Wang.gura yabu yabu wang.gura
Juwi i barrgoni o Juwi i barrgoni

Ces paroles font partie du récit des deux frères **Argad,** responsables de la métamorphose des humains en oiseaux au cours d'une cérémonie. Au moment où se disent les paroles ci-dessus un groupe d'hommes est étendu sur le sol, serrant des boomerangs sur leurs poitrines, puis sous leurs bras et contre leurs côtes. Les puissants mots sacrés des chants de la Loi chantés au-dessus d'eux pénètrent **Argad** et les autres hommes étendus sur le sol. Ils sont agglutinés, prenant des positions semblables aux bébés naissant dans le bush. La transpiration venant du dessous de leur bras est sacrée et elle est frottée pour pénétrer dans le bois des boomerangs.

Ce fragment du chant d'**Argad** décrit uniquement cette phase des événements et fait seulement référence à la place d'**Argad** près d'un homme du clan **wang.gura** (corneille). Pour un **munnumburra** par contre, ce récit suffit pour reconstruire tous les détails de la scène, mais c'est à ce seuil de compréhension de ce qui est **mamaa** (secret et sacré) que nous, étrangers, devons rester. Ceci contraste avec avec les textes très «libres» des chants populaires profanes, composés comme de simples morceaux de musique et de distraction, tels les chants **gulowada** teintés de ragôts et de romance; les chants du **Wunan** ne doivent jamais etre modifiés, au risque d'atténuer leur signification profonde. D'où notre réticence à donner ici des traductions plus détaillées des paroles des chants **Wunan** qui figurent dans le récit d'**Argad,** pages 106 et 107, comme d'autres extraits contenus dans ce livre.

Les mots des textes des chants **Wunan,** conservés par une longue tradition musicale, reflètent la sensualité et la clarté de la pensée **Gwion.** Leur musique est indissociable des gens vivant au cœur du pays aujourd'hui.

GLOSSARY

agula dangerous and ghostly spirit creature

Algi one of the original matriarchs portrayed at **Alyaguma** receiving a tribute gift of many spears covering her reclining body

alnguru spear-shaft of bamboo

Alyaguma sacred waterhole beneath waterfall with a wall of many revered paintings including vital image of **guloi** (native plum tree); place where the **Gwion** hunter **Yandama** rested when his knee became weak and failed him

amalad minia greetings with respect or hello, as in "I see your shining forehead"

amalar single member of **Jungun moiety** group and **skin** title for associated flora and fauna; *pl* **brramalar**

ambalaru human footprints or tracks on ancestral pathway

ambiliji see **maba**

amurangga man

Anaut.ngarri country and people associated with wind, permanently named after **Jillinya**

andarri local Ring-tailed Possum, living evidence of ancestor **Andarri** who originally spoke the **Ngarinyin** language

angga bark bowl or flat surface, e.g. **Wunan** stone table

anggurun Woollybutt tree *(Eucalyptus miniata),* a dominant species of savannah woodland across the northern Kimberley with bright orange **maniwan** flowers producing fine honey

anjum lotus or water-lily with a big leaf

arawari drawing or mapping in the earth with a finger

argad Brown Falcon *(Falco berigora),* living evidence of two **Gwion** brothers called **Argad,** responsible for humans becoming birds

Arnhem Land continental Australia, west of the Gulf of Carpentaria; homelands of numerous indigenous language groups preserving aspects of **Wunan** laws

Arrernte indigenous language group in central Australian desert, connected to Kimberley by **Wunan** cultural exchange routes

arri humans

arririn see **gundilli**

arru freshwater eel, one of five sacred water animals of **Wanjina Gulingi,** living evidence of **Arru wanjina** represented in icon at **Alyaguma**

Badjayei sacred song expression

balbrangi balbri ancient song to summon clans together for a law council; performed wearing **nguniri** (ancestral hairbelt) to compel distant people to arrive at the point where the songman stands

Balgo place on the western edge of the Tanami desert; location of indigenous language groups

Balmirriya see **Walamba**

banad local "bush turkey" or Australian Bustard *(Ardeotis australis);* any hardwood boomerang with an elbow or "number 7" shape similar in profile to the neck and erect head of the bird; beaked boomerang carried in dances as an emblem of ancestral times

banbangi see **balbrangi balbri** and **gulbrungi**

Banggal the late David **Mowaljarlai;** of **Wodoi skin** from **Brrejirad dambun;** cultural translator and published educator; **munnumburra** within **ornad moiety; gi** (spiritual connections) with **jirad** (native hibiscus) and **Gwion Gwion**

Bangmorro family whose members trace their descent to **Ngegamorro wanjina**

banman expert interpreter of dreams; mystic or sorcerer knowing secrets associated with lightning; medicine expert or doctor

bararu.ru place where rituals occur; dancing ground

bare vagina; **Jillinya's** legacy to all women

Barilamma location in fossilised reef of the Napier Range where **Jebera** fugitive rested and became immortalised in a large painted icon as an emu hoarding **golani** (fruit)

Barraru.ngarri country and people of the clan named after ceremonial peace-making events, containing **Walamba wanjina** and closely connected to **Galeru.ngarri dambun**

barrij to arise, get up and become active

belnged sulphur-crested Cockatoo, living evidence of **Belnged Kamali** clan

Bimbidora sacred place where **Yandama** killed a **gundilli** (wallaby) and cooked it in a stone oven surrounded by a ring of **jallala** (signal stones); location of **yalmalnyu malngud** power

Binbin original incarnation of **Walamba** (red kangaroo ancestor) who first appeared with all-white body near **Guringi**

binja winja white cowrie shell, often worn as a costume highlight centred on a belt attached to a **mudurra** (wig); with pearl-shell, an item of **Wunan** exchange into the centre of the continent

Binjiraregu sacred area of the north-west coast linking places of origin of **Wunan** laws and **Jillinya;** location for early **walu.ngarri** (ceremony) participated by **Walamba**

Binjirri a destination for **Walamba** as above

birrawudi ritual procession when boy initiates are carried on men's backs. This important stage of the **walu.ngarri** normally happens on the afternoon of the second day, just before sundown. All afternoon, lines of men and women dance in rings orbiting the stone seat where the songmen sit. These **munnumburra** sing day and night, always in the middle, while they conduct the procedures of the **walu.ngarri.** The boy initiates sit on the ground beside the songman's seat in the company of their "aunties", close female relatives of the opposite **moiety.** The intensity of the singing and dancing has a profound effect on the young initiates. As the final day ends, all the men of the **moiety skin** opposite to that of the initiates, form a long line, and the boys are lifted onto their "uncles" backs. The boys lie on their backs facing backwards while being carried along. **Birrawudi** dances commence when the men stamp their feet to make the ground shake and march in a line while making a loud **dududu,** louder than emus. Each **ngawarra wanggi** initiate rides on his elder's shoulders in the ritual procession of the **birrawudi**

birrina "coming together" dance, linking men and women in public event

Biyad.ngerri one ancestral title for **Walamba,** during stages of reincarnation along his **dulwan** (pathway)

biyu ladder or scaffold

boab common baobab *(Adansonia gregorii),* tree providing fibres made into an all-purpose string or cord to construct nets for trapping game by the first **Gwion** hunters

borror Frogmouth Owl, living evidence of **Borror Kamali** clan

brad first light when an orange band spreads across the predawn horizon; correct time for circumcision; direction for skulls of the departed to face

breb-brenya song expression ordering everyone to get up to commence the **walu.ngarri**

brilgi cicatrise body scars; arrangements of fine marks in the skin emblematic of eel, turtle, fish, water-goanna and crocodile as signs originating from the **wanjina** of these five sacred water animals; markings that distinguish fully initiated male and female **munnumburra** after ritual encounters, when the living animal is placed on the body; permanent evidence of participation in rituals with the living animals during which **mamaa** sacred songs (secret to these private rituals only) are sung in the presence of the person attaining the scars, so that the power of the songs enters the person

briyal arm, and a measurement of its length

brramalar plural of **amalar**

Brrejalnga country and people of the water-chestnut clan; region under the custodianship of **Ngarjno**

Brrejirad country and people of the native hibiscus clan; region with territory adjoining the northern side of the Prince Regent River; ancestral land of **Banggal**

brrornad plural of **ornad**

Brrunjini sacred location where sharing of meat laws began; associated with the grey kangaroo ancestor **Yara,** and marked by a stone oven and a tall **jallala** (signal stone)

Bunaba neighbouring Kimberley language group

Bundiwin pair of male lightning deities named **Jundiwan** and **Mul.ngirri**

bunja rock overhang or shelter preserving paintings

bunja mamaa sacred sanctuary or secret storage place of **maya.ngarri**

bunji any form of hook or barb on any object, such as at the tip of a **nyarndu** (spear-thrower); wooden point sharpened to fit into the hollow end of a spear-shaft, prior to using a spear-thrower such as a **woomera**

bunun.guli song expression for being released from a blood ritual; status of initiates when they are free to travel between **dambun** again

buren clan members departing a **Wunan** place

burrin.burrin Rainbow Bee-eater *(Merops ornatus)*

burroi Brown Goshawk or Collared Sparrowhawk, living evidence of **Burroi Kamali** clan

burrunba large Australian foraging crane *(Grus rubicundus)* known as Brolga, also garanguli

coolamon colloquial term for a shallow dish or concave container made from light wood

corroboree colloquial term for indigenous ceremony

dadall Long-tailed Finch, living evidence of **Dadall Kamali** clan

dal.gnana fan-shaped palm *(Livistona eastonii),* harvested for preservable flour made of starch from immature leaf stalk from heart of young palms

dambun clan regions allocated by the first **Kamali** council when originating law at **Dududu.ngarri;** pattern of land titles inherited by **Ngarinyin** that define the network of exchange with their neighbours

darrawani little finger; footprint; the durable quality of indelible **Gwion** paintings as deep stains in sandstone

degulan Frilled Lizard, living evidence of ancestor **Degulan** who followed the ritual practice of **Wiji.ngarri** at **Wudmangu** by performing **walu.ngarri** near **Winjagin** and elsewhere, thus widening the distribution of **Wunan** songs

didiyii expression of finality and farewell; cry of all participants of both sexes at the conclusion of **wir.nganyen**

dindiwal Peregrine Falcon, living evidence of **Dindiwal Gwion** clan

dinjid small tree supplying digging sticks; constant sniffing with a runny nose, symptoms like influenza; a punishment for vandals of the living evidence of **Dinjid wanjina**

dududu noise of stamping emus or thumping sound of dancing feet

Dududu.ngarri deep gap in the land formed by three Emu clan men when fleeing the **Wunan** stone table; general location name for the site in **Guru.ngongo dambun** where the **Gwion** ceased to be nomadic

Duduk.ngunga site of a new stone seat for songmen marking the ring-dancing ground of a **walu.ngarri** held at **Marranba.bidi** in 1995

dudu-narawi ceremonial ground, literally where dancers stamp their feet loudly

dulwan pathway created by ancestors; one moral direction; walking in the living bush

dulwan mamaa sacred pathway of secret evidence, distributed across the country

dulwan nimindi pathway of knowledge and flow of ideas through continuous education

duma see **waluwi**

dumbi Masked Owl, nesting in either caves or trees, often observed feeding on rodents and insects among grass on ground, living evidence of **Dumbi Kamali** clan

durran Red-tailed Black Cockatoo *(Calyptorhynchus banksii),* living evidence of **Durran Kamali** clan

emmalen ghost of an individual; free spirit

gaama tunnel in the bank of a river used as a burrow by turtles and crocodiles

gadiya Kriol English term for non-indigenous Australians

gagul red pigment or red ochre paint (see **jimbri**)

galambi Great Egret *(Ardea alba),* large white heron

Galeru.ngarri country and people of the northern rain clan under the custodianship of **Nyawarra**

gallid any barbed or multi-pronged wooden spear; fishing spear with five sets of parallel barbs, when twirled between palms makes ripples attracting fish towards the spear that can then be gaffed by its barbs when the spear is jerked

galuman bamboo used for spear-shafts

galwa unidentified species of bush with a yellow flower

galwadi malleable resin stirred to the consistency of clay for shaping and molding the forms of **mudurra**

galwal see **nguniri**

gambul see **julwungi**

Gananinjal place south of **Warmun** where the selfish fugitive **Jebera** was executed

gandad stone knife

gangan pair of song-sticks clapped as rhythm instruments

ganjal Black Kite *(Milvus migrans)* bird, living evidence of **Ganjal Kamali** clan

ganmangu long bulbous yam; variety of yam cultivated in stone walled gardens

garabri see **mandi**

garagi carry-all wallet or bag; bucket made from paperbark or hide

garan.garan diving waterbird, Eurasian Coot, living evidence of **Garan.garan Kamali** clan

garramarra saltwater

Gawanali public surname of **Ngarjno**

Gelngu region where **Wodoi** and **Jungun** visited the workshop of **Wibalma**

gerd skin hanging under the penis, foreskin before circumcision

gi personal spiritual connections between human and land and **wanjina**

gimbu reddish-brown stone; raw material for the sharpest spear-points invented by **Gwion;** circumcision and cicatrise scalpel

gingu hollow-ended shaft of a spear made from native bamboo

goanna colloquial term for a variety of Monitor Lizards and skinks

golani small dark native currant *(Vitex glabrata);* ritual fruit loaf from the crushed and cooked fruit; matching size and colour of currant and eye pupil, visual metaphor for the common law of **Wunan;** fallen fruit excellent as emu bait; dark emu shape in Milky Way beneath Southern Cross representing **Jebera** bent over with spear in his spine; celestial source of all water on earth

golani muna a wooden dish made from stringy bark

goro.goro Blue-winged Kookaburra, living evidence of **goro.goro Kamali** clan
gorrodoo Magpie Lark (Grallina cyanoleuca), living evidence of **Gorrodoo Kamali** clan; also **gri gri**
Gubu.ngarri dambun territory of king brown snake ancestor who left fossilised faeces as **onmal** (white paint)
gudmerrermeri song expression for grabbing hold of each other's hands to form a line, before moving in the direction of the **birrawudi** dance
gulbrungi song expression of a most sacred nature performed only when wearing a **nguniri** (ancestral hairbelt) noose around the neck; a telepathic command to distant people, compelling them to arrive at the actual point where the singer stands
guli blood
Gulilli fearsome female **wanjina** of termites, resident in a deep gorge pool
gulin to bear children or breed offspring
Gulingi primary creator of all life and a force invigorating the cosmos; bringer of rain impregnated with lightning; influential force for general fertility and dispersal of **wungud** (life essence) in water; supreme **Wanjina** of snake form
Guli.ngulindi see **malarrin**
guli wodoi fine red ochre; precious residual blood of ancestor **Wodoi**
guliwud marked and engraved spear-thrower with burin tool tip attached with wax at opposite end to barb that fits into the shaft of a spear; **woomera** carved from hardwood like ironbark into flattened ovoid forms
guloi sweet green native plum *(Terminalia carpentariae)*, a popular food with harvest songs when fruit ripens during wet season; the "life tree", symbol of birth and regeneration revered in numerous rock-paintings, (e.g. icon at **Alyaguma**) as visual metaphor for education and continuing culture
gulowa sister-in-law
gulowada non-sacred songs of social comment and love
gumaa vegetable resin or gum
gumba.lawal White-quilled Rock-Pigeon (*Petrophassa albipennis*), rare species endemic to the Kimberley, nests on ledges in rocky gorges and hills, probable ancestor of cosmopolitan pigeons, living evidence of **gumba.lawal Kamali** clan; one bird that still responds to its **Wunan** name
gumbaru yellow ochre or iron oxide pigment; residue of ancestral frog excreta
gunan stick of dry wood used to create fire from friction
gundilli small river Agile Wallaby *(Macropus agilis)* known in law as first wallaby hunted with **nyarndu** (spear-thrower) and cooked in stone oven by **Gwion** hero **Yandama** (as celebrated in icon at **Alyaguma**)
guranguli see **burrunba**
gurin denticulated stone blade
Guringi north-west coastal sanctuary of **Jillinya**
guriwin medicinal sap from bloodwood tree
Guroni ancestral kangaroo matriarch, wife of **Walamba,** represented by a conical mountain, her permanent **wungud** place
guru.amalad minia expression of greeting for a large group or humanity as a whole
Guru.ngongo dambun region
Gwion used here as general term for artist ancestors of the **Ngarinyin,** known as "inventors" (to acknowledge the introduction of **nyarndu** and stone tools such as sharp **gimbu**); another title for the **Jenagi Jenagi** and **Munga.nunga**
Gwion Gwion originally the mysterious "cave bird" who used its beak to wipe blood across the surface of stone and so began painting; sacred name when repeated mimics the bird's call but if ignorantly spoken out of sacred context may provoke ancestral wrath
Gwion Gwion formal title of human artists of and fine rock-paintings, the first nomadic people spreading out across a land without boundaries who began **Wunan** law

jaawa common Koel or "rainbird", living evidence of female ancestor **Jaawa** who punishes children if they vandalise bird nests containing eggs
Jadgud.gude one of a series of titles for reincarnations of the red kangaroo ancestor **Walamba**
jalba utility shoulder bag of string or hide
Jalbanuma mountain formed when **Jebera** man dropped his shoulder bag while escaping after he stole **golani** from the law table
jalgud variety of yam
jalgun small skirt of hide or fibre string worn by women; short bustle of emu down worn by women in the **walu.ngarri** (ring-dance)
jalim.baran dancing wand or baton tipped with feathers
jaljalbi running while carrying things in bag
jalla vibrant green algae found in fresh running water, used as incense for the stimulation of the imagination of a newborn child; evidence of the circulation from water to the upper atmosphere of **wungud** (life essence) from **Wanjina Gulingi,** and a sign of the cycle of creative energy in water and rain
jallala standing stones erected as a warning sign marking a sacred place; array of stones marking and mapping historical events
Jalmi see **Algi**
jalnga water chestnut; vegetable growing in wetlands and river margins
jarrgun small flat potato
jebera common flightless Emu *(Dromaius novaehollandiae)* known by its booming voice and stamping footsteps, living evidence of the **Jebera** clan
Jebera Emu clan ancestor from Tanami desert who stole from the **Kamali** council and was executed for breaking the sharing law of **Wunan**
jegabi image of the human form
Jenagi Jenagi another title for **Gwion** artists; literally the "wanderers" or nomads who became messengers of law; "messengers" who began the exchange of sacred **maya.ngarri**
Jillinya the Great Mother of everyone, also known as **Mumuu;** mother of all **Gwion** and the provider of all vegetables; primordial matriarch who gave women their genitals with the gift and power of birth; "big law woman" from **Guringi** associated with **mandzu** (praying mantis) and spirit power of wind
jimbila quartz spear-point of common unspecified type
jimbri red mineral pigment for painting
jirad native hibiscus, symbol of the **dambun** of **Banggal,** hence the regional title **Brrejirad**
jirrgal vegetable fibre string used to weave bags and fasten **mudurra** (wig)
jowul sharpened sticks or wooden staffs; spear-shafts trimmed from sapling; thin wood skewers used to draw blood during the ring-dance, publicly distracting initiates before the imminent shock of their circumcision
jugarrun "tie it up"
juiban the north-western race of the Great Bower Bird
julai see **julungi**
julungi long sinew from kangaroo
julwungi kangaroo tail cleaned and dried as a strap used as cord (e.g. for binding together spear-shafts)
Jumbowulla matriarch (see **Algi**)
jumubumuru freshwater Black Bream, living evidence of **Jumubumuru wanjina** – one of five central to the origin and formation of humans in water
junba songs and narrative dance following visions by composers; contemporary theatrical performances combined with acoustic and electrical music
jun.bii kangaroo or human shinbone
Jundiwan one of the paired forces that leads a thunderstorm, revered together as lightning deity **Bundiwin**
jungi anthill or termite mound built in many forms and colours depending on geological location; sacred ground protected by spirit woman **Gulilli**; coloured earth refined by termites used as women's intestinal medicine
jungun Australian Owlet-nightjar *(Aegotheles cristatus),* diminutive nocturnal predator busy pouncing on insects from low branch; small owl face with big eyes ringed in black, well camouflaged, looking like a possum while sleeping by day in tree hollows, living evidence of **Jungun,** one of two **Gwion** heroes who, with **Wodoi,** was seminal in starting the **Wunan;** common title for the **amalar** side of the two **moiety** groups inter-related with local flora and fauna
junjun all evidence of **Wunan** law in the natural world and human culture; residual marks of ancestors in land and art that resonate in **Ngarinyin** society; proof of **Wunan** history in numerous paintings on rock, cupoles, spear-sharpening grooves and tool-grinding marks in rockshelters; extensive stone-arrangements as narrative diagrams in country and connecting across the land; ancestral song language of archaic words used as music of heritage only by fully initiated **munnumburra**
jurull bird, living evidence of **Jurull Kamali** clan
juruma fine as talcum medicinal ash processed from the fibrous bark of the white flowering swamp corkwood tree *(Sesbania formosa),* coagulant prepared in advance for healing circumcision and initiation wounds

Kamali seminal grouping of **Gwion** lawmakers who gathered around the stone table at **Dududu.ngarri;** order of stones around table forming a ring of clans, named after birds, who ceased to be nomadic and adopted **dambun** titles following **Wunan** conference on law; first inheritors and declarers of central **dambun** regional titles. They are currently represented by the **Kamali Land Council** with offices located in Derby under the Chairmanship of **Paddy Neowarra (Nyawarra)**
kane-kane looking down
karabri see **mandi**
Kunmunya coastal site of a former mission
Kuri Kuri ancestral title

Laajmorro title of Milky Way **wanjina** imaged with one arm
Laundi ancestral title for old man wearing full **mudurra** observed by **Nyawarra** in the late-1940's
lulwa any gift large or small ranging from ritual presentations to relatives in mourning to a toy present for a baby; a tribute of sacred material offered to ancestors celebrating generosity in the **Wunan**
lulwa wunandi ritual presentation of gifts during **Wunan** events and offerings to matriarchs and **wanjina**
Luma a desert margin district south of the Kimberley plateau, with indigenous groups connected by **Wunan**
lung.gudengari see **banad**

maba a revered old man, relieved of further responsibility in **Wunan** affairs when symptoms of blindness take hold
mabajiri a more formal title of reverence for **maba**
Mabo a recent colloquial term for Australian native title rights, derived from a landmark case in the High Court of Australia which acknowledged native title rights of Eddie Mabo over his Torres Strait island. This seminal case overturned two centuries of *the terra nullius* (empty land in Roman law) status previously maintained by colonial authorities, thus opening the way for future mainland native title claims. These include the pending claims of the authors' representative organisation, the **Kamali Land Council.** Titled after the original **Gwion** lawmakers around the stone table at **Dududu.ngarri,** the current claim follows the traditional boundaries of **Gwion dambun** regions with hereditary titles and symbols
majarumba the beauty that grabs hold of our eye with the inspiring health of youth
malai an emphatic greeting of respect
malgara fire made when hunting kangaroo, to singe off its fur and to cook the fresh meat. Large branches are burnt to form a bed of coals for baking the kangaroo in a shallow earth oven
mallara frangipani form of white flower *(Gardenia spp.)* perfumed like gardenia; leafy shrub favouring rocky hillsides and ridges near **wanjina;** green leaves burnt for incense smoke during announcements identifying visitors and songs of respect before approaching **wanjina** and sources of **wungud**
mamaa anything respected as sacred or secret ancestral evidence; warning pertaining to all things which are untouchable or forbidden; cultural connections fully protected by law; sacrosanct quality of places where major creative and historical events occurred; sources of spiritual charisma of marks or art or specific animals with totemic ancestral connections
mamalan footprints left in sandy ground
mamandu sticky red sap of rough-barked mulberry-like tree provides fixative and dye used to paint and stain many indelible **Gwion** figures onto rock surfaces
mambi triangular girdle skirt worn by women in **Gwion** paintings; mother's ceremonial skirt inherited by daughter
mamul essential form of sacred objects exchanged as **wulari** and **maya.ngarri** (transmitted knowledge)
manbata fringed white waterlily with small ovoid leaf
mandi crescent-shaped boomerang; pairs are clapped together for keeping rhythm of songs
mandzu praying mantis *(mantis sp.)*, living evidence of **Jillinya**
mangarri food and sharing; connecting obligations of hospitality and respect between relatives
mangiwarunga a seminal meeting or the initial gathering that commences a ceremony
Manirri ancestral country
maniwan orange tasselated flowers of **anggurun** (tree)
manjilarri sacred object crafted by **Wibalma** then removed by **Wodoi** and **Jungun** to share with all the people; a known source of justice meaning "running without help because the relentless power of law pursues you"
Maraja ancestral country
margi honeyeater family of birds, living evidence of **Margi Kamali** clan
marguli sacred song form
Marranba.bidi permanent settlement of **Ngarinyin** relatives on the King Edward River
marririn green-foliage-coloured Red-winged Parrot *(Aprosmictus erythropterus)*, living evidence of **Marririn** who stopped **Ngerdu** (crocodile **wanjina**) from possessing fire in the water so it can always be shared by everybody on dry land
maya.ngarri messages through sacred objects; secret or private forms of incised and painted boards preserving primary

cultural concepts; abstracted law symbols circulated as messages of law; also ritual **mamul** objects exchanged as **wulari** throughout **Wunan** network; an ancient cultural practice linking indigenous peoples across central and tropical Australia
menda stone hand-axe
min min min min onomatopoetic expression for ripples spreading across the surface of water, produced by the spinning tip of a gaff spear when the shaft end is twirled between the palms of the hand
mob colloquial collective term for a class of animals, many people, a district group, or local members of a **dambun**
modeden tracks of animals real and painted; marks on pathway to place of totemic source
modu anyi footprints of an animal or person on the move
moiety anthropological term for two halves of a social system; equal divisions of a population through cross-marriage relationships; the basis of **Ngarinyin** terminology for complex social structures with linguistically divided symbolic associations between all living things and between each half of their human representatives
molu the middle position of a clan leader when acting as a link in a chain of **Wunan** exchange
molu bidingarri role of authority when clan leaders transfer **maya.ngarri** between neighbouring **dambun** or on towards distant regions
molu ijirinari custodial role for **munnumburra** ensuring continuity of cultural exchange according to traditional routes of the **Wunan** system
mondollo body paint applied across the forehead and following the line of the jaw
Morrongo Morrongo country and people of **wamma** (native tobacco); clan under the custodianship of **Ungudman** of the **Jungun moiety**
Mowaljarlai (David Mowaljarlai, died 1997); public surname of **Banggal**
mudurra sculptured wig or headdress of various shapes and sizes recorded in **Gwion** painting to recent times; distinct graphic motif common to cultural traditions of other indigenous peoples across Australia and Papua
mullawundin forked lightning, and a potent magical influence for **banman** sorcery
Mul.ngirri title given to a lightning spirit that causes medium level lightning strikes that immediately follow the storm front, paired with **Jundiwan**
Mumuu sacred name for the Great Mother **Jillinya,** "a big word" in **Ngarinyin**
mun the imagination
Munga.nunga visionaries by name; **Gwion** title for ancestors acknowledged as social visionaries and originators of **Wunan** law; expert stone-tool makers and communicators of knowledge
Munggundu wanjina associated with the formation of the earth from plasma, whose icon is revered at **Alyaguma;** connected through meaning with pliable gum from bloodwood tree sap and resin
munilla body painting across the torso
Muni yalla ancestral blood-daughter of **Yemben wanjina**
Munja coastal settlement in Collier Bay north of Derby, a site of former mission where **Ngarinyin** refugees were sent from inland to join local **Wororra**
munnumburra senior woman or man fully initiated and well educated in **Wunan** law; experts responsible for supervising rituals, and preserving **Wunan** law
munya gesture of warning

nabun camp-fire for domestic cooking
Naiya second phase of lightning during a cyclonic storm, associated with a female identity as wife to the leading pair of **Bundiwin** (lightning brothers)
nambud burlwin song expression for joining dancers
Nenowatt family surname associated with **Bararru.ngarri dambun** and custodians of the **Walamba** sanctuary
Neowarra (**Paddy Neowarra,** chairman of the **Ngarinyin** Aboriginal Corporation); public surname of **Nyawarra**
ngallad glittering quartz-like stone reflecting light, easily fractured into flakes used for fine spear-points
ngangurr warra boy during first initiation stage when painted with **onmal** (white spots) like **wodoi** (Spotted Nightjar) before circumcision
Ngarinyin language group with "soft" and "hard" dialects, first spoken by a ring-tailed possum man known as **Andarri** on the **Jungun** side and **Wad.munna** on the **Wodoi** side
Ngarjno ancestral name of Laurie **Gawanali** of the **Wodoi skin** from **Brrejalnga dambun,** expert songman and **munnumburra** who is **ornad** in **moiety** relationships, with **gi** (spiritual connections) to **jalnga** (native water chestnut), custodian of king brown snake **wanjina** icon
ngawarra wanggi title for male initiate during second stage wearing ancestral hair **jirrgal** string around forehead for the first time; body image of two black rings with white dots around torso encircling each shoulder to represent each **moiety** group dancing the **walu.ngarri;** the painted rings are made from intense black **wulngon** (charcoal) mixed with **wurd.ngun** (bird fat), are painted over a body first smeared with **jimbri** (red blood), and are finished with lines of **onmal** (white dots)
Ngegamorro wanjina who loved **Wurrumurru** and began a family to which members of the family **Bangmorro** trace their descent
ngerdu small freshwater crocodile *(Crocodylus johnstoni)*, living evidence of **Ngerdu**, the crocodile **wanjina** who tried to keep fire for himself by taking it underwater
ngi.ornad of the **Wodoi skin** or **ornad moiety**
ngolo ngolo walu.ngarri song phrase "come, walk along"
ngoru inner sacred breath of life; an essence inside water given by **Wanjina Gulingi;** attribute of potency for **maya.ngarri** (sacred objects)
ngowrun expression "of the sacred wind" (see **ngoru**)
nguniri precious rope of woven ancestral hair depicted in **Gwion** art and worn by **munnumburra** when performing **gulbrungi** (powerful songs) that announce a ceremony and compel everyone to attend
nimindi belonging to all, of everyone, such as knowledge
niyan.gawa ancient expression of inexact origin, retained in the **Jebera** narrative by **Ngarinyin** speakers when the selfish man asks "who me", believed to have its source in the distant Tanami desert area (see **Unggumi**)
Njumillibulli see **Algi**
nollabiallu groups of men or women painted for the **walu.ngarri,** singing songs while walking up to the ring-dance ground
norgun concave palette worn into stone for grinding **mamandu** bark to extract red liquid as paint
Nudu.nudu Kamali clan title
numanda to "wake up" from sleep
numbila song term for moving quickly
nu meri expression for concentrating, listening carefully
numurangga woman
nyamalar expression of greeting
Nyamanbiligi blind wife of **Wibalma**
nyamun-buna keeping oaths made; not going against the law because of the trouble and punishment it would bring; staying quiet and keeping secret
nyarndu hooked stick used as a spear-thrower cut from the stem of a corkwood tree or riverbank pine *(Nauclea orientalis)*; prototype spear-thrower giving hunters extra thrust to pierce the thick hides of emu and kangaroo; common motif of **Gwion** painting
nyarra self-referring pronoun
nyarrama clan members talking in a **Wunan** meeting
Nyawarra ancestral name of **Paddy Neowarra** of **Wodoi skin** from **Galeru.ngarri dambun;** community leader and **munnumburra** who is **ornad** in **moiety** relationships; **gi** (spiritual connections) include rain and frogs and **Walamba** (red kangaroo) as living symbols
nyawarra black basalt rocks; also the **gi** (spiritual connections) of **Nyawarra** and source of his name
nyirri gunduba curled up in sleep
nyonor female members of **ornad moiety (Wodoi skin)** in marriage relationship with opposite **amalar** (see **nyamalar**)

Olgi title given to minor forms of lightning that occur as a storm front passes; title attributed to a boy following **Naiya**
onmal white paint processed from kaolin and exposed pipe-clay
ornad moiety name of **Wodoi skin,** *pl* **brrornad**
oru liwarad expression for the shape of kangaroo ears, erect while listening, shape of flanged **mudurra** (wig)

Pijantjatjara central desert language group, southern neighbours of the **Arrernte** and **Anangu,** also connected to **Wunan** laws originating in the Kimberley

quoll marsupial native "cat" with distinctive white spots

Romul see **Algi**

skin colloquial term for a **moiety** system of binary associations; social duality reflecting the sharing of blood between **Wodoi** on one side and **Jungun** on the other, through the inter-marriage of their children

Uluru the massive red monolith in the central desert of Australia, a landmark symbolic for **Anangu** and other indigenous language groups connected by the laws of **Wunan**
umralu denticulated stone blade used as a spear-point
Unggumi Tanami desert language that may be the source of the expression **niyan.gawa** used in the **Ngarinyin** narrative about **Jebera**
ungia waterlily with hanging roots
Ungudman ancestral name of **Paddy Wamma** of **Jungun skin** from **Morrongo Morrongo**; expert naturalist and **munnumburra** with **amalar moiety** relationships; **gi** (spiritual connections) include freshwater crocodile and **wamma** (native tobacco); source of his public name
urilimul armlet or girdle

wadba single shaft solid wooden fighting spear with two rows of carved barbs facing both directions making them painful to remove
wade song expression "all together, come on"
wad.munna Ring-tailed Possum on the **Wodoi** side, known as **andarri** on the **Jungun** side
walamba Antilopine Wallaroo *(Macropus antilopinus)* red kangaroo living animal of **wanjina,** living evidence of **Walamba wanjina** who reconstructed his body from scraps left by dogs after they ate him; originally known as **Binbin**, he survived by repeating the process through eight reincarnations, changing his name along the way until finally becoming **Wudmi.mulimuli**
walbo gudina sacred song expression related to circumcision
walbud tri-pointed belt-girdle of marsupial hide worn by **Gwion** males
walgunu fertility stones containing **wungud** (sacred essence); egg-shaped stones that levitate and move freely during the night
Wallagari Merrbini long curving lagoon, formed when **Walamba** threw down his **banad** (boomerang), and sat down painted in red ochre
Wallagunda the entire Milky Way; a body of light forming the ultimate creator of the earth
walmarro see **gundilli**
walu.di deep permanent river water and lagoons
walu.ngarri initiation ceremonies including the ring-dance of men and women; public events before circumcision with songs originally composed by **Wiji.ngarri** and first performed at **Wudmangu**
waluwi a local Blue-tongued Lizard, living evidence of **Waluwi** female ancestor who sacrificed herself to save her children in a flood
wamba nervous; an expression of concern
wamma native tobacco; regional symbol for **Morrongo Morrongo dambun;** homeland of **Ungudman**
Wamma (Paddy Wamma); public surname of **Ungudman**
wandagi arm-band around bicep, normally a wide strap cut from kangaroo hide, tightly bound with string and painted with **onmal;** a single bright white cowrie shell may also be attached to it with string for ritual events
Wangalu title of old man wearing **mudurra** (wig) observed by **Nyawarra** in his youth
wa.ngara long string or hide skirts ending with tassels worn only by women
wanggi status of initation from youth to marriageable age
wang.gura glossy black Torresian Crow (Corvus orru) with raucous calls and fearless behaviour often ubiquitous and busy camp scavengers, living evidence of **Wang.gura** – **Kamali** clan title for **Worrora** coastal people for inter-related western neighbours of the **Ngarinyin** – often referred to as the "sunset mob"
Wanjina creative power manifesting **wungud** (the essence of all life circulating through the earth, the water and the sky) as an influence of the supreme being **Wanjina Gulingi;** numerous other local **wanjina** have multiple associations with animals and plants, and enshrine identites of deified ancestors who formed country
wanjina fertile source situated where ancestral creative spirits imaged themselves as bas-relief and colour in rock as sites of renewal; term for re-painted icons on white ground with distinctive haloed head forms without mouths,
wanjina "water people", local title for indigenous people of the Kimberley, particularly the **Ngarinyin, Wila Wila, Wororra, Wunambul** language groups
warid wani mumal small flat stone heated in warm ashes, used as an anvil to heat slowly and straighten a bamboo spear-shaft. Great care must be taken not to overheat and dry the bamboo, or split it by bending it when cold. The temperature of the anvil stone is carefully controlled, to radiate heat into the bamboo, until the shaft is judged ready to bend. Then the shaft is gradually straightened with firm downward pressure onto the anvil stone, allowing a craftsman to prudently eliminate many subtle defects
Wari.ngarri dambun region
waringi de.de song phrase connecting the growth of young children and a yellow flowering shrub
Warlpiri indigenous central desert language group connected by the laws of **Wunan**
Warmun indigenous community east of the Kimberley, on the north-western margin of the Tanami desert; a district title for "sunrise **mob**"; easterley groups connected by **Wunan**

warrana Wedge-tailed Eagle *(Aquila audax)* and major predator of wallaby and kangaroo

warrngon see **windji jaman**

Wibalma Gwion author of sacred objects who lived at **Gelngu** and kept sacred knowledge to himself until the intervention of **Wodoi** and **Jungun** revealed his wealth of **maya.ngarri** (sacred objects)

Wiji.ngarri Northern spotted Quoll (Dasyurus hallucatus), nocturnal carnivorous marsupial, aggressively pounces on any reptile, rat or insect prey in sight, with pads on the hindfeet to grip smooth sandstone surfaces, living evidence of **Wiji.ngarri** composer of the first **walu.ngarri** (ring-dancing ceremonies of both sexes, preliminary to male circumcision); ancestor who suffered from sores on his body signified by white spots on living animal

Wila Wila northern coastal neighbours of the **Ngarinyin** represented by **jallala** (signal stones) at **Dudu.ngarri**

wilmi mobile spirals of mist over streams of **wungud**; visible evidence of resident spirits of future children

windji jaman to anoint and paint the human body as image; also **warrngon**

Winjagin mountain standing out as a monolith on the savanna of **Morrongo Morrongo** (area under the custodianship of **Ungudman**)

winjangun small camp fire

winjin torrential rains sent by **Gulingi** that begin the humid monsoon season extending from November into February; time when **guloi** (fruit) mature

winya song expression of determination to perform dances during **Wunan** events

wir.nganyen the second phase of initiation following **walu.ngarri;** series of **Wunan** songs introducing male initiates to sacred animals and culminating with private circumcision rituals

wodoi familiar Australian Spotted Nightjar or nighthawk *(Eurostotodus argus)* distinguished by white spots and a bright white window on wings; sleeps camouflaged among litter on the ground during the day and gracefully hawks on the wing at night, eating insects, living evidence of **Wodoi,** one of two **Gwion** cohorts who by agreement with **Jungun** originated the sharing of land and blood through marriage as **Wunan** law; common title for anyone **ornad** related in the **moiety** system

Wodoi.ngarri dambun clan region named after **Wodoi**

wongai senior woman initiated in the law, with full knowledge of **Wunan** rituals and songs

woomera colloquial term for spear-thrower (see **nyarndu**)

Wororra coastal language group, western neighbours of the **Ngarinyin**

worri-unbin flowing words going around among people during conversation; dialogue circulating through **Wunan**

Wo.wa Kamali clan title

wowarra Common Bronzewing Pigeon *(Phaps chalcoptera)*, living evidence of **Wowarra** – title for **Kamali** clan celebrated as the fastest runners, led by pair of responsible men who chased and speared **Jebera** for breaking the **Wunan** law

Wudjawudja.ngarri dambun clan region

wudma female small river wallaby *(Macropus agilis)*. An infant wallaby, still being carried in the marsupial pouch of a **wudma,** is never eaten, following a ban originated by the **Gwion** hunter **Yandama** (see **gundilli**)

Wudmangu location where **Wiji.ngarri** composed the original **walu.ngarri** songs; revered place surrounded by streams where a stone seat was first used to position the songman in the middle of a ring-dance

Wudmi.mulimuli the last title assumed to **Walamba**

wudu moving around

wuduwan see **mandi**

Wulamu early **Gwion** clans who came to the **Wunan** table from the direction of the sunrise; people of the deserts over the horizons to the east of the **Ngarinyin**

wulari sacred objects moving as **maya.ngarri** through **Wunan** network

wuludi deep and permanent waterholes, rivers and billabongs; green water where childrens spirit's rise as **wilmi** (mist), designated sacred water places where the **wungud** (essence of life) from **wanjina** resides

Wunambul neighbours of the **Ngarinyin,** closely related in language and history

Wunan the sharing Law; ancient agreements that ended nomadism by fixing family **dambun** estates and by establishing **moiety** division of society into two cross-marriage groups originating from the pledge of **Wodoi** and **Jungun** to unify their blood; binary order of classification between **brrornad** and **bramalar moiety** "tribes" or **skins** with marriage arranged between **ornad** and **amalar** (male) or **nyonor** and **nyamalar** (female) individuals; original model of multiple versions of extant **moiety** kinship systems connecting every living thing within a cultural network; layout and pattern of land

wunanbri spatially widespread routes of exchange of sacred objects and rituals and sanctified gifts and songs

wunandi ongoing ethos of **Wunan** law

wunan.gu calling people together for the **Wunan**

wunbanburan unchanging ethics in **Wunan** law as **lulwa** (gift) from **Munga.nunga** ancestors; ethical foundation for any legal obligations

wungarun ironwood, tree of the hardest timber

wunginunna pool of dark water, in Milky Way and on earth

wungud energy or essence of living things; primary life-force common in all forms of life created by **wanjina;** life circulating within water giving structure and form to all things from protozoa to humans; any physical or spiritual essence that influences humans or animates, reflects, sustains and motivates life; evidence of various **wanjina;** faint traces of **Gwion** paintings are considered rich with the essence of life and may also be called **wungud**

wungurrurun mamandu palette in stone (see **norgun**)

wunindid traditional law from ancients; also **wunanbri wunindid naga** law in the process of passing through the **Wunan**

wunindid naga enduring influence of **Wunan** law through the ages

wura.wura Partridge Pigeon *(Petrophassa smithii)*, camouflaged in shaded undergrowth with yellow skin around the eye, signifying resident of the grass-covered woodlands of northern Kimberley

wurd.ngun body fat of any bird used as wood preservative for utensils and weapons

Wurrumalu blood son of water goanna **Yemben wanjina**

Wurrumurru female long-neck turtle ancestor, loved by **Ngegamorro wanjina**

yalmalnyu malngud forbidden areas near sacred ground which are dangerous to humans and animals, normally a quicksand, bog or swamp. Such a place is imbued with a deadly force, and considered **mamaa** (secret). The action of taking the life of some animals when law was created resulted in sacred deposits of a beneficent nature residing alongside a dangerous one. As a result of the original law events, deposits of fresh water and distinctive landforms also remain as **junjun** (evidence of their actions)

yalungarri alternative term for white pigment (see **onmal**)

yamalad minia term of greeting, acknowledging the individual face of a person, more literally "I see your shining forehead"

Yandama famed hunter whose icon celebrates the use of a **nyarndu** (spear-thrower); icon of hunter at **Alyaguma** with three, not five, fingers to signify ancestral links between bird and human; **Gwion** hero responsible for cooking **gundilli** (wallaby) in stone oven, and creating several sacred sites linked with one name **Alyaguma**

yangudi adolescent girls with developing breasts

yara Common Wallaroo *(Macropus robustus)*, locally known as the plains or "grey hill kangaroo", living evidence of **Yara;** law originating at a stone oven near **Binjirri** where ancestor **Yara** was eaten by wild dog people; kangaroo butchering protocol and song that spread southwards and eastwards until ultimately adopted in central Australia

yarrad human bones of the recently deceased left under a protective pile of loose stone for more than a year until ants and the weather clean the skeleton. Mourners must wait until all traces of sinew are gone and the bones bleached before preparing them for their final interment in a cave recess. Each bone is carefully washed and cleansed, and then wiped with **wurd.ngun** (bird fat) before being coated with **gagul** (red paint).

yemben sleek grey water goanna, living evidence of **Yemben wanjina,** blood son of **Ngegamorro**

yidmunggul emu hide cloak or epaulets worn off the shoulders; distinctive motif of **Gwion** painting

Yirrbal adopted son of ancestral **Ngegamorro wanjina,** de facto brother of **Yemben**

Yowinjella Kamali clan title from the Pheasant Coucal bird

Yullamaiya old man wearing **mudurra** (wig) observed by **Nyawarra** (see **Laundi**)

yululun attached feathers and wings worn as adornment and emblem

yungulli water lily of the lotus family

yururu.mal necklaces of feather and string

GLOSSAR

agula gefährliches Geisterwesen
Algi mächtiges, weibliches Ahnenwesen; auf den Felsmalereien von **Alyaguma** als liegende Figur dargestellt; ihr Körper ist von einer Vielzahl von Speeren bedeckt, die sie als Geschenk erhält
alnguru Speerschaft aus Bambus
Alyaguma heilige Wasserstelle unterhalb eines Wasserfalls mit zahlreichen sakralen Felsbildern, unter anderem einer besonders beeindruckenden Darstellung des **guloi**-Baums; der Ort, an dem sich der **Gwion**-Jäger **Yandama** ausruhte, als er wegen seines schmerzenden Knies nicht mehr weiterkonnte
amalad minia respektvolle, freundschaftliche Begrüßung; wörtlich übersetzt „Ich sehe deine glänzende Stirn"
amalar einzelnes Mitglied der **Jungun moiety** und innerhalb dieser Gruppe **(skin)** eine übliche Bezeichnung für die ihr zugeordneten Pflanzen und Tiere; *pl* **brramalar**
ambalaru menschliche Fußspuren oder Fährten auf dem Pfad eines Ahnenwesens
ambiliji siehe **maba**
amurangga Mann
Anaut.ngarri Land und Leute des Wind-Clans, benannt nach **Jillinya**
andarri australischer Gleitbeutler, lebende Manifestation des Ahnen **Andarri,** der als Erster die Sprache der **Ngarinyin** benutzte
angga Schale aus Rinde; ebene Oberfläche wie etwa die steinerne Platte des **Wunan**-Tisches
anggurun langblättriger Eukalyptusbaum *(Eucalyptus miniata)*, eine in der Baumsavanne der nördlichen Kimberley-Region häufig vorkommende Art, deren orangefarbenen Blüten **(maniwan)** guten Honig liefern
anjum großblättrige Lotosblume oder Seerose
arawari mit dem Finger ein Bild oder eine Landkarte auf den Boden zeichnen
argad Habichtfalke *(Falco berigora)*, lebende Manifestation von zwei **Gwion**-Brüdern namens **Argad**, die dafür verantwortlich waren, dass die Menschen in Vögel verwandelt wurden
Arnhem Land nordaustralische Region westlich des Carpentaria-Golfs; Heimat zahlreicher Aborigine-Stämme, die die Aspekte des **Wunan**-Gesetzes bewahren
Arrernte in der zentralaustralischen Wüste beheimatete Stammesgruppe, die durch Pfade des kulturellen Austauschs mit dem **Wunan**-Gesetz verbunden ist
arri Menschen
arririn siehe **gundilli**
arru Aal, eines der fünf heiligen Wassertiere des **Wanjina Gulingi**, lebende Manifestation des **Arru wanjina**, der auf dem Felsbild von **Alyaguma** dargestellt ist

Badjayei Ausdruck aus den heiligen Liedern
balbrangi balbri alter Gesang, mit dem die Clan-Gruppen zur Beratung über das Gesetz zusammengerufen werden, wobei der Sänger einen **nguniri** (Gürtel aus den Haaren der Ahnen) trägt. Dieser soll dafür sorgen, dass Leute aus der Ferne sich an den Ort begeben, wo der Sänger steht
Balgo Ort am westlichen Rand der Tanami-Wüste, in dem verschiedene Aborigine-Stämme leben
Balmirriya siehe **Walamba**
banad australischer „Buschtruthahn" oder Wammentrappe (*Ardeotis australis*); jede Art von Hartholz-Bumerang in Form eines gebeugten Arms oder einer Sieben, der an den hochaufgereckten Kopf und Hals dieses Vogels erinnert; ein Hakenbumerang, wie er heutzutage zur Erinnerung an die Zeit der Ahnen bei bestimmten Tänzen getragen wird
banbangi siehe **balbrangi balbri** und **gulbrungi**
Banggal der inzwischen verstorbene David **Mowaljarlai**, ein Mitglied der **Wodoi moiety** aus dem Brrejirad **dambun;** Kulturvermittler und durch verschiedene Veröffentlichungen bekannt gewordener Lehrer; **munnumburra** der **ornad moiety** mit spirituellen Verbindungen **(gi)** zum australischen Hibiskus **(jirad)** und dem Vogel **Gwion Gwion**
Bangmorro Familie, die ihre Abstammung auf den **Ngegamorro wanjina** zurückführt
banman Traumdeuter; Mystiker oder Zauberer, der die Geheimnisse des Blitzes kennt; Heilkundiger oder Arzt
bararu.ru Ort, an dem Rituale stattfinden; Tanzplatz
bare Vagina; **Jillinyas** Vermächtnis an alle Frauen
Barilamma Teil eines versteinerten Korallenriffs im Napier Range, wo sich **Jebera** auf der Flucht ausruhte und auf einem Felsbild in Gestalt eines großen Emus mit einem Vorrat an **golani**-Früchten verewigt ist
Barraru.ngarri Land und Leute, benannt nach einem rituellen Friedensschluss; Heimat des **Walamba wanjina** und eng verbunden mit dem **Galeru.ngarri dambun**
barrij sich erheben, aufstehen und tätig werden
belnged Gelbhaubenkakadu, lebende Manifestation des **Belnged-Kamali**-Clans
Bimbidora heiliger Ort mit einem Steinkreis aus **jallala**, an dem **Yandama** ein Wallaby erlegte und in einem Erdofen briet; Ort, an dem sich **yalmalnyu-malngud**-Kräfte wirken
Binbin ursprüngliche Verkörperung des Roten-Känguru-Ahnen **Walamba**, dessen Fell bei seinem ersten Auftreten in der Nähe von **Guringi** ganz weiß war
binja winja weiße Kaurimuschel, die oft als Schmuck an einem Riemen befestigt wurde und eine **mudurra** zierte; neben Perlmuscheln ein wichtiges Tauschobjekt, das nach den Regeln des **Wunan** bis weit ins Landesinnere gehandelt wurde
Binjiraregu heilige Region an der Nordwestküste, die den Ursprungsort der **Wunan**-Gesetze mit **Jillinya** verbindet; **Walamba** nahm hier an einer **walu.ngarri**-Zeremonie teil
Binjirri Ort, der wie der vorherige mit **Walamba** assoziiert wird
birrawudi rituelle Prozession, bei der die männlichen Initianden auf den Rücken der Männer getragen werden. Diese wichtige Phase des **walu.ngarri**-Rituals findet in der Regel am Nachmittag des zweiten Tages statt, unmittelbar vor Sonnenuntergang. Den ganzen Nachmittag lang umtanzen Männer und Frauen in Kreisen den steinernen Sitz der Sänger. Diese **munnumburra** singen Tag und Nacht, stets im Mittelpunkt, und leiten den **walu.ngarri.** Die Initianden sitzen am Boden neben dem Sänger, gemeinsam mit ihren engen weiblichen Verwandten aus der anderen **moiety.** Die Intensität des Gesanges versetzt die jungen Initianden in eine Art Trance. Wenn sich der letzte Tag der Zeremonie dem Ende zuneigt, stehen alle Männer der anderen **moiety** in einer langen Reihe den Initianden gegenüber, und die Jungen werden auf den Rücken ihrer „Onkel" gehoben. Die Jungen liegen auf dem Rücken, den Blick rückwärts gewandt. Der **birrawudi**-Tanz beginnt damit, dass die Männer mit den Füßen stampfen, bis die Erde bebt, und dann laufen sie in einer Reihe mit einem lauten **dududu**-Stampfgeräusch, lauter als das der Emus. Bei der rituellen Prozession des **birrawudi** ruht jeder **ngawarra wanggi,** jeder Initiand auf den Schultern der älteren Männer.
birrina Tanz; öffentliches Ereignis, bei dem Männer und Frauen zusammenkommen
Biyad.ngerri einer von mehreren Namen, die **Walamba** auf verschiedenen Stufen der Wiedergeburt auf seinem **dulwa** trug
biyu Leiter oder Gerüst
boab oder Baobab *(Adansonia gregorii)* Baum, aus dessen Fasern sich Schnüre oder Seile für verschiedene Verwendungszwecke herstellen lassen, beispielsweise für die Netze, mit denen die ersten **Gwion**-Jäger dem Wild nachstellten
borror Eulenschwalm, lebende Manifestation des **Borror-Kamali**-Clans
brad der erste Lichtschein, wenn sich der Horizont in der Morgendämmerung orangerot färbt; der richtige Zeitpunkt für die Beschneidung; Ort, dem die Schädel der Verstorbenen zugewandt werden
breb-brenya Liedzeile, mit der alle Teilnehmer aufgefordert werden, mit dem **walu.ngarri** zu beginnen
brilgi rituelle Ziernarben. Diese Narben bilden ein feines Muster auf der Haut, das an die Hautzeichnung der fünf heiligen Tiere der **wanjina** erinnert: Aal, Schildkröte, Fisch, Wasserwaran und Krokodil. Die Narbenmuster sind Zeichen der vollständig initiierten männlichen und weiblichen **munnumburra** nach rituellen Begegnungen, bei denen das lebende Tier auf den Körper gelegt wird. Die Narben sind das unauslöschliche Zeugnis der Teilnahme an diesen Ritualen, bei denen in Anwesenheit der Person, die die Narben empfängt, bestimmte heilige **(mamaa)**, ausschließlich für diese privaten Rituale bestimmte Lieder gesungen werden. Dadurch geht die Kraft, die den Liedern innewohnt, auf die **munnumburra** über
briyal Arm und ein davon abgeleitetes Längenmaß
bramalar Plural von **amalar**
Brrejalnga Land und Leute des Wasserkastanien-Clans; das Gebiet steht unter der Obhut von **Ngarjno**
Brrejirad Land und Leute des Hibiskus-Clans; das Gebiet grenzt an das Nordufer des Prince Regent River; Stammesland der Familie von **Banggal**
brrornad Plural von **ornad**
Brrunjini heiliger Ort, Ursprungsort der Gesetze über das Teilen der Jagdbeute, die mit dem grauen Känguruahnen **Yara** in Verbindung gebracht werden; der Ort wird markiert durch einen Erdofen und einen hohen Gedenkstein **(jallala)**
Bunaba benachbarte Sprachgruppe in der Kimberley-Region
Bundiwin zwei männliche Blitzgottheiten namens **Jundiwan** und **Mul.ngirri**
bunja Höhle oder Felsvorsprung, in dessen Schutz sich Felsmalereien erhalten haben
bunja mamaa heilige Stätte oder geheimer Aufbewahrungsort von **maya.ngarri**
bunji jede Art von Haken oder Widerhaken, etwa an der Spitze einer Speerschleuder **(nyarndu);** eine hölzerne Spitze, die in das hohle Ende eines Speerschafts greift, bevor er mit einer Speerschleuder **(woomera)** geworfen wird
bunun.guli Liedzeile, die die Beendigung eines Blutrituals ankündigt; Status der Initiierten, wenn sie sich wieder frei durch verschiedene **dambun** bewegen dürfen
buren Clanmitglieder, die sich von einem **Wunan**-Ort entfernen
burrin.burrin Regenbogenspint *(Merops ornatus)*, ein Vogel aus der Familie der Bienenfresser
burroi brauner Hühnerhabicht oder Bänderhabicht, lebende Manifestation des **Burroi-Kamali**-Clans
burrunba großer australischer Kranich *(Grus rubicundus)*, Brolgakranich

coolamon im australischen Englisch gebräuchliche Bezeichnung für einen Teller oder eine Schale aus leichtem Holz mit einer charakteristischen Vertiefung in der Mitte
corroboree im australischen Englisch gebräuchliche Bezeichnung für die Zeremonien der Aborigines

dadall Spitzschwanzamadine (eine Finkenart) lebende Manifestation des **Dadall-Kamali**-Clans
dal.gnana Fächerpalme *(Livistona eastonii)*, aus deren unreifen, stärkehaltigen Blattstängeln ein Mehl gewonnen wird
dambun Gebiete, die die Clans auf der ersten **Kamali**-Ratsversammlung von **Dududu.ngarri,** bei der das Gesetz ins Leben gerufen wurde, zugewiesen bekamen; traditionelles System der Landeigentümerschaft bei den **Ngarinyin,** das den Austausch und Handel zwischen ihnen und ihren Nachbarn regelt
darrawani kleiner Finger; Fußabdruck; Unauslöschlichkeit der **Gwion**-Gemälde, die tiefe, dauerhafte Spuren im Sandstein hinterlassen haben
degulan Kragenechse, lebende Manifestation des Ahnenwesens **Degulan,** der die von **Wiji.ngarri** in **Wudmangu** erfundenen Rituale fortführte, indem er den **walu.ngarri** bei **Winjagin** und andernorts aufführte und so für die Verbreitung der **Wunan**-Gesänge sorgte
didiyii Ruf des Abschieds und der Unwiederbringlichkeit; er wird zum Abschluss des **wir.nganyen**-Rituals von allen Teilnehmern ausgestoßen, männlichen wie weiblichen
dindiwal Wanderfalke, lebende Manifestation des **Dindiwal-Gwion**-Clans
dinjid kleiner Baum, dessen Äste als Grabstöcke dienen; eine ständig laufende Nase, Symptome wie bei einer Grippe; Strafe für jemanden, der der lebenden Manifestation des **Dinjid wanjina** Schaden zufügte
dududu stampfendes Geräusch von laufenden Emus oder tanzenden Füßen
Dududu.ngarri tiefe Schlucht, die entstand, als drei Männer aus dem Emu-Clan vor der **Wunan**-Ratsversammlung am Steintisch flohen; Bezeichnung für den heiligen Ort im **Guru.ngongo dambun,** an dem die **Gwion** ihr Nomadendasein aufgaben
Duduk.ngunga Standort eines neuen Steinsitzes für die Sänger auf dem Tanzplatz von **Marranba.bidi,** wo 1995 eine **walu.ngarri**-Zeremonie stattfand
dudu-narawi Platz für Zeremonien, wörtlich übersetzt „ein Ort, an dem die Tänzer mit den Füßen stampfen"
dulwan Pfad, der von den Ahnenwesen geschaffen wurde; moralische Richtschnur; Weg durch die lebendige Welt des Buschs
dulwan mamaa heiliger Pfad mit den geheimen Spuren der Ahnenwesen, die überall im Lande verteilt sind
dulwan nimindi Pfad des Wissens und ein fortlaufender Erziehungsprozess, bei dem Ideen weitergegeben werden
duma siehe **waluwi**
dumbi Maskeneule, nistet in Höhlen oder Bäumen und ist oft bei der Jagd auf Nagetiere und Insekten im Gras zu beobachten, lebende Manifestation des **Dumbi-Kamali**-Clans
durran Rabenkakadu (Calyptorhynchus banksii), die lebende Manifestation des **Durran-Kamali**-Clans

emmalen Geist eines einzelnen Menschen; freier Geist

gaama tunnelförmiger Schildkröten- oder Krokodilbau in der Uferböschung eines Flusses
gadiya im umgangssprachlichen Englisch der Aborigines die Bezeichnung für einen Australier, der nicht zur indigenen Bevölkerung gehört
gagul rotes Pigment oder rote Ockerfarbe (siehe **jimbri)**
galambi Silberreiher (*Ardea alba*), großer weißer Reiher
Galeru.ngarri Land und Leute des im Norden beheimateten Regen-Clans; das Gebiet steht unter der Obhut von **Nyawarra**
gallid jede Art von Holzspeer mit Widerhaken oder mehreren Spitzen; Fischspeer mit fünf parallel angeordneten Spitzen mit Widerhaken, der zwischen den Handflächen gedreht wird, so dass die dabei entstehenden Wellen Fische anlocken, die in den Widerhaken hängen bleiben, wenn der Speer mit einem Ruck aus dem Wasser gezogen wird
galuman Bambus für Speerschäfte
galwa nicht näher identifizierter Busch mit gelben Blüten
galwadi leicht formbares Harz, das durch Rühren eine lehmige Konsistenz erhält und zum Formen und Modellieren der **mudurra** dient
galwal siehe **nguniri**
gambul siehe **julwungi**
Gananinjal Ort südlich von **Warmun,** wo der habgierige **Jebera** auf der Flucht getötet wurde
gandad Steinmesser
gangan zwei Holzstäbe, die zur rhythmischen Begleitung von Gesängen aneinander geschlagen werden
ganjal Schwarzmilan *(Milvus migrans)*, lebende Manifestation des **Ganjal-Kamali**-Clans
ganmang.gu längliche Jamswurzel, die in von Steinmauern umgebenen Gärten gezogen wird
garabri siehe **mandi**

garagi große Mappe; Beutel oder Eimer aus Paperbark-Rinde oder Leder
garan.garan tauchender Wasservogel, Blässhuhn, lebende Manifestation des **Garan.garan-Kamali**-Clans
garramarra Salzwasser
Gawanali offizieller Nachname von **Ngarjno**
Gelngu Gegend, in der **Wodoi** und **Jungun** die Werkstatt von **Wibalma** besuchten
gerd Haut, die an der Unterseite des Penis herabhängt, die Vorhaut vor der Beschneidung
gi persönliche spirituelle Verbindungen zwischen Mensch, Land und **wanjina**
gimbu rötlich brauner Stein; Ausgangsmaterial für die schärfsten Speerspitzen der **Gwion;** Skalpell für Beschneidungen und für das Einritzen von rituellen Ziernarben
gingu Speerschaft aus Bambus, der am Ende hohl ist
goanna im australischen Englisch gebräuchliche Bezeichnung für verschiedene Warane und Skinke
golani kleine, dunkle Frucht (*Vitex glabrata*); rituelle Nahrung in Gestalt eines Brotes aus den zerdrückten und gekochten Früchten; wegen Übereinstimmung in Größe und Farbe zwischen der Frucht und der menschlichen Pupille eine visuelle Metapher für das allumfassende **Wunan**-Gesetz; heruntergefallene Früchte sind gute Emuköder; dunkler emuförmiger Schatten in der Milchstraße unter dem Kreuz des Südens symbolisiert den vom Speer getroffenen **Jebera,** der sich vornüber beugt; himmlische Quelle allen Wassers auf der Erde
golani muna hölzerne Schale aus Eukalyptusrinde
goro.goro Blauflügel-Kookaburra, lebende Manifestation des **Goro.goro-Kamali**-Clans
gorrodoo australische Elsternart (Grallina cyanoleuca), lebende Manifestation des **Gorrodoo-Kamali**-Clans; auch **gri gri**
Gubu.ngarri dambun Gebiet des braunen Königsnatter-Ahnen, von dessen früherer Anwesenheit vielerorts versteinerter Kot zeugt, der als **onmal**-Farbe verwendet wird
gudmerrermeri Liedzeile, die die Tänzer dazu auffordert, sich an der Hand fassen und eine Reihe zu bilden, bevor sie sich in die für den **birrawudi**-Tanz vorgeschriebene Richtung drehen
gulbrungi Liedzeile mit besonders heiligem Inhalt, die nur von jemandem gesungen wird, der eine **nguniri**-Schnur um den Hals trägt; telepathische Aufforderung an weit entfernt lebende Menschen, die sie zwingt, sich genau an den Ort zu begeben, an dem der Sänger steht
guli Blut
Gulilli Angst einflößender weiblicher Termiten-**wanjina,** der in einem zwischen Felsen verborgenen tiefen Wasserloch haust
gulin Kinder gebären oder Nachwuchs hervorbringen
Gulingi Schöpfer allen Lebens und eine Kraft, die dem Kosmos innewohnt; Bringer von Regen und Blitz; Kraft, die überall für Fruchtbarkeit und für **wungud** im Wasser sorgt; höchster **wanjina** in Schlangengestalt
Guli.ngulindi siehe **malarrin**
guli wodoi feiner roter Ocker; wertvolle Überreste vom Blut des Ahnen **Wodoi**
guliwud verzierte und geschnitzte Speerschleuder mit einer mit Wachs befestigten, meißelartigen Spitze am hinteren Ende, die in den Schaft eines Speers greift; aus Hartholz, etwa dem Holz des Eisenbaums, geschnitzte Speerschleuder **(woomera)** in abgeflachter ovaler Form
guloi süße, grüne australische Pflaume *(Terminalia carpentariae)*, die in der Regenzeit reif wird und ein beliebtes Nahrungsmittel bei den Erntegesängen ist. Der **guloi**-Baum als „Baum des Lebens", ein Symbol für Tod und Wiedergeburt, findet sich auf zahlreichen Felsbildern, zum Beispiel in **Alyaguma,** und ist ein Sinnbild für den schrittweisen Erwerb und die Weitergabe von Wissen
gulowa Schwägerin
gulowada weltliche Gesänge über alltägliche Begebenheiten und die Liebe
gulug Höhle oder Tunnel in Sandbänken an oder in Flüssen
gumaa Pflanzenharz oder Gummi
gumba.lawal Weißspiegeltaube *(Petrophassa albipennis)*, eine seltene Spezies, die nur auf Felsvorsprüngen in Felsenschluchten und im Gebirge der Kimberley Region nistet; vermutlich die Ahnherrin der weltweit verbreiteten Tauben; lebendige Manifestation des **Gumba.lawal-Kamali**-Clans; Vogel, der noch immer auf seinen **Wunan**-Namen hört
gumbaru gelber Ocker oder gelbes Eisenoxid-Pigment; Überreste von den Ausscheidungen des Frosch-Ahnen
gunan Reibholz zum Feuermachen
gundilli Flinkwallaby *(Macropus agilis)*; nach der Tradition das erste Wallaby, das von dem **Gwion**-Helden **Yandama** mit einer Speerschleuder **(nyarndu)** erlegt und im Erdofen gebraten wurde; ein Ereignis, das auf einem Felsbild in **Alyaguma** festgehalten ist
guranguli siehe **burrunba**
gurin gezahnte Steinklinge
Guringi Heiligtum der **Jillinya** an der Nordwestküste
guriwin heilkräftiger Saft des Blutbaums (Kino-Gummibaum)
Guroni mächtige Känguru-Ahnin, die Ehefrau von **Walamba,** repräsentiert durch einen Kegelberg, Sitz ihres **wungud**
guru.amalad minia Grußformel für eine größere Gruppe von Menschen oder für alle Menschen
Guru.ngongo dambun Stammesgebiet
Gwion bezeichnet hier allgemein die künstlerisch tätigen Ahnen der **Ngarinyin,** die auch „Erfinder" genannt werden, weil ihnen die Einführung der **nyarndu** (Speerschleuder) und bestimmter Steinwerkzeuge wie der scharfen **gimbu** (Speerspitze) zugeschrieben wird; eine andere Bezeichnung für die **Jenagi Jenagi** und **Munga.nunga**
Gwion Gwion ursprünglich der geheimnisvolle „Höhlenvogel", der seinen blutigen Schnabel an den Wänden einer Höhle abwischte und so das erste Felsbild schuf; heiliger Name, der, wenn man ihn wiederholt, den Ruf des Vogels nachahmt; außerhalb des religiösen Kontexts gesprochen kann das die Ahnen erzürnen
Gwion Gwion formelle Bezeichung der **Ngarinyin** für die Schöpfer und ihre Felsbilder, die ersten umherwandernden Bewohner einer Region ohne Begrenzungen, die das **Wunan**-Gesetz begründeten

jaawa Koel oder Regenvogel, lebende Manifestation des weiblichen Ahnenwesens **Jaawa,** das Kinder bestraft, wenn sie Vogelnester mit Eiern beschädigen
Jadgud.gude einer von mehreren Namen, die der Känguru-Ahne **Walamba** im Zuge seiner Wiedergeburt annahm
jalba Schultertasche aus Schnüren oder Leder
Jalbanuma Berg, der entstand, als **Jebera** auf der Flucht seine Schultertasche fallen ließ, nachdem er die **golani** vom Tisch des Gesetzes entwendet hatte
jalgud Jamswurzelart
jalgun knapper, von Frauen getragener Schurz aus Leder oder Faserschnüren; kurzer Federbausch aus Emudaunen, wie ihn die Frauen beim **walu.ngarri**-Kreistanz tragen
jalim.baran Tanzstab oder Taktstock mit federverzierter Spitze
jaljalbi laufen und dabei Dinge in einer Tasche transportieren
jalla leuchtend grüne Süßwasseralge, die im fließendem Wasser gedeiht – wenn man sie verbrennt, ergibt sie einen Weihrauch, der die Phantasie eines neugeborenen Kindes anregt; sichtbarer Beleg für das Strömen der **wungud** (Lebenskraft) die vom **Wanjina Gulingi** ausgehend durch das Wasser in die Atmosphäre gelangt, ein Zeichen für den Kreislauf der Schöpfungsenergie in Wasser und Regen
jallala aufrecht stehende Steine als Warnung vor einem heiligen Ort; Arrangement von Steinen zur Kennzeichnung von historischen Schauplätzen und wichtigen Ereignissen
Jalmi siehe **Algi**
jalnga Wasserkastanie, essbare Pflanze, die in Feuchtgebieten und an Flussufern wächst
jarrgun kleine flache Kartoffel
jebera flugunfähiges Emu *(Dromaius novaehollandiae)*, das für seine laute Stimme und seine stampfenden Füße bekannt ist, lebende Manifestation des **Jebera-Kamali**-Clans
Jebera Ahnenwesen aus dem Emu-Clan der Tanami-Wüste, das bei der **Kamali**-Ratsversammlung einen Diebstahl beging und seinen Verstoß gegen das **Wunan**-Gesetz des Teilens mit dem Leben bezahlte
jegabi Darstellung einer menschlichen Gestalt
Jenagi Jenagi andere Bezeichnung für die **Gwion**-Künstler; wörtlich übersetzt die Wanderer oder Nomaden, die zu Botschaftern des Gesetzes wurden; „Botschafter", die mit dem Austausch der heiligen **maya.ngarri** begannen
Jillinya Urmutter allen Lebens, auch bekannt als **Mumuu,** die Mutter der **Gwion** und Schutzherrin aller essbaren Pflanzen; uralte mächtige Ahnenherrin, von der die Frauen ihre Geschlechtsorgane und die Gebärfähigkeit erhielten; die „große Mutter des Gesetzes" aus **Guringi,** assoziiert mit der Gottesanbeterin **(mandzu)** und der Kraft des Windes
jimbila häufig vorkommende Speerspitzen aus Quarzgestein
jimbri rotes Malpigment auf Mineralbasis
jirad australischer Hibiskus; Symbol des **dambun** von **Banggal,** das den davon abgeleiteten Namen **Brrejirad** trägt
jirrgal Schnüre aus Pflanzenfasern zur Herstellung von Taschen und zum Befestigen von **mudurra**
jowul spitze Stöcke oder Holzstäbe; Speerschäfte aus dem Holz junger Bäume; dünne Holzspieße, mit denen die Tänzer einander beim Kreistanz kleine blutende Wunden zufügen, um die Initianden von dem bevorstehenden Schock der Beschneidung abzulenken
jugarrun zusammenbinden
juiban der in Nordwestaustralien vorkommende Große Bowervogel
julai siehe **julungi**
julungi eine lange Kängurusehne
julwungi gereinigte und getrocknete Sehne des Känguruschwanzes; dient als Schnur, mit der man zum Beispiel Speerschäfte zusammenbindet
Jumbowulla Muttergottheit (siehe **Algi**)
jumubumuru schwarze Brasse, lebende Manifestation des **Jumubumuru wanjina,** einer von fünf **wanjina** mit zentraler Bedeutung für den Ursprung und die Entstehung des Menschen im Wasser
junba Lieder und Tanzdarstellungen, die sich an visionären Vorstellungen von musikalischen Schöpfern orientieren; zeitgenössische Aufführungen arbeiten dabei sowohl mit akustischen als auch mit elektrischen Instrumenten
jun.bii Schienbein eines Kängurus oder eines Menschen
Jundiwan eine der stets gemeinsam auftretenden Kräfte, die ein Gewitter hervorbringen und zusammen als Blitzahnenwesen **Bundiwin** verehrt werden
jungi Ameisenhaufen oder Termitenhügel, deren verschiedene Formen und Farben von der Bodenbeschaffenheit abhängen; heiliger Ort, der unter dem Schutz der Geistfrau **Gulilli** steht; farbige, von Termiten verarbeitete Erde, die die Frauen als Heilmittel gegen Darmbeschwerden verwenden
jungun australischer Zwergschwalm *(Aegotheles cristatus)*, ein kleiner nachtaktiver Raubvogel, der sich von niedrigen Ästen auf Insekten stürzt; mit seinem kleinen Eulengesicht und den großen, schwarz geränderten Augen sieht er aus wie ein Opossum, wenn er tagsüber in hohlen Baumstämmen schläft; lebende Manifestation von **Jungun,** einem der beiden **Gwion**-Helden, der zusammen mit **Wodoi** die **Wunan**-Gesetze ins Leben rief; Bezeichnung für die **amalar**-Seite der beiden **moieties,** die untrennbar mit der lokalen Flora und Fauna verbunden sind
junjun alle Belege für das **Wunan**-Gesetz in Natur und menschlicher Zivilisation; von den Ahnenwesen im Land und in der Kunst hinterlassene sichtbare Zeichen, die das Leben der **Ngarinyin** beeinflussen; Belege für die Geschichte des **Wunan** in zahllosen Felsbildern und von Steinwerkzeugen hinterlassenen Kratzspuren auf Felsen und in Felsunterständen; überall im Land anzutreffende Stein-Arrangements und Diagramme, die Geschichten erzählen und Verbindungen zueinander herstellen; die Sprache der uralten Lieder, wie sie nur von vollständig initiierten **munnumburra** verwendet wird
jurull Vogel, lebende Manifestation des **Jurull-Kamali**-Clans
juruma die talkumfeine heilkräftige Asche aus der faserigen Rinde des weißblühenden *Sesbania-formosa*-Baums; wird als Blutgerinnungsmittel bei Beschneidungs- und Initiationsritualen eingesetzt

Kamali ursprüngliche Gesetzgeber der **Gwion,** die sich um den Steintisch von **Dududu.ngarri** versammelten; ein Steinkreis um einen Tisch als Sinnbild einer Versammlung der verschiedenen nach Vögeln benannten Clans, die ihr Wanderleben aufgaben und im Anschluss an die Beratung über das **Wunan**-Gesetz **dambun**-Namen annahmen; die Ersten, die die **dambun**-Namen erbten und für sich beanspruchten. Die Clans werden heute repräsentiert vom **Kamali Land Council** mit Sitz in Derby, an dessen Spitze **Paddy Neowarra (Nyawarra)** steht
kane-kane nach unten blicken
karabri siehe **mandi**
Kunmunya Küstenort, an dem sich eine Missionsstation befand
Kuri Kuri Ahnentitel

Laajmorro Titel des Milchstraßen-**wanjina,** der einarmig dargestellt wird
Laundi Name eines alten Mannes mit **mudurra** (Perücke), den **Nyawarra** in den späten vierziger Jahren beobachtete
lulwa jede Art von Geschenk, gleichgültig wie groß, von rituellen Gaben für trauernde Angehörige bis hin zu einem Spielzeug für ein Baby; heilige Gaben, die man den Ahnen als Tribut darbringt, als Sinnbild für die Freigiebigkeit, die Teil des **Wunan** ist
lulwa wunandi rituelle Gaben im Rahmen von **Wunan**-Ritualen und Opfergaben für weibliche Ahnenwesen und **wanjina**
Luma Gebiet am Rande der Wüste südlich des Kimberley-Plateaus, bewohnt von Aborigines, die zum **Wunan** gehören
lung.gudengari siehe **banad**

maba angesehener alter Mann, der von seiner Verantwortung für das **Wunan** entbunden ist, weil er erblindet
mabajiri eine förmlichere, ehrerbietigere Anrede für einen **maba**
Mabo eine heute geläufige Abkürzung für die bahnbrechende Entscheidung des High Court of Australia von 1992, in dem die Besitzansprüche des Aborigine Eddie Mabo auf seine Insel in der Torresstraße anerkannt wurden. Dieses wichtige Urteil setzte die 200 Jahre lang gültigen *terra-nullius*-Status außer Kraft, wonach Australien bei der Landnahme der Kolonisten nach römischem Recht unbewohntes Land war, und bereitete so den Weg für weitere Landrechtsklagen auf dem australischen Kontinent. Dazu gehören auch die anhängigen Verfahren des Gremiums, für das die Autoren stehen, des **Kamali Land Council.** Dieser Rat, der seinen Namen nach den ursprünglichen Schöpfern des Gesetzes erhielt, die sich um den steinernen Tisch von **Dududu.ngarri** versammelten, stützt sich bei seinen Forderungen auf die von den **Gwion** festgelegten überlieferten Grenzen der **dambun,** die bezüglich ihrer Gebietsaufteilung und ihrer traditionellen Symbole über die Generationen hinweg verbindlich geblieben sind
majarumba Schönheit und Gesundheit der Jugend, die dem Betrachter sofort ins Auge springt
malai freudige, respektvolle Begrüßung
malgara ein Feuer während der Kängurujagd, mit dem das Fell abgesengt und das frische Fleisch gegart wird. Große Zweige werden entzündet, und auf der entstehenden Glut brät man das Fleisch in einem flachen Erdofen
mallara eine weiße, nach Gardenien duftende Jasminart *(Gardenia spp.)*; grüner Busch, der bevorzugt an felsigen

Hängen und auf Bergkämmen in der Nähe der **wanjina**-Felsbilder gedeiht; grüne Blätter, die zum Zeichen, dass Besucher kommen, als Weihrauch bei ehrfürchtigen Gesängen verbrannt werden, bevor man sich den **wanjina** und den Quellen des **wungud** nähert
malu Bergkänguru
mamaa alles, was als heiliges oder geheimes Zeichen der Ahnen gilt; Warnung, die alles betrifft, was unberührbar oder verboten ist; kulturelle Verbindungen, die unter dem Schutz des Gesetzes stehen; Unverletzlichkeit von Orten, die Schauplatz wichtiger schöpferischer und historischer Ereignisse waren; Quellen spiritueller Kräfte von bestimmten Zeichen oder Kunstwerken oder Tieren mit einer totemistischen Verbindung zu den Ahnen
mamalan Fußspuren im Sand
mamandu klebriger Saft eines Maulbeerbaums, der Fixiermittel und rote Farbe für viele dauerhafte Felsmalereien der **Gwion** liefert
mambi dreieckiger Lendenschurz, den die Frauen auf den Felsbildern der **Gwion** tragen; zeremonieller Schurz, der von der Mutter auf die Tochter vererbt wird
mamul Grundform der heiligen Gegenstände, die als **wulari** und **maya.ngarri** zur Übermittlung von Wissen ausgetauscht werden
manbata gezackte weiße Seerose mit kleinen ovalen Blättern
mandi halbmondförmiger Bumerang; ein Paar, das aneinander geschlagen wird, gibt bei Gesängen den Rhythmus an
mandzu Gottesanbeterin *(mantis sp.)*, lebende Manifestation der Urmutter **Jillinya**
mangarri Nahrung und Teilen; Gemeinschaft stiftende Verpflichtung zu Gastfreundschaft und Respekt unter Verwandten
mangiwarunga die entscheidende erste Versammlung, mit der ein Ritual beginnt
Manirri Stammesland
maniwan die quastenförmigen, leuchtend orangefarbenen Blüten des **anggurun**-Baums
manjilarri von **Wibalma** geschaffener heiliger Gegenstand, den **Wodoi** und **Jungun** raubten, um ihn zu teilen; Quelle der Gerechtigkeit – es bedeutet so viel wie „ohne Hilfe fliehen, weil die erbarmungslose Kraft des Gesetzes einen verfolgt"
Maraja Stammesland
margi Vogelfamilie der Honigfresser, lebende Manifestation des **Margi-Kamali**-Clans
marguli heiliger Gesang
Marranba.bidi permanente Siedlung von mit den **Ngarinyin** verwandten Aborigine-Gruppen am King Edward River
marririn laubgrüner Rotflügelsittich *(Aprosmictus erythropterus)*, lebende Manifestation von **Marririn**, der verhinderte, dass das Krokodil **Ngerdu** das Feuer mit unter Wasser nahm und so dafür sorgte, dass alle es auf dem trockenen Land miteinander teilen können
maya.ngarri durch heilige Gegenstände übermittelte Botschaften; geheime oder private Formen geschnitzter und bemalter Hölzer, auf denen grundlegende kulturelle Vorstellungen überliefert sind; abstrakte Symbole des Gesetzes, die als **wulari** innerhalb des **Wunan**-Netzes im Umlauf sind; uralte kulturelle Gemeinsamkeit, die die Aborigines der tropischen Regionen im Norden mit den zentralaustralischen verbindet
menda Steinaxt
min min min min lautmalerischer Ausdruck für die Wellen, die sich auf der Wasseroberfläche bilden, wenn man den Schaft eines ins Wasser getauchten Speeres zwischen den Handflächen dreht
mob im Aborigine-Englisch Bezeichnung für eine Gruppe von Tierarten, Menschen, Bewohnern eines Verwaltungsbezirks oder eines **dambun**
modeden echte oder gemalte Tierfährten; Zeichen auf dem Pfad zum Ursprung eines Totems
modu anyi Fußspuren eines Tieres oder eines Menschen auf Wanderschaft
moiety ethnosoziologischer Begriff für jeweils eine Hälfte eines zweigeteilten sozialen Systems; Unterteilung einer Gesellschaft in zwei gleiche Hälften mit festen Heiratsregeln; in der Sprache der **Ngarinyin** die Grundlage der Terminologie für komplexe soziale Strukturen mit sprachlich geschiedenen symbolischen Assoziationen unter allen Aspekten der Natur und den beiden Hälften der menschlichen Gesellschaft
molu Mittlerstellung eines Clan-Anführers, wenn er als Bindeglied der Kette des **Wunan**-Austausches fungiert
molu bidingarri Autorität eines Clan-Anführers, wenn er **maya.ngarri** zwischen benachbarten **dambun** oder in weiter entfernte Regionen weitergibt
molu ijirinari Wächterfunktion der **munnumburra**, die für die Kontinuität des kulturellen Austausches auf den traditionellen Routen des **Wunan**-Systems sorgen
mondollo Gesichtsbemalung quer über die Stirn und um das Kinn
Morrongo Morrongo Land und Leute des **wamma-** bzw. Tabak-Clans, dem **Ungudman** von der **Jungun moiety** vorsteht
Mowaljarlai (David Mowaljarlai, 1997 verstorben), amtlicher Nachname von **Banggal**
mudurra Kopfschmuck oder modellierte Perücken in verschiedenen Formen und Größen, die in der Kunst der **Gwion** bis in die jüngste Vergangenheit zu sehen sind; eindeutiges grafisches Motiv, das die Verbindung zu anderen alten Kulturen von Australien und Papua erkennen lässt
mullawundin gespaltener Blitz, der dem **banman** magische Kräfte verleiht
Mul.ngirri Name eines Blitzgeists, der Blitzschläge mittlerer Stärke verursacht, denen unmittelbar ein Unwetter folgt; tritt gemeinsam mit **Jundiwan** auf
Mumuu heiliger Name für die Urmutter **Jillinya,** „ein großes Wort" in der Sprache der **Ngarinyin**
mun Phantasie
Munga.nunga Visionäre; Bezeichnung für die **Gwion**-Vorfahren, die als Schöpfer einer neuen Gesellschaftsordung und der **Wunan**-Gesetze gelten; Meister im Anfertigen von Steinwerkzeugen und Wissensvermittler
Munggundu wanjina, der mit der Entstehung der Erde aus dem Plasma in Verbindung gebracht wird; sein Bild wird in **Alyaguma** verehrt; assoziiert mit einem weichen Gummi aus dem Saft und Harz des „Blutbaums" (bloodwood)
munilla Körperbemalung am Oberkörper
Muni yalla leibliche Tochter des **Yemben wanjina**
Munja Küstensiedlung an der Collier Bay nördlich von Derby, ehemals eine Missionsstation, in der **Ngarinyin**-Flüchtlinge aus dem Inland zusammen mit den dort ansässigen **Wororra** angesiedelt wurden
munnumburra eine vollständig in die **Wunan**-Gesetze eingeweihte und darin bewanderte ältere Frau oder ein älterer Mann; Experten, die für die Durchführung von Ritualen und das Bewahren der **Wunan**-Gesetze verantwortlich sind
munya warnende Geste

nabun Lagerfeuer zum Kochen
Naiya zweite Phase eines Unwetters, weibliches Wesen und Frau im Gefolge der **Bundiwin,** der beiden Blitzbrüder
nambud burlwin Liedzeile, mit der die Tänzer aufgefordert werden zusammenzukommen
Nenowatt Familienname, der mit dem **Bararru.ngarri dambun** assoziiert wird; Hüter des **Walamba**-Heiligtums
Neowarra (**Paddy Neowarra,** Vorsitzender der **Ngarinyin** Aboriginal Corporation); amtlicher Name von **Nyawarra**
ngallad glitzernder, quarzartiger Stein, der sich besonders gut zur Herstellung von Speerspitzen eignet
ngangurr warra Junge, der vor der Beschneidung in der ersten Phase der Initiation, mit weißen **onmal**-Flecken bemalt wird, so dass er aussieht wie ein **wodoi** (Gefleckter Nachtfalke)
Ngarinyin Sprachfamilie mit „weichen" und „harten" Dialekten, den Überlieferungen nach erstmals von einem Mann aus dem Gleitbeutler-Clan gesprochen, der auf der **Jungun**-Seite **Andarri**, auf der **Wodoi**-Seite **Wad.munna** heißt
Ngarjno Stammesname von Laurie **Gawanali**, einem **Wodoi** aus dem **Brrejalnga dambun**, erfahrener Sänger und **munnumburra, ornad** im **moiety**-System, mit spirituellen Verbindungen **(gi)** zu **jalnga** (Wasserkastanie); Hüter des Bildes des Königsnatter-**wanjina**
ngawarra wanggi Bezeichnung für einen Jungen während der zweiten Phase der Initiation, bei der er zum ersten Mal eine **jirrgal** um die Stirn trägt. Die Körperbemalung aus zwei schwarzen Kreisen mit weißen Punkten um beide Schultern symbolisiert den Tanz der beiden **moieties** bei der **walu.ngarri**-Zeremonie. Die Farbe für die schwarzen Kreise ist eine Mischung aus schwarzer Holzkohle **(wulngon)** und Vogelfett **(wurd.ngun).** Die Farbe wird auf den vorab mit roter Farbe **(jimbri)** eingeriebenen Körper aufgetragen dann und mit einem Muster aus weißen Punkten **(onmal)** ausgefüllt
Ngegamorro wanjina derjenige, der in **Wurrumurru** verliebt war und eine Familie gründete, von der die Mitglieder der **Bangmorro**-Familie ihre Herkunft herleiten
ngerdu kleines Süßwasserkrokodil *(Crocodylus johnstoni)*, lebendes Zeugnis des **Ngerdu wanjina**, der versuchte, das Feuer für sich zu behalten und es mit unter Wasser zu nehmen
ngi.ornad der **Wodoi skin** oder **ornad moiety** zugehörig
ngolo ngolo walu.ngarri Liedzeile: „Komm, lass uns gehen"
ngoru der innere, heilige Atem des Lebens; eine dem Wasser innewohnende Kraft, die vom **Wanjina Gulingi** gespendet wird; Attribut der Macht der **maya.ngarri**
ngowrun „zum heiligen Atem gehörig" (siehe **ngoru**)
nguniri kostbare Schnur aus dem Haar der Ahnen, wie man sie auf den Bildern der **Gwion** sieht und wie sie heute von den **munnumburra** getragen werden, wenn sie **gulbrungi** singen, die magischen Lieder, die zum Ritual rufen und die Teilnahme aller verlangen
nimindi etwas, das allen gehört, zum Beispiel das Wissen
niyan.gawa alter, angeblich aus der weit entfernten Tanami-Wüste stammender Ausdruck unklarer Herkunft, Bestandteil der von den **Ngarinyin** erzählten Geschichte vom selbstsüchtigen **Jebera**, wenn dieser fragt „Wer, ich?" (siehe **Unggumi**)
Njumillibulli siehe **Algi**
nollabiallu Gruppen von Männern oder Frauen, die für den **walu.ngarri** bemalt sind und auf dem Weg zum Tanzplatz ihre Lieder singen
norgun flache, schüsselartige Vertiefung in einem Stein, in der **mamandu**-Rinde zerrieben wird, um rote Farbe zu gewinnen
Nudu.nudu Name eines **Kamali**-Clans
numanda aus dem Schlaf erwachen
numbila Ausdruck aus den Liedern, bezeichnet eine rasche Bewegung
nu meri sich konzentrieren, aufmerksam zuhören
numurangga Frau
nyamalar Grußformel
Nyamanbiligi die blinde Frau des **Wibalma**
nyamun-buna einen gegebenen Schwur halten; nicht gegen das Gesetz verstoßen, weil das Schwierigkeiten und Strafe nach sich ziehen würde; ruhig bleiben und Geheimnisse bewahren
nyarndu aus dem Stamm des Korkholzbaums oder der Flusskiefer *(Nauclea orientalis)* geschnittener, mit einem Haken versehener Stock, der als Speerschleuder dient; Vorbild für alle späteren Speerschleudern, die dem Speer so viel Schwung verleihen, dass er die dicke Haut von Emus oder Kängurus durchdringt; ein häufiges Motiv auf den Felsbildern der **Gwion**
nyarra rückbezügliches Pronomen
nyarrama Clanmitglieder, die sich bei einer **Wunan**-Versammlung beraten
Nyawarra Stammesname von **Paddy Neowarra,** von **Wodoi skin** des **Galeru.ngarri dambun;** Stammesältester und **munnumburra, ornad** im **moiety**-System, mit spirituellen Verbindungen **(gi)** unter anderem zu Regen, Fröschen und dem Roten Riesenkänguru **(Walamba)** als lebenden Manifestationen
nyawarra schwarze Basaltfelsen; die heilige **gi**-Verbindung von **Nyawarra** und sowie Ursprung seines Namens
nyirri gunduba zum Schlaf zusammengerollt
nyonor Frau der **ornad moiety (Wodoi skin),** verheiratet mit einem **amalar** der anderen Hälfte (siehe **nyamalar**)

Olgi Bezeichnung für die kleineren Blitze bei einem durchziehenden Gewitter; Name eines Jungen im Gefolge der **Naiya**
onmal weiße Farbe, hergestellt aus Kaolin und Pfeifenton
ornad moiety Name der **Wodoi skin**, *pl* **brrornad**
oru liwarad Ausdruck für die zum Horchen aufgerichteten Ohren eines Kängurus; Form bestimmter **mudurra**

Pijantjatjara Sprachgruppe der zentralaustralischen Wüste, südliche Nachbarn der **Arrernte** und **Anangu,** ebenfalls zum Geltungsbereich der **Wunan**-Gesetze gehörig, die in der Kimberley-Region ihren Ursprung haben

quoll Tüpfelbeutelmarder, australische „Katze", Beuteltier mit auffällig weißgeflecktem Fell

Romul siehe **Algi**

skin umgangssprachlicher Ausdruck für die spezifischen Gruppen des zweigeteilten **moiety-Systems**; eine dualistische Sozialstruktur, die den Bund zwischen **Wodoi** und **Jungun** durch Heiraten zwischen ihren Kindern widerspiegelt

Uluru gewaltiger roter Monolith in der zentralaustralischen Wüste, ein Naturwunder, das für die **Anangu** und andere Sprachgruppen, die durch die **Wunan**-Gesetze verbunden sind, symbolische Bedeutung hat
um.ralu gezahnte Steinklinge, die als Speerspitze Verwendung findet
Unggumi Sprache der Tanami-Wüste; mögliche Quelle des Ausdrucks **niyan.gawa,** der in der Erzählung der **Ngarinyin** über **Jebera** vorkommt
ungia Seerose mit hängenden Wurzeln
Ungudman Stammesname von **Paddy Wamma;** Angehöriger der **Jungun skin** aus **Morrongo Morrongo**; ausgezeichneter Naturkenner und **munnumburra** mit Beziehungen zur **amalar moiety;** spirituelle Verbindungen **(gi)** unter anderem zum Süßwasserkrokodil und zu **wamma,** der australischen Tabakpflanze, von der sich sein offizieller Name herleitet
urilimul Armbinde oder Gürtel

wadba einschäftiger Kampfspeer aus massivem Holz mit zwei Reihen von geschnitzten, in beide Richtungen weisenden Widerhaken, die dafür sorgen, dass er sich nur schwer wieder herausziehen lässt
wade Liedzeile: „und jetzt alle zusammen"
wad.munna der Name der **Wodoi** für den Gleitbeutler, der bei den **Jungun** als **andarri** bekannt ist
walamba Rotes Riesenkänguru *(Macropus antilopinus),* lebende Manifestation des **Walamba wanjina**, der seinen eigenen Körper aus den Überresten wieder zusammensetzte, nachdem Hunde ihn zerrissen hatten; sein ursprünglicher Name war **Binbin**, und er wiederholte diesen Vorgang durch acht Wiedergeburten und wechselte mehrfach den Namen, bis er schließlich **Wudmi.mulimuli** hieß
walbo gudina ein Ausdruck aus den sakralen Liedern, die bei den Beschneidungsritualen gesungen werden
walbud dreieckiger Lendenschurz aus Beuteltierleder, wie ihn die männlichen **Gwion** trugen
walgunu Fruchtbarkeitssteine, die **wungud** enthalten, die heilige Lebensessenz; eiförmige Steine, die sich den Überlieferungen nach in der Nacht vom Boden erheben und durch die Luft schweben

Wallagari Merrbini lange, geschwungene Lagune, die entstand, als **Walamba** seinen Bumerang **(banad)** auf den Boden schleuderte und sich, bemalt mit rotem Ocker, hinsetzte
Wallagunda die gesamte Milchstraße, ein Lichtgebilde, das der eigentliche Schöpfer der Erde ist
walmarro siehe **gundilli**
walu.di tiefer, permanenter Flusslauf oder Lagune
walu.ngarri Initiationsriten, darunter der Kreistanz der Männer und Frauen; öffentliches Ritual vor der Beschneidung mit Liedern, die von **Wiji.ngarri** komponiert und erstmals in **Wudmangu** gesungen wurden
waluwi Blauzungenechse, lebende Manifestation der **Waluwi,** eines weiblichen Ahnenwesens, das sich bei einer Überschwemmung für seine Kinder opferte
wamba nervös; Ausdruck der Besorgnis
wamma australischer Tabak, das Symbol des **Morrongo Morrongo dambun,** der Heimat von **Ungudman**
Wamma (Paddy Wamma); amtlicher Nachname von **Ungudman**
wandagi um den Bizeps getragene Armbinde, in der Regel ein breiter Streifen Känguruleder, der fest mit einer Kordel zusammengebunden und mit **onmal** angemalt wird; bei Ritualen kann auch mit einem Stück Schnur eine einzelne weiße Kaurimuschel daran befestigt sein
Wangalu Name eines alten Mannes mit **mudurra,** den **Nyawarra** in seiner Jugend beobachtete
wa.ngara lange Schnur- oder Lederschürze mit Quasten, die nur von Frauen getragen werden
wanggi Lebensphase von der Jugend bis zum heiratsfähigen Alter
wang.gura an der Torresstraße vorkommende Krähenart (Corvus orru) mit glänzend schwarzem Gefieder, heiserem Schrei und unerschrockenem Auftreten, als Aasfresser oft in der Nähe der Lager anzutreffen, lebende Manifestation des **Wang.gura;** Clanname der **Wororra,** der an der Küste ansässigen westlichen Nachbarn und Verwandten der **Ngarinyin,** die oft auch als „Sonnenuntergangs-Leute" tituliert werden
Wanjina abstrakte schöpferische Kraft; in ihr manifestiert sich das **wungud** (die Essenz allen Lebens, von der die Erde, das Wasser und der Himmel durchdrungen sind) als Wirken des höchsten Wesens, des **Wanjina Gulingi.** Eine Vielzahl von anderen, lokalen **wanjina** sind mit Tieren und Pflanzen assoziiert und verkörpern sakrale Ahnenwesen, die die Landschaft geformt haben
wanjina Quelle der Fruchtbarkeit und Erneuerung, an dem die schöpferischen Ahnenwesen als Basrelief oder farbiges Gemälde auf den Felsen konkret Gestalt angenommen haben; Bezeichnung für immer wieder neu gemalte sakrale Bilder auf weißem Grund mit charakteristischem strahlenförmigen Kranz um den Kopf und mundlosen Gesichtern
wanjina water people (wörtlich: **wanjina** Wassermenschen) lokale Bezeichnung für die Aborigine-Bevölkerung der Kimberley-Region, insbesondere die Sprachgruppen der **Ngarinyin, Wila Wila, Wororra** und **Wunambul**
warid wani mumal ein in warmer Asche erhitzter kleiner flacher Stein, der als Amboss dient, auf dem ein Speerschaft aus Bambus langsam erhitzt und gerade gebogen wird. Die Arbeit erfordert große Sorgfalt, denn durch zu starke Überhitzung wird der Bambus zu trocken, und er bricht, wenn man ihn in zu kaltem Zustand biegt. Die Temperatur des „Ambosses" wird genau kontrolliert, sodass er den Stab gleichmäßig erwärmt, bis der richtige Zeitpunkt zum Biegen erreicht ist. Dann wird der Speerschaft mit kräftigem Druck auf den „Amboss" gepresst und langsam gerade gebogen, wobei ein geschickter Speermacher viele kleine Unregelmäßigkeiten vorsichtig glätten kann
Wari.ngarri dambun Stammesgebiet
waringi de.de Liedzeile, die das Heranwachsen der Kinder mit den gelben Blüten eines Busches in Verbindung bringt
Warlpiri Sprachgruppe der zentralaustralischen Wüste, die zum Geltungsbereich des **Wunan-Gesetzes** gehört
Warmun Stammesgruppe östlich der Kimberley-Region, am Nordwestrand der Tanami-Wüste; Bezeichnung für die „Sonnenaufgangsleute", die zum Geltungsbereich des **Wunan-**Gesetzes gehören
warrana Keilschwanzadler *(Aquila audax),* ein großer Raubvogel, der Wallabies und Kängurus erlegt
warrngon siehe **windji jaman**
Wibalma zu den **Gwion** zählender Schöpfer von heiligen Gegenständen **(maya.ngarri),** der in **Gelngu** lebte und das heilige Wissen für sich behielt, bis **Wodoi** und **Jungun** auftauchten und die **maya.ngarri** an die Öffentlichkeit brachten
wiji.ngarri Tüpfelbeutelmarder (Dasyurus hallacatus), nachtaktiver Raubbeutler, der alle Arten von Reptilien, Ratten oder Insekten frisst, wobei ihm die weichen Ballen seiner Hinterfüße Halt auf dem glatten Sandstein geben, lebende Manifestation von **Wiji.ngarri,** dem Schöpfer der rituellen **walu.ngarri** (Kreistänze von Männern und Frauen, die der männlichen Beschneidung vorausgehen) Ahnenwesen, dessen Körper mit Wundmalen übersät war, die durch das weiß getupfte Fell des lebenden Tieres versinnbildlicht werden
Wila Wila in der Küstenregion lebende nördliche Nachbarn der **Ngarinyin,** dargestellt durch **jallala** (Gedenksteine) in **Dudu.ngarri**
wilmi spiralförmige Nebelschwaden, die über Bächen mit **wungud** schweben; sichtbares Zeugnis der Geister ungeborener Kinder, die im Wasser wohnen
windji jaman den menschlichen Körper salben und bemalen, im Zusammenhang mit einem Bild auch **warrngon**
Winjagin Monolithfelsen in der Savanne von **Morrongo Morrongo,** einer Region, die unter der Obhut von **Ungudman** steht
winjangun kleines Lagerfeuer
winjin heftiger Monsunregen, den der **Wanjina Gulingi** schickt und mit denen die von November bis Februar dauernde Regenzeit beginnt; die Zeit, in der die **guloi** reifen
winya Liedzeile, die die Entschlossenheit der Tänzer bei **Wunan-**Zeremonien ausdrückt
wir.nganyen zweite Phase des Initiationsrituals nach Abschluss des **walu.ngarri;** Folge von **Wunan-**Liedern, die die Initianden mit heiligen Tieren vertraut machen und an deren Ende die im Verborgenen vorgenommene Beschneidung steht
wodoi weit verbreiteter australischer Gefleckter Nachtfalke *(Eurostotodus argus)* mit auffälligen weißen Sprenkeln und einem leuchtend weißen Fleck auf den Flügeln; schläft tagsüber zwischen Blättern und Gras getarnt auf dem Boden und macht nachts im eleganten Flug Jagd auf Insekten, lebende Manifestation von **Wodoi,** einem der beiden wandernden **Gwion,** der zusammen mit **Jungun** die **Wunan-**Gesetze des Teilens von Land und Blut durch Heirat begründete; eine häufige Bezeichnung für jeden, der innerhalb des **moiety-**Systems zur **ornad moiety** zählt
Wodoi.ngarri dambun Stammesgebiet, benannt nach **Wodoi**
wongai gesetzeskundige alte Frau, vollständig initiiert in die Rituale und Lieder des **Wunan**
woomera im australischen Englisch gebräuchliche Bezeichnung für eine Speerschleuder (siehe **nyarndu**)
Wororra in der Küstenregion lebende westliche Nachbarn der **Ngarinyin**
worri-unbin Gesprächsfluss in der Unterhaltung; gesprochene Worte, die im Geltungsbereich des **Wunan** zirkulieren
Wo.wa Name eines **Kamali-**Clans
wowarra Gemeine Bronzeflügel-Taube *(Phaps chalcoptera),* lebende Manifestation von **Wowarra** und Bezeichnung für den **Kamali-**Clan, der wegen seiner schnellen Läufer gefeiert wird, weil zwei seiner Anführer **Jebera** verfolgten und hinrichteten, als dieser das **Wunan-**Gesetz gebrochen hatte
Wudjawudja.ngarri dambun Stammesgebiet
wudma - weibliches Flinkwallaby *(Macropus agilis).* Junge Kängurus, die noch in der Tasche einer **wudma** getragen werden, werden niemals gegessen – ein Verbot, das auf den **Gwion-**Jäger **Yandama** zurückgeht (siehe **gundilli**)
Wudmangu der Ort, an dem **Wiji.ngarri** die ursprünglichen Lieder für den **walu.ngarri** erschuf; ein von Bächen umflossener heiliger Ort, an dem der erste steinerne Sitz für den Sänger in der Mitte des Kreises der Tanzenden stand
Wudmi.mulimuli der letzte Name von **Walamba**
wudu im Kreis gehen
wuduwan siehe **mandi**
Wulamu frühe Clans der **Gwion,** die aus der Richtung des Sonnenaufgangs an den **Wunan-**Tisch kamen, Bewohner der Wüste jenseits des Horizonts im Osten der **Ngarinyin**
wulari heilige Gegenstände, die als **maya.ngarri** im Geltungsbereich des **Wunan** zirkulieren
wuludi tiefe, permanente Wasserlöcher, Flüsse und Teiche; grünliches Wasser, aus dem die Geister von Kindern als **wilmi** (Nebelschwaden) aufsteigen; heilige Wasserstellen, in denen sich das **wungud-**Lebenselixier der **wanjina** befindet
Wunambul Nachbarn der **Ngarinyin,** die sprachlich und geschichtlich eng mit ihnen verwandt sind
Wunan Gesetz des Teilens; uralte Übereinkünfte, mit denen durch die Festlegung der **dambun** (Stammesland), die Zeit des Nomadentums endete; Aufteilung der Gesellschaft und aller Lebewesen in zwei **moieties,** zwischen denen Ehen möglich sind, auf der Grundlage des Schwurs von **Wodoi** und **Jungun,** ihr Blut zu verbinden; System der binären Klassifizierung nach **brrornad** und **brramalar moiety** oder **skin,** wobei männliche **(ornad** und **amalar)** und weibliche **(nyonor** und **nyamalar)** Mitglieder ihre Ehepartner aus der jeweils anderen **moiety** wählen; Vorbild für eine Vielzahl von **moiety-**Einteilungen, die alles Lebendige in einem allumfassenden kulturellen Netzwerk verbinden; Aufbau und Muster des Landes
wunanbri weit verzweigte Routen des Austauschs von heiligen Gegenständen und Ritualen sowie rituellen Geschenken und Liedern
wunandi das **Wunan-**Gesetz in seiner praktischen Anwendung
wunan.gu das Zusammenrufen zum **Wunan**
wunbanburan unveränderliche ethische Grundätze im **Wunan-**Gesetz, ein Geschenk **(lulwa)** der **Munga.nunga;** die ethische Grundlage aller gesetzlichen Verpflichtungen
wungarun Eisenbaum mit besonders hartem Holz
wunginunna ein Wasserloch mit dunklem Wasser in der Milchstraße und auf der Erde
wungud Energie oder Lebensessenz; ursprüngliche Lebenskraft, die allen Formen des von **wanjina** geschaffenen Lebens innewohnt; Lebenskraft im Wasser, die allen Dingen Struktur und Gestalt verleiht, vom Einzeller bis zum Menschen; jede Art von physischer oder spiritueller Essenz, die Menschen beeinflusst oder Leben fördert, reflektiert, erhält und motiviert; Spuren des Wirkens verschiedener **wanjina;** selbst schwache Spuren von **Gwion-**Malereien gelten als reich an Lebensessenz und können ebenfalls **wungud** genannt werden
wungurrurun mamandu Steinpalette (siehe **norgun**)
wunindid traditionelles Gesetz der Ahnen, als **wunanbri**
wunindid naga ein Gesetz auf dem Weg durch das **Wunan**
wunindid naga der nachhaltige Einfluss des **Wunan** durch alle Zeitalter
wura.wura Schuppenbrusttaube *(Petrophassa smithi),* die mit ihren gelb umrandeten Augen gut getarnt im schattigen Unterholz der grasbewachsenen Waldgebiete der nördlichen Kimberley-Region lebt
wurd.ngun Körperfett von Vögeln, dient zur Pflege und Konservierung von hölzernen Utensilien und Waffen
Wurrumalu leiblicher Sohn des Wasserwaran **Yemben wanjina**
Wurrumurru Schlangenhalsschildkrötenahnin, in die sich der **Ngegamorro wanjina** verliebte

yalmalnyu malngud verbotene Umgebung in der Nähe eines heiligen Ortes, die für Mensch und Tier gefährlich werden kann, meist Treibsand oder Sumpf. Ein solcher Ort ist durchdrungen von einer tödlichen Macht und gilt als **mamaa** (geheim). Wo bei der Schöpfung des Gesetzes Tiere ihr Leben lassen mussten, entstanden heilige Orte mit guten Kräften in unmittelbarer Nachbarschaft zu gefährlichen. Als Folge der ursprünglichen Ereignisse, die am Anfang jedes Gesetzes standen, bleiben auch Wasserstellen und charakteristische Merkmale des Landes als Belege **(junjun)** für das Wirken der Ahnen zurück
yalungarri andere Bezeichnung für weiße Farbpigmente (siehe **onmal**)
yamalad minia Grußformel für einzelne Personen, wörtlich übersetzt „ich sehe deine glänzende Stirn"
Yandama berühmter Jäger, dessen Bild den Gebrauch der Speerschleuder **(nyarndu)** zeigt; dargestellt mit drei statt mit fünf Fingern zum Zeichen der uralten Verbindung zwischen Vögeln und Menschen; **Gwion-**Held, der als Erster ein **gundilli** (Wallaby) in einem Erdofen briet und damit eine Reihe von heiligen Stätten schuf, die mit dem Heiligtum von **Alyaguma** verbunden sind
yangudi junge Mädchen mit sich entwickelnden Brüsten
yara Gemeines Wallaroo *(Macropus robustus)* oder graues Bergkänguru, verbunden mit einem Gesetz, das an einem Erdofen in der Nähe von **Binjirri** seinen Ursprung hat, wo der Ahne **Yara** von wilden Hundemenschen gefressen wurde; die Regeln für das Töten von Kängurus und das damit verbundene Lied breiteten sich nach Süden und Osten und schließlich bis nach Zentralaustralien aus
yarrad die Gebeine der Verstorbenen werden ein gutes Jahr lang unter schützenden Steinen verwahrt, bis die Ameisen und das Wetter die Knochen gereinigt haben. Die Hinterbliebenen müssen warten, bis alle Reste von Sehnen verschwunden und die Knochen gebleicht sind; erst dann werden die Gebeine zur letzten Ruhe in einer Höhle vorbereitet. Jeder Knochen wird sorgfältig gewaschen und gereinigt, dann mit **wurd.ngun** (Vogelfett) eingerieben und schließlich mit **gagul** (roter Farbe) bemalt
yemben grauer Wasserwaran, lebende Manifestation des **Yemben wanjina,** des leiblichen Sohns von **Ngegamorro**
yidmunggul Mantel oder an den Schultern getragene Epauletten aus Emuleder; charakteristisches Motiv in der Malerei der **Gwion**
Yirrbal Adoptivsohn des **Ngegamorro wanjina,** de facto Bruder des **Yemben**
Yowinjella Kamali-Clan, der auf den Spornkuckuck zurückgeht
Yullanmaiya alter Mann, den **Nyawarra** mit einer **mudurra** gesehen hatte (siehe **Laundi**)
yululun Schmuck oder Emblem aus Federn oder Vogelflügeln, die zu rituellen Zwecken getragen wird
yungulli Seerose aus der Lotos-Familie
yururu.mal Halsschmuck aus Federn und Schnur

GLOSSAIRE

agula esprit dangereux et fantômatique
Algi une des matriarches originelles peinte à **Alyaguma,** où elle reçoit comme tribut de nombreuses lances qui couvrent son corps incliné
alnguru manche de lance en bambou
Alyaguma point d'eau sacré en dessous d'une cascade qui possède une paroi aux peintures vénérées, comprenant l'image de **guloi** (prunier sauvage) ; lieu où le chasseur **Gwion Yandama** s'est reposé lorsque son genou a faibli et ne lui a plus obéi
amalad minia salut respectueux ou plus familier tel que, par exemple, « je vois ton front brillant »
amalar membre de la **moitié Jungun** et nom de **skin** pour la flore et la faune qui y sont associées ; pluriel : **brramalar**
ambalaru empreintes de pas ou traces sur le chemin ancestral
ambiliji voir **maba**
amurangga homme
Anaut.ngarri territoire et peuple associés au vent dont le nom a été donné d'aprés **Jillinya**
andarri opossum à la queue annelée, preuve vivante de l'ancêtre **Andarri** qui parla le premier la langue **Ngarinyin**
angga récipient en écorce ou surface plane comme par exemple la table en pierre **Wunan**
anggurun eucalyptus au tronc velouté *(Eucalyptus miniata)*, espèce dominante des arbres de la savanne du nord du Kimberley aux **maniwan** (fleurs de couleur orange vif) qui donnent un excellent miel
anjum lotus ou nénuphar à grande feuille
arawari dessiner ou tracer un plan sur le sol avec un doigt
argad faucon brun *(Falco berigora)*, preuve vivante des deux frères **Gwion** appelés **Argad** qui sont responsables de la transformation des humains en oiseaux
Arnhem Land partie du continent australien à l'ouest du golfe de Carpentarie ; région où de nombreux groupes de langues indigènes conservent des aspects des lois **Wunan**
Arrernte langue d'un groupe du désert central australien lié au Kimberley par les routes d'échanges culturels **Wunan**
arri humains
arririn voir **gundilli**
arru anguille d'eau douce, un des cinq animaux aquatiques sacrés du **wanjina Gulingi,** preuve vivante du **wanjina Arru** qui est représenté dans une peinture à **Alyaguma**

Badjayei expression d'un chant sacré
balbrangi balbri composition vocale ancienne pour convoquer la réunion des clans pour le conseil de la Loi ; interpétée en portant une **nguniri** (ceinture ancestrale en cheveux tressés) qui a la fonction d' obliger les personnes qui se trouvent au loin à venir près du chanteur
Balgo lieu situé à la bordure ouest du désert de Tanami ; emplacement de plusieurs groupes liguistiques
Balmirriya voir **Walamba**
banad outarde ou « dindon du bush » *(Ardeotis australis)* ; tout boomerang en bois dur coudé ou en forme de 7, qui de profil est semblable au cou et à la tete dressée de l'oiseau ; boomerang à bec porté aujourd'hui pendant les dances comme symbole des temps ancestraux
banbangi voir **balbrangi balbri** et **gulbrungi**
Banggal David **Mowaljarlai,** aujourd'hui décédé ; il était de peau **Wodoi** et du **Brejirad dambun ;** traducteur et éditeur d'ouvrages éducatifs; **munnumburra** de moitié **ornad ;** avait des **gi** (liens spirituels) avec le jirad (hibiscus indigène) et l'oiseau **Gwion Gwion**
Bangmorro famille dont les membres établissent leur généalogie jusqu'au **Ngegamorro wanjina**
banman expert qui interprète les rêves ; mystique ou sorcier connaissant les secrets liés à la foudre ; médecin ou qui a des connaissances en médecine
baobab arbre *(Adansonia gregorii)* fournissant des fibres transformées en ficelle ou corde à tout faire, les premiers chasseurs **Gwion** s'en servaient pour fabriquer des pièges en filets
bararu.ru endroit où ont lieu des cérémonies rituelles, terrain de danse
bare vagin ; l'héritage que **Jillinya** a laissé à toutes les femmes
Barilamma emplacement dans le récif fossilisé de Napier Range où le fugitif **Jebera** s'est reposé et a été immortalisé dans une grande peinture sous la forme d'un émeu stockant des **golani**
Barraru.ngarri région et clan dont le nom a été donné à la suite de cérémonies de pacification englobant le **Walamba wanjina** et intimement liées au **Galeru.ngarri dambun**
barrij paraître, se lever et devenir actif
belnged cacatoès à la crête vaporeuse et brillante, preuve vivante du clan **Belnged Kamali**
Bimbidora lieu sacré où **Yandama** tua un **gundilli** (wallaby) et le cuisit dans un four en pierre entouré d'un cercle de **jallala** (pierres dressées) , un emplacement du pouvoir des **yalmalnyu malngud**
Binbin première incarnation de **Walamba** (ancêtre kangourou de couleur rouge) qui est apparu pour la première fois avec un corps blanc albinos prés de **Guringi**
binja winja cauri blanc souvent porté comme décoration pour donner plus d'éclat à un costume que l'on met au centre d'une ceinture attachée à une **mudurra ;** avec la « pearl shell » (coquille d'un mollusque de la famille des Ficidae) c'est un objet important dans les échanges **Wunan** dans le centre du continent
Binjiraregu endroit sacré sur la côte nord-ouest reliant les emplacements de l'origine des lois **Wunan** et de **Jillinya ;** lieu où **Walamba** participa à la **walu.ngarri** (cérémonie)
Binjirri une destination pour **Walamba** comme ci-dessus
birrawudi procession rituelle lorsque les garçons attendant leur initiation sont portés sur le dos des hommes. Cette étape importante de la cérémonie **walu.ngarri** a lieu normalement l'après-midi du second jour juste avant le coucher du soleil. Toute l'après-midi, des hommes et des femmes en file indienne dansent autour du siège en pierre où les chanteurs sont assis. Ces **munnumburra** chantent jour et nuit, toujours au centre, pendant qu'ils dirigent le déroulement de la **walu.ngarri.** Les garçons s'assoient sur le sol à côté du siège du chanteur avec leurs « tantes » – des parentes proches de la **moitié** opposée. L'intensité des chants et des danses a un profond effet sur les jeunes. Quand la journée finale touche à sa fin, tous les hommes de l'autre **moitié** et de **skin** opposée aux garçons forment un long rang et les garçons sont placés sur le dos de leurs « oncles ». Les garçons sont portés en étant tournés vers l'arrière. Ces danses **birrawudi** commencent lorque les hommes tapent du pied pour que le sol tremble et qu'ils marchent en ligne tout en faisant le bruit sourd **dududu** plus bruyamment que les émeus. Chaque initié **ngawarra wanggi** est porté sur les épaules de ceux qui l'ont dirigé dans la procession rituelle de la **birrawudi.**
birrina « être ensemble », danse qui rapproche hommes et femmes dans une cérémonie non secrète
Biyad.ngerri un titre ancestral de **Walamba** pendant des étapes de sa réincarnation le long de son **dulwan** (chemin)
biyu échelle ou échafaudage
borror oiseau nocturne (de la famille des Podargidae) , preuve vivante du clan **Borror Kamali**
brad premier rayon apparaissant lorsqu'une bande orange s'étire à l'horizon avant l'aube ; moment de la circoncision ; direction vers laquelle on oriente le crâne des morts
breb-brenya chant ordonnant à tout le monde de se lever et de commencer le **walu.ngarri**
brilgi incisions cicatricielles ; arrangements de fines marques sur la peau qui sont des emblèmes de l'anguille, de la tortue, du poisson, du goanna d'eau et du crocodile qui ont comme origine les **wanjina** de ces cinq animaux sacrés aquatiques ; marques qui distinguent les hommes et les femmes **munnumburra** qui sont complètement initiés aprés des rencontres rituelles où l'animal vivant est placé sur le corps ; preuve permanente de la participation à des rituels avec les animaux vivants pendant lesquels des chants **mamaa** (sacrés) qui sont uniquement secrets à ces rituels privés sont chantés en présence de la personne que l'on scarifie, ces chants ont un pouvoir qui pénétre entre dans le **briyal** (bras) de la personne et ceux-ci marquent également la durée de la cérémonie
briyal bras humain et mesure dérivée de celui-ci
brramalar pluriel d'**amalar**
Brrejalnga désigne le pays et le peuple du clan des marrons d'eau ; région sous la garde de **Ngarjno**
Brrejirad désigne le pays et le peuple du clan hibiscus dont le territoire est contigu à la partie nord de la rivière Prince Regent ; terre ancestrale de **Banggal**
brrornad pluriel d'**ornad**
Brrunjini lieu sacré où les lois du partage de la viande ont débuté ; associé à l'ancêtre kangourou gris **Yara,** indiqué par un four en pierre et une haute **jallala** (pierre levée)
Bunaba groupe lingistique jouxtant le Kimberley
Bundiwin paire de divinités masculines foudre appelés **Jundiwan** et **Mul.ngirri**
bunja surplomb en pierre ou abri ayant des peintures
bunja mamaa sanctuaire secret ou emplacement secret où l'on garde les **maya.ngarri**
bunji toute forme de crochet ou de picot présent sur n'importe quel objet, comme par exemple l'extrémité d'un **nyarndu** (propulseur) ; pointe en bois taillée pour rentrer dans l'extrémité creuse d'un manche de lance avant l'utilisation d'un propulseur tel qu'un **woomera**
bunun.guli chant pour être libéré d'un rituel de sang ; stade où les initiés sont libres de voyager à nouveau entre les **dambun**
buren membres de clan quittant un site **Wunan**
Burrin.burrin oiseau arc-en-ciel *(Merops ornatus)*
burroi faucon brun ayant une marque sur le cou, preuve vivante du clan **Burroi Kamali**
burrunba grande grue fouisseuse d'Australie *(Grus rubicundus)* appelée brolga ou **garanguli**
coolamon terme familier pour désigner un plat peu profond ou un récipient concave en bois léger
corroboree terme familier pour désigner une cérémonie indigène

dadall fringillidé à longue queue, preuve vivante du clan **Dadall Kamali**
dal.gnana palmier en forme d'éventail *(Livistona eastonii)*, récolté pour obtenir une farine faite de l'amidon tiré de la tige jeune du coeur des jeunes palmiers
dambun régions claniques attribués par le premier conseil **Kamali** lorsque la loi a été créée à **Dududu.ngarri ;** type de droits sur le territoire hérité par les **Ngarinyin** déterminant le réseau d'échange avec les voisins
darrawani petit doigt ; empreinte de pas ; la nature durable des peintures indélébiles **Gwion** comme marques profondes dans le grès
degulan lézard à collerette, preuve vivante de l'ancêtre **Degulan** qui a suivi la pratique rituelle de **Wiji.ngarri** à **Wudmangu** en interprétant une **walu.ngarri** près de **Winjagin** et à d'autres endroits élargissant ainsi la répartition des chants **Wunan**
didiyii expression d'adieu et de fin de cérémonie; les pleurs de tous les participants des deux sexes à la fin du **wir.nganyen**
dindiwal faucon pélerin, preuve vivante du clan **Gwion Dindiwal**
dinjid petit arbre qui est source d'approvisionnement de bâtons à fouir ; reniflement constant lorsque le nez coule ; symptômes grippaux ; punition pour les vandales de la preuve vivante du **Dinjid wanjina**
dududu bruit de battement de pieds d' émeus ou son que produisent les pieds d'un danseur
Dududu.ngarri trouée profonde dans le paysage faite par trois hommes du clan Émeu lorsqu'ils ont pris la fuite de la table de pierre **Wunan ;** nom général du lieu dans le **dambun** de **Guru.ngongo** où les **Gwion** ont cessé d'être nomades
Duduk.ngunga emplacement d'un nouveau siège en pierre pour les chanteurs indiquant le terrain de la danse circulaire d'une **walu.ngarri** qui s'est tenue à **Marranba.bidi** en 1995
dudu-narawi terrain cérémoniel, littéralement où les danseurs tapent du pied en faisant du bruit
dulwan chemin créé par les ancêtres ; une direction morale ; marcher dans le bush
dulwan mamaa chemins sacrés de la preuve secrète répandus dans tout le pays
dulwan nimindi chemins de la connaissance et déroulement des idées à travers une éducation continue
duma voir **waluwi**
dumbi chouette masquée faisant son nid dans des cavernes ou des arbres qu'on voit souvent se nourrir de rongeurs et d'insectes sur les étendues d'herbe, preuve vivante du clan **Dumbi Kamali**
durran cacatoès noir à queue rouge (Calyptorhynchus banksii), preuve vivante du clan **Durran Kamali**

emmalen fantôme d'un individu ; esprit n'obéissant pas à une règle

gaama galerie dans la rive d'une rivière utilisée comme terrier par les tortues et les crocodiles
gadiya mot en créole-anglais pour désigner une personne non-indigène d'Australie
gagul pigment rouge ou peinture ocre rouge, voir **jimbri**
galambi grande aigrette *(Ardea alba)*, gros héron blanc
Galeru.ngarri désigne le territoire et les membres du clan septentrional de la pluie sous la garde de **Nyawarra**
gallid toute lance en bois à picots ou dents multiples ; harpon de pêche ayant cinq séries de picots parallèles qui, entortillés entre des feuilles de palmier font des rides dans l'eau attirant le poisson vers la lance jusqu'à ce qu'il puisse être attrapé par les picots lorsque l'on tire la lance brusquement
galuman bambou utilisé dans la fabrication des manches de lance
galwa espèce non identifiée de buisson à fleurs jaunes
galwadi résine maléable que l'on remue jusqu'à ce qu'elle ait la consistance de l'argile et qu'on utilise pour donner forme et modeler une **mudurra**
galwal voir **nguniri**
gambul voir **julwungi**
Gananinjal lieu situé au sud de **Warmun** là où l'égoïste et fugitif **Jebera** a été exécuté
gandad couteau en pierre
gangan paire de claves servant à imprimer le rythme
ganjal faucon noir de couleur brun foncé *(Milvus migrans),* preuve vivante du clan **Ganjal Kamali**
ganmangu long igname bulbeux ; variété d'igname cultivée dans les jardins entourés de murs de pierres
garabri voir **mandi**
garagi sac à tout transporter ; seau en écorce de paperbark ou en peau d'animal
garan.garan oiseau d'eau plongeur ; foulque eurasien ; preuve vivante du clan **Garan.garan Kamali**
garramarra eau de mer

Gawanali nom de famille public de **Ngarjno**
Gelngu région où **Wodoi** et **Jungun** sont allés à l'atelier de **Wibalma**
gerd peau en dessous du pénis ; prépuce avant la circoncision
gi liens spirituels personnels entre les humains, la terre et les **wanjina**
gimbu pierre brun-rougeâtre ; matière première pour la fabrication des pointes de lance les plus tranchantes inventées par les **Gwion ;** scalpel pour la circoncision et l'incision
gingu manche à l'extrémité creuse d'une lance faite en bambou australien
goanna terme familier pour désigner certaines espèces de lézards moniteurs et de scinques
golani petite baie sombre *(Vitex glabrata)* ; nourriture rituelle qui se présente sous la forme d'une tranche de baies écrasées et cuites ; la comparaison de la taille et de la couleur semblables de la baie et de la pupille de l'œil ; métaphore visuelle du **Wunan ;** baie tombée de l'arbre, excellente comme appât à émeu ; constellation de la forme d'un émeu foncé dans la Voie lactée en dessous de la Croix du Sud représentant **Jebera** courbé avec une lance dans la colonne vertébrale ; source céleste de toute eau sur la terre venue du ciel
golani muna plat fait en écorce fibreuse
goro.goro kookaburra à ailes bleues ; preuve vivante du clan **Goro.goro Kamali**
gorrodoo passereau blanc et noir (Grallina cyanolenca), preuve vivante du clan **Gorrodoo Kamali,** également **gri gri**
Gubu.ngarri territoire de l'ancêtre serpent brun roi qui a laissé des matières fécales fossilisées utilisées comme **onmal** (peinture blanche)
gudmerrermeri modulation du chant lorsqu'il faut se prendre la main les uns les autres et se mettre en file avant de se diriger vers une danse **birrawudi**
gulbrungi chant le plus sacré interprété uniquement par les hommes portant une **nguniri** (cordelette ancestrale en cheveux) autour du cou ; un ordre télépathique à des gens éloignés qui les obligent à venir à l'endroit où le chanteur se tient
guli sang
Gulilli redoutable femelle **wanjina** des termites résidant dans le profond bassin d'eau d'une gorge
gulin donner naissance à des enfants ou engendrer sa descendance
Gulingi premier créateur de toute vie et la force vitale animant le cosmos ; celui qui apporte la pluie avec de la foudre ; force influente pour la fertilité et la dispersion du **wungud** (l'essence de vie) dans l'eau ; **wanjina** de classe supérieure ayant la forme d'un serpent
Guli.ngulindi voir **malarrin**
guli wodoi ocre rouge fin sang de l'ancêtre **wodoi**
guliwud propulseur gravé ayant une pointe en forme de **burin** triangulaire fixé par de la résine à l'autre extrémité du picot et qui peut s'adapter au manche de la lance ; **woomera** sculpté dans du bois dur comme par exemple du bois de fer de forme lenticulaire
guloi prune verte sucrée *(Terminalia carpentariae)* ; nourriture très appréciée étant le thème de chants de récolte pendant la saison humide ; symbole de naissance et de régénération vénéré dans de nombreuses peintures rupestres (par exemple l'image peinte à **Alyaguma**) comme symbole visuel de l'éducation et de la permanence de la culture
gulowa belle-sœur
gulowada chants profanes sur la société et l'amour
gulug tunnel ou cavité dans un banc de sable
gumaa résine végétale ou gomme
gumba.lawal pigeon de roches au plumage blanc *(Petrophassa albipennis)* qui fait partie des rares espèces indigènes du Kimberley faisant leur nid sur les rebords des gorges rocheuses et coteaux ; ancêtre probable des pigeons du monde entier ; preuve vivante du clan **Gumba.lawal Kamali,** oiseau qui garde encore son nom **Wunan**
gumbaru ocre jaune ou pigment de l'oxyde de fer ; résidu des excrétions fossilisées d'une grenouille
gunan bâton en bois sec utilisé pour faire du feu par friction
gundilli petit wallaby de rivière *(Macropus agilis)* connu dans la loi comme le premier wallaby chassé avec un **nyarndu** (propulseur) et qui a été cuit dans un four en pierre par le héros **Gwion Yandama** (comme il est commémoré dans une peinture à **Alyaguma**)
guranguli voir **burrunba**
gurin lame en pierre denticulée
Guringi sanctuaire de **Jillinya** sur la côte nord-ouest
guriwin sève médicinale tirée d'un eucalyptus à sève rouge
Guroni ancêtre matriarche kangourou ; femme de **Walamba** représentée par une montagne de forme conique, lieu permanent de son **wungud**
Guru.amalad minia salutation à un grand groupe ou à l'humanité dans son ensemble
Guru.ngongo dambun territoire
Gwion utilisé ici comme terme général pour désigner les ancêtres artistes des **Ngarinyin**, connus comme les « inventeurs » (pour reconnaitre l'introduction des **nyarndu** et des outils en pierre comme par exemple les tranchantes pointes de lances **gimbu**) ; un autre titre pour les **Jenagi Jenagi** et les **Munga.nunga**
Gwion Gwion désigne originellement le mystérieux « oiseau des cavernes » qui utilisa son bec pour étaler du sang sur la paroi d'une pierre et ainsi est à l'origine de la peinture ; nom sacré qui quand il est répété imite le bruit de l'appel de l'oiseau, mais si cela est fait par ignorance en dehors du contexte sacré, cela peut provoquer la colère ancestrale
Gwion Gwion titre formel pour désigner les artistes humains auteurs des peintures rupestres, le premier groupe nomade qui s'est dispersé dans une terre sans frontières et qui a débuté la loi **Wunan**

jaawa coucou à longue queue ou oiseau de pluie, preuve vivante de l'ancêtre femelle **Jaawa** qui punit les enfants qui saccagent les nids d'oiseaux contenant des œufs
Jadgud.gude un des titres qui désignent les réincarnations de l'ancêtre kangourou roux **Walamba**
jalba sac à lanière en corde ou en peau d'animal
Jalbanuma montagne apparue à l'endroit où **Jebera** a laissé tomber son sac pendant qu'il s'enfuyait aprés avoir volé le **golani** à la table de la Loi
jalgud variété d'igname
jalgun petite jupe en peau ou en fibres portée par les femmes, courte tournure en plumes d'émeu portée par les femmes dans la **walu.ngarri** (danse circulaire)
jalim.baran baguette de danse ou bâton à la pointe ornée de plumes
jaljalbi courir en portant des choses dans un sac
jalla algue de couleur verte vive qu'on trouve dans l'eau fraîche, utilisée comme encens pour stimuler l'imagination d'un nouveau-né ; preuve de la circulation de l'eau vers une plus haute atmosphère du **wungud** (essence de la vie) du **Wanjina Gulingi ;** également un signe du cycle de l'énergie créative présente dans l'eau et la pluie
jallala pierres dressées comme signe d'avertissement indiquant un endroit sacré ; alignement de pierres marquant et délimitant les lieux d'événements historiques
Jalmi voir **Algi**
jalnga marron d'eau ; légume poussant dans les zones humides et aux bords des rivières
jarrgun petit tubercule plat
jebera émeu commun qui ne peut voler *(Dromaius novaehollandiae)* connu pour sa voix retentissante et ses battements de pieds; preuve vivante du clan **Jebera**
Jebera ancêtre du clan Émeu du désert de Tanami qui a volé au conseil **Kamali** et qui a été exécuté pour avoir enfreint la loi du partage du **Wunan**
jegabi image de forme humaine
Jenagi Jenagi un autre nom pour désigner les artistes **Gwion ;** littéralement « les vagabonds » ou nomades qui devinrent les messagers de la Loi ; « messagers » qui ont commencé l'échange des **maya.ngarri** sacrés
Jillinya la Grande Mère de tous, également connue sous le nom de **Mumuu ;** mère de tous les **Gwion** et qui a donné les légumes aux humains ; matriarche primordiale qui a donné aux femmes leurs organes génitaux et le pouvoir d'enfanter; « grande femme de la Loi » originaire de **Guringi** associée à **mandzu** (mante religieuse) et à l'esprit de la puissance du vent
jimbila pointe de lance en quartz de type courant
jimbri pigment rouge d'origine minérale utilisé pour peindre
jirad hibiscus australien; symbole du **dambun** de **Banggal**, d'où le nom de la région **Brrejirad**
jirrgal cordelette en fibre végétale utilisée pour tresser des sacs et attacher les **mudurra** (coiffes)
jowul baguettes aiguisées ou bâtons en bois; manches de lance taillés dans un jeune arbre; fines baguettes de bois utilisées pour faire couler du sang pendant la danse circulaire détournant l'attention des jeunes initiés avant le choc imminent de leur circoncision
jugarrun ficeler quelque chose
juiban l'espèce du nord-ouest du passereau *(chlamydera nachialis)*, voisin des oiseaux de paradis
julai voir **julungi**
julungi long tendon de kangourou
julwungi tendon de queue de kangourou nettoyée et séchée pour faire une courroie utilisée comme corde (par exemple pour fixer les pointes de lance aux manches)
Jumbowulla matriarche, voir **Algi**
jumubumuru brème noire d'eau douce, preuve vivante du **wanjina Jumubumuru ;** un des cinq **wanjina** à l'origine de la création des humains dans l'eau
junba chants et récits dansés qui suivent les visions des compositeurs ; représentations théatrales contemporaines combinées à de la musique accoustique et électrique
jun.bii tibia de kangourou ou d'humain
Jundiwan une des forces couplées qui provoque un orage, révérées ensemble comme étant la divinité éclair **Bundiwin**
jungi fourmilière ou termitière de formes et couleurs diverses suivant la nature du sol ; terrain sacré protégé par l'esprit femme **Gulilli ;** terre colorée réduite en poudre par les termites et utilisée comme médicament intestinal par les femmes
jungun engoulevent australien *(Aegotheles cristatus)*, petit prédateur nocturne qui passe son temps à bondir sur les insectes dans les branches basses; il a une petite tête de hibou avec de grands yeux cerclés de noir pouvant leurrer parfaitement par sa ressemblance avec un opossum quand il dort le jour dans le creux des arbres ; preuve vivante de **Jungun,** un des deux héros **Gwion** qui, avec **Wodoi** était à l'origine du **Wunan ;** nom commun pour désigner le côté **amalar** des deux groupes de **moitié** liés à la flore et la faune locales
junjun désigne toutes les preuves du **Wunan** dans le monde naturel et l'humanité ; marques laissées par les ancêtres dans le paysage et l'art qui ont un sens dans la société **Ngarinyin ;** preuve de l'histoire du **Wunan** dans de nombreuses peintures sur roche, coupoles, sillons pour aiguiser les lances et dans les marques laissées par le façonnage par usure des outils dans les abris sous roches ; vastes alignements de pierres qui forment des dessins narratifs dans le paysage et se répandent d'un bout à l'autre du pays; langage ancestral dans les chants composé de mots archaïques utilisé comme héritage musical uniquement par les **munnumburra** complètement initiés
jurull oiseau, preuve vivante du clan **Jurull Kamali**
juruma poudre à usage médical aussi fine que du talc obtenue de l'écorce fibreuse de l'arbre à liège de marécage à fleur blanche *(Sesbania formosa)*; coagulant préparé à l'avance pour cicatriser les plaies de circoncision ou d'initiation

Kamali groupe des **Gwion** initiateurs de la Loi qui se sont rassemblés autour de la table de pierre à **Dududu.ngarri ;** disposition des pierres autour de la table symbolisant un cercle des clans dont les noms viennent d'oiseaux et qui ont cessé d'être nomades et ont choisi des noms de **dambun** aprés la réunion sur la loi des **Wunan ;** premiers héritiers et proclamateurs des noms des **dambun** de la zone centrale. Ils sont actuellement représentés par le **Kamali Land Council** qui a des bureaux à Derby sous la présidence de **Paddy Neowarra**
kane-kane regarder vers le bas
karabri voir **mandi**
Kunmunya emplacement d'une ancienne mission sur la côte
Kuri Kuri titre ancestral

Laajmorro nom du **wanjina** à un bras représenté dans la Voie lactée
Laundi titre ancestral pour désigner un vieil homme portant une **mudurra** complète comme **Nyawarra** en a vu à la fin des années 1940
lulwa tout cadeau, grand ou petit, qui peut aller de présentations rituelles aux parents en deuil à un jouet pour un bébé ; un tribut d'objets sacrés offerts aux ancêtres célébrant la générosité dans le **Wunan**
lulwa wunandi présentation rituelle de cadeaux pendant les réunions **Wunan** et offrandes aux matriarches et aux **wanjina**
Luma frange désertique au sud du plateau du Kimberley où des groupes indigènes sont liés aux **Wunan**
lung.gudengari voir **banad**

maba un vieil homme vénéré, libéré de toute responsabilité supplémentaire dans les affaires **Wunan** quand les symptômes de cécité surviennent
mabajiri un titre plus formel de respect pour **maba**
Mabo expression familière récente pour parler des droits du Native Title australien se référant à une décision de la Haute Court d'Australie qui a fait date en reconnaissant les droits fonciers indigènes d'Eddie Mabo sur son île du détroit de Torres. Ce cas remit en cause le statut de *terra nullius* (« terre inhabitée » en droit romain) en vigueur pendant deux siècles et maintenue par les autorités coloniales, ouvrant ainsi la voie à de futures revendications de titres fonciers sur le continent. Cela inclut les revendications en instance de l'organisation représentant les auteurs : le **Kamali Land Council.** Appelé ainsi d'après les premiers **Gwion** initiateurs des lois autour de la table de pierre à **Dududu.ngarri,** la revendication en cours suit les frontières traditionnelles des régions des **dambun Gwion** avec ses titres héréditaires et ses symboles
majarumba la beauté qui capte notre regard et qui a l'allant stimulant de la jeunesse
malai salut avec emphase de respect
malgara feu qu'on fait quand on chasse le kangourou pour brûler ses poils et cuire la viande fraîche. Des grosses branches sont brulées pour former un lit de charbons pour cuire le kangourou dans un four peu profond dans la terre
mallara fleur blanche du type des frangipaniers *(Gardenia spp.)* au parfum semblable à celui du gardénia ; arbuste feuillu préférant les pentes rocheuses et les bords des falaises près des **wanjina ;** feuilles vertes brûlées comme encens pendant les annonces identifiant les visiteurs et les chants de respect avant d'approcher des **wanjina** et des sources de **wungud**

malu kangourou des collines
mamaa toute chose respectée comme preuve ancestrale sacrée ou secrète ; avertissement relatif aux choses intouchables ou interdites ; liens culturels protégés par la Loi ; caractère sacré des lieux où des événements majeurs de la création et historiques se sont déroulés ; source de l'aura spirituelle de repères, d'art ou d'animaux particuliers ayant des liens totémiques ancestraux
mamalan empreintes de pied dans le sable
mamandu sève rouge collante tirée d'une sorte de mûrier à l'écorce rugueuse qui fournit un fixatif et une teinture utilisée pour peindre et colorer de nombreuses figures **Gwion** indélébiles sur des surfaces rocheuses
mambi tournure de jupe triangulaire portée par les femmes dans les peintures **Gwion ;** jupe cérémonielle que la fille hérite de sa mère
mamul forme essentielle des objets sacrés échangés comme **wulari** et **maya.ngarri** (connaissance transmise)
manbata nénuphar blanc à petite feuille de forme ovoïde
mandi boomerang en forme de croissant ; frappés par paires, ils donnent le rythme pendant les chants
mandzu mante religieuse *(mantis sp.)*, preuve vivante de **Jillinya**
mangarri nourriture et partage ; obligations d'hospitalité et de respect entre ceux qui ont des liens de parenté
mangiwarunga réunion importante ou rassemblement initial qui ouvre une cérémonie
Manirri pays ancestral
maniwan fleurs oranges en grappe de l'**anggurun** (arbre)
manjilarri objet sacré confectionné par **Wibalma** qui a ensuite été enlevé par **Wodoi** et **Jungun** pour être partagé entre tous ; une source connue de justice qui veut dire « courir sans être aidé car le pouvoir implacable de la Loi te poursuit »
Maraja pays ancestral
margi espèce d'oiseaux qui mange du miel, preuve vivante du clan **Margi Kamali**
marguli forme de chant sacré
Marranba.bidi lieu d'habitation permanent de parents des **Ngarinyin** sur la rivière King Edward
marririn perroquet vert aux ailes rouges *(Aprosmictus erythropterus)*, preuve vivante de **Marririn** qui a empêché **Ngerdu** (crocodile **wanjina**) de posséder le feu dans l'eau. Ainsi le feu puisse être toujours partagé par tout le monde sur la terre
maya.ngarri messages à travers les objets sacrés ; formes de tablettes incisées et peintes secrètes ou personnelles conservant les principes culturels fondamentaux ; symboles abstraits de la Loi qui circulent comme messages de la Loi ; sont également des objets rituels **mamul** échangés comme **wulari** à travers le réseau **Wunan ;** une ancienne pratique culturelle qui relie les peuples indigènes du centre du continent aux zones tropicales
menda hachette en pierre
min min min min onomatopée qui désigne les rides produites à la surface de l'eau par le tournoiement de la pointe du harpon quand on fait pivoter son manche dans les paumes de la main
mob expression familière pour désigner un groupe, une bande, que ce soit pour une catégorie d'animaux, beaucoup de gens, un groupe régional ou les membres locaux d'un **dambun**
modeden traces d'animaux réelles ou peintes ; marques sur un chemin menant à l'emplacement d'une source totémique
modu anyi empreintes d'un animal ou d'un humain en migration
moitié (*moiety* en anglais) terme anthropologique qui désigne les deux **moitiés** d'un système social dualiste ; divisions égales d'une population à travers des relations de mariages croisés entre les deux groupes ; la base de la terminologie **Ngarinyin** dans ses structures sociales complexes comportant une symbolique linguistique associant toutes les choses vivantes à une des deux **moitiés** des humains
molu position d'intermédiaire qu'a un chef de clan quand il joue le rôle de lien dans la chaine des échanges **Wunan**
molu bidingarri rôle d'autorité quand les chefs de clan transfèrent les **maya.ngarri** entre les **dambun** voisins ou vers des régions éloignées
molu ijirinari rôle de gardien pour les **munnumburra** assurant la continuité des échanges culturels selon les directions traditionnelles du système **Wunan**
mondollo peinture corporelle appliquée sur le front et suivant les lignes de la mâchoire
Morrongo Morrongo désigne les gens et le territoire du clan **wamma** (tabac indigène) ; clan sous la garde d'**Ungudman** appartenant à la **moitié Jungun**
Mowaljarlai (David Mowaljarlai, décédé en 1997) ; nom de famille public de **Banggal**
mudurra coiffes de formes et de tailles variées représentées dans les peintures **Gwion** jusqu'à une époque récente ; motif graphique commun aux traditions culturelles d'autres peuples indigènes en Australie et en Papouasie
mullawundin éclair ramifié et influence magique puissante dans la sorcellerie pratiquée par les banman
Mul.ngirri nom donné à un esprit éclair qui provoque de la foudre d'une intensité moyenne juste après le début d'un orage allant en paire avec **Jundiwan**
Mumuu nom sacré de la Grande Mère **Jillinya,** « un mot important » dans la langue **Ngarinyin**
mun l'imagination
Munga.nunga « visionnaires », nom **Gwion** pour désigner des ancêtres reconnus comme les visionnaires et les fondateurs des lois **Wunan ;** spécialistes dans la fabrication des outils en pierre et communicateurs de connaissances
Munggundu wanjina associé à la formation de la terre à partir du plasma dont les représentations peintes sont vénérées à **Alyaguma ;** lié dans sa signification à la malléabilité de la sève rouge et de la résine de l'eucalyptus bloodwood
munilla peinture corporelle sur le torse
Muni yalla fille ancestrale du **wanjina Yemben**
Munja lieu d'habitation côtier dans la baie de Collier au nord de Derby, emplacement d'une ancienne mission où les réfugiés **Ngarinyin** du centre ont été envoyés pour se joindre aux **Wororra** qui habitaient là
munnumburra femme faisant partie des aînées ou homme complètement initié et instruit dans la loi **Wunan ;** spécialistes chargés de superviser les rituels et de conserver intacte la loi **Wunan**
munya geste d'avertissement

nabun feu de camp pour la cuisson
Naiya seconde phase d'éclairs pendant un cyclône, associé à une identité de sexe féminin comme femme des deux **Bundiwin** (frères foudre) qui viennent en premier pendant un orage
nambud burlwin chant pour les danseurs qui rejoignent le groupe déjà formé
Nenowatt nom de famille associé au **dambun Bararru.ngarri** et dont les membres sont les gardiens du « sanctuaire » de **Walamba**
Neowarra (**Paddy Neowarra**, président du conseil aborigène **Ngarinyin**) ; nom de famille public de **Nyawarra**
ngallad pierre brillante ressemblant à du quartz réflechissant la lumière qui se casse facilement en lames qu'on utilise comme pointes de lance
ngangurr warra garçon lors de la première étape d'initiation quand son corps est peint de taches blanches avec de l'**onmal** comme un **wodoi** (engoulevent tâcheté) avant la circoncision
Ngarinyin groupe linguistique avec des dialectes à vocales douces et dures, langue parlée pour la première fois par un homme-opossum à queue annelée connu sous le nom d'**Andarri** du côté **Jungun** et **Wad.munna** du côté **Wodoi**
Ngarjno nom ancestral de Laurie **Gawanali** qui est de **skin Wodoi** et qui vient du **dambun Brrejalnga,** chanteur confirmé et **munnumburra** qui est de **moitié ornad,** ayant des **gi** (liens spirituels) avec **jalnga** (marron d'eau) et qui est le gardien de l'image peinte du **wanjina** serpent-roi brun
ngawarra wanggi nom pour désigner un initié pendant la seconde phase portant une cordelette ancestrale en cheveux **jirrgal** autour du front pour la première fois ; peinture corporelle consistant en deux cercles noirs à points blancs sur le torse encerclant chaque épaule qui symbolise chacune des deux **moitiés** dansant la **walu.ngarri ;** la peinture utilisée pour les deux cercles est faite avec le noir intense du **wulngon** (charbon de bois) mélangé à de la **wurd.ngun** (graisse d'oiseau), ces deux cercles sont peints sur un corps qui a été d'abord enduit avec du **jimbri** (rouge) et sont ensuite finis avec l'ajout d'**onmal** (points blancs)
Ngegamorro wanjina qui aimait **Wurrumurru** et qui est à l'origine d'une famille à laquelle les membres de la famille de **Bangmorro** font remonter leur origine
ngerdu petit crocodile d'eau douce *(Crocodylus johnstoni)*, preuve vivante de **Ngerdu,** le crocodile **wanjina** qui essaya de garder le feu pour lui en l'emportant sous l'eau
ngi.ornad de **skin Wodoi** ou de **moitié ornad**
ngolo ngolo walu.ngarri expression dans un chant qui signifie « viens, promène toi »
ngoru souffle de vie intérieur de nature sacrée ; essence dans l'eau donnée par le **Wanjina Gulingi ;** attribut de puissance pour les **maya.ngarri** (objets sacrés)
ngowrun expression signifiant « du vent sacré » , voir **ngoru**)
nguniri précieuse cordelette en cheveux ancestraux tressés représentée dans l'art **Gwion** et portée par les **munnumburra** quand ils interprètent les **gulbrungi** (chants puissants) annoncant une cérémonie et obligeant tout le monde à y assister
nimindi appartenir à tous, venant de tous, comme par exemple la connaissance
niyan.gawa expression ancienne d'origine incertaine, gardée dans le récit de **Jebera** par les gens parlant le **Ngarinyin** quand l'homme égoïste demande « qui moi ? » ; on pense qu'elle vient de la région du désert de Tanami, voir **Unggumi**
Njumillibulli voir **Algi**
nollabiallu groupes d'hommes ou de femmes avec des peintures corporelles pour les **walu.ngarri,** chantant tout en marchant vers le terrain de la danse circulaire
norgun palette concave creusée dans la pierre pour piler l'écorce **mamandu** pour en extraire un liquide rouge servant de peinture
Nudu.nudu Kamali nom de clan
numanda se réveiller
numbila terme dans un chant impliquant un déplacement rapide
nu meri expression signifiant « se concentrer », « écouter avec attention »
numurangga femme
nyamalar expression pour saluer
Nyamanbiligi la femme aveugle de **Wibalma**
nyamun-buna tenir un serment ; ne pas aller contre la Loi à cause de la punition que cela entrainerait ; rester silencieux et garder un secret
nyarndu bâton avec appui à l'extrêmité servant de propulseur de lance, taillé dans le tronc du « corkwood tree » (arbre australien de bois de liège) ou de conifère australien *(Nauclea orientalis)* ; c'est le modèle de propulseur donnant aux chasseurs une force de poussée supplémentaire pour percer les peaux épaisses d'émeus et de kangourous ; motif courant des peintures **Gwion**
nyarrama membres d'un clan parlant dans un meeting **Wunan**
Nyawarra nom ancestral de **Paddy Neowarra** qui est de **skin Wodoi** et du **Galeru.ngarri dambun ;** ayant des **gi** (liens spirituels) incluant la pluie, les grenouilles et **Walamba** (kangourou rouge) comme symboles vivants
Nyawarra rochers noirs en basalte ; également les **gi** (liens spirituels) de **Nyawarra** et origine de son nom
nyirri gunduba se recroqueviller en dormant
nyonor membres du sexe féminin de **moitié ornad (skin Wodoi)** dans leurs liens de mariage avec la **moitié amalar,** voir **nyamalar)**

Olgi nom donné à des formes mineures d'éclairs qui ont lieu au moment du passage d'un front d'orage ; nom donné à un garçon qui suit **Naiya**
onmal peinture blanche tirée du kaolin et de l'argile claire dite terre à pipe existant en affleurement
ornad nom de la **moitié** qui est de **skin Wodoi,** pluriel **brrornad**
oru liwarad expression pour désigner la forme des oreilles de kangourou dressées quand ils sont à l'écoute ; forme d'une **mudurra** (coiffe) à rebord

Pijantjatjara groupe linguistique du désert central, voisins méridionaux des **Arrernte** et des **Anangu**, également lié aux lois **Wunan** originaires du Kimberley

quoll marsupial aux points blancs caractéristiques dit martre tachetée

Romul voir **Algi**

skin (anglais, « peau ») terme familier pour désigner un sytème de **moitié** fait d'associations binaires ; dualité sociale reflétant la partage du sang entre **Wodoi** d'un côté et **Jungun** de l'autre à travers les mariages entre leurs enfants

Uluru énorme monolithe rouge dans le désert central australien, point de repère symbolique pour les **Anangu** et d'autres groupes linguistiques indigènes liés par les lois **Wunan**
umralu lame en pierre à picots utilisée comme pointe de lance
Unggumi langue du désert de Tanami qui est peut-être à l'origine de l'expression **niyan.gawa** utilisée dans l'histoire de **Jebera**
ungia nénuphar aux racines pendantes
Ungudman nom ancestral de **Paddy Wamma** qui est de **skin Jungun** et de **Morrongo Morrongo ; Ungudman** a des connaissances trés poussées de la nature, il est **munnumburra** et de **moitié amalar** dans ses liens de parenté ; ses **gi** (liens spirituels) incluent le crocodile d'eau douce et **wamma** (tabac indigène) ; origine de son nom public
urilimul brassard ou tournure

wadba lance de combat d'un seul tenant en bois dur possédant deux rangées de picots taillés dans les deux directions et très douloureuse lorsqu'on la retire
wade expression dans les chants signifiant « tous ensemble, venez »
wad.munna opossum à la queue annelée du côté **Wodoi,** connu sous le nom d'**andarri** du côté **Jungun**
walamba antilopine wallaroo *(Macropus antilopinus)*, nom donné à un kangourou rouge, animal symbole d'un **wanjina,** preuve vivante du **Walamba wanjina** qui a reconstruit son corps à partir des restes laissés par les chiens après qu'ils l'eussent mangé ; originellement connu sous le nom de **Binbin,** il a survécu en recommençant ce procédé à travers huit réincarnations, changeant de nom en chemin pour finalement devenir **Wudmi.mulimuli**
walbo gudina expression sacrée dans un chant en relation avec la circoncision
walbud sorte de tournure-ceinture à trois pointes faite en peau de marsupial portée par les hommes **Gwion**
walgunu « pierres de fertilité » renfermant de la **wungud** (essen-

ce sacrée) ; pierres en forme d'œuf dont on dit qu'elles se soulèvent et bougent en toute liberté pendant la nuit
Wallagari Merrbini long et sinueux lagon qui s'est formé quand **Walamba** a jeté son **banad** (boomerang) et s'est assis le corps recouvert d'ocre rouge
Wallagunda la Voie lactée dans son ensemble; masse lumineuse formant le créateur suprême de la terre
walmarro voir **gundilli**
walu.di eau profonde et permanente de rivière ou de lagon
walu.ngarri cérémonies d'initiation incluant la danse circulaire des hommes et des femmes ; événements publics avant la circoncision comportant des chants composés à l'origine par **Wiji.ngarri** et interprétés à **Wudmangu**
waluwi un lézard à langue bleue, preuve vivante de l'ancêtre de sexe féminin **Waluwi** qui s'est sacrifiée pour sauver ses enfants lors d'une inondation
wamba nerveux ; expression d'anxiété
wamma tabac indigène, symbole régional du **dambun Morrongo Morrongo,** la région d'**Ungudman**
Wamma (Paddy Wamma) ; nom de famille public d'**Ungudman**
wandagi brassard autour du biceps, c'est normalement une large bande en peau de kangourou fermement attachée avec une cordelette et peinte avec de l'**onmal** ; un seul cauri blanc peut y être attaché avec de la ficelle pour des rituels
Wangalu titre d'un vieil homme portant une **mudurra** (coiffe) que **Nyawarra** a vu dans sa jeunesse
wa.ngara jupe longue de ficelle ou de cuire avec des pompons portées uniquement par les femmes
wanggi étape d'initiation allant de la jeunesse à l'âge du mariage
wang.gura corneille de Torres noire et brillante (Corvus orru) aux cris d'appel stridents et au comportement téméraire que l'on trouve souvent affairée à nettoyer les restes d'un campement, preuve vivante de **Wang.gura,** nom du clan **Kamali** pour les **Wororra** de la côte et donné par les voisins de l'ouest qui sont en relation réciproque avec les **Ngarinyin** et qu'on appelle souvent « les gens du couchant »
Wanjina puissance créatrice portant le **wungud** (source de toute vie circulant sur terre, dans l'eau et dans le ciel) en tant qu'influence de l'être suprême **Wanjina Gulingi** ; de nombreux autres **wanjina** locaux ont de multiples associations avec des animaux et des plantes et conservent les identités d'ancêtres divinisés qui ont formé le pays
wanjina lieu où les esprits ancestraux créateurs se sont représentés sous la forme de gravures et de couleurs sur les rochers et qui est un site de renouveau ; terme pour désigner les images repeintes sur un fond blanc qui ont des têtes entourées d'un halo caractéristique et sans bouches ; le nom **wanjina,** « peuple d'eau » désigne les peuples indigènes du Kimberley, particulièrement les groupes linguistiques **Ngarinyin, Wila Wila, Wororra** et **Wunambul**
warid wani mumal petite pierre plate chauffée dans des cendres chaudes ; on l'utilise comme enclume pour chauffer lentement un manche de lance en bambou afin de le redresser. On doit faire très attention de ne pas trop chauffer et sécher le bambou ou le fendre en le courbant quand il est froid. La température de l'enclume en pierre est soigneusement contrôlée pour diffuser la chaleur dans le bambou jusqu'à ce que le manche soit considéré comme prêt à être courbé. Ensuite, le manche est progressivement redressé en appuyant fermement vers le bas sur l'enclume en pierre ce qui permet à l'artisan d'éliminer petit à petit un certain nombre de légers défauts
Wari.ngarri dambun territoire
waringi de.de dans un chant, expression liant la croissance des jeunes enfants et un arbuste à fleurs jaunes
Warlpiri groupe linguistique indigène du désert central lié aux lois **Wunan**
Warmun communauté indigène à l'est du Kimberley sur la bordure nord-ouest du désert de Tanami ; un nom de région pour « les gens du soleil levant »; groupes de l'est liés aux **Wunan**
warrana aigle audacieux ou aigle à longue queue *(Aquila audax)*, principal prédateur des wallabys et des kangourous
warrngon voir **windji jaman**
Wibalma Gwion créateur d'objets sacrés qui vivait à **Gelngu** et qui gardait la connaissance sacrée pour lui tout seul jusqu'à l'intervention de **Wodoi** et de **Jungun** qui ont découvert sa richesse en **maya.ngarri** (objets sacrés)
wiji.ngarri (Dasyrus hallucatus) marsupial tacheté carnivore nocturne bondissant sur n'importe quel reptile, rat ou insecte en vue et qui a sur ses pattes arrière des coussinets lui permettant de s'aggriper aux surfaces grèseuses ; preuve vivante de **Wiji.ngarri,** compositeur de la première **walu.ngarri** (cérémonie de la danse circulaire pour les deux sexes préliminaire à la circoncision) ; ancêtre qui souffrait de plaies sur son corps, symbolisées par des points blancs sur le corps du marsupial
Wila Wila voisins sur la côte plus au nord des **Ngarinyin** représentés par des **jallala** (pierres dressées) à **Dudu.ngarri**
wilmi spirales mobiles de brume sur les cours d'eau de **wungud** ; preuve visible des esprits qui habiteront les enfants à naître
windji jaman oindre et peindre le corps d'un humain comme une image ; également **warrngon**
Winjagin montagne ressortant comme un monolithe dans la savane de **Morrongo Morrongo** (région sous la garde d'**Ungudman**)
winjangun petit feu de camp
winjin pluies torrentielles envoyées par **Gulingi** qui marquent le début de la saison humide qui dure de novembre à février ; époque à laquelle le guloi (fruit) arrive à maturité
winya modulation de chant pour exprimer la volonté d'interpréter des danses pendant les événements **Wunan**
wir.nganyen seconde phase de l'initiation aprés la **walu.ngarri** ; séries de chants **Wunan** présentant aux initiés les animaux sacrés et se terminant par les rituels de circoncision en dehors des spectateurs
wodoi engoulevent tacheté ou faucon nocturne, oiseau australien familier *(Eurostotodus argus)* reconnaissable à ses points blancs et une tache très blanche sur ses ailes ;qui dort caché parmi les détritus sur le sol durant la journée et qui déambule gracieusement la nuit en mangeant des insectes ; preuve vivante de **Wodoi** une des deux **moitiés Gwion** qui par un accord avec **Jungun** fut à l'origine du partage de la terre et du sang à travers le mariage comme loi **Wunan** ; nom courant pour quiconque est **ornad** dans le système de **moitié**
Wodoi.ngarri dambun région clanique appelé d'aprés **Wodoi**
wongai ainée initiée à la Loi qui connait tous les rituels et chants **Wunan**
woomera terme familier pour désigner un propulseur (voir **nyarndu**
Wororra groupe linguistique de populations de la côte, voisines des **Ngarinyin** à l'ouest
worri-unbin les mots qui viennent pendant une conversation ; dialogue concernant les **Wunan**
Wo.Wa Kamali nom d'un clan
wowarra pigeon de couleur brune *(Phaps chalcoptera)*, preuve vivante de **Wowarra,** nom d'un clan **Kamali** renommé pour ses coureurs, les plus rapides, menés par deux hommes dignes de confiance qui ont poursuivi et transpercé d'un coup de lance **Jebera** pour avoir enfreint la loi **Wunan**
Wudjawudja.ngarri dambun région clanique
wudma petit wallaby femelle de rivière *(Macropus agilis)*. Un bébé wallaby encore porté dans la poche marsupiale d'une **wudma** ne peut être mangé depuis un interdit introduit par le chasseur **Gwion Yandama,** voir **gundilli**
Wudmangu endroit où **Wiji.ngarri** a composé les premières chansons **walu.ngarri** ; lieu vénéré entouré de torrents où pour la première fois un siége en pierre fut utilisé pour placer le chanteur au centre de la danse en cercle
Wudmi.mulimuli le dernier nom attribué à **Walamba**
wudu se déplacer
wuduwan voir **mandi**
Wulamu clans **Gwion** très anciens dits « du soleil levant », qui sont venus à la table **Wunan** ; peuples des déserts à l'est des **Ngarinyin**
wulari objets sacrés circulant comme le **maya.ngarri** au sein du réseau **Wunan**
wuludi points d'eau profonds et permanents, rivières et bassins ; eau de couleur verte d'où les esprits des enfants s'élèvent sous forme de **wilmi** (brume) ; points d'eau sacrés où le **wungud** (essence de vie) des **wanjina** réside
Wunambul voisins des **Ngarinyin,** desquels ils sont proches par la langue et l'histoire
Wunan loi du partage ; accords anciens qui mirent fin au nomadisme en fixant les **dambun** (domaines) familiaux et en établissant la division en **moitiés** de la société (deux groupes de mariage croisé qui a pour origine le pacte de **Wodoi** et **Jungun** pour unir leur sang) ; ordre de classification binaire entre les membres des tribus selon les **moitiés brrornad** et **brramalar** ou les **skin** avec des mariages arrangés entre les hommes **ornad** ou **amalar** et les femmes **nyonor** ou **nyamalar** ; modèle de nombreuses versions de systèmes de parenté utilisant la division par **moitiés** liant toutes les choses vivantes au sein d'un réseau culturel ; agencement et disposition de la terre
wunanbri voies d'échanges trés étendues des objets sacrés, des rituels, des dons et des chants
wunandi nature de la loi **Wunan**
wunan.gu appeler les gens à se rassembler pour le **Wunan**
wunbanburan principes moraux immuables dans le **Wunan,** considérés comme un **lulwa** (don) des **Munga.nunga** (ancêtres) ; base morale pour tout devoir préscrit par la Loi
wungarun bois de fer, arbre au bois le plus dur
wunginunna nom d'un plan d'eau sombre dans la Voie lactée et sur terre
wungud énergie ou essence des choses vivantes ; force de vie originelle propre à toutes les formes de vie crées par les **wanjina** ; vie circulant dans l'eau, donnant structure et forme à toutes les choses allant des protozoaires aux humains ; toute essence physique ou spirituelle qui influence les humains ou anime, reflète, maintient ou suscite la vie ; preuve de divers **wanjina** ; les restes délavés de peintures **Gwion** sont considérés comme riches en essence de vie et peuvent également être appelés **wungud**
wungurrurun mamandu palette en pierre, voir **norgun**
wunindid loi traditionnelle venant des anciens ; également **wunanbri wunindid naga** signifiant une loi en train de traverser le **Wunan**
wunindid naga influence persistante de la loi **Wunan** à travers le temps
wura.wura genre de perdrix *(Petrophassa smithii)* qui se cache dans des broussailles et sous-bois ; il a la peau jaune autour de l'œil ; on le rencontre en nombre important dans les étendues boisées herbues du nord du Kimberley
wurd.ngun graisse de n'importe quel oiseau utilisée comme agent de conservation pour le bois des ustensiles et des armes
Wurrumalu frère de sang du **wanjina Yemben (goanna** ou lézard d'eau)
Wurrumurru ancêtre tortue femelle qui était aimée par le **Ngegamorro wanjina**

yalmalnyu malngud endroits interdits prés d'un terrain sacré ; considérés comme dangereux pour les humains et les animaux, ce sont généralement des sables mouvants, un marécage ou un marais. Un tel endroit est imprégné d'une force mortelle et considéré comme **mamaa** (secret). Le fait d'ôter la vie à certains animaux quand la Loi fut créée aboutit à ce que des dépots sacrés se retrouvent à côté d'autres qui sont dangereux. À la suite des premiers événements relatifs à la Loi, des dépots d'eau fraîche et de certaines formes définies du paysage demeurent également **junjun** (preuve de ce qui s'est produit)
yalungarri terme pour désigner du pigment blanc, voir **onmal**
yamalad minia expression de salut qui induit la reconnaissance de l'individualité d'une personne ; plus littéralement: « je vois ton front brillant »
Yandama célèbre chasseur dont l'image commémore l'utilisation du **nyarndu** (propulseur) ; peinture du chasseur à **Alyaguma** avec trois et non cinq doigts pour indiquer les liens ancestraux entre l'oiseau et l'homme ; héros **Gwion** qui a cuit un **gundilli** (wallaby) dans un four en pierre et qui a créé plusieurs sites sacrés liés au nom d'**Alyaguma**
yangudi adolescentes pubères
yara wallaroo commun *(Macropus robustus)*, connu localement comme kangourou commun ou kangourou gris des collines, preuve vivante de **Yara** ; loi qui débuta à l'emplacement d'un four en pierre près de **Binjirri** où l'ancêtre **Yara** a été mangé par les hommes-chiens sauvages ; protocole pour dépecer un kangourou ; chant qui s'est étendu vers le sud et l'est et a finalement été conservé en Australie centrale
yarrad os des gens récemment décédés, que l'on laisse sous une pile protectrice de pierres non cimentées pendant plus d'un an, jusqu'à ce que les fourmis et les changements climatiques aient complètement nettoyé le squelette. Les parents en deuil doivent attendre qu'il n'y ait plus de traces de tendons et que les os soient blancs avant de les préparer pour leur inhumation finale dans un recoin de caverne. Chaque os est soigneusement lavé et nettoyé, il est ensuite essuyé avec de la **wurd.ngun** (graisse d'oiseau) avant d'être enduit de **gagul** (peinture rouge)
yemben goanna d'eau gris et luisant, preuve vivante du **Yemben wanjina,** fils de sang de **Ngegamorro**
yidmunggul cape en peau d'émeu ou couvre-épaule ; motif caractéristique de la peinture **Gwion**
Yirrbal fils adoptif du **Ngegamorro wanjina,** frère de facto de **Yemben**
Yowinjella nom d'un clan **Kamali** qui descend du faisan
Yullamaiya vieil homme portant une **mudurra** (coiffe) vu par **Nyawarra,** voir **Laundi**
yululun plumes et ailes portées comme décoration ou emblème
yungulli nénuphar de la famille du lotus
yururu.mal colliers fait avec une cordelette et des plumes

CAMERA   KAMERA   LUMIÈRE

Photography: Jeff Doring
p. 160 Southern Cross: © David Malin
p. 35 malarra smoke: Jon Rhodes
p. 206, p. 207 walu.ngarri dancers; p. 233 d, e (betacam): Bruce Blake
p. 123 e, p. 189 d, e, f, p. 206, p. 207 Ngarjno at walu.ngarri (16mm): John Whitteron
Original colour laboratory Colorpro: John Finlay

When our publisher Ludwig Könemann first looked at the photographs in Sydney and responded: "Yes! images with extended captions", I instantly wanted to reward his enthusiasm for the concept. Since then we have been in the careful hands of Sally Bald and her capable team at Könemann Verlag, to bring this first edition to fruition. The editor wishes to acknowledge the professional services and cooperation of various people during several stages of film production, and many collaborators during the ongoing process of producing documentary media. The first stage of filming was made possible with the assistance of the Australian Film Commission. The editor remains grateful for the legal advice of Michael Frankel and Greg Duffy. Among those from the start, Roberta Friedman, Alan Rumsey, Jennifer Isaacs, and later Jean-Pierre Beaux, Paul Tacon, Pamela Scott, Jean-Patrick Razon, Peta-Lyn Farwagi, John Clegg and others, I thank all for their encouragement. Deep respect has grown with the advice and generosity of those who have supported me personally throughout this long project: Gary Warner, Ben Churcher, Lindi Harrison, Graeme Ward, and Pierre Brochet. I say thanks to Alexander Nettlebeck for introducing me to Pierre Brochet, my left hand on this book from beginning to end, and Marie-Odile Brochet for providing mangarri in Paris while completing the work. And for my true brother Ray, brother Carl, and my loyal sister Ann, no star is lost, no words are enough. Sometimes my thoughts will be camping again with Banggal, inside his country. When we started on the dulwan as a team of five, Nyawarra said not to trust anyone. Nyawarra has truly been solid black rock, it has been a privilege to work together. I hope professor Ngarjno will forgive any mistakes in the text, and know maba Ungudman will stay young "or what!" and the munnumburra remain invaluable friends who love this country together. JD

Als unser Verleger Ludwig Könemann die Fotos in Sydney zum ersten Mal sah und ausrief: „Genau! Bilder mit ausführlichen Legenden", war ich sofort angesteckt von seiner Begeisterung. Seither haben Sally Bald und ihr engagiertes Team vom Könemann Verlag uns tatkräftig dabei unterstützt, diese erste Buchausgabe unseres Materials zu verwirklichen. Der Herausgeber dankt all denen, die ihm während der verschiedenen Stadien der Filmarbeiten und bei dem laufenden Projekt der Bild- und Tondokumentation mit Rat und Tat zur Seite gestanden haben. Möglich wurden die ersten Filmaufnahmen durch die Unterstützung der Australian Film Commission. Mein Dank gilt Michael Frankel und Greg Duffy für die Beratung in Rechtsfragen. Roberta Friedman, Rumsey und Jennifer Isaacs, die von Anfang an dabei waren, sowie Jean-Pierre Beaux, Paul Tacon, Pamela Scott, Jean-Patrick Razon, Peta-Lyn Farwagi, John Clegg und anderen, die später dazustießen, danke ich für den Mut, den sie uns gemacht haben. All denen, die mich während dieser langen Arbeit persönlich begleitet haben – Gary Warner, Ben Churcher, Lindi Harrison, Graeme Ward und Pierre Brochet –, schulde ich tiefen Respekt für ihren Rat und ihre Großzügigkeit. Ich danke Alexander Nettlebeck, dass er mich mit Pierre Brochet bekannt gemacht hat, meiner linken Hand bei dem ganzen Buch von der ersten bis zur letzten Minute, und ich danke Marie-Odile Brochet für das mangarri, mit dem sie uns während der abschließenden Arbeiten in Paris bewirtet hat. Und für meinen wahren Bruder Ray, Bruder Carl und meine treue Schwester Ann ist kein Stern verloren, kein Wort zuviel. In Gedanken werde ich manches Mal wieder mein Lager mit Banggal im Busch aufschlagen, in seinem Land. Als wir uns zu fünft auf den Weg machten und den dulwan beschritten, sagte Nyawarra, ich solle niemandem trauen. Nyawarra war ein schwarzer Fels in der Brandung, und es war mir eine Ehre, mit ihm zusammenzuarbeiten. Ich hoffe, Professor Ngarjno läßt Nachsicht walten, wenn der Text noch Fehler enthält, ich weiß, maba Ungudman wird jung bleiben, „was denn sonst!", und die munnumburra werden für immer Freunde bleiben, verbunden durch die Liebe zu diesem Land. JD

Quand notre éditeur, Ludwig Könemann, vit pour la première fois les photographies à Sydney et répondit : « Oui ! Que des images avec des longues légendes. », je voulus dès cet instant récompenser son enthousiasme pour ce concept. Depuis lors nous avons été choyés par Sally Bald et sa compétente équipe chez Könemann, pour mener à bout l'édition de ce livre. L'auteur tient à souligner le professionalisme des services et de la coopération de plusieurs personnes lors de la production du film, et de nombreux collaborateurs durant le processus – en cours – de production du matériau documentaire. La première étape de prises de vues a été rendue possible grâce au soutien de l'Australian Film Commission. L'auteur exprime sa gratitude envers Michael Frankel et Greg Duffy. Parmi eux, dès le début il y eut Roberta Friedman, Alan Rumsey, Jennifer Isaacs, puis Jean-Pierre Beaux, Paul Tacon, Pamela Scott, Jean-Patrick Razon, Peta-Lyn Farwagi, John Clegg et d'autres ; je les remercie tous pour leurs encouragements. Mon respect va envers ceux qui m'ont personnellement supporté tout au long de ce projet, me prodiguant conseils et générosité : Gary Warner, Ben Churcher, Lindi Harrison, Graeme Ward et Pierre Brochet. Je remercie Alexander Nettlebeck de m'avoir présenté Pierre Brochet, ma main gauche sur ce livre du début à la fin, et Marie-Odile Brochet qui m'a procuré de la mangarri à Paris alors que nous achevions le travail. Et pour mon vrai frère Ray, mon frère Carl, et ma loyale sœur Ann, que rien, pas même des mots, ne suffirait à remercier. De temps en temps, mes pensées seront avec Bangal, quelque part dans son pays. Quand nous entamèrent, à cinq, le dulwan, Nyawarra nous dit de ne faire confiance à personne. Nyawarra a été comme un solide roc noir, cela fut un privilège de travailler avec lui. J'espère que le professeur Ngarjno pardonnera d'éventuelles erreurs dans le texte, et je sais que maba Ungundman restera jeune « ou quoi ! » et les munumburra restent d'inestimables amis qui aiment ensemble ce pays. JD

The editor recognises the partnership of the Ngarinyin community and their Wororra and Wunambul neighbours during the recording of material for this book. On the advice of the Ngarinyin Aboriginal Corporation, we first acknowledge some of their relations and supporters including deceased relatives, who passed away during this time. We first name some of those relatives indirectly involved, followed by those who were present at the Duduk.ngunga events of 1995, including some of the young people who continue Ngarinyin education.

Der Herausgeber dankt den Ngarinyin und ihren Nachbarn, den Wororra und Wunambul, für die Zusammenarbeit während der Aufzeichnung der Materialien zu diesem Buch. Nach Rücksprache mit der Ngarinyin Aboriginal Corporation danken wir an erster Stelle einigen ihrer Verwandten und Unterstützer, darunter auch jene, die während der Entstehungszeit gestorben sind. Wir nennen zuerst einige der Verwandten, die indirekt beteiligt waren, und im Anschluß daran diejenigen, die bei der 1995 abgehaltenen Zeremonie von Duduk.ngunga zugegen waren, unter anderem einige der jungen Leute, die in der Tradition der Ngarinyin erzogen werden.

Nous sommes reconnaissant de la contribution de la communauté Ngarinyin et de leurs voisins les Wororra et les Wunambul durant la collecte des matériaux qui constituent ce livre. Sur les conseils de la Ngarinyin Aboriginal Corporation, nous remercions d'abord leurs relations et soutiens, ainsi que les parents, qui sont décédés durant ce temps. Nous nommons d'abord certains de leurs parents indirectement impliqués, suivis par ceux qui étaient présents aux événements de Duduk.ngunga en 1995, y compris certains des jeunes gens qui poursuivent leur éducation Ngarinyin.

Henry Mowaljarlai, Francis Dalby, Alfie White, Wilfred Gunak, Stanley Nyandi, Ronson Bangmorro, James Bangmorro, Kenny Oobagooma, Janet Oobagooma, Keith Nenowatt,
JUN.GUN - Theresa Bear, Pansy Nulgit, Dorothy Chapman, Susan Bangmorra, Maisie Martin, Bruce Ernott, Edmund Ngerdu, Samson Morlumbun,
Scottie Martin, Donny Dolan, Jeffrey Burgu, Nathan Nulgit, Alison Burgu, Marshall Morlumbun, Neville Morlumbun, Matthew Nyandu, Andrew, Angus...
WODOI - Maisie Bear, Lucy Ward, Paul Chapman, Campbell Allanbra, Jason Nenowatt, Jessica Nenowatt, Clinton Bangmorra, Kane Nenowatt,
Claude Mowaljarli, Benjamin Mowaljarlai, Alphonse Buck, Darryl Nandoo, Jennifer Nandoo, Ruby Angburra, Marilyn Smith, Leonnie Nenowatt
Deborah Bangmorra, Yvonne Bangmorra, Jillian Bangmorra, Danielle Bangmorra, Kasia Bangmorra, Simone Bangmorra...

and don't forget the beauty and the beautiful
Banggal

und vergiß nicht die Schönheit und das Schöne
Banggal

et n'oublies pas la beauté, ce qui est beau
Banggal

We have to look after the song and the country
In the bush... secret place
Nyawarra

Wir müssen die Gesänge und das Land behüten
im Busch... ein geheimer Platz
Nyawarra

Nous devons protéger les chants et le pays
dans la brousse... un lieu secret
Nyawarra

BIBLIOGRAPHY   BIBLIOGRAPHIE   BIBLIOGRAPHIE

Akerman, K., *A note on rock art in the Kimberleys*, in: Mankind 10(3), 1976, p. 183-4.

Blundell, V. and Layton, R., *Marriage, myth and models of exchange in the West Kimberleys*, in: Mankind 11, 1978, p. 321-245

Bradshaw, Joseph, *Notes on a recent trip to Prince Regent River*, in: Geographical Society of Australia, Victorian Branch Proceedings 9/2, 1892, p. 90-102.

Brancusi, Constantin, *Aphorisms*, in: Rumanian Review 19/1, 1965, p. 117-120.

Capell, A., *Kimberley cave painting myths*, Oceania and Linguistic monographs 18, Sydney 1972.

Chaloupka G., *Journey in Time*, Sydney 1993.

Coate, H.H.J. and A.P. Elkin, *Ngarinyin-English Dictionary*, Oceania and Linguistics monographs 16, Sydney, 1974.

Crawford, I.M., *The Art of the Wandjina*: *Aboriginal cave paintings in Kimberley, Western Australia*, Melbourne 1968.

Godden, E., Malnic, J., *Rock Paintings of Aboriginal Australia*, Sydney 1982.

Isaacs, J. (ed.), *Australian Dreamings. 40,000 years of Aboriginal History*, Sydney 1980.

Layton, R., *Australian Rock Art*: *a new synthesis*, Melbourne 1992.

Love, J.R.B., *Mythology, totemism and religion of the Worora tribe of northwest Australia*, in: report of the Australian and New Zealand Association for the Advancement of Science 22, 1935, p. 222-231.

Morphy, H., *Ancestral Connections, Art and an Aboriginal System of Knowledge*, Chicago 1991.

Mowaljarlai, D. and Peck, C., *Ngarinyin cultural continuity: a project to teach the young people the culture including the re-painting of Wandjina rock art sites*, in: Australian Aboriginal Studies 1987(2), p. 71-78.

Mowaljarlai, D., Vinnicombe, P., Ward, G.K. and Chippendale,C., *Repainting of images on rock art in Australia and the maintenance of Aboriginal culture*, in: Antiquity 62, 1988, p. 690-696.

Mulvaney, J., kamminga, J., *The prehistory of Australia*, Sydney 1999.

Roberts, R.G. et al., *Luminescence dating of rock art and past environments using mud-wasp nests in northern Australia*, in: Nature 387, 1997, p. 696-699.

Schulz, A.S., *North-west Australian rock paintings*, Memoirs of the National Museum of Victoria 20, 1956, p. 7-57.

Vinnicombe, P., *Site Management problems and prospects in the Kimberleys*, in: Sullivan, H. (ed.) Visitors to Aboriginal sites: access, control and management, Canberra 1974.

Ward, G.K., *Obituaries: D. Mowaljarlai O.A.M. 1925-1997*, in: Australian Aboriginal Studies 1997/2, p. 78-84.

Wilson, Ronald, *Bringing them home. Report on the National Inquiry into the Separation of Aboriginal and Torres Strait Islander children from their families*, Human Rights and and Equal Opportunity Commission, Sydney 1997.

Woolagoodja, S., *Lalai dreamtime: Aboriginal poems as told by Sam Woolagoodja*, trans. M.Silverstein. Sydney 1975.

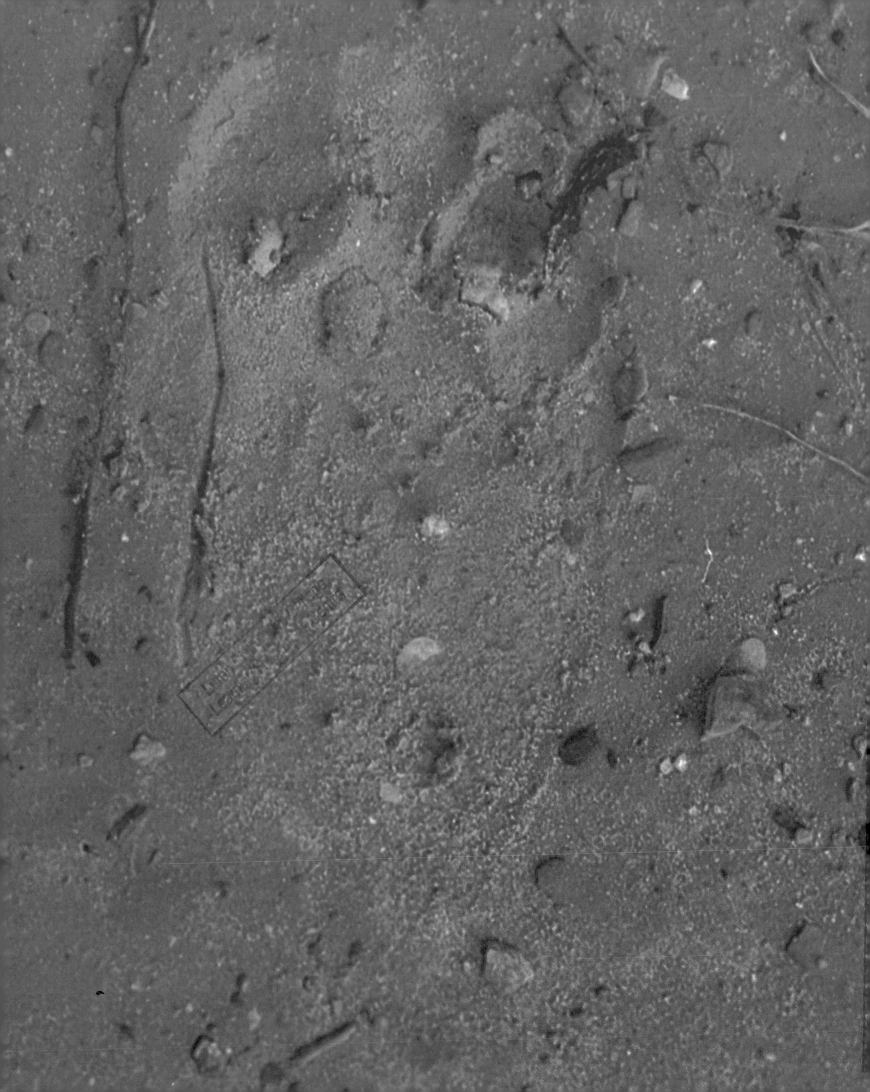